Introduction to Business Organisation

SECOND EDITION

121BSS

prepared by:

Tracey Holker

Coventry University

ISBN 13:   9781121255432

The McGraw·Hill Companies

McGraw-Hill Custom Publishing

www.mcgrawhillcreate.co.uk

Published by McGraw-Hill Education (UK) Ltd an imprint of the
McGraw-Hill Companies, Inc., 1221 Avenue of the Americas, New
York NY 10020.

ISBN: 9781121255432

Introduction to Business Organisation
SECOND EDITION

Contents

Credits

What is a Business Organisation?

Chapter ONE

Defining Management

Chapter contents

❖ LEARNING OBJECTIVES

After studying this chapter you should have a general overview of management and managers. In particular you should be able to:

❖ **define*** the essential role of management and differentiate managers from operatives and specialists

❖ **explain** the concepts of transformation, added value and organising people

❖ **distinguish** between management processes and management functions

❖ **compare and contrast** different types of managers when classified by ownership, relation to line functions, seniority etc

❖ **identify** three general management skills and explain how their importance changes at different levels of management

❖ **list** three characteristics of management work and 10 management roles

❖ **list** the three competences sought most frequently by employers

❖ **describe** the main psychological characteristics of typical managers

❖ **compare** the approach and management style used several decades ago with the approach and management style used today

* *Explanation of terms such as define, describe, describe briefly, compare and contrast, list, analyse etc. are given on the website associated with this book.*

CASE 1.1 *Managing birds or bytes?*

Arthur Darfor is an owner-manager of an ostrich farm at Oudtshoorn in South Africa. He is responsible for the work of eight farmhands who need to be allocated work such as feeding or moving the birds to breeding paddocks. At times their work needs to be monitored closely to ensure that the correct temperatures and hygiene standards are maintained in the incubators. Since breeding is seasonal, Arthur needs to plan his flock carefully so that his farm is fully utilised throughout the year. He also needs to plan the supply of "lucerne", which is a key part of the birds' diet. Many of his decisions are routine, but the timing of sending the birds to market is a key judgement as the prices for both feathers and ostrich meat need to be predicted. The income produced must be budgeted carefully to ensure that cash is available to meet labour and other costs until another flock of birds is sent to market.

Karen Bede is the team leader of a group of six computer programmers working for a software company based in Berkshire, near Windsor Castle. Every week she allocates the parts of a larger program to each programmer and checks the code they produce. The work needs careful planning to ensure that the parts fit together and the costs stay within the budget agreed with the client. Karen often needs to juggle demands and prioritise tasks in order to meet deadlines. A considerable amount of her time is spent writing progress reports and attending meetings so that the middle managers in her organisation can integrate the work of several teams like hers.

Managers play a very important role in our society but, unlike many other occupational groups, such as teachers, builders or doctors, managers do not form a single homogeneous group. They work in many different ways, at many different levels in many different types of organisation. It is therefore important to understand both the similarities and the variations in management. This chapter aims to do this by answering, the question "What is management?" in four sections:

1.1 Definition of management

The basic transformational role of management

A simple definition of management is "using resources in an efficient and effective way so that the end product is worth more than the initial resources". This definition has the advantage that it focuses upon the crucial role of management to transform inputs into outputs of greater value. This is shown in Figure 1.1.

The simple definition has a drawback: it is too inclusive. According to this definition, a cow chewing the cud would be an excellent manager since it eats a cheap resource, i.e. grass, and converts it into a more valuable product (milk). The definition includes practically every adult: a vagrant collecting cigarette stubs, a student working in a library and a lone programmer debugging information technolgy (IT) code would qualify as a manager. A definition so wide is useless because it does not differentiate a subset of people who are

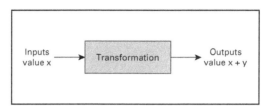

FIGURE 1.1 The fundamental transformation process

clearly managers. Many people identify the management of *other people* as the defining characteristic of management. Mary Parker Follett (1941) defined management as:

> 66   Getting things done by other people.   99

More recently Stewart (1967) described a manager as:

> 66   Someone who get things done with the aid of other people.   99

This emphasis on the management of other people provides a good way to differentiate between managers, operatives (workers who work directly upon raw materials or information or who directly provide personal services) and specialists (workers who use their skills and knowledge to enable other people to do things). Specialists such as neurologists, lawyers or financial analysts may have equal or higher status and salaries than managers. However, they will not be managers until they are responsible for the work of other people such as a clinical team or a group of junior investment analysts.

The simple definition of a manager needs a final improvement. It needs to specify what is meant by "more value". Resources can be combined in ways that merely make the workers feel happy or they can be combined in ways that merely give managers pleasure. However, managers work within organisations and the phrase "more value" means "more value" in terms of the organisation's goals. When all these ideas are taken into account management can be defined as:

> 66   the activity of getting other people to transform resources so that the results
> add value to the organisation in terms of reaching its organisational goals.   99

As we saw in Case 1.1, despite the fact that Arthur and Karen are working in very different environments (different countries, different industrial sectors and different technologies), the processes they use – planning, organising, staffing, deciding, budgeting – are very similar. The only major difference is that Karen spends time reporting and communicating to others. In both cases, these managers are using other people to transform resources so that the end product has greater value than their inputs.

Indices of managerial effectiveness and types of transformations

In the commercial world organisational goals are usually framed in monetary terms. The effectiveness of managers is often gauged by the percentage return on capital. For example, a manager who uses £1 million of resources to produce a product worth £1.2 million will, other things being equal, be a better manager than one who uses £1 million to produce a product

CRITICAL THINKING 1.1 *Is management necessary?*

People in many organisations, such as hospitals, frequently complain that there are too many managers and management has major **disadvantages**:

- *It consumes a great deal of working time*. Time spent in meetings means that there is less time for direct work. Policy documents and memos also consume time. Further, reports and records are often viewed as distractions.

- *It is expensive*. Managers are often highly paid. It is often argued that it would be better to use this money to employ more operatives, buy better equipment or pay higher salaries.

- *It pursues selfish goals*. Sometimes managers take decisions that benefit their own interests and status (e.g. empire building) rather than adding or behaving fairly.

Sometimes, even effective management is a bad thing because it is used to pursue evil ends such as improving the efficiency of gas chambers or the marketing of fraudulent financial services. A management guru, Peter Drucker, once commented, "So much of what we call management consists in making it difficult for people to work".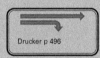

Drucker p 496

Although these arguments are persuasive, management has two *huge* **advantages**:

- *It enables big achievements*. Management often enables the work of very large numbers of people to be co-ordinated so they can achieve things beyond the reach of individuals or small amorphous groups.

- *It increases efficiency and reduces waste*. This means that resources can be conserved or used to create extra value.

These huge advantages mean that management is clearly necessary. If management is abandoned totally our lives would revert to a Neathandrial existence. So, it is best to use management with care. Leading thinkers such as Peter Drucker conclude that management is an evil necessity!

worth £1.1 million. Similarly, a managing director who takes over a company that is valued at £50 million and turns it into a company worth £55 million after one year is, other things being equal, a better managing director than one who takes over the same company and destroys value so that it is worth only £45 million one year later.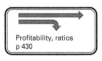

Profitability, ratios p 430

In many situations, financial indices are far too crude. They need to be supplemented by other information such as the number of people managed. The value added per employee is a common index of a manager's efficiency. For example, a manager who employs five people to convert £1 million of resources to products worth £1.2 million is probably doing a better job than a manager who employs 20 people to convert £1 million of resources to products worth £1.2 million – even though they add the same value (£200 000). Each person employed by the first manager is adding £40 000 value per year, while each person employed by the second manager is adding only £5 000 – probably not enough to cover their wages and other costs. Unless the second manager is able to obtain a subsidy from the government or other parts of the organisation, their unit will not be viable and the 20 jobs will eventually disappear – with enormous consequences for the 20 employees and their families.

Value added per emploee p 307

These examples have been drawn from the commercial world because they are clear. Similar indices can be used in other types of organisation but value will be expressed in non-monetary units. For example, in the university sector a unit of performance will be FTE (full-time equivalent) per member of staff, in the theatre the unit of performance may be the number in the audience per performance, while in the health sector a hospital manager may be judged on the number of successful operations per surgeon per year. Table 1.1 lists some of the transformations where managers can add value to resources they consume.

Industry	Transformation	Means of transformation
Education	Makes students more valuable by adding to their knowledge, intellectual ability, skills and, perhaps, enjoyment of life	Lectures, tutorials, practicals, books, webinars, tests, exams, etc.
Transport and communication	Alters the position of physical things to a location where they are more valuable	Air-flights, lorry journeys, courier services, postal system
Media	Transmits information from the mind of originator to the mind of someone who finds it valuable	Newspapers, radio, TV, computer games, the Internet
Manufacturing	Changes the physical form of objects or chemicals into a more valued shape	Bending, cutting, joining, heating, assembling, etc.
Storage and warehousing	Holds things until a time when they are more valuable	Warehouses, depots, data stores
Exchange	Transfers the ownership of an object or commodity to someone who places a higher value upon it	Wholesale and retail organisations, merchanting organisations, exchanges such as the Stock Exchange, legal conveyancing
Health care	Removing or ameliorating illnesses	Hospitals, clinics, surgeries
Government	Improving security and infrastructure for the population	Parliaments, councils, armed forces, police services, Quangos

TABLE 1.1 Examples of various management transformations

Management processes, management functions and other perspectives of management

Once the basic concept of management (as the process of organising other people to transform resources so value is added) is understood, many questions arise:

- who are managers?
- where do they work?
- what processes are used to transform resources?
- what are management functions?
- what is involved in a management career? Etc.

This book divides the topic of management into four parts.

In *Part 1* we take **a broad look at managers and the context in which they work**. It considers different types of managers: all managers are not identical and it is essential to know the different types. It also considers the skills that managers need. The next chapter concerns contexts in which managers work:

- the institutional context
- the organisational context
- the international and the global context

There is a fourth important context – the historical context. This is so big that, for convenience, it is given a chapter on its own (Chapter 3).

Part 2 covers **management processes**. They are the *activities* performed by the majority of individual managers in order to transform resources. For example, almost all managers make plans and supervise their staff. The main management processes are planning, organising, staffing and making decisions. Often management processes can be performed adequately without detailed levels of specialist knowledge. For example, a manager may be able to motivate staff without having studied psychology to degree level.

Part 3 covers **management functions**. These are distinct areas *of management practice* that involve only a fraction of all managers. For example, in most large organisations less than 10 per cent of managers are directly involved in marketing or looking after the organisation's money. People working within a management function will usually need specialised training or experience in order to perform the intricate, high-level tasks within their function. For example, a manager in the human resource (HR) function will need specialised training in order to devise an appraisal system that will be applied to the whole organisation. Managers working within a function often belong to relevant professional organisations. For example, a manager working within the HR function is likely to belong to an institute of personnel and will have studied for its qualifications. Similarly a manager working within the finance function is likely a member of an institute of accountancy. The main management functions are marketing, operations, HR, finance and the information function. It is vital to keep the distinction between management process and management functions clear. Some academics use the words interchangeably. But there is a clear distinction in the minds of practising managers. **Management processes** are the activities which individual managers use in order to get other people to transform resources to a greater value. **Management functions** are the ways that managers are grouped within an organisation to achieve specialist tasks.

Part 4 covers two issues that are personal to an individual manager's understanding of management. It includes topics such as behaving ethically, avoiding management 'cons' and evaluating the scientific merit of articles and papers that are written about management.

The interrelationships between these topics is shown in Figure 1.2, which, in effect is a plan of this book. In principle, all management processes are relevant to all management functions, which is why there is a shaded area in Figure 1.2 connecting processes to functions. However, some management processes are particularly relevant to certain functions For example, a manager working within the HR function is likely to spend a large proportion of his or her time on staffing processes, while a manager working within the finance function will spend a large part of their time dealing with budgeting processes – which is why there are arrows indicating explicit links between, say, staffing and HR and budgeting and finance.

Even the complicated structure shown in Figure 1.2 is a simplification. A further perspective is needed – the viewpoint of academic disciplines that underlie many management processes, functions and topics. The main management disciplines are sociology, psychology, economics and quantitative methods. Marketing, for example draws on each discipline. A manager in the marketing function may use economics and sociology to identify unexploited markets. He or she may use psychology to ensure that advertisements

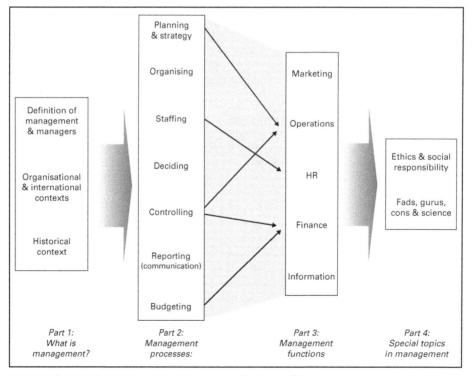

FIGURE 1.2 Relationship between management processes, functions and topics

have the maximum impact in the minds of customers. He or she may also use quantitative methods to predict the number of future sales. Unfortunately, even a superficial treatment of academic functions is impossible in a book of this size. However, textbooks covering academic disciplines are readily available elsewhere. Often these topics are the subject of specific courses at college or university. On their own, these courses can appear fragmented, but if they are related back to Figure 1.2 a unifying framework for the study of management will be clear.

1.2 Varieties of manager

Many schools of management tend to assume that all managers are the same. In fact there are many different kinds of manager. The types of managers can be classified in many ways. The main ones are:

1 *relationship to ownership*: owner managers, entrepreneurs and intrapreneurs

2 *levels in organisation*: junior, middle, senior

3 *relationship to operations*: line, specialist and project managers, and functional and general managers

Managers categorised by *ownership*: owner-managers, entrepreneurs and intrapreneurs

"**Owner-managers**" are, perhaps, the archetypal form of manager where the management and the ownership of the organisation is the same. It was probably the dominant form of management before the Industrial Revolution. However, with the rise of limited companies and government organisations, a specialist cadre of people emerged to manage organisations on behalf of other people. People can own an organisation even when they are patently unsuitable to manage it. Walker and Webster (2006) note that "for many small business owners . . . managerial skills may not be well developed and, more importantly, the recognition of the need to participate in skills development may not be obvious, even though the chances of business survival are higher in business owners who have participated in some form of training or skills development". Perhaps these people have inherited an organisation from previous generations. Perhaps such people have saved money all their lives and have used their savings to purchase an organisation in order to provide an income in retirement. Professional managers, on the other hand, can be selected and trained specifically for the job.

Today most owner-managers exist in small firms and will be involved in most, if not all, activities. They keep their finger on the pulse by walking round the firm and directly observing the state of affairs. As an organisation grows beyond, say, 50 employees, the demands and the complexity of communication are too much for one person to control directly and the organisation will tend to hire professional managers.

Many, but not all, owner-managers started as **entrepreneurs**. An entrepreneur is someone who identifies a business opportunity – by seeing a gap in the market, a technological development or a commercial change. Once the opportunity is identified an entrepreneur will take a moderate risk to initiate a business venture to exploit it. A classic example of an entrepreneur would be James Dyson. He noted that current vacuum cleaners became less efficient as the dust bag filled. He developed a new type of vacuum cleaner that did not need a dust bag. Dyson took a calculated risk and used his own money to fund the early developmental stages. Then he spent considerable time and effort convincing bankers who specialise in funding new developments (venture capitalists) to provide further funds that would pay for later development and the set-up costs for a factory. Other examples of entrepreneurial successes are Amazon book distribution, and Lastminute.com travel reservations. Perhaps the most successful entrepreneur of all time has been Bill Gates, who founded the software colossus Microsoft. There are also many examples of successful entrepreneurs in China and Singapore (Dana, Hamilton and Wick, 2008; Tang, 2010).

CASE 1.2: *A modern entrepreneur – Peter Cuddas*

Peter Cuddas was born in Hackney. His father was a meat porter and his mother an office cleaner. Peter left school at 15 and went to work in the telex room at the Western Union where he would type out instructions to transfer money from one country to another. He learned two important things: how to type and how financial markets worked. He became a trader and prudently saved his bonuses. By the time he was 36 he had paid off the mortgage on his house. He spotted a gap in the market. Most trades in foreign exchanges were so complicated and expensive that few people were able or willing to engage in them. Peter Cuddas invested £10 000 of his savings to set up CMC, an innovative firm that simplified trading and which lowered the cost. In the mid-1990s he grasped the potential of Internet trading. He invested £½ million in IT and broadened its scope to include trading in commodities, shares and currencies. His fairly simple trading system also allowed investors to dabble in more risky products such as contracts for difference. The commission he charges can be as low as 0.1 per cent. Simplicity and low charges attracted huge numbers of customers. His business grew, around the globe. Peter Cuddas is believed to be the richest man in the City of London and he enjoys a very opulent lifestyle. He has also made generous charitable donations and has established a foundation which makes grants to charities that help disadvantaged young people.

Small firms (under 500 employees) account for a disproportionate number of innovations. Birch (2000) suggests that small firms are responsible for 55 per cent of all innovations and 95 per cent of radical innovations. Fast-growing businesses, sometimes nicknamed "gazelles", produce twice as many product innovations per employee as larger firms. Unfortunately, entrepreneurs do not have a guarantee of success. Small entrepreneurial organisations have a high failure rate. Perhaps 60–80 per cent of small businesses fail within five years.

In recent years the importance of entrepreneurs to the economic well-being of a country has been more appreciated. Many large employers have been investing in machinery or moving their factories to countries where labour costs are low. Governments have been looking to entrepreneurs to start up new businesses which will replace the jobs being lost from large organisations.

Entrepreneurs frequently set up businesses in two sectors: business services and restaurants – presumably because the "entry costs" are low in these sectors. They are often "corporate refugees". They have either been the victims when a large organisation has downsized or they are people who feel uncomfortable with the restrictions imposed by corporate life. Whatever their background, entrepreneurs follow one of five main tactics:

1 **Start a new business**: this means the entrepreneur is in total control and can form the business in any way he or she prefers. Starting a new business can take a long time to produce a profit.

2 **Buy an existing business**: an existing business can be obtained fairly cheaply if the former owner wishes to retire or sell the business for other personal reasons. Existing businesses carry much less risk. However, it will be more difficult for entrepreneurs to mould these to their own preferences.

3 **Buy a franchise**: in a franchise an entrepreneur buys the right to produce or distribute a product or service which has already been developed. Franchises carry much less risk than marketing a totally new product (Castrogivanni and Justis, 2007). However, the person taking on the franchise will have much less freedom because he or she will need to operate procedures determined by the owners of the product. Perhaps the most famous franchises are McDonald's, and some hotel chains such as Holiday Inns.

4 **Be incubated**: some venture capitalists, government organisations and universities have incubator units where a number of entrepreneurs are gathered in close proximity, probably in a "science park". The parent organisation provides facilities such as premises and secretarial support in return for a share in the equity. The proximity of other entrepreneurs means that they can share information and business leads.

5 **Be spun off**: sometimes good ideas emerge within organisations. However, it may not be appropriate for the large organisation to exploit the idea. The large organisation may therefore produce a spin-off company which is staffed by its former employees. They usually buy their materials and, perhaps, patents from the parent organisation. The parent organisation may provide support such as guaranteed sales for the entrepreneur's output. A typical spin-off situation would be where an employee of a large glass producer develops a new type of double glazing. A double-glazing unit or division would provide the glass producer with a distraction that could mean a loss of focus from its core activity. The double-glazing company could, however, be spun off. The new company might use the parent as a source from which to buy raw materials and, maybe, to identify contacts as potential customers.

Obtaining sufficient finance is a significant problem for most entrepreneurs. In essence there are two sources of finance: debt financing and equity financing. In **debt financing** (see page 415) an entrepreneur will approach a bank, other institutions or wealthy individuals and obtain the required capital at a rate of interest. Sometimes the money is borrowed from family and friends. If the money is borrowed from commercial sources, the rate of interest may be high because the risk of failure may also be high. Commercial sources of finance are likely to demand extra surety such as a claim on the entrepreneur's house. In **equity financing** (see page 417) money is obtained in exchange for a share in the ownership of the new organisation. Often the funds are provided by venture capital firms such as 3i. If the firm fails the venture capitalists lose money, but if it succeeds they make big profits. Usually a venture capital company will only provide money if it has reasonable expectations of a high rate of return. This is because the return from successful companies must outweigh the losses they might make from unsuccessful ones. However, using a venture capital company brings the additional advantages of advice, It would be wrong to think that all entrepreneurs work in small companies. Some large organisations realise that it is often necessary to act like a small firm. They value the entrepreneurial spirit and give entrepreneurs scope to work (Drucker, 1985). Entrepreneurs who work within a large company are called **intrapreneurs**. Some large organisations take proactive steps to encourage intrapreneurs. They set up small units where groups of people are able to work on new ideas creatively and without formality. Sometimes, these units are called "**skunk works**". Perhaps the best-known skunk work was a fiercely independent and sometimes anarchic unit set up by Apple Computers that developed the famous Macintosh computer which was state-of-the-art and user-friendly.

Financing p 413

Managers categorised by *level* in organisation: first-line managers, middle managers and senior managers

Managers may be divided into first-line managers, middle managers and senior managers.

First-line managers are also called junior managers, supervisors, overlookers, team leaders or foremen/women. First-line managers are responsible for directing the day-to-day activities of operatives. They have substantial spans of control but their range of responsibility is quite narrow. Their responsibility is restricted to ensuring that their team of operatives is achieving performance targets. Often first-line managers will be directly responsible for machinery and materials. The objectives of first-line managers are usually clear. Their success in achieving objectives is clear-cut and apparent within a short period of time (i.e. their **time span of discretion** is low). First-line managers frequently work at a frenetic pace, often needing to attend to a new issue every one or two minutes. An important part of the role of a first-line manager is to listen to the concerns of the people they manage (their **direct reports**) and relay these concerns to more senior managers. Similarly, they need to be aware of the wider organisational objectives and translate these into terms that are relevant and understandable by their direct reports. First-level managers are usually recruited from the ranks of operatives. They would be expected to be able to perform the job they supervise as well as manage it.

CRITICAL THINKING 1.2 *Why do business schools ignore first-line managers?*

First-line managers are the most junior level of management. And their contribution to an organisation cannot be overstated. However, their contribution is often taken for granted or ignored – especially by business schools and theorists.

▶ Look in the index of most management texts and magazines – junior managers are hardly mentioned except in passing. Why is this so? Perhaps the writers lack the practical experience to understand what first-line managers do? Perhaps, writers and academics are a bit snobbish or megalomaniac. Perhaps, the simple truth is that it is easier to write about grand things such as strategy without appreciating the need for someone to translate the strategy into action.

Recently, the role of first-line managers has expanded. They are now expected to perform many of the activities previously required of middle managers. The main reasons are flatter organisational structures, greater use of computer information systems and a marked trend to better training and recruitment of first-line managers.

Middle managers manage first-line managers. They will have titles such as Head of Recruitment or Head of Payroll or even Head of Procurement! One of the major trends in recent years has been reduction in the number of middle managers. Their number has often been reduced by as much as 30 per cent. This has been achieved by using computers to do many middle-management tasks and by training first-line managers to do some (hitherto) middle-management tasks.

The key activities of middle managers are co-ordination and liaison. They transmit information up and down the hierarchy and across the various functions in the organisation. They convert the strategies and objectives set by senior managers into specific actions and plans which must be implemented by first-line managers. Often they are required to find creative ways to achieve objectives. They will have a fairly wide remit and will spend most of their time on organisational activities rather than operations. Middle managers will spend a great deal of time in meetings with other middle managers. The pace of middle management work is less frenetic. Typically they will have about nine minutes to concentrate on a problem before they need to attend to another matter. In some large organisations there may be several layers of middle managers. The four excellent vignettes of middle managers given by Rouleau and Balogun (2010) are a good read!

Senior managers are sometimes called "top managers" or "C-suite managers". They will generally have the word "Chief" in their job title – such as Chief Executive Officer (CEO), "Chief Financial Officer" (CFO) or "Chief Knowledge Officer" (CKO). Senior managers are often called directors, president, chief officer or controller. Except in very large organisations they will report to the most senior person in the organisation, such as the Chairman or the President or the Principal. Senior managers are primarily concerned with future strategy and developing a "vision" for the organisation. They then need to communicate their vision effectively *so that other people within the organisation are motivated towards its achievement.*

Senior managers are responsible for the performance of large units or the organisation as a whole. They need to be particularly sensitive to trends and developments in the outside environment. Much of their time is spent in meetings with other senior managers, important people from the external environment and middle managers, as well as acting as figureheads for the organisation.

> ### CRITICAL THINKING 1.3 *C-suite inflation*
>
> Job titles containing the word "Chief" are very desirable and they seem to be multiplying like rabbits! *The Economist* (2010, 6/26/2010 p 70) calls it "job title inflation". It notes that some companies have *four* CEOs. Southwest Airlines has a Chief Twitter Officer (CTO), Kodak, Coca-Cola and Marriott hotels have Chief Blogging Officers (CBOs) and Kodak also has a Chief Listening Officer (CLO). Someone could offer a prize to the first organisation with both CXO and CZO – whatever they may be.

Managers categorised according to their *relationship with production*: line and specialist managers

Line managers are directly responsible for producing goods or services. Sometimes, they are called "production managers" or "operations managers" but this title should not be interpreted narrowly since most line managers these days produce services rather than material goods. In a factory, the line manager will be the supervisor, the head of the production department or the head of the manufacturing unit. In a call centre, line managers will be the section supervisor, the floor manager and the call centre manager. Line managers' actions play a clear, identifiable part in the performance of the organisation. Often line managers have large spans of control. Many line managers regard themselves has being at the "sharp", "front end" of management.

    Specialist managers are sometimes called staff managers or enabling managers. Typically they are found in finance, HR, purchasing or technical service functions. Specialist managers often have only a narrow range of expertise but, within that restricted range, their knowledge is deep and detailed. For example, a line manager will be one of the first people to notice that productivity has declined and will use their working knowledge to eliminate possible causes (e.g. poor operative training) and to identify obsolete machinery as the major problem. Engineering specialists and financial specialists will then be involved to design a better machine and to obtain necessary money to fund it, although the line manager will retain the central role of co-ordinating their specialist efforts. Some specialist managers may have formal authority over line managers. These usually involve control functions designed to prevent errors – especially when environmental health and safety are involved. They have the power to overrule line managers and, if necessary, shut down production. Similarly, quality control managers will have a right to overrule line managers if they feel that the output is below the required standard.

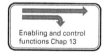

Enabling and control functions Chap 13

    New initiatives and major changes are usually developed and brought to fruition by a **special project team**. For example, a financial services organisation that decides to offer a new tele-banking service would probably set up a team consisting of a line manager from its existing services, an HR specialist, a legal specialist and an IT specialist. This team would meet on a very regular basis to produce plans, organisational structures, procedures and training systems until the new service was up and running. It would then hand over to a line manager and disband. When the organisation undertakes another project a fresh team of different members would be constituted. The person in charge of such a team is usually called a "**project manager**". Sometimes organisations hire special managers who are employed by the organisation only for the time (the interim) it takes to finish a project. This usually occurs when the project requires specialist expertise which is not provided by anyone in the organisation. **Interim managers** are also used when people cannot be spared from their other duties. Interim managers may also be used to substitute for existing managers if they suddenly become unavailable due to ill health or other causes. Interim managers usually have a considerable track record in management which has given them a wide range of experience which they can deploy rapidly and effectively when they are called into a company. Interim managers need to "hit the ground running".

1.3 Skills and abilities needed by managers

The skills needed by managers have been studied by a large number of researchers. Probably the most influential studies have been carried out by Katz, Mintzberg and McClelland. Other important studies have centred upon management competencies and the psychometric qualities of managers.

Katz's three broad skills and management level

Katz (1974) divided management skills into three broad groups:

1 **Conceptual skills**: the ability to view situations broadly, think analytically and to solve problems. Often conceptual skills involve breaking problems into smaller parts and understanding the relationships between these parts. Sometimes this is called a "helicopter view".

2 **Interpersonal skills** involve the ability to work effectively with other people and teams within the organisation. They involve listening carefully to the views of other people and tolerating differing perspectives. Communication is a very important interpersonal skill but others include the ability to motivate people and generate the appropriate psychological atmosphere. Interpersonal skills also embrace political acumen – which is needed to be able to build a power base, establish the right connections and the ability to enhance one's own position.

3 **Technical skills** consist of specialised knowledge of an industry or a process. Technical skills can involve engineering, scientific, financial or legal knowledge. Knowledge of IT systems, markets and commercial procedures are also kinds of technical skill. Often technical skills are obtained initially through formal education and are then developed by formal training.

Figure 1.3 shows how the mix of these three skills changes according to a manager's position in the hierarchy.

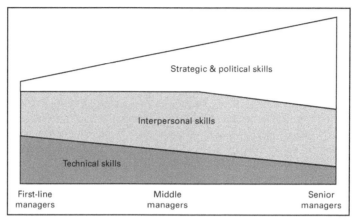

FIGURE 1.3 Changes in management skills according to managerial level

First-line managers require high technical skills in order to get their operatives to transform resources into more valuable products. Good technical skills are often the *basis* for a higher career. However, as a manager rises in the hierarchy, detailed technical skills become less important. A computer programmer, for example, must know the ins and outs of the computer language that is used. However, a chief executive needs a less detailed understanding but he or she must understand the contribution which IT can make to the organisation.

The most important skills for *middle managers* are the interpersonal skills. Many technically competent people who are promoted into middle management fail because their interpersonal skills are insufficient. Sometimes people with brilliant financial skills rise to high positions within an organisation only then to fail because they antagonise so many people that their position becomes untenable. While interpersonal skills assume their maximum importance at middle management level they are also very important at all other levels.

Conceptual and political skills are highly important at *senior levels*. Managers at the top of the organisation encounter complex, ambiguous, longer-term problems. They need to be able to understand the many components of a problem and find accurate, long-term, solutions.

Changes in the skills needed at different management levels cause much heartbreak. First-line managers who have exceedingly good technical ability can become very frustrated when they are passed over for promotion in favour of a colleague who has better interpersonal skills. Similarly, very successful middle managers may be promoted to senior levels only to find that they no longer enjoy their jobs because they do not have conceptual skills.

Katz's analysis has important implications for management training and education. It suggests that introductory courses should focus on technical skills with an appreciation of interpersonal and conceptual skills. Courses for senior managers, however, should focus upon conceptual skills.

Mintzberg and the nature of managerial work

Probably the most famous study of the skills needed by managers was conducted by Henry Mintzberg (1973). His study is a classic example of research using **structured observation**. He observed each of five chief executives for five days. Mintzberg noted that the work of the chief executives was characterised by three features: brevity, variety and fragmentation.

Management work primarily consists of a series of *brief episodes*. Mintzberg carefully recorded the duration of each episode. He found that, on average, each episode would last nine minutes. Less than 10 per cent of managerial episodes last longer than an hour. The average for chief executives included six minutes for each of numerous telephone calls. This was counterbalanced by scheduled meetings which tended to last 68 minutes. By some standards nine minutes is a long time. Previous research into the work of first-line managers (foremen) suggested that they attended to 583 incidents per day – less than one minute for each incident. The duration of a managerial episode seems closely related to the level of management. The more senior the level, the longer the duration of an activity. This is in sharp contrast to the assumptions made by many management educators who emphasise that managers should spend extended periods of analysis and reflection before they take action.

Management work is also characterised by *variety*. This is in contrast to many other jobs such as a general practitioner (GP) The average time a GP devotes to each patient is about nine minutes. But for each patient the GP will be dealing with a medical problem. However, each nine-minute episode completed by a manager is likely to vary from the previous one: the first episode may involve a financial problem; the second may involve a customer; the third may involve disciplining a subordinate; and the fourth may involve a mechanical problem that is affecting production. The range of activities which managers need to complete suggests that their education should be broad and multidisciplinary with a wide range of knowledge and skills.

The third characteristic of managerial work is *fragmentation*. Managers are rarely able to complete a task in one go. Often, they will spend nine minutes dealing with a problem – perhaps by ascertaining the nature of the situation and requesting further information. They will then deal with several totally different issues. Later in the day they may return to the initial problem, absorb the new information and request further clarification. The problem will be revisited, perhaps during the next day, when a decision will be made. Mintzberg also noticed that managers *prefer live* action. They much prefer talking to people and observing situations. They dislike static, formal and written work. Much of this dislike was based upon the fact that formal media are slow. With the possible exception of email, by the time a written report is composed, typed and checked it is likely to be out of date. Further, people are more circumspect when writing things down: they are more likely to be diplomatic and disguise the true facts and causes.

Mintzberg noticed that managers routinely perform 10 major roles. He groups the roles under three major headings:

Interpersonal roles centre upon dealing with other people:

   1 **Figurehead**: this is probably the most basic managerial role. Most managers act as a symbol of their unit because they have the formal responsibility. They are therefore

obliged to perform a ceremonial duties such as welcoming guests or presenting retirement presents. In other cases a manager must formally sign legal documents.

2 **Leader**: it is a manager's responsibility to induce people to do things they would otherwise let lapse. They must inform, motivate and guide subordinates to perform activities that contribute to the organisation's goals. A manager must act as a role model for his or her subordinates.

3 **Liaison**: managers have a vital function in linking their own group to other groups. Their role in vertical communication (forming a channel between their own subordinates and senior management) is demonstrated in most organisational charts. With middle and senior managers the vertical communication role is masked by the importance of horizontal communication. A large proportion of a middle manager's time is taken up by liaising with other middle managers in the same organisation. A large proportion of a senior manager's time involves liaising with senior people from other organisations. Often this is a source of complaint from junior managers who frequently feel that senior managers should spend more time liaising with them.

Informational roles involve the key management activities of obtaining and receiving information. Once information has been obtained it must be passed on to people who can use it. Informational roles are:

4 **Monitor**: managers are continuously seeking information about the performance of their **area of responsibility** (**AoR**). They do this by making frequent, informal tours of inspection (walking the job), discussions with other people and by reading trade press. Further, they are bombarded with information from suppliers, customers, regulatory authorities (e.g. health and safety) and other stakeholders. They must sift information to identify relevant trends.

5 **Disseminator**: once information has been collected it must be transmitted to subordinates for action.

6 **Spokesperson**: a spokesperson is similar to a disseminator but, while the disseminator directs information internally within the organisation, a spokesperson directs information outside the organisation to keep the general public informed. The chances are it will be a manager, and probably a senior manager, who performs this task.

Decisional roles concern the choices made in the allocation of resources, the direction to follow and how to negotiate with other organisations.

7 **Entrepreneur**: a manager often acts as an initiator and designer of change. Often the entrepreneurial roles stem from a manager's ability to authorise action. This allows them to spot opportunities and to galvanise their unit into appropriate action.

8 **Disturbance handler**: unforeseen events may send progress violently off-target. A disturbance handler takes action to get progress back on track. Typical disturbances are sudden departure of staff, accidents such as a fire or when a major customer takes their business elsewhere. Disturbances usually have a sudden onset and managers usually give them priority. Often the first reaction is to "buy time", which is used to find a solution.

9 **Resource allocator**: usually a manager has more possibilities than their resources can match. They therefore exercise judgement when allocating resources to some activities and not to others. This power gives a manager ultimate control without the necessity of being involved in the detailed preparatory work. The process of delegation involves considerable power because it contains the authority to choose one individual over another. The choice process communicates to the whole unit the preferences a manager will reward. Delegation is a clear manifestation of power because the manager can give the work to a second person if the first choice does not live up to expectations.

10 **Negotiator**: a manager will nearly always be involved in a major negotiation with an external organisation. Normally the manager will lead the other negotiators. In part the negotiation role flows from the role of figurehead, but it also involves the spokesperson and the resource allocator roles since only a manager can commit the resources that are implicit in the negotiated solutions.

McClelland and managerial needs

David McClelland (1971) was interested in managers' needs. He was particularly interested in achievement motivation. Achievement motivation is the need to do something quicker, better or more efficiently. McClelland maintained that if a society had a high proportion of people who were motivated by achievement the society would grow faster. Using an ingenious method of gauging motivation by analysing street ballads he was able to show that the Industrial Revolution in the UK was preceded, 50 years earlier, by a surge in the level of achievement motivation of the British population. Similarly, the relative economic decline of Britain in the first part of the twentieth century was preceded, 50 years earlier, by a fall in the level of achievement motivation in the British population.

McClelland studied achievement motivation in executives of companies in the USA, Finland, the UK, India and Australia. He obtained a very robust finding. Companies who had executives with high level of achievement motivation made more innovations, filed more patent applications and grew faster. McClelland was also interested in the motives for power and affiliation. He found that people who rose to senior levels in large organisations showed a distinct motivational pattern which he called the **Leadership Motivation Profile** (**LMP**). People who rise to the top of large organisations tend to have a high need for power, a moderate need for achievement and a low need for affiliation.

Managerial competencies

During the 1980s many organisations were keen to identify the skills, abilities, attitudes and other characteristics which made managers competent at their jobs. Boyatzis (1982) called these attributes "competencies". Organisations tried to determine the competencies needed so that they could recruit people who already had the required competencies or who could be trained to achieve them. Many organisations produced their own list of competencies. The lists used different words to describe the competencies but often they were referring to the same attributes. Bristow (2001) analysed the lists which were used by over 60 different organisations. Table 1.2 is based on his results.

20 **Part 1:** What is management?

Competency	Components	%
1 Communication	Written communication, oral communication	97
2 Self-management	Personal effectiveness, self-control, self-discipline, self-confidence, resilience	75
3 Organisational ability	Organisational awareness, delegation, control, structure	68
4 Influence	Impact others, networking, negotiation	67
5 Teamwork	Team membership, team leadership	60
6 Interpersonal skills	Relationships, dealing with individual people	58
7 Analytical ability	Conceptual thinking, problem-solving	58
8 Results orientation	Achievement focus, concern for effectiveness	55
9 Customer focus	Customer service, customer orientation	53
10 Develop people's potential	Enabling others, coaching	53
11 Strategic ability	Vision, breadth of view, forward thinking	52
12 Commercial awareness	Business acumen, market awareness, competitor awareness	48
13 Decision-making	Decisiveness, evaluating options	48
14 Planning	Planning and organising, action planning, task planning	40
15 Leadership	Providing purpose and direction, motivating others	40
16 Self-motivation	Enthusiasm for work, achievement drive, commitment, energy, drive, will to win	35
17 Specialist knowledge	Expertise, professional knowledge, functional expertise, operational understanding	35
18 Flexibility	Adaptability, mental agility	32
19 Creativity	Innovation, breakthrough thinking	32
20 Initiative	Proactivity	31
21 Change orientation	Change management, openness to change	23

22 Dealing with information	Information gathering, information processing	20
23 Concern for quality	Quality focus, concern for excellence	20
24 Reliability	Accuracy, disciplined approach, procedural compliance, attention to detail, systematic	18
25 Ethical approach	Integrity, commitment to social and economic equity, valuing people	13
26 Financial awareness	Financial judgement, cost awareness	12
27 Negotiating skills		7
Other		15

TABLE 1.2 Competencies demanded of graduates

Interpersonal skills dominate the competencies a manager needs. (This conclusion is supported by the Chartered Institute of Personel Development's *Learning and Development Survey 2009* (CIPD, 2009a) which identify interpersonal and communication skills as the most important attributes for recruits.) Seven of the top 10 competencies concern relations with other people. Communication skills are particularly important and tower above all other competencies. This suggests that the priority in both self-development and management training should be given to interpersonal and intra-personal skills. Once these competencies have been developed, precedence should then be given to organisational skills, analytical ability and a results orientation.

Psychometric profiles of managers

Managers have been completing psychometric tests of intelligence and personality for many years as part of a selection procedure or career counselling. The results reveal a consistent pattern.

Managers need to be more intelligent than average and their intelligence score correlates with their managerial level. The average IQ score for the population as a whole is 100. Typically, a first-line manager will have an IQ of about 109 which would put them in the top 27 per cent of the population. A typical middle manager will have an IQ of about 119 (top 10 per cent of the population) while a typical senior manager will have an IQ of about 124 (top 5 per cent of the population). This pattern is not perfect and there will be a spread of scores either side of these averages. Nevertheless, "tests of cognitive ability", commonly known as intelligence tests, are good predictors of management ability. Personality tests are moderately good predictors of managerial performance but there is a wider spread of scores about the averages. Personality is more complex and difficult to measure. Research indicates that there are five main aspects of personality. They are:

- extroversion (relating to people)
- stability (feelings and emotions)

- conscientiousness
- tough-mindedness
- openness to new ideas

CRITICAL THINKING 1.4 *What? No Freudian personality?*

You might be surprised that this section on the personality of managers makes no reference to the ideas such as the id, the ego and the superego that were "invented" by Sigmund Freud. Today, few psychologists regard Freud as much more than a historical curiosity. Indeed, some such as Crews (2003) regard Freud as an unscientific fraud who "reconstructed" a few famous case studies to fit his theories. For example, it is claimed that he mis-diagnosed a case of tuberculosis as a psychological illness (conversion reaction). Medawar (1975) suggested that the psychoanalytic theory of personality was a most stupendous intellectual confidence trick of the twentieth century. Nevertheless, some academics continue to promulgate his theories despite the lack of substantial evidence. Old theories die hard – especially when they tell a simplified but interesting story. Another example of a theory which persists without much empirical support is Maslow's hierarchy of needs, which is discussed in Chapter 7.

Typically managers, especially production managers, tend to be *moderate extroverts*. They are lively and sociable without going "over the top". Moderate extroverts enjoy jobs involving a variety of tasks and where they need to make quick practical decisions involving people. This is consistent with Mintzberg's view that the managerial job involves brevity, variety and fragmentation. There are, however, some exceptions to this rule. Managers of specialist functions such as R&D, quality control or finance may be less extroverted and perhaps even a little introverted.

Managers are usually *emotionally stable*. This enables them to cope with a torrent of emotional situations and gives them the resilience to bounce back after setbacks. Again, there are some exceptions to this rule. Project managers and some managers in the finance function may have average stability and may even be a little "touchy".

Almost all managers are *conscientious*. They have a sense of duty and they have a clear self-image to which they adhere. This often means that they are reliable and their work is well organised and considerate of other people. The few exceptions to this rule are usually seen in managers working in highly competitive, dealing or merchanting situations.

Finally, managers tend to be moderately *tough-minded* – they are prepared to take responsibility, push proposals through and get things done. They will face conflict but they will not actively seek it.

The level of *open-mindedness* is often related to the industry in which they work. Traditional industries which are "close-coupled" to the market and which produce a fairly standard product with high efficiency and at low cost tend to suit people with a personality that is down to earth and focuses on concrete information. On the other hand, academia, the media, advertising and fashion industries tend to favour a personality that exults in new ideas.

Writers such as Dumaine (1993) believe that the skills needed by managers are changing in order to match contemporary demands. Table 1.3 shows the contrasts between what Dumaine calls the old manager and the new manager.

Old manager	New manager
Thinks of self as manager or boss	Thinks of self as sponsor, team leader or internal consultant
Follows chain of command	Deals with anyone necessary to do job
Works within existing structure	Changes structure according to environment
Makes decisions alone	Involves others in decisions
Hordes information	Shares information
Masters single discipline, e.g. finance or marketing	Masters broad array of disciplines
Demands long hours	Demands results

TABLE 1.3 Differences between old and new managers

1.4 Careers in management

Understanding management careers is important because the behaviour of managers differs according to their career stage. Furthermore most management careers have had drastic changes in the last decade and these changes have had big impacts on individual and organisations. Indeed, career development is a major preoccupation of most managers. In 2007 Velthouse and Kadogan asked managers to rank management issues in order of importance. Career development was in seventh place out of 22 issues – higher than planning, ethics and diversity. A good understanding of the importance of careers can be obtained by first studying traditional careers and then studying modern management careers.

Traditional management careers

Traditional management careers tended to follow a standard path such as those described by Super (1990), Levinson (1986) or Schein (1978) and they are described in more detail on the website that accompanies this book. Super's career stages are the best known and they are shown in Figure 1.4.

24   **Part 1:** What is management?

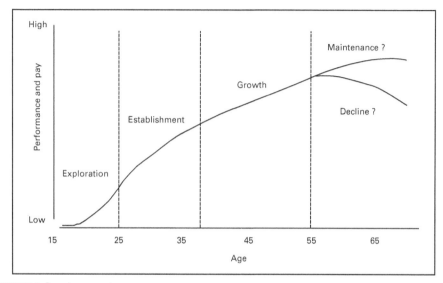

FIGURE 1.4 Super's career stages

Super envisaged adult careers as passing through four main stages. From the age of leaving education until about the age of 25 many people explore a range of jobs without much commitment. Super calls this stage the stage of exploration. At about the age of 25 people settle down and build up experience as individual performers in, say, a single management function. In the mid-thirties people have often shown their ability and they are promoted to managing a group of people. They extend the range of their expertise into, say, two additional functions so that by the time they are 47 they will be regarded as broad-based managers who are knowledgeable in three or more functional areas. From the age of 47 the upward trajectory continues for a while but there is soon a divergence. People either continue to maintain their position or they start to decline. Those who maintain their position will expand their experience into extra functions, slowly arriving at the point when they have *some* experience in a majority of functions. Alternatively, those who decline will lose out in relative terms as the organisation and the world moves on. They will be analogous to the person who steps off an escalator that is moving onwards. Often the clearest examples of Super's stages were seen in bureaucracies where there is a strict ladder of promotion and progression. Such careers are known as **bureaucratic careers**.

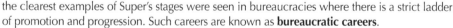

Management
functions Chap 13

Modern management careers

Super, Levinson and Schein formed their ideas in middle of the twentieth century when careers were fairly predictable, stable and **bureaucratic** careers. However, the rate of organisational change in the 1980s and 1990s bought about major changes. Modern careers are much less stable. People often stay in a job for less than four years before they either change employer or type of work. Nowadays people can expect as many as 10 job changes and several episodes of redundancy during a career. Handy (1989) likened today's world of work to a shamrock in which there are three types of worker (Figure 1.5). There is a small group that forms an inner core of an organisation. They have permanence and stay with an organisation over long periods. They largely conform to the traditional pattern of bureaucratic careers. There is also a contractual fringe of people who are employed on a fee-paying basis for specific pieces of work. Often, they are employed on a repeat-contract basis, working for many organisations. Finally, there are the hired helps – people who are employed on a casual basis, when and where the need arises.

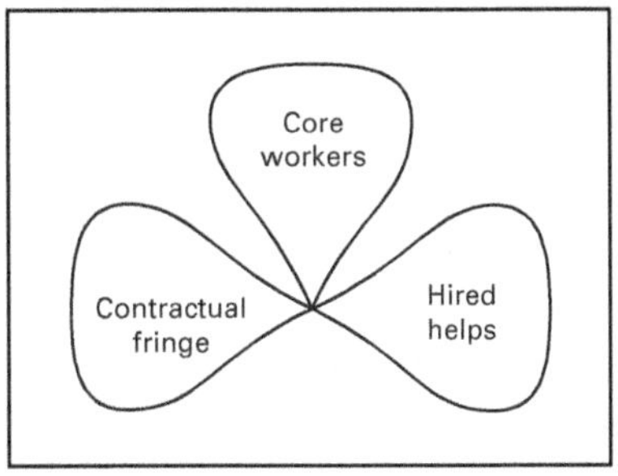

FIGURE 1.5 Handy's shamrock

This relative impermanence of employment has important implications. In the past long-term employees were key organisational assets. It was in the organisation's interests to develop and improve their skills and abilities. Nowadays, this logic is less forceful. Why spend money on developing managers when, in four year's time, they will be working for someone else? The responsibility has shifted. Today, it is the individual who must ensure that their skills and experience improve so they will be able to obtain the next job or contract. People need to ensure their own "**employability**".

Arthur and Rouseau (1996) used the term **boundaryless** to describe such careers because there seemed to be few boundaries – there is high job mobility across employers and between different types of employment. People would use their networks of contacts to find different and new employment. Often, career moves were lateral rather than upwards. Many people in boundaryless careers enjoyed less certainty and gave less loyalty. A boundaryless career is characterised by two dimensions: physical mobility (from employer to employer); and psychological mobility (from one type of work to another). Hall (1996) observed the same trends but characterised careers in a slightly different way. He identified a **protean career –** after the Greek sea-god who would change his character in order to avoid someone capturing him and telling him what to do. A protean career is the one where the person, not the organisation is in charge. As in Schein's work a person's subjective core values are the main criteria. A protean career is also characterised by two main dimensions: the degree to which it is driven by *values* and the degree to which it is *self-directed*. The progress of protean careers is shown in Figure 1.6 (Based on Hall, 1996), which can be compared with Super's career stages given in Figure 1.4.

A typical career span has now shifted upwards and spans, say 20–70 years rather than 15–65. Also there are four or more related but distinct sub-careers. Each sub-career shows a recurrent sequence of exploration, trial, establishment, mastery and further exploration in

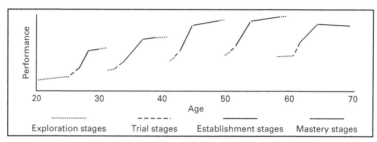

FIGURE 1.6 Protean careers

anticipation of the next career move. There are, however, subtle differences in the stages at different ages. For examples, the trial stage during a person's twenties is likely to be longer than in later years and the establishment stages are particularly steep during a person's forties and fifties.

CASE 1.3: *Duncan Bannatyne's protean career?*

The career of Duncan Bannatyne, entrepreneur and celebrity "angel" on BBC's *Dragon's Den,* is usually quoted as an example of a career that does not follow a customary path. From a relatively modest background he joined the Navy at the age of 15 but was dishonourably discharged at the age of 20. He then tried a number of jobs which included welding, bakery and the car trade. At the age of 29 he started his entrepreneurial career by purchasing an ice-cream van. He grew this business and sold it at a profit. He then moved on to other areas such as nursing homes and finally health clubs, bars, hotels and property. He has also worked as a writer and television star. In addition, he has made notable contributions to charities such as a hospice for Romanian orphans and Comic Relief. Certainly his career has been restricted by few boundaries. Further, proteus-like, he has changed his career in a fluid and flexible way.

However, it can also be claimed that his career has followed a trajectory in line with Super's career model – exhibiting great flexibility *exploring* many different kinds of career up to the age of 29. Then he became an entrepreneur and an entrepreneur he has remained the rest of his life. Perhaps he was a little late settling down: many men make their fundamental choice of career at about the age of 25. Bannatyne *established himself* as an entrepreneur during that time when he owned the nursing homes. The main period of *growth* in his fortune occurred between his late thirties and his mid-fifties. In the last five years he has been successful in *maintaining* and even improving his career.

This introduction to managerial careers has been very brief and has only focused upon crucial concepts. Practical advice on topics such as:

- getting a job
- managing your boss
- getting promotion

CRITICAL THINKING 1.5 *What's the use of management books?*

Superb managers such as Bolton, Watt or Richard Branson, were very successful even though they have never read a management book or studied management at college or university. Catastrophic managers, such as Skilling, CEO of Enron (USA's largest corporate failures) and Stanley O'Neill (CEO who steered Merrill Lynch into the disastrous sub-prime market), read many management texts while studying for their MBAs at Harvard Business School

Practical experience influences about a third of managerial success by giving direct exposure to management situations. In particular, it teaches how to implement specific projects and procedures. However, practical experience has two major disadvantages:

- *It is often very slow* and it takes many years to amass enough, especially when practical experience is accumulated in just one or two organisations.
- *It may provide a very limited perspective.* Managers may become very proficient in a limited range of situations but have little knowledge of other circumstances. They may develop a bigoted view that their limited perspective is universal. This may reduce their ability to adapt.

Management texts can play a small role in developing practical experience by giving practical cases and "toolkits" of practical tips.

Management texts usually contain a great deal of information which reinforces lectures and seminars and they can help obtain higher grades. They also give a wide, more flexible, view of management. Good textbooks have two further advantages:

- *They develop critical thinking which is a paramount skill.* Texts can give examples of flawed thinking and can outline scientific principles to evaluate management research.
- *They explain principles of ethics and social responsibility* that are often unclear when embroiled with practical, day-to-day activities.

Management texts have a useful role, especially for students who are keen to obtain good grades. In practice, however, texts need to be supplemented by experience and a substantial helping of good luck.

- making success of a promotion
- winding up a career

is given in the website *www.mcgraw-hill.co.uk/textbooks/mikesmith* that accompanies this book.

This chapter has focused closely upon the essential nature of management work, the ways that the different types of managers can be classified. It has also described some of the key characteristics that managers need. These are absolutely crucial elements in understanding management. Despite their importance they are inadequate. Management does not occur in a vacuum. It occurs within various contexts and these contexts play a very important part in determining the shape and form that management takes. There are at least four important contexts:

- the types of organisation in which managers work
- the organisational context
- the international context
- the historical context

Each of these contexts needs to be understood in greater detail. The types of organisation, the organisational context and the international context are discussed in Chapter 2. Dumaine's work highlights the fact that management is not static. It changes over time. In order to understand management it is necessary to have a basic knowledge about its history and how it has changed in the past. The historical context of management is discussed in Chapter 3.

Activities and further study

Essay plans

Prepare plans for the following essays:

1 Compare and contrast the work of managers and non-managers.
2 Compare and contrast management processes with management functions
3 To what extent are managers, and their work, the same?
4 What skills and abilities do managers need in order to perform their work effectively?

Compare your plans with those given on the website associated with this book.

Web activities

1 Go to the website associated with this book and download the spreadsheet containing a sample of 100 activities performed by managers. Use the adjacent column on the spreadsheet to classify each activity according to its management process. Use the initials:

P = planning
O = organising
S = staffing
D = deciding
C = controlling
R = reporting (communicating)
B = budgeting (money and time)

Use the sort function to rearrange the activities according to the management process involved. Work out the percentage of time that managers spend on each process and answer the following questions:

- Which two activities take up most management time?
- The sample of a hundred activities was obtained from managers in manufacturing. To what extent would you expect the results to differ if the sample had been obtained from managers in a service industry?
- To what extent would you expect results to differ according to the level of managers involved?

Compare your answers with those given on the website associated with this book.

2 Use the Web to research the career of an entrepreneur in whom you are interested.

3 Self-management is a key skill which is not covered in depth in this book. Spend an hour surfing Youtube viewing appropriate clips. Remember, time management is an important skill. Some appropriate clips might be:

- how to keep a job: self management skills
- Daryl Cross – time management
- time management and the 80–20 rule
- 10 time management tips
- YP – Young Professional Time Management Tips
- why time management doesn't work

Experiential activities

1 Form a discussion group to examine one or more of the following topics:

- the changes that have occurred in management work during the past 40 years (i.e. during the working life of someone who is just retiring)
- the changes that are likely to occur in management work during the next 40 years (i.e. during the working life of someone who is just starting a career)
- the skills needed for management work (start by brainstorming the skills and competencies needed) and writing them on a flip chart. Then list the skills and competencies according to their importance. Finally, compare your group's list with list of competencies from organisations – for example, see the list on page 20

2 Interview a manager (use your network of friends and relatives to identify someone who would help) and ask about:

- the people they supervise
- the people to whom they are responsible
- the way they spend their time at work

On the basis of this information decide whether they are junior, middle or senior managers. Also decide whether they are general or specialist managers. You should also identify the function (e.g. marketing, operations, finance, HR, etc.) in which they work. Check your decisions by asking your interviewee to name their management level and their management function.

3 Arrange (perhaps with the help of your college, university or careers service) to observe a practising manager at work for one or two days. In advance of your visit read Henry Mintzberg's (1973) book *The Nature of Managerial Work* (or at least a summary of it!). Keep notes on the roles that the manager occupies and the duration of his or her "working episodes". Compare your notes with the findings by Mintzberg.

Recommended reading

Recommended readings will improve your understanding and be useful for assignments, seminars and tutorials. They will also guide your personal development and career.

1 Mintzberg, H.H. (1973) *The Nature of Managerial Work*, New York: Harper and Row. An old but classic text that has stood the test of time. It is usually sufficient to:

- quickly read the sections on the different management schools. Make a mental note of the general contents so that you can refer to them in the future
- read (but do attempt to memorise) the sections describing the 10 major management roles
- read the sections on brevity, variety and preference for action

A long read – at least four hours – interesting and of average difficulty. Highly recommended.

2 Rouleau, L. and Balogun, J. (2010) "Middle managers, strategic sense making and discursive competence", *Journal of Management Studies*, early view, 30 March. Gives four vignettes of entrepreneurs and the tasks of middle managers. Useful for seminars.

3 Katz, R.L. (1974) "Skills of an effective administrator", *Harvard Business Review*, **52** (94). Another classic text, which will help you understand the different levels of management and the skills that they require.

4 Hall, D.T. (1996) "Protean careers of the 21st century", *Academy of Management Executive*, **10** (4), 8–16. An excellent article which contrasts careers as viewed by Super with modern careers. Particularly good for developing your own career and understanding modern management.

5 Hindle, T. (2008) *Guide to Management Ideas and Gurus,* London: Economist Books. This is like an encyclopedia where management topics and leading thinkers are arranged in alphabetical order. It is easy reading. Highly recommended and relevant to all chapters. If you are studying management for more than a year, this book would be a good buy!

Chapter TWO

Organisational Structures and Teamwork

Chapter contents

❖ LEARNING OBJECTIVES

After studying this chapter you should be able to suggest ways of structuring jobs, managing teams and arranging them into an organisation. In particular, you should be able to:

❖ **define** the organising process and **differentiate** between formal organisational structures and informal ones

❖ **explain** how you would design a job using the concepts of: division of labour – authority and responsibility– span of control – ergonomics

❖ **describe** the types of teams, team roles and the factors that make teams effective

❖ **describe** the following ways of scheduling work: flexitime – compressed working week – homeworking and teleworking – job sharing – contingency working – office sharing and hoteling

❖ **briefly explain** the concept of functional organisational structures and **differentiate** between tall and flat structures

❖ **briefly explain** the concept of divisional structures and **itemise** the three main ways of creating divisions

❖ **draw a diagram** of a matrix organisational structure

❖ **draw a diagram** of network organisational structures

❖ **explain** the concepts of learning structures and itemise their five main characteristics

❖ **draw up a substantive table** that systematises the advantages of functional, divisional, matrix and team structures

❖ **itemise** four ways of co-ordinating the activities teams within an organisation

❖ **itemise** five main dimensions of organisational structure

---

CASE 5.1: *Organisational restructuring at Pilkington in Australia*

Pilkington is a world-renowned maker of glass, now owned by Nippon Sheet Glass. One of its manufacturing plants is in Dandenong, Australia.

The factory had a very traditional organisational structure with workers at the bottom and senior managers at the top. The normal flow of information was from the top downwards. Top management set standards and objectives which were then communicated down the hierarchy. This structure resulted in many employees feeling they were given orders by managers who had little knowledge of things that were happening on the "factory floor". The hierarchical structure was largely responsible for strong divisions between "them and us". Labour relations were poor and at the time the plant was shut by strike action. The plant was also losing its competitive advantage against other glass-makers.

Pilkington decided to implement major changes in the organisation at Dandenong. Work was reorganised into three business units: making, cutting and warehousing. Within these divisions employees were organised into work teams which participated in setting standards and working methods. The main information flow was reversed and passed from employees to team leaders to team supervisors and upwards to the plant manager.

An evaluation showed that the changes in organisational structure had resulted in higher morale, greater industrial harmony, higher customer satisfaction and increased employee productivity.

Source: based on B. Barrett, C. Cook and M. Williams Pilkington, "An organisation in transition" http://www.thomsonlearning.com.au/higher/management/waddell/2e/media/Case_Pilkington.pdf.

In a one-person set-up there is no need for organisation: the one person does everything. As soon as more people are involved the process of organising becomes essential–otherwise people will complete tasks at random using whatever resources are at hand and in ignorance of what others are doing. Chaos will ensue. While *planning* determines *what* tasks need to be done in what sequence, *organising* determines *who* completes the tasks and the *resources needed*. Planning and organising are interrelated. For example, many action plans involve a certain amount of organising.

The subject of organising includes a number of interesting topics such as team-working, organisational change and organisational structures which can be studied in isolation. However, it is much better to cover them in a logical order. The obvious starting point is to *define the process of organising* and to *recognise the two main branches, formal and informal organisation*. The most basic aspects of work are the activities that need to be performed in order to add value. Hence, the most basic aspect is to organise these activities into jobs (i.e. *job design*). The next stage is to arrange the jobs into coherent groups that can be performed by *teams of people*. In their turn, teams of people can be placed within an *organisational structure* that helps deliver its strategy. Unfortunately, the world is not static and even a good initial organisational structure will need to be amended to suit a different business environments. Hence the subject of organising does not finish with a study of the

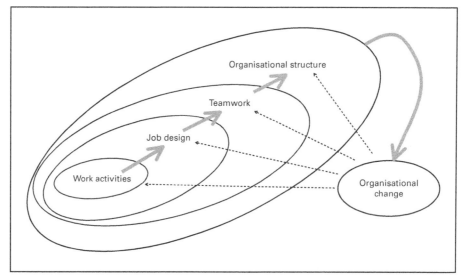

FIGURE 5.1 The relationship between the subtopics of the organisational process

organisational structure. It finishes, instead, with the topic of *organisational change*. This logical arrangement of organising is shown in Figure 5.1.

The topics interact with each other. For example, organisational change will influence the activities that are performed, the way that teams function and the way an organisation is structured. The six topics cover a great deal of information. In order to make it easier to absorb, they are split into two chapters. This chapter covers the first four of these topics. The next chapter deals with organisational change and all its uncertainties.

5.1 Definition of organising and organisational structures

Many definitions do not make the distinction between planning and organising sufficiently clear. One of the clearest definitions is:

> 66 Organising is the process of determining who will perform the tasks needed to achieve organisational objectives, the resources to be used and the way the tasks will be managed and co-ordinated. 99

Four points from this definition need to be noted. Organising:

- **Is *not* primarily concerned with specifying goals and tasks**. However, the way in which things are organised will have a bearing on the tasks which can be attempted and the degree to which they are achieved.
- **Is concerned with the allocation of the tasks** to specific people or groups of people.

- **Is concerned with the co-ordination of the efforts** of several people needed to complete large tasks.
- **Concerns resources and other people**. It may involve budgets, territories, production facilities or intellectual abilities.

Many of the issues concerning organisational structure were illustrated in Case 5.1.

5.2 Formal and informal organisational structures

An *organisation chart* is a representation of an organisation's formal structure – the official arrangement of work positions within an organisation. The distinction between the *formal* organisation and the *informal* organisation is important but, when set up, they may be very similar. In practice the formal structure is soon modified by friendships, the personalities of individuals and the networks which develop. The "grapevine" is an important component of an informal organisation. The informal organisation often allows people to use shortcuts and obtain information or take action which would otherwise be impossible and is particularly important during times of change and stress. The informal organisation meets the psychological needs of individuals. However, the informal side of organisations has disadvantages: it may take on a life of its own and work towards goals which are different from the formal goals: information "on the grapevine" may be inaccurate or distorted; and informal organisation can be used to exclude certain people and their ideas. The formal organisation is made up of jobs and the structure in which the jobs are placed. The first step in understanding the formal structure of an organisation is to understand the fundamentals of job design.

The grapevine p 287

5.3 Job design

The most fundamental aspect of organising is to decide what people are required to do as part of their job. This process is called *job design*. Six main aspects need to be considered:

1 specialisation
2 authority
3 span of control
4 ergonomics
5 work schedules and
6 worker involvement in job design

Specialisation and division of labour

Job design assumes that some workers will specialise in certain activities while other workers will specialise in different ones. *Specialisation* means that each worker only does a part of what is needed to make a product, deliver a service or complete a task. It is sometimes called *division of labour*. Up to a point it leads to greater efficiency and economies of scale because:

- Individuals can quickly develop high level of skills in certain activities.
- People can be employed in those activities where they have natural ability. Their potential can be exploited more fully.
- Employees do not waste time changing from task to task.
- Jobs are often simplified and can be allocated, at less cost, to workers with lower skills.

Extreme specialisation is seen in some assembly lines where employees are required to do a single task, repetitively, but with a high level of speed and efficiency. Unfortunately, high levels of specialisation have disadvantages:

- Highly specialised jobs are boring and tend to demotivate people. Employees rarely see a finished product; they tend to have no pride in their work.
- Teamwork and creativity are inhibited.
- Employees only have a restricted range of skills. They cannot be redeployed to deal with bottlenecks elsewhere. Further, these employees are vulnerable to changes. When changes occur these employees are likely to be dismissed or need retraining.

In general, job design seeks to achieve a balance between the advantages and disadvantages of specialisation. Figure 5.2 indicates that optimum productivity is achieved at intermediate levels of specialisation.

Jobs should be designed to avoid negative effects of specialisation and include factors which motivate workers. Hackman and Oldham (1980) suggest that people will be motivated if a job:

- Requires the use of different skills rather than the repetitive use of one or two skills (*skill variety*).

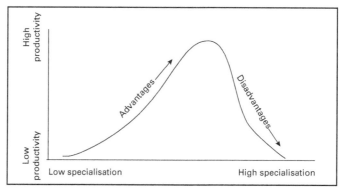

FIGURE 5.2 Specialisation and productivity

- Allow a person to do a complete job rather than a small part. Workers are then more likely to be motivated by a sense of pride (*task identity*).

- Allows people to understand the contribution their work makes to the goals of the organisation or its importance to colleagues or customers (*task significance*)**.**

- Gives freedom, discretion and independence in the way that the work has to be done – providing that the correct results are achieved (*autonomy*).

- *Provides feedback* on a worker's effectiveness. Sometimes feedback is *extrinsic* in the sense that people are told by others how well they are performing. In other jobs feedback is *intrinsic* because the job itself provides information about success or failure.

Often these principles are applied to improve specialised jobs which are believed to be demotivating. The jobs are examined using a special questionnaire and those areas that are found to be deficient are improved by, say, including new activities or developing a systematic method of feedback.

It is widely recognised that, nowadays, the greatest asset of most organisations is the knowledge generated and held by its employees. Many jobs should therefore be designed so that expanding and recording the organisation's knowledge base is an explicit component. Knowledge management is explained in more detail in Chapter 18.

Knowledge management p 452

Authority and responsibility

Authority is the formal power to make decisions, marshal resources and give instructions to others. Authority is a characteristic of a job rather than a characteristic of an individual – it remains the same even if a job is held by a different person. Early management theorists considered authority in depth. They viewed from a feudal perspective: all authority was held by top management and it was successively delegated to lower ranks. Authority was therefore determined by one's position in a management hierarchy.

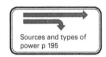
Sources and types of power p 195

The modern view of authority is rather more complicated. Subordinates often refuse to obey the authority of a superior who is incompetent. Subordinates may join forces and use the informal organisational structure to thwart the authority of a new or insecure manager. Subordinates who have particular expertise may exercise more authority than those in superior positions. For example, a chief executive may follow the judgement of a human resource (HR) manager when selecting key members of staff because the HR manager has a higher level of expertise. Job descriptions usually specify limits of authority. For example, a job description might state that a manager can only authorise overtime up to a certain level.

Traditionally authority was closely guarded. It was believed that employees at lower levels were basically idiots who could not be trusted. This meant that time was wasted because subordinates repeatedly referred matters to their superiors and waited for decisions. Many decisions were made by superiors who had neither up-to-date information nor specialist expertise. The modern trend is to push authority as far down the organisation as possible so that decision-making is quicker and based on better information. This trend is called **empowerment.**

Responsibility is the converse of authority. A manager's "area of responsibility" (AOR) is the domain of resources over which she or he has authority. It is the duty of a subordinate to perform a task that has been given to him or her. However, this duty only exists if the employee, in turn, has authority over the resources needed to do the job. Job design must achieve the correct relationship between authority and responsibility.

Span of control

Responsibility for the work of other employees is a special kind of authority. The number of employees supervised is called the "span of control". Traditionally it was argued that about six subordinates was the optimum span of control. If a manager is responsible for more employees there is the danger of "communication overload". However, research has indicated that the span of control depends upon a number of factors such as environmental stability. In highly stable situations with few complexities and exceptions, the span of control can be higher, perhaps extending to 20, 30 or even 50 subordinates. The latter situation occurs on production lines making highly standardised products. High spans of control are possible when an organisation has a clear system of values, where a boss and subordinates work in close proximity, or where there is an efficient computer system that captures and collates key management information. The increasing use of information technology may be one of the reasons why, in recent years, the spans of managerial control have increased. In more changeable situations, where different products are made to meet the needs of individual customers, smaller spans of control may be better.

Ergonomics and job design

Ergonomics is a specialised area of psychology. It aims to ensure that jobs are designed in a way that makes them suitable for human beings to perform. This means that workplaces should minimise harmful effects. Machines should be designed in a way which makes accidents impossible. For example, a metal-cutting machine can avoid accidental amputation of a hand by making sure that the cutting blades do not operate until a guard is in place and the worker's hands are safely out of the way while pressing two buttons that are placed well outside the danger area.

Ergonomics plays an important role in the **design of instrument displays**. For example, the pilot of an aircraft must monitor many dials. Many scientific experiments have been conducted to ensure that a cockpit display is laid out to maximise the ease of reading and to minimise the risk of confusion. One of the most recent concerns of ergonomists is the design of computerised workplaces. They should be constructed so that the working position does not create problems from poor posture, glare or repetitive actions that result in repetitive strain injury (RSI).

Ergonomists try to establish the patterns of **shiftwork** which do least damage to long-term health. Working very long hours (48 hours or more per week for more than nine weeks) carries long-term health risks. Studies conducted as long ago as 1918 showed that the output of people who work very long hours is less than those who work to a more reasonable schedule.

Work schedules

In traditional agricultural economies work schedules were determined by seasonal cycles of night and day. With the Industrial Revolution and invention of artificial lighting, work schedules tended to involve long shifts of 12 hours or more. Such long hours were often counterproductive and shorter hours with more holidays became the norm. In the middle of the twentieth century the stereotypical work schedule followed a "nine to five" pattern – although probably only a small proportion of the working population actually worked that schedule. In the closing decades of the twentieth century work schedules became more varied and included flexible working hours, a compressed working week and homeworking.

- **Flexitime** is probably the most common variation on the "standard" working week. It allows workers some autonomy and discretion in the hours that they work – provided that the total hours worked is sufficient. Flexitime employees must usually be present for certain core hours such as 10.00 a.m. to 3.00 p.m. It is very popular with secretarial and administrative staff. Flexitime often increases productivity because it decreases absenteeism and lateness. *Employees* like flexitime because it allows them to balance the competing demands of work and home. However, some *managers* may question an employee's motivation and commitment if they use flexitime too liberally.

- **Compressed working week** is another variation on the "standard" working week. Employees have longer working days in return for more days when they do not work. The most common form is for employees to work ten hours for four days in return for having a weekend break of three days. Some employees then choose to take a second job. The compressed working week is ideally suited to the domestic arrangements of some employees. However, many people are fatigued during the last two hours of the 10-hour working shifts and their concentration and attention may suffer.

- **Homeworking** and **teleworking**. Working at home, or in the fields near to home was once the most common form of work. In many industries, such as assembling small products or packing goods, working from home persisted for many years. The increasing availability of computers has led to a new variety of homeworking–teleworking. In teleworking an employee works at home but is linked to "the office" via the Internet. In addition, they attend "the office", say, one day a week for meetings and social events. The archetypal form of telecommuting is employees who are engaged in data input. Some *advantages* of teleworking are:

    - *Low overheads* – a firm does not have to provide office space, heating and lighting. These costs are usually borne by the teleworker.

    - *Reduction of labour shortages* – firms can employ people who would otherwise be outside the labour market. Teleworking often allows employers to recruit people with domestic responsibilities or who do not wish to commute to work.

    - *Increased productivity* – research suggests that teleworking can increase productivity by 25 per cent. Part of this saving is due to lower absenteeism and lower labour turnover. Some of the saving may be due to a reduction in time spent on social activities at work and the fact that employees are not fatigued by commuting.

Some *disadvantages* of teleworking are:

- Teleworkers may feel that their *careers suffer* because they are not as visible to important people in the organisation.
- *Home circumstances may interfere* with teleworking and increase the stress placed upon teleworkers. Teleworkers may find the *home-work interface* very difficult and will work very long hours in order to complete assignments.

- **Job sharing** – the concept of job sharing is self-explanatory. The duties involved in one job are shared, usually, by two people. Sometimes they work on different days of the week. Sometimes one person works in the morning while the other person works in the afternoon. Frequently the people who share the job are friends, indeed, sometimes husband and wife. If the job is complex, it is important to arrange a "handover" period where the sharers co-ordinate. From the employee's point of view job sharing may be an excellent way of combining work with domestic responsibilities or leisure. From the employer's point of view job sharing reduces the impact should an employee fall ill. Some people maintain that there is an increase in productivity because each person will achieve more than their proportionate share of the job. Apparently this is particularly true when the job involves creative work: a job shared between two people may well produce 20 per cent or more ideas than a single employee.

- **Contingent workers** – casual workers who are hired as and when there is sufficient demand are called contingent workers. There is nothing new about contingent working. In agricultural economies many people were hired during the harvest period and their employment ended once the crops were gathered. In the past, dockyard workers were employed when ships arrived and dismissed when cargoes had been unloaded. Universities employ large numbers of contingency seminar leaders to cope with increased student numbers. Managers who are hired for specific projects are often called "interim managers". The provision of many contingent office workers is highly organised by "temping agencies". Many contingent workers are paid low wages but the temporary nature of their work may be convenient for them. Costs of using contingent workers from an agency may be high because an agency charges a sizeable commission to cover the expense of recruiting and maintaining a register of temporary employees. Nevertheless, the costs of employing "temps" may be an efficient way of meeting peaks in demand.

Operational planning p 102

- **Office sharing and hoteling**. Providing employees with a workplace or office is expensive. It is particularly expensive if the workplace requires specialist equipment or if it is located in the centre of a major city. To make matters worse, individuals may only use their workplace for a part of the time. For example, a sales manager may only use his or her office during the mornings. During the afternoon he or she may be accompanying sales representatives "on the road". Therefore it may be possible to allocate an office to two sales managers. One uses it in the morning and is "on the road" during the afternoon while the other is "on the road" during the morning and in the office during the afternoon.

Hoteling takes the idea a step further. A firm can have a number of desks or offices. Staff can book a desk or an office when it is needed in a way that is analogous to booking a hotel room when it is needed for a day or, for some purposes, only an hour! These arrangements are often used by major consultancy firms that have premises in prestigious but expensive centres of major cities. Providing consultants with their own accommodation would be prohibitively costly. Each might occupy an office for only a few hours each week since most of their time is spent at the premises of their clients. The system of booking an office or desk space for short periods is called **"hot-desking"**.

CRITICAL THINKING 5.1 *Hot desks and employer commitment*

A hot-desking employee will be given a trolley to keep files and other equipment. It will be stored, cheaply, in a depot. When the consultant needs an office one will be reserved, the trolley will be taken from the depot to the allocated desk and a computer will route telephone calls to them. When they complete their work the desk will be vacated, the trolley returned to the depot and the desk space allocated to another consultant. From the firm's point of view, hot-desking is an excellent proposition – it slashes accommodation costs. Further, it inhibits employees wasting time luxuriating in their own office rather than spending time with clients on work that generates fees. However, the impact on employees can be very negative. Hot-desking may generate annoyance. Time is often wasted by the process of reserving a desk, and trolleys may arrive late or be delivered to the wrong desk. Perhaps the most damning criticism of hot-desking is that it hardly engenders a feeling that the organisation has a long-term commitment to an employee. Hot-desking may reduce organisational commitment. After all, if the organisation provides them with so little back-up, they may as well become a "Fred in a shed" and "poach" clients from his or her employer.

The way that jobs are designed has changed. In the past jobs were usually designed by managers who then explained them to workers. Nowadays, workers are often encouraged to be proactive and take the initiative in shaping their own job designs. It is perhaps surprising that people at lower organisational levels seem to have the greatest freedom in shaping their own jobs. There is evidence that jobs have become more stressful. In addition, interaction with other people form important activities. Daniels and de Jonge (2010) suggest that workplace social support and job control help to reduce excessive job demands. An excellent source of recent findings on a job design is given in a special issue of *Journal of Organisational Behaviour* (see Grant *et al.*, 2010).

Worker involvement in job design

In the classical view of job design a job is objectively defined, in great detail, by management so that a job is objective and independent of the person who performs the work. This may have been accurate the days of Ford when mass production required people to produce identical things with great efficiency. Today, this is rarely the case. Jobs are conceived as broad roles which give incumbents a great deal of latitude and allow them to interpret and perform the work. Workers are usually involved in the process of producing a job description: indeed many workers are allowed to define their own jobs. It is commonplace for organisations to encourage workers to "sculpt" their jobs by stretching and contracting its boundaries, often redefining it in idiosyncratic ways. This has advantages: it motivates workers and it makes them more flexible. However, it can lead to "untidy organisational structures" that are difficult to communicate and it makes some activities such as equitable appraisals quite difficult (see Lievans, Sanchez, Bartram and Browne, 2010). Further, management needs extra vigilance to ensure that all essential activities are covered.

In some jobs, such as sales, an individual works predominantly on their own, occasionally reporting to their boss and perhaps delegating work to an assistant. However, such jobs are rare. Most jobs involve working with other people in a team. Therefore, once a job has been properly designed, the next step is to arrange jobs into groups that can be performed by teams and it is important to describe how these teams can work.

5.4 Teams and teamwork

Teams exist in most organisations but, as Elton Mayo discovered in the bank wiring room at the Hawthorne electrical plant, they can restrict output and productivity. However, the opposite can also be true. A good team that is well managed can be very good at transforming resources into more valuable products. Clearly every manager needs a good understanding of teams and teamwork. The topic can be divided into five major sections:

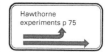

Hawthorne experiments p 75

- advantages and disadvantages of teams
- types of teams
- composition of teams and team roles
- stages of team development
- characteristics of effective teams

We now consider each of these sections in greater detail.

Advantages and disadvantages of teams

Teams exist in most organisations because they have many *advantages*. The main ones are:

- Groups of people working in co-operation can often *achieve more* than the same number of people working individually. This was discovered thousands of years ago when men learnt that they could hunt and kill more and bigger animals when they worked as a group.

- People can *learn new skills* from other people. This means that ideas which benefit an organisation can spread faster. Further, in teams, the ideas of one person can *stimulate* other people to have more and better ideas (synergy)

- Working in teams satisfies human "belongingness needs" and this may increase worker motivation.

A major *disadvantage* of teams is the *time and effort it takes to weld individuals into a team.* Energy needs to be spent communicating the organisation's objectives and methods, and inculcating organisational values. More time is needed to maintain a group. Time must be allowed for team members to communicate with each other – mainly at meetings. Time will also be spent 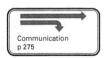 on meeting the social and emotional needs such as resolving arguments or arranging social events. The energy taken to form and maintain a team means, inevitably, that there is less energy to complete the team's task. There is a third disadvantage of teamworking: **social loafing**. Some members of the team "do not pull their weight". They make the calculation they can get away with doing less work and yet receive full pay. Social loafing can be reduced by good leadership and incentives such as team bonus schemes.

Types of teams

Teams take many forms. Sometimes, as in the airline industry, a team takes the form of a **crew** – a group of people who have rarely met but they can work effectively because they have been thoroughly trained and understand their duties. These teams may only last as long as a work shift. Sometimes, teams take the form of **project teams** who are dedicated to a particular objective. Often the members of these teams are drawn from different department so that they encompass a wide range of skills. Project teams are frequently used to develop new products or services. They are frequently found in the IT industry where, say, they will be tasked to devise a system and write a computer program for a client. Quality circles are another kind of project team where a major role is to communicate and advocate new ideas. The duration of a project team will depend on the precise project but, in general, they last 3–15 months. **Production teams** are a 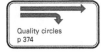 group of people who produce an established good or service, in considerable quality. They usually last a long time, perhaps years (see CIPD, 2009b). Classic examples are construction teams or healthcare workers. A more specialist example might be legal teams who work together to deal with the legal side of, say, a merger or acquisition.

    Virtual teams are a relatively new and have come into prominence because of the Internet or Intranet. Members of virtual teams may rarely meet and may work in different buildings, countries or continents. They will communicate by telephone, computer or teleconferencing. The geographical distances between members means that managing virtual teams is particularly difficult: they are prone to misunderstandings on fundamental issues. **Self-managing teams** are another, relatively new, form of teamworking. They are also called **semi-autonomous workgroups** and **self-directed teams**. A self-managing team is given a task where quantity, quality and cost are clearly specified. The team then decides, by

---

CASE 5.2: *The C-suite teams at Goldman-Sachs etc.*

The C-suite team (senior people whose job title includes the word "chief") is probably the most important team in any organisation. A classic example emerged in the financial giant, Goldman Sachs. In 1976 the managing director died and his position was filled by two people, John Weinberg and John Whitehead. They were friends and they found it easy to co-operate to run the firm for eight years and set a precedent. Henry Paulson was member a later C-suite who ran Goldman Sachs with two chief operating officers (COOs) and then he became US Treasury Secretary. Similar C-suite teams are seen in many other major companies, such as Coca-Cola, Microsoft and Wal-Mart. Starbucks once had an H2O team made up of three chiefs whose Christian names were **H**oward, **H**oward and **O**rrin. The C-suite team in Seagate (disk-drive maker) has four members: CEO, COO, CFO and a vice-president in charge of marketing and strategy.

Small, high-ranking, teams are necessary because a single person does not have enough ability to focus attention, acquire new capabilities, process information or take on the diverse roles needed at the head of a large organisation. Bruce Chizen, CEO of Adobe Systems has said, "my job is simply too big for any one person".

Members of a C-suite team are usually *complementary*. Generally the CEO is good at dealing with external matters such as politics and public relations, while the COO is good at dealing with internal matters such as procedures and operational matters. Often, one or more members of a C-suite team will act as a diplomat and a "good cop" while others act aggressively as "bad cops". Similarly, one member of a team acts as a "guardian" who preserves what is good in the organisation, who tries to *pull* things together within the organisation, while another member acts as an entrepreneur who tries to *push* the organisation into new things. Members of C-suite teams usually have complementary expertise. Although they are general managers they only have detailed experience in one or two business functions such as sales and marketing or, say, R&D plus operations. Some *advantages* of C-suite teams are:

- There is a diversity of thought and talent.
- While decisions take longer to make, they are usually superior.
- There is an effective constraint on strong egos that are found at the top of organisations.

C-suite teams also have *disadvantages* such as:

- Members may pursue incompatible goals and they may have incompatible styles.
- People lower down the organisation sometimes wonder to whom they should talk or listen.
- It is much more difficult to make changes at the top because members of a C-suite team are likely to join forces to resist changes they dislike.

Source: based on Miles, S.A. and Watkins, M.D. (2007) "The leadership team: complementary strengths or conflicting agendas?", *Harvard Business Review*, **85** (4), 90–97.

themselves, how to fulfil the task – e.g. the order and pace at which sub-tasks are completed and which team members perform different roles. Self-managing teams can be thought of as the opposite of the assembly-line system where managers decided, in minute detail, the sequence in which a car should be assembled. *Individual workers* would then be give specific tasks to perform at a pace determined by the conveyor belt which was controlled by management. A classic example of self-managing teams is Volvo's production system at their Uddvalla plant in the 1960s where a team of assemblers stayed with a car as it moved through the assembly process on a special jig. The team put the whole car together and they obtained much higher job satisfaction.

CRITICAL THINKING 5.2 *What is wrong with self-managed teams?*

In the closing decades of the twentieth century most management thinkers romanticised the virtues of teamworking – especially the virtues of self-management teams. "However, most of these experiments, even in Volvo, have been terminated and traditional assembly systems have been reintroduced" (Contu, 2007). The reversion to traditional assembly systems has been attributed to lower productivity in self-managed workgroups but variability in quality also played a part in their demise. Higher unemployment in Sweden meant that it was easier to get employees to work on assembly lines and vested interests in traditional methods were happy to reassert themselves. Others have pointed out that, even in their heyday, most self-managed teams had limited discretion and could not, for example, hire or fire workers, nor could they change suppliers or redesign components.

Barker (1993), for example pointed out that teamworking has a darker side and that managers were using teams as an invisible form of control. Group dynamics were doing management's job for them. Peer-group pressure was being harnessed to shape a worker's behaviour so that it was in line with the organisation's objectives. Team members themselves would identify and discipline colleague who failed to meet targets. Time and motion study may have been formally abandoned but "the stopwatch" still resides in the team (see Alder, 1993).

Composition of teams and team roles

A team will consist of a relatively small (about 6–12) number of workers drawn from relevant functions. Generally, it is better to choose members who share the same goals and that those goals are consistent with the organisation's goal. Within this basic constraint, it is better that the team members are quite diverse so that many different types of expertise and viewpoints are available. For example, in IT, an ideal software development team would contain someone who is good at structuring systems (an "IT architect"), someone who is good at detailed logical thinking (an analyst), someone who is good at graphics and design and someone who is good at implementing the final result and deploying the software in different business locations. The exact composition of members will depend on the task facing the team.

Teams needed to complete management tasks have been studied extensively, especially by R.M. Belbin (2004). He identifies nine team roles – which he defined as "a tendency to behave, contribute and interrelate with others in a particular way". Three of the nine roles are *outward oriented and creative*:

- **Plants** are managers who sow the seeds of an idea within the group. They then encourage the seed to develop into a flower. Plants are good at solving problems, are imaginative but sometimes unorthodox. However, they may not pay sufficient attention to detail and they may be so wrapped up in their ideas that they do not communicate them to others.

- **Resource investigators** forage inside and outside the organisation for opportunities and useful contacts. They are usually enthusiastic extroverts who like to communicate with others. Unfortunately they can be over-optimistic and they may not follow through with projects, skipping from idea to idea.

- **Shapers** make a team "shape-up" to challenges and the task ahead. Left on their own, other team members will be happy to have a good time. Shapers are happy to challenge this. They are also prepared to challenge established ideas or people. They are dynamic and thrive on pressure. They have the drive and courage to tackle obstacles. Unfortunately they may offend people and provoke anger. A team containing two or more shapers is likely to be turbulent!

Two of the nine roles are oriented to *dealing with people:*

- **Co-ordinators** make good chairpersons, clarifying goals and encouraging sound decision-making. They are usually good at delegating tasks to others. However, they can offload too much work to others and they may be very manipulative.

- **Teamworkers** help maintain good relations in a group and they help to repair damage caused by disagreements. They listen carefully to others. They are perceptive, diplomatic and avoid friction. In addition they are happy to give up some of their own interests in order to co-operate with others. However, teamworkers may be indecisive in a crisis.

The remaining four roles are oriented towards the *tasks facing the team*:

- **Monitor-evaluators** weigh up situations in a sober way that takes account of the major options. They take a long-term view and avoid distraction by minor issues. They have good judgement. However, they may give the impression that they lack drive and their balanced, careful approach means they are unlikely to enthuse or inspire other people

- **Specialists** are often technical people who provide expert knowledge and skills. They will be single-minded and dedicated to their profession or trade. Specialists may only contribute on technical points where they are sure of themselves – indeed they may dwell too much on technicalities

- **Implementers** are organised, reliable and efficient. They are good at dealing with the practicalities of turning ideas into results. Dependability and discipline are their watchwords. However, they may be slow to respond to new ideas and they can appear to be inflexible.

- **Completer-finishers** are team members who are concerned with things that may go wrong. They are painstaking and conscientious in searching out errors or omissions. They will focus themselves and other team members on deadlines. Unfortunately, they may be anxious and worry too much. This may lead them to keep things under their own control rather than delegating them.

Most managers will be good at two or more of these roles. It is important to avoid teams where everyone suits the same role. Indeed, in an ideal team, every role would be covered by at least one member.

Stages of team development

Tuckerman (1965) and Tuckerman and Jensen (1977) reviewed a number of studies of small teams and noted that team behaviour was not the same throughout the time the team existed, but would pass through a sequence of five stages:

- Stage 1: **forming** is the initial stage when the team first comes together. Team members are forming impressions of each other and trying to ensure that they are being accepted. During this stage the team will be trying to establish the details of their task and the ways they can operate in order to achieve objectives. The team will look to the formal team leader for guidance and direction. Substantial resources will be directed towards interpersonal issues and team productivity will be mediocre.

- Stage 2: **storming** occurs as team members start to vie with each other for position or to get their ideas accepted. They may openly challenge each other and the leader. Alliances may form and cliques may battle for supremacy. Conflict and confrontation rule the day and productivity is low. The team gains a better understanding of itself and its task. Eventually, compromises are made and the team is ready to progress to the next stage.

- Stage 3: **norming** happens as the team clarifies its task and starts to develop its own way of doing things. They come to value each others' different strengths. There is a growing sense of togetherness and there may be some social activities which will repair the damage to relationships that arose during the storming stage. There is less need to devote resources to clearing ambiguity or conflict. Productivity rises to reasonable levels.

- Stage 4: **performing** is the stage where the team is free to concentrate on the task in hand. There is synergy between team members. Although disagreements occur, there will be accepted ways of reconciling them so that they are only a minor distraction from the task. Members get on with their jobs with only a low level of instruction or communication. Most of the team's energy is focused on the task and productivity is high.

- Stage 5: **mourning** is sometimes called "adjourning" or "deforming". This final stage was added by Tuckerman and a colleague after an analysis of more research. Having completed the task, the team members go their separate ways, being redeployed to other teams. They will probably be proud of their achievements and happy to have made new friends. They may feel a sense of loss when the team ends. Sometimes there may be a reluctance to move on to new things.

Some teams omit certain stages. Experienced airline cabin crew rarely go through the storming or mourning stages. Similarly some teams become mired in the storming stage and never reach the performing stage – especially when there are two or more members who consider themselves "prima donnas". Sometimes teams go backwards. For example, if there are new team members a high-performing team may revert to the storming stage. Nevertheless, Tuckerman's stages are very useful. Managers need to remember that team performance is a process and that one of the aims of a good leader is to help the team pass quickly and easily through the first three stages. Managers should also be watchful in case a team regresses – in which case some action will be needed to get the team back to the performing stage. In some cases, managers may need to remind colleagues who loiter too long in the mourning stage that it is time to move on.

Characteristics of effective teams

There has been a great deal of speculation about the characteristics of an effective team. Many writers suggest that effective teams should be small since social loafing is more prevalent in large teams. Others have argued that trust between members is the hallmark of a good team. It has also been argued that a key characteristic is group cohesion. It is easy to see why a group that sticks together may be effective *provided* its values and goals coincide with the values and goals of the organisation. If a cohesive group's values and goals are antagonistic to the organisation, it will hinder an organisation achieving its aims. In the 1960s and 1970s a great deal of industrial strife arose, partly, because highly cohesive groups pursued goals that were contrary to the goals of management.

Ground-breaking research by Campion, Papper and Medsker (1996) and Campion Medsker and Higgs (1993) involved high-quality empirical studies. They found that the main characteristics of effective teams were, in order, the:

- **Processes used by the group.** Teams which: (1) believed that they were efficient and could be effective; (2) who supported each other when difficulties arose; (3) shared work in a way that ensured little social loafing or "free-riding"; and (4) where there was good communication and co-ordination between members, tended to be very effective teams.

- **Interdependence** was, according to Campion *et al.*, the second most important factor in determining a team's effectiveness. This includes such things as whether bad performance by one person would have knock-on effects for the work of other team members (task interdependence) and goal interdependence. It also covers the interdependence of the feedback that each team member receives.

- **Task design.** Teams whose work was structured according to the principles of researchers such as Hackman and Oldham (1980) were also likely to be effective teams. These teams were allowed a high degree of self-management and there was a high level of participation by all team members. Their work also involved a variety of tasks rather than a monotonous concentration on a single tasks.

- **Group context** in terms of their training, the support given by management and the level and quality of communication with other teams was the fourth most important determinant of group effectiveness.

■ As expected the **composition of the team** was related to effectiveness but the strength of the relationship was weaker than the relationship for the previous factors. There was a weak tendency for heterogeneous teams and flexible teams to be more effective. The results concerning group size were a little more complex. It would appear that team size is important with lower-level jobs but much less so at higher levels.

Very few organisations have only one team. Indeed, large organisations may have hundreds of teams. They cannot be structured in a random way. The next section explains the different ways that teams can be arranged into an organisational structure.

5.5 Types of organisational structure

Even when jobs are properly defined and work groups assembled they cannot be arranged at random. It is necessary to put jobs and work groups in a structure so that they do not duplicate each other and, collectively, they cover all the things an organisation needs to do in order to add value. A good organisational structure also helps communication and the sharing of knowledge. If there is a good organisational structure it much easier to establish "who should be told about what". There are many ways of structuring jobs. The main ones are:

■ functional structures
■ divisional structures (regional, product, client)
■ matrix structures
■ network structures
■ learning structures

Business process re-engineering (BPR) is a detailed way of looking at how an organisation is structured and then restructuring it to be more efficient. It was a popular management fad of the 1990s (Micklethwaite and Wooldridge, 1996). Further details of BPR are given on the website associated with this book.

Functional structures

The usual way to organise jobs is to group them according to their function. A function is an intended purpose. For example, the purpose (function) of the brain is to think and the purpose (function) of the skeleton is to support the body. Similarly, the function of the production department is to make goods or services while the function of the sales department is to sell those goods.

Most organisations have a number of functions. The major functions are marketing and sales, operations (production), human resources, finance and the knowledge function. These are covered in detail by later chapters. Most organisational functions are based on jobs that share a similar purpose. For example, the common purpose of selection, training, personnel planning and safety is the management of human beings. Hence, an interviewer, a management trainer, the personnel planning officer and a safety officer might be grouped into the HR function. Similarly, the common element of paying suppliers, paying employees, raising money on the stock market and obtaining payment from customers all concern money, and the people whose jobs involve these activities might be grouped into the financial

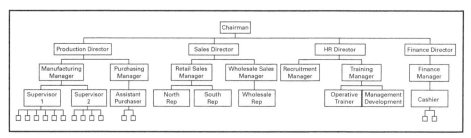

FIGURE 5.3 A flat functional structure

function. A functional structure brings together people with similar expertise. This means that they can advise and support each other. A functional structure normally engenders loyalty in its members. Organisation by function is depicted by a classic organisation chart of a small manufacturing business, shown in Figure 5.3.

This organisation has a *flat structure* and is typical of many manufacturing organisations with large spans of control and where a small number of people manage the work of many operatives. Some administrative and clerical organisations also have flat structures. For example, in government departments collecting taxes a few senior officials will supervise the work of many people who process tax returns.

Some organisations have *tall structures* where each manager has only one or two subordinates. Tall structures are found in specialist organisations where the activities of one person are interrelated with to the activities of others. A typical tall structure is depicted in Figure 5.4. It would be characteristic, for example, of a consultancy designing software.

Functions differ from organisation to organisation. A manufacturing organisation will have functions similar to those shown in the first organisational structure. In a retail organisation such as Homebase there will be no production function but a very large sales function. In a regulatory organisation, such as the the Health and Safety Executive, there will be neither a production nor sales function but there will be large technical and legal functions. Functional structures work well when an organisation recurrently processes large batches of a few standard products.

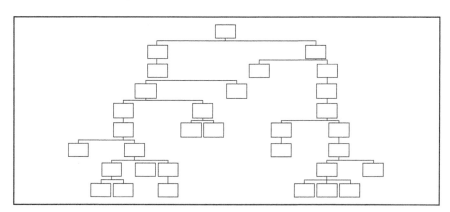

FIGURE 5.4 A tall functional structure

Functional organisational structures have a number of *advantages*:

- **Operational efficiency is high**. There is tight, centralised control. Responsibilities are clearly defined and understood.
- **Similar jobs are grouped**. People doing similar tasks can support each other and develop considerable expertise. Work groups are cohesive.
- **Employees have a clear career structure.**
- **Economies of scale are obtained**. Resources are used efficiently. Specialised equipment is located where it is needed most and fewer items of equipment need to be bought.

Unfortunately, functional structures also have *disadvantages*. Loyalties develop to the function rather than to the organisation. People put the goals of their own groups before the goals of the organisation. Functional groups may develop narrow perspectives that lead to conflict with other functions. For example, the sales function may blame the manufacturing function for producing poor products, while the manufacturing function may blame the sales function for not selling products energetically. The narrow viewpoints of functions are often called "functional chimneys" that lead to a "blame culture" and poor communication. Decision-making slows because choices are referred to higher levels where responsibilities for the functions converge.

Functional structures also lead to "empire building" by managers. They enhance the prestige of their jobs by expanding the numbers inside their function – irrespective of the contribution extra workers might make.

Divisional structures

Large organisations are often structured into self-sufficient divisions. Divisions are often like mini-businesses within a larger business. For example, in a bank there may be a retail division, an Internet division and a commercial banking division. Similarly, a large legal partnership may have separate divisions for different types of legal work, such as commercial property, intellectual property, litigation and family law. Divisions have a number of *advantages*:

- **Clear identification** of costs, profits and the contribution a product is making to an organisation's success. The responsibility for poor performance can be pinpointed. Managers of a division are highly motivated to respond to their customers and their environment.
- **Justification of dedicated facilities**. Decision-making is speeded up and changes to customer needs can be met quickly. An organisation that is divided into divisions is likely to be flexible and adaptable.
- **Co-ordination within divisions** is usually easy because a division is likely to consist of a small number of units and employees (Baron and Greenberg, 1990).
- **Divisions can focus on particular areas of business** and build up the specific expertise needed.
- **Structural changes are easier**. Failing divisions can be closed and new, profitable, divisions can be opened.

- **Divisions provide a training ground for general managers**. Each division will have managers who are concerned with integrating a whole business unit. When a new manager is needed at corporate level, there are likely to be a number of suitable candidates in the various divisions.

Divisional structures have *disadvantages*:

- **Facilities are duplicated**. For example, a New Zealand organisation structured into regional divisions may have three separate accounts departments: one in the North Island and one in the South Island and a further accounts department at corporate headquarters. It might be more efficient to have one accounts department for the whole country.

- **Divisions may become too autonomous**, following their own vision and strategy rather than those of the organisation.

- **Divisions may also be subject to "empire building".** "Divisional chimneys" may develop.

In large organisations the advantages of structuring operations into divisions usually outweigh the disadvantages. The divisions can be based upon many characteristics – mainly region, product, customer and process. Usually there is a hybrid structure combining an appropriate mix of divisional structures. However, it is useful to know the pure types:

- **Regional divisions** are based on geographical proximity. They are very common in organisations involved in retailing, distribution and transport. They are also common in service organisations such as hospitals, highway maintenance and schools. Multinational organisations are often organised on a regional basis such as North America, Europe, Middle East and Asia and Australia. Organisations structured into regions have the key advantage that decisions can be made at a local level where personnel have first-hand local knowledge. Further, they often reduce transport costs. Unfortunately, regional structures may not give managers the wider, general experience needed to operate at a national or global level: they only have experience of their own region. A typical regional structure is shown in Figure 5.5.

- **Product divisions** group activities making similar products or services. They have a major advantage that a business unit can specialise in a technology or market and develop a high level of expertise. Figure 5.6 gives an example of a chemical organisation structured according to its products.

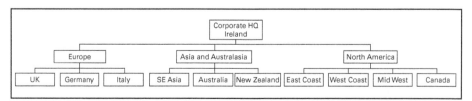

FIGURE 5.5 A regional divisional structure

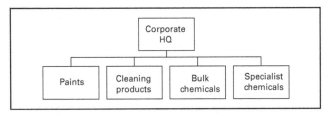

FIGURE 5.6 A product divisional structure

■ **Client divisions** group jobs and activities according to their customers. This is common in service organisations such as hospitals and prison services. It is also common in consultancies and organisations making sophisticated equipment. For example, a hospital may be structured into A&E, paediatrics, obstetrics and geriatrics. Organisations supplying a handful of powerful clients will set up a division for each client. Client divisions are able to serve the special needs of customer groups. In a commercial setting, an organisation structured into divisions may be able to build customer loyalty which gives them a competitive advantage. A major disadvantage of client divisions is that many clients have common needs, yet the divisions duplicate facilities when meeting the needs of each separate group.

Matrix structures

Matrix structures aim to avoid functional and divisional chimneys by making sure that subunits co-operate. At the same time they try to maintain the advantages of specialisation. In many ways, matrix structures can be thought of as a mixture of functional and divisional structures. They have been defined as "a structure in which the tasks of the organisation are grouped simultaneously along two organising dimensions". Figure 5.7 shows a typical matrix structure where functions are shown along the top of an organisation chart while divisions, in this case product divisions, are placed down the side.

A distinctive feature of a matrix organisation is that each person appears to have two bosses. They have a function boss who is in charge of their function and who has authority over professional matters such as promotions and salary, and they have an operational boss who has day-to-day authority relative to working on a specific project. The operations boss and function boss need to co-ordinate their demands. Some matrix structures are even more complex. They attempt to place employees in a three-dimensional matrix of, say, functions, products and client base. Such complex matrix structures are often impractical.

Many medium and large organisations have adopted a matrix structure. The main *advantages* are:

■ **Co-ordination is increased and gross duplication is avoided**. Often a matrix structure enables an organisation to achieve several objectives simultaneously.

■ **Employees have varied work and they gain wide experience**. Matrix structures may allow a higher level of worker participation.

■ **A cohesive organisation** results from the interaction of employees from different functions or divisions.

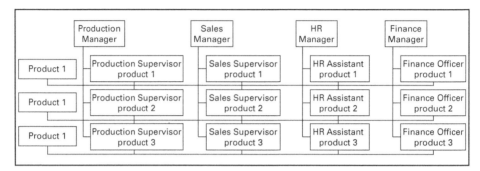

FIGURE 5.7 A matrix organisational structure

■ **A more adaptable and flexible organisation** results from the richness of the contacts between employees. It can readily adapt to changes in the business environment.

The major *disadvantages* of a matrix organisation are:

■ **Confusion arises** when a functional boss and a project boss fail to co-operate or, worse, when they engage in a power struggle. People in a matrix structure are sometimes confused about where their main responsibility lies.

■ **Much time is consumed** by complexities of co-ordination. Matrix structures may lead to more discussion than action.

■ **Employees feel isolated** from the colleagues with whom they have a natural or professional affinity.

Network structures

Network structures are a modern innovation. They are sometimes called "boundaryless organisations". They have similarities with "strategic alliances" and "partnering arrangements".

In a network structure (see Figure 5.8), a small core of employees has responsibility for the general organisation, communication, finance and perhaps one other function where it excels, such as design. All other aspects are subcontracted to outside suppliers. Core workers co-ordinate the outside suppliers so that the final product can be delivered. For example, an entrepreneur may invent a new self-sealing can that prevents fizzy drinks going flat. Instead of setting up a sizeable organisation to manufacture and market the product, the entrepreneur enters an arrangement with an existing Malaysian manufacturer.

This saves expense. There is no need to acquire expertise in container manufacturing. The entrepreneur could also enter into an alliance with a sales and marketing organisation based in New York – saving the time and trouble of setting up a sales organisation. The entrepreneur would also hire three or four core workers who would manage relationships with the suppliers. Naturally, the training and salary administration of the core workers would be outsourced to a specialist agency based in Delhi.

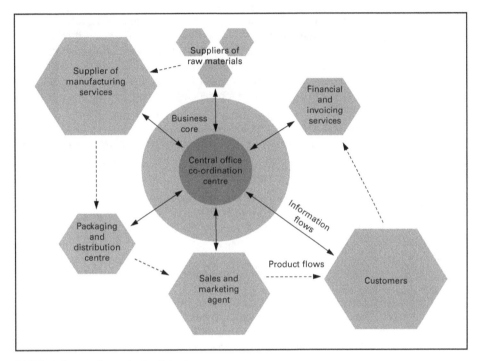

FIGURE 5.8 A network organisational structure

Network organisations are particularly common in the clothing, computer and publishing industries. Network or boundaryless organisations are free to find subcontractors anywhere in the world. The network can be changed rapidly in response to market demand. If a product is not selling, a contract with the producer can be terminated. A new contract can be struck with another producer who makes a more profitable or attractive product. In a sense, a network structure is a **modular organisation** where the components can be removed or added according to demand.

There are three main kinds of network structures:

1 **Internal networks** exist within large organisations that need to retain full control in order to achieve high quality or to meet statutory requirements. They often set up subgroups with responsibility for supplying various products or services to "internal customers". The subgroups operate like mini-organisations. Usually they act independently as a separate profit centre. They negotiate prices and conditions of supply with their internal customers. However, the organisation maintains sufficient control to prevent them defecting to another organisation or refusing to supply their internal customers. Most of the power is with the internal customers since they are usually free to source their requirements from the open market.

2 **Stable networks** rely on outsourcing. Suppliers are chosen with care. The objective is to establish strong, long-standing relationships. Suppliers have a high level of loyalty and

commitment to the core organisation, which in turn will act in a slightly paternalistic way to ensure the health of their key suppliers. The core organisation may give help with financing and research and development. These relationships may be called "organisational partnerships". But the power lies with the core organisation. When necessary, the core organisation switches to a cheaper supplier. The partner supplier, on the other hand, usually becomes too dependent upon the core organisation to resist their demands.

3 **Dynamic networks** are characterised by outsourcing most operations. They consist of many alliances and partners. Partners change rapidly and there is little loyalty.

The physical headquarters of a network structure may be small: in extreme cases it may simply consist of a room with a computer and communications equipment. This type of network structure is often called a "**virtual organisation**". Virtual organisations can locate and relocate very quickly in any country that suits their temporary requirements. The supreme example of a virtual organisation is eBay where a relatively small number of people manage a computer and financial system which links to huge numbers of buyers and sellers.

Small entrepreneurial firms may find that a network structure enables them to match the power of large organisations since they are able to "buy in" facilities and services at will. Other organisations adopt a network structure in order to concentrate on key strengths (core competences) and will leave other aspects to outside organisations chosen on the basis of core strengths that complement the strengths of the central organisation.

The main *advantages* of network structures are that they:

- **Enable organisations to manufacture and market globally**. A network structure can often achieve large results from meagre resources.
- **Give flexibility to redefine an organisation rapidly** in the search for markets.
- **Enable efficiency**. A network organisation will have little administration and low overheads. There may be no need for a traditional hierarchy.

The *disadvantages* of a network structure include:

- **Loss of control**. Many decisions will be made by subcontractors. Further, actions will be fragmented amongst subcontractors. Long-term suppliers may be unstable because subcontractors are able to switch to another organisation who can offer better terms. Loss of control often means an increase in uncertainty. Long-term projects may become difficult to plan and organise. Loss of control may mean loss of key components overnight.
- **Employee loyalty may decrease** because there is little identification with the central core.

Learning structures and knowledge management

Management gurus such as Peter Drucker (1997) (see pages. 497–505) suggest that for today's organisations, the knowledge they contain is their major asset. This knowledge includes patents, copyrights, trade secrets and contacts. The majority of such knowledge is inside the heads of employees. Senge's (1990) book, *The Fifth Discipline*, emphasised the need to structure an organisation in a way that maximises its ability to increase the capital of knowledge it holds by adopting a "learning structure". A learning structure uses its people, values and systems continuously to change and improve performance-based experience (Senge, 1990). This places a high value on learning from the experience of customers, suppliers, partners and contractors. Learning structures seek out learning opportunities whenever and wherever they can.

A learning structure shows five main characteristics:

- **Employees share the same vision of the organisation**. They will have participated in the formation of the vision and will therefore be willing to consent to the actions needed to bring it about. If the vision is clear, people are able to identify and solve problems in order to achieve that vision.

- **Employees understand how the whole organisation operates**. Understanding how the organisation works as a system helps individuals work in a succession of project teams while maintaining a sense of perspective.

- **Employees are willing to discard the old ways** – in particular, views on controlling staff change. Managers in learning structures think of control as a co-operative process. Rather than having control *over* subordinates, managers exercise control *with* subordinates. People are not a cost that needs to be minimised. Their knowledge, experience and creativity are regarded as the organisation's main asset. An atmosphere of respect and trust creates an environment where it is safe to experiment. Mistakes are accepted not punished. They are an inevitable part of taking necessary risks needed to learn, grow and improve. People are expected to "push the envelope" on the understanding that sometimes things will go wrong and they will not be blamed.

- **Employees feel confident of their position** within the organisation. They are able to discuss ideas openly and frankly, without taking defensive positions. Features which emphasise status differences (car-parking spaces, separate restaurants and differences in dress) are eliminated.

- **Information is distributed widely**. Everyone can obtain information about budgets, expenses, schedules and other databases. People can see for themselves how their actions and ideas contribute to organisational goals. Communications are fluid. People can email any other person in the organisation.

Although learning structures are particularly efficient at generating knowledge, in fact, it is generated in all organisations and in many cases it is the organisation's most valuable asset. Hence it must be managed as effectively as an organisation's human resources or finances. Knowledge management is explained in more detail in Chapter 18.

Knowledge management p 452

Co-ordination within organisational structures

Structuring an organisation involves placing people in groups and then arranging the groups into some kind of logical order. On its own, this is not enough. There must be some mechanism that enables the groups to relate to each other so that their activities harmonise.

This process is called "co-ordination". In this context it refers to the quality of collaboration between groups or departments. All organisations require some co-ordination. In very small organisations this can be provided by one person, usually the owner, who directly supervises all activities. In large organisations, especially international ones, specific methods of co-ordination need to be built into the organisational structure. The main methods are:

- **A hierarchical arrangement of authority** means that someone is available to tell groups what they must do in order to work harmoniously with other groups. The higher authority arbitrates in disputes and issues plans or instructions to ensure that groups work towards the organisation's goals in a mutually helpful way.
- **Standardisation** helps co-ordination by simplifying the situation so that compatibility and interchangeability are increased. Standardisation covers procedures, inputs and outputs.
- **Personal contact**, where one person speaks to people from other groups, allows each group to be aware of events in the other group. This means that they are able to adjust their own activities in a way that helps themselves, the other group and the organisation as a whole. Often personal contact is formalised and certain people are given the specific responsibility of keeping one group informed of events in another group. These roles are usually called "liaison posts". For example, one member of the engineering department may have an official responsibility for liaising with the sales department.
- **Computer information systems** are playing an increasingly important role in the co-ordination of organisations. Data from one group can be automatically passed to other groups that need to be kept informed. Indeed, with automated information-sharing, a receiving department has data almost as quickly as the group that generates it. Moreover, the information on organisational intranets often allows every employee to see the progress an organisation is making towards it production, sales or financial targets.

5.6 Major organisational dimensions

The characteristics of an organisation can vary in many ways. The main variations concern size, role variety, centralisation, formalisation, mechanistic or organic systems, and environmental uncertainty. Often these factors are related. For example, large organisations tend to be more mechanistic than small ones. Each of the six major characteristics of organisations needs further explanation.

Size

Size is a very significant, self-explanatory, organisational dimension. Large organisations tend to have a more formal structure, usually based on functions or departments. Large organisations also tend to have many hierarchical levels. The size of an organisation is usually measured in two ways: the number of employees or its financial value (usually **market capitalisation** which is the value of a single share on the stock exchange multiplied by the number of shares in existence).

Role variety

Some organisations are very simple and have only two jobs: the manager and the aides who do all kind of work, as and when needed. Other organisations have many different jobs which are quite distinct. Sometimes, role variety is also called "specialisation". Role variety centres upon interchangeability. If many employees can be substituted there is little role variety. Tyler (1973) developed a mathematical index of role variety.

Centralisation

Centralisation is the concentration of power. The opposite is "decentralisation", "autonomy" or "participation". If all power is in the hands of one person the organisation is highly centralised. If members of an organisation have equal power the organisation is highly decentralised. A highly centralised organisation is characterised as follows:

- Decisions, even quite minor ones, will be referred to senior managers.
- Plans, even operational plans, will be drawn up without the participation of junior staff.
- Information will be "hoarded" by managers and only be given reluctantly to subordinates.
- There will be stringent control procedures to ensure that operations are carried out exactly in the prescribed way. Employees have little discretion.

Formalisation

Formalisation (see Reimann, 1974) is the extent to which expectations and norms are made explicit. In theory, formalisation applies to both written and oral communication. In practice, formalisation is the level to which rules, procedures, instructions and other communications are written. Formalisation is related to concepts such as routinisation (Hage and Aiken, 1968, 1969) and standardisation. Routinisation is the degree to which roles are structured. Roles are routinised when tasks are simplified and repeated. The degree of standardisation in an organisation can be measured by counting the number of repetitive sequences.

Mechanistic or organic systems

Burns and Stalker (1961) noted that organisations often operate in one of two ways. Some operate much like an efficient machine devised by scientific managers and administrative theorists. In these **mechanistic organisations** tasks are divided into small parts that are organised in a logical sequence. Senior levels of management exercise downward control using precise instructions and rules which minimise discretion. Boundaries of responsibility are clearly defined and often related to technical expertise and knowledge. Mechanistic organisations seem to work well in stable situations – especially when products or services are mature and produced in high volume. In the second type of organisation things are less predetermined. In these **organic organisations** there is a degree of disorganisation and fluidity that is analogous to the flexibility seen in the cells of living material. There are few prescriptive job descriptions, rules and regulations are kept to a minimum and employees are often expected to use their initiative. Communications within these organisations tend to be horizontal between colleagues rather than upwards towards senior management. Organic organisations seem to work best in volatile situations where the market or technology is changing rapidly and frequent adjustments mean that long production runs are infrequent.

Environmental uncertainty

Lawrence and Lorsch (1969) maintain that a major difference between organisations is the uncertainty of their environments. Organisations, such as manufacturers in the computer industry, operate in an uncertain environment where new developments and market trends can emerge overnight and then completely change the organisation's operations. Ambiguity is often highest in the political arena where political leaders do not spell out their requirements clearly. Public services also suffer from competing demands. A prison service, for example, must strike a balance between the need to restrict the activities of prisoners in order to make the community safer and the need to expand the activities of prisoners in order to rehabilitate them into society. A final component of environmental uncertainty includes the quality and speed of feedback. In an uncertain environment it is vague and slow.

Other significant dimensions of an organisation's culture are its attitude towards risk (to what degree it will tolerate actions that might go wrong), innovation (the emphasis it places on making improvements) and rules (the number of rules it has, whether they are written down and the severity of punishment when rules are broken). Space constraints mean that they cannot be described here but details can be found in the website associated with this book.

5.7 Organising toolkit

- Design jobs carefully. Do not over-specialise. Make sure the job has motivating elements. In management jobs, make sure the span of control is reasonable – especially in organisations that produce complex, interrelated product or services (pages 114–121).
- Make the authority and responsibilities of every job crystal clear (pages 116).
- Make sure that all equipment, including IT equipment, is ergonomically designed (page 117).
- Choose appropriate work schedules for each job. Consider adopting less traditional schedules such as teleworking, job-sharing, contingent workers, office-sharing and hoteling (page 118).
- Organise jobs into teams. With lower level jobs, keep teams relatively small. Help them to be effective by making sure they adopt the right processes, their work is interdependent and contextual factors are right (page 127).
- Make sure teams share the same basic outlook but then choose members so that they have a wide range of backgrounds and experience (page 128).

140 **Part 2**: Management processes

- Check the styles of team members. Make sure that they do not all have the same style. If possible, choose members so that there is at least one person who can discharge each of the major roles (page 128).
- Choose an organisational structure that suits your organisation's size, product and methods. Do not ignore newer structures such as network structures (page 133)
- Using five-point scales (very high, high, middle, low, very low), indicate where your organisation would lie on the six major organisational dimensions. Next estimate where your organisation is now. If there is any discrepancy between the two, sketch out ways of reducing the discrepancy (page 137).

Activities and further study

Essay plans

Prepare plans for the following essays:

1 What are the advantages and disadvantages of work specialisation?
2 Do charities have organisational structures?
3 What are the different ways in which work can be scheduled?
4 What are recent trends in structuring organisations and why have they changed from traditional structures?

Web activities

1 Search the Internet for organisational structures. You should try a number of organisations including governmental and charity organisations. Some useful examples of organisational structure are given by:

- Parker Pens – a structure very largely based on geographical regions – why? Try www.competition-commission.org.uk.
- Gillette – a complicated structure which uses both product group and geographical regions.
- Nomura Research Institute – a service organisation largely based on customers and products. Try http://www.nri.co.jp/english/company/org.html.
- Serious Fraud Office – a governmental structure based on procedural responsibilities. Try http://www.sfo.gov.uk/about/structure.asp.
- For a really complex organisational structure look at the organisation chart for Microsoft, which can be found at: http://www.directionsonmicrosoft.com/sample/DOMIS/orgchart/sample/orgchart. html.

2 You might also try to locate the organisational structure for a "virtual organisation" such as Amazon or eBay.
3 Log on to the website associated with this book and access the file containing the organisation chart exercise. Examine the chart, locate the errors and a draw a new chart which does not contain errors.

Experiential activities

1 Draw up a job description for your role as a student. Compare your result with the model answer given on the website associated with this book.

2 With a group of fellow students discuss the different ways that work can be scheduled. Allocate one of the following roles to each member of the group:

- single unmarried worker
- married worker
- married worker with young children
- worker who is a single parent with young children

Each person should then examine the following work schedules and describe the impact it would have on their work and domestic lives:

- traditional nine to five schedule
- flexitime schedule
- compressed working week
- job share

Recommended reading

1 Oldham, G.R. and Hackman, J.R. (2010) "Not what it was: the future of job design research", *Journal of Organizational Behaviour*, **31** (2/3), 463–480. These veterans of job design speculate on the future of research and theory of organisational design. A difficult read but highly recommended. This issue of the journal is devoted to job design.

2 Miles, S.A. and Watkins, M.D. (2007) "The leadership team: complementary strengths or conflicting agendas?", *Harvard Business Review*, **85** (4), 90–98. This considers the way that top management should work as a team. There is a good section on succession planning and transitions within senior management teams.

3 Barker, J.R. (1993) "Tightening the iron cage: concertive control in self-management teams", *Administrative Science Quarterly*, **38** (3), 408–437. This makes the point that high commitment of a team increases demands on members. This article won an award for its scholarly contribution. It is a long read (two hours or more) which delves into the concept of organisational control.

4 Ortenblad, A. (2004) "The learning organisation: towards an integrated model", *The Learning Organisation*, **11** (2/3), 129–144. An excellent discussion of concept and vagueness of "learning organisations", this offers a good review of literature on: organisational learning; learning at work; learning climate and learning structure. A challenging read; stop at page 135.

Chapter THREE

The Organisational Context

Chapter contents

❖ LEARNING OBJECTIVES

After reading this chapter you should have a clear knowledge of the world in which managers work. You should also have some appreciation of how the management context influences the way that managers work. In particular you should be able to:

❖ **list** at least five types of commercial organisations, three types of voluntary organisation and three types of public sector organisation. You should be able to name two specific examples of each

❖ **briefly describe** the advantages and causes of organisational culture

❖ **define** organisational culture and list, with examples, two main components

❖ **briefly describe** one- and two-dimensional ways of categorising organisational culture

❖ **describe** the work of Hofstede and Trompenaars and give some examples

of the differences they found between countries

❖ **briefly describe** the difference between high context cultures and low context cultures

❖ **give** five examples of possible cultural misunderstanding in non-verbal communications

❖ **identify** four different types of legal systems and outline the impact this has on judicial and financial systems

❖ **define** globalisation and list the possible problems of globalisation

❖ **identify** five different stages of globalisation and put them in order on a scale simple–complex

Most aspects of management are generic, and good managers can use their skills in a wide range of situations. Managers do not operate in a vacuum and they need to adjust the way they work according to:

- the *type of organisation* where they work, e.g. sole trader, conglomerate or charity
- the *culture of the organisation* where they work
- the *national culture* of the unit or organisation where they work
- *globalisation* and its impact on organisations

These contexts have an important influence on what managers do, how they do it and the quality of both home and work life. A sole trader will need to cope with all aspects of management from basic operational activities to long-term strategic activities. The first part of this chapter outlines the different types of organisation where managers work. The simplest type involves sole traders. Sole trader, Dave Banks, is unusual because his work is very specialised and technical. But in many other ways he is typical of sole traders.

CASE 2.1: *Dave Banks – an interesting sole trader*

Dave Banks is a sole trader specialising as a geological consultant in hydrogeological aspects of ground water. For example, he measures the purity of wells, streams and ponds, and advises how to eliminate impurities such as copper or zinc from the acid drainage caused by abandoned mines. He also uses deep boreholes to circulate water within strata where heat can be extracted. He has worked in London, Durham, Merseyside, Anglesey, Sudan, Zambia and Bucharest. A part of his work consists of training courses and research – in collaboration with the universities of Newcastle upon Tyne, Leeds and Tomsk, Russia. Like many "high-end sole traders" the visibility in all his work is promoted by authoring books (Banks, 2008).

His history shares many characteristics with "high-end" sole traders. He obtained a BA in natural sciences from Cambridge and went on an MSc in hydrogeology at Birmingham. He then gained practical experience at Thames Water authority in Reading and became a hydrogeologist. He obtained wider experience as a senior hydrogeologist in a global engineering consultancy that helps design infrastructure projects such as London Crossrail and hydroelectric projects in Laos. That company played an important role in the construction of the Mulberry harbours that were vital in the D-Day landings. Sole traders need a wide range of experience. In Dave Banks's case this included a review of water supply and sanitation in Darfur, Sudan. From 1998 until 2008 was a sole trader under the name of Holymoor, based in Chesterfield, Derbyshire. In 2008, the business grew sufficiently to justify converting Holymoor to a limited company, still operating out of Dave's home.

The way Dave works and his career are quite different to, say, that of a sales manager in a multinational organisation such as Rekitt-Benckisser (see Case 2.4). However, both travel extensively. They both experience many different national cultures and the impact of globalisation.

34   Part 1: What is management?

A junior manager in a pharmaceutical firm and a junior manager in a charity will share many attributes: they both need to transform resources so that they add value, they will both have frenetic pace of work – attending to a new thing every few minutes – and they will both have noticeably above average intelligence. However, their contexts, one in a leading edge technology puplic limited company (PLC) and the other in a world-class charity, will mean that they must manage differently. The former will have a lot of authority because he or she has formal power over wages or promotion. The latter will have little power over volunteers and he or she must be more aware of social and ethical issues. Similarly, there will be many similarities between a senior manager in a UK public enterprise and a similar organisation in, say, the Middle East. They will both be responsible for strategic decisions and have long timescales of discretion. However, cultural differences will mean that the former will be able to take decisions quickly, based on detailed written sources whilet the senior manager in the Middle East will need to proceed much more slowly in negotiations and to take non-written information such as family relationships or the location of meetings into account.

The other main contextual perspective on management, the historical context, is so big that it is described separately in the next chapter.

2.1 Types of organisation

Managers work in many different kinds of institutions. In broad terms these institutions can be grouped into three categories: commercial, voluntary and public sector. Below is a list of the main types of institutions in each group. Many of the types are well known or self-explanatory. Readers familiar with this subject can merely scan the list and perhaps read some of the more unusual entries such as limited partnerships, conglomerates and virtual organisations.

Commercial institutions

- **Sole traders** (often 'called Fred in a shed') are people who run a one-man or a one-woman band. They handle all aspects of the organisation and are responsible to only themselves. Often, sole traders work from home. Sole traders are personally responsible for the debts they incur. Technically, sole traders are not managers: they are not usually responsible for the work of others – unless, of course, their trade is organising events and other people.

- A **franchise** is an arrangement between the owner of a product or service and a franchisee who owns the limited rights to make or sell it. The product is usually unique or has a strong brand image. The franchisee is relieved of the risk of developing and marketing the product, and often benefits from advice and supervision. However, the franchisee usually has to pay a substantial purchase price and a continuing proportion of the profits. Perhaps the best-known franchise in the world is the McDonald's fast-food chain.

- **Owner-managers** – the main difference between owner-managers and sole traders is that the former will employ other people. There are a large number of owner-manager organisations, especially in retailing. Most owner-managers employ up to 50 people. Above this limit it becomes increasingly difficult for one person to control all aspects of an organisation. Consequently, when organisations employ more than 50 people, it is likely that professional managers will be employed.

- **Partnerships** involve two or more people who jointly act as owner–managers. The key aspect of a partnership is the personal and unrestricted liability of each partner for the debts and obligations of the firm – whether or not he or she specifically agreed to them. One partner can be made personally liable for the business debts incurred by another partner. Partnerships are common in organisations providing professional services in architecture, accountancy and law. Many management consultancies are partnerships and there may be dozens or even hundreds of international partners. Generally, however, the number of partners is fewer than six. A well-known partnership, the John Lewis Partnership, is quite unusual since all employees who have a substantial length of service are partners. Many large organisations started as partnerships. Examples include Hewlett & Packard, Goldman & Sachs and Marks and Spencer. Eisner (2010) examines 10 effective partnerships and the reasons why they succeeded.

- **Limited partnerships** have existed in continental European countries and the USA for some time. They now exist in the UK. In limited partnerships each partner is only liable for the organisations debts to the extent of the capital they may contribute or agree to contribute.

- **Private companies** are owned by a small number of shareholders and the shares are not traded to the public. Private companies have the advantage that they are not required to make stringent disclosures of financial information. This involves less cost and it gives greater confidentiality. Many private companies start as owner-manager organisations. The original owner-manager may have passed some ownership to friends, family and business acquaintances. One of the most famous private companies is the BMW organisation.

- **Public limited companies** are owned by thousands of shareholders and the shares are traded to the public. In order to protect the public these organisations are required to submit detailed, stringent accounts. Public companies are often traded on national stock exchanges such as LSE (London) and NYSE (New York). Sometimes the stock exchanges specialise in various sectors of the economy such as technology (NASDAQ). Some public companies are set up merely to trade in the shares of other companies. These are usually called investment trusts. Large public companies, usually in the top 100 companies, are referred to as "blue-chip" companies**.** Obtaining a quotation is a long and costly procedure that involves establishing a track record and producing Articles of Association that regulate the way a company is governed. This elaborate process inhibits small or medium-sized organisations from obtaining a quotation. Consequently, small and medium companies are often listed on the Alternative Market (AIM). Belonging to the Alternative Market is less onerous and acts as a halfway house to a full listing.

- **Holding companies** are organisations that own a number of other companies. Often they have assets of many billions of pounds or dollars but they employ only a small number of people – most of the work is performed by the employees of subsidiary

36 **Part 1**: What is management?

organisations. Most holding companies own subsidiaries that are related in some way. Sometimes there is a vertical structure whereby, for example, one subsidiary mines the raw materials, another subsidiary processes the raw material and a third subsidiary retails the product to the public. Sometimes there is a horizontal structure whereby, for example, one subsidiary manufactures a product in the southern region, another manufactures it in the northern region' etc. Conglomerates are usually large organisations and are often called corporations or groups. They are usually a type of holding company where the subsidiaries are involved in different industrial sectors. Conglomerates are usually formed when one company takes over several other companies in order to diversify risk, improve its market position or make additional use of plant and machinery. The formation of conglomerates was frequent between 1960 and 1980. Well-known conglomerates include AEG-AG, Agfa-Gevaert Group, Lever Brothers, Broken Hill Proprietary Company (BHP) and Virgin.

CASE 2.2: *A Virginal conglomerate*

In 1970, with pizazz and razzmatazz, Richard Branson founded Virgin Mail Order. The Virgin Record Shop, in Oxford Street followed close on its heels in 1971. Since then it has grown into a mature conglomerate. At the centre, Virgin Management Ltd consists of a relatively small number of people who are organised into specialist teams in London, New York and Sydney. They attend to three main activities:

- fastidiously number crunching the conglomerate's financial ratios to ensure assets get the best return
- analysing markets and spining public relations to maximise the value of the Virgin brand
- managing human resources so that Virgin's units are able to attract talented employees

The brand proved very successful and flexible. Today the Virgin conglomorate has more than 300 companies worldwide and employs many people in over 30 countries. The subsidiaries operate in a very wide range of sevice sectors. They include:

- transport (Virgin Atlantic Airways, Virgin Trains)
- telephone (Virgin Mobile India, Virgin Mobile France, etc)
- media (Virgin Radio International, Virgin Megastore, Virgin Books)
- vacations (Virgin Holidays, Virgin Experience Days, Virgin Balloon Flights, etc)
- finance (Virgin Money, Virgin Money Giving, Virgin Voucher)
- beverages(Virgin Drinks, Virgin Wines)

The Virgin conglomerate aims to provide better value than established competitors. Its name implies purity and lack of sexual experience. Some businesses, such as Virgin Bride – selling wedding dresses – were not successful. The oxymoronic subsidiary 'Virgin Condoms' was withdrawn after it failed!

- **Multinational corporations** are organisations that maintain significant, simultaneous, operations *in several countries* but are based in one home company. Well-known examples of multinational companies include the Kerry Group (Ireland), Shell Oil (Britain and Netherlands) and Nestlé (Switzerland).

CASE 2.3: *The Kerry group – an Irish multinational*

The Kerry group originated as a federation of farmer of co-operatives in County Kerry, western Ireland. In 1972 it joined forces with a state-owned dairy company and a US company that specialised in milk protein. The new company financed a new factory and initially focused on dairy processing. It grew organically over four decades and now has annual sales of about €4.5 billion.

It is not a conglomerate because it is focused in a single industrial sector, food products. A major advantage is its technological lead in the manufacture of food ingredients and flavours, which means that it sells products to other manufacturers who make crisps, sauces and beverages. The Kerry group also manufactures consumer goods that are well-known brands such as Wall's Sausages, Denny, Mattessons and Cheesestrings.

The Kerry group's headquarters remains in the delightful town of Tralee but it has a global reach. It employs over 20,000 people in 140 countries that cover Europe, North America, South America, Australasia and Asia. It has factories in over 20 countries.

- **Virtual companies** are a relatively new kind of organisation. They occur when the various departments or components of an organisation are physically divided and separated by distances of miles. The component units may be separately owned. The separate components are linked together by computers and IT connections, which means that the separate components can work together as if they were one organisation. For example, a bookseller could set up a central computer that receives Internet orders. The computer could then search the inventories of several book wholesalers to locate a copy of the relevant book. It could then initiate the wholesaler's dispatch of the book to the customer. Finally, the computer could arrange to debit the customer's bank account. As far as the customers are concerned, they would be dealing with a large bookseller holding a huge inventory of books. In fact, they are dealing with a sophisticated computer system that links various components.

- **Mutual organisations and co-operatives** are business association created for the mutual benefit of members. Often these are trading associations or financial institutions. In the UK they are sometimes called building societies or unit trusts. In the USA they are often called mutual funds. A co-operative is a legal entity that is owned and controlled by those who work for it or use it. There is usually some form of profit-sharing and the directors and managers are accountable to the members.

Voluntary institutions

- **Charities** are institutions or organisations set up to provide help, money and support to people and things in need. Many charities are small and are staffed by volunteers.

However, some charities have huge turnovers equalling those of substantial commercial organisations. Examples of large charities are the National Trust, Oxfam and Médecins sans Frontières. Much more about managing charitable institutions is given on the website associated with this book.

- **Clubs and associations** exist to increase the enjoyment of members. Some are managed by volunteers and are quite small. However, some clubs are large and employ professional managers. Some famous clubs are the MCC (Marylebone Cricket Club), the Garrick, the Liverpool Athenaeum and the Royal Channel Islands' Yacht Club. Some clubs become huge commercial successes and convert into commercial organisations. Typical examples include Manchester United Football Club and the Automobile Association.

- **Trade associations** and **professional bodies** are organisations which seek to protect and foster the interests of certain occupational groups and companies. To some extent they are very similar to political pressure groups since their aim is to increase the power of their members. These organisations can be substantial and wield considerable influence. They may also employ numerous managers. Associations fostering the interests of trades are usually called unions. Typical examples include the Communication Workers Union, and UNISON. Professional bodies tend to be called associations or societies. Typical examples include the Law Society, the British Psychological Society and the British Medical Association. Companies which share similar interests usually form a trade association to protect and foster their interests. Frequently they are called associations, federations or chambers. Typical examples include the Knitting Industries Federation, the Building Material Producers National Council and the Newspaper Publishers' Association. Usually trade associations and professional bodies start off as voluntary organisations but as their reputation and power increase it becomes virtually compulsory for members of the trade to enrol. For example, it is virtually impossible for a doctor or lawyer to practise unless they are a member of their professional body.

- **Political parties** and **pressure groups** aim to obtain sufficient power to change society. They aim to persuade other people to adopt and support their views so that they are then able to control resources they do not actually own. Senior managers in these organisations usually need a high level of charisma.

Public sector organisations

- **Government departments** employ many managers. Usually these managers are responsible to representatives who are directly elected. The range of government departments is enormous. They include the diplomatic service, the armed forces, revenue collection, education and health. Usually government organisations are divided into two groups: central government and local government.

- **Public enterprises** are created by statute to govern nationalised businesses. Perhaps the most famous public enterprise is the Bank of England. Other public enterprises include the German Federal Railway and the Tennessee Valley Authority. These organisations do not have share capital and are owned by the government.

- A **quango** is a quasi autonomous non-governmental organisation. They are semi-public administrative bodies which are set up by a government to achieve a "public good". Some are financed directly by a government and others are financed by a levy, which is often compulsory. A key feature of quangos is that the members are appointed, directly or indirectly, by the government and thus provide the government with huge powers of patronage. Quangos are often called agencies, commissions or councils. Typical examples of quangos are Health Service Trusts, the Health and Safety Executive, the Commission for Racial Equality and the Equal Opportunities Commission. Some lesser-known and esoteric quangos include the Crofters Commission, the Home Grown Cereals Authority and the Unrelated Live Transplant Regulatory Authority.

2.2 Organisational cultures

Apparently similar organisations can have quite different cultures. For example, a manager of a provincial newspaper will have quite a different work environment from that of a manager of a national newspaper based in London – even though they work in the same industry, produce a similar product and use similar technology. A great deal of the difference can be explained by the culture of the two organisations. One of the best-known definitions is given by Schein (2004):

> 66 the pattern of basic assumptions that a given group has invented discovered or developed and therefore taught to new members as the correct way to perceive think and feel in relation to problems. 99

In other words, culture is "the way we do things round here". Schein's definition focuses upon the intangible aspects of culture. However, as Figure 2.1 shows, it has both tangible and intangible components.

Tangible aspects of culture include the physical layout of the organisation. For example, an organisation with a culture that emphasises status might have separate canteens for

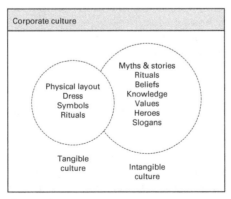

FIGURE 2.1 Components of corporate culture

managers and workers. The intangible aspects of culture are usually more important and more numerous. They include shared values, shared knowledge and a fund of shared stories of past events and heroes.

Organisational cultures perform very **useful functions**. They help integrate the organisation and make sure that all members are "on the same wavelength". They help communication and give a sense of purpose. It has been claimed that a strong corporate culture helps to increase performance efficiency. However, research by Kotter and Heskett (1992) suggests that the relationship between corporate culture and performance is weaker than earlier claims suggest.

Corporate cultures do not happen at random. Schneider (1987) believes that the main *cause of a culture* is the personality and style of the person who sets up the organisation. If the founder has a fluid, ethical style with an interest in basics (e.g. Anita Roddick, founder of Bodyshop) the organisation will be imbued with a fluid, ethical culture that emphasises products. This initial culture is then transmitted to future generations by the ASA process: first, the organisation **a**ttracts applications from people who hold similar values. It then **s**elects those who adhere most closely to its cultural norms. Finally, there is a process of **a**ttrition whereby employees who do not fit into the culture are encouraged to leave. Schneider's ASA theory does not fully explain the *transmission of organisational culture*. There is a socialisation process by which newcomers are taught the appropriate way of doing things and receive rewards, such as promotion, when they perform according to the organisation's culture.

Organic versus mechanistic cultures

Half a century ago Burns and Stalker (1961), identified two main kinds of organisational culture: mechanistic and organic. In **mechanistic cultures** the organisation is like a machine with everything tightly controlled and very predictable. Jobs are closely defined and highly specialised. Efficiency is paramount. These organisations were often appropriate in the mass-production and relatively stable environments of the first half of the twentieth century. However, mechanistic organisations have one big disadvantage: they are often inflexible and stifle innovation; a combination that can be fatal in a rapidly changing world. **Organic organisations** are like living things. They tend to grow and develop into new forms, they respond to their environments and, perhaps, may be a little messy or chaotic. Organic organisations thrive on problem-solving and innovation. Jobs are defined loosely and many regulations are informal. Organic structures are better adapted to a fast-changing world.

In the1960s and 1970s organisational psychologists identified many dimensions of organisational culture. Some are shown in Table 2.1. The list is still relevant today: it gives dimensions that can be taken into account when writing assignments or preparing discussions on organisational culture. The list is too long to be used in its entirety: it will be necessary to focus on three or four of the most relevant factors. Questionnaires to measure these organisational characteristics are described by Smith (1981). Generally it is better to use established questionnaires in projects rather than develop something new. It will then be possible to compare results between studies.

Organisational characteristic	Authors of relevant questionnaires
Organisational context (history, origin)	Pugh and Hickson (1976)
Location, geographical distribution, size, ownership and control, etc.	Pugh and Hickson (1976); Litwin and Stringer (1968)
Organisational structure	Reimann (1974);
Role variety; specialisation	Tyler (1973)
Role conflict; role ambiguity	Rizzo, House and Lirtzman (1970); Hage and Aiken (1968); Reimann (1974)
Centralisation	Reimann (1974); Hage and Aiken (1968); Pugh and Hickson (1976)
Decision-making style (participation, timeliness, level, etc.)	Likert (1967); House and Rizzo (1972); White and Ruh (1973)
Control processes and tolerance of error	Likert (1967); House and Rizzo (1972); Hage and Dewar (1973); Payne & Pheysey (1971)
Orientation towards the wider community	Payne and Pheysey (1971)
Innovation and risk	Litwin and Stringer (1968); Payne and Pheysey (1971)

TABLE 2.1 Some aspects of organisational culture

Strong versus weak cultures

A number of writers (Collins and Porras, 1994; Deal and Kennedy, 1982; Perrow, 1979; Schein, 2004) suggest that one of the most important distinction concerns **strong** and **weak** cultures (Table 2.2).

STRONG organisational cultures	WEAK organisational cultures
■ Most people have basic beliefs and values that *agree* with the organisation's values	Subcultures or people within an organisation have values and beliefs that are different or conflict with the organisation's values
■ Values and beliefs are *consistent* and coherent	Values are vague or contradictory
■ Values and beliefs are *comprehensive* and cover most things	Values are patchy

TABLE 2.2 A contrast between strong and weak organisational cultures

A strong culture has been defined by Robbins (1998) as

66 one that is internally consistent, is widely shared, and makes it clear what it expects and how it wishes people to behave 99

It was generally thought that strong organisational cultures were better than weak ones – especially in volunteer organisations and charities. A strong culture means that people are "on the same wavelength". They can communicate speedily, they act as a cohesive group, they do not challenge organisational decisions and so these decisions can be made very quickly. Often, strong cultures are led by charismatic leaders. However, some writers such as Schein (2004) have noted that strong cultures can be dysfunctional. The strong structure tends to foster a conservative approach. New ideas have difficulty gaining a foothold and people therefore have difficulty thinking "outside the organisational box". Others have noted that "groupthink" is prevalent in strong organisational cultures. Perrow (1979) believed that strong organisational cultures could be coercive and manipulative because aggressive behaviour may be used to enforce conformity.

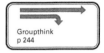

Groupthink
p 244

In an organisation with a weak culture people follow their own ideas beliefs and customs. This may be beneficial in innovative organisations or those organisations whose environment changes rapidly. This can work effectively *provided* that there are clear common goals – otherwise there may be little sense of direction as different parts of an organisation pull in different directions. The organisation may respond to this situation by using rules or extra supervision – which may alienate many employees.

The competing values framework (Cameron and Quinn)

Cameron and Quinn (2006) developed a framework based on the idea that organisational cultures largely arise from two values, each of which have two poles that compete with each other: they are:

- Flexibility, dynamism and discretion which is important in organisations that must change and adapt

versus

- Control and stability which is important in organisations that succeed by operating in a standard, structured and predictable way

- External orientation which is seen in organisations who are sensitive to the external environment and external competitors

versus

- Internal orientation where building unity and integration are major concerns

In the time-honoured way beloved by many organisational theorists, Cameron and Quinn placed two dimensions on a grid to produce four quarters. Each quarter was said to represent an organisational culture, as shown in Figure 2.2.

A **clan culture** is sometimes called a collaborative culture. A well-documented example is given by the courier company, DHL (Chan, 1997). It often gives the feeling of a family firm.

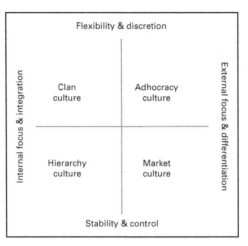

FIGURE 2.2 Cameron and Quinn's competing values framework

Goals are achieved by consensus and agreement by involving as many people as possible in decision-making. Loyalty and cohesion are highly valued. In return, the organisation looks after employees – frequently helping them to develop their potential for promotion. An organisation with a clan culture tends to have a flat structure with diffused authority. Co-ordination is achieved via shared ideas and values rather than rules and regulations. Clan relationships engender a feeling of safety which, in turn, encourages flexibility and growth. Most employees prefer clan cultures. A classic example of an organisation with a clan culture is the John Lewis Partnership.

Hierachy cultures are sometimes called *control cultures*. They tend to be seen in large or bureaucratic organisations such as tax offices or government. They may also be seen in large manufacturing organisations such as Toyota and McDonald's. People in these organisations will use standard operating procedures (SOPs) to produce large numbers of products or services that have a lot of similarity. Also, it is likely that there are a large number of clearly defined management levels. Promotion often depends upon an employee's ability to know and navigate their way around a set of rules. These organisations tend to occur in stable business environments,

Adhocracy cultures are sometimes called *creative cultures*. They tend to be seen in organisations that transform ideas and data rather than things (e.g. Google) and in entrepreneurial organisations. They are also seen in aerospace, IT, the media, consultancy and advertising. Organisational charts are either transitory or non-existent. Similarly the allocation of office space changes very frequently. In an adhocratic organisation the management tends to respond to urgent problems rather than planning to avoid them. Adhocractic cultures have very little structure and are very flexible. This enables them to exploit new ideas and technologies so that they quickly capture market share.

Organisations with **market cultures** are sometimes called *competitive organisational* cultures. They value stability and control but they focus closely on the external market.

Often they face severe competition from organisations at home or abroad. They are transactional. Astute relations with suppliers, customers, unions and law-makers are vital. They strive to compete by being excellent in managing relations through partnership and positioning. Performance, in terms of profitability, market share or customer base is paramount!

For convenience, this discussion of organisational culture has assumed that all organisation show only one, pure, culture. Nothing could be further from the truth. In fact, most organisations are amalgams of different cultures, albeit one type of culture might predominate. Further, different parts of the same organisation may have different cultures. For example, the finance function may, rightly, have a hierarchy (control) culture, while the salesforce have a market (competitive) culture. Divisional managers will have the unhappy task of reconciling such differences. Finally, this discussion has focused on the major trends in thinking on organisational cultures. However it should be noted that other writers consider issues such as risk-taking, teamwork, attention to detail, time orientation and a proactive approach to change to be important issues.

Relevance of organisational culture

Academic writings on organisational culture are relevant for three reasons:

- **Managers need to understand the culture of the organisation that employs them.** Even if they are technically proficient, intelligent and have the "right" personality and skills, they need to deploy these assets in a way that is appropriate to their organisational culture. For example, managers in an adhocratic organisation may be brilliant in devising rules and procedures but they are unlikely to succeed. Using their intelligence to be creative and adaptive would be better.

- **Managers need to foster an organisational culture that is appropriate to their business environment.** For example, a manager in an industry that is stable and where the unit costs are vital should encourage a control culture rather than an adhocracy.

- **Organisational culture matters in mergers and acquisitions.** A large proportion of mergers and acquisitions fail. The main reason for such failures is incompatible organisational cultures. When mergers or acquisitions are contemplated, due attention must be given to the congruence between organisational cultures or the ways in which the cultures of one (or both) organisations can be changed.

Organisational change p 143

2.3 National cultures

A large organisation such as IBM will have its own organisational culture but, since it operates in many countries, it will also need to take international cultures into account. The dominant western management style focusing on the achievement of overt results in the shortest possible time does not go down well in some countries. It is impossible to follow the western pattern of working 9 a.m. to 5 p.m., Monday to Friday in many parts of the world. In some countries a siesta is taken between noon and 4 p.m. and work then continues until, say, 8 p.m. In other countries Friday or Saturday are holy days when businesses are closed. In many western countries enthusiastic shaking of hands between negotiators is a sign that a deal has been reached; in some countries in the Middle East it is a sign that serious negotiations are about to begin. These differences are of great interest to multinational organisations. IBM, for example, commissioned a Dutchman, Geert Hofstede, to study such differences in 72 countries. His book *Culture's Consequences*, published in 1980 made him the most famous researcher in the field. Hofstede (2005) likens national cultures to "software of the mind". In essence he claims that there are five main dimensions to international cultures, which are fully described on Hofstede's website: *www.geert-hofstede.com*. In approximate order of size, they are:

- **Power distance (PD)** – the extent to which a culture accepts an unequal distribution of power. In high power distance cultures some people in an organisation will have much more power than others and this will be accepted.

- **Individualism (IDV)** – the opposite of collectivism. In individualistic cultures, the ties between individuals are loose and everyone is expected to look after themselves and their families.

- **Masculinity (MAS)** – the extent to which people are assertive, ambitious, competitive and wanting to accumulate wealth or possessions.

- **Uncertainty avoidance (UA)** – a culture's dislike of uncertainty and risk. It indicates the extent to which a culture programs its members to avoid unstructured, unusual, unknown situations.

- **Long-term orientation (LTO)** only emerges from data from students in 23 countries – mainly those with a Confucian heritage. When detected, it concerns perseverance over a long time. Things do not need to be rushed and another opportunity is to be expected – *mañana!*

Hofstede and other researchers have collected scores for many countries and they are available from his website. Figure 2.3 illustrates the results from the UK, Australia, Brazil, the Middle East and China.

It is no surprise that the cultures of the *UK* and *Australia* are very similar. They are characterised by a very high scores on individualism. This indicates that individual rights are very highly valued and that individuals tend to form a large number of looser relationships. The high score on masculinity suggests that people will be assertive and competitive. Low scores on long-term orientation suggest that punctuality is expected and that decisions can be made fairly rapidly (but not as rapidly as in the USA). Change can also be made more rapidly than in many countries. *China* has a very high score for long-term orientation, which means that people feel little need to rush when making decisions or friends. China also has a low score on individualism and things tend to be seen from a group perspective. Loyalty to one's group or family is paramount The high power-distance scores suggests a high level of inequality of power in Chinese society. Large power-distance and uncertainty avoidance indicates a society that has restricted upward mobility. Rules, laws and regulations are developed by those in power to reinforce their own control. In an effort to eliminate uncertainty, strong rules and regulations are often implemented. *Brazil* has a cultural profile similar to other Latin American countries. It has a very low

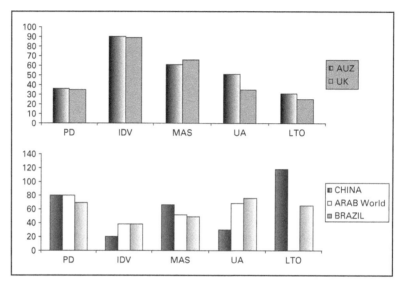

FIGURE 2.3 Scores of selected countries on Hofstede's cultural dimensions

individualism score which indicates a collectivist approach to many things. Further, it is a society that tries to eliminate uncertainty, sometimes using strict rules and regulations. The moderately high score for power-distance suggests an acceptance of inequality in society. Contrary to the "macho" stereotype of South American countries, Brazil's moderate score on masculinity is not of particular note. An excellent site containing Hofstede profiles for many countries is *www.cyborlink.com*.

CRITICAL THINKING 2.1 *Hofstede's critics*

Hofstede's work on international cultures is not universally accepted. There are five main criticisms (Jones, 2007 – a good read!):

- Surveys are not sufficiently sensitive measures of deep values. Hofstede (2002) rebutted this criticism by pointing to supporting studies using other methodologies.

- Cultures are not homogeneous – most nations are made up of subcultures whose characteristics are hidden when national averages are used. Hofstede attempted to rebut this by asserting national averages are usually the only data that are available and they are better than nothing.

- Some dimensions, especially masculinity, change according to "political influences" from time to time. Hence results change from decade to decade and results of Hofstede's 1980 study are now obsolete. Hofstede's rebuttal points out that the roots of a culture are centuries old and do not change significantly within a few decades.

- Results were based on one company (IBM) and could not provide information on the cultural system of a country. Hofstede attempted to rebut this by claiming that differences between national cultures were apparent by studying the same organisation in different countries.

- Four or five dimensions are not enough to capture the richness of cultures. Hofstede replies that many of the additional suggestions correlate highly with his dimensions and therefore amount to the same thing. More cultural dimensions are possible but they will be less important.

- The analysis was inadequate because some questions were used on more than one scale and many statistics were based on a small sample of 40 datapoints (countries). This means correlations are multiplied and subject to huge random error. However, other people have replicated Hofstede's work and found four dimensions that were very similar.

Jones concludes that the majority of Hofstede's findings have weathered the storms of time and will be a good guide to culture.

Hofstede's work has been so influential that it has overshadowed other important work on international culture. For example, the dimensions of international culture have also been studied by Trompenaars (1993). Trompenaars's research was more systematic and scientific. It involved 15 000 people from 47 countries. He came to the view that cultures differed in three main ways: relationships between people, attitudes towards time and attitudes towards the environment.

Relationships between people is the most complex way that cultures differ. Trompenaars differentiated five sub-dimensions:

- **Universalism vs particularism** reflects a culture's emphasis on rules and their consistent application (universalism) or its emphasis on flexibility and bending the rules depending upon the person and his or her circumstances (particularism).

- **Individualism vs collectivism** concerns the emphasis a culture places upon the individual and his or her rights and responsibilities (individualism) or the interests of the group and achieving a consensus of opinion (collectivism).

- **Unemotional vs emotional** is the degree to which a culture stresses detachment and objectivity in decision-making (unemotional) or whether subjective feelings are a part of decisions (emotional). This dimension may be related to universalism versus particularism.

- **Specific vs diffuse** is the extent to which a culture stresses in-depth, intense relationships (specific) or a wider range of superficial relationships (diffuse). Again this may be an aspect of universalism versus particularism; universalism is more likely when there are diffuse relationships.

- **Achievement vs prescription** reflects the extent to which a culture rewards people on the basis of their achievement or their social standing, celebrity and connections.

Trompenaars' second major dimension of cultural differences was the *way that time was viewed* – particularly the way that the present is viewed in relation to the past. Western cultures tend to see time as a linear **synchronic** dimension. There is a clear past, present and future. Present time is precious and must not be wasted. Decisions need to be taken quickly without losing time. In **sequential** cultures, time is a passing series of recurring events where opportunities will recur. Consequently there is a relaxed attitude to time and appointments – a philosophy of *manyana*.

Trompenaars' third dimension of cultural differences focuses on the *relationship with the environment*. In **inner-directed** cultures people see themselves as separate from the environment and attempt to control it for their personal benefit. On the other hand, in **outer-directed** cultures people see themselves as a part of nature. They try to live in harmony with nature and are more likely to "go with the flow".

Hall (1976) also studied international cultures and divided them into low-context and high-context cultures. **Low-context cultures** are typified by the UK, Canada, Germany and the USA. Important communication uses the written and spoken word. A message will be encoded very precisely. To decode the message the recipient needs to listen and read very carefully. **High-content cultures** include Japan and many Mediterranean countries. Only a part of the message is communicated in words. The rest must be inferred from contextual cues such as physical setting, the body language and even previous history. High-context communication takes considerable time. People from low-context cultures may not understand this and they may be perceived as pushy, hurried and even rude.

Other researchers contrast the way that different countries view **conflict** and **harmony**. Some organisations, especially those based in Australia and the UK, regard disagreement as a healthy sign. Employees are encouraged to discuss openly their reservations and conflicting views. There is a cultural belief that suppressing disagreements leads to longer-term problems and prevents good ideas from being adopted. Some organisations based in Asian countries have cultures that emphasise harmony. There is a cultural belief in preserving present methods and fostering traditional social relationships. Organisational cultures may also differ in a way that they deal with severe competition from home and abroad.

At a more specific and practical level differences in verbal and non-verbal communication can plague meetings where people from different national cultures are present. Some examples (see Dubrin, 2003) are:

- UK managers understate positive emotions. The comment "not bad at all" is likely to be interpreted by Americans as lack of enthusiasm.
- UK managers dislike personal questions and tend to stand further from people during business meetings.
- French managers expect to be greeted by formal titles for a number of meetings until everyone is well acquainted.
- The American "OK" symbol using the thumb and fore finger is a vulgar gesture in Spain and many Latin American countries.

- Attempts to impress Brazilian managers by greeting them in Spanish will be counterproductive. The language of Brazil is Portuguese!
- Shaking hands or embracing at the start of the meeting is considered offensive by the Japanese.
- Presenting small gifts when conducting business with Japanese managers is acceptable but it is offensive behaviour when conducting business with Chinese managers.
- In Arab countries, it is rude to sit down in a way that shows one's host the bottom of your feet or shoes.

National legal and financial contexts

International managers must also work within the context of national differences in legal and accounting systems. Briefly, there are four main types of legal system:

- **Codified law** is sometimes called civil law where a nation sets up a legislature to devise a comprehensive set of laws based upon their view of justice and morality. Countries with codified law include Brazil, France, Germany, Japan, Mexico, the Netherlands and Switzerland. Civil law starts with abstract ideas that aim to formulate general rules for the future. These general ideas become more specific and practical as they are developed. It is a "top-down system". The archetypal example is the Roman code set up by Emperor Justinian. Napoleonic and Germanic codes are other examples. Trials are dominated by an elite of judges who have a high level of independence from politicians. Juries are sometimes used in important cases.

  Financial context: countries with codified law tend to favour raising finance by credit: from banks, rich families or the state. Gearing is usually high. Often, even listed companies rely heavily on these sources. The banks etc. usually appoint several board members. Consequently, they will have inside knowledge of an organisation's financial situation. The need for legal safeguards and formal financial reports is usually less. Therefore, in these countries there are fewer accountants and accounting rules give greater focus to taxation issues (Nobes and Parker, 2006).

- **Common law** is mainly developed by judges who make specific decisions in response to specific situations. These decisions are taken into account in making further judgements, i.e. they set a precedent for future cases. Gradually a consistent system is built up to cover most situations. Sometimes the legislature will intervene to systematise judgements and remove anomalies. It is a "bottom-up" system. In the courtroom, career layers are as influential as career judges and they are very independent from politicians. Juries are very important in deciding matters of fact. Countries using a system of common law include the UK, Australia, Cameroon, Ghana, India, Ireland, Malaysia, New Zealand, Pakistan and the USA.

  Financial context: countries using common law tend to favour raising finance by offering equity such as via the stock market. For example, for every million Germans there are 7.9 listed companies whereas there are 44.4 listed companies for every million people in the UK. Consequently, gearing will be relatively low (107 per cent for the UK but 236 per cent for Germany). In order to protect shareholders, requirements for reporting a company's finances will be high and it will be necessary to employ hordes of accountants who need to grapple with *both* taxation and financial issues.

- **Islamic law** is sometimes called **religious law** and it is based in religious writings such as the Qur'an. Lawyers play a relatively minor role and the judges have religious training as well as legal training. Juries are not allowed and the courts are not very independent of religious leaders. Sharia law has some similarities to common law in the sense that it is based on previous cases and precedent. Indeed, it has been suggested that English common law was inspired by Islamic law. There are two main branches of Islamic Law; Sunni and Shia. The classic example of a legal system based on Islamic law is Saudi Arabia but there are many other examples in the Middle East and northern and eastern Africa.

  Financial context: for many years the development of financial institutions in countries that adopted Islamic law was severely restricted by the sharia's prohibition against payment or collection of interest. However, experiments with Islamic banking during the 1960s has resulted in over 300 Islamic banking institutions. A number of ways are used to overcome the ban on interest. For example, instead of charging interest on a loan to buy property, the lender buys the property and then sells it back at a higher price (the original price plus the equivalent of interest) and the original owner repays this higher price over a number of years. Other approaches involve banks giving depositors "a gift" or paying "rent" rather than interest.

- **Socialist law** is sometimes called communist law, which, like codified law, is based on statutes devised by a legislature. Party members play an important part in deciding disputes so the courts have only limited independence from politicians and juries are rarely used for important cases. The primary example of a country using socialist law is the Soviet Union.

  Financial context: in a pure socialist state, the state owns and controls all financial resources. However, it was usually convenient for the state to set up several banks. Usually there would be at least a state bank, such as the Russian Gosbank (which handled all significant transactions) and a people's savings bank such as the Russian Sberbank. There may be other banks for specific purposes such as construction (Stoybank) and foreign trade (Vneshtorgbank). However, most socialist states now also have commercial banks or at least have allowed investors to purchase a share in previously state-owned banks (e.g. a Hong Kong billionaire was allowed to buy a 20 per cent stake in the Bank of China). Despite such relaxation the state still controls the economy and may fiercely restrict foreign control. For example, in China there are A and B shares. Foreigners have a restricted ability to trade in A shares which are more numerous.

To make matters more complex some countries have a mixture of the two systems. For example, most of Canada adopts common law while Quebec uses codified law. Scandinavian countries have a system that is a *mélange* of common law and codified law, as does Scotland. China has a mixture of socialist law and codified law (derived largely from the German version) and Hong Kong follows the English common law.

Yet more complications are added by specific pieces of legislation, especially in employment legislation where there may be differences in legal aspects of industrial relations, security of employment, equal opportunities and health and safety. There are also major differences in company law.

2.4 The global context and globalisation

This chapter has set out the contexts in which managers need to work. It started with the relatively small issues of the type of organisation and the organisational context and worked its way up to international contexts. A generation ago, this would have been sufficient. Few managers would have to work or deal with more than two or three countries. Today things are different. It is not unusual for managers to deal with a dozen countries across several continents because trade has become global.

Definition and history of globalisation

There are many definitions of globalisation such as:

> A de-coupling of space and time, emphasising that with instantaneous communications, knowledge and culture can be shared around the world simultaneously.

> A process in which geographic distance becomes a factor of diminishing importance in the establishment and maintenance of cross-border economic, political and socio-cultural relations.

A more succinct definition by Fitzroy (2001) defines globalisation as:

> A worldwide drive towards a globalised economic system dominated by supranational corporate trade and banking institutions that are not accountable to democratic processes or national governments.

These definitions highlight the strong influence of communications, the shrinking of geographical distances and the flow of resources across national boundaries, together with globalisation's impact on political systems. They reflect the impact that globalisation has on virtually every person on the planet. As early as 1962 McLuhan recognised that the world had become "a global village". In the past, humankind existed in villages where they had personal knowledge of other people and events. McLuhan, considering the spread of radio communications in the 1920s, claimed that with the new media we could have the equivalent knowledge of people on the other side of the world. Today, we learn of far-off events, such as an earthquake in Haiti, almost as quickly as we learn of events in our own community. In this sense, the world is now one large village.

Reasons for and advantages of globalisation

The reasons for globalisation are simple. Different countries have different advantages that allow them to make things more cheaply and better than other countries. For example,

Saudi Arabia can produce oil, Australia cannot. Australia can graze sheep, Saudi Arabia cannot. It makes sense for Saudi Arabia to concentrate on extracting oil and buying sheep from Australia. If all countries focus upon what they do best and trade with other countries for things they do less well, the whole world is better off: petrol gets cheaper and so do lamb chops! Barriers to trade make the world less efficient. While these principles are true, the real situation is more complex.

The reasons for globalisation at the *organisational level* are similar but they show themselves in the form of economies of scale, bigger markets and exploitation of resources:

■ In many situations there are **economies of scale** if a service or product is made in high volumes. Often the market in one country is not big enough so organisations try to get customers from other countries. Indeed, in some industries it would not be economic to attempt *any* production on the basis of national demand. For example, despite the fact that it is situated in the USA, the biggest single market for aircraft, Boeing would not have developed the 747 if other markets were closed. Even if it captured 100 per cent of the American market it would not have sold enough aircraft to cover development costs. At a more mundane level there are huge advantages if global suppliers, such as Rekitt Benckiser, produce fast-moving consumer goods.

CASE 2.4: *Reckitt Benckiser – a truly globalised company*

When Isaac Reckitt rented a starch mill in Hull, on the east coast of England, in 1840 he could not have dreamt that he would be a founding father of one of the most globalised companies on the planet. Today, Reckitt Benckiser is a very successful player in the fast-moving consumer goods (FMCG) market. Fast-moving consumer goods are low-cost products that sell very quickly. They include toiletries, cleaners and soft drinks. The market is very competitive and Reckitt Benckiser's competitors include giants such as Unilever, Procter & Gamble and Colgate-Palmolive. People may not have heard of Reckitt Benckiser but it is almost certain that they have used its products. The company derives about 80 per cent of its income from 17 "power products" which include Dettol, Clearasil, Strepsils and Harpic. Fifteen million of its products are sold every day.

The company's headquarters is in Slough, near London Airport. However, its reach is truly global. Its products are sold in approximately 200 countries and it has offices and factories in over 60 countries. The C-suite executives (those who have the word "Chief" in their job title) has a global composition too. The chief executive is Dutch. This is not particularly exceptional since a substantial proportion of global companies have CEOs from the Netherlands. (The country has a historical global outlook. One of the first global organisations was the Dutch East India Company. Perhaps people from a small country are forced to think internationally!) Further, the nine-member executive committee includes seven different nationalities.

In an article for the *Harvard Business Review* (Brecht, 2010, p.103 – a good read) the CEO, Bart Brecht, describes how they built a company "without borders". In every country Reckitt Benckiser has employees of many nationalities: the UK business is run by an Italian;

the German business is run by an American; the American business is run by a Dutchman; the Russian business is run by a Frenchman and so on. Forty-nine different nationalities are represented in the top 400 managers. This level of globalisation among senior executives requires streamlined organisational policies. There is only one employment contract and there is only one set of rules covering the remuneration, pension rules, medical plans, etc. However, Reckitt Benckiser funds whatever schooling an employee chooses for their children. All this makes international transfers easily. The company has a distinct approach with students who have studied in a "foreign country". It may help them get work permits in the country where they have been studying because the fact that they have travelled to study mean they are internationally minded. Many companies assume that, after a "tour" abroad "expats" will return home. Reckitt Benckiser does not make this assumption. It focuses on placing executives in the best job for them, regardless of country.

A major advantage of the international variety at Reckitt Benckiser is the synergy to develop new projects. For example, a brand manager in Korea noticed that some stores were using an automatic scent disperser. It was crude but he thought it could form a new product. Further development was a substantial gamble for Reckitt Benckiser. The price would be higher than existing products; the company would have to develop expertise in electronic interval timers. Consumer tests were very positive. Within 12 months Air Wick Freshmatic was "flying off the shelves" in 30 countries and Reckitt Benckiser had overseen the building of a new factory in China where it could be mass produced. There are now many variations that are sold in 85 countries and the product generates well over £200 million per year for the company.

- Other organisations "go global" when they have **saturated their home market**. McDonald's is a classic example. It had fully exploited the economies of scale when there were, say, five or six restaurants within a 50-mile radius of any sizeable town and the American market was saturated. The only alternative to stagnation was to establish restaurants abroad in the UK, Australasia, Hong Kong and even, eventually, in France and Russia.

- Some companies "go global" in search of **cheaper resources**. The colonial powers established their empires in order to have cheaper access to gold, sugar, cotton, tobacco, tea or rubber. A few companies still establish overseas operations in order to have cheap access to physical resources such as gasoline, aluminium or timber. However, today firms may "go global" to gain access to cheap labour for, say, call centres or producing trainers.

   Relocations are usually greeted warmly by recipient countries. Although the wages paid by multinational companies are usually much lower than in an organisation's "home" country, they are usually significantly higher than wages in the recipient country – bringing advantages for both workers and their country. In other cases organisations have moved production facilities to less-developed countries because they have less onerous regulations. For example, Union Carbide has been accused of having lower safety and environmental standards at its plant in Bhopal than in a similar plant in West Virginia.

■ Some organisations "go global" to **provide a 24-hour service**. By siting offices in each of the three main time zones (London, New York and Tokyo) they will be able to trade throughout the day.

CASE 2.5: *Footloose and in search of cheaper labour*

In the past few decades firms such as Nike, Bennetton, Gap, Motorola and Dyson have moved manufacturing units to places such as Taiwan, the Philippines, Mexico and Malaysia in search of cheaper labour. More recently many manufacturing organisations have moved their production plants to China where labour costs are only a fraction of those in the developed world. Another example of an organisation seeking lower labour costs is Volkswagen's decision to move the production of its Polo cars to Bratislava, Slovakia. Years previously it moved production of Ibiza cars to Spain in order to avoid the high costs of labour in Germany. By 2002 Spanish labour costs had risen. Volkswagen then decided to move some production to Bratislava. Similarly, many American corporations such as Microsoft sited administrative centres dealing with billing and issuing licences in Ireland in order to take advantages of lower labour costs and government inducements. However, now that Irish labour costs have risen, these companies are relocating their administrative centres to Asia. Indeed, in 2004 Ireland became the second largest exporter of technology jobs worldwide. The most globalised countries in the world are Belgium, Austria, the Netherlands and Switzerland (KOF, 2010).

Stages of globalisation

Organisations rarely jump from domestic operations to operations on a truly global scale. Usually a company's path follows a discernible pattern with six main stages, but companies do not necessarily pass through all six stages.

The first step is usually **importing** supplies from another country. Nowadays, this is very easy. Later an organisation may **export** goods by setting up a **website** or **advertising** in another country. More proactively, it can employ **agents**. Employing an agent needs to be managed with care so that the agent is motivated towards selling the organisation's products rather than promoting a large number of other products – including those of a competitor!

In a **licence agreement** a local company is allowed to use specialised knowledge and processes (e.g. a patent) to make a product or produce a service. Licensing agreements offer a relatively easy method of global expansion. Licences are operated by people from the second country who use their own resources and capital. However, when the agreement expires, the second company may set up as a competitor. A **franchise** is a special kind of licence.

Joint ventures represent the next stage of globalisation and they often give companies quick access to new markets because they can use existing distribution channels. They also provide quick access to increased production capacity. Possibly the main advantage of a joint venture is sharing the risk. Unfortunately, about half of all joint ventures experience difficulties. These usually arise if there is a large imbalance in the expertise, where one partner's contribution is disproportionate or where integration and control is poor.

CASE 2.6: *Examples of joint global ventures*

Airbus is a classic example of a large-scale joint venture. The American giant, Boeing, was so dominant that companies outside the USA were not be able to mount an effective challenge. However, large aircraft manufacturers in France, Germany, England and Spain formed a joint venture that would be able to build a new series of aircraft (such as the super jumbo A380) and overtake Boeing in world markets. Bilateral joint ventures, where one company finds one partner in a host country, are more usual. For example, in 2004 Siemens Mobile signed a contract with Shenzhen Huawei Technology Company, one of China's leading telecommunication equipment manufacturers, to develop wireless-based communication products.

Acquisition is a bold globalisation strategy. It involves buying an existing organisation in another country. For example, a relatively small UK oil exploration company Paladin PLC was able to expand into the Timor Sea off north-west Australia by purchasing existing interests from the Australian multinational BHP Billiton. Acquisitions provide very speedy and full control over resources in another country. These include trained personnel, their tacit knowledge, an existing customer base and, perhaps, well-known brands. Unfortunately, acquisitions frequently fail.

Finally, an organisation may expand by starting and **developing their own foreign operations**. For example, when, in 1911, the Ford Motor Company wanted to expand outside the USA it set up an entirely new manufacturing operation at Trafford Park in Manchester. Today such developments are often called greenfield ventures. Greenfield ventures have the advantage that the new organisation can be set up in exactly the way the parent organisation wishes. Governments will often offer substantial inducements. The main disadvantage with a greenfield venture is that it takes a considerable time to mature.

When more than 25 per cent of an organisation's sales are derived outside its country of origin it is known as a **multinational corporation** (**MNC**). Technically, a multinational corporation is the same as a **transnational corporation** (**TNC**). However, the latter term tends to be used with large organisations operating on a truly global scale and where the majority of their income is outside the country of origin. A classic example of a transnational organisation is Nestlé, where over 98 per cent of its income is generated outside its country of origin, Switzerland. Philips is another example of a transnational company. It is estimated that Philips earns over 94 per cent of its income outside the Netherlands.

CRITICAL THINKING 2.2 *Pitfalls of globalisation?*

Organisations that operate in several countries encounter difficulties. In many countries the *infrastructure* of roads, telecommunications and education may make production difficult. In parts of the world such as some African countries political *instability* can pose a threat. A change in the composition of the ruling faction can wipe out a huge investment or make trading difficult.

Languages can cause problems – especially in marketing and advertising. Some excellent examples of advertising gaffes are given in Table 2.3.

Product	Intended message	Translated message
Coors Beer	"Turn it loose"	"Drink Coors beer and get diarrhoea"
Budweiser Beer	"Drink Bud light"	"Filling, less delicious"
General Motors car	"Body by Fisher"	"Corpse by Fisher"
Nova car	Nova	"Doesn't go" (Non Va)

TABLE 2.3 Unintended cultural misunderstandings (see New Mexican, 1994; Ricks and Mahajan, 1984)

2.5 Globalisation toolkit

Toolkit

Managers cannot afford to adopt an ethnocentric view that their own country's business methods are superior. The best approach is to retain the best from their own culture but also benefit from good things in other cultures. There are three main implications of globalisation: implications for organisations, implications for managers abroad and implications for negotiations.

Organisational implications of globalisation

The implications of globalisation for organisations divide into opportunities and challenges. A major opportunity is the ability to source raw materials from around the world. This gives greater choice and possibly higher-quality inputs at a lower price. Another opportunity is access to markets in other countries. An organisation that operates in another country must:

- Choose the **correct form of presence**: licensing, franchising, joint ventures, acquisition or greenfield development.
- Be familiar with **local customs, beliefs and laws**. In particular, organisations must be familiar with the local law governing workers.
- Use the organisation's **networks of contacts** to obtain informal information about the destination country, e.g. neighbouring organisations that are already operating in the destination country.
- be prepared to **modify** the organisation's management style to provide a better fit with the culture of the host country
- provide existing employees with **language training**. Managers should be given *acclimatisation training* to minimise "culture shock". Further details of content of acclimatisation training is given on the website associated with this book. Significant public announcements or **advertisement**s in another language should be *checked with at least two local speakers* who do not know the expatriate manager's home language

Implications of globalisation for managers

The implications of globalisation for managers sent to a **host** country mirror many of the implications for organisations. *Managers* should attend acclimatisation training to learn about the culture of the host country. It is important that they adapt to the local culture rather than try to re-create their home culture. An individual manager will need to adapt his or her management style to take into account differences on the dimensions identified by Trompenaars and Hofstede.

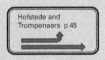

Hofstede and Trompenaars p 45

Implications of globalisation for negotiators

Implications of globalisation for **negotiators** are fewer but more acute since they have a relatively short time to achieve success. They must remember that other cultures have

58   **Part 1**: What is management?

 different perspectives on time. Negotiations in a host country will probably take longer than equivalent negotiations at home. There may be a protracted period of establishing friendship and rapport that is punctuated by ceremonial occasions such as giving gifts or formal meals. It is vital that negotiators familiarise themselves in advance with local custom and the formalities of introductions, visiting the homes of their counterparts and closing negotiations. Negotiators should also familiarise themselves with the local euphemisms that their counterparts may use to say "no" or to decline an offer.

Activities and further study

Essay plans

Prepare plans for the following essays:

1 Compare and contrast *one, named* unidirectional classification of organisational cultures with Cameron and Quinn's classification.

2 Compare and contrast Hofstede's analysis of national cultures with Trompenaar's classification.

3 What are the main reasons why organisations "globalise"?

4 What are the main difficulties facing organisations that globalise. Illustrate your answer with at least three specific examples.

Web activities

1 Use *Yellow Pages* or the Web to locate two specific examples, preferably from your own area or region, of the following types of organisations in which managers work. Enter their names in a table such as the one that follows:

Type of organisation	Example 1	Example 2
Franchises		
Limited partnerships		
Holding companies		
Conglomerates (not Virgin!)		
Multinational corporations		
Virtual companies		
Trade associations		
Quangos		

2 Choose two countries that you think you might visit, or work in, in the future. Visit Geert Hoftstede's website (www.geert-hofstede.com) and look up the the cultural profile of these countries. Compare these profiles with that of your own country.

3 Visit www.cyborlink.com, scroll down to bottom of page and choose the two countries you nominated in the previous exercise. Using this information make a list of two important things that you would have to adapt concerning each of:

- your appearance
- your behaviour
- communications
- doing business

Look at the page for your home country. Using the same headings, list three things you think might surprise foreign visitors.

Experiential activities

1 Form a discussion group that contains students from other countries.
   - Write a list of things you would expect foreign student to find unfamiliar or difficult about coming to your country. Then ask the foreign students to list things they actually found different or difficult. Compare and discuss the two lists
   - Write a list of the things that you would expect to find difficult if you were to stay in the foreign students' country. Ask them to produce a list of the things they would expect you to find difficult. Compare and discuss the two lists
2 Read Chan's (1997) article ("The corporate culture of a clan") to obtain a fuller understanding of a clan culture.
3 Choose four organisations you know – preferably organisations where you have worked. Consider each in turn. Decide whether each had a culture of adhocracy, hierarchy, clan or market.
4 Choose four family members or friends who are working. Read them the sections of this chapter that describe adhocracy, hierarchy, clan or market cultures. Ask them to decide the type of subculture where they work.

Recommended reading

1 Brecht, B. (2010) "Building a company without borders", *Harvard Business Review*, April, 103–106. Gives useful insights into globalisation and how a major multinational, Reckitt Benckiser, operates.
2 Schneider, B. (1987) "The people make the place", *Personnel Psychology*, **40** (3), 437–453. A classic paper explaining how organisational cultures arise and persist. It contain useful sections on career choice. Hard in places but the sections on Mischel can be skipped.
3 Chan, A. (1997) "Corporate culture of a clan", *Management Decision*, **35** (2) 94–92. A description of the organisational culture of the DHL parcel delivery company (in Hong Kong).
4 Jones, M. (2007) "Hofstede – culturally questionable?", Oxford Business and Economics Conference, Oxford, 24–26 June, http://ro.uow.edu.au/commpapers/370. Follow the link to a good précis of Hofstede's work and its critics. Good references.

Organisational Behaviour - Role of Management

Chapter FOUR

The Historical Context

❖ LEARNING OBJECTIVES

After reading this chapter you should be able to trace the development of managerial theory and practice. You should be able to explain how economic, technological and social factors of a period influence management thought. You should be able to identify and date the main schools of management such as scientific management, contingency theory and systems theory. In particular you should be able to:

❖ **describe** scientific management and the work of F.W. Taylor

❖ **describe** the work of classical administrative theorists – especially the work of Fayol and Weber

❖ **list** the seven management processes identified by Fayol and **explain** the distinction between a management process and a management function

❖ **explain** the basic philosophy of Fordism and explain the management techniques involved

❖ **briefly describe** "post-Fordism" and the reasons why it arose

❖ **explain** the Hawthorn experiments and **evaluate** the influence of the Human Relations School of Management

❖ **draw diagrams** depicting three types of organisational system

❖ **explain** the concepts of feedback, entropy and synergy

❖ **evaluate** the contributions of Fiedler and Woodward

CASE 3.1: *PROTON City of the future – or of the past?*

Malaysian car manufacturer Perusahaan Otomobil Nasional Berhad (better known as PROTON) is currently building Proton City (tagged "City of the future") which is due to be completed in 2020. Its vision statement is "To be a self-contained eco-sensitive, intelligent city with superior technological and educational capabilities . . . which provide . . . living environment that enriches its multicultural community". Proton City is a vision of a futuristic city combining work, education, health care, but the idea may not be new at all. In the early nineteenth century Robert Owen, an enlightened Scottish mill owner, who set up a textile mill in New Lanark, south of Glasgow. New Lanark combined improved working and living conditions and an enlightened attitude towards its employees which produced a rise in productivity and profitability. Like Robert Owen's vision, Proton City is a community where the workforce lives and works in conditions to nourish their productivity. It features:

- enlightened and fair working conditions
- modern, living accommodation
- state-of-the-art amenities including healthcare (hospitals etc.) and education (schools, universities, etc.) that instill the company's vision and enlightened ethos

Proton City may be hundreds of years and thousands of miles from New Lanark, but it is the historical descendant of Robert Owen's ideas in its aims of providing a progressive model of industry that benefits workers, owners and the country.

Henry Ford once famously said that "History is bunk". Recent writers have suggested that history is like driving using the rear-view mirror. At a superficial level these views may be true – history tells us about the past. Most people, especially managers, are more concerned with the present and the future. However, there are three good reasons why managers need a basic grasp of the history of their profession. First, it is important to learn the terms and ideas that are used by other managers. A brief study of the history of management is a good way to learn what they mean. Further, knowing how the terms arose helps to ensure that they are used intelligently and within their proper context. Second, history allows management to be seen in perspective. This has two advantages. It stops people taking a narrow view of management where their actions are based on limited personal experience. History also helps managers identify and react to longer-term trends. Third, managers in the past have learned from both mistakes and sucesses. Knowledge of history can mean that some of these lessons can be learned without the inconvenience of making them. Avoiding mistakes is useful but it is even better to reduce the waste of "reinventing the wheel" and cherry-picking past successes.

3.1 Early beginnings

Management is not new. It has existed ever since humans started to undertake tasks in groups. The hunting of mammoths by groups of Neanderthals required some managerial activity. The high priests of the Sumerian Empire managed agricultural estates and developed writing specifically to record resources for purposes of taxation. The Egyptians used fairly advanced management techniques to build the pyramids. Druids used management skills to build Stonehenge.

The Romans were great and systematic managers. Their soldiers were organised into cohorts, managed by senior centurions, which in turn were organised into legions and armies. The Roman Catholic Church (in terms of longevity, the most effective organisation of the western world) adopted a management structure leading from the parish priest to the Pope.

Machiavelli tried to improve the management skills of his bosses, the Medici princes of Renaissance Florence. Jay (1967) believes Machiavelli's works are "bursting with urgent advice and acute observations for top management of the great private and public corporations all over the world". All these historic examples of management were unsystematic. Management became more rigorous with the start of scientific management.

3.2 Scientific management (rational goal)

Scientific management is sometimes known as the Rational Goal School of Management and it emerged with the Industrial Revolution. There were three reasons why management became more important as the Industrial Revolution progressed:

- Larger units of economic activity became more common. Previously the family or a group of families was the predominant unit of economic activity. Large organisations were exceptional and usually associated with government, armies or religion.

- Industry requires greater specialisation of labour. Industrial processes were more complex and required high expertise. Employment in agriculture depended upon a few generic skills which most agricultural workers could perform as and when they were required.

- Factories and machinery were costly and often could only be financed by the combined savings of groups of people. This led to the development of the limited company where investors' liability was limited to the money they had staked in the institution. The person managing the enterprise may or may not have been the same as the person or people who owned it.

Many of the management techniques that are taken for granted today were developed by the grandfathers of scientific management, such as Bolton and Watt or Arkwright.

CASE 3.2: *Management ideas that can be traced back to Bolton and Watt*

Bolton and Watt, the grandfathers of scientific management were pioneers. They built a factory to manufacture steam engines in Birmingham in 1800. Existing systems of manufacturing were based on the craft workshops, which were disorganised and inefficient. Bolton and Watt adopted a scientific, analytical approach to increase productivity by making work easier to perform:

- They made a systematic analysis of the market for steam engines and the rate at which steam engines needed to be produced.

- They designed their factory to provide an efficient flow of work on the basis of these estimates. The speeds of the various machines were studied and adjusted to provide the desired rate of output. Each stage was broken down into a series of minor operations which could be analysed systematically. The basics of time-and-motion study were developed at Bolton and Watt's factory.

- They developed a wage system which was based on the work done. The output for each job was estimated and workers who exceeded the estimate received a bonus while those who did not achieve the estimate received a wage cut. This system can be thought of as the forerunner of later piece-rate systems.

- They introduced an accounting system which kept track of material costs, labour costs and finished goods. The accounting system also recorded indirect costs. It also allowed management to pinpoint inefficiencies and waste so that productivity could be improved.

Another grandfather of scientific management was Richard Arkwright whose contributions to management are described on this book's website.

F. W. Taylor – the father of scientific management

The scientific approach was taken up with enthusiasm in the USA, where workers were often seen as mere parts of a large machine. One of the pioneers of scientific management was Frederick W. Taylor. Taylor is most famous for his work at Midvale Steel and then the Bethlehem Steel Company. He studied jobs more scientifically than Bolton and Watt. He determined how much work could be expected from an operative each day. Previously management had relied upon tradition and workers had kept their output low to reduce the demands on them. Taylor used a more scientific approach to establish what a good worker should achieve. In one case, Taylor studied men loading pig iron into railway wagons: the average was 12.5 tonnes per day. Taylor calculated that if men worked 42 per cent of the time they should be able to achieve 47 tonnes per day. Taylor then chose a man called "Schmidt" and supervised him very closely, telling him exactly what to do and when. Note that Taylor was a reasonable man. He did not expect labourers to graft 100 per cent of the time. He scheduled substantial rest periods. At the end of the first day Schmidt had loaded 47.5 tonnes of pig iron. After a short period of training other men on the shift also achieved the target of 47 tonnes. Another experiment at Bethlehem Steel concerned shovelling iron ore and coal. When men were working with iron ore the load was very heavy but when they were working with coal the load was much lighter. Taylor's experiments showed that most material was moved when the shovel load was 21 lb. At that time workers provided their own shovels and they tended to use the same one irrespective of the material moved. Taylor provided a series of shovels – a small one for heavy material and a larger one for lighter material – so that the load was always constant at 21 lb. The average tonnage moved per labourer per day rose from 16 to 19. At a consequence the number of labourers needed fell from about 400 to 140. Taylor was sufficiently enlightened to pass on some of the increased productivity to the labourers. Wages increased from $1.15 per day to $1.88 – a rise of 63 per cent. In 1911 Taylor wrote his classic book *Principles of Scientific Management* and in 1912 he spoke before a congressional committee investigating systems of management. On the basis of these achievements Taylor was named the "father of scientific management".

CASE 3.3: *Taylor's lectures on management, 1907–1915*

Wrege (2008) gives a delightful and very readable description on the background to Taylor's lectures on management. Taylor built an opulent Georgian mansion with beautiful gardens and large rooms near Philadelphia in 1905. In 1906, Taylor's health was poor and he was advised to work only two-and-half-hours per day. In 1907 he started giving lectures at his home and they continued until his death in 1915.

Taylor's friend Maurice Cook arranged for his lectures to be recorded by a court stenographer and eventually they became the basis for a chapter of Taylor's (1911) well-known book *Principles of Scientific Management*. The lecture was highly standardised and was virtually identical each of the frequent times it was delivered – but no matter how often it was heard, it was always interesting and stimulating and showed a progressive viewpoint.

Lilian Gilbreth attended many times and described it carefully. The audience assembled in the early morning in the beautiful large living room and was greeted by Taylor and then his two young sons. The lecture lasted two hours and Taylor very much objected to interruptions, but he did allow questions when he had finished. He took one-and-a-half hours talking about handling pig iron and shovelling, with which everybody was familiar. Taylor then spent 15 minutes talking on slide rules where the audience was bombarded with terms such as "cuts", "gears", "variables", "formulas", etc. until the audience was in a muddled frame of mind.

Some of the sons and daughters of the scientific management movement were Frank Gilbreth and his wife Lillian, a psychologist. The Gilbreths studied the hand movements of bricklayers in minute detail. By eliminating repetitions and movements which served no purpose they were able to reduce the number of movements needed to lay a brick from 18 to 5. Some movements were eliminated by training bricklayers, others by improving materials (e.g. making sure that the mortar was at the proper consistency so that bricklayers did not need to "tap down" each brick) and by providing equipment such as a stand to hold the bricks so that the bricklayers did not need to stoop to pick up each brick. These improvements meant that the number of bricks a person could lay in an hour rose from 120 to 350. The analyses conducted by the Gilbreths were so detailed that they needed to use slow-motion photography. Gilbreth and his wife developed a system which characterised all operative work in terms of 17 basic motions such as "reach", "grasp", "hold" and "position". They called these basic movements "Therbligs".

Fordism and post-Fordism

Fordism

Henry Ford was another son of the Scientific Movement of Management. His major contributions were between, say, 1903 and 1926. At that time technology had devised attractive new products such as the motor car, but they were expensive luxury items built by craftsmen. Even though "the masses" of America were more prosperous than ever, a motor car was beyond their reach. In 1901 Ransom Olds used a stationary production line to bring down costs and produce the first mass-produced car, the "Oldsmobile". Henry Ford refined these ideas and developed a new line of thought. If better production methods could reduce costs, more people could buy the product. If more people bought a product, the economies of scale would bring costs down further and demand would grow. More people would be employed so more people could afford cars and so on. There would be an accumulation of wealth and economic activity. The idea of efficient mass production and mass consumption lies at the heart of Henry Ford's contribution to management. A number of things were necessary in order to reduce costs so that "the masses" could afford products. They were:

- **Standardisation, interchangeability and precision**. Henry Ford sought to standardise as much as possible. Every component would be designed to be as efficient and as economical as possible. It would have very exact specifications so that its performance would be precise and employees would not have to spend time making adjustments for each individual item. Any one of a specific component could be fitted to any car. If one proved defective, it could be replaced by one that worked well. Components could be manufactured in very large numbers, at low costs. Ford's standardisation is epitomised by his statement that the consumer could have "any colour of car so long as it was black" – he had established that black paint dried quicker than other colours. This together with bulk buying of only one colour shaved costs so that the price of cars could be brought within the reach of more people.

- **Simplicity and specialisation.** Henry Ford analysed the manufacturing process in fine detail. Even complex assemblies were divided into a series of very simple actions such as (1) placing an axle in position, (2) putting a wheel hub on the axle, (3) tightening two top screws and (4) tightening two bottom screws. Workers would be trained to perform just one of these specialist actions. This reduced training costs and it could be accomplished by less skilled workers. Further, time was not wasted changing tools – again reducing costs. Specialisation was extreme. An employee would have only one task, such as putting a bolts on a wheel. He did not order parts, repair equipment, check quality, keep the work area clean or even understand what the assemblers on either side were doing (Womack, Jones and Roos, 1990).

■ **Syncronisation and conveyor belt production.** Because production was broken down into small standardised steps they could be syncronised into a smooth, efficient sequence. One of Henry Ford's innovations was **the conveyor belt system** which is also called a **production line**. Previously, mechanical power, such as in the textile industry, had been produced by huge central steam engines or even waterwheels. It was transmitted to the workplace by cumbersome and inefficient systems of gears and belts. Henry Ford used electric motors. This energy could be placed much nearer the workshop and could power a series of conveyor belts. The belt brought work to the workers – saving the cost of the time they would take to walk between units. Further, the speed of the belt could be set at a pace which just, and only just, allowed enough time for workers to complete their small, monotonous tasks. However, it saved the time that workers might spend idling.

All of these innovations were implemented at Ford's Model-T plant at Highland Park in Michigan in 1914. Productivity increased tenfold and the price of cars was halved – bringing their purchase within reach of more people-volume increased and so did economies of scale and profits. The workers benefited too. Wages rose from $2.34 per day to a breathtaking $5.00 per day. So more workers could afford to buy cars for themselves – thus increasing volumes, the economies of scale and profits. The Ford Motor Company quickly became the biggest company in the world and retained that position for decades.

A business model yielding such fantastic results could not be ignored. It was copied with enthusiasm by competitors and many other industries in the USA. Ford already had a factory near Manchester and the techniques were quickly transferred to the UK before the factory was relocated to Dagenham in 1931.

Other countries rushed to adopt Ford's principles. This was especially true in Germany (some of Ford's ideas were based on Prussian principles of administration) and, ironically, the anti-capitalist state of the Soviet Union (standardisation, uniformity and the promise of a better future for the masses, if properly planned and controlled, were especially appealing to Stalin and his colleagues). It also attracted attention in Italy. In about 1929 an Italian Marxist philosopher, jailed by the Fascists, noted the spread of Ford's influence. Gramasci (see Levy and Egam 2003) considered the Ford "model" to be a ploy by the bourgeoisie to obtain hegemony by making concessions. He termed the phrase "Fordism". Fordism, fuelled by the demands of war and subsequent aspirations of "the masses" for a more affluent life swept into its heyday, say, 1950–1970, when it was very dominant as large corporations provided masses of people with many standard products at prices they could afford. It could not last. Fordism, in all its mighty glory had inherent problems.

CRITICAL THINKING 3.1 *What was wrong with Fordism?*

There were at least two major problems with Fordism:

Inflexibility resulted from centralisation and specialisation. Changes needed to be referred to HQ and this took time. Alfred P Sloan, chairman of rival General Motors allowed divisional managers to make decisions. They came up with a bigger range of products, and quicker decision-making meant better adjustment to changes. Customers wanted more choice and many preferred cars, made by competitors, that were not black. General Motors overtook Ford as the number one car-maker in the late 1920s.

Working practices were monotonous. There were considerable hidden personal and social costs. Large numbers of "bored" workers were easy to organise into unions to stand up for their rights. Strikes could cause mayhem in a rigid and tightly scheduled assembly line. The negative aspects of monotonous working practices were satirised by Charlie Chaplin in the film *Modern Times*.

Post-Fordism

Among others, a Russian economist, Nilolai Kondratiev (1935), controversially noted that there are long-term economic cycles lasting about 54 years. This is the time it takes for a major set of innovations to pass through four phases: prosperity following the innovation, recession, depression and recovery. He identified three waves in modern times:

- Kondratiev wave 1: *c.*1800–50, cotton processing technology
- Kondratiev wave 2: *c.*1850–1900, steam power, railways, steel, etc.
- Kondratiev wave 3: *c.*1900–50, motor cars, petrochemicals, etc.

So, it should have been no surprise that a major change, from Fordism, was due in the 1960s. Almost on cue, major changes started and they became very apparent in the 1970s. This led to an era called post-Fordism. The changes were fuelled by several developments:

- The market for cars, petrochemicals and electricals became mature and saturated. Additional volumes to provide greater economies of scale were hard to find. People wanted more and better services rather than material possessions.
- Boundaries between social classes became less important. Many blue-collar workers became more affluent than many white-collar workers. The many different groups were not satisfied with a limited range of products.
- Computers and IT made it easier to identify a myriad of trends and to set up production to cater for these trends. Modern robotics meant that the production line could be easily modified, Indeed, modern robotics mean that production could be achieved without assembly lines of the type built by Ford.

Post-Fordian managers developed flexible organisations with fewer managerial levels, smaller corporations, where many activities were outsourced. This was Kondratiev's fourth wave and it was based on electronics and consumer goods. Kondratiev's fifth wave started in the 1990s and it was based on the Internet, wireless technology and biotechnology. It is expected to reach its high point about now!

The continuing contribution of scientific management

Writers today tend to minimise, or even disparage, the contribution of scientific managers. However, their great contribution is clear when it is set against the historical context of their times when industry was very labour intensive and productivity was very low. Scientific managers, and Henry Ford, tackled the most pressing managerial problem – to increase efficiency and productivity. Today we take their efforts for granted. We automatically assume that workers will be properly selected, trained and equipped. Scientific managers were primarily concerned with productivity of manual workers in heavy industry. The importance of heavy industry to the economy has decreased substantially in the century since the heyday of Taylor, Ford and Gilbreth. Nevertheless, scientific management retains an important role. The Gilbreths' contributions are an integral part of operations management and industrial engineering. Their ideas are fascinating and still used in many different ways. If they were alive today Frank and Lillian Gilbreth would be overwhelmed to see how much their work is the foundation for a great deal of contemporary management (Mousa and Lemark, 2009).

Equipment manufacturers conduct studies to ensure that their products are suited to people's capabilities. For example, designers of computer software will check that screen images are legible. Similarly, manufacturers of mundane military equipment such as boots and socks will conduct studies to ensure that their products are designed to allow soldiers to march long distances without producing footsores. Designers of control panels for complex chemical plant will go to great lengths to ensure that the control displays are easy to understand and that warnings of danger are unmistakable. Today studies in scientific management are usually covered by the discipline of ergonomics – the science of work.

The quantitative school of management

Scientific management and the basic ideas of Taylor reached a second peak, in a slightly different form, between 1940 and 1980 and it operated under different names such as the **Quantitative School** or **management science**. There were, however, important differences. Taylor was largely concerned with physical work, whereas the Quantitative School focused upon managerial decisions. While Taylor used very straightforward analytical techniques, the Quantitative School used very sophisticated methods of analysis. In many areas the Quantitative School is still strong today.

During the Second World War garguantian quantities of men and material were deployed against the enemy. Governments were keen to obtain a military advantage by deploying men and materials in the most effective way. They employed scientists, mathematicians and statisticians to study a problem in a rational, quantitative, scientific way. For example, it was imperative to defeat the U-boats' menacing convoys. Depth charges were a main method of attack. Many questions needed to be answered for a destroyer to make a successful attack.

70   **Part 1:** What is management?

How many depth charges should be used against a single submarine? Too few might not result in a "kill" while the use of too many might mean there were insufficient to attack other submarines in the pack. At what depth should the fuses be set to explode? What would be the most efficient pattern of scattering the depth charges? Scientists and mathematicians studied the kill rates for various situations and derived an attack plan which would result in the greatest number of submarine kills per depth charge. More recent, civilian, problems are illustrated by a retail organisation which wants to know the optimum density for its outlets. If each outlet serves a large area, a large number of consumers will be within range and profits will be high – except for the fact that large catchment areas involve high transport costs and management supervision becomes costly and difficult. Further, wide spacing of outlets might allow competitors to establish themselves. On the other hand, retail outlets too close to each other yield small catchment areas. The question arises "what is the optimum density of retail outlets". The company might conduct a study and its mathematicians might produce the formula:

$$\text{Profit (in millions)} = r \times 2 + (r^2 \times \pi) - (r^3 \times 0.5)$$

It is then possible to construct the following table:

Catchment radius (miles)	1	2	3	4	5	6	7	8	9
Expected profits (£m)	23	49	75	98	116	125	122	105	70

From the table it is clear that the catchment area of retail outlets should have a radius of 6 miles. Therefore shops should be set 12 miles apart so that the catchment areas touch but do not overlap.

The Quantitative School of Management had a great influence upon quality management which emphasises setting standards, samples, measurement and the use of statistical methods to detect batches that were faulty. This developed into a very numerically based statistical process control (SPC) and a six sigma approach which aims to ensure that there are less than four defects per million products (see Fisher and Nair, 2009). The Quantitative School of Management also had important influences on the development of queuing theory and "just-in-time" production methods. The Quantitative School uses algorithms and game theory to reach solutions. It aims to provide the best possible decision and it is usually applied to problems that are too complex to be solved by common sense. When managers are asked to solve complex problems without the aid of qualitative models they tend to settle for solutions which are satisfactory (**satisficing**) rather than the best possible solution (**optimising**).

SPC and TQM
p 374

The quantitative approach is often called **operations research** (**OR**). The quantitative approach is characterised by three features:

- *mathematical models*, linear programs and statistical trend analysis to identify patterns that can be projected into the future to make forecasts

- *simulations* to determine the impact of different decisions – often these simulations take the form of spreadsheets to examine "what if" scenarios where the impact of several variables can be studied
- *specialised techniques* such as algorithms, critical path analysis and just-in-time methods to help managers determine key dates and identify likely bottlenecks

The Quantitative School is a far cry from the techniques developed by Taylor. Nevertheless they share the aim of making behaviour more predictable, more productive and more machine-like. The quantitative approach has made enormous contributions to management decisions, especially decisions concerning planning and control.

CRITICAL THINKING 3.2 *Problems with quantitative methods*

Quantitative methods are not as perfect as they seem.

- They may be less precise than they seem. They often rely on data which are estimated by managers and other people who may have a vested interest in providing distorted information. These estimates can be substantially awry and unreliable.

- The assumptions used in the models developed by the quantitative managers may be wrong. Because these assumptions appear scientific they are difficult to identify and correct.

- Quantitative methods may place an unreasonable emphasis on economic effectiveness. They may miss more subtle goals such as satisfaction, enjoyment and justice because intangible psychological states are very difficult to quantify.

Some critics go further and complain that the Quantitative School gives too narrow a view of management. Other critics maintain that it is not a school at all. Mathematics and statistics are used in many sciences such as engineering and medicine but they are not a school of thought.

3.3 Classical (administrative) theorists

Scientific managers, and Ford, were concerned predominantly with managing operatives and labourers. They said very little about management itself. The classical theorists were largely senior managers in large organisations who turned their minds to analysing the processes of management.

Henry Fayol

Probably the most important classical theorist was Henry Fayol. Fayol was the general manager of a large French mining company. He was primarily concerned with "administrative principles" that apply to the organisation as a whole. Fayol identified the key processes which managers needed to perform. If a manager performed these functions properly, he would be effective. The main processes of management according to Fayol were: planning, organising, commanding, co-ordinating and controlling. Since his time Fayol's list has been amended and the main processes of management are now seen to be:

- planning
- organising
- staffing
- deciding
- controlling
- reporting
- budgeting

The processes can be remembered by the acronym POSDCRB. Each of the processes will be considered in much greater depth in Part 2 on management processes. Fayol also identified a number of management principles. It has been argued (Yoo, Lemak and Choi, 2006) that they are important constituents of modern competitive strategies – cost leadership and differentiation (CL and DF respectively below). Fayol's management principles were were:

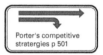

Porter's competitive stratergies p 501

- **Division of labour** – up to a point people should specialise in performing certain tasks so that they can build a high level of expertise (CL).

Specialisation p 114

- **Authority and responsibility** – the right to give orders and expect them to be obeyed. Authority usually arises from a manager's role. Sometimes, authority arises from the person's abilities such as intelligence, expertise, charisma or general character. This kind of authority is sometimes known as "informal" or "personal" authority. A good manager should have both formal and informal sources of authority. Fayol was keen to link authority with responsibility. When a manager uses power to issue an instruction, he or she is responsible for the consequences. If the course of action leads to success, the manager should be rewarded and if it leads to failure the manager should be punished. Later writers referred to Fayol's concept as the *"parity of authority and responsibility"* (CL).

Types of power p 195

- **Discipline** – involves obedience, diligence, energy, correct attitude and respect.
- **Unity of command** – everyone should have one, and only one, boss (CL).
- **Scalar chain of command** – there should be a clear hierarchy which runs from the bottom of an organisation through to the top. This ensures the integrity of the organisational structure and unity of command. Generally, communications should follow the hierarchical route. However, Fayol recognised that if every piece of information needed to go from the bottom of an organisation to the top and then down again to the bottom,

the delays would be unacceptable. Fayol therefore introduced the "gang-plank" principal whereby people at the same level within an organisation could communicate with each other (CL).

- **Unity of management** – efforts and plans should be in pursuit of the same objective.
- **Subordination of individual interests to the common good** – the goals of the organisation should take precedence over the goals of individuals or groups.
- **Remuneration of staff** – employees should be fairly rewarded for what they do.
- **Centralisation** – the degree of initiative which is left to individuals or groups. Centralisation is neither good nor bad: it depends on the organisation, its environment and goals. Every organisation must strike the appropriate balance
- **Order** – the correct position for equipment should be determined and equipment should be kept in that position (a place for everything and everything in its place).
- **Equity** – managers should be friendly and fair. They should show good sense and good nature.
- **Stability of staff** – staff turnover is disruptive and incurs costs. It should be minimised so staff can develop required skills and commitment to the organisation (modern thinking is that excessive stability produces rigidity and should therefore be carefully controlled) (DF).
- **Initiative** – employee initiative is an asset to all organisations, especially when times are difficult. Initiative is the ability to conceive and execute a new plan when existing plans are not satisfactory.
- *Esprit de corps* – refers to the harmony among people within the organisation so that morale is high (DF).

Max Weber and bureaucracy

Max Weber was a classical theorist who focused on administrative processes. Weber was struck by the inefficiencies of the old semi-feudal structures where people had loyalties to their patrons rather than to the organisation. This led to conflict and inefficiency. Weber attempted to provide guidelines for a rational organisation which had rules so that the organisation performed predictably and consistently. He envisaged organisations managed in an impersonal, rational way. He called these organisations "bureaucracies". Weber attempted to improve routine office operations in a way similar to Taylor's improvement of labour operations. According to Weber an ideal organisation would be characterised by six facets:

- Jobs are **specialised** and have **clear definitions** of their authority.
- Jobs are arranged in **hierarchical order** in which each successive level has greater authority and control.
- Personnel are selected and promoted on the basis of **merit**. Personnel are given adequate training.
- Acts and decisions are **recorded in writing**. Proper records form the memory of an organisation and the use of precedents ensures equality of treatment.

■ A **comprehensive set of rules** which cover almost all eventualities. Employees are expected to keep to the letter of these rules and apply them impartially – irrespective of the rank and position. This meant that employees, customers and citizens would not be subject to the whims of individual employees and people would be treated fairly.

■ **Management is separate from ownership** of the organisation.

Bureaucratic organisations have been heavily criticised because they become inflexible. Rules confine initiative and lead to demotivated employees. Some writers have identified the phenomena of **bureau pathology** in which unrealistic and irrelevant rules are set. When employees fail to observe these rules, yet more rules are developed to control non-conformance. The additional sets of rules alienate employees further and provoke more non-conformance – which triggers yet more detailed rules and so on. Over time, the original purpose of the rules is forgotten and the rules become ends in their own right. Strict observance of the rules may serve administrative officials well because it offers security – as long as they obey rules they are safe from criticism. However, the rules may not be in the interests of the organisation's clients. Weber is also famous for his identification of the link between prosperity and the Protestant work ethic. He noted that according to Protestant culture and dogma hard work was sanctified by God. Thus Protestant people work harder. A scattergram where countries are positioned on two axes, the proportion of the population that is Protestant and the gross domestic product (GDP) per head of population shows a clear trend. There is a clear correlation between Protestantism and national wealth. Protestant countries such as the UK, the USA and Germany tend to be wealthier than countries such as Mexico, Italy and Spain.

CRITICAL THINKING 3.3 *Was Weber wrong?*

A paper by Becker and Ludger (2009) suggest that Weber was mistaken. The Protestant ethic emphasised the importance of individuals studying and reading the Bible. This meant that Protestant countries had a higher rate of literacy which in turn meant people were more productive. Becker and Ludger tested their hypothesis by studying the percentage of Protestants in provinces of Prussia, the level of literacy and average income. When literacy is taken into account there appears to be no relationship between Protestantism and economic success.

This is a very good example of the great problem of interpreting correlations. There may be a clear relationship between two things but this does not mean that one thing (e.g. Protestantism) necessarily causes another (e.g. economic success). There could be a hidden, unsuspected phenomena (e.g. literacy) that is more important. Further, a causal relationship might be the other way around. For example, higher incomes could make it more favourable for people to be literate, and more inclined to be Protestant.

3.4 Human relations

Scientific managers thought of employees as machines. They sought to improve the efficiency of the "human" machines. Even during the heyday of scientific management, some people were not convinced that human beings were like machines. They argued that human beings had special characteristics. The human relations school goes back at least to the days of Robert Owen, a Scottish mill owner, who criticised contemporary managers for buying the best machines and then hiring the cheapest labour. He set up a textile mill in New Lanark, south of Glasgow, where he established better working conditions for his employees and noted a rise in productivity.

The work of Robert Owen was influential but it did not employ techniques that were explicitly scientific. One of the first people to use scientific methods to investigate the characteristics of human beings in work situations was a German, Hugo Munsterberg. He noted that the scientific managers emphasised physical skills but ignored mental skills. Munsterberg was way ahead of his time. During the first decade of the 1900s he identified the major trend in the nature of work which is still evident today: work becoming less dependent on physical skills and more dependent on mental skills. Munsterberg developed tests which could identify workers who had the mental skills demanded by a job – especially higher-level jobs. Munsterberg also tried to establish the psychological conditions that produce highest productivity. In many ways Munsterberg was the link between the scientific managers and the human relations school of management.

Elton Mayo and the Hawthorne experiments

Elton Mayo followed Munsterberg's lead. He tried to find psychological conditions that would give higher levels of productivity among workers at the Hawthorn electrical plant near Chicago which, among other things, manufactured light bulbs. The work of Mayo and his colleagues has been described by Roethlisberger, Dixon and Wizght. (1939) and criticised by Parson (1974), Adair (1984) and Diaper (1990). The company was keen to prove that good lighting improved the performance of operatives. Mayo and his colleagues established two groups of workers. One was a control group. The other was an experimental group and the level of illumination at their workplace was varied. As the level of illumination rose so did productivity. However, most people were surprised when productivity also rose when illumination was reduced. Evidently, the actual level of illumination was not a key factor. Other experiments suggested that workers were responding not to the levels of illumination but to the attention which management was devoting to workers. These studies are famous for identifying the "Hawthorne effect".

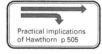

Practical implications of Hawthorn p 505

The Hawthorne effect was a very, very important discovery. However, a second finding from the Hawthorne studies was equally important. Mayo and colleagues observed workers in the bank wiring room where connections on electrical equipment were soldered (nowadays such connections are a part of microchip's design). The time-and-motion department established that an efficient worker should be able to solder 7312 connections per day. However, workers generally completed about 6300. Mayo and his colleagues wondered why output was lower than expected – was it because the time-and-motion department had set a target that was too high? Mayo came to the conclusion that **informal social norms** were responsible. The men, and indeed their immediate supervisors, believed that 6300 connections was a fair day's work. If anyone made significantly more connections than 6300, they were called a "rate buster" and were punished by sarcastic comments and a hard punch on the top of their arm – a process called "binging". If anyone made fewer than 6300 connections they were called a "chiseller" and subjected to similar sanctions. This was not the machine-like behaviour that scientific managers expected. Machines do not form coalitions to set and enforce their own standards of output. The work of Mayo in the bank wiring room showed that managers need to take account of social and psychological factors such as social norms and group dynamics. The bank wiring room studies pointed to the importance of teamworking.

Teamworking
p 121

Barnard and Follett

Other experts refined and developed ideas demonstrated in the Hawthorn studies. Mary Parker Follett (1941) argued that the management of people was the very essence of management. She defined management as "getting things done by other people". She advocated abandoning traditional bureaucratic organisations and their demotivating disadvantages. She argued, we should harness the potential of people. She suggested that management's main task is to encourage people to form self-governing groups that are empowered to solve commercial and industrial problems. This advice contradicted the principle of "specialisation" advocated by the scientific managers. Mary Parker Follet also offered advice on conflict resolution. Whereas scientific managers believed senior managers should work out the best possible solutions to the problem and then cajole employees to implement that solution, she suggested it is better to bring conflicting groups together and allow them to work out their own solutions.

Chester Barnard was president of the New Jersey Bell Telephone Company. He stressed the need for managers to obtain the co-operation of employees so that they would work towards adding value to the organisation rather than their own goals. He maintained that the best way of obtaining employee co-operation is to communicate effectively and hence create a harmonious working atmosphere. Again, this was in direct contradiction to Taylor and Ford's approach which implied that working atmosphere is irrelevant to the performance of machines.

The Human Relations School has had an enormous, evangelical impact on management practice. Nevertheless, it is open to criticism.

CRITICAL THINKING 3.4 *What were the weaknesses of the Human Relations School?*

Many of the early experiments were less scientific than they seemed. For example, the Hawthorn studies were very poorly controlled and many factors were left to vary at random. In other cases the changes introduced for human relations reasons were introduced at the same time as other changes such as higher wages.

> Consequently, it is not possible to identify with certainty the causes of improvements. Other critics point out that the Human Relations School has too narrow a focus, which excludes aspects such as equipment, planning and organisations that are an undoubted part of management.

3.5 Systems theory

During the 1950s people became increasingly suspicious of theories which, while true, only explained a part of the management task. In 1961 Koontz complained that there was "a management theory jungle". Systems theorists aimed to correct the situation by considering organisations as a whole in the same way medics need to consider the human body as a whole rather than a collection of separate functions such as excretion, breathing and thinking. Each part of an organisation would have an impact on other parts. *The whole organisation can only work effectively if the individual parts work effectively and co-operate.* A system is usually defined as a set of interrelated parts that function as a whole to achieve a common purpose.

The simplest system is a **closed system** that operates in isolation to its environment. A closed system is depicted in Figure 3.1. Closed, simple, systems tend to be called "linear systems ". In linear systems events occur as management plans them without too much interference from the outside environment.

This means that the outside environment is usually stable and, with effort, can be understood and predicted. In a linear system it is usually clear what actions (levers) must be taken in order to achieve a given goal.

Many early management theories tended to operate on the basis that organisations were closed, linear, systems. As an approximation, this was almost true. A century ago technological developments were relatively slow to make an impact. Communications and ideas travelled slowly. Further, physical barriers and tariffs meant that outside competition was low. Modern organisations tend to be complex **open systems.** The defining characteristic of an open system is that it interacts with its environment via feedback loops. This is shown in Figure 3.2.

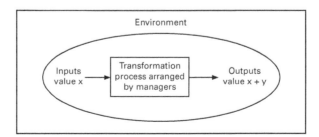

FIGURE 3.1 A simple closed system

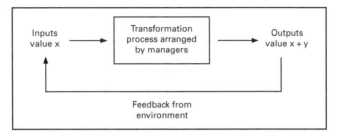

FIGURE 3.2 A simple open system

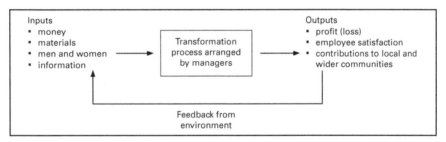

FIGURE 3.3 An open system showing some inputs and outputs

Systems theorists spend considerable effort specifying inputs and outputs in detail. Often inputs are specified in classical terms of money, machines and men and women. However, information resources are important to most modern organisations and are added as an important input. Traditionally the main output of an organisation has been its profit (or loss).

However, a modern list would also include employee satisfaction and contribution to the local and wider community. A modern systems view is given in Figure 3.3.

Figure 3.4 shows a very simplified view of the environment. In reality the environment is complex. On the **supply side**, managers need to be alert to the demands of employees, suppliers, shareholders and lenders. On the **demand side** they need to be aware of markets, pressure groups, new competitors and changes in consumer tastes. There are also a number of factors that might affect both the demand side and the supply side. For example, a poorer economic climate might mean that there are fewer customers, which will make the managerial task more difficult. However, a poorer economic climate might also aid managers by making suppliers and employees more co-operative. Similarly, government regulations and new technology can also affect the inputs and the outputs of an organisation.

Figure 3.4 illustrates the concept of **stakeholders**. A stakeholder is any person or group that is affected by an organisation's activities. As the diagram shows, stakeholders include employees, suppliers, customers, clients, pressure groups, the local community, competing organisations and government. These are in addition to the more obvious stakeholders

Introduction to Business Organisation, Second Edition

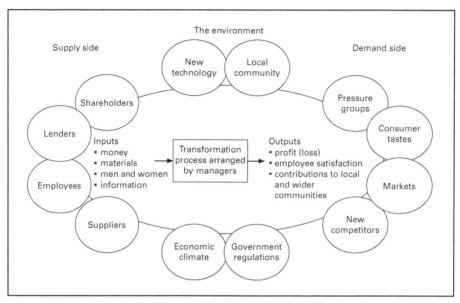

FIGURE 3.4 A complex open system

who have a formal financial interest – the shareholders, lenders and creditors. In many ways managers, especially senior managers, need to achieve a successful balance between competing demands of the organisation's stakeholders.

Closed systems tended to be linear systems in which the outcome of any action would be highly predictable. Complex open systems, such as that shown in Figure 3.5, are generally non-linear systems with less certainty. In a non-linear system managers may be able to predict the short-term consequences within their organisation but it is very difficult for them to predict wider, longer-term consequences.

Open systems contain feedback loops. They are much less predictable and decisions can have quite unexpected consequences. Figure 3.5 represents only a fraction of the complications that exist: it shows only one organisation, one competitor and one government. However, there are feedback loops both within, and between, the three organisations.

Suppose there is a major technological advance. Suppose also that organisation A detects the technological change and uses it to improve production so that quality is increased by 50 per cent and costs are reduced by 50 per cent (not an unlikely scenario in the computer industry!). In a closed system this would bring enormous benefits to organisation A because it would be able to dominate its market with superior goods at a lower price. However, in an open system the situation may be quite different. A competitor would be more likely to monitor websites, newspaper articles and the promotional literature and to detect organisation A's actions. The competitor might respond in a number of ways. If it was larger and richer it might engage in a **predatory price war** designed to starve organisation A of funds so that it could not exploit the new product. Alternatively, the competitor could

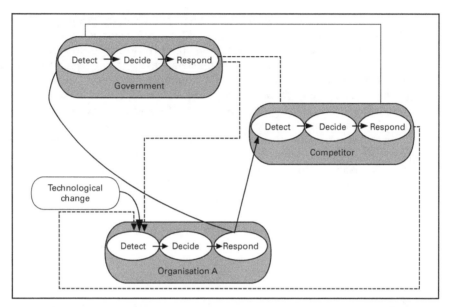

FIGURE 3.5 An open system showing competitors, government and feedback

decide to meet the challenge "head on" by embracing the same technological advance and developing a similar product. Finally, the competitor could abandon hope, exit that market and concentrate on its other products. Organisation A is unlikely to know which of these alternatives its competitor will choose.

Government would also detect increased revenues and it would decide upon some course of action. It might decide to levy a windfall tax; it might decide to write off organisation A's extra capital expenditure on favourable terms. In the interests of greater employment the government could also offer organisation A help in developing export markets. It will be difficult for organisation A to predict exactly which combination of decisions will be made by its competitor and the government. Most modern organisations tend to be more like non-linear systems than linear ones.

Feedback mechanisms are generally believed to be good. As organisations put more information on the Internet, or intranet, the rate of feedback both within and between organisations has accelerated. However, **excessive feedback** can, as any acoustic engineer will verify, be dysfunctional. The feedback mechanisms can amplify the consequences of each decision so that the level of noise in the system is so great that it becomes intolerable. The systems approach to management emphasises three other concepts: entropy, synergy and subsystems.

Entropy is the tendency for a system to run down, decay and become chaotic unless it receives energy, regular inputs and maintenance. The duration of decay will be influenced by the organisation's size: small organisations usually reach the point of extinction before larger ones (survival of the fattest). **Synergy** is the extra value that is produced when two parts of a system interact. For example, in isolation, even an excellent production department will not generate extra value, because it will have to rely on customers calling in person to buy a product. In isolation even a superb sales team will not generate extra value, because it will have nothing to sell. However, the combination of an excellent production department and a superb sales department can add considerable value.

Except for one-person concerns, organisations are not amorphous structures where all parts perform the same tasks in the same way. Usually they are split up into **sub-systems**. For example, some people in an organisation will attend to financial matters, others to purchasing supplies and materials and others still will attend to personnel matters, and so on. Technically sub-systems are defined as relatively homogeneous parts of a system that depend on one another. Sub-systems must be managed and co-ordinated and the impact of one sub-system have upon other systems must be understood. Unfortunately several sub-systems may conflict and the conflict may divert energy

Organisational functions pp 316–436

3.6 Contingency theory

The systems approach to management emphasises that most modern organisations are open systems which need to respond to their environment. Contrary to the ideas of scientific management, administrative management and the human relations schools (which all implied there was one best way to manage – *if only it could be identified*) systems theory implies that the style of management needs to be responsive to (contingent upon) an organisation's environment.

To an extent the contingency theory of management has its roots in research into leadership. Many research programmes were conducted but they tended to produce different results. It was concluded that the style of leaders is contingent upon the circumstances of their group. (Later re-analyses suggest that, to an extent, this was false. There is a clear tendency for leaders to be more intelligent, stable, conscientious and assertive than most people.)

Fiedler's contingency theory of leadership

Fiedler, Chemers and Mahar (1978) measured whether members of a group had good or poor *relationships* with each other. They also measured whether the group had a clear *task* or an ambiguous task. Finally, they measured the extent of the leader's *formal power*. Fiedler categorised groups into eight types. He then looked at the leadership styles that were preferred by each kind of group. The results are shown in Figure 3.6.

Group relationships	Good	Good	Good	Good	Poor	Poor	Poor	Poor
Tasks structure	High	High	Low	Low	High	High	Low	Low
Position power	High	Low	High	Low	High	Low	High	Low
Situational control	Very high							Very low
Appropriate leader style	Task-oriented style			Relationship-oriented style			Task-oriented style	

Figure 3.6 Fiedler's contingency theory of leadership style

Fiedler's results indicate that when the situational control is either very high or very low a leader should emphasise the task which faces the group. However, when the situational control is in the middle range a leader should emphasise the maintenance of good relationships among group members.

Woodward

Another classic investigation which supports the contingency view of management was conducted by Woodward (1965). She investigated three groups of manufacturing companies. One group was classified as "unit and small batch production". In this group products were made in small quantities – often to the specifications of individual customers. The products included designer furniture, luxury yachts and specialist cars. In some ways these firms were like craft organisations because they relied heavily upon individual skills and the quality of the products. The second group was termed "large batch and mass production". These organisations made large quantities of standard products such as computer disks, standard cars and everyday washing machines. The work was heavily mechanised and routinised. The third group were termed "continuous process". Highly sophisticated machines did most of the work, which continued 24 hours a day. Employees had the task of maintaining and checking the machines. This group included brewers, oil refineries and steel-makers. Woodward and her colleagues collected a wide range of data about the organisations. They noted systematic differences in managers' spans of control (see Figure 3.7).

The differences in spans of control could be explained readily by the differences in the complexity of information involved. In the continuous process manufacturing work was high level, intricate and each worker undertook separate tasks. Hence, managers could only keep track of the activities of a relatively few number of employees. In mass production most workers were producing similar or identical products. Hence managers could keep track of a relatively high number of employees.

Many of the terms and ideas introduced in this brief history of management are still in use today. For example, most management courses and texts use terms such as "span of control", "open systems" and "stakeholders". The management processes first outlined by

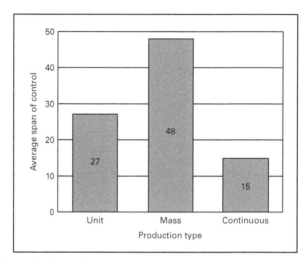

FIGURE 3.7 Span of control and type of production

Fayol are still considered important – even though the details have been heavily modified and improved. Consequently, the next part of this book is devoted to providing a more up-to-date and detailed description of planning, organising, staffing, deciding, controlling, reporting and budgeting.

CRITICAL THINKING 3.5 *Management history – not bunk for Bill Smith*

When presented as a mere chronology of past events, history conforms to Ford's dictum that "history is more or less bunk". It is a phrase that enables many consultants to charge high fees for reinventing the wheel. Good history is more than a chronology. It involves the integration of past events, people, situations and understandings into theories that explain *why* the events occurred. Intelligent use of these theories helps managers understand their current situations. This understanding can help them make successful improvements that are more effective than random restarts.

For example, Bill Smith looked into the history of quality management which included individual topics such as quality control, total quality management (TQM) and zero defects outlined by previous pioneers such as Deming, Juran, Ishikawa and Taguchi. He cherry picked key historical ideas such as the importance of:

- measurement of important things
- continuous improvement

- entire organisational commitment to quality – especially top management
- statistical process control (SPC)

Bill Smith was not content to simply mimic historical ideas, he integrated and built on them. History stimulated him to add:

- a focus on achieving measurable and quantifiable financial returns and making decisions made on the basis of verifiable data rather than guesswork
- methods of ensuring leadership structures that emphasised strong and passionate support for quality – a hierarchy of quality champions that included "yellow quality belts", "black quality belts" and "master black quality belts".

Bill Smith built on history to devise the "six sigma" quality system that was implemented in Motorola and has since saved the company billions of dollars. The "six sigma system" born of history is used by two-thirds of Fortune's top 500 companies.

Activities and further study

Essay plans

Prepare plans for the following essays:

1 Compare and contrast the contribution of F.W. Taylor (scientific management) with those of Elton Mayo.

2 Explain why the management schools of scientific management, administrative theorists, human relations and contingency theory evolved when they did.

3 Evaluate the extent to which modern managers use scientific management, administrative theory and human relations theory.

4 Was Fordism good or bad?

5 Outline the main aspect of systems theory and relate the concepts to a specific organisation that you have researched.

Compare your plans with those on the website site associated with this book.

Web activities

Use the Web to locate:

1 The first example of measuring the time it took workers to perform certain operations.

2 The contribution of Eli Whitley to an efficient factory system.

3 Who studied the economies achieved from specialisation of labour by studying workers manufacturing pins?

4 Why were civil servants in the USA forbidden to use stop watches (until 1949) after F.W. Taylor was questioned by a special committee of the US House of Representatives (1911–12)?

5 The company that first used a "production line".

6 Page 68 describes three 'long-term' or 'Kondratiev' waves. There has since been a fourth wave and it is said we are starting a fifth wave. Use the Web to identify details of these later waves: what they are, their technological base, and their start and end dates.

7 To whom the concept of "operational research" is attributed. Where did he work?

8 What is Fielder's "cognitive resource theory". To which school of management does it belong?

Experiential activities

1 Draw a time line stretching from 1800 to the year 2000. Position the following schools of management onto this time line: contingency theory, operational research, scientific management, human relations and administrative theory.

2 Choose an organisation you know well and identify all the possible stakeholders. Then classify the stakeholders into three types: supply side, demand side and others.

3 Arrange a debate with other students to discuss the motion "On the whole, observing bureaucratic principles brings benefits to an organisation".

4 Hold a seminar discussion on "the value of studying the history of management".

Brainstorming p 235

5 Hold a brainstorming session on "the likely developments in management practice in the next 30 years".

Recommended reading

1 Wrege, C.D. (2008) "F. W. Taylor's lecture on management, June 4, 1907", *Journal of Management History,* **14**(3), 209–213. A delightful, very readable description of the background to Taylor's lectures on management.

2 Becker, S.O. and Ludger, W. (2009) "Was Weber wrong? A human capital theory of Protestant economic history", *Quarterly Journal of Economics*, **124**(2), 531–566. A long and tedious paper but it is a good example of how sociologists can empirically examine and revise historical ideas.

3 Hartford, T. (2009) "How social science ends up as urban myth; the undercover Economist", *Financial Times*, 13 June; and Economist (2009) "Finance and economics: light work: questioning the Hawthorne effect", *Economist*, 6 June, **391**(8634), 74. Some of the well-established management ideas (e.g. the Hawthorne effect) are less solid than we think because their imperfections are forgotten.

Chapter FIVE

Leading and Leadership

Chapter contents

❖ *LEARNING OBJECTIVES*

After studying this chapter you will have a realistic and detailed view of leading people in work situations. You will understand how leaders, followers and situations interact to influence the leadership. You will also appreciate the complexity of the subject. In particular you will be able to:

- ❖ **critically evaluate** the concept of leadership

- ❖ **describe in detail** types of leaders and leadership styles

- ❖ **explain in detail** the relationship between leaders and the characteristics of their followers

- ❖ **explain in detail** the relationship between leaders and the situations in which they operate

The management process of staffing aims to maximise the effectiveness and potential of employees. It uses four main methods. Three of these methods (selecting, training and motivating) were discussed in the previous chapter. The fourth main method of maximising the effectiveness of staff is leading. Fundamentally, leading is about one person changing the direction and behaviours of other people, often in times of adversity, by using personal influence.

CASE 8.1: *Terry Leahy – Tesco's finest*

There are many surveys and books which attempt to define a business leader. A good place to start is to consider Terry Leahy, CEO of Tesco from 1997 to 2011.

In 1924 Jack Cohen bought tea from a supplier called T.E.S (T.E. Stockwell) and added the first letters of his own name (CO) to form the brand of Tesco. It operated at the bottom end of the market, by "piling it high and selling it cheap". Before Leahy took over, it was still firmly in the second rank of supermarkets below Sainsbury's and Marks & Spencer. He began to move it to its now well-established pole position in the supermarket sector with a number of significant developments. He introduced the Tesco's Clubcard and the upmarket "Finest' brand", and developed its market-leading Internet service. Today, from its headquarters in Cheshunt, it is the UK's largest private sector employer with 1000 stores and 23 7000 employees and is the second largest food retailer in the world when measured by profits.

Sir Terry was born in Liverpool and studied at what is now part of Manchester Business School – earning money during vacations by stocking shelves in Tesco stores. Almost by chance he obtained a junior management post at Tesco but rose to be marketing chief and finally CEO. He abandoned Tesco's strategy of apeing Sainsbury and Marks & Spencer's and devised the Clubcard scheme which both increased loyalty and yielded data that could be mined to reveal customer trends. He also led the way in international developments, with strategic alliances in India and China. In 2003, 2005, 2006 and 2009 Leahy and his "Cheshunt mob" were one of the most admired group of managers (*Management Today*, December 2009 – a very easy but interesting read).

Leahy's leadership style is not flashy – he defined a leader as someone "who takes you further than you would go on your own". Key aspects of his leadership philosophy include:

- *Vision, values and culture* are more important than strategies or marketing tactics and they should come from staff. He promoted listening to customers, specifically initiatives like cashiers calling for help if there is more than one customer in a queue, and made sure that all Tesco managers have access to customer concerns. He himself visited a store at least once a week to listen to staff and customers.

- *Encouraging and growing future leaders*. Leahy was quick to point out that Tesco's success was not all his own, acknowledging that it was a team effort. "I don't believe you can lead by central control or diktat; certainly we don't at Tesco. How can I sit in my office and micro-manage almost 350 000 people around the world?" He did not settle for one leader, he wanted thousands of them. As a result, Tesco devoted a

▶

great deal of time, energy and money developing staff. Leadership was also found in customers. Leahy said that if you allow them, customers will take you further than you can go on your own

- *Keeping things simple*. People need to understand what is expected of them and how they can contribute. This does not come from management jargon but from simple thoughts, simply communicated in a way that relates to the jobs that people have to do. For leaders to grow and develop they need a clear framework.

Leahy's tenure is proof of his leadership. The average CEO remains for four years while Leahy was CEO of Tesco for 14 years. Further, when the Board sought to replace, him, they chose another Liverpudlian, Philip Clarke – except Leahy supported Everton while Clarke supports Liverpool FC! (*Economist*, 2010).

Henry Newbolt's poem "Vitai Lamparda" reflects the classic image of heroic leadership. There is a battle in the desert where the army has formed a defensive square that has been "broken" by the enemy:

> The sand of the desert is sodden red -
> Red with the wreck of the square that broke
> The gatling's jammed and the colonel dead,
> And the regiment blind with dust and smoke.

Clearly, the situation is dire. Annihilation threatens. Fortunately someone remembers how they were inspired by the captain of the cricket team on the playing fields of Eton and shows leadership, calling out to his fellow soldiers, "Play up! Play up! And play the game!" The men remember the stoicism and fortitude they learnt while playing cricket at school. They rally, reform the square and prevail over the enemy - all thanks to the call from a true leader of men.

Wow! If leadership can bring about fantastic changes like that, it is little wonder that every CEO on the planet wants more leadership. After all, you just select the right types and then send them on a week or so's outward bound course somewhere on Bodmin Moor or the Lake District and get them to play a modern equivalent of cricket. Voila! Even a pathetic organisation will be redeemed. Unfortunately, in reality, leading people is less heroic and much more complex. Further, not everyone realises that leadership has its dark side.

A competent worker who is motivated can produce acceptable results. When targets are easy and the situation is static they have the momentum to churn out results without intervention from others. However, the momentum is not enough when things become difficult or where a change of direction is needed. An external force is required to alter the direction or to continue in the face of adversity. One external force is leadership. Organisations are very keen to foster leadership; if teams are properly led they will achieve more. Managers therefore need to know about leadership.

8.1 Definition and concept of leadership

The central concept of leadership is *power to influence others and get them to do things they otherwise would not do.* It is often the ability to get people to follow a vision of a better state of affairs. Probably the best formal definition of leadership is:

 . . . . a social influence process that involves determining a group's objectives, motivating behaviour in aid of these objectives and influencing group maintenance and culture.

(Lewis, Goodman and Fandt, 1995)

Differentiation from 'management'

Sometimes, a key role of a definition is to clarify it's distinction from something similar. Clearly, leadership and management are not the same things. Table 8.1 draws on the writings of Mintzberg (1998), Kotter (2001) and others to contrast *leadership* and *management*.

Leaders' *strategies*	Managers' *strategies*
Having the *vision* to take a *long-term* view in order to shape the organisational *cultures* by persuading *followers*	Achieving the *objectives* in the *shorter term* and *enacting* requirements which *achieve stability* by *giving instructions to subordinates*
Leaders' *methods*	**Managers' *methods***
Adopts a *proactive* approach using *charisma* and *passion* to make people *emotional* and *excited* so that they can be *sold* a mission which *transforms* their efforts towards work	Adopts a *reactive* approach using *formal authority*, *logical arguments* or *monetary rewards* which people will *transact* for their efforts towards work
Leaders' *motives*	**Managers' *motives***
Strives towards future *achievements*	Takes *action* to achieve specific *results*
Leaders' *actions*	**Managers' *actions***
Takes *risks*, uses *conflict* and frequently breaks *rules*	Minimises *risks*, avoids *conflict* and usually devises *rules*

TABLE 8.1 A contrast between leaders and managers

CRITICAL THINKING 8.1 *Management versus leadership – a false dichotomy*

Table 8.1 is clearly an oversimplification because it only has two categories. In fact there is a spectrum in which people can take intermediate positions. Furthermore, at a superficial level it gives a dangerous impression that management is bad and that leadership is good: the words used for leaders are less restrictive and more inspirational. This is unreasonable. Leadership deploying all the above characteristics has taken some organisations into zany, unpredictable, directions which destroyed

Two dimensions of leadership pp 205–206

value for stakeholders (e.g. shareholders, employees and government tax revenues). A closer inspection of the table indicates that leadership is primarily concerned with nice things such as dealing with people and liberating their potential, whereas management focuses on less exciting activities such as getting tasks done. As we shall see later in this chapter, there is considerable evidence that good leaders pay attention to both people *and* tasks. Mintzberg (1998 – an excellent read) points out that leading people, especially professional people, is a covert activity and that leaders do a lot more hands-on managing than one might expect. Covert leadership means managing routine things in a nuanced way. In 2009 Mintzberg asserted that "We're over-led and under-managed" and that "corporate America has had too much fancy leadership disconnected from plain old management". He turns the knife further by writing, "Too many leaders fancy themselves above the messy, but crucial work of managing".

In general, management is about coping with complexity and managing things, whereas leadership is about influencing people and coping with change. Most people dislike being managed but they want to be led.

Main components of leadership

At first sight leadership might appear a single topic but as Figure 8.1 shows it is more complex and has at least three components.

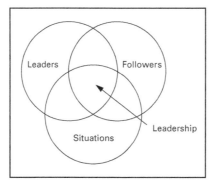

FIGURE 8.1 The components of leadership

Obviously, there must be *leaders*. Second, there must be *followers* since it is impossible to lead no one. Third, leaders and followers do not exist in a vacuum – there must be a *situation*. The relationship between these components is shown in Figure 8.1. Leadership exists where these three components intersect. The next sections of this chapter examine each of these main components in greater detail.

8.2 Leaders

An assembly of strangers will have equal positions and it will be leaderless. Very soon, one or more people will start to take a more dominant role and **leaders will emerge**. These people will exercise more **power** over decision-making and the allocation of resources. The power these leaders exercise will arise from different sources and several **types** of leaders are possible. Further, leaders have their own **traits** (characteristics) and **style**. The sub-topic of "leaders" can therefore be divided into five subsections:

- leader emergence
- leader power
- leader traits
- leader types
- leader style

Leader emergence

In many work settings the leader is appointed by superiors. These are **formal leaders** who have official power. Generally, their official power is sufficient to maintain their position. However, if a formal leader has the wrong characteristics or the situation becomes chaotic another member of the group becomes the de facto, **informal leader**. Informal leaders can emerge in other situations. For example, in a volunteer organisation, a formal leader might not be appointed and an informal leader will emerge. Similarly, a group of army recruits will have a formal leader (a corporal) but, among themselves, one private will emerge as the informal leader of the group.

Curtin (2004) used Tuckerman's (1965) framework of group development to explain the process of leader development. During the formation stage, a number of members announce their "candidacy" for the leader position. During the conflict stage two or more leaders pass the "candidacy threshold" and conflict with each other as they vie for position. Hollander (1961) suggested

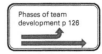

that these candidates build up "idiosyncrasy credits" by helping the group accomplish its task and meeting the group's expectations. The candidates must be both innovative and conformists (see Stone and Cooper, 2009): they must innovate to provide novel solutions but these solutions should not be so drastic that they appear impractical. The nature of the task can play an important part in deciding who emerges as a leader. If the task is very specialised and technical, the candidate with most expertise in the area will have a strong advantage. The candidate's social skills also play an important part. Emergent leaders tend to talk more and give more instructions to others. They are also careful to monitor their own behaviour and use the information to choose from a range of resactions (see Eby, Cader and Noble, 2003). They are also good at managing the emotions within their group (Pescosolido, 2002), clarify ambiguities and catalyse the group to act in a cohesive way. (Smith and Foti, 1998). They suggest that leaders who emerge show a strong tendency to be intelligent, dominant and have a strong belief in their own abilities to change things.

Several authors suggest that emergent leaders tend to have a narcissistic streak (Brunell *et al.*, 2008). In some ways narcissistic tendencies may be counter-productive once a leader is established. This demonstrates the important point that the qualities needed to emerge as a leader may be different from the qualities needed to be an effective leader.

Leadership power

Leaders have power. They are able to deploy resources, decide which team members should reap the most rewards and, to a large extent, have the power to choose the tasks attempted by the group. It is important to understand the basis on which this power is derived. Writers (e.g. French and Raven, 1960) have distinguished four main sources of leadership power.

- **Position power** is sometimes called **legitimate power** or **formal power** and it stems from a manager's position in the organisation. Often this power will be written down and enshrined in job descriptions. Position power may overlap with other sources of power because a position in a hierarchy will usually give a person control of both intellectual and material resources.

- **Reward power** is the ability to bestow or withhold things that other people desire. Typical rewards are pay and promotion. Rewards also include the allocation of desirable jobs and recognition. Managers can use these rewards to influence behaviour. **Coercive power** is one particular type of reward power. It is the ability to dispense punishments. Typical punishments include verbal reprimands, pay penalties or even dismissal.

- **Expert power** is based on knowledge and special expertise. It is often derived from possession of a central position within a communication network which provides up-to-date and, often, confidential information. Expert power may not always reside with managers. Frequently, expert power resides with technical specialists. For example, a relatively junior IT specialist may eclipse a senior manager when a problem involving computers needs to be solved.

- **Referent power** is based on popularity and esteem. It is the power associated with interpersonal attraction, and often involves admiration and the willingness to accept someone as a role model.

It should be remembered that power in itself is neither good nor bad. It is the uses to which power is put that matters.

Traits and skills of leaders

Managers are keen to identify the characteristics that leaders possess. If these leadership traits can be identified then organisations can either select people who have these traits or they can use training and development to give leadership traits to their employees. In this way the level of leadership in an organisation can be improved. Many researchers have tried to meet this need and identify the characteristics of leaders. Initially, this research was not very fruitful because different studies highlighted different characteristics. These differences led researchers to the initial conclusion that there was no single set of traits which leaders held in common. However, in 1991 Kirkpatrick and Locke reviewed the research and came to the conclusion that leaders tended to show the following traits:

- **Energetic and tenacious** – leaders tend to have a high need for achievement and want to get ahead in their work and career. They are prepared to take the initiative to make things happen.
- **Want to lead other people** – leaders are happy to assume responsibility and to seek power, not for its own sake, but in order to achieve their goals.
- **Honest, trustworthy and well organised** – leaders are good at obtaining and keeping the confidence of other people. They usually keep their word.
- **Intelligent and verbally fluent** – leaders are able to analyse situations accurately, solve problems and make sensible decisions
- **Self-confident and interpersonally skilled** – leaders are able to cope with setbacks and take hard decisions. Leaders are usually emotionally stable.
- **Commercially astute** – leaders understand their organisation and its business environment. They accumulate considerable information about their organisation's vision strategy, technologies and procedures.

Other researchers have built on this. Judge *et al.* (2002) examine the traits of leaders using the five-factor theory of personality. They found that leaders tended to be extroverted, conscientious, stable and open to experience. This combination of personality factors correlated fairly highly with holding leadership positions. Apparently, the agreeableness of a leader did not correlate with leadership success – leaders may well be self-centred monsters! Judge *et al*'s. (2002) research gives strong, quantitative support for the trait theory of leadership.

More recently, Sternberg (2007) suggested that leaders were not characterised by single traits but a confluence of traits that reinforce each other. They were **W**isdom, **I**ntelligence and **C**reativity (WICs):

- *Wisdom* involves having the right values and having tacit knowledge of the organisation and its business environment. It also includes being able to appraise social situations with accuracy.
- *Intelligence:* Sternberg did not use the term "intelligent" in a conventional sense. He used it to mean practical intelligence – the set of skills and dispositions needed to solve everyday problems. Practical intelligence requires the ability to apply previous experience in order to select, shape and adapt to environments – rather than solving academic or abstract problems.
- *Creativity* involves skills and dispositions for generating new ideas and novel products. Sternberg emphasised that there were many types of creativity which range from simply redefining the situation to reconstructing and redirecting the organisation.

Luthans and Aviolo developed the concept of an **authentic leader** which seems to be one of the emerging pillars of leadership research today. Authentic leadership is defined as "a process that draws from both positive psychological capacities and a highly developed organisational context, which results in both greater self-awareness and self-regulated positive behaviours . . . fostering positive self-development". Authentic leaders have four main characteristics:

1 **Balanced processing** is the way leaders objectively analyse data before making a decision.

2 **Internalised moral perspective** is the way that a leader is guided by internal moral standards and the way that a leader uses these same standards to regulate their own activities.

3 **Relational transparency** is an open and truthful way of dealing with other people. It also includes sharing information openly and having emotional responses that are appropriate to the situation – i.e. avoiding inappropriate displays of emotion.

4 **Self-awareness** is the extent to which a leader understands their own strengths and weaknesses and the way that they make sense of the world.

Scales to measure each of these four facets have been developed. Luthans and Aviolo's work is based upon positive psychology and aims to offer a more effective way of developing leaders.

Most of this research on leader characteristics can be summarised in the idea of **positive psychological resources** (Luthans and Avoilo, 2003). It suggests that leaders can build up a positive profile in many ways, i.e. intelligence, personality and experience. The lists given in previous paragraphs merely demonstrate the huge range of the possible components of positive psychological resources. This suggests that there are many ways in which leadership effectiveness can be improved. Luthans and Aviolo's positive resource approach is quite different to previous work, which was based on a deficit-reduction model, i.e. where it was important to discover a leader's weaknesses and then work out how they can be strengthened.

Excellent information on leaders is contained in a special edition of the *American Psychologist* in January 2007. In particular it contained an article by Stephen Zaccaro which helps make some sense of the plethora of lists of the traits of leaders. Zaccaro makes the distinction between *proximal* and *distal* traits. Distal traits are basic long-term characteristics that are difficult to change. Proximal traits are similar to skills. They involve distal traits which have been modified by experience. Figure 8.2 (based on Zacccaro, 2007) shows the traits of leaders which help them to develop appropriate skills and expertise. These skills and expertise, together with environmental factors, influence how well the leader manages their team. This in turn influences whether the person will emerge as a leader, their effectiveness while they are a leader and, ultimately, whether they will be promoted to higher leadership positions.

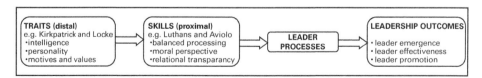

FIGURE 8.2 Zaccaro's model of how traits affect leader performance

> **CRITICAL THINKING 8.2** *Do researchers understate links between traits and leader effectiveness because they only think in straight lines?*
>
> The relationship between personality traits (both distal and proximal) with leadership may be understated. Researchers generally use statistics that can only detect linear relationships. They often miss more subtle, curvilinear relationships. A classic example concerns the trait of assertiveness. Ames and Flynn (2007) performed a subtle analysis on "what breaks a leader". They found that people in leadership positions who had either low assertiveness or very high assertiveness were not effective. Low assertiveness means that other group members set an agenda that may be against the team's interest. High assertiveness can bring instrumental rewards in the short term. In the long term they can be costly in relationships that are needed for success. This means that at least some traits have a curvilinear relationship with leader success. However, most research will miss such relationships because they only use statistics, such as correlations, which can only detect linear relationships.

Finally, there is the question of whether people are born with leadership traits or whether they learn them from their experiences. Arvey *et al.* (2007) suggest that approximately 30 per cent of the differences between leaders is hereditary. The remaining differences are caused by environmental factors such as the availability of role models and early opportunities for leadership development.

Types of leader

Even though leaders may have many characteristics in common, there are many differences in the way that they carry out their role. Therefore authors have been able to identify many different types. One way of organising the types of leader is to categorise them according to three interrelated facets: the leader's source of authority, the change they produce or their style of behaving.

Leaders types classified by source of their authority

Many distinctions between the different types of leader are focused upon their source of authority to act as leaders. Authority for leadership can arise from a *higher source or from God*. The classic example is a **hereditary ruler** or a religious leader such as the Pope or the Grand Ayatollah who are elevated to supreme religious leadership by the highest levels of our hierarchy. This type of leadership is not very important in commercial organisations but it is occasionally encountered in small, owner-occupied organisations. At one point it seemed as though the Ford organisation might be led by a hereditory ruler (see Case 8.2).

Other types of leader draw their *authority from their organisations*. The distinction between **formal leaders** and **informal leaders** has already been noted (page 194). The authority of formal

---

CASE 8.2: *Edsel Ford: a rare example of hereditary leadership*

Edsel was Henry Ford's only child and it was Henry's wish that he should take over his father's business. In 1919 he became the company president. Unfortunately, key decisions were contested and overruled by his father but eventually he was able to persuade him to manufacture a new car which was a commercial success and helped reverse flagging sales. Edsel favoured faster and flashier cars and expanded the motor company's overseas car production. He died in 1943 and his father took back the presidency of the Ford Motor Company.

In 2009 Toyota needed to rejuvenate the company. Hereditary leadership came into action; the founder's grandson, Akio Toyoda became the company's president.

---

leaders arises from their official position within a hierarchy and the scope of their power is formally set out in writing. The weakness of formal leadership is that people in a formal role may not have characteristics such as intelligence, personality, training or experience to exercise leadership required of them.

Many types of leader draw their *authority from the consent of their followers.* Greenleaf (1977) identified **servant leaders** who devote themselves to fulfilling the needs and desires of their group. If they fail to do this there is a danger that they will be overthrown by someone who is better at this task. Servant leaders emphasise trust, understanding, co-operation and the ethical use of power. By fulfilling followers' needs servant leaders maximise their followers' potential and hence the achievements of the group. Perhaps the archetypal servant leader is the parish priest whose *raison d'être* is to serve his flock and lead them to righteousness. Most democratically elected leaders are also servant leaders. The characteristics of servant leaders have been well studied. Spears (2004) applied a scattergun approach and identified 10 traits: listening, empathy, healing, awareness, persuasion, conceptualisation, foresight, stewardship, commitment and community building. Russell and Stone (2002) were more structured. They suggested that the characteristics of a servant leader fell into two categories:

1 Functional characteristics, which help get the job done, include: honesty, trustworthiness, service orientation and appreciation.

2 Social characteristics (accompany attributes) maintain the social structure of the group and include: listening, credibility, encouraging others, teaching others and delegating.

The concept of a servant leadership is related to the **path – goal theory of leadership** proposed by House (1971). In essence, the theory maintains that a leader should adopt a style that helps subordinates attain their goals – provided the goals are consistent with the aims of the organisation. In general, this means that a leader should clarify a follower's *path to goals and increase the relevance of rewards* obtained when the goals are reached. Clarification of the path involves:

■ helping followers define the goals they should reach within those roles

■ increasing followers' confidence that they can achieve the goals

Increasing the relevance of rewards involves:

- learning the followers' needs
- ensuring that a follower receives his or her reward when goals are achieved

House believed that good leaders are capable of different styles and they vary their approach according to the followers' needs. The path–goal theory of leadership has several points in common with expectancy theory.

Cole (2004) also distinguishes **functional leaders** who secure their leadership position because they serve the purposes of their group. The source of their authority is also the consent of their group. However, the concept of functional leader is much narrower than the concept of servant leader. Functional leaders simply adapt their behaviour to meet the competing needs of the task at hand. Servant leaders look to the future well-being of their followers. Groups grant **situational leaders** authority for a short period of time when they are facing difficult circumstances. When circumstances return to normal, previous leadership roles are resumed. The classic fictional example is the butler, the Admirable Crichton, who assumes leadership over his lords and masters because, when they are shipwrecked, he is the only one with practical skills. When they are rescued he relinquishes leadership to his lords and masters.

Several types of leaders derive their *authority from themselves*. **Principle-centred leaders** gain their authority from their own moral and ethical values. Covey and Gulledge (1992) identified a type of leader who recognises and keeps to principles such as even-handedness, fair dealing, honesty and trust. It is practised from the inside to the outside at all levels (personal, group and organisational). The leader often exercises self-discipline and self-denial and tries to improve their own character and competence. People recognise the goodness of principle-centred leaders and therefore consent to follow them.

Charismatic leaders are sometimes called **visionary leaders** and they include great leaders of the past such as Alexander the Great, Boadicea, Churchill, Mother Theresa, Gandhi and Martin Luther King. Charismatic leaders draw their authority from their abilities to awe-inspire people. They have a personal "presence", a vision and the ability to enthuse followers towards that vision. These charismatic leaders can have a dramatic effect on the lives of their followers. Such leaders were first identified by Weber (1947) who defined charisma as a "quality of an individual personality by virtue of which he is considered extraordinary and treated as endowed with supernatural or exceptional forces or qualities". Both charismatic leaders and transformational leaders (see below) raise their followers' aspirations and activate their higher-order values such as altruism. The followers identify strongly with their leaders, which makes them positive about their work so that they try to exceed simple transactions and standard expectations (see Aviolo Walumbwa and Weher, 2009). The notion of charismatic leaders belongs to the "great man" (masculine intended) theory of leadership where great leaders are born and cannot be developed or trained. Often, in the fullness of time, charismatic leaders turn out to have fundamental flaws.

Transformational leaders are less exceptional and revered than charismatic leaders. According to Bass (1985), transformational leaders form a clear view of the future and they are able to achieve a step change in the performance of their followers. This is often achieved by radically changing the way that followers see a situation or their organisation. Transformational leaders usually raise the self-esteem of individual followers and pay attention to their development needs. This contrasts with charismatic leaders who require followers to sacrifice their own needs in favour of "the cause". The exact nature of transformational leadership is summarised in a paper by Bono and Judge (2004). Bono and Judge found that charisma was related to the leader's personality. Transformational leaders tended to be stable extroverts. Transformational leadership has five main components:

- **Charisma** consists of two sub-components: idealised influence and inspirational motivation. **Idealised influence** involves high standards of moral and ethical conduct so that transformational leaders are held in high regard and engender loyalty in followers. **Inspirational motivation** starts with a strong vision for the future which is based on values and ideals. This generates an enthusiasm among followers. Sometimes, idealised influence and inspirational motivation are combined to produce charisma.
- **Intellectual stimulation** involves challenging organisational norms and pushing people to develop inspirational strategies and challenging existing norms.
- **Individual consideration** refers to the way that leaders recognise the talent and also the concerns of group members.
- **Management by exception** refers to how a leader monitors performance and takes corrective action. Having set standards, the leader adopts a passive approach and only intervenes when problems become serious.
- Transactional leaders **establish** goals and then they guide their followers to pursue their plans – largely by means of giving rewards when the plans are executed properly.

Effective leaders can induce followers to do bad things. Ineffective leaders can let bad things happen. Lipman-Blumen (2005) identified a dark type of leader – the **toxic leader**. Toxic leaders are individuals who have destructive behaviours and dysfunctional personalities. They generate serious and enduring poisonous effects on the groups they lead. A classic example of an extremely toxic leader would be Adolf Hitler. Adolf is not an isolated example: think of leaders such as Robespierre, Stalin, Pol Pot and Sadam Hussain!

Toxic leaders are not necessarily proactive like Hitler, Stalin, Pol Pot or Radovan Karadzic. Some leaders may be toxic because they fail to act or are ineffective. Inactive toxic leaders are difficult to identify but British Prime Ministers such as Stanley Baldwin or Neville Chamberlin might be considered. Toxic, inactive leaders in commerce and industry are even harder to identify because they are sheltered by their organisations. Would any organisation be willing to admit it is led by an idiot? Kellerman (2004) identifies seven types of toxic leader:

- incompetent leaders who lack skill or motivation
- rigid leaders who reject new ideas because they are unbending
- intemperate leaders who lack self-control
- callous leaders who are uncaring and unkind
- corrupt leaders who lie cheat or steal
- insular leaders who disregard the welfare of people outside their group
- evil leaders who commit atrocities and who use pain as an instrument of power

---

CASE 8.3: *Koresh's toxic leadership in Waco*

Another example of a more recent, proactive toxic leader is David Koresh, leader of the Davidian religious sect. Koresh had a borderline personality disorder and he manipulated people in very small increments. He pulled them deeper and deeper into his power without them knowing where they were going or being aware of the consequences. There were allegations of sexual abuse and other misconduct: he released a video claiming he had been told by God to procreate with the women of his group to establish a house of "Special People". Couples dissolved marriages so that Koresh could have sex with ex-wives. There was some evidence of child abuse. He believed that the government was the enemy of the Davidians. After a long series of legal disputes over his leadership, criminal activity and stockpiling of weapons, Texan authorities in Waco felt forced to act and attempted to execute a search warrant. Koresh anticipated the raid. He had prepared defences and ordered some followers to arm and take up defensive positions. Shots were exchanged and then a ceasefire was arranged. For 51 days the siege of Waco ensued during which Koresh allowed the "release" of some children. Texan authorities used proactive techniques such as sleep disturbance, crushing cars and driving tanks over the graves of sect members – not an especially bright move when dealing with people with border personality disorders! The FBI, fearing further atrocities such as abuse of children, planned a "relief operation". When Koresh's Davidians opened fire the FBI punctured walls so that people could escape and they used a lot of teargas. No one left. Fires broke out. Some say sect members were prevented from escaping. Many were buried alive by rubble or suffocated by the effects of fire. Seventy-five of Koresh's followers died. Nine survived. No doubt, Texan authorities were imperfect. But, no doubt more people would have lived without Koresh's toxic leadership.

One explanation for the behaviour of toxic leaders is that they believe they are specially chosen or have a special mission. On that basis they believe they should not be bound by normal rules or ethical standards.

A number of researchers have examined whether gender is relevant to leading people. There was a general assumption, promulgated by war films, novels and poems that leadership is a "man thing". Research by Powell, Butterfield and Bartol (2008) suggests this stereotype is not true. Indeed, in their study, MBA students judged descriptions of females who were transformational leaders more highly than identical descriptions of males who were also transformational leaders. However, research by Ryan *et al.* (2007) suggests that some differences do exist. When women achieve leadership positions they may experience "a glass cliff" – they tend to be put in more risky leadership positions where the chances of failure are higher.

Leader style

Types of leader can also be based on the way that they treat subordinates. This is a very big topic which deserves its own section. The way that leaders treat subordinates is usually called leader style.

Many researchers have investigated leader style. At first, investigators studied a *single dimension* of management style – participation. As early as the 1930s Lewin, Lippet and White (1939) examined leadership style in boys' clubs. They distinguished three leadership styles:

1 **Democratic leaders** (sometimes called **participative leaders**) gave their group clear guidance but they did not dominate the situation. They encouraged input from group members so that they felt engaged. This lead members to be more motivated and creative. They were also careful to take the views of the group into account in any decision.

2 **Laissez-faire leaders** (sometimes called **delegative leaders**) played a minimal role. They made sure of the basics, such as venue and timing, but otherwise provided little input. They offered little guidance and left all decisions to the group members.

3 **Authoritarian leaders** provided very clear expectations. They told a group what it had to do and how it had to do it. They made decisions unilaterally.

Lewin *et al.* set up groups with these three types of leader. They then examined how productive the groups were. Democratic leaders had the most productive groups. Findings for autocratic leaders were mixed. When the leader was present the productivity of the groups was almost as high as the productivity of the Democratic group. However, when, inevitably, the leader was not physically present there was a dramatic fall in productivity. Consequently, their overall productivity was lower. The least productive was the laissez-faire group. More recent research (Skogstad *et al.*, 2007) has demonstrated how destructive laissez-faire leadership can be – especially in a stressful work situation where there was bullying.

In 1958 Tannenbaum and Schmidt refined Lewin *et al.*'s ideas. Instead of seeing leadership style in terms of clear-cut groups they saw it as a continuum stretching from authoritarian at one end to participative at the other. Further, Tannenbaum and Schmidt gave specific instances of the behaviour of managers at various points on this continuum. For example, a very autocratic leader would tell subordinates what to do; a fairly democratic leader would consult with his or her group and a very democratic leader would engage in joint decision-making.

A little later McGregor (1960) suggested that managers could adopt one of two leadership theories. **Theory X**, held by autocratic managers, maintains that workers are lazy, unreliable and need to be told what do. **Theory Y**, held by democratic managers, says that workers naturally enjoy work and are most productive when they have made a contribution to decisions.

Likert (1979) identified four management styles (which he called systems) that can be arranged on a single dimension:

■ System 1, **exploitative-authoritative style** where the leader is autocratic, rarely delegates, guards information jealously, manages by edict and uses punishment as the main way of motivating people.

■ System 2, **benevolent-authoritative style** where the leader adopts the same autocratic style but uses rewards to motivate instead of punishment.

■ System 3, **consultative style** where the leader has some trust in workers and permits some teamwork. Workers will be consulted over decisions but the final decision is taken by the leader.

■ System 4, **participative group style** where the leader has a high level of trust and confidence in workers. Decisions are made in a participatory way. Information flows in all directions.

The leadership styles identified by Lewin, Tannenbaum and Schmidt, McGregor and Likert are very similar, as shown in Figure 8.3.

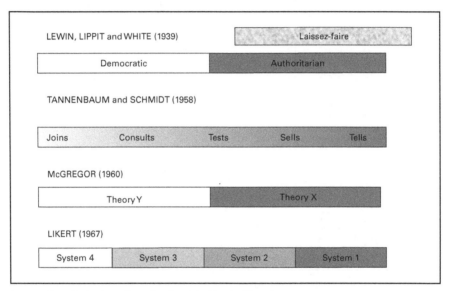

FIGURE 8.3: A synthesis of one dimensional models of leadership style

All four models have authoritarian at one end and democratic leadership at the other. They differ however in the number of categories. All except Lewin, Lippit and White imply that leaders must have a style. Lewin, Lippit and White's model has a management style that is close to nothing (laissez-faire). The one-dimensional approach to leader styles was an advance but it had two problems. *First*, as already been noted, these models of leading imply leaders must be active. *Second*, the dimension democratic–authoritarianism is complex and might be concealing more fundamental dimensions.

Two important studies into leadership style were conducted at Ohio State University and the University of Michigan. The Ohio studies looked for dimensions of leadership, while the Michigan studies looked for differences between leadership in high-performance and low-performance units. Although their aims were different the two studies came to much the same conclusion – that there are two major dimensions of leading: the emphasis a leader places on *people* and the emphasis a leader places on the *task*. As Figure 8.3 shows, other researchers have located similar dimensions but have used slightly different names. Blake and Mouton (1964) put the two dimensions into graphical form and created the well-known **managerial grid** (the diagrammatic part of Figure 8.4). There they were able to divide the grid

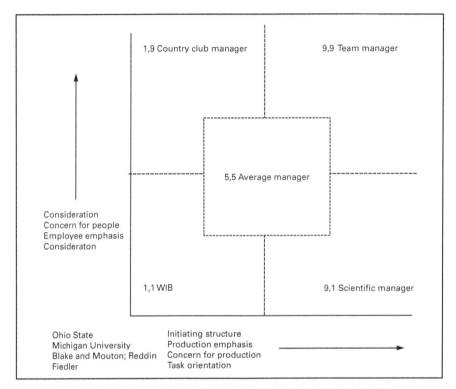

1,9 Country club manager   9,9 Team manager

5,5 Average manager

Consideration
Concern for people
Employee emphasis
Consideraton

1,1 WIB   9,1 Scientific manager

Ohio State   Initiating structure
Michigan University   Production emphasis
Blake and Mouton; Reddin Concern for production
Fiedler   Task orientation

FIGURE 8.4 Managerial grid showing relationship with other two-dimensional models of leadership

into five areas representing five main leader styles. A leader who stressed both the personal side of the team and the task was called a 9,9 "team manager". A leader who stressed task but ignored the personal side was called a 9,1 "scientific manager". A leader who stressed the personal side, ensuring that employees enjoyed their work while ignoring the task they were supposed to do, was called a 1,9 "country club manager". A leader who stressed neither the task nor the people was called a 1,1 WIB (weak inefficient bastard). Of course, most leaders were somewhere in the middle of the extremes and would be called a 5,5 "average manager".

Reddin (1970) adapted the basic 2 × 2 grid in two ways. He changed the names of the types of leader and then he added an extra dimension to show what the style would be for average, good and poor leaders. Reddin's grid is shown in Figure 8.5.

Thus, a "country club" manager in the 2 × 2 grid could be a "developer", helping people to exploit their talents or a "missionary", simply being nice to people – depending upon how effective they were as leaders. Similarly an effective "scientific manager" would be a "benevolent autocrat" whilst an inefficient "scientific manager" would be an autocrat. Reddin's 3D grid is useful in reminding us that most leadership styles can be made better or worse depending upon the skill of the leader.

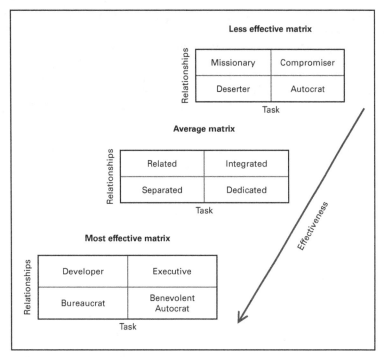

FIGURE 8.5 Reddin's 3D grid

8.3 Leaders and followers

Even a combination of leader characteristics *and* leader style fails to give a good understanding of leading in work situations. Something is missing. Sometimes a task-oriented style works, while at other times a person orientation (followers) is better. Hersey and Blanchard (1982) focused upon the importance of the followers.

Hersey and Blanchard started with the familiar two-dimensional grid inherited from the Ohio and Michigan studies which is based on task orientation and consideration. *First*, they translated the two dimensions into behavioural terms. Task-oriented leaders give explicit directions, whereas leaders with a lower task orientation let followers get on to work in their own way. Similarly, highly considerate leaders give followers lots of support. Figure 8.6a shows how this changed the basic 2×2 grid. *Third*, Hersey and Blanchard inserted the approach leaders should adopt to support their followers. The result is shown in Figure 8.6b.

Fourth, Hersey and Blanchard considered the development level of followers. Experience and commitment are key factors. Followers with neither experience nor commitment are poorly developed (D1), while followers who are both experienced and committed are highly developed (D4). Other combinations produce groups D2 and D3. Hersey and Blanchard matched the development level to the appropriate type of leadership support. The results are shown in Table 8.2.

Fifth, Hersey and Blanchard matched the appropriate support style for each of the four categories of follower. A key aspect of Hersey and Blanchard's approach is that all team members are *not* the same. An interesting but frequently overlooked implication of Hersey and Blanchard's work is that there is a category of worker who require no leadership (D4, the experienced and committed group). Following this one stage further might point to

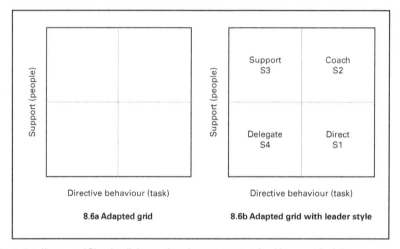

FIGURE 8.6a & b Hersey and Blanchard's integration of management style with support for followers

the conclusion that organisations should concentrate upon developing the experience and commitment of workers rather than developing the leader! However, the broad conclusion of Hersey and Blanchard's work is that different groups need to be supported with different styles. The **theory of vertical dyad linkage** took this notion a stage further.

The vertical dyad linkage theory is also known as the **leader–member exchange theory (LMX)**. Several theories imply that leaders relate to followers equally and as a whole as shown in Figure 8.7a. But, as everyone who has been a member of any group knows, this is untrue.

Liden and Graen (1980) suggest that leaders *behave* differently to different followers – a series of dyadic relationships. Each dyad is different: some are characterised by trust, others may be characterised by tolerance or hate or respect, etc. Further, an "in group" will receive confidential information, participate in decisions and be given extra responsibility. The "in group" believe they owe their membership to their competence rather than preferment. Leaders foster and protect their "in group". For example, when senior managers change jobs they often take members of their "in group" with them. Members of the "out group" may be treated differently – like temporary employees – within formal guidelines. They resent the "in group" and believe that they owe their position to bias or even nepotism. Dyads can

Type of follower			
Hersey Blanchard **UNDEVELOPED (immature)**		**DEVELOPED (mature)**	
D1	**D2**	**D3**	**D4**
Enthusiastic beginners Committed to their work but lacked experience and competence	**Disillusioned workers** Some experience and competence but lacking commitment and motivation	**Reluctant contributors** Some experience and competence but lacking confidence	**Peak performers** Experienced and competent, committed and motivated
Suitable styles			
Hersey Blanchard			
S1 – Directing	S2 – Coaching	S3 – Supporting	S4 – Delegating
Tannenbaum and Schmit			
Tell	Sell	Participate	Delegate
Blake and Mouton			
9, 1 Scientific management	9, 9 Team management	1, 9 Country club management	1, 1 WIB

TABLE 8.2 Hersey and Blanchard's matching of leader style to follower development (maturity) and comparison with other theories

have a self-fulfilling prophecy. The "in group" member receives more from the leader so, in accord with Adam's equity theory, they give more to the leader, perform better because of their inside knowledge and so receive more favour in return. A member of the "out group"

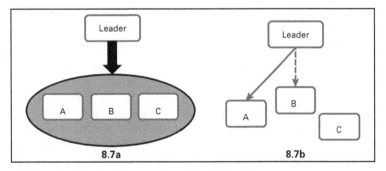

FIGURES 8.7a & b Simplistic leader-follower and dyad linkage leader-follower

receives less, gives less and then receives even less. Improving dyadic relationships is one key to good leadership.

The relationship between leader and follower starts as soon as they first meet. From then, the relationship proceeds in three main stages:

1 When a new member joins they are immediately evaluated by the leader and are given, what the leader considers, appropriate opportunities to demonstrate capability.

2 Leader and follower negotiate a role and the rewards that will ensue from its successful performance. Leader and follower extend trust. Subsequent perceptions, especially by the leader, that trust has been misplaced has critical consequences. If a leader feels betrayed, the follower will be demoted to the "out-group".

3 Successful relationships are routinised. The behaviours of leader and follower are consolidated so that each other's expectations are met consistently. Similarity between leaders and follower's personality and values are probably significant.

It is important to note that the vertical dyads may extend in chains. The leader will have a dyadic link with his or her leader and the follower may have a dyadic link with her or his followers. The network of dyads engulfs the whole organisation.

The vertical dyad linkage theory suggests that similarities of personality and values may be important in fostering a strong leader-follower relationship. Giberson, Resick and Dickson (2005) indicate a substantial correlation between leaders and followers in terms of:

■ *personality traits* of agreeableness (.35), conscientiousness (.35) and extroversion (.34)

■ *values* concerning benevolence (.42) and aesthetics (.35)

Similarities between leader and follower probably result from Schneider's ASA theory (**a**ttracting similar people, **s**ocialising new people to be similar and the **a**ttrition of people who differ). Research shows that followers are attracted to leaders on the basis of **prototypicality** – that is, they are drawn to leaders who are exemplars of the groups they belong to or want to join (Aviolo, Walumbwa and Weber, 2009).

Schneider's ASA theory p 40

Some researchers (e.g. Bresnahan and Mitroff, 2007) liken the way relations between a leader and follower develop to the way attachment develops between mother and child – as described by John Bowlby (1988) in his classic book *A Secure Base: Parent Child Attachment and Healthy Human Development*. An "adult attachment" theory could set the concept of leadership on a stronger footing. An examination of any such similarities could produce a stunning dissertation or thesis.

In a similar vein, House's (1971) path–goal theory also emphasised relevance to vertical links and servant leadership. He suggests a major role of a leader is to help followers achieve individual and team goals. Leaders do this by clarifying goals and removing obstacles. The extent to which leaders enhance followers' paths to their goals varies from dyad to dyad. If leaders frequently default in minor situations, or catastrophically default in major situations, their position may become insecure. Deposing leaders has not been widely researched. It is another aspect of leadership that could form an excellent essay, dissertation or thesis.

> **CRITICAL THINKING 8.3** *It's the results that matter – not the leadership style!*
>
> Some writers (see Fulop and Linstead, 1999) suggest the traditional emphasis on leadership styles have been overzealous. They point to Peltz's (1952) comments, partly endorsed by Kanter (1983), that if a leader "has considerable influence within his organisation . . . he will achieve concrete benefits for them . . . not his good intentions, but his actual accomplishments are what pay dividends in employee satisfaction." It suggests that many followers may, like Machievelli, adopt the ethic that might is right and counsel a leader to "never mind your style, bring us results that justify the pain of being your follower!"

8.4 Situations and leading

An understanding of leading would be incomplete if the relationship between leaders and situations is ignored (see Figure 8.1). Several of the writers we have already cited include the situation in their models of leader style. For example, House (see above) believed that leaders are capable of different styles and they vary their approach according to the situation. He identified four leader styles, each appropriate for various situations. The four styles and the situations, which should be compared and contrasted with those suggested by Hersey and Blanchard, are:

- *Directive leadership* – providing instructions and guidance about methods, standards and rules. This is suitable in ambiguous situations where the leaders need to clarify situations to increase the probability of success.

- *Supportive leadership* – a friendly approach that is sensitive to the concerns and emotions of followers. This is suitable in stressful situations.

- *Participative leadership* – listening carefully to the opinions and suggestions of followers. This is suitable for complex problems where no single person has all the information or expertise.

- *Achievement-oriented leadership* – showing confidence in followers' abilities to meet challenges. This is suitable where creativity is important and where mistakes are accepted as an engine of growth and development

Fiedler's analysis of leader styles incorporated both follower and situations (such as whether the group's task was structured, the power of the leader's position, and the degree of control a leader has over the situation). Figure 8.8 illustrates the influence of the leader's situational control.

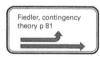

Fiedler, contingency theory p 81

If a leader has either low control or high control, a task-oriented leader style is indicated. If a leader has moderate control, a style emphasising consideration may be better. A great example of the integration of situational variables with leadership styles is given by Vroom and Jago's analyses of the way that leaders should make decisions.

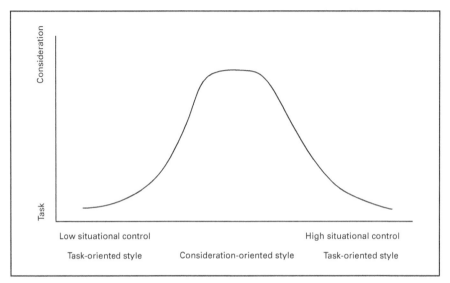

FIGURE 8.8 Fiedler's contingency theory of leadership style and situational control

Vroom and Jago's (1988) analysis of a leader's decision-making shows that situational variables such as: technical correctness, the structure of a problem and the adequacy of the information available to the leader are very important.

Vroom and Jago decision p 230

To make matters even more complex, organisational variables can play a great part in determining a leader's success. This aspect of leadership has not been extensively researched but there is considerable anecdotal opinion. An exception is the work by Wasserman, Anand and Nohria (2001). They found that the leadership of chief executives has the greatest impact when there are few opportunities available but there are plenty of surplus resources. Presumably, under these circumstances skilled leaders are able to choose the right opportunity and then have the luxury of deploying massive resources to exploit it.

CRITICAL THINKING 8.4 *Face-to-face leaders versus electronic leaders*

Today, one of the most stark situational factors is whether the leader meets their group on a face-to-face basis or whether they lead a virtual group communicating by emails and videoconferencing, etc. Zaccaro and Bader (2003) give an excellent overview of the similarities and differences in these situations. Xiao *et al.* (2008) found that when the team leader is physically present they have a great influence on communications. When the leader was communicating by electronic means, the balance of communications between the leader, senior members and junior members was more balanced. Followers in face-to-face groups are more cohesive, have more energy and have greater acceptance of group decisions than followers where groups communicate electronically.

Sometimes, situational variables may be called **leadership substitutes**, **leadership neutralisers** and **leadership enhancers** (Howell *et al.*, 1990). Other researchers use the term **moderator variables**. There are at least three kinds of substitutes for leadership:

- *Getting workers to lead themselves* by instigating self-managed work teams, obtaining guidance from colleagues and involving colleagues in making decisions. These establish group goal-setting.
- *Select and develop mature employees* who have motivation and experience (i.e. professional employees). These changes aim to remove the need for a leader by empowering employees.
- *Develop automatic (intrinsic?) reward systems* that motivate appropriate behaviour in a way that does not involve leaders. These establish highly formalised plans, standard operating procedures and clear areas of responsibility. These changes clarify the situation and so remove the need for a leader to arbitrate when there is ambiguity or role conflict.

Other ways of *enhancing* leadership include increasing employees' dependence upon the leader by giving the leader greater control of rewards and resources. Organisations may also enhance leadership by improving the image of the leader by involving them in important projects or bestowing symbols of approval.

Post-heroic leadership

Notions of charismatic leaders and transformational leaders reached their height in about 1990. Doubts began to set in.

- Were there were enough people with charismatic qualities to be leaders in all organisations?
- Transformational leaders might change things for the worse (some transformational leaders became associated with greed, ruthlessness and lining their own pockets).
- There were examples were heroic leaders did not actually help the organisation to add value – some led their organisations to bankruptcy.
- Organisations were becoming too big and complex to be led by a single leader no matter how charismatic or transformational. This was particularly true of organisations in the knowledge industry.

Mintzberg (2010) is not impressed by the contribution made by heroic leaders. Top organisational performance is "a question of building strong institutions, not creating heroic leaders. Heroic leaders get in the way of strong institutions". Consequently, organisations started to think about leadership in more realistic terms. Their conclusions led to what is known as **post-heroic**

leadership or **distributed leadership.** The concept of post-heroic leadership was identified by Huey in 1994. It abandons ideas of leaders acting as heroes, single-handedly saving the followers from the perils of the organisational jungle (Pearce and Manz, 2005). The heroic image of leadership was fostered by the popular press, which prefers stories that are exciting, broad-brush and simple. It ignores the mundane reality where good leadership is boring, detailed, complicated and almost invisible to those outside the organisation. The square that broke probably reformed and won the day not because a brave soul had cried "play-up, play up and play the game". It probably won the day because a recruiting sergeant had conscientiously selected good cadets, lowly officers had spent hours training squaddies in defensive tactics and because some lowly clerk had remembered to order reserve supplies of bullets. The concept of post-heroic leadership has six main characteristics:

- Workers are encouraged to develop *their own expertise and commitment to their work.* Considerable resources are devoted to "growing" people and making them effective. Hence the organisation has a large proportion of "exemplary followers".
- Post-heroic leaders want other people to *take responsibility and become empowered.* They actively seek input from other people – even at the expense that they themselves may become dispensable.
- Exemplary followers have *the resources to solve their own problems.* They do not need a hero to intervene and save them.
- The post-heroic leader devotes time and effort to *develop an organisational culture* where information is widely shared and where people are expected to be exemplary in taking responsibility for adaptation and innovation.
- Exemplary followers take an *active part in determining strategies.*
- Followers *share the limelight* when there is success (and they also share some of the "ordure" when things go wrong).

An excellent introduction to post-heroic leadership is given by Crevani, Lindgren and Pakendoff (2007). Post-heroic leadership has major implications for leadership research. In the future, researchers will need to focus upon teams rather than individuals. Further, leadership will need to be investigated, *in situ,* by quantitative field studies rather than survey techniques (Lindgren and Packendorff 2009).

CRITICAL THINKING 8.5 *Post-heroic leadership – Planet Utopia?*

It is easy to understand why the concept of post-heroic leadership has such allure. Management's romance with heroic leadership was clearly overheated. Overheated romances eventually come back down to earth. A theory on the rebound can be as unrealistic as a relationship on the rebound. Post-heroic leadership may work in a minority of situations familiar to academic writers: research groups, boards of studies, consultancy organisations. Such situations involve intelligent, educated, professional, motivated people. Further, there is the luxury of time for analysis (sometimes, to the point of paralysis). Such luxurious situations may not be abundant

▶

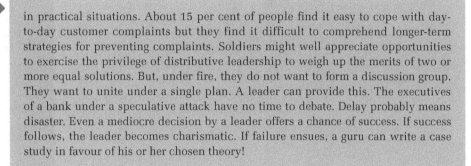

in practical situations. About 15 per cent of people find it easy to cope with day-to-day customer complaints but they find it difficult to comprehend longer-term strategies for preventing complaints. Soldiers might well appreciate opportunities to exercise the privilege of distributive leadership to weigh up the merits of two or more equal solutions. But, under fire, they do not want to form a discussion group. They want to unite under a single plan. A leader can provide this. The executives of a bank under a speculative attack have no time to debate. Delay probably means disaster. Even a mediocre decision by a leader offers a chance of success. If success follows, the leader becomes charismatic. If failure ensues, a guru can write a case study in favour of his or her chosen theory!

Other important perspectives on leadership

A chapter of this kind can do no more than cover the main themes of a vast topic. However, it is important not to lose sight of a number of other issues. For example, it is interesting to speculate on the differences between *men and women leaders*. As more women earn well-deserved leadership positions, this is an issue of increasing importance. There is some evidence that women leaders are particularly good at motivating and communicating with their teams. They also tend to lead in an interactive, collaborative way. It has been suggested that the post-heroic type of leadership is linked to the way in which women leaders operate because it emphasises the skills of relating to other people. Another up-coming topic is the issue of *virtual leaders* and how they may differ from traditional leaders. Teleworking and other technological advances mean that more people are working away, sometimes continents away, from their leaders. Nobody yet fully understands how this affects leadership style.

CRITICAL THINKING 8.6 *Leadership – philosophical, cynical and scientific views*

Philosopher Noam Chomsky (1999) has a critical view of leading. The definition at the beginning of this section shows that, fundamentally, leadership involves one person influencing other people to do things they otherwise would not do. Put another way – *manipulation of other people is at the heart of leadership*. This manipulation can be for evil as well as good. It is questionable whether leadership should have received such positive, romantic attention during the last half century. Chomsky questioned whether it is right for us to abrogate our own responsibility to think for ourselves. Many people are happy to be "told what to do". Further, many people may believe that leaders are merely those who help them on the path towards their existing goals. Unfortunately, Chomsky argues, the social system has its ways of inducing people to adopt goals that most benefit the leaders. In essence, Chomsky argues that leadership is undemocratic.

Cynics attack leadership from another direction. They contend that good *leadership is merely a matter of good luck and attribution theory*. Leaders are highly visible and therefore they are thought to be responsible for the success or failure of the organisation whether or not they actually have power or influence. A clear example of the cynics' case is managers of football teams. If the team has a successful season, the manager is lauded. If the team has bad luck (injuries, bad draws against opponents or treachery from the club chairperson), the manager gets fired. More scientifically, Bligh *et al.* (2007) found that followers tended to heap blame on leaders if they thought that their work environment was poor even when their leaders were not particularly culpable. Cynics advise that leadership success boils down to: "first be lucky and then be very skilful in persuading others that your efforts were the most relevant factor". To cynics a good leader is merely someone who happens to be on the winning side and who is sufficiently guileful to claim the credit. And, as everyone knows, winners get to write history.

CRITICAL THINKING 8.7 *Flaws in leadership research*

"Leadership agnostics" think that we know much less about management than we believe. Many "findings" about leadership are questionable. Research uses poor criteria. Most of the research depends on measuring subjective ratings of the satisfaction of followers. Yes, satisfaction of followers is very important – but so is the value added to resources consumed. Very few studies use objective measures such as the organisation's fitness to meet challenges from the environment or the value an organisation adds to the resources. Further, leadership is there to improve the bottom line measures. Few studies have even attempt to measure the *difference* (distance travelled) any leader makes to things that really matter.

8.5 New directions for leadership research

Researchers have been studying for decades the same questions about leading, such as: What are the qualities of leaders? What are the types of leaders? How do situations affect leadership? Hackman and Wagerman (2007) suggested reframing the topic of leadership:

1 Instead of asking "whether leaders make a difference" we should be asking *"under what conditions do leaders matter?"* Post-heroic leadership downplays the impact of leaders. They are merely a part of a system that is sometimes subject to so many constraints that not even the most charismatic leader can have any effect. The question therefore arises "under what circumstances can leaders play an important role?"

2 Instead of asking "what are the traits of successful leaders" we should be asking *"how do the personal attributes of leaders interact with the situation to influence the*

outcomes?" It is now agreed that neither traits nor situations are sufficient to explain leader effectiveness. It is the interaction between the two that matters. The interactions may be unbelievably complex. If there are just three traits and just three situational variables there are at least 243 different types of interactions. Is it humanly possible for leaders to have the brainpower to process all the combinations in a practical setting? If it is not possible then the value of this line of research is very limited!

3 Instead of asking "is there a single dimension that determines good leaders from bad leaders?" we should be asking *"is good leadership qualitatively different from bad leadership?"* There are many social and psychological phenomena where two different dimensions are needed to distinguish good from bad. For example, the effect of rewards upon people is qualitatively different from the effects of punishment. A similar situation may be relevant to leaders.

4 Instead of asking "how do leaders and followers differ?" we should be asking *"how can everyone in an organisation be considered to be both leaders and followers?"* Leaders must have followers. But lesser leaders must follow bigger leaders – and so on ad infinitum. Under some circumstances followers, such as the Admirable Crichton, emerge as leaders. There is no clear-cut line between leadership and followership.

5 Instead of asking "what should be taught on leadership courses?" we should be asking *"how can leaders be helped to learn?"* Leaders manage situations with the help of mental models they have built up over many years. Leaders need to be helped to build up mental models as accurately and as quickly as possible. Leadership training must teach managers to examine their own mental models, check their accuracy and the degree to which they transfer to novel situations.

Hackman and Wageman's questions are a fitting note on which to end this section on leadership. It is hoped that their questions are answered before the next edition of this book is due to be written.

8.6 Leadership toolkit

A leadership toolkit needs to give two kinds of advice: how to be a leader and how to manage leaders.

Toolkit for leaders

- Have a clear vision about where and how you want your group to go. Communicate this vision enthusiastically and lucidly.
- Be a good role model. Act intelligently, energetically and with integrity.
- Do not rely on a single source of power. Usually you will need to supplement reward power with, say, expert power or referent power.
- Adapt your approach to the *situation* that you face. For example, in very easy or very difficult situations it may be best to be directive.
- Adapt your approach to the characteristics and, especially, the needs of your followers. Do not assume that all followers have either the same needs or the same relationships with you.
- Pay attention to the two main dimensions of leadership: focus on the task your group needs to perform and at the same time focus on personal issues such as the relationship between yourself and team members and also the relationships between the various members of the team.

Toolkit for managing leaders

- Do not rely on leadership too much. There are many situations where even the best leadership makes no difference. If you rely on good leadership alone, there might be chaos if your leaders move to another, competing, organisation. It is safer to rely on good procedures that select and develop committed, mature and competent workers.
- Beware that leadership is much less effective in groups that communicate predominantly by electronic means.
- Be careful to align formal leadership with informal leadership by appointing formal leaders who have, or who can gain, respect.
- Arrange to select staff who have leadership qualities: intelligence, integrity, creativity, etc. However, it is often the combination of qualities that matters. The combination must add up to a significant level of competence that can deal with difficult situations.
- Make sure that leaders have effective control over rewards and sanctions which are valued by their followers.
- Beware "toxic leaders" who might influence their group to follow bad pathways that might damage the organisation.

Toolkit

Activities and further study

Essay plans

1 Choose a business leader and describe their career in the context of the issues raised in this chapter.

2 To what extent are leaders born not made?

3 What are the characteristics of effective leaders? (Top tip: inevitably this will involve regurgitating many of the lists of research findings but you need to do much more than this. Compare and contrast the lists, and synthesise them. You can add value with a short discussion about how leader effectiveness is defined at the start of the essay. You could also make the point, with examples, that leader effectiveness depends on the situation and the followers. You should then refer back to this discussion of effectiveness at least three times during the remainder of the essay.

3 What is post-heroic leadership and how did the concept arise?

4 The dark side of leadership.

5 Is leadership necessary?

6 What is the difference between management and leadership?

Web activities

1 Use the Web to research successful business leaders such as Warren Buffet, John C. Bogle, Inguar Kamprad, Ratan Tata and Alan Bond. Also research the leadership of Rosa Parkes. Synthesise the information in a table and speculate on the commonalities of business leaders.

2 Use the Internet to locate and research the career of one toxic leader who interests you. List the ways that they have damaged their organisations and suggest ways that their colleagues and followers might have been able to limit the damage they caused.

3 Go to: psychology.about.com/library/quiz/bl-leadershipquiz.htm and complete the quiz on leadership style. Do not take the results too seriously but as you answer the questions try to identify the leadership dimensions they are attempting to measure. Also note that the quiz is fairly typical of those used on management development courses. Consider the psychometric properties quizzes like this should have.

4 Go to http://www.leadership-expert.co.uk/7-tips-to-transform-leadership/ and read seven useful tips on becoming a good leader. This site also has a range of good information on other topics such as "how to gain your first loyal follower", and "do leaders and credit cards mix?"

5 Use the Internet to locate three examples of "toxic leaders" or "narcissistic leaders". The example of Adolf Hitler is too obvious to be counted amongst your examples. On the basis of your research, work out the advice you would give an organisation on how to avoid employing toxic or narcissistic leaders.

Experiential activities

1 In a seminar, nominate four members and four business leaders (such as Michael Eisner, Harinda Singh, Gordon Wu and Meg Whitman). Allocate a business leader to each seminar member and arrange a balloon debate for the next seminar.

2 Choose an effective leader that you know well and list the personal qualities that you think helped them to be an effective leader. Compare your list with the list of characteristics of effective leaders that are given in this chapter. You can extend this experiential activity by doing the same thing with a leader who you consider to be ineffective.

3 Imagine that you are in a leadership position. What style of leader do you think you would be?

4 Go to your learning resources centre (i.e. library) and ask your learning resource facilitator (i.e. librarian) to direct you to a hard copy of *Annual Review of Psychology, 2009*. Turn to page 421 and browse the article on "Leadership: current theories, research, and future directions". This is not easy reading but it will help develop skills that will be useful throughout the remainder of your course and, maybe, the rest of your life. First, do not dwell on details. Look at the section headings and sample the odd paragraph, here and there. Next, choose a section (about a page long) that interests you most and read it carefully. You may need to read it several times, perhaps separated by a day or more. The style is abstract and very difficult for a newcomer to assimilate. Nevertheless, persevere. No pain, no gain! The skills you are learning will be of immense benefit when completing future assignments. Despite the difficult style, try to relate your chosen section to what you have heard in your lectures and what you have read in this or other books. Think how you could use this information and references in future assignments. Write down the names of three or four researchers whose publications are quoted. Look at other chapters and note those which may be relevant to your studies of management (hint: pages 451 and 475 – and there are at least two other chapters relevant to management). *Annual Reviews of Psychology* are the gold standard of concise, up-to-date information. Topics are renewed on a cycle of about three years. *Annual Reviews of Psychology* should be one of your top resources when researching an essay, assignment or work project. *Remember that!* There are annual reviews in other subjects relevant to management (e.g. sociology). Locate at least three of them.

5 Use this chapter to identify as many different types of leader as possible. Write each different type on a file card and then shuffle the cards. Ask a friend to arrange the cards

into groups so that the leader-types in each group are similar in some way. Then ask your friend to explain what the leaders in each type of group have in common. Repeat this exercise with several other friends, and finally on yourself. Then consider whether the many different types of leader mentioned in the literature could usefully be grouped into a smaller number of categories.

Recommended reading

1 Curtin, J. (2004) "Emergent leadership: case study of a jury foreperson", *Leadership review*, **4**, 75–85. A delightful paper, available on the Internet, which describes how a leader emerged in a jury. It is an example of a methodology (participant observation) which is rarely used in management research.

2 Sternberg, R.J. (2007) "A system's model of leadership: WICS", *American Psychologist*, **62** (1), 34–32. This is the trait theory of leadership reincarnated in a modern, slightly more sophisticated, guise! The paper incorporates most modern theories of leadership. Many other excellent articles on leadership will be found in same issue of *American Psychologist*.

3 Zaccaro, S.J. (2007) "Trait-based perspectives of leadership", *American Psychologist*, **62** (1), 6–16. This is good account of the trait theory of leadership. It emphasises patterns of traits and gives a new model.

4 Mintzberg, H.H. (2009) "We're over-led and undermanaged", *Business Week*, 17 August, **4143**, 68. An iconoclastic article suggesting that too much emphasis has been placed on leadership. Stimulating thoughts!

Managing Change

Chapter SIX

Planning and Strategy

Chapter contents

Classical management theorists (see Chapter 3) identified seven main management processes. The first process is planning. It can be considered under eight main headings:

❖ LEARNING OBJECTIVES

After studying this chapter you should have a clear understanding of the planning process. You should be able to see the topic of "strategy" in its context as a key and early part of a bigger chain of activity. You should also be able to make a balanced judgement on the advantages and pitfalls of planning. In particular you should be able to:

- ❖ **define** planning and **list** the five main stages in the planning process
- ❖ **define and differentiate** between mission and vision statements
- ❖ **differentiate** strategic plans from tactical and operational plans
- ❖ **produce** SWOT and PESTLE analyses for an organisation you know well
- ❖ **compare and contrast** the dangers of three strategies: choose one strategy concerning size, one concerned with customers and one strategy concerned with adaptation

- ❖ **explain** the nature of tactical plans and their place in the planning cycle
- ❖ **explain** the nature of operational plans and their place in the planning cycle
- ❖ **explain the reasons** for using PERT charts and **draw** an illustrative example
- ❖ **describe briefly** single-use, standing and contingency plans
- ❖ **discuss in detail** the advantages and disadvantages of planning

---

CASE 4.1: *Advantages of planning an assignment*

Imagine you've been set a student assignment to produce a report within a week on the impact of computers on marketing. If you dislike planning, you might immediately start work by borrowing a library book on computers and then spend the next two days extracting relevant information. You then need to borrow a book on marketing, but find that it is on loan and the recall will take two days. After the book becomes available, it takes a day to extract and integrate the relevant information and to word process the assignment. Unfortunately, on the evening before the deadline you discover that your printer has run out of ink and paper. By the time you've got your hands on ink and paper the deadline has passed. By contrast, one of your fellow students has carefully noted the future deadline, anticipated the need for both books and ordered them from the library simultaneously. At the same time this student checks the supplies of ink and paper and tops up her stocks in advance. Consequently she does not waste three days' waiting time. The assignment is submitted on the fourth day and the remainder of the week is free to spend on leisure activities.

4.1 Definition of planning and the various types of plan

A plan is a scheme which specifies the future resources and actions that an organisation needs in order to perform in an efficient way. It involves anticipating future requirements and challenges. It also involves sequencing future resources and actions to minimise the delay and waste which could arise if events were allowed to take their natural pace and chronological order. A basic but relevant example of how planning increases effectiveness was given in Case 4.1, which illustrated the essential features of planning. They are:

- a goal – the desired future states an organisation intends to achieve
- an analysis of resources and stages
- an arrangement of the stages to minimise delay and waste

There are six main kinds of plan. Figure 4.1 shows they are linked together in a consistent and logical way.

The whole planning process should start with an analysis of the organisation's mission and this feeds into successive types of plan which become increasingly more detailed and practical. The diagram wrongly implies that planning is a top-down process. Indeed, the planning process may start that way. But all stages of the process need to be influenced by consultation and feedback from subsequent stages. Once the general framework has been established, each of the main kinds of plan needs to be considered in more detail.

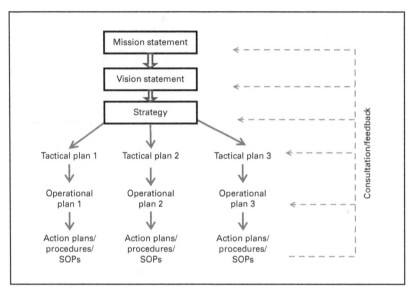

FIGURE 4.1 The relationship of the six main kinds of plan

4.2 Mission statements and visions

M ission statements and visions are often mistaken for each other or the terms are used interchangeably. Even when a distinction is made some people believe that planning should start with a mission statement while others believe it should start with a vision. Generally, planning should start with an organisation's **mission statement**, which is a succinct statement of *the reason for the organisation's exisitence*. Sometimes this is called the organisation's *overarching purpose*. When a mission statement refers to a group of related organisations it is often called a **team charter**. A mission statement should be short (three or four sentences) and it should form a memorable image which gives focus to the organisation's activities and employees. The mission statement usually refers to the present purpose of the organisation and is intended for use by all stakeholders, both internal, such as employees, and external, such as customers, suppliers and the government. A mission statement often contains:

- a statement of core values or ethics
- target customers or market and, sometimes, corporate relationships
- the products or services offered and the geographical region of availability
- expectations for growth or profitability

Mission statements should avoid hyperbole and bragging. Some inspired mission statements include the following:

- "High Quality Care for All" – British National Health Service
- "Make People Happy" – Disney Corporation
- "Ford will democratize the automobile" – Ford Motor Company (*circa* 1920)

A **vision statement** is a picture of what the organisation is likely to be at a time in the future when it is performing its mission in an effective way. It sets out the organisation's chosen way of achieving its purpose. It is perfectly possible for two organisations to have identical missions but very different visions. A good example is different churches. They may have identical missions, e.g. to redeem as many souls as possible by bringing people nearer to God. However, one church may have a vision of doing this by providing hostel accommodation to "down-and-outs" while another church may have a vision of achieving the same purpose by reading bible stories and providing Sunday services. Vision statements are longer and may, for a large and complex organisation, stretch to several pages. They are powerful pieces of communication that attempt to inspire employees. Indeed, the main readership will be employees and others (such as suppliers or regulators) who have a close and enduring contact with the organisation. Vision statements will often have specific dates stating when various components of the vision will be realised. All this should help the organisation communicate its core values and sense of direction to active stakeholders. Much criticised, but highly readable, research by Peters and Waterman (1988, see page 500) suggests that a key feature of outstanding companies is that employees share a core ideology and sense of direction.

CRITICAL THINKING 4.1 *Problems with mission and vision statements*

Mission and vision statements are usually full of lofty language, superlatives and rhetoric which aim to position an organisation on high moral ground. However, they have been criticised as a managerial fashion of the 1990s. Many reek of condescension and give the impression of "the great and the good" hypocritically setting moral standards for the "lower social orders".

Enthusiasm for vision statements and strategy can be overdone. For example, KPMG (a global organisation providing accountancy and other services and which employs over 140000 professional people in 146 countries) takes vision statements and strategy very seriously. So seriously that, in 2001, a company song was written and sung at a consultants conference in Frankfurt. The chorus went

66 KPMG – We're as strong as can be
We dream of power and energy
We go for the gold, together we hold
Onto our vision of global stratergy 99

The other verses and some rather scathing comments on the song can be accessed on http://www.theregister.co.uk/2001/03/08/kpmg_rocks_the_world_not/.

> Boddy (2002a) points out that vision statements can fail to recognise an organisation's capabilities. Unrealistic statements can blind an organisation to commercial realities. They may also make employees cynical of management claims.

Mission and vision statements are often confused. Table 4.1 contrasts the two types of statement.

Facet	Mission statement	Vision statement
Order in planning sequence	First	Second
Length in sentences	3 or 4 sentences	5 or more sentences
Whether factual or inspirational	Factual	Inspirational
Primary readers	All stakeholders	Mainly employees and close partners
Time orientation	Present statement of intent	Future statement of organisation

TABLE 4.1 Mission statements contrasted with vision statements

Once missions and visions have been formed, it is possible to get down to the nitty-gritty of planning. In principle, there are three other major types of plans:

- strategic plans
- tactical plans
- operational plans

These are covered in some detail in the next sections. Other, more specialised types include standing plans, single-use plans and contingency plans and are described later.

4.3 Strategic plans

What are strategic plans?

Strategic plans specify the major objectives of an organisation. They are derived from the vision statement. Strategic plans may be thought of as an organisation's overall master plan that will shape its destiny and achieve its vision. They indicate the direction an organisation needs to take. Indeed, some people call strategic plans "directional plans". Strategic planning is a complex and multidimensional activity that can be viewed in many ways. Figure 4.2 indicates the way the topic is structured in this book. The figure shows that strategy is fundamentally a part of planning.

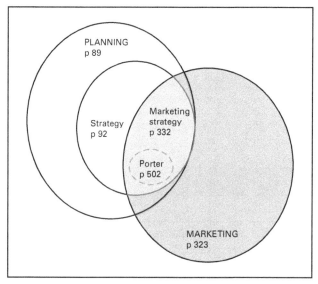

FIGURE 4.2 The relationship between planning, strategy and marketing

Treated separately, strategy is emasculated: it can be irrelevant if it is not related to an organisation's mission or goals and it has little effect if there is no follow-through with tactical and operational plans. Yet, strategy is also a vital part of marketing and much of the research on strategy has been written by marketers. So, even though strategy belongs within planning, there is an overlap with marketing. We explore marketing strategy more fully on pages 332–336.

Within marketing strategy there is the very important contribution of guru Michael Porter. His contribution to strategy is best seen in the context of other management gurus. Porter's excellent contribution to strategic planning is therefore described in Chapter 20.

To avoid cluttering Figure 4.2, other aspects of planning such as missions, visions, tactical and operational plans, etc. have been omitted (see pages 332–336). Similarly, important aspects of strategy such as methods of producing strategies or types of organisational strategies have been omitted from the figure (see pages 94–97).

The aim of any strategy is to guide the organisation to areas where the organisation will find it easiest to achieve its objectives and where it can resist challenges from competitors. To do this it must identify its **competitive advantages** which are sometimes **key success factors**. They are also sometimes called **core competences** or **critical success factors**, depending upon the consultant giving the seminar! A competitive advantage is a medium- or long-term factor where the organisation has such strength that its competitors are deterred from entering its market. Ideally, organisations should have several layers of competitive advantage so that other organisations can see that even if they penetrate or neutralise one they still face a daunting challenge. Ideally, the competitive advantage should be restricted to just one organisation or only a small group of organisations. Competitive advantages give an organisation an edge over its rivals. They enable an organisation to transform resources more efficiently than similar organisations. An organisation with a competitive advantage may be able to achieve superiority, so that it is difficult for other organisations to copy. Competitive advantages are those facets of the organisations which are costly and time-consuming for others to develop so that a competitor's "entry price is high". Typical competitive advantages are:

- cost leadership
- brand recognition
- technological superiority
- uniqueness

Examples of cost leadership would be the John Lewis Partnership, "who are never knowingly undersold" and the do-it-yourself, (DIY) chain B&Q, who refund 110 per cent of the difference if a local supplier sells the same item at a lower price. Marks & Spencer once had a competitive advantage in the quality of their clothes. IBM also had a competitive advantage in the field of mainframe computers, but this advantage evaporated when personal computers became common.

The last two examples illustrate that competitive advantages are not permanent. Companies may seek to sustain a competitive advantage by using patents, trademarks and copyrights. However, the most effective methods of maintaining a competitive advantage include:

- improvements and innovations to produce "layers of technological advantage"
- economies of scale which allow for cost-cutting
- "strategic alliances" with suppliers which deny raw materials to competitors

All of these approaches seek to make the entry price for competitors daunting.

Counteracting threats to a competitive advantage requires a system of **competitive intelligence** that scans the business environment for information about the activities of competitors. The vast majority of competitive intelligence is available from public sources. The expansion of the Internet means that information on new competitor activities is available much more quickly!

Another major aim of strategic planning is to direct an organisation towards promising markets. Consequently, marketers have devised additional methods of identifying aids to strategic planning which include the BCG matrix, the GE matrix and the Ansoff matrix. Michael Porter's work on the way that organisations and nations can develop a strategy for achieving competitive advantage is very important.

A good example of a strategic plan is given by Luton and Dunstable Hospital which is highlighted in Case 4.2.

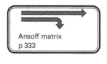

Ansoff matrix
p 333

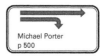

Michael Porter
p 500

Methods of producing strategic plans

Strategists use many methods to identify an appropriate strategy. Probably the best-known method is a **SWOT analysis** which covers four main features that involve internal and external factors.

CASE 4.2: *Strategic planning in the NHS*

The British National Health Service (NHS) is a huge organisation. It employs more people than any organisation on the planet except the China's People's Liberation Army. The NHS is a stable organisation: it has a steady income, no competitors and the demands placed on it are relatively easy to predict. However, changes (such as building a new hospital or department) take many years to complete. All these factors mean that the NHS must produce strategic plans, and any strategic plan is unlikely to be overturned by sudden changes in its environment.

Luton and Dunstable are two large towns situated either side of the main motorway, about 30 miles north of London. In 2005 the area (population of about 300 000) is served by a medium-sized hospital which offers an accident and emergency (A&E) department, specialist treatments (such as neurophysiology or intensive care of babies) and minor medical procedures (such as removal of some skin growths).

Luton and Dunstable Hospital draws up a strategic plan every five years (sometimes called "quinqennial planning"). The 2006–10 strategic plan includes:

- Providing services for a catchment population of 500 000. The increase reflects two factors: natural population growth and offering specialist services to a wider area – in the neighbouring county of Hertfordshire.

- Making the A&E department quite separate from other services. This specialisation will increase expertise and make A&E provision more accountable.

- Providing more treatments away from the hospital, in places that are more convenient to patients. More patients, especially the elderly, will be treated in their own homes or in their own communities, such as their local GP surgeries.

- There will be an effort to add more value by constraining costs to a level that can be afforded.

The "architects" of Luton and Dunstable Hospital's strategic plan needed to take account of many different factors. It might be useful to pause and think of the factors you would take into account if you were one of the planners.

Factors *internal* to the organisation:

1. **Strengths** may include closeness to customers, management expertise and other skills, financial strength, branch network, market position and brand image.

2. **Weaknesses** are often the opposite of the strengths. They may include poor reputation, out-of-date equipment, inadequate R&D, difficult markets, poor industrial relations and poor communications.

Factors in the *external* environment:

3. **Opportunities** can arise from either strengths or weaknesses. Often they occur from a change in technology, legislation or markets where there is a gap.

4 **Threats** usually arise from competition – especially new entrants in the market and substitution products, shortage of resources (including skilled labour) and new government regulations.

SWOT analysis is easy to use, especially by those with little knowledge of strategic planning. However, it can be unsystematic and it is easy to miss important factors. **PESTLE analysis** is more comprehensive and gives a good checklist of important strategic factors. PESTLE is not in opposition to SWOT. Indeed, the PESTLE factors can be used to identify strengths, weaknesses, opportunities or threats. The PESTLE checklist has six main factors:

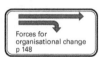

Forces for organisational change p 148

1 **Political factors** such as government stability, privatisation/, government regulation and control, or health issues

2 **Economic factors** such as phases of the business cycle, economic growth, interest rates, inflation, labour costs and unemployment rates

3 **Sociocultural factors** include population trends, educational levels, lifestyles and changes in consumer tastes and values

4 **Technological factors** include new discoveries, new production methods, better communications, technology transfer

5 **Legal factors** include changes in the law concerning employment, companies or business regulation

6 **Environmental factors** include discovery of new supplies of energy or raw materials, shortages of water, etc. climate change nationalisation

Sometimes PESTLE analyses is too involved. Consequently some organisations, such as UNISON and the Highways Agency, use an abbreviated version called PEST analysis.

CASE 4.3: *Unison's PEST analysis*

In Chapter 2 it was noted that trade associations and unions employ significant numbers of managers. Unison is Europe's largest public sector trade union and it has over 1.3 million members working in jobs such as librarians, social workers, secretaries and school meals supervisors. In order to represent the interests of its members it needs to develop a strategy key areas. For example, Unison used PEST analysis to develop its strategy towards immigration:

- **Political factors** are important because immigration is an emotive issue that can generate sensational press coverage which can lead to actions by politicians. Political pressures are greatest in locations where the migrant population is high and can impact on, say, the provision of housing, health and education. Government decisions such as reducing funding for legal aid can have unanticipated effects on the ability of migrant workers to uphold their rights.

- **Economic factors** play an important role in developing a strategy towards immigration. For example, most migrants come to the UK from countries that pay lower wages. Further, it is claimed that immigration adds 0.5 per cent to the UK's gross domestic

▶

product (more than £6 billion). The level of immigration is correlated to the business cycle – highest in booms and lowest in recessions.

- **Social factors** relevant to immigration include an ageing population which without immigration would mean a smaller number of workers to support pensioners. Difficulty in communicating in English is often another significant social factor relevant to immigration.
- **Technological factors** have a huge impact on the actions of immigrants and the appropriate strategy. For example, automation has reduced the demand for less skilled workers, transport to the UK is much cheaper and improvements in telecommunications have made it easier for immigrants to discover job opportunities and maintain contact with their home countries.

This PEST analysis has helped Unison develop an effective strategy to help immigrants. This includes political lobbying, disseminating statistics, shaping employment legislation and providing information in 11 different languages.

Source: based on *Times 100 Case Studies*.

Alternative strategies

Once an organisation has analysed position and competitive advantages, it must decide upon the appropriate strategy. Many different kinds of strategy have been identified by writers such as Miles and Snow (1978), Mintzberg (1987) and Porter (1996, 2001). The following section categorises the main types of strategies according to size, focus, customers and adaptation/innovation. In addition there are some miscellaneous strategies.

Strategies concerned with size:

- **Globalisation:** expanding into other countries.
- **Industry dominance:** capturing such a large part of a market that there is little room for competitors.
- **Growth:** to obtain economies of scale and market dominance. Growth can be:
  - organic (natural) growth of present business
  - acquisition (takeover) of other organisations
  - merger with other organisations.
- **Retrenchment** is a defensive strategy aimed at increasing efficiency by reducing the size of an organisation. It takes several forms including:
  - downsizing – usually by removing middle managers and support staff
  - selling parts of the organisation to refocus on core competences
  - liquidation – closing parts of an organisation to eliminate debt (bankruptcy) or to realise assets (asset stripping).

Strategies concerning focus aim to stop an organisation spreading itself too thinly:

- **Core competences:** restricting activities to those the organisation does best. Often this means selling minor parts of the organisation.
- **Geographical focus:** restricting activities to a well-defined area so that regional dominance is achieved.

Strategies concerning *customers* focus on building a clear difference from its competitors in the minds of its consumers:

- **Product differentiation**: making a product appear different to others.
- **Cost leadership**: offering a product or service cheaper than competitors – by increased efficiency or "squeezing" suppliers.
- **Imitation**: following the ideas of a market leader and not incurring risk or development costs.
- **High speed**: delivering services to customers more quickly than competitors.

Strategies concerning *adaptation and innovation* reflect how the organisation intends to respond to changes:

- **Prospectors** innovate and follow new opportunities. They bear a risk in return for prospects of substantial growth.
- **Defenders** attempt to hold a position in a declining market by emphasising existing products. This strategy may end in terminal decline.
- **Analysers** "follow the leader when things are good". These organisations usually maintain the stability of their key products while expanding a few promising areas pioneered by others. Analysers will also follow the imitation strategy and make goods that are clones of the market leaders' products.
- **Reactors** only respond to competitive pressures when there is a danger to their survival. Reactor organisations often do not have any other strategy and only change as a last resort.

Miscellaneous strategies:

- **Employee talent** involves finding and retaining able people.
- **Strategic alliances** involve collaborating with other organisations – especially in marketing and sales where the same infrastructure can be used to sell non-competing products from different companies.

Strategies are not mutually exclusive. Many organisations, especially large ones, will use a combination. For example, they may retrench older and less profitable parts while expanding more profitable parts.

Some people are sceptical of strategic plans, they suggest that such plans are only useful in hindsight. Advocates of strategic plans forget those that have gone wrong. For instance, one of the biggest business failures in recent decades has been the fall of the Marconi Company, a fall which has been blamed on bad strategy. This is explored in Case 4.4.

CASE 4.4: *Strategies that failed – Marconi and the Royal Bank of Scotland*

Under the chairmanship of Arnold Weinstock the General Electric Company (GEC) was a jewel in the crown of British industry: steadfast, calculating every risk with precision and making oodles of money out of such things as defence contracts. It had a cash pile of more than £2 billion – a massive sum in 1999. Lord Arnold Weinstock retired and was succeeded by George Simpson, who was keen on grand strategies. He saw GEC's future in terms of the high-technology communications market. His intention was to exploit the use of micro mirrors as optical switches to bounce signals around the Internet and become a serious rival to the likes of Cisco, the American computer colossus.

The bold strategic plan had everything – selling off the old defence businesses, rebranding with the new name Marconi, relocation of the communication business's headquarters to Pennsylvania in order to be nearer the world's largest communications market. The plan was implemented with gusto. High-technology communication companies were bought as if they were gold mines.

Simpson was so dazzled by the strategic plan, he failed to notice that communications companies were actually going out of fashion! The dotcom bubble burst. Worse, customers such as such as BT were short of cash after bidding for hugely expensive mobile phone licences and were cutting back on equipment purchases. Other companies such as Nortel and Ericsson were not blinded by their strategic plan. They saw the downturn and reacted appropriately. Simpson did not. The Marconi spree continued. Inevitably, the share price crashed. The company had a debt pile of £2.5 billion and many underperforming assets. A former GEC executive commented "as destructions of shareholder values go, I cannot think of another case that even approaches this". Simpson was replaced. Thousands of innocent workers lost their jobs and wished ruefully for the profits made in the boring old days before Simpson's "innovative", "exciting", "far-seeing" strategic plan.

The Royal Bank of Scotland (RBS) was founded in 1727 and under prudent management grew steadily to become a major British bank. In the late 1990s Sir Fred Goodwin (known as 'Fred the shred' because of his reputation for ferocious cost-cutting) joined the company and subsequently became CEO. Sir Fred and colleagues developed a strategy of aggressive expansion. In 2000, Fred led a successful hostile takeover of NatWest, a bank that was three times the RBS's size. Fred's Napoleonic strategy of expansion led to a $1.6 billion minority stake in the Bank of China. Analysts regarded his strategy as risky in case of inclement financial weather. Some shareholders accused him of megalomania. Goodwin promised to avoid further acquisitions and to focus on growing the group organically. But a harsh financial winter, the global liquidity crisis, developed in 2007. Goodwin and his colleagues continued the strategy of expansion and took over parts of a large Dutch Bank, ABN Amro. The victory stretched the RBS's resources beyond the limit. ABN Amro had underwritten many dodgy debts in America. The RBS was in real trouble, and was bailed out by the British government. 'Fred the shred' was shredded – he resigned but refused to forfeit any of his (circa £700 000 per annum) pension.

The two cases have remarkable similarities. Both were very respected and stable organisations before they adopted aggressive strategic planning. The strategies were championed by powerful and dominating men. In both cases the strategies were continued even though there were clear signs that the business environment had changed. Alas, in both cases, thousands of loyal workers lost their jobs and shareholders such as pension funds lost a lot of money. In the RBS's case the taxpayer, including the families of readers of this book, were hard hit too!

CRITICAL THINKING 4.2 *Criticisms of strategic planning?*

Mintzberg (1994) suggests that strategic planners often make fallacious assumptions:

1 They assume an organisation can, with sufficient skill, *predetermine the future*. In fact, the business environment is so dynamic and interactive that the future cannot be estimated with any precision. It is likely that a strategic plan will be blown off course. Strategic plans reached their zenith in times of greater stability. They are less useful in today's turbulent environment.

2 They assume that *planners have an objective view*, detached from current political intrigues and beliefs of the organisation. In fact, strategists are as immersed in subjectivity and political intrigues as anyone else. Their strategies are not as objective as they would wish.

3 They adopt a formal approach involving ticking boxes on checklists in the belief that *standard procedures will produce the best plans*. In fact, a good strategy requires flair, imagination, insight and creativity, which tend to be stifled by a formal approach. It is necessary to think "outside the box".

Mintzberg acknowledges that organisations may have deliberate, *intended strategies* but these will be buffeted and blown about by forces that subsequently emerge in the environment. The *realised strategy*, the events that actually happen, may be quite different. Perhaps the most sensible approach is an *incremental strategy*. An incremental strategy occurs when an organisation takes sensible, case-by-case decisions that gradually merge to form a strategy. An incremental strategy emerges via unstructured, unpredictable, organic processes rather than a series of clinical steps. This organic approach often produces the strategy that is more appropriate to the environment.

Kay (1996) suggests that strategic planning has a formal impossibility. If good strategic planning can be reduced to a set of procedures and checklists, most organisations would be able to produce a good strategy. If all organisations have good strategies then there is little or no competitive advantage in having one!

4.4 Tactical plans

Tactical plans are also called *functional plans* or *intermediate plans*. They translate a firm's strategic plan into specific goals for organisational subunits. For example, a strategic plan may call for a 10 per cent increase in the market share. This depends on detailed tactical plans for each of the sales, production and finance departments. Tactical plans are usually concerned with *how* things are done whereas strategic plans are usually concerned with *what* is done.

Tactical plans need to be co-ordinated with each other and with the strategic plan. They usually have a timescale of one to five years. This contrasts with strategic plans and visions which generally have a timescale of 10 years or more. Strategic plans primarily involve top managers, whereas tactical plans primarily involve middle managers.

One of the main tools of tactical planning is the Gantt chart. These are particularly useful because they show how related operational plans are progressing. An idealised Gantt chart associated with a marketing department's tactical plan to increase sales by 10 per cent is given in Figure 4.3.

This example is highly simplified but it does demonstrate the main features of a Gantt chart. A complete Gantt chart would include holidays and other activities. It would also show progress to date and other events. Often each of the main programmes shown on a Gantt chart would be accompanied by a detailed action plan.

Period (week) No	1	2	3	4	5	6	7	8	9	10	11	12	13
Month	June			July				August				September	
Week	wk 2	wk 3	wk 4	wk 1	wk 2	wk 3	wk 4	wk 1	wk 2	wk 3	wk 4	wk 1	wk 2
STAGE													
1. NEW BROCHURE													
1.1 consultation stage	■	■	■										
1.2 design stage				■	■		■						
1.3 production stage								■	■				
2 EXHIBITION STAND													
2.1 designing new stand						■							
2.2 produce new stand										■	■		
2.3 assemble stand in exhibition													■
3 SALES STAFF TRAINING													
3.1 design training conference								■					
3.2 book venue & accommodation	■												
3.3 arrange for seperators			■	■	■	■							
3.4 conference													

FIGURE 4.3 An example of a Gantt chart

Much less research and thought has been devoted to tactical plans than to strategic plans. The reasons are open to speculation. Perhaps it is because academics, writers and researchers find the heady world of high-level strategy much more exciting. Perhaps they do not have sufficient practical knowledge – an essential requirement for tactical planning.

4.5 Operational plans

Definition of operational plans

Operational plans are sometimes called **action plans** or **production plans**. They are the most detailed level of planning, and specify the actions or results which individuals or small groups must achieve. Operational plans are very specific. For example, they may specify that a production line should produce 150 objects per week, a sales representative should obtain orders worth £100 000 per month or that a consultant should recruit two new clients every quarter. Operational plans should be linked to tactical plans. Operational plans are short term. They have a time span of several months but they can involve time intervals that are as short as a week or less. Operational plans involve first-line managers and should incorporate suggestions and input from employees at lower levels.

Good operational plans are essential to the efficient functioning of an organisation. They affect all employees on a day-to-day basis. They state the results which must be achieved so that tactical and strategic plans come to fruition. Clear, unambiguous communication of operational plans is essential. While strategic plans and tactical plans are not altered over long periods, operational plans constantly change – even though much of this change is cyclical. Operational plans often incorporate rules and **standard operating procedures (SOPs)**. These procedures are often contained in an operations handbook.

Action plans

The prime tool for operation planning is the action plan. These first divide large goals into small discreet stages, which are then placed in the optimum sequence and completion dates are estimated. Sometimes, action plans allocate responsibility for the completion of the stages. Table 4.2 gives a simplified example of an action plan, starting 1 June, for producing a new brochure. This was one of the three projects included in the Gantt chart in the previous section on tactical plans. A comparison between the Gantt chart and the action plan will shows that the latter is more detailed and specifies the results that must be achieved by individuals.

Gantt charts and action plans are fairly simple and popular methods but may not be adequate for complicated projects where there are many interrelated activities. **PERT charts** are often used in these circumstances. PERT is an acronym of Program Evaluation and Review Technique. A PERT chart is a flowchart that shows the sequences, durations and timings of events needed to achieve an objective. PERT charts can be thought of

Action plan for new brochure			
Stage		**Completion date**	**By**
1	Review present brochure	1 June	MA
2	Discuss needs and ideas with sales force and small number of customers	21 June	MA & MD
3	Discuss needs and ideas with marketing director	28 June	MA & MD
4	Produce specifications for new brochure and submit to marketing director for approval	7 July	MA & MD
5	Produce draft brochure	21 July	CW
6	Discuss draft brochure with marketing director, sales force and small number of customers	28 July	MA & MD
7	Dispatch revised draft to printers	1 Aug	MA
8	Correct proofs	14 Aug	MA
9	Receive copies of new brochure from printer	21 Aug	MA

TABLE 4.2 Example of action plan
MA = marketing assistant MD = marketing director CW = copywriter

as complicated versions of Gantt charts which are complicated and are produced by computer programs. PERT charts consist of activities which have a start, duration and completion point. Usually completion points are called "milestones". The start point of an activity is usually governed by the completion of a previous activity. Events which govern the start of an activity are usually called "**dependencies**". The preparation of a lecture provides a simple example of the process of structuring a PERT chart. The activities are shown in Table 4.3.

A computer can compile the information into a PERT chart such as that shown in Figure 4.4.

A key feature of a PERT chart is the "critical path" which indicates the shortest time in which the project can be completed. The critical path is emphasised by thicker lines or use of colour. Activities along the critical path *must* be completed to time. If they are not, the project will not finish on time. The timing of activities that are not on the critical path is less crucial. Some delay can be tolerated. The tolerable level of delay is called "**the float**". In our example, the timing of locating own books is not crucial. It can be performed any time before the library books are obtained. In fact there is a float of two and a half days.

Activity	Duration	Dependency
A. Check syllabus	½ day	None
B. Order and collect library books	½ day	Activity A
C. Locate own books	½ day	Activity A
D. Read and note relevant material	3 days	Activity B,C
E. Write lecture notes	3 days	Activity D
F. Prepare visual aids	1 day	Activity E
G. Prepare handouts	2 days	Activity E
H. Duplicate handouts	½ day	Activity F
I. Assemble all materials	¼ day	Activities E, F, H
J. Deliver lecture	1hr	Activity J

TABLE 4.3 Data for a PERT chart

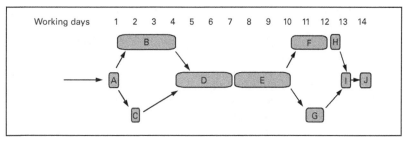

FIGURE 4.4 Example of a simple PERT chart

Other plans: single-use plans, standing plans and contingency plans

Sometimes it is useful to distinguish between single-use plans and standing plans:

Single-use plans are devised to meet unique situations and are never used again. For example, a pharmaceutical company setting up a new production plant will have elaborate plans covering the construction of buildings, the cash flow and the recruitment of employees. Even if another production plant is commissioned, the circumstances will have changed so much that the original plans will be useless.

Standing plans are used when a task reoccurs. For example, the pharmaceutical company may make a range of medicines, manufacturing a stock of each medicine on a cyclical basis. Thus, for example, it will have a standing plan for the manufacture of an anti-cancer medicine, a standing plan for the manufacture of a medicine to combat high blood pressure and a standing plan to manufacture a medicine to reduce inflammation of joints. Standing plans have the advantage of ensuring consistent standards and methods.

Contingency plans are needed because the business environment can change rapidly, making it difficult to plan for the future with certainty. Hence, many organisations develop parallel plans to cover likely eventualities. Two or more parallel plans which are in place and activated if certain conditions arise are called contingency plans. For example, a company that is extending its production facility may have two contingency plans: one will come into operation if the new plant is ready on time, while the other will be used if there is a significant delay. Similarly, a company bidding to take over another company will have two plans: one will be used if the takeover bid is successful and the other will be used if its bid fails. Contingency plans enable organisations to respond to events in a flexible way.

4.6 Management by objectives (a synthesis of types of plan?)

Strategic, tactical, operational, single-use, standing and contingency plans do not add value unless they are co-ordinated. Management by objectives (MBO) is a system which aims to integrate all types of plans into a coherent system where each is linked explicitly to the level above and ultimately, to an organisation's mission. Management by objectives, was embraced very enthusiastically in the 1970s. Today it is ubiquitous but implemented in a more subtle and less mechanistic way.

Management by objectives starts with the goals of someone's boss – often called "key results". The boss' key results are examined and the ways that a worker should contribute to them is identified. These are developed into key results for the worker. If he or she has subordinates, the worker's key results are examined to identify the subordinate's key results and so on. Therefore, MBO is a top-down system where one person's goals are linked to the goals of their boss and the goals of any subordinates. Ultimately everyone's goals are linked to organisational mission.

For example, an organisation's strategic plan may lead to a service manager's key result of servicing 100 customers per month. If there are four service units, the service manager will discuss their key result with each of the four first-line managers. Taking other factors such as the stringency of service contracts and the availability of service providers into account, the service manager and first-line managers will agree individual targets. For example, the four first-line managers may agree to service 30, 30, 25 and 15 customers, respectively. The first-line managers with the highest targets may have agreed an above-average contribution because they are in charge of a production lines with up-to-date equipment and experienced staff. The first-line manager with the lowest target may manage services staffed by trainees and where much machine maintenance is needed. However, as a group, the four first-line managers will service the 100 customers the service manager needs in order to achieve his or her key result that is linked to the organisation's mission.

At the end of the month each manager and subordinate will meet to discuss performance. Any shortfall is examined and its reason identified. The shortfall may not be the fault of the subordinate. It could be that the initial target, or perhaps the strategy, are too ambitious – in which case they should be reduced. It could be the shortfall was caused by an unreliable supplier – in which case the purchasing department would be asked to improve the supply chain. Finally, it could be that the manager omitted to communicate a key piece of information – in which case the manager should seek to improve communication skills. In some cases it is important to note the five characteristics of MBO, and extra information about them is given on the website associated with this book.

Research results and MBO

Management by objectives is consistent with research by occupational psychologists such as Locke *et al.* (1981), which proposed that people perform better when they are given specific goals that are moderately, but not excessively, challenging. However, many people are unenthusiastic about the effectiveness of MBO. Research concerning participation in decision-making is less positive. It would seem that the level of the difficulty of the goals is much more important than the way the goals are set (Latham and Saari, 1979). In general, research indicates that MBO is highly effective and is likely to produce productivity gains in over 90 per cent of cases (Rogers and Hunter, 1991). Rogers and Hunter's study emphasised the importance of top-management commitment. When their commitment to MBO was high the average productivity gain (56 per cent) was higher than the productivity gain when top-management commitment was low (6 per cent).

CRITICAL THINKING 4.3 *Weaknesses of MBO*

The original enthusiasm for MBO is somewhat diluted because it has at least five *weaknesses*:

1 MBO distorts an organisation by focusing upon measurable things which are not necessarily important things. Behaviour linked to targets increases but the gains may be at the expense of equally important, less measurable activities such as setting a good example or helping others. Often, these activities are called "corporate citizenship".

2 Implementation and operation of MBO absorbs a great deal of managerial effort. Sometimes MBO produces excessive paperwork and managers may spend more time devising criteria, drawing up action plans and preparing for appraisal meetings than actively managing others.

3 In the longer term, MBO encourages managers to set lower goals. Once managers realise that successive cycles of MBO will result in ever-increasing targets, they become wise and set themselves easier goals.

4 MBO might work in the UK, the USA, the Netherlands and Australia where there is a high work ethic and where people are accustomed to working towards goals in an independent way. However, there is doubt whether it works in other cultures that have different values (Hofstede, 1980).

5 MBO does not work well where rapid change is the norm. MBO was developed in the 1950s when there was a more stable business environment. Nowadays a dramatic, overnight change can make such plans obsolete.

4.7 Advantages and disadvantages of planning and strategy?

Most people agree that the advantages of planning far outweigh the disadvantages. Plans are *advantageous* because they:

- **Give direction and focus to organisational activities** – provided the plans are well communicated. Without plans people will make decisions in isolation and ignore the goals that need to be achieved.
- **Indicate the required standard of performance**.
- **Improve speed of decision-making**. Instead of referring matters higher and waiting for a reply, a manager can consult a plan and make a quicker decision.
- **Plans allow lower levels of staff to participate in making decisions**.
- **Give context** and an explanation of many decisions which are handed down from senior management.
- **Minimise waste and redundancy** by foreseeing future difficulties and therefore taking action to circumvent them.
- **Focus attention on the future** and the way an organisation must marshal its resources. Without plans people may be content to "rest on their laurels".

However it is clear that plans and strategies have *three disadvantages:*

- Strategies are **only useful with hindsight.** Advocates of strategy ignore strategic plans that have gone wrong. For example, two of the biggest business failures in recent decades has been the fall of the Marconi Company and the RBS. The falls of Marconi and the RBS were explored further in Case 4.4.
- Strategies **consume large quantities of management time** and effort that would be better spent elsewhere. If the organisation operates in a very turbulent environment or if it operates in a very predictable and constraining environment, strategies have limited value. It is better to simply make sure that the organisation is very adaptable so that it can respond appropriately whatever happens.
- Strategies can **induce rigidity**, because their designers become too committed to them. Instead of responding to the environment, strategists are likely to argue that their plans will work "if only" the organisation will provide more resources. Continued failure may lead to the claim that the strategy is correct and the difficulties are only short-term aberrations. Yet further failure may lead to the claim that the strategy is fine but it was implemented in the wrong way. Eventually it dawns that a new strategy is needed but by that time the organisation may have "done a Marconi or an RBS!"

The inevitable conclusion is that managers *must* use plans to their full advantage. Nevertheless, they should beware of devoting too much time perfecting plans to the nth degree and they should abandon plans when there is clear evidence that they are inadequate or if the environment has changed. Plans are excellent servants but are very dangerous masters!

4.8 Planning toolkit

- Most disadvantages of planning are because of *inflexibility*. Hence planners should ensure a flexible environment which values learning and continuous improvement.

- The goals contained in plans are important. *Goals should be ambitious but not unreasonable.* The goals will be more practical and easier to understand if the people required to implement the plans are involved in setting the goals. Generally speaking, plans should be constructed "bottom-up" rather than "top-down".

- *Timescales of plans should be realistic.* They should take account of:
  - illnesses and holidays
  - staff training
  - daily, seasonal and other variations in workload
  - rotation of staff into different jobs so that versatility and motivation are enhanced

- *Planning specialists should not be aloof experts* working in a distant planning department. Rather, they should be facilitators who assist a group to formulate their own workable plans.

The importance of planning was identified very early in the history of management. However, tasks need to be organised into jobs. Jobs must be organised into a coherent structure. Staff must be willing and able to implement the plans and the plans must be communicated effectively. The next chapters describe other important management processes such as organising, staffing and communicating.

Activities and further study

Essay plans

Prepare plans for the following essays:

1 Compare and contrast two methods of producing organisational strategies.
2 Select a local organisation (perhaps your college or university department, perhaps a charitable organisation or club that you know well) and conduct both a SWOT analysis and a PESTLE analysis for that organisation.
3 Compare and contrast mission statements and vision statements.
4 Compare and contrast strategic plans, tactical plans and operational plans.
5 Evaluate the benefits and disadvantages of planning.

Web activities

1 People often confuse mission statements and vision statements. Log on to the website associated with this book and and access "Web Based Exercise 2: Missions and Visions". Then complete the table that contrasts the two types of statement. When you have finished compare your answer with the model which is also given on the website.
2 Log on to the website associated with this book and access "Web Based Exercise 3: Planning Techniques". Follow the instructions and produce an action plan and a Gantt chart. When you have finished compare your work with the model answer which is also given on the website.
3 Search the Internet for mission statements – perhaps the mission statement of your employer, university or college. To what extent do you think people in the organisation find a mission statement useful in achieving organisational goals? Ask six members of the organisation whether they are aware the mission statement exists. Ask those who are aware of its existence what the mission statement contains.
4 Search the Internet for more information about the Marconi case study (hint: wikipedia. org and news.bbc.co.uk are good places to start).

Experiential activities

1 Write a mission and vision statement for yourself!

2 Imagine that you are a member of a consultancy group that helps other organisations install management by objectives. You have received an enquiry from a small organisation that employs 100 people and has 12 managers. They invite you to give a 20-minute presentation to explain MBO. Prepare this presentation and deliver it to a group of fellow students.

3 Make a list of the six most important goals you wish to achieve in the next year. Examine these goals critically for their technical merit as objectives:

- Are they clear?
- Are they quantifiable?
- Are they realistic, etc.?

(Hint: it may be useful to visit websites such as www.smc.qld.edu.au/goals.htm or www.goal-setting-guide.com/smart-goals.html.)

4 Visit the Preactor website (http://www.preactor.com/online-demo/data/english/ standard%20demo/online-demo.html) to gain an impression of the complexity of operational planning. After a wooden introduction the demonstration shows how complex Gantt charts are set up to control production.

Recommended reading

1 Porter, M.E. (1996) "What is strategy?", *Harvard Business Review*, 61–78. November–December, A long, tedious paper which is a little outdated. Nevertheless it gives a clear distinction between effectiveness and strategic positioning. It also give many examples of company strategies. Highly recommended.

2 Collins, J.C. and Porras, J.I. (1996) "Building your company's vision", *Harvard Business Review*, September–October, 65–77. This article outlines the construction of vision statements and examples from well-known companies.

3 Furst, P. (2010) "Planning is the architect", *Industrial Engineer*, **42** (2), 44–50. A practical example of the importance of planning. Read from page 46 onwards.

4 Stoller, J. (2010) "The world according to Gantt", *CMA Management*, **84** (5), 33–35. This article outlines the significance of Gantt charts in managing projects and helping stakeholders communicate with each other. It also gives details of IT packages which can construct Gantt charts.

Chapter SEVEN

Organisational Change

Chapter contents

❖ LEARNING OBJECTIVES

After reading this chapter you should be able to recognise the need for organisational change and the different types of change that may be necessary. You should also be aware of some of the stages of change and the methods that change agents may use. You should be able to identify some of the factors that may make organisational change effective. Finally, you should be aware of some of the criticisms levelled against writers and researcher on the subject of organisational change. In particular, you should be able to:

- ❖ **explain** why organisational change may be necessary
- ❖ **list** at least four covert ways that people can sabotage organisational change
- ❖ **describe** at least four dimensions of change situations and suggest at least one way that these dimensions may converge
- ❖ **describe** in detail Lewin's three phases of organisational change and describe at least one other writer's categorisation of the phases of change
- ❖ **explain** the ethical issues that may be involved in organisational change

- ❖ **list** three techniques of changing the way an organisation analyses and solves problems, and two techniques of changing organisational structures
- ❖ **describe** at least four techniques of changing behaviour in organisations
- ❖ **describe** the role of change agents
- ❖ **explain** the difficulties of evaluating the success of organisational change
- ❖ **list** at least six factors that are thought to help the success of organisational change
- ❖ **explain** at least three serious criticisms of research into organisational change

Organisational change is in itself not new. The following statement may sound familiar.

> 66 We trained hard . . . but it seemed that every time we were beginning to form into teams we would be reorganised. I was to learn later in life that we tend to meet any new situation by reorganising; and a wonderful method it can be for creating the illusion of progress while producing confusion, inefficiency and demoralisation. 99

You may be surprised to discover that its author is believed to be a Roman soldier, Petronius Arbiter. No doubt the builders of the pyramids and the scribes of Hammurabi voiced similar complaints. However, the business environment always changes and an organisation that does not change with it will encounter great difficulties. This can be true of high-technology and nimble organisations such as Nokia.

CASE 6.1: *Nokia's organisational change – from manufacturing galoshes to mobile phone behemoth to ailing multinational*

Many owners of Nokia phones produced by the largest Finnish company will be amazed at the changes that it and its organisation have experienced. They will also be amazed at the changes it needs to make in order to survive in the face of recent commercial developments.

In brief, Nokia was founded (near the Nokianvita river) in 1896 as a manufacturer of rubber galoshes. Shortly after the First World War, it took over an insolvent electricity company, in order to ensure its electricity supply. Over the next few decades it changed its organisation to focus upon the manufacture of electricity cables. It reorganised again after 1967 when it became an industrial conglomerate. When mobile telephone technology developed in the 1990s, the organisation changed by divesting many peripheral products to concentrate on the manufacture of mobile phones. This was a shrewd organisational change and by 1998 it became the world's largest mobile phone manufacturer. Its handset (Nokia 1100) was the world's best selling mobile phone – indeed the world's best consumer electronics product. The company reorganised again after troubles in the network equipment division. It shed large numbers of staff and moved production from a factory with high costs in Germany to a factory with lower costs in Romania.

Shortly after the appointment of a new CEO (Olli-Pekka Kallasvuo – known as OPK) in 2006 the behemoth encountered a storm that threatens it hegemony. Six months later Apple unveiled the smart mobile phone, the iPhone. Since then Nokia has been on a downhill run and its profit margins have dived from 15 per cent to 7 per cent. Google and Blackberry produced competing products. Nokia took time to unveil the N8 model which despite its spin, is perceived as a mere "catch up". Nokia's slowness to change its organisation in response to a commercial challenge is blamed on its CEO's cautious and inward-looking approach. However, the people of Finland share some of the blame because they are unwilling to condone drastic changes in an organisation they deem to be a national treasure.

Nokia can regain ground. If it skilfully uses the techniques of organisational change, it can produce an equivalent transformation of its change from making rubber shoes to a leading manufacturer of mobile phones. The challenges facing the senior management of Nokia are discussed in the Schumpeter column of the *Economist* 8 July 2010, 396 (8694), page 65.

Obviously, managers need the skills, described in the preceding chapter, such as designing jobs, encouraging teamwork and devising an organisational structure which are vital to establishing an organisation. But, even if they establish a perfect organisation, it will only be a matter of months before they need to use their understanding of how to change their organisation to cope with changes in their environment.

6.1 Definition and reasons why organisations change

Change simply means "altering the state or direction of something". It does not necessarily imply either innovation or improvement. Change can be for better or for worse. It can also be backwards. Organisational change therefore means:

66 Altering the state and direction of an organisation – for better or for worse, forwards or backwards 99

While technically correct, this definition is somewhat cynical. Although many changes are bad and regressive, probably a larger number are good and progressive and lead to progress. This means that change should be generally welcomed but we should be wary of adopting changes that follow "the flavour of the month" or "changes that are made for "change's own sake".

When organisations are set up they are usually fit for purpose and in step with their environment. Forces soon emerge which tend to slow the organisation down so that it starts to lag behind the environment. Organisations must change – otherwise they become outdated, uncompetitive and eventually they are either taken over or disbanded.

CRITICAL THINKING 6.1 *Is change faster nowadays?*

It is often claimed that the pace of change is faster today than ever. This claim needs to be taken with a pinch of salt – *cum grano salis* as Petronious might have said! The dissolution of the monasteries was a huge change that took only five years. The urbanisation of Manchester saw its population grow from 22 000 in 1772 to 75 000 (an increase of 340 per cent) just 28 years later. Colonialisation of the Australian continent was assured in a generation or two. The rate of change imposed upon Japan after its defeat in 1945 was phenomenal. It would seem that each generation believes that its rate of change is the fastest in history. The belief that today's change is faster than ever is bolstered by writers and consultants who have a vested interest in increasing their opportunities and fees. Any bets that Petronius and his colleagues were claiming financial allowances because the Empire was expecting so many changes of them?

Organisational change is not rare. It is estimated that a typical establishment is reorganised every three years (CIPD, 2010). Petronius may have had an easy time in his day!

Resistance to change

Vested interests are a force that prevents organisations changing at a pace to match their environments. For example, if a change means that Manager B's department is likely to grow faster than Manager A's department, Manager A may hinder the change. Inertia is another force that retards change. Change requires extra effort and some individuals will not want to put in the extra energy. Some people interpret a request to change as a criticism of their current methods. Still others will be reluctant to change because the end result is less predictable – the uncertainty makes them anxious. Paradoxically, one of the most powerful forces against change is an existing, very efficient organisation. Tim Mannon a senior executive with Hewlett Packard is widely quoted (e.g. Hoff, 1995) as saying, "The biggest single threat to our business today is staying with a previously successful business model one year too long". Managers of a successful business will usually be perplexed when they are told they need to change!

There are two main *foci of resistance* to change: content and process.

1 *Content resistance* occurs when workers object to what is being changed such as a new salary structure, new equipment, new job descriptions or the introduction of new pension arrangements.

2 *Process resistance* occurs when workers are content to accept the change but object to the way it is being introduced: they may be prepared to adopt new working methods but object to them being imposed without discussion. Similarly, they may be content with a new salary system but object if it is applied too quickly.

The *form of resistance* can vary widely. Sometimes change will be resisted on an *individual* basis by not attending meetings where change is discussed or simply continuing with old ways despite instruction to use new methods. Sometimes *groups* can resist change. Workers can form alliances to protest against change or they can collectively withhold useful information. In extreme situations trade unions may organise strikes in protest at "new working practices". Resistance can also be *passive* where workers quietly refuse to respond to initiatives. More seriously it can be *active* where workers sabotage attempts to change by spreading false information or misusing or damaging equipment. The difference between direct and indirect resistance is an important distinction. **Direct resistance** in terms of protests, arguments or withdrawal is uncomfortable but at least the change agents know it exists. Subtle **indirect resistance**, is a more dangerous foe. Change agents may not even realise that information is being withheld or that "political manoeuvring" is going on behind the scenes.

CRITICAL THINKING 6.2 *How to spot change blockers*

Resistance to change is quite common so it is important to be able to recognise it and take appropriate action. Keen (1981) identified seven tactics people may use to block change. They are:

1 **Divert resources** to other projects so that the change is starved of support. Staff involved in the change are given competing priorities. At a crucial moment

▶

essential equipment has to be shared with another department – preferably a department in a remote location. Superb diversions include commissioning research, writing long reports, holding many meetings and arranging fact-finding tours – preferably abroad.

2 **Insist enthusiastically that the project is "done properly".** Everyone's views must be canvassed and reconciled. Contradictory views will emerge and a heated conflict between rival proponents will slow or kill a project.

3 **Be vague.** Use long, convoluted communications couched in general, grandiose and abstract terms. At all costs, avoid specific goals with specific timetables.

4 **Encourage inertia** by commissioning research, waiting for the completion of another project, waiting until the "time is ripe" or until an important (and preferably very, *very* busy) person is consulted and persuaded to back the project.

5 **Ignore interpersonal issues** during the early stages. This will ensure that misunderstanding and animosities incubate and grow to the point where they later jeopardise success.

6 **Damage the credibility of those leading the change.** Spread gossip concerning those championing the project. It is particularly important to spread the gossip among supporters of the project champion. This can be done very skilfully by pretending to be outraged by a scurrilous rumour and pretending to defend the project champion.

7 **Avoid overt hostility to the change.** Overt hostility alerts change champions and allows counter-measures to be deployed.

Whatever the reason, focus or form, resistance acts as a kind of magnetic force that retards the rate at which the organisation moves forward with its environment. Inevitably, it begins to fall behind.

Forces in favour of change

Kurt Lewin (1951), a seminal management theorist, developed "field theory" which posited that for change to occur there must be a stronger force in favour of change and this force must be felt by the people in an organisation. He called this "perceived need for change". There are two main types of factors that can create a perceived need for change: internal forces and external forces. **Internal forces for change** are factors within the organisation. Some are inevitable. The people within the organisation change: they grow older; they get bored with current methods; they learn that some current methods do not work; some powerful people get weaker and some weak people gain confidence; new recruits arrive with new ideas or demands. Other internal forces for change are less certain. The values of the organisation may change so that, for example, it may wish to foster more equal opportunities or adopt a more collaborative management style. The organisation might also decide to change its mission. Further, it is possible that the R&D department devises a new method or product.

Every author has their own list of **external forces for change**. It seems best to offer a more organised list, given in Table 6.1, which is based on the PESTLE model of strategic planning.

PESTLE strategic analysis p 96

PESTLE category	Examples of external forces for organisational change
Political	■ Change of government favouring, e.g. private sector or expenditure on, say, rail infrastructure ■ Decrease in size of traditional working-class vote ■ Decrease in power of trade unions ■ Collapse of communism in Russia ■ Opening up of market in China
Economic	■ Credit crunch ■ Cuts in government expenditure ■ Greater regulation of banking and lending ■ More equal/unequal distribution of wealth ■ New competitors, international competition ■ Capital markets and exchange rates
Social	■ Ageing population ■ Higher levels of education ■ Greater emphasis on equality
Technical	■ New technologies and production methods ■ New products and services
Legal	■ Changes in safety legislation ■ Changes in employment legislation ■ Local planning constraints ■ International treaties
Environmental	■ Climate change and recycling ■ Better transport and communications ■ Stricter regulation of pollution

TABLE 6.1 Forces attracting organisations to change

The balance between the three forces is crucial. Figure 6.1 illustrates Lewin's **field force analysis**.

If the forces of resistance are bigger than the combined internal and external forces for change, it is unlikely that the organisation will change. Indeed, in a few situations the organisation might regress to a previous form. However, if the combined forces for change are bigger than the forces of resistance, then it is highly likely that organisational change will ensue.

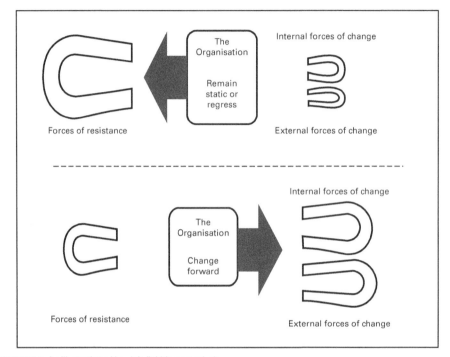

FIGURE 6.1 An illustration of Lewin's field force analysis

6.2 Types of organisational change

Organisations may attempt many different types of change. For example, one organisation may, foolishly, attempt a total reorganisation in a matter of three weeks while another, only slightly less foolishly, may only strive to accomplish one piffling change in a decade. The different types of organisational change can be classified into five main groups – which are not mutually exclusive:

1 **Episodic versus continuous change** (Weick and Quinn, 1999) is probably the most important concept concerning types of change. Most of the present discussion has implied episodic change where there is organisational inertia and where infrequent major decisions are made to institute a specific changes. This is not the ideal situation. In a perfect organisation, change would be a process of continual adaptation. *Episodic change* tends to be dramatic and is largely driven by external events. It usually follows Lewin's three stages of organisational change and there is one or more champions at senior level who initiate and propel the change throughout the whole organisation.

Lewin's three stages of change p 152

2 **Continuous change** is self-explanatory: it is like evolution. It is an endless process of constant modifications in day-to-day work practices that is driven

by pragmatic sensitivity to the work environment. Changes tend to emerge from the situation and usually amount to a redirection of what is already under way – but the cumulative effect can be huge. Change agents adopt the role of a sense-maker who recognises and reframes the current situation. The change agent will also spend time enabling a wide range of people to improvise and learn.

3 **Minor versus incremental change** (Marshak, 1993) lists four types of change in ascending order of how drastic they were: he called them metaphors. A *fix and maintain* change is not very drastic. It involves tweaking the system with minor adjustments or perhaps adding a few extra resources to cope with a minor problem. It does not involve anything fundamental. It is analogous to running repairs on your car. A *build and develop* type of change is also based on the belief that the present structure is fine but it is capable of improvement – which can be achieved by learning and consultation. For example, an organisation may improve production methods by enriching jobs, empowering workers or using new technology. It is analogous to improving your car's aerodynamics by fitting a new spoiler. A *move and relocate* change involves a transition that alters basic parameters within the organisation. Top management is certain to be involved. An obvious example would be to move the headoffice to a cheaper, out of town location. Similarly, the changes that follow a merger or outsourcing a function, such as payroll, would count as a move and relocate change. It is analogous to replacing your car with a new one with four-wheel drive to enable you to travel across country. A *liberate and re-create* type of change is the most drastic. The organisation is transformed by a complete rethink of mission vision and methods. The organisation almost reinvents itself. A good example would be when IBM changed drastically from a manufacturer selling mainframe computers to large organisations to a manufacturer of personal computers sold to private individuals. Sometimes such changes are called "morphing". A liberate and create change is analogous to giving up car travel in favour of helicopter transport.

4 The **organisational level** of the change can also be used to classify changes. This classification is often related to the "minor versus radical" dimension described in the previous paragraph. Some changes affect only individual jobs (micro-change) whereas others might affect a department and still others might affect the organisation as a whole (macro-change). Unfortunately, the situation is not so simple because changes at organisational level are very likely to produce changes in individual jobs – and vice versa. It may be better to view this categorisation of changes as a categorisation of where the changes start (Child, 2005). Sometimes this way of characterising changes is called **narrow vs broad changes**.

5 The distinction between **planned change** and **emergent change** is made by many writers (see Burns, 2004a). Early writers on organisational change, such as Kurt Lewin, focused on planned change which usually starts at the top. As described in the previous chapter, top managers devise a strategy to achieve the change which is then translated into tactical plans and, ultimately, action plans. Often, management will appoint or hire a change agent who has responsibility of ensuring the change takes place. In essence, planned change is "top-down change" where senior managers decide how their organisation must develop – although they will use participation and consultation to achieve their aims.

During the 1980s it became apparent that planned change had a number of shortcomings. For example, planning takes a great deal of time and the time needed is not available in turbulent environments when change is rapid and continuous: a few managers at the top of an organisation need a lot of time to understand all the complexities. By the time plans are finalised, the situation has changed!

Consequently attention turned to *emergent change* where a decentralised organisation continually changes itself. Weick (2000) notes, "Emergent change consists of ongoing accommodations, adaptations, and alterations that produce fundamental change without *a priori* intentions to do so". It occurs when workers devise new methods in their day-to-day work dealing with problems and opportunities. Often these changes go unnoticed. Emergent change is predominantly "bottom-up". A good explanation of planned and emergent change, together with a case study showing that the two approaches are not mutually exclusive is given by Burns (2004b)

As Table 6.2 shows, there are many similarities between these characterisations. It seems that authors have been using different words to write about the same things.

Types of change		
Planned change **Name** ■ Episodic change ■ Radical change ■ Top-level change ■ Planned change	***Major proponent*** (Wieke and Quinn, 1999) (Marshak, 1993) (Child, 2005) (Burns, 2004b)	***Emergent change*** ■ Continuous change ■ Incremental change ■ Lower-level change ■ Emergent change
Characteristics ■ Major and infrequent ■ Macro-change ■ Top management – who may experience information overload. May therefore be slow to react ■ Organisational learning ■ Acceptance problems		■ Constant and small ■ Micro-change ■ All levels – many people to share information and avoid overload. May therefore be quicker to react ■ Individual learning ■ Easy acceptance
Suggested name **Command change**		**Devolved change**

TABLE 6.2 A synthesis of the types of organisational change

Clearly, different authors have been describing the same dimension where, at one end, is a centralised type of change that originates with senior managers – and all that implies. This can be called *command change*. At the other end of the dimension, change is initiated - more or less spontaneously – by many people throughout the hierarchy. This can be called *devolved change*.

An interesting, rather different, and pragmatic classification of change has been suggested by Senior and Flemming (2006). Organisational change is classified according to:

1 the rate at which change occurs (discontinuous, continuous, etc.)
2 how it comes about (planned, emergent, etc.)
3 the scale of the change (fine-tuning, incremental adjustment, etc.)

Their book is a useful practical guide that gives greater detail than could be given in this wider-ranging text.

6.3 The phases of change

Change rarely happens instantly. It usually occurs over a period of time and it is likely to pass through phases. Writers (surprisingly perhaps) agree what these phases are! This section first describes the grandfather of change phases – Lewin's three-phase model – and then outlines some others which have particular merit.

Lewin's three phases of organisational change

The most frequently quoted stages of the change were developed long ago by Kurt Lewin (1947). He said there are three stages of change: unfreezing, changing and re-freezing.

Unfreezing aims to dissolve existing attitudes and positions. Essentially, it involves emphasising and strengthening the need to change so that the forces for change outweigh those in favour of the status quo. The main techniques for the unfreezing stage involve communication and can be described as three stages:

- *First*, many reasons for the change are assembled. These reasons will then be translated into words, examples and images which resonate with employees. The reasons to resist change will also be mentioned, because research suggests that giving both sides of an argument is more persuasive and much more effective against subsequent counter-arguments.

- *Second*, reasons for change are communicated by many media, such as meetings, memos, newsletters and presentations. It is important that employees should not be passive recipients. It is better if they play an active part. A standard tactic is to co-opt likely opponents of change to the planning and delivery of the change (provided the opponents are neither numerous nor powerful).

- *Third*, negotiations will be needed with powerful figures who resist the changes. It may be necessary to offer a trade or compromise which compensates for any negative effects. If all else fails, the bad consequences of blocking change can be pointed out. Explicit or implicit coercion carries enormous risks but it may be appropriate where speedy change is necessary.

Once a situation has been unfrozen, the **actual change** can start to take place. Change agents and organisational development (OD) consultants have evolved techniques to help. The main techniques include: survey feedback, team-building and process consultation plus large-group interventions. Some of these techniques are described in the next section.

The change stage sometimes uses small-scale projects in which the new methods can be perfected and the results used to reassure other employees.

When actual change has taken place it must be consolidated – otherwise the organisation may drift back to earlier methods. Lewin called this the **re-freezing phase**. It may involve altering the organisation's pay systems to reward adherence to the new situation. The organisation's culture may need to be altered to support the new system. Above all, the new systems and methods must be routinised so that they become habitual.

CRITICAL THINKING 6.3 *What is wrong with Lewin's stages?*

Lewin's stages contain a great deal of sense but they are not perfect. There are two major criticisms:

1 While it is useful for planned (command) change, it does not cope well with emergent (devolved) change. It is easy to envisage how to unfreeze, change and re-freeze applies when the process is being directed from the top towards a clear set of objectives. It is exceedingly difficult to see how 'unfreeze, change and refreeze' applies when there are lots of small impromptu, continuous changes. Most organisations desire continuous change. Re-freezing will only store up problems for the future. Currently, emergent change is probably more important than planned change.

2 Lewin's three-stage process is incomplete. It ignores, for example, the vital, opening part of change – deciding what to change and how. Similarly, it ignores the closing parts of a change process – checking how effective the change has been and whether it was the correct change in the first place.

Other models of the stages of change

The shortcomings of Lewin's three-stage process led many others to develop their own list of stages. It is easy to produce a list, and numerous writers have risen to the task. Many of the lists have modest scientific merit; they are only conjecture and experience from a few case studies. Hussey (2000) produced a six-stage approach to organisational change using the mnemonic "EASIER":

1 **E**nvisioning – developing a coherent view of the future
2 **A**ctivating – making sure others understand and share vision
3 **S**upport – helping people overcome the problems they encounter
4 **I**mplementing – planning and executing the change process
5 **E**nsuring – checking that the change is being implemented
6 **R**ecognising – and rewarding those involved

Kotter (1995) divides organisational change into eight stages The first two stages and the last stage are omitted from many models. Kotter's stages are derived from errors observed in organisational change projects. Kotter's eight stages and the errors associated with them are:

1 **Establish urgency**: identify crises, potential crises or opportunities. (Error – not kick-starting the change project.)
2 **Create guiding coalition**: establish a powerful group, encourage them to work as a team. (Error – not getting a critical mass of organisational power to support the changes in a coherent way.)
3 **Develop vision and strategy**. (Error – with no clear aims and objectives the change process will drift and meander.)
4 **Communicate the vision of change**: use all media, the guiding coalition act as role models. (Error – seriously under-communicating to people who are essential to the changes.)
5 **Broad-based action**: remove obstacles, encourage new ideas, risk-taking. (Error – allowing obstacles, especially recalcitrant managers, to remain.)
6 **Generate short-term, visible, wins**: reward the people involved. (Error – people become demotivated and cynical if they have to wait years to see positive results.)
7 **Consolidate gains and use them to produce more change**: use increased credibility to hire, promote and develop those who will help change and reinvigorate the process with new projects etc. (Error – declaring victory too soon can undermine future change.)
8 **Anchor changes in the organisational culture**: articulate links between changes and success, ensure leadership succession. (Errors – failing to make the link between success/survival and the changes; not ensuring the next generation of managers support the changes.)

Hannagan (2002) presents four stages of the change process, with has a different perspective. Instead of providing a "road map" for the change agents it focuses upon the emotions of the people involved:

1 **denial** that change is needed
2 **resistance** to change
3 **exploration** of the possibilities offered by change
4 **commitment** to the new changes

Bullock and Batten (1985) reviewed the literature and generated a general list of stages of change. Parker, Wall and Jackson (1998) outline the stages of a change process involving job design.

The time taken for an organisation to pass through all of these stages varies widely, depending on the change attempted, the people involved and the change techniques that are used. However, change usually takes much longer than people estimate – often more than twice as long. Managers face the challenge of shortening the time taken to change but without an undue rush that may jeopardise the whole process.

6.4 Techniques of changing organisations

Change agents and others do not simply "swan about" saying nice things to workers and even nicer things to top management. They employ a number of Organisational Development techniques. An Internet search will reveal hundreds of techniques but many come down to standard techniques that have been given a unique "spin" by consultants in order to appeal to prospective clients. OD techniques can be divided into three categories: problem analysis, changing structure and changing behavior. The final category is much bigger than the others.

OD techniques for analysing problems

Briefly, OD techniques of problem analysis and diagnosis include surveys and **focus groups** as well as forcasting and planning techniques such as "what if" scenarios of **contingency planning**. They also include **business process engineering**.

Business process engineering p 493

OD techniques for structural change

Role analysis examines the expectations inherent in worker's positions. Roles are scrutinised to identify ambiguities such as reducing costs while also maintaining customer satisfaction. **Analysing the structure of jobs and enriching** them is another important OD technique. The outcomes of these processes help change roles and jobs for the better.

Hackman and Oldham p 115

OD techniques for behavioural change

Changing behaviour always involves ethical issues. If people will be affected by a change, perhaps losing their job, they should at least be allowed to participate in the decisions. Indeed, in many countries there is a legal requirement to involve workers in any large change that could result in redundancy. Further, changing people's behaviour can become mere Machiavellian manipulation. If exploitation is to be avoided, worker participation should be on the basis of informed consent. Participation usually helps the change process because it helps gain support. Further, it helps communicate people's role in the change process and what the new structure will require from them. But, participation has grave dangers. It is inevitably time-consuming and it gives determined opponents an opportunity to slow or sabotage the change. Assuming that the ethical and practical problems are resolved, behavioural change can be achieved by one or more techniques such as action research, team-building exercises and process consultation, large-group interventions and survey feedback.

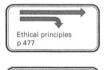

Ethical principles p 477

Tactics of resisting change p 146

Action research

Action research was pioneered by Lewin. It sprang from the idea that much academic research led only to the production of books which were of limited practical use. He suggested that a small group of workers (and often, an academic from a local university) study a practical issue at the place of work.

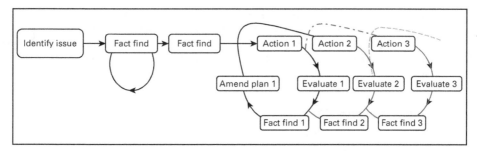

FIGURE 6.2 Lewin's action research cycle

Their work proceeds in cycles. The first step is to identify an issue. The second is to obtain as much relevant information as possible. When this is reviewed, gaps are identified and more fact-finding may be undertaken. When the group is happy with their knowledge they make a plan to solve the issue and initiate the first step of action. After a short time, the consequences are evaluated. More information is obtained, the plan is revised and the cycle is continued, as shown in Figure 6.2.

The essence of action research is that managers learn from experience and that it inculcates managers with a scientific approach. It teaches them to work in groups, 'theorise' and then test their theories in a flexible empirical way.

CRITICAL THINKING 6.4 *What is wrong with Lewin's action learning cycle?*

The action research approach has been criticized by writers such as Elliot (1991) and Winter (1987) They argue that action research:

- gives insufficient emphasis to analysis and it implies that fact-finding and implementing are straightforward processes

- is not very rigorous in scientific terms. People who undertake action research often have insufficient training. Action research is often used in a partisan way to further someone's self-advantage

- tends to ignore the cultural and psychological context of the issues explored. In itself, correct knowledge does not lead to change

---

Team-building

Team-building is designed to weld people into a cohesive group which works effectively, and is particularly important when changes bring together collections of strangers. Indeed, many change processes in mergers and acquisitions bring together people who were previously competitors or even enemies. It is essential to remove old attitudes or rivalries. Team-building involves providing information about how effective teams function. Also, it will usually include sessions on behaviours that make teams ineffective. Participants who are taught these skills are organised into groups and given a "team task". They are observed by a facilitator who leads a discussion on how well the group operated as a team.

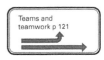

Teams and
teamwork p 121

Process consultation

Process consultation is nothing to do with production processes. It is an aspect of team-building. It is generally used when a team is inefficient. The team analyses how it can improve the way it works. It examines how group norms are formed, how the group members perceive each other's roles and how decisions are made. For example, a facilitator might start by observing the way that a team tackles a specific problem. The facilitator then guides a team's discussion of its performance. It is important to note that the facilitator will not diagnose the problem unilaterally. Their role is to help the team diagnose its own problems. However, the facilitator will ensure that the team does not overlook important facts. They will also help the team to recognise and correct its own prejudices. For example, the facilitator might point out that the team spent a lot of time obtaining information which was already known to an unpopular member who was excluded. The team might then conclude that its effectiveness was being diminished because of personal prejudices and informal cliques. An examination of the team's prejudices and social structure follows before deciding on remedial action.

Team-building and process consultation are expensive: they require a high number of facilitators. They generally produce permanent changes in specific, but small, areas of an organisation. These techniques often produce gradual, incremental changes.

Large-group interventions

As the name suggests, these are often used in big organisations where it would be expensive and take too much time to cover everyone in a series of small groups. Organisational development consultants have developed ways of intervening on a large scale (Dannemiller and Jacobs, 1992). Large-scale interventions aim to change a whole system in a relatively short period. They bring together, say, 300 participants for three days in a large hotel. Participants are drawn from all sections of the organisation and may, sometimes, include suppliers or clients. There will usually be a number of set presentations which aim to give as much information as possible about the nature of the change. There will also be a number of group discussions led by facilitators. Often these events finish in activities where participants are required to show their commitment to the change and in the development of personal action plans which will help the change.

Because large-scale interventions involve many people, they can bring about major and profound changes in favourable situations where there is basic agreement on the content and processes of change. They can harness pressures to help change because everyone in the organisation will have been involved and everyone will be involved at the same time. Momentum for change can be established. However, large group interventions are not good at removing deep-seated objections to change.

Survey feedback

Survey feedback is one of the most powerful OD techniques. It has five stages. *First*, the main worries about the change are identified. *Second*, a questionnaire is designed to measure people's attitudes. *Third*, the questionnaire is given, on an anonymous basis, to a large sample. In fact, the questionnaire is usually sent to all employees. This makes it clear that the change will affect the whole organisation. *Fourth*, replies are analysed and the main results are distributed to everyone. *Fifth*, results are discussed by groups of employees, who are asked to produce recommendations.

Survey research has an obvious role in clarifying employees' views. However, its feedback also has useful by-products. The construction of the questionnaire forces an organisation to clarify the main issues. Further, completing the questionnaire helps to educate employees. In addition, the process emphasises the importance of participation and it allows people to feel that they have been consulted. Survey research works best when the findings of the survey lead to specific actions which can then be reported back to those who took part – especially reporting back "quick wins". Survey feedback is a relatively cheap way of involving a large number of people. It can lead to a rapid change.

Change agents

Many organisations employ outsiders (third parties) to help them implement change. They are often called change agents and there are two main types: commercial consultants and academics – although some change agents may be "in-house" professionals from headquarters. The main *advantages* of using external change agents is that they appear neutral (they have not been involved in previous inter-organisational power struggles) and their specialist expertise (they will have gained experience from their involvement with change in other organisations). The main *disadvantages* of external change agents may depend upon whether they are consultants or academics. Some consultants may have a hidden agenda to create more work for themselves and some may seek to impose a standard solution, used with previous clients, rather than developing a tailor-made solution. Some academics, on the other hand, may have a poor grasp of the realities of working life and their teaching or research commitments may mean they cannot devote sufficient time to the change project. Change agents, as outsiders, may encounter hostility from workers who may see them as either mercenaries or management lackeys. Kanter (1984) identified three sets of skills needed by change agents. *First*, good change agents must have a thorough knowledge of the types and techniques of change. They must also be good at adapting their knowledge to the needs of particular organisations. *Second*, they need to have good communication skills (acting, listening and speaking) to persuade people to adopt change – writing reports, giving presentations or taking part in group exercises. They are also likely to be good at understanding and using the power structure within the organisation. *Third*, a good change agent will be good at managing problems that arise from interventions such as participation. These skills determine whether a change program is successful. However, as the next section shows there are other factors involved in success or failure.

Success factors in organisational change

Organisational change is a very risky business. Some writers estimate that about 70 per cent of attempts at organisational change fail. This grim statistic, however, raises the question: "what is meant by success of organisational change?" Following the major theme of this book that management is "organising people so they add value", the success of organisational change is:

 changing the structure, behavior or culture of an organisation so that the new form adds more value than the old form. **"**

However, this simplistic definition conceals problems:

1 It requires measuring the added value to an organisation both before the change and after the change. This rarely happens. The better pieces of research, however, may take two measures of a restricted range of indicators but miss other areas. For example, they may measure an increase in the value of the profit made but omit damage to the firm's reputation or the environmental impact of the change.

2 It begs the question, "value to whom?" An organisational change may increase value to shareholders and even other employees but it may also make other workers redundant. For example, in 2009, the John Lewis Partnership changed the location of its distribution centre from Stevenage to Milton Keynes. Undoubtedly this added value for customers and other partners. But, did it add value for the "partners" who thought they were secure but who lost their jobs? Such changes can be justified on the *ethical* grounds of the greater benefit to a large number of people. But, does this amount to a violation of "partners" rights and the "tyranny of the majority"? Reports suggest that the John Lewis move was a success. In the 1990s many people in many organisations lost their jobs as a result of business process engineering. Many of these change programmes were not successful and people lost their jobs needlessly.

Business process engineering p 493

Utilitarianism and rights p 468

Many evaluations of organisational change ignore these wider considerations and focus upon the question: "did the change bring about the aims that were stated at the start of the change?" Using this limited criterion many people have sought to identify *critical success factors*. Moss Kanter (1983) looked at the success of organisational change in 10 companies. Her sample was minuscule. However, she came to the momentous conclusion that there are two main approaches to change: integrative and segmental. In the **integrative approach** organisations welcome change as an opportunity and are prepared to adopt a high level of change. They foster new ideas and view change in a holistic way: they are prepared to attempt change that might affect the whole organisation. In the **segmental approach** organisations tend to attempt change only within certain limits or certain segments of the organisation. Change is divided into easily managed and predictable compartments. Kanter found that organisations with an integrative approach were better at assimilating innovative ideas.

A quick Internet search yields an endless and disorganised array of lists of specific factors that lead to successful change. The following selection is based on By's excellent paper

(2005) which compared Kanter, Stein and Jick's (1992) "Ten commandments for executing change", Kotter's (1996) "Eight-stage process for executing change" and Luecke's (2003) "Seven Steps". The requirements of successful organisational change appear to be:

1 **A good change strategy** that is based on the analysis of the organisation and its need for change. Energy and commitment should be mobilised through joint identification of business problems and their solutions.

2 **A shared vision and a common sense of direction** is developed and widely communicated.

3 **A sense of urgency** where a clear line is drawn under the organisation's past shape and methods.

4 **Political support** is marshalled by forming a guiding coalition of powerful people and then identifying and supporting strong leaders.

5 **A detailed implementation plan.** This will include developing enabling structures (new posts, new committees, new communications, etc.) and empowering people to take action.

6 **Communicate, communicate, communicate** – in a direct and honest way.

7 **Anchor the new approaches in the organisation**. Reinforce the change by rewarding those who develop and maintain it. Institutionalise the change with formal policies, systems and organisational structures.

Other important aspects of successful organisational change include generating short-term wins and focusing on results rather than activities. Luecke (2003) suggests starting by changing the periphery of the organisation and allowing changes to spread to other units without undue pressure from the top. Naturally, an important feature of organisational change is to monitor and adjust both the strategy and the methods in response to problems and issues that emerge.

CRITICAL THINKING 6.5 *The Wild West of organisational change*

In some ways the topic of organisational change is like the Wild West: everyone agrees that it is important and contains many riches, but it is chaotic, lawless and contains lots of cowboys and cowgirls!

It certainly contains many riches. For example the UK's spending watchdog, the National Audit Office (2010) reported that the central government machinery, as recommended by management gurus, is in a constant state of change. There were 90 reorganisations in four years at a cost of more than £1 billion. Yet, the National Audit Office found that these expensive changes could not demonstrate value for money. The situation is likely to be worse, but hidden, in the private sector where there is no parliamentary opposition and no public scrutiny by an equivalent of the National Audit Commission. A cynic might wonder how much longer we can afford the mania for change.

Research in this area seldom reaches the scientific standards set out in Chapter 19. *First*, the sample sizes used in research are often miniscule. Moss Kanter's (1983) study is highly respected but is based on a sample of merely 10 organisations. While it may be difficult to obtain large samples of *organisations*, it remains true that conclusions based on small samples are highly unstable and often incomplete. For instance, had Kanter used a larger sample she might have detected more than two (integrative and segmental) approaches to innovation.

Second, measures used by researchers are sometimes weak and amount to little more than subjective opinions. Even when objective scales or questionnaires are used, their reliability and validity are not established. In many studies there are no checks on the validity of questionnaires and we are left relying on the words of the researchers.

Third, the views we do have are organised in a chaotic way. For instance, many researchers produced multiple lists of the stages of organisational change (seven were duly listed on pages 152 – 154). Each list has some differences and similarities with other lists. This gives unnecessary confusion and duplication. It is as though each researcher has found some nuggets – some real gold, some fools' gold. Nobody has had the sense to separate them and then give true nuggets a consistent name. It is equivalent, but less obvious, to calling the same thing "gold", "aurum" and "bullion". In scientific terms the topic of organisational change is pre-Linnaean and pre-Mendeleevian.

In the end, the management processes of planning and organising are useless unless the organisation has people who are willing and able to implement the plans and fill the roles within the organisation. The management process of "staffing" aims to ensure that the organisation has employees that will do these things and is the subject of the next chapter.

Toolkit

6.5 Change toolkit

- Identify the major "environmental change" that has affected your work in the past six months. Identify a change that you must make in order adapt to the altered work environment. If the change you have chosen is negative, regressive or unethical choose another one.
- Identify *sources* of resistance (content and process) to the proposed change. Identify the *tactics* of resistance which opponents might use.
- Identify an appropriate change stratergy (Lewin or Hussey or Kotter, or Hannagan?).
- If possible, choose an integrative approach to change that affects several aspects of your organisation.
- Choose appropriate OD tools to bring about the change.
- Ensure that the change process will produce at least two "short-term wins".
- Communicate, communicate, communicate – especially the vision and urgency.
- Make sure you have the support of powerful people in your organisation.
- Have a detailed plan for implementing the change.

Activities and further study

Essay plans

Prepare plans for the following essays:

1 To what extent is the topic of organisational change a coherent academic subject?
2 Evaluate the contributions of Kurt Lewin to the topic of organisational change.
3 Compare and contrast the different types of organisational change.
4 Describe and synthesise at least three different writers' analysis of the phases of organisational change and explain why these are important to managers.
5 Describe and compare the OD techniques of action research, team-building and survey feedback.
6 What factors would help to make an organisational change project successful?

Web activities

1 Kurt Lewin has been called the grandfather of organisational change. Use the Internet to find information about him and to build up a picture of his contribution to the topic.
2 Enter the terms "success factors" and "organisational change" into your search engine and locate the lists produced by a number of organisations. Compare these lists and evaluate their scientific basis. Decide whether each list is more like a marketing tool or a scientifically based list.
3 Search for an example of organisational change in your local area or in a sector of the economy that interest you. Appropriate search terms might be the name of your area, retailing, manufacturing and "organisational change". Searching a database of newspapers or journals will produce the best results.

Experiential activities

1 Choose an organisation that you know well and think of a change that it might consider (your present educational establishment or an organisation where you have worked would be good choices). List the following forces:

- possible forces of resistance against the change
- possible internal forces in favour of the change
- possible external forces in favour of the change

2 Think of a change that you would like to make in an organisation that you know well. Decide how you would evaluate whether such a change is successful. List the OD techniques that you would use in order to bring this change about.

3 Find someone (friend or family) who has recently experienced an organisational change in the place where they work. Ask their opinions about:

- the need for change
- the phases the change went through
- the various OD techniques that were used
- the contribution and effectiveness of any external change agents (if any)
- their evaluation of the effectiveness of the change
- their view of the fairness of the change

4 Organise a mini-debate on the motion that "Most organisational change is motivated by senior management's need to be seen doing things rather than a genuine need for change". Speakers for and against the motion have a maximum of five minutes to make their cases. The maximum contribution from other people is two minutes. A vote is taken at the end of the mini-debate.

Recommended reading

1 By, R.T. (2005) "Organisational change management: a critical review", *Journal of Change Management*, **5**(4), 369–380. This article describes the different types of change, the characteristics of change and how it comes about. Integrates these aspects with the work of major theorists.

2 Bacon, N., Blyton, P. and Dastmalchian, A. (2010), "The impact of organizational change on steelworkers in craft and production occupational groups", *Human Relations*, **63**(8), 1223–1248. A difficult paper which is an antidote to the belief that organisational change is easy. It gives a detailed analysis of the impact of organisational change in steelworks at Teeside and Scunthorpe. Start reading at the new section on page 1227 – and the section on research sites. Then read result sections on: team design; attitudes; job quality; work pressure and job satisfaction. Do not get bogged down in statistics or complicated tables.

3 Boomer, G. (2010) "Managing change: clarity reduces resistance", *Accounting Today*, July–August, p. 32. Common sense advice for accountants on how to manage change.

Chapter EIGHT

Staffing – Selecting, Developing and Motivating People

Chapter contents

❖ *LEARNING OBJECTIVES*

After studying this chapter you should be able to **explain** the importance of three of the four main staffing processes (the way all managers relate to staff) and **make a preliminary distinction** from human resource management (the specialist activities undertaken by a group of experts). You will also be able to **outline** the main ways in which managers recruit, train and motivate their staff. In particular you will be able to:

- ❖ **list** the four main stages involved in selecting employees

- ❖ **evaluate** the advantages and disadvantages of four scientific methods of selection – especially their accuracy

- ❖ **list** three main categories of training methods

- ❖ **describe briefly** each of six methods of "off the job" training

- ❖ **explain** the difference between training and development

- ❖ **describe briefly** the concepts of learning skills, self-awareness and 360-degree feedback

- ❖ **explain** the importance of motivating employees

- ❖ **compare and contrast** three theories of motivation

Once an organisation's strategic plans have been laid and an appropriate structure devised, the next step is to fill the organisation with workers and to treat them in a way which maximises their contribution. This latter stage is called **staffing**. It is also called **people management** but a pedant would point out that this alternative term is misleading since managers are only responsible for maximising the performance of their staff, not people in general.

CASE 7.1: *Investing in People at Eversheds*

Eversheds is a huge law firm which employs more than 2000 lawyers and advisers in more than 20 locations in the UK, Europe, the Middle East, Africa and Asia. It recognises the importance of managing all its staff as effectively as possible and has achieved recognition by Investors in People (IIP) - which promotes high standards in staffing procedures. With the aid of an organisation-wide survey, Eversheds identified the key areas in managing its staff. Among other things, the organisation uses the following methods to harness their employees' talents:

- comprehensive induction programmes
- regular development reviews
- training and development
- a wide range of internal communications such as intranet and briefing sessions
- a "Careers Pathway" scheme for non-lawyers
- 360° feedback

For four years in a row, Eversheds has been voted as one of the top UK employers (*Sunday Times* annual surveys). Its internal employee survey indicates that 78 per cent of its staff believe the firm is a great place to work.

Most analyses of management work show that dealing with staff is *the* main management process. No matter whether they work in operations, sales, marketing or even IT, *all* managers need to maximise the potential of workers. It will be an exceptional day if a manager does not meet at least one member of their staff. This contrasts with other processes such as planning, organising and budgeting. At certain times of the year a manager can go for days without performing any of these processes. Staffing may be divided into four major topics: selecting, training, motivating and leading. The first three are discussed in this chapter, while leading is covered in Chapter 8.

There are important reasons why these topics do not appear in Chapter 16 which covers human resource (HR) management. Selecting, training, motivating and leading are management processes that *every* manager must perform. The primary responsibility for each aspect of staffing lies with the manager not the organisational function. Of course, the HR department can help with facilities or technical advice, but it is the manager's responsibility to select suitable people, to give them proper training and to motivate them and, as the next chapter shows, it is vital that the manager gives his or her team proper leadership. The message is loud and clear: selection, training, motivation and leadership of staff is the primary responsibility of the manager. Although there are close links between staffing and HR there are additional dangers in treating them together. First, there may be confusion about who is responsible for what. Managers might be able to blame poor motivation on the HR department, while the HR department might blame managers for poorly designed *systems* of appraisal or remuneration. Further, if staffing is simply considered as an aspect of HR, it will be difficult to compare and contrast its contribution relative to other processes such as planning or organising. Similarly, it will be more difficult to compare and contrast the contribution of the HR function with that of other functions such as marketing or finance.

7.1 Definition and introduction to the staffing process

The purpose of the staffing process is to produce effective workers. Figure 7.1 shows that the process starts with designing a job and then producing a job description. The next stage is to select workers who have most of the skills that are needed. However, it is probably impossible to find employees that have exactly all the right skills. Further, jobs change and, usually, extra skills are needed in the future. It is necessary to fill the gap between the skills that workers have and the skills that they need by training and development. When these

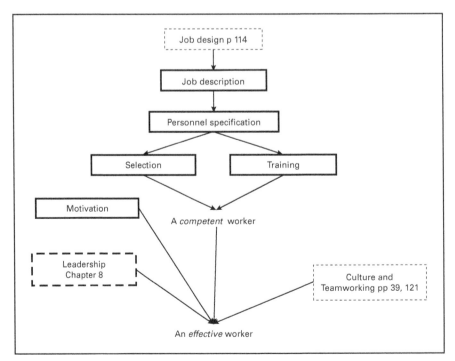

FIGURE 7.1 The process of producing effective workers

steps are completed effectively, the organisation will have competent workers that are able to do the job. However, workers may not use their abilities to the full. Their managers need to motivate them and lead them for their potential to be realised. In addition, the manager needs to provide a conducive organisational climate and an effective team.

This chapter briefly explains job descriptions and personnel specifications. It then gives substantial details on the selection, training, motivation and leadership of workers. More information on designing jobs, providing a conducive organisational climate and managing an effective team are covered elsewhere in this book as indicated in Figure 7.1.

7.2 Job descriptions and personnel specifications

The production of job descriptions and personnel specifications does not arise out of thin air. They are based on the way that jobs are designed. Technically, job design is a part of the organising process described in an earlier chapter. In practice jobs are usually designed with a combined effort of the HR and the operations functions – with perhaps a contribution by the finance function. Once jobs have been designed it is necessary to fill them with suitable workers. The first stage is to produce a **job description** which sets out what workers need to do. The purpose of the job description is to set out the key results a worker must achieve. A job description also covers the type of workplace, pay and other conditions of employment, and it will indicate where the job fits into the organisational structure (e.g. identifying the manager to whom the worker is responsible). In most countries, it is a legal requirement to give an employee a written job description. It should be noted that job descriptions are about the *job to be done*, not the people who occupy the job.

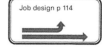

Job design p 114

Personnel specifications are based upon the job description and they concern the *people* who occupy the job. They identify the knowledge, skills, abilities and other characteristics which a person must have in order to perform the job in a competent way. In other words they specify the ideal person for the job. A personnel specification can take many formats. One very basic method of producing personnel specification uses Roger's seven-point plan (Roger,1953), which groups requirements under seven headings. The job description is used to identify the essential and desirable characteristics of workers. *Essential characteristics* are those which are central to the job and which would be difficult or expensive to develop by training. *Desirable characteristics* are those which are important to the job but which might be developed with appropriate training. A table which gives a simplified personnel specification for a sales representative of a software company is given on the website which accompanies this book.

Great care should be taken to avoid unfairness and discrimination. For example, it would generally be unfair to include a candidate's height in a personnel specification. Men are generally taller than women and a height requirement would differentially exclude more women than men. This would normally constitute unfair discrimination but there are exceptions if a person's height is relevant to performing the job. Similarly, personnel specifications should not imply that women candidates might be unsuitable because they would be responsible for the care of children.

> ### CRITICAL THINKING 7.1 *When height is a valid qualification for a job*
>
> In a famous case in the USA it was declared illegal for a police force to demand that recruits should be taller than 1.75 m (5 feet 10 inches) because this would exclude many women and members of some ethnic groups such as Hispanics who could be competent police officers. However, the police force *was* allowed to demand that recruits should be taller than 1.65 m (5 feet 6 inches) since shorter officers might endanger themselves and colleagues because they would not be sufficiently tall to shoot a pistol over the top of a car (this is America!).

7.3 Recruiting and selecting (employee resourcing)

Recruitment and selection concerns the supply of suitable employees and is sometimes referred to as **employee resourcing**. Good recruitment and selection can easily raise productivity by 10 per cent and give an organisation a competitive edge. Good selection has two stages:

- attracting a field of candidates
- choosing among candidates

In addition, good selection often involves giving applicants a realistic preview of the job.

Recruitment

The aim of recruitment is to attract about eight credible applicants for each post. If there are fewer than eight there might not be enough to allow a good choice. If there are many more, it will be difficult to give each candidate full and proper consideration. Some ways of attracting applicants are:

- internal notices and emails
- government employment agencies
- private employment agencies
- headhunters (executive search agencies)
- advertisements in the local press, national press and professional journals
- careers fairs and college visits

The choice of media will depend upon the exact situation. Many senior management jobs are advertised in the national press and professional journals. Very senior management posts will seek applicants using executive search agencies. The use of "headhunters" is very expensive (about 33 per cent of the first-year salary). But the service is very confidential and it is most likely to locate able people who are not actively searching for the job – because they are busy being successful in their present job. Whichever medium is chosen, care must be taken to ensure that the advertising is fair. Advertising a job solely in a magazine such as *FHM* or *GQ* is likely to be unfair because, presumably, few women read these magazines. Advertising a vacancy using internal notices or by word of mouth of existing employees may also be discriminatory since it is less likely that minority groups will learn that a vacancy exists.

CASE 7.2: *Selection of technical managers*

Bristol-Myers Squibb is a world-famous pharmaceutical company. It has a large production plant near Dublin airport in Ireland. A major expansion meant it needed to employ more than 40 technical managers who would be responsible for producing medicines to impeccable quality standards. Because requirements were so high the company decided to engage in a textbook selection exercise in order to obtain the best possible recruits.

First, the jobs of technical managers were analysed to identify the precise characteristics the managers would need. This was a substantial exercise involving more than 60 interviews with senior managers and currently successful managers. A selection system was devised to measure the exact characteristics needed to perform the job.

Applicants were first screened on the basis of their application forms. Those who survived were invited to a mini-assessment centre where they completed:

- two tests of high-level mental ability (verbal reasoning and numerical reasoning)
- a personality test to check, among other things, conscientiousness and emotional stability
- an in-tray test to check how well they could handle written administrative tasks
- a group discussion to check their ability to communicate and work in a team
- a situational interview seeking their reactions to realistic situations they might face
- a technical interview with the potential line manager to check their technical knowledge

The system proved very successful and it was used with hundreds of applicants. It was calculated that the improved selection system saved the organisation over €6 million during the time that the cohort of technical managers would work for the company.

Selection

When a field of candidates has been assembled, it is necessary to **choose the best person** for the job. Many selection methods exist. Cook (2009) noted that three methods predominate. They are known as **the classic trio**:

1 application forms and CVs
2 interviews
3 references

While these methods are widely used they are not very accurate. A traditional interview, for example, is about 4 per cent better than chance in selecting the best candidate. References

CRITICAL THINKING 7.2 *Lies, damn lies and cvs*

A good example of a deceitful CV is the nutritionist who advised the England football captain, Alan Shearer, for two years. When she tried to negotiate a sponsorship deal with Lucozade, a sharp-eyed executive noted that her documents were false. Due to ill health she had dropped out of a degree course and subsequently forged degree and diploma certificates. She obtained work at *two* private health clinics before joining Newcastle United.

Another example is an eye surgeon who was sacked on the spot when it was discovered that his application had omitted to mention a disciplinary offence and had covered it up by supplying two false references. Medical and allied professions seem particularly prone to this problem. One organisation that vets the applications of nurses found 24 bogus claimants within a period of nine months.

In 2002 a leading English clergyman, dean of Portsmouth Cathedral, resigned because he had falsely claimed a PhD.

Lies on CVs and application forms are tragic. They are discovered by reference checks. The perpetrator is disgraced and suffers the financial penalty of unemployment and subsequent reduction in earning power.

are no better but they are a useful way of checking basic facts, dates and job titles of previous employment. Perhaps surprisingly, it is estimated that about one in seven CVs contains blatant lies: the original copies of licences, certificates or diploma's, etc. should be inspected.

Because the classic trio of selection methods are so poor, many organisations use more modern methods such as psychometric testing which we discuss shortly. But just because the classic trio are flawed does not mean that they should not be used at all – they do fulfil other purposes. If candidates know that references will be checked, they tend to be more truthful when filling out application forms or writing CVs. Candidates expect to be interviewed and feel cheated if they are not given a chance to make their own case (even if, in doing so, they do themselves a disservice). Further, interviews are fairly efficient at giving candidates information about the job and starting their orientation towards the organisation. One of the best solutions is to put any interview at the very end of the selection process where it can do the least damage, since at that stage any of the surviving candidates will be reasonably well qualified.

CRITICAL THINKING 7.3 *The long-known weakness of traditional interviews*

The lack of accuracy of traditional interviews has been known since 1929 when Hollingworth asked 12 experienced sales managers to interview 56 applicants. He ensured that the interviewers ranked the applicants independently. If interviews are any good, there should be some correspondence between the ratings – for

▶

example if an applicant is in the top 10 for one interviewer they should be in the top 10 for other interviewers. The actual results were appalling. There was very little correspondence between the rankings. For example, one applicant was top of one interviewer's ranking but fifty-third on the ranking of another interviewer. The conclusion is clear: with traditional interviews your chances of being offered a job very much depend on who is your interviewer.

Modern selection methods

Psychologists and others have been developing better selection methods for almost a century. Some of the most accurate methods of choosing employees include psychometric tests, work samples, structured interviews and biodata. However, as Table 7.1 shows, no single method is perfect and it is usually better to use a combination of methods in, say, an assessment centre. Methods used to select among candidates must be sensitive, reliable, valid and fair.

Psychometric tests

These are samples of behaviour which are highly standardised so that everyone is given precisely the same instructions and time to complete the same tasks. The answers are also evaluated in a standard way. Psychometric tests are more objective than other methods. Broadly speaking, two kinds of tests are used in selection: tests of mental ability and tests of personality.

- **Mental ability** is the ability to *process information quickly and accurately*. It is fairly stable after the age of about 18. Tests of mental ability have been used for 100 years or more. They are highly reliable (a typical reliability correlation is 0.9 – about the same relationship as the length of your right arm to your left arm). Scores of mental ability tests usually correlate about 0.53 with future success. In managers the correlation is higher at about 0.58. Mental ability is a vital factor in job success because it enables people to learn the job more quickly and to respond better to changes or unusual events.

- **Personality** is the *style in which things are done* and is moderately stable after the age of about 30. Tests of personality are rather less reliable than ability tests. A typical test–retest correlation will be about 0.75. Personality tests are useful predictors of job performance and correlate about 0.4 with future job success. Personality is less accurate than mental ability in predicting job performance because equal success can be achieved by people with different styles. Further, up to a point, people can mould jobs to suit their personality. Honesty tests are a particular type of personality test. They attempt to predict whether a future employee will participate in theft or other antisocial activity such as drug-taking. Honesty tests are most frequently used in retail organisations.

	Use			Accuracy/Validity	
100%		**1.0**			
90%	Traditional interviews	0.9			
80%	CVs and letters of application	0.8			
70%		0.7			
				Intelligence and *integrity*	(0.65)
60%		0.6		*Intelligence* and *structured interviews*	(0.63)
				Intelligence and *work sample*	(0.60)
				Work sample tests	(0.54)
50%		0.5		Intelligence tests	(0.53)
				Structured interviews	(0.51)
43%	References			Job knowledge tests	(0.48)
				Integrity tests	(0.40)
40%		0.4		Personality tests	(0.40?)
				Assessment centres	(0.37)
30%		0.3		Biodata	(0.33)
				Conscientiousness	(0.31)
22%	Mental ability tests			References	(0.25)
20%	Personality tests	18%	0.2	Traditional interviews	(0.15)
13%	Work samples			Years education	(0.15)
13%	Graphology	0.1		Interests	(0.14)
8%	Assessment centres			Years job experience	(0.09)
2%	Astrology			Graphology	(0.0)
0%		0.0		Age	(0.01)

TABLE 7.1 The use and accuracy of methods of selection

Work samples

These are carefully worked out exercises which aim to be mini-trials of the job. For example, an applicant for the job of a carpenter would be provided with a standard piece of wood and a standard set of tools. A set time is allowed to produce a piece of work entailing a range of joints and cuts. The exact nature of the task is determined by a prior analysis of the joints and cuts which differentiates between good and bad carpenters. Work samples for management jobs include:

- **Written analysis** of a business problem on the basis of a set of files.
- **A presentation** on a business topic to an audience.
- **A group exercise** which mimics a management meeting.
- **A role play**, e.g. a candidate is asked to study an errant employee's file and conduct a disciplinary interview with that employee.

Work samples are among the best methods of selection and usually correlate 0.54 with subsequent job performance.

Structured interviews

These are much better traditional interviews. Structure means *all candidates are asked more or less the same questions* and, consequently, better comparisons can be made. Further, structured interviews are based on the job description and *only ask questions concerning work behaviour*. For example, an applicant sales representative might be asked how they would respond to the following, realistic, situation:

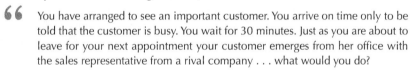

> You have arranged to see an important customer. You arrive on time only to be told that the customer is busy. You wait for 30 minutes. Just as you are about to leave for your next appointment your customer emerges from her office with the sales representative from a rival company . . . what would you do?

The applicant's answer would be compared to a carefully calibrated set of model responses and a score would be allocated. An applicant would be asked how they would respond to five or six of these situations. This particular kind of structured interview is known as a "situational" interview. If properly prepared, situational interviews can be good predictors of future job performance and can rival work samples in their accuracy. Some people say that situational interviews are "verbal work samples".

Biodata

This is a way of collecting information, usually by a questionnaire, about the course of a person's life. Typically the data include educational qualifications, hobbies, memberships and work experience. The data are then used in a carefully derived formula that calculates a person's probability of success. Credit scoring and the calculation of insurance premiums are specific varieties of biodata. Biodata has a moderately good correlation with future job performance. It is very useful as a first sift when there are many applicants for a job.

Assessment centres

Many organisations, especially large ones, use a combination of methods. Candidates are asked to attend for a whole day when they will be asked to, say, complete tests of mental ability and personality, take part in a discussion group, write a report and participate in a situational interview. Combinations of methods such as this are called **assessment centres**. At senior management level they may be more intensive and last two days or even a week. Because assessment centres use several methods, the weaknesses of individual methods have chance to iron themselves out. However, assessment centres are expensive and may cause disruption to both the candidates and the assessors within the organisation.

Because there are so many methods of selection the question arises "which one to use?" A consultant graphologist would probably claim that graphology is best; a firm specialising in interview training would probably suggest using interviews; while a pychometrician might recommend psychometric tests. Before an organisation can choose the best candidate, it must decide on the characteristics that make a good method. The four main characteristics of good selection are:

- **Sensitivity**: it must differentiate between different candidates. If a method gives the same score to every person it is useless. References, for example, are often not very helpful because a very large majority of referees maintain that their applicant is very good.

- **Reliability**: it must give consistent results – otherwise the choice of candidate would depend upon the day on which they were chosen. Reliability is often measured using a correlation. A correlation of 1.0 means that a candidate will always achieve the same score, while a correlation of 0.0 will mean that the scores of a candidate will vary at random. For example, the scores of ability tests are very reliable and achieve a correlation of 0.9 or more. This means that a candidate will achieve a very similar score if they complete an ability test a second time. The reliability of traditional interviews is much less, and a typical correlation would be 0.3. This means that, while there would be a slight trend for candidates to obtain similar scores, far more would depend upon the person who interviewed them.

- **Validity**: does the selection method accurately predict which candidates will be successful? Validity is usually established by collecting scores at the selection stage and correlating them with the later job performance.

- **Fairness:** does not necessarily mean that all groups can do their job equally well. However, it does mean that those people from different groups who are likely to be equally good at doing a job are equally likely to be selected. For example, perhaps only 10 per cent are women who are able to carry a human body down a long ladder; however, these women should have an equal chance of being hired as a firefighter as men who can do the same thing.

Occupational psychologists have been studying the use and accuracy of different methods of selection for over 90 years and are able to provide the general results contained in Table 7.1.

It will be little surprise that the traditional methods of interviews, application forms or letters and references (Cook's classic trio) are the most frequently used methods of selection. There are, however, interesting national differences. In most countries the use of graphology is rare, at about 3 per cent. However, in France approximately 40 per cent of organisations use this technique and this has a marked effect upon the average figure shown in Table 7.1.

Indeed, the use of graphology outside France is largely restricted to subsidiaries of French companies. On average, references are used as a part of selection in 43 per cent of cases; there are, however, notable national differences. The use of references in the UK is very prevalent and is used by about 74 per cent of companies, but its use is much less common in other countries.

The right-hand side of Table 7.1 indicates the accuracy (validity) of the methods of selection. It is based largely upon the paper of Schmidt and Hunter (1996). Results gathered over the last 90 years indicate that the traditional and most prevalent methods of selection are not very accurate (valid). Traditional interviews, for example, have a validity of about 0.15.

More modern methods such as work samples, intelligence tests and situational interviews are far more accurate and have validities in excess of 0.50. While this is a big improvement, it should be noted that modern methods of selection are still far from perfect and many selection errors are still made.

The selection process should give applicants **a realistic preview of the job**. In other words, at the end of the selection process a candidate should have a realistic picture of what the job involves. If they have an unrealistic picture of their future jobs they are likely to leave within a few weeks and the organisation will have to bear the extra costs of recruiting another replacement. Realistic job previews (RJPs) can be provided by giving applicants information in brochures or handouts. An RJP can also be arranged by asking candidates to watch a video or by providing a tour of the workplace and allowing questions to existing employees.

7.4 Training and development (employee development)

The aim of selection is to ensure that employees arrive with the skills, knowledge and abilities (competencies) that are needed. However, selection is never perfect. Usually new employees have most, but not all, the required competencies. Managers must arrange training and development as a way of making up the gap between actual and required competencies. Training and development (nowadays there is a tendency to call this **employee development**) can be divided into five major topics. Managers need to know sufficient about each topic in order to follow a systematic approach and choose the most appropriate approach such as the best method of off-the-job training. The training and development of employees should follow a systematic process, shown in Figure 7.2.

In practice, training and development involves five major aspects:

1 assessing training needs

2 induction training

3 on-the-job training

4 off-the-job training

5 management development

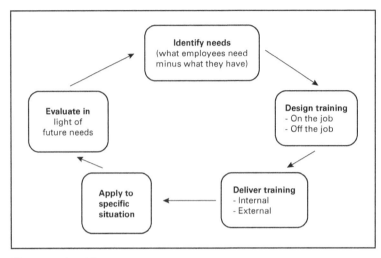

FIGURE 7.2 The systematic training system

Assessing training needs

Assessing *training needs* usually proceeds in three stages.

1 The *strategic plan is inspected and the major HR implications are identified.* For example, a strategic plan may aim for a 20 per cent increase in market share. To achieve the increase it may be necessary to arrange training for existing sales staff, recruit four extra sales representatives and seven production operatives together with two additional administrative staff. Sometimes, this process is called **human resource planning**.

2 Capabilities of existing or new employees are evaluated against the capabilities that will be needed. The difference is often called **the training gap**.

3 Arrangements are made to **provide the training and development** which will close the training gap. Most external recruits will need induction training. In essence, other training is into on-the-job training and off-the-job training. Managers need to know enough about the methods and their advantages and disadvantages in order to make appropriate choices.

Induction training (orientation training)

Induction training aims to familiarise a newcomer with the organisation. It usually covers details which are taken for granted by existing employees. It may include arrangements for receiving wages, conditions of employment, grievance procedures, refreshment facilities and car-parking arrangements. It aims to remove initial problems for new employees and reduce the probability that they leave within the first few weeks. Induction training will usually include information about the company, its history, its structure and products. This information is an important element of fostering company loyalty and ensuring that a new employee becomes an effective employee. Finally, induction training usually tries to communicate the culture and ethos of the organisation.

On-the-job training

On-the-job training is the oldest and simplest type of training. Since time immemorial new female recruits were told to "sit by Nellie" and watch what Nellie does and male recruits have been told to "stand by Sid" and be similarly observant. On-the-job training requires little preparation and there are few obvious costs. Further, it is very realistic so there are no transition problems when a trainee is transferred to production. Nevertheless, this type of training has major problems: it is inefficient and costly. Costs are, however, hidden and secrete themselves in lower production by Nellie and Sid and longer training times. In addition, Nellie or Sid may teach the trainee bad habits!

Other forms of on-the-job training are better and are very useful after initial training. Their success depend on careful planning and availability of a **mentor** who discusses work with the trainee and ensures appropriate lessons are drawn. First, the mentor determines what the trainee already knows. Often the mentor will then demonstrate the job to the trainee. In other cases the mentor will arrange for someone else to give instruction. Instruction will cover one point at a time. The trainee will be asked questions to check learning has taken place. When the trainee has fully understood the task, he or she will be asked to try it out by themselves. Once the trainee has gained confidence further guidance can be given. Finally, the trainee is left to perform the job unaided. Initially the performance of the trainee should be monitored at regular intervals but later this can be reduced.

This basic approach to on-the-job training is used in two main contexts: job rotation and special assignments. **Job rotation** is useful with new recruits, such as graduates, who have little previous experience of work or the organisation. It involves moving trainees through a series of jobs in different departments. For example, a graduate trainee may spend the first month in the production department, the second month in the sales department, and so on. Job rotation is an excellent way of allowing new recruits to build up knowledge of the organisation. It produces a flexible workforce and allows trainees to make informed decisions about the direction of their future careers.

Special assignments are used with longer-serving employees. Generally a review of training needs for a specific employee reveals a development need. An assignment, different to present duties, which allows new knowledge and skills to be acquired is found. For example, the strategic plan of a financial service company may envisage expansion into foreign markets. A review may reveal an existing personnel manager has no experience of foreign cultures. The organisation may therefore arrange a special assignment in which the individual is seconded for six months to the personnel department in, say, Singapore. Sometimes it is possible to arrange a special assignment in another organisation.

Off-the-job training

Many managers shun off-the-job training that is conducted away from the workplace and outside their immediate control. This can disrupt the normal flow of work. Off-the-job training may strain their budget with substantial out-of-pocket expenses. Further, off-the-job training involves decisions about how it should be delivered such as:

- night school
- day release

- block release
- special seminars and workshops
- correspondence courses
- online, interactive training

The most appropriate method depends upon circumstances. For example, a day-release course for printing-machine engineers may be appropriate for trainees who work close to a suitable college. However, commuting and travelling times would make day release inappropriate for similar engineers who work in outlying areas. They might find block release courses (a week's residential course, for example) more suitable. Similarly, much will depend on the ability and motivation of trainees. Generally, night-school courses and correspondence courses are only suitable for people who are *very highly* motivated.

Off-the-job training may involve a wide range of instruction methods. The main methods are:

- **Lectures** are a very cost-effective method because their size is limited only by the size of the lecture theatre. Lectures can be very good at introducing a topic, identifying the structure of a subject and highlighting the key points. Lectures are not a good medium for consolidating detailed learning. Lectures have an intrinsic drawback: they are usually boring. Communication between lecturer and learner is usually one-way only. **Classes and seminars** are costly. Their size is usually limited to a maximum of about 16 students. Classes are based upon the question and answer technique. They are interactive and are able to maintain interest while consolidating detailed learning. **Role plays** require trainees to act out situations – usually situations involving decisions or interpersonal reactions. **Discussion groups** are used when training focuses upon changing or developing attitudes. A relevant topic will be introduced by a skilled leader. The group will then be invited to discuss the topic. The leader inconspicuously rewards positive attitudes and ignores negative ones. For example, a training session on ethnic diversity might include a discussion group on racial prejudice. Whenever a participant expresses tolerant attitudes, the discussion leader signals approval and encourages the participant to amplify their ideas. The contributions of participants with intolerant attitudes are accepted politely, but with minimal comment.
- **Case studies** are a very popular method of management development. Students are given background data and the details of the specific problem. They are then asked to discuss the situation and recommend a course of action. The actions actually taken and their actual consequences are then revealed. Students are able to compare their suggestions with the action actually taken. They also try to analyse the situation to evaluate why the organisation's actions did, or did not, work.
- **Online training** is a medium that has many potential advantages. Typically, trainees can use online training at any time convenient to them. The flexibility of online training means that there is no disruption of the normal workflow. At its simplest, online training will involve a screen containing text. When this has been read, the trainee completes, say, a multiple-choice test and they are immediately given a score which shows whether the material has been learned successfully. Online training can have more sophisticated features. For example, a video clip can be used instead of text. In some situations, online training can be highly interactive and it can branch according to decisions made by the trainee. Online training is very useful when there is a clear set of objective "facts"

▶

CRITICAL THINKING 7.4 *Are case studies shared ignorance?*

Although the case study method is used in many top management courses, it has strong critics who maintain that the method results in "shared ignorance". There is an assumption that the person who creates a case study is an objective and knowledgeable expert. In fact, most problem situations involve a number of explanations. The person who creates a case study will choose the explanation which suits her or his purposes and it can never be known whether or not they have chosen the correct explanation.

Students like case studies because they *seem* realistic. In fact, most case studies are oversimplifications and the solutions proffered rarely have empirical evidence of their effectiveness. Indeed, shortly before its collapse in shame and ignominy, business schools around the world used more than a dozen Harvard Business School case studies that hyped and praised the innovation of Enron and the Enron business model (Curver, 2003). In effect, these case studies were teaching bad business methods. More details of the Enron collapse are given in Chapter 19. This is not an isolated example. Case study writers from Harvard Business School extolled the virtues of the "new architecture" formed by the Royal Bank of Scotland after its acquisition of NatWest Bank (Fred the shred, again!) – within a short time the bank was in trouble and had to be rescued by the British government (Broughton, 2008).

It is highly likely that readers of this book will be required to critique at least one case study during a management course. Some guidance on evaluating case studies is given on pages 505-506.

that a trainee must learn. For example, audiovisual training is a good way of training computer programmers to diagnose problems and faults. However, the set-up costs are high. This means that it is only appropriate where there are many trainees. The high set-up costs also mean that this training is appropriate only where the material is unlikely to change for a significant period of time. Indeed, critics complain that audiovisual training is inflexible, because the costs of making adjustments are so high. Initially, trainees like online training. However, the most able trainees quickly become bored and complain that it is too repetitive and pedestrian.

Management development

Training implies learning *specific knowledge, procedures or skills* to meet *existing* challenges. Development implies the *improvement of a more general capability* which can be used to meet *future* situations. Management development is therefore a broader concept than management training. In most circumstances people in the first two years of their management career should spend at least four weeks on development courses. Thereafter, experienced managers should spend about two weeks per year on development activities. The two most prominent aspects of management development are **learning skills** and **self-awareness**.

Learning skills are an important aspect of "knowledge management". In a dynamic and rapidly changing world it is impossible to specify and train people to solve all the problems they might encounter. It is much better to train people in *ways* of solving problems so that they can solve-problems themselves, as and when they arise. This means that managers need to be aware of their own style of learning and any of their weaknesses in problem-solving. Probably the most famous analysis of problem-solving was made by Kolb and Fry (1975). They viewed problem-solving as a continuous cycle (Figure 7.3) with four main stages:

- **Concrete experience** occurs when a person performs an action and then directly experiences the results of that action in their specific situation.
- **Observation and reflection** follow from concrete experience. An individual tries to understand why the result followed from the action in that particular situation.
- **Abstract conceptualisation** involves extending the lessons from a particular situation to a more generalised idea of how the action and the result might be linked in a wide variety of situations.
- **Active experimentation** involves seeking out new circumstances in which to test the general ideas generated in the previous stage.

Active experimentation produces a new set of concrete experiences which set the cycle in motion again. According to this analysis management learning is a continuous cycle in which ideas become more and more accurate. Kolb found that individuals differed in their approach to problem-solving. Some would emphasise concrete experience while others would emphasise active experimentation, etc. However, effective learners need to be proficient at all stages of the cycle. A weakness at any one stage will slow down the whole learning process. It is therefore important for managers to locate their area of weakness

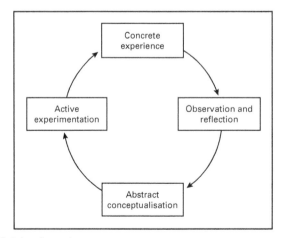

FIGURE 7.3 Kolb and Fry's learning cycle

and develop it to the level of their ability at the other stages. A number of people including Honey and Mumford (Honey, 1982) have adapted Kolb's ideas.

Self-awareness is very important in leaders (see Chapter 8). It can be developed in a number of ways. Sometimes it is achieved by special training courses (**T groups**) where a workgroup sets aside, perhaps, two days to discuss their perceptions of each other. Each group member becomes, in turn, the focus of the training. The other group members give their frank and open views of that person and any inaccurate perceptions are challenged and discussed. Often the sessions are stormy but, it is claimed, at the end of the training the workgroup will have fewer personal misunderstandings. Self-awareness training can sometimes make vunerable participants upset and distraught – if you are trying hard but only just succeeding it does not help if others repeatedly tell you so!

360-degree feedback is another way of increasing a person's awareness of their strengths and weaknesses. A questionnaire measuring the competencies the organisation believes are necessary is produced. The questionnaire is then circulated to a person's boss, their colleagues and their subordinates and it is completed anonymously. The results are compiled and fed back to the individual so that she or he will be aware of how they are perceived by other people. The feedback will clearly indicate areas where other people believe they are strong and where they are weak. A manager will then be in a position to take action to improve areas of weakness.

7.5 Motivating

Motivation is the *energy* which enables people to achieve an organisation's objectives. Motivations are sometimes called **drives**. An organisation can recruit and select very able people and train them so that they have the appropriate knowledge: the result (as we saw in Figure 7.1) is a competent worker who is able to do a job. But without motivation they will do nothing – their skills and abilities need to be activated by some kind of motivation. Motivation determines the *goals* a person attempts to achieve, the *energy* that is devoted to attaining the goal and the *persistence* with which the goal is pursued.

Motivation can be increased in many ways. Probably the most effective way is to design a job so that people derive intrinsic enjoyment in their work and are keen to do it. This aspect of motivation was covered by the section on job design in the previous chapter on organisational processes. However, it is often necessary to use other techniques to add extrinsic motivation to a job. Extrinsic motivation can be provided by factors such as pay, recognition or social pressure. Extrinsic motivation can also be provided by a person who is either a formal or informal leader of a group.

Motivating job characteristics p 115

Theories of motivation

Many theories of motivation have been put forward. Some popular theories, such as Maslow's (1970) hierarchy of needs and Herzberg's two-factor theory, have not been supported by scientific evidence. However, equity theory, expectancy theory and goal-setting theory are particularly relevant to managers.

CRITICAL THINKING 7.5 *What is wrong with Maslow and Herzberg?*

Sometimes, inaccurate theories which make a nice, memorable story become entrenched in the literature and are regurgitated from author to author long after they are disproved. Maslow's theory of motivation is a classic example. It is still taught on many management courses and described in many management textbooks. Maslow studied a group of atypical, very successful men and came up with a theory that there are five types of motivation and that they are arranged in a certain hierarchical order. None of this has been supported by academic research. Since 1977, it has been known that there is little evidence for either the existence of five types of motives or their hierarchical ordering (Korman, Greenhouse and Badin, 1977).

Similarly, the job enrichment theories developed by Herzberg are still taught on management courses and described in management textbooks. Herzberg claimed that there were two types of motivation: motivating factors and hygiene factors. Hertzberg's theory was enormously influential in enriching jobs. However, his conclusion was reached on the basis of poor research – he asked two questions and should not have been surprised that he received two separate types of answers. Further, the apparent existence of two types of motivation could have arisen from attribution theory rather than motivation theory: we tend to attribute good things to ourselves (motivation factors) and bad things to other people or our environment (hygiene factors) (Lock, 1976; Wall, 1973).

Equity theory

Equity theory was put forward by Adams in 1965. It is a very simple theory which states that people try to balance what they put into a job with what they get from it. If the rewards from a job are less than the effort they expend, they will reduce their effort to restore the balance. On the other hand, if the rewards are noticeably higher than the effort they expend they will increase their effort in order to restore the balance. The implications of equity theory are straightforward. If an employer wishes to increase motivation, wages should be raised and employees will then increase their effort in order to maintain the balance. Unfortunately, research suggests that the situation is not quite so simple. It would seem that, while equity theory is correct in predicting that a decrease in rewards will be met with a decrease in effort, an increase in rewards does not necessarily guarantee an increase in effort.

Expectancy theory

Expectancy theory is one of the dominant theories of motivation. It starts by noting that different people value different things. In an employment context, some people are motivated by money, some by status, while others are motivated by security. This means that one of the first steps in increasing motivation is to identify those rewards which are valued by a specific individual.

Expectations play a crucial role in determining how hard people will work. Two expectations are particularly important. The first is the expected probability of achieving the level of performance demanded. This is called the *effort–performance expectancy*. It is the answer to the question, "If I make the effort, how likely is it that I will achieve the performance required?" For example, a salesperson might have a target of 100 sales per month. The effort–performance expectancy is the chance a salesperson perceives that they have of achieving that target, provided they make the effort. They may believe that their chances are good (high effort–performance expectancy) and consequently they will work hard to achieve that target. However, the salesperson may believe that the target is too ambitious or the market is in recession, and consequently no matter how hard they work they will not achieve that target (low effort–performance expectancy). Consequently they will not be motivated to make the required effort.

The second expectation concerns the link between performance and reward (**performance–reward expectancy**). It answers the question, "If I achieve my target performance what is the likelihood that I will be given my reward?" For example, a salesperson might believe that achieving their target is certain to result in a large bonus (high performance–reward expectancy). On the other hand, the salesperson might believe that the organisation's word cannot be trusted and that, even if the sales target is achieved, a bonus will not be given (low performance–reward expectancy). The situation is shown in Figure 7.4.

Expectancy theory has clear indications for managers who wish to maximise the motivation of their staff:

- Do not assume that everyone is motivated by money. Work out the rewards that each person values and offer these as incentives.
- Make the performance required absolutely clear. Specify exact behaviours.
- Make sure that performance targets are considered to be reasonable and attainable with extra effort. Make sure that employees know that achieving the target performance will be rewarded. Never renege on a promise of a reward – it will lower, probably irrevocably, the performance–reward expectancy.

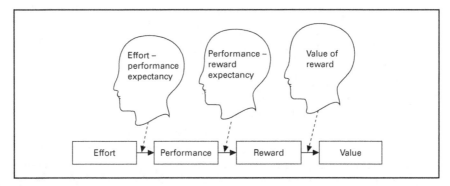

FIGURE 7.4 The expectancy theory of motivation

Goal-setting theory

The basics of goal-setting theory were developed by Locke (1968) and claims have been made that it has more scientific support than any other approach to motivation (Pinder, 1984). The basics of goal-setting theory are very simple: people are motivated and work harder when they are set difficult, but not impossible, goals. Goals focus people's attention on required behaviour and allow them to mobilise their efforts in a clear direction. Moreover, goals often boost people's commitment so that they will persevere longer in the face of difficulty.

The nature of the goals is a crucial factor in their ability to motivate. People are motivated when:

- Goals are *difficult but realistic* and within the capabilities of employees. Often, goals should be set using the performance of existing employees as a guide. For example if the top 15 per cent of sales representatives obtain average monthly sales of £80 000, a target of £80 000 can be set for all sales representatives. *Vague goals* such as "work very hard" do not motivate people as much as specific goals that specify quantity, quality and timescale. A specific goal for a lumberjack might be to fell 40 trees (quantity) per day (timescale) with side branches removed and delivered to central logging depot (quality).
- *People are committed to goals* and regard them as reasonable. Some researchers say that goals should be set in a participative way but others maintain that delegated goals are just as effective.

7.6 Staffing toolkit

Toolkit

- Make absolutely sure that your methods of recruitment and selection are as fair as possible and that they do not discriminate against people on the grounds of gender, sexual orientation age or disability.
- A great deal of effort can be saved if jobs are designed so that responsibilities are clear and motivating. Every job should have a job description and a personnel specification. Be careful to make sure that these documents are kept up to date and are used when making decisions about selecting staff or training them.
- Use modern selection methods because they are much more accurate (but still far from perfect) than the classic trio: interviews, references and CVs. If you decide to use any of the classic trio for other reasons, put them at the end of the selection process where they can do least harm.
- Ensure that staff are properly trained and that there is an adequate training budget – both for expenses and the time needed for training. Make sure that training is relevant to an employee's present job or a likely future job – consult the job description, the person specification and any other relevant documents such as recent appraisal forms.
- Take responsibility for your own training. Do not leave it to your employer. It is more important to you than it is to them. You get a lifetime's worth of benefit from training and

development. They only get a few years' benefit. In your first two years of employment this should be at least four weeks per year. Later, it should be at least two weeks per year. Above all else, make sure that you develop your ability to learn and adapt (check your learning style). If you can learn and adapt you will get maximum benefit from later experience

- Pay employees reasonable rates. If you underpay they will become demotivated and reduce their efforts or engage in counterproductive practices. Set clear, ambitious but reasonable goals. Establish the things that motivate individual employees and then offer individualised incentives. Do not assume that everyone is motivated by pay. Make the links between effort, performance and rewards clear. Do not renege on rewards that have been earned.

Activities and further study

Essay plans

Prepare plans for the following essays:

1 Choose a job that interests you. Describe how you would recruit someone for this post. (This does not include the selection phase.)

2 Evaluate scientific research on the validity of different methods of personnel selection

3 What is fairness in recruitment and selection? How would you establish whether a selection method was unfair

4 Describe how three different theories of motivation can give practical guidance to managers wanting to motivate their subordinates

Web activities

1 Look up the local website of Saville-Holdsworth Ltd (SHL), e.g. www.shl.com/shl/nz, www.shl.co.za or www.shl.com/SHL/hk or shl.com. Follow the trail site map; candidate helpline; practice tests; you will then be able to do some of their psychometric tests on line. The site also contains a lot of excellent information about selection and assessment.

2 Look up other sites that give information about recruitment. One good source is the site at the University of Cape Town: www.careers.uct.ac.za/students/careering/articles/selection.pdf. Often the sites of major employers give details of their selection methods. A good one is Qantas's site www.qantas.com.au/infodetail/about/employment/QTests.pdf. Beware: there are many poor sites offering unscientific tests or which use tests as a part of a sales ploy.

3 Go to the website http://www.nelsoncroom.co.uk and look at the material concerning online training.

4 Kolb and Fry's learning cycle may be the most well-known example. However, other good descriptions of how managers learn are available. Use the Internet to locate at least two other cycles. Evaluate the cycles you locate and identify their similarities and differences with Kolb and Fry's system.

Experiential activities

1 Write two sentences about yourself under each heading of Roger's seven-point plan.

2 Think of a job that you would like to do in, say, three years' time. List the skills and knowledge needed to do that job. Then rate yourself on whether you have the knowledge and skills at present. For each area where there is a gap identify the training you will need and identify a suitable training method.

3 Imagine that you have been asked by your present employer, university or college to develop a one-day induction programme for people joining your organisation. Work out what training you would give.

Recommended reading

1 Clarke, L.A. and Roberts, J. (2010) "Employer's use of social networking sites: a socially irresponsible practice", *Journal of Business Ethics*, 95, 507–525. This article discusses the unethical practice of using social networking sites such as Facebook to obtain information for hiring and firing decisions.

2 Mason, R. and Power, S. (2009) "360° appraisal: a simple pragmatic solution", *Clinical Governance: An International Journal*, 14(4). A straightforward, practical example of the use of 360-degree feedback to improve the performance of hospital consultants.

3 Eliott, E.M. and Williams, F.P. (1995) "When you no longer need Maslow: exchange professionalism and decentralisation in the management of criminal justice agencies", *Public Administration Quarterly*, 19(1). Pages 74–78 criticise need theories (such as Maslow's or Hertzberg's) and suggests that situational variables asre underemphasised.

Chapter NINE

Decision-making

Chapter contents

❖ *LEARNING OBJECTIVES*

After studying this chapter you should be able to **explain** why managers need to make decisions, the ideal way in which they should be made and **give some of the reasons** why the ideal is not always attained. In particular you will be able to:

❖ **list** two major ways that decisions may vary

❖ **distinguish** between programmed and non-programmed decisions

❖ **discuss in detail** different styles of making decisions

❖ **describe in detail** the seven main stages of rational decision-making

❖ **describe** five ways of generating alternative solutions to organisational problems

❖ **explain in detail** how alternative solutions to organisational problems can be evaluated

❖ **draw up** a decision matrix for a major choice you may need to make

❖ **describe briefly** six common faults in making decisions

Managers never have enough time, money, staff or other resources. If managers obtain what they think are enough resources, their minds turn to new, more demanding goals which require yet more time, money or staff, etc. This is a good thing. It means that managers are proactive and accept the challenge of continuing improvement. However, the perpetual shortage of resources requires frequent decisions between the available options. Decision-making is therefore an important management process.

CASE 9.1: *A good "bad decision" to clean microwave ovens*

Reckitt Benckiser's boffins devised a fantastic product to clean microwaves. A little sachet is placed into the microwave and when the oven heated, the sachet popped, spreading the cleaner around. When the cycle finished, the sachet could be used as a cloth to wipe the microwave oven. Decisions to develop and trial the product seemed brilliant. Reckitt decided to support the product, and because the organisation had several super-brands it was secure enough to innovate in this way. But sensibly, Reckitt Benckiser decided to limit the risk of launching a new product by thorough market testing. Unfortunately, consumer tests proved that people do not actually want to clean their microwaves very often – perhaps because microwaves are no longer expensive items. So the product failed. Reckitt Benckiser did not castigate those involved. The initial decision to support the product was not good. But, it encouraged innovation, developed management skills and fostered the right culture of market research. Not a bad decision after all.

Decision-making is not an isolated management process. It is closely linked to planning. Senior managers constructing strategic plans need to make important decisions which are often based on incomplete data and ambiguous situations, and they may have momentous outcomes. It may be many years before the outcome is known. A wrong strategic decision may cause severe pain such as dismissal of key executives or other employees. Junior managers following operational plans certainly make many more decisions but they are less significant and based on clearer, unambiguous information. Further, the correctness of their decisions will be obvious very quickly (sometimes within minutes) and if they are wrong it will be possible to take relatively painless remedial action.

Leaders also make many decisions. If he or she chooses, say, wrong goals, adopts the wrong style or decides to trust the wrong follower they are likely be replaced or usurped. Poor decision-making can affect many other areas of management. Wrong financial decisions can alienate shareholders. Wrong human resource (HR) decisions can affect employees. Wrong decisions are inevitable. Within limits they should be tolerated because organisations which relish "blamefests" discourage innovation. Organisations that control acceptable bad decisions can learn and prosper. Managers who make occasional bad decisions learn lessons and they work harder to redeem themselves. Decisions can also be both good and bad, as Case 9.1 illustrated.

Clearly decision-making is complex and involves many activities – especially making decisions in a rational way, using varied decision-making techniques and avoiding problems in making decisions.

9.1 Definition and types of decision

The definition of a decision is no intellectual challenge. It simply means:

> 66　Making a choice about something.　99

It usually carries connotations that the choice is significant and will have long-term consequences. Decisions can concern an object such as choosing the most cost-effective commercial software package. It can also concern people. For example, at the end of the selection process an employer must choose the most suitable candidate. A decision can also involve abstract notions and ideas such as strategic objectives or an organisation's moral standards.

The simplest decision is whether or not to accept a single possibility. A decision with only one option is often called **Hobson's choice**, after a sixteenth-century stable owner who had a local monopoly of hiring horses in Cambridgeshire. To make sure the best horses were not overworked Hobson rotated the position of the horses within the stable. Anyone wishing to hire a horse had to accept the horse in the stall nearest the door – "take it or leave it". A modern example of a single-option decision might be granting an employee compassionate leave. This is positive because it helps the individual and demonstrates social responsibility. However, it also has negative consequences for employees who need to cover for another's absence and, possibly, customers who may need to wait longer. Another example of a single-option decision is whether or not to purchase software at exorbitant prices from a monopoly supplier.

Most decisions involve a choice between several things. A decision between two things is usually called a **dilemma**. The two objects of a dilemma are not necessarily negative. In the fourteenth century the French philosopher Jean Buridan noted a dilemma between two positive things could have dire consequences. "Buridan's Ass" was both hungry and thirsty. Fortunately it was close to a pile of hay and an equal sized trough of water. Unfortunately, the ass was exactly halfway between the two positive rewards. The ass died because it could not decide whether it preferred the hay to the water and consequently did not move from the mid-point. A modern equivalent of Buridan's ass is a student who locates two very desirable job opportunities and who has only has enough time to apply for one of them. He or she takes so much time agonising over which one to choose that the deadlines for both applications are exceeded.

Dilemmas, however, are usually associated with a choice between two negative things. In Greek mythology captains of ships sailing the narrow strait of Messina between the toe of Italy and the island of Sicily had to make a choice between Scylla and Charybdis. On the one side of the straight there was a monster, Scylla, who regularly ate sailors who passed by and on the other side was a monster, Charybdis, whose huge mouth swallowed water to create an engulfing whirlpool. Modern negative dilemmas involve being caught between "the devil and the deep blue sea" or being "between a rock and a hard place". Modern managerial dilemmas often follow a dramatic fall in market share after which managers must choose between dismissing some loyal employees or running the risk of the organisation becoming bankrupt. A less sympathetic case is the dilemma facing directors of large banks, who must choose between facing a storm of public protest or the loss of key employees who might defect to the competition if they do not receive a large bonus.

A **false dilemma** arises when people think there are only two options when, in fact, there are more. A **trilemma,** for example, involves three options. The so-called **Warnock's dilemma** is actually a quintelemma. Warnock made a post on an intranet forum in the year 2000 but there was no response. He then had to decide between five possible alternatives in order to understand the lack of reaction. The five alternatives were:

1 The original post was perfect – no follow-up comments were necessary.

2 The original post was rubbish – no one could be bothered to reply.

3 Nobody read the original post – for various reasons.

4 Nobody understood the original post but would not ask for clarification - perhaps because they feared appearing stupid.

5 Nobody cared about the original post.

Warnock noted that the real reason why there was no response to the original post was probably an amalgam of all five alternatives. (Warnock's plight has even given rise to a new verb: to be "Warnocked" is to make a post on a discussion group or blog and not receive a reply.)

Decisions are sometimes described as a series of sequential activities, smoothly transforming into one another. In real-life situations decisions are characterised by lack of clarity, pressure and situation of factors such as risk-taking and politics. Consequently, much decision-making in innovation deviates from rationalists models. Decision-making often takes the form of garbage-can decision-making (Styhre *et al.*, 2010). This brief description of the complications in making decisions discusses the dimensions of clarity, the decision situation and the pressure.

CASE 9.2: *To tea or not to tea*

Elmwood Fine Teas started in 1990 as a tea room set in a mansion in Kentucky. In a short time it became a local institution and achieved recognition as one of the British Tea Council's best tea places in the world. Thousands of people went to enjoy a formal British tea of sandwiches, scones, cakes and, of course, tea. Two gift shops and an art gallery were added. They did well – visitors usually made purchases after drinking their afternoon teas. The owners diversified. They started wholesaling tea and published books with gourmet recipes. Soon the wholesaling and publishing became bigger than the tea rooms and the owners found that running all aspects of the business was too much. They had to make a decision whether or not to close the tea-rooms and concentrate on wholesaling and publishing.

Major factors in the decision were:

- The impact on the local community. The tea room had become a tourist feature, earning money for the local community.
- The tea room accounted for 40 per cent of the total income.

- Money would be needed for investment in the publishing and wholesale business.
- The tea room was an important aspect of the brand.

After considerable deliberation the tea rooms were closed. The mansion was sold (with stipulations that tea rooms could not be re-opened and the mansion's image could continue as the company logo). The owners are pleased with their decision. The wholesale business is prospering and more books are being published.

Source: based on Wellner (2006)

Clarity

Some decisions, such as the choice of a photocopier are straightforward. The objective is clear, the decision criteria well known, the information concerning the photocopiers is objective, the problem is well structured and the organisation has procedures for handling this kind of decision. This type of decision is called a **programmed decision**. Programmed decisions often require little thought and may be delegated to less senior employees. Usually:

- they are repetitive and routine
- they have existing precedents. Managers do not need to establish new methods and can rely on those which were successful in the past
- they are well structured
- they have solutions that are well known or obvious
- they have a high degree of certainty of the outcome
- most, if not all, of the required information is available

"Non-programmed decisions" are the opposite. They are non-routine, require original thinking and they are usually taken at a senior level. It has been argued that the increasing uncertainty and volatility of the business environment has increased the proportion of non-programmed decisions. Sometimes, non-programmed decisions can involve unusual or life-threatening situations. Strategic decisions are also usually non-programmed.

CASE 9.3: *Healthy Pepsi*

Most people associate PepsiCo with the manufacture of sugary drinks, crisps and other fatty, salty snacks. In 2010, the boss of the company, Indra Nooyi decided that Pepsico should become a part of the solution to the public health challenge of obesity – not one of its causes. It was decided to reduce the salt in its biggest brands by 25 per cent within five years. Similarly, it was decided to withdraw sugary drinks from schools around the world within two years. In part, the decisions were motivated by social responsibility. In part, they were motivated by a wish to avoid the company going the way of tobacco firms and being held responsible by governments for health problems associated with their products.

These decisions are excellent examples of non-programmed decisions. They were the result of complex factors in the business and social environment. The company had rarely made such wide-raging changes in the formulation of its products. The decision was made at the very top of the organisation. Some of the production technology needed to bring about the change has yet to be perfected. The decision was made with incomplete knowledge of the relevant decisions by the company's arch rival Coca-Cola. Most important of all, the reaction of customers is uncertain and hence the reaction of investors might be jittery.

Reducing calorie, salt and fat consumption is only one aspect of preventing obesity. Increasing calorie burn is another. "Why aren't we going after computer and cable-TV companies for creating a sedentary lifestyle?" asks Ms Nooyi.

Source: *Economist, 25 March 2010*

In many cases managers cannot be certain of the outcome but they are able to calculate their chances of success or failure with some accuracy. The probability of failure is known as **risk**. Risk is not necessarily a bad thing – it is often associated with higher returns. However, it needs to be managed carefully. It often needs to be spread across different projects or investments so that the failures of some will be compensated for by the success of many others. A cardinal principle of risk management is that the combined level of risk should not jeopardise the fundamental stability of the organisation.

CRITICAL THINKING 9.1 *Lehman Brothers' risk busts the bank*

Lehman Brothers provides a salutary lesson in accepting a combined level of risk that could jeopardise an organisation's existence. Lehman Brothers was once the fourth largest investment bank in the USA. It specialised in securitising the risks that people might default on their mortgages. Basically, this involved amalgamating lots of poor risks on the basis that only a small proportion would actually fail. The collective risk of these bundles can be quantified and the bundles can be sold to others or held as investments. It is not clear why Lehman held so many of these bundles (securities). Some say it was a deliberate investment decision. Others say that they could not sell all the securities they had created. The bank managed to hide its huge level of risk for a long time. But when the mortgage market turned, the truth leaked out. Lehman brothers had to devalue these assets which meant its reserves were so low that other banks would not lend it the money it needed to continue. The bank went bankrupt, hastening a global financial meltdown.

A decision-maker may have clear goals but may not be able to calculate accurately the risks attached to the alternative solutions. These situations are uncertain. **Uncertainty** is usually defined as the inability to calculate the probability of failure. It arises from two sources: the absence of information and the complexity of the environment. For example, a marketing manager may make an uncertain decision because the size of the potential market is not known. An uncertain decision may also be made when the size of the potential market is well established but there are so many factors influencing purchasing decisions that it is impossible to predict the number of sales.

Ambiguity represents the lowest level of clarity. It usually exists when a decision-maker is not clear about the goals. Ambiguity also arises when the alternatives are difficult to define. Sometimes, there is ambiguity in whether a manager should be making a decision at all. Ambiguity means that a manager cannot be clear whether he or she is tackling the right problem or evaluating the right alternatives. Hence it is impossible to even estimate the probability of success.

In general, decisions that are clear are likely to be successful. The relationships between the five concepts related to clarity (programmed decisions, certainty, risk, uncertainty and ambiguity) and other factors are given in Figure 9.1.

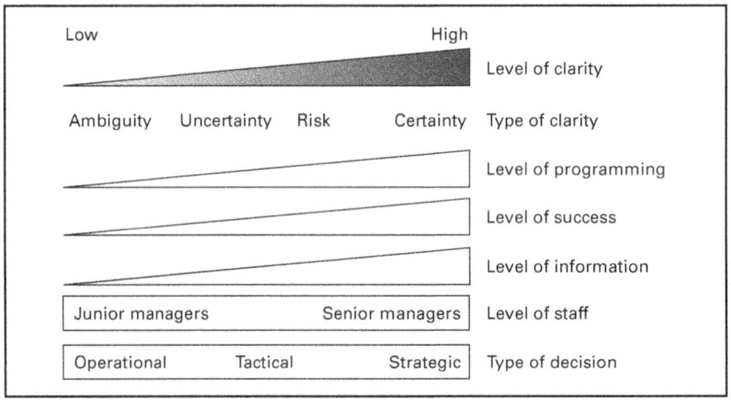

FIGURE 9.1 Correlates of decision clarity

Pressure

Decisions also vary according to the degree of pressure involved. Pressure is largely independent of clarity since a manager can be under pressure whether or not the decision involves a clear, programmed problem or an ambiguous, non-programmed problem. Pressure in decision-making has three main aspects: time, conflict and organisational politics.

Many decisions are made under **time pressure**. Sometimes the time pressure is caused by a decision-maker's lack of planning and foresight. Sometimes managers may not have the experience or ability to foresee a routine, predictable problem. Sometimes the time pressure is generated by an unpredictable event such as an accident or the resignation of a key employee. A crisis arises when there is a major threat which must be resolved quickly. Most managers find crises are stressful but many thrive on the excitement and activity. In crisis situations, decision-makers may not be able to consult others. Consequently, they may not be aware of all possible solutions and may not be able to reconcile differences of opinions. Many organisations attempt to reduce pressure on the managers in times of crisis by providing "disaster training". This aims to teach decision-makers how to remain cool under pressure and how to deal with the media. It also encourages them to anticipate how they would deal with a number of disaster scenarios.

Pressure may also be generated by **conflict** between opposing groups. Conflict may generate strong emotions that interfere with judgement. However, a moderate level of conflict may improve the quality of decisions because it tends to ensure that a wider range of alternatives is considered. Dealing with conflict situations needs a high level of social skill in order to avoid long-term antagonism between contenders.

Conflict is often the consequence of **organisational politics**. Ideally, decisions should be based on a totally objective analysis of facts. In many situations judgements are distorted by favouritism, coalitions, alliances and the desire to please superiors. In these circumstances the pursuit of power and influence may become more important than the correctness of the decision. Organisational politics are more likely to affect ambiguous and uncertain decisions where there are conflicting viewpoints. Dean and Sharfman (1996) found that organisational politics tend to reduce the effectiveness of decision-making. However, it is possible to defend the inclusion of "political factors" on the grounds that, if they are taken into account, the implementation of a decision will be easier because it meets less opposition.

The results of Dean and Sharfman support the generally held view that pressure interferes with decision-making. Pressure tends to produce tunnel vision and restrict the number of alternative solutions considered. Moreover, pressure uses up mental capacity so that less is available to diagnose the problem and evaluate alternatives. Other factors which reduce the quality of decisions are described in Section 9.5

9.2 Styles of decision-making

Managers approach decision-making in varied ways. Often, the decision-making style adopted by managers will reflect their personality. For example, some managers are cautious and favour solutions that carry little risk, while others are adventurous and favour decisions which carry a high risk. Similarly, some managers are decisive and reach conclusions swiftly while others take a long time and will not come to a conclusion until all the information is available.

Perfectionists tend to make decisions slowly. Rigid people often fail to consider all alternative solutions – especially those solutions which include novel elements. Intelligence has a major impact on decision-making. Generally, intelligent people make better decisions more quickly because they process a wide range of information speedily. However, a combination of intelligence and perfectionism can slow down the decision-making process. Such people like to gather vast quantities of information and analyse it exhaustively. Sometimes this can lead to "paralysis by analysis".

Rowe, Boulgarides and McGrath (1994) considered all these aspects and came to the conclusion that there are two main dimensions which govern decision style. They are shown as the axes in Figure 9.2. The first dimension deals with *tolerance for ambiguity*. Some managers like to deal with situations where the objectives are clear, the alternatives are easily understood and the information is objective. These managers dislike ambiguity. They value order and consistency. Other managers are happy to deal with situations that are ill-defined and which can be tackled in a large number of ways. They have a tendency to see problems in a wider perspective and they revel in the freedom which ambiguity may give. The second dimension concerns *rationality*. Some managers are very rational and stick to reasoning with objective information. They make their decisions in a logical and sequential way. Others are more *intuitive* and go by their "gut feelings". They tackle a problem from many angles and may use unorthodox, even zany, methods. Rowe, Bulgarides and McGrath used a combination of these two dimensions to identify the four decision-making styles shown in the quadrants of Figure 9.2.

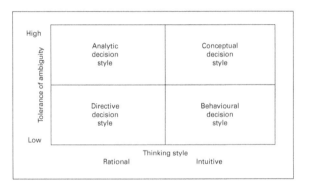

FIGURE 9.2 Rowe, Boulgarides and McGrath four decision-making styles

A manager with an *analytical style* will collect as much data as possible – preferably objective data from a management information system. She or he will consider the alternatives in a clinical, objective way and try to choose the optimum solution. Their decisions will usually be technically very competent. A manager with a *conceptual style* will try to see a problem in perspective and will try to understand the general principles that will give a broad approach. They will collect a large amount of data but they will use information obtained from people as well as that obtained from a management information system. Their decisions will often be unusual and creative. A manager with a *directive style* will often appear efficient and practical. They usually make decisions very quickly because they simplify the situation, deal with a restricted range of information and consider only a narrow range of conventional alternatives. A manager with a *behavioural style* is usually concerned with other people's feelings and the impact a decision has upon colleagues and employees. They obtain the majority of their information by talking to others on a one-to-one basis.

It must be emphasised that few people are pure examples of these four styles. Managers may tend towards one of the styles, but they will generally adopt other styles when the situation demands. In fact, the situation in which a decision is taken has a considerable influence upon the style that is appropriate. Vroom and Jago (1988) tried to be more specific. Their work involves three main components: an analysis of decision styles, an analysis of decision situations and a procedure for linking styles and situations.

Vroom and Jago did not use the classification of management styles developed by Rowe, Boulgarides and McGrath. Instead, they developed their own classification based upon how autocratic or democratic a manager was:

- A **very autocratic** manager (A1) makes decisions entirely on their own using the information available.
- A **fairly autocratic** manager (A2) makes decisions on their own but will obtain information from subordinates.
- A **fairly consultative** manager (C1) discusses decisions with *individual* subordinates and will obtain their ideas. However, this manager will make the decision on their own and the decision may or may not incorporate the views of subordinates.
- A **very consultative** manager (C2) discusses decisions with *subordinates as a group*. However, the decision will be made by the manager on their own and it may or may not incorporate the views of subordinates.
- A **very democratic** manager (G2) is very group oriented. The group will play a major part in identifying the problem, diagnosing the situation, suggesting alternatives and choosing the final course of action. This manager accepts and implements the alternative chosen by the group.

When Vroom and Jago examined decision situations they identified eight important situational variables which are:

- the requirement for decision to be technically correct   (DQ)
- the importance of employee commitment   (DC)
- the adequacy of the leader's information   (LI)
- the structure of the problem   (DS)
- probability of employees' commitment to autocratic decision   (EC)
- degree to which employees' goals are congruent with those of the organisation   (EG)
- the probability that employees will disagree among themselves over the preferred alternative   (ED)
- the degree to which employees have enough information to make a good decision (EI)

Note: the abbreviations have been changed from Vroom and Jago's diagram in order to make it clear which factors relate to the decision (D), the leader (L) or the employee (E). Vroom and Jago simplified these characteristics into two levels: high or low. They were then able to draw up the algorithm shown in Figure 9.3 to identify the appropriate decision style.

Vroom and Jago's diagram is very elegant but it is probably too complex to be of much use to practising managers. Two very general conclusions may be that structured decisions and employee commitment may slightly favour autocratic styles.

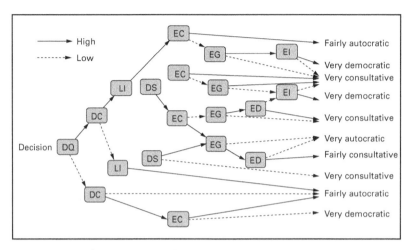

FIGURE 9.3 Vroom and Jago's decision-making algorithm

Often, differences in decision-making style boil down to whether decisions are made by an individual or a group. **Group decision-making** has a number of advantages:

- Groups have a *greater resources* such as a "pool" of knowledge and experience that can be brought to bear on any decision. They have a broader perspective and many minds have more processing power than a single mind.

- Interaction between group members may result in *synergy* where ideas are cross-fertilised to produce a better result.

- People are *more likely to support a decision* if they are involved in making it.

- Group decision-making serves as an important *communication channel*.

- Group decision-making serves important *"political" functions*.

Unfortunately, group decision-making also has a number of *disadvantages*:

- Groups usually work much more slowly than individuals.

- Decisions made by groups may be less optimal because of many compromises that are necessary to maintain group cohesion. At its worst a decision made by a group may simply represent the "lowest common denominator".

- Group decision-making may undermine managerial authority.

The style of decision-making is important – especially for the way that a decision is accepted by other people and its appropriateness to the situation. But the style of a decision does not give an adequate picture. It does not give much detailed guidance on the practical details of *how* to make a decision. Fortunately, details of how to make an ideal decision are set out by the rational decision paradigm which is described in the next section.

CRITICAL THINKING 9.2 *What's the use of Vroom and Jago's model?*

Vroom and Jago's model of decision-making style is very elegant and intellectually interesting. It has spawned a great deal of research and comment from academic thinkers. However, do the practical results justify all the research time, the trees pulped to make paper or the carbon dioxide emitted as researchers jet from conference to conference to discuss their findings. The model is simply too complex for practical situations.

It is hard to imagine managers learning Vroom and Jago's decision tree to the extent that they can use it spontaneously. It is even harder to imagine a manager adjourning a meeting convened to make an important decision in order to consult Vroom and Jago's diagram. It may be argued that the value of Vroom and Jago's model is less direct and that it has a great deal of benefit for management training. The evidence to support this is difficult to find.

A search of the PsychLit database for the past decade (2000–2010) did not reveal a single case where the performance of actual managers was improved by training based on the Vroom and Jago model. Some findings based on simulations with MBA students or on people's perceptions of *satisfaction* were located – but not on the *actual performance* of managers. One study (Duncan, LaFrance and Ginter, 2003) found that commanding generals in the American Civil War who made decisions in a way that is consistent with the Vroom-Yetton model of decision-making were more successful in achieving the objectives of their campaign. This is interesting but of marginal relevance. Clearly generals in the American Civil War (1861–65) were not using this decision model and neither had they attended any training courses based upon Vroom, Jago or Yetton's work.

9.3 The rational decision paradigm – decision-making in ideal circumstances

Most organisations are keen to make rational decisions. The rational decision paradigm sets out what they should do under ideal circumstances. The rational decision paradigm is sometimes called the **classical decision-making process** and **the rational comprehensive method**. It is illustrated in Figure 9.4.

Each of the stages as identified in the rational decision paradigm needs to be discussed in detail.

Detecting a problem

The most crucial step in good decision-making is to recognise that a decision needs to be made. It goes without saying that if the need for a decision is not identified then an appropriate choice of action cannot be taken. Most decisions stem from two main causes: a desire to exploit a new opportunity or a need to correct a problem.

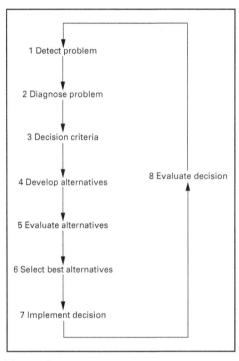

FIGURE 9.4 The rational decision paradigm

New opportunities often arise from technological developments such as biotechnology. They can also arise from sociological developments such as changes in the age distribution of the population or in social attitudes.

Problems are situations where there has been a failure to meet established goals. It is easy to dismiss such failures as minor blips which should go away of their own accord. It is easy, and often justifiable, to claim that a failure is the result of someone else's actions and should be resolved by them. Problems needing decisions arise from four main sources:

- **a disturbance** caused by unpredictable factors such as a sudden resignation by an existing employee, the interruption of supplies by bad weather or the discovery of theft and fraud

- **a decline in performance** such as increased levels of waste, poorer machine utilisation, higher expenses. Gradual, insidious declines often present the greatest difficulties because they are easier to rationalise, overlook or deny

- **deviation from plan** such as a delay in commissioning new equipment, failure to achieve planned market share, or even an overproduction of merchandise

- **competitive threats** such as new competitors, the expiry of patents or the development of substitution products

Diagnosing an opportunity or problem

Once an opportunity or problem has been recognised it must be *defined* and the nature of the problem *diagnosed*. Sometimes a problem is diagnosed at a very superficial level and a decision is made to treat the symptoms of the problem rather than its real cause. For example, a manager may conclude that a decline in sales is due to lack of effort by the sales force. He or she may then decide to retrain sales staff. However, the real cause of the problem may be that the product is out of date and competitors are offering products that are more market friendly.

A very simple approach to problem diagnosis is to ask, *"who is doing what to whom?"*. A rather more sophisticated method is to ask what, where, when, how, who, what and why? Less cryptically the questions are:

- *What* is the evidence that a problem really exists?
- *Where* does the problem appear to arise?
- *When* does the problem appear to arise?
- *How* urgent is the problem?
- *Who* is most involved with the problem?
- *What* factors (people, departments, organisations, processes) are related to the problem?
- *Why* did the problem occur?

When a problem has been diagnosed, it is always worth checking the analysis with people who are not involved in the situation and who will not share the same assumptions. This results in a more robust diagnosis. It is very important to communicate the problem definition to people involved in subsequent stages, otherwise they will be basing their efforts on implicit and slightly different assumptions. Chaos may ensue.

Establishing decision criteria

Establishing the criteria for a good decision is a vital stage of the decision-making process. It is often overlooked. Many people do not develop decision criteria until *after* alternative solutions have been identified. This has a big disadvantage. Decision criteria may then be distorted to favour one of the alternatives instead of being thought out in an objective way. Hence the decision may be subconsciously biased towards a faulty, subjective choice. Frequently used decision criteria are:

- financial costs or benefits
- physical resources needed
- human resources needed
- quantity (more production)
- quality (better products)
- certainty of desired outcome (risk)
- acceptability to others
- appropriate timescale
- reliability (e.g. low maintenance)
- compatibility with organisational culture and values

The combination of criteria used to decide between alternative solutions will depend on the exact nature of the problem. For example, an organisation deciding which photocopier to purchase may choose to base its decision upon cost, reliability, quantity (sheets per minute) and delivery time.

Once decision criteria have been established, their relative importance is assessed. For example, the weight given to the decision criteria for the photocopier might be: reliability 0.4, delivery time 0.3, quantity 0.2 and cost 0.1.

Developing alternatives

It is important to generate several alternative solutions so that the best one can be chosen. If the decision is important, special techniques may be used to produce alternatives. The main techniques are:

- **Employee suggestion schemes** encourage everyone in the organisation to produce new ideas. Many suggestion schemes are moribund and either produce no suggestions or only trivial ones. Good suggestion schemes are usually found in organisations which stress creativity and which give substantial rewards for good ideas.

- **Idea quotas** are used to ensure a steady flow of new proposals. Some companies require each employee to propose at least one improvement to quality, efficiency or service every month. Idea quotas need to be supported by a range of incentives and a commitment by management to implement a large number of the suggestions made.

- **Brainstorming** was a very popular method of generating ideas in the 1970s and 1980s and is still used today. A meeting of, say, six people would meet specifically to generate a large number of ideas. Every member is expected to provide new thoughts – no matter how zany or bizarre. The *number* of ideas generated is emphasised. Participants are expected to "freewheel" and build on the ideas of others in a spontaneous, uninhibited way. Criticism, sarcasm or judgemental comments are not allowed. Since written notes appear formal and may slow the process, brainstorming sessions are often recorded. Some people doubt the value of brainstorming. They point to findings from social psychologists which indicate that creativity is often a solitary process. The presence of other people, even in a brainstorming situation, tends to increase the quantity of routine rather than truly novel ideas. In group situations many people are reluctant to make radical suggestions because they fear the disapproval or ridicule of others.

- **The nominal group technique** attempts to overcome some of the difficulties that arise from group dynamics and is more controlled than brainstorming. Members first write down their individual ideas. During this stage they are not allowed to speak to other participants. Each member then presents one idea to the group. The ideas are not discussed but are merely summarised on a flip chart. In the final stage group members rate each alternative. They are not allowed to speak to each other during this process. Nominal groups are useful when complex, controversial decisions need to be made. They are also useful in situations where assertive members are likely to dominate a discussion. Computer versions of nominal groups in which members communicate by email can also be used. An added advantage of using email is that contributions can be made anonymously.

- **The Delphi technique** is similar to the nominal group technique. However, participants do not meet in person. Instead, participants write out their ideas, which are collated and fed back to the group in an anonymous form. Participants are asked to give revised estimates which, in turn, are again collated and fed back. The process is repeated until some kind of group consensus is achieved. Initially the Delphi technique used paper questionnaires but today it is more usual to use email.

Evaluating alternatives

The fifth stage of decision-making involves *collecting and collating relevant information*. For example, data concerning reliability, productivity, delivery time and cost of photocopiers could be obtained from rival manufacturers. The accuracy of the information is important. It makes sense to cross-check information from several sources. It would be better, for example, to cross-check the details given by photocopier manufacturers with information from organisations which have already purchased their photocopiers.

More complex decisions such as where to site a factory or whether to develop a new product will require a great deal of information – often more information than a human brain can store. Consequently computers and *management information systems* may be used to assemble, collate and present the information. Generally **management information systems** track four kinds of information:

Information systems
p 438

- **production data**, e.g. number of units produced, the number of clients processed, machine utilisation or levels of waste recovery
- **financial data** such as present and future cash flow, invoices outstanding, investments
- **commercial data** such as sales, stock levels and perhaps competitor activity
- **personnel data**, e.g. employee numbers, seniority, location and training

Management information systems usually produce routine, monthly or weekly, reports and only alert managers when events deviate from a plan (**exception reporting**). However, managers who are making major decisions are able to request specific reports which contain the information they need. Programmes which produce these specific reports are often called "decision support systems". Decision reports have a tighter focus than general reports and they will attempt to filter out routine and irrelevant information. Decision reports need to deliver high-quality information which is up to date and comprehensive. Further, the information needs to be presented in a way that is easily understood by the people who are making the decisions.

Many decisions are made against an uncertain background. The data used by decision support systems often contain estimates containing a margin of error. Decision support systems may therefore include a "sensitivity analysis" (sometimes called a "what if" analysis) that will take account of a range of possibilities. Typically, a sensitivity analysis consists of three sub-analyses: first, the analysis is performed on the best estimates available. This will be called the "central prediction". Second, an analysis using optimistic estimates, which assume everything goes well, is performed. Third, an analysis using pessimistic estimates, which assume that things go wrong, is performed. Sensitivity analyses are vital if a wrong decision could jeopardise the survival of an organisation or have other very serious consequences. They allow the decision-maker to see whether a decision could send the organisation out of business.

Evaluating alternatives is a particularly crucial stage of the rational decision paradigm and a number of methods have been devised to help managers. The main methods are:

- gut feelings
- heuristics
- PMI analysis
- decision matrices
- hat analysis

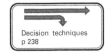

Decision techniques
p 238

Each of these methods is a very important aid in choosing the best alterative and they are considered in detail in the next main section (9.4).

Implementation

Even correct decisions are useless unless they are implemented. The first stage of implementation is to communicate the decision to those who need to take action. This is much easier if these people have previously participated in making the decision. One specific person should be made responsible for carrying a decision to fruition. Implementation is often a question of using the techniques of tactical and operational planning.

Tactical and operational
planning pp 101–105

Evaluation

The implementation process should be monitored to check whether a decision produces good results. Sometimes it may be necessary to adjust the way that the decision is implemented or it may be necessary to adjust the decision itself – in extreme circumstances it may even be necessary to abandon or reverse the decision in the light of subsequent events. The lessons learned during evaluation should be used to improve later decisions. The last disadvantage is very important. As long ago as 1957 the Nobel prizewinner Herbert Simon pointed out that people are not entirely rational. Their rationality is limited by their brainpower to store, manipulate and communicate with information. It is also limited by people's perceptions and emotions. In other words decision-making is limited by bounded rationality. Herbert Simon noted that managers tend to accept the first reasonable solution that occurs. This is called **satisficing** and it is very common. Satisficing means accepting a solution which meets minimum requirements. It is the opposite of **optimising** which is the acceptance of the solution that provides the best possible answer.

Ariel Rubinstein (1998, p.16) gives details of experiments which show how some decisions are not rational. They also shows how our limited memory, the sources of information we choose and working in groups puts boundaries on rational thinking when making decisions.

One consequence of bounded rationality is that decision-makers may try to simplify the situation and use "rules of thumb", called **heuristics**. Heuristics are simplifications and shortcuts which allow decisions to be made quickly without constantly stopping to ponder. Typical examples of heuristics are "never schedule activities for more than two-thirds of the

> ## CRITICAL THINKING 9.3 *What is wrong with the rational decision paradigm?*
>
> The rational decision paradigm is very logical and systematic. In theory it will produce the best possible decision. However it has a number of disadvantages:
>
> - It works best if the problem is clear and unambiguous. Further, it needs clear preferences which make it possible to order the criteria and then rank the alternatives upon the criteria.
> - It works best if the problem and the problem situation are fairly stable over time.
> - It is time-consuming.
> - It requires a lot of information which is assumed to be accurate, measurable and accepted by all.
> - It assumes that decision-makers are totally rational and that organisational politics do not impinge upon decisions.

time available" or "always allow a 20 per cent overrun on building projects". Gigerenzer and Selten (2002) cast an interesting light upon heuristics. They suggest that heuristics are a rational response to bounded rationality because they allow decision-makers to cope speedily with complex decisions. Further, they contend that heuristic rules often lead to better decisions than the rational decision-making paradigm.

The consequences of bounded rationality and other problems are discussed in a later section on the problems of decision-making.

9.4 Decision-making techniques

A large number of techniques have evolved to help managers make prompt and accurate decisions. The main methods are: gut feelings, heuristics, PNI analysis, decision matrices and thinking hats.

- **Gut feelings** are sometimes called **gut instincts**. They are usually vague feelings that something will turn out right or, perhaps, turn out wrong. They often arise from the brain subconsciously accessing memories of similar situations. They are also closely related to a person's values and beliefs. Gut feelings often have a high emotional content which originates from some of the primitive areas of the brain. Gut feelings are frequently encountered when a decision involves a high level of ambiguity. Many people can cite instances where their gut instinct led them to a good decision. This evidence is anecdotal and probably relies on selective memory of instances where successes are remembered and failures are forgotten. In fact, gut instinct probably has a slightly higher than chance probability of success. This may be due to a self-fulfilling prophecy where an emotional belief in a decision leads to greater effort and persistence which, in turn, leads to success. It would be a very rash manager who relied upon gut instinct to make major irreversible decisions.

- **Heuristics** are much better than gut instinct. They are simple rules based on experience. A classic heuristic is **the Pareto principle** (the 80/20 rule): 80 per cent of success is obtained from 20 per cent of activities – or, in this context, 20 per cent of the information will yield a decision that is 80 per cent accurate.

- **PNI analysis** is a very simple decision-making technique which can be used in decisions on whether or not to take up a single option. It involves constructing a table with three columns as shown in Figure 9.5. The positives, negatives and interesting aspects of the single option are inserted into the relevant columns. When the table is complete, a judgement is made as to whether the positives outweigh the negatives. If the difference is small, the entries in the "interesting" column are used as a tie-breaker.

- **Decision matrices** are a relatively sophisticated tool that involves five stages. First, criteria and their weights are arranged at the top of the matrix while alternative solutions are listed down the side. Figure 9.6 demonstrates how a decision matrix can be used to choose the best photocopier. The relevant criteria are: reliability (which, because of its importance, is given a weighting of .4); delivery time (weighting .3); quantity (sheets per minute, weighting .2) and cost. There are four potential photocopiers which in this example are labelled A, B, C, D. Second, using a nine-point scale, each photocopier is rated on each criterion. In the example, copier B is highly reliable and is given a rating of 9, while copier A is very fast and is also given a rating of 9. Third, the ratings are multiplied by the weight for each criteria. For example copier C has a rating of 3 for reliability which is weighted .4 and therefore they weighted reliability is 1.2 (3×1.2). Fourth, the weighted ratings, are added and the total entered in the final column. In this example, photocopier B is the best choice because it has the highest total ($6.0 = 3.6 + 0.9 + 1.4 + 0.1$).

The decision matrix is very useful: it makes clear that copier B is the best choice but it might have been rejected because it is expensive and the delivery time was poor. A less systematic decision process might have chosen the poorer photocopier C because it was cheap.

- **Hat analysis** is a metaphor inspired by Gilbert and Sullivan's operetta, *The Mikado*, in which Pooh-bah, the "Lord High Everything Else" (General Manager?) has many roles:

Positives	Negatives	Interesting

FIGURE 9.5: A simple PNI table

	Reliability (0.4)	Weighted reliability	Delivery (0.3)	Weighted delivery	Quantity (0.2)	Weighted quantity	Cost (0.1)	Weighted cost	TOTAL weights
Copier A	5	2.0	1	0.3	9	1.8	3	0.3	4.4
Copier B	9	3.6	3	0.9	7	1.4	1	0.1	6.0
Copier C	3	1.2	9	2.7	1	0.2	9	0.9	5.0
Copier D	1	0.4	7	2.1	3	0.6	5	0.5	3.6

FIGURE 9.6 Example of decision matrix

first Lord of the Treasury, Leader of the Opposition, Paymaster General, etc., etc. To avoid confusion about the role he was occupying at any one time he would wear a distinctive hat. In decision-making, hat analysis is useful in complex decisions that must be viewed from many perspectives. Separate members of the decision team are given various "hats" and are asked to evaluate alternative solutions according to the perspective of their hat. Sometimes, however, a single person, like Pooh-Bah, is asked to wear several hats in succession. There are several versions of this technique. For example, in one version there is the "white hat" who is responsible for examining data and gaps in knowledge; the "red hat" inspects any alternative using gut instinct and emotion; the "black hat" inspects possible solutions with a dark mien (pessimistic, cautious, defensive) etc. A more managerial focus uses hats based on PESTLE:

PESTLE p 96

– *Pink hat* examines alternatives from a political (both internal and external) perspective.
– *Emerald hat* views things from an economic perspective.
– *Silver hat* considers the sociological point of view.
– *Turquoise hat* is responsible for exploring technological issues.
– *Ebony hat* considers environmental issues.
– *Lavender hat* examines legal issues.

Hat analysis does not lead to a specific decision in a mechanical way – as do decision matrices. But it does ensure that most of the relevant factors are taken into account so that decision-makers can integrate them in an organic way.

CASE 9.4: *BodyCheck decides on its cardio equipment*

BodyCheck is the main gym in Glossop – a Pennine town between Manchester and Sheffield. It had a good number of exercise bikes, treadmills and cross-trainers that were in perfect working order and would last a good few years. However, the equipment was past its prime. Management recognised the need to make a decision about its replacement. External factors played a part in the decision: the economic climate was subdued so the gym would be able to negotiate a good price with suppliers and "state-of-the-art" machines would sustain the gym's premier status in the town. Replacing the cardio equipment involved a significant investment of over £120,000. It also required a subsequent decision about which machines to buy. But, how should that decision be made? Gut instinct was not appropriate – it was a major choice which could not be reversed with ease. Further, there are few, if any, heuristics concerning gym equipment. Gym equipment involves few political, economic, sociological, technological, etc. issues – therefore "hat analysis" was not appropriate. In this situation, a decision matrix is an ideal technique.

Soundings with other gyms and a scan of the trade press identified four possible suppliers: M, N, O and P. Staff at BodyCheck identified four decision criteria: safety, function (providing appropriate exercise), cost and reliability. Safety was identified as the most important criteria and it was weighted .5 so that no other factor could overwhelm it. Weightings given to other criteria were: function .3, reliability .1 and cost .1. These weights illustrate interesting points. *First*, some criteria are much more important than others – in this case safety is paramount. *Second*, it is better to limit the number of criteria, otherwise minor criteria have so little weight that they add more complications than their importance justifies. BodyCheck then rated suppliers on the criteria and multiplied the ratings by the weights to produce the decision matrix shown in Figure 9.7.

	Safety (0.5)	Weighted safety	Function (0.3)	Weighted function	Cost (1.0)	Weighted cost	Reliability (1.0)	Weighted reliability	TOTAL weights
Supplier M	9	4.5	6	1.8	8	0.8	9	0.9	8.0
Supplier N	9	4.5	9	2.7	6	0.6	9	0.9	8.7
Supplier O	8	4.0	8	2.4	6	0.6	6	0.6	7.6
Supplier P	9	4.5	8	2.4	5	0.5	7	0.7	8.1

FIGURE 9.7: BodyCheck's decision matrix

The decision matrix showed that the best equipment was provided by supplier N and the worst was provided by supplier O. The decision matrix also revealed some interesting aspects. All total scores were high and this indicates that generally cardio equipment is good. Although safety was strongly weighted, it played an insignificant role in the decision because the equipment of all suppliers was very safe. Further, cost on its own would not

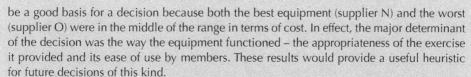

be a good basis for a decision because both the best equipment (supplier N) and the worst (supplier O) were in the middle of the range in terms of cost. In effect, the major determinant of the decision was the way the equipment functioned – the appropriateness of the exercise it provided and its ease of use by members. These results would provide a useful heuristic for future decisions of this kind.

The final aspect of BodyCheck's decision process was to evaluate its decision. The performance of the new cardio equipment was monitored and members were asked for their opinions. Fortunately, only fine-tuning of some aspects of the equipment was needed.

9.5 Common problems in decision-making

It is rare for the decision-making paradigm to be followed in its pure form. Sometimes certain phases will be omitted. Often it is necessary to cycle through the paradigm several times before the best decision is made. Frequently other factors intervene to create decision making faults. Managers may try to be logical but their efforts are bounded by the capacity of their thinking power and also by their emotions and attitude. Generally, there is more information than a human brain can process. Consequently people will choose to attend to some information and ignore other information. The way that people make this choice is often called "orienting response" and is a major influence on how decisions are made (see Weber and Johnson, 2009).

Another major issue is the way that people assess the probabilities of various outcomes. Recent research suggests that we process information in two ways. First, there is an automatic, intuitive and emotional process (gut feeling?). Second, there is a slower, analytical, deliberate and logical process. Kahneman (2003) suggests that the second system is used to supervise and correct wrong, intuitive, judgements made by the emotional system. There seem to be systematic errors in decisions about time and money: people are much more optimistic about the time they will have available in the future than the money that will be available. People also overestimate the difficulty of adjusting to lifetime changes such as moving home to somewhere 1,000 miles away, not achieving promotion, or receiving a big windfall. In general, people are not very good at predicting future events: the accuracy of political predictions made by pundits is not much better than chance (Tetlock, 2005). The decision-maker's characteristics can also influence the probabilities attached to future events. In many situations and contexts women are more risk averse than men – possibly because they are more aware of emotions, and emotional discomfort magnifies perceptions of risk. Risk-takers tend to have certain personality characteristics: they tend to be extrovert, stable and open people who have low scores on conscientiousness and agreeableness. Risk-taking is also associated with sensation-seeking. People who are good with basic mathematics and probability tend to have better judgement of probabilities (see Weber and Johnson, 2009 for references). Kahneman and Klein (2010) disagree about the use of gut feelings when making decisions but, in most circumstances, relying on "gut feelings" to make important choices is very dangerous. Kahneman and Renshon (2007) explain that in conflict situations there are systematic distortions of decision-making which mean that the hawks (the hardliners) usually win - often with disastrous consequences!

The list of individual findings seems endless and is of doubtful use for individuals with bounded rationality. Fortunately, a more useful list of common errors in decision-making have evolved over the decades. They are: procrastination, anchoring, escalation of commitment, groupthink and communication failure.

Procrastination

Procrastination is the tendency to delay decisions without a valid reason. It is sometimes called dithering and is personified as the "thief of time". Procrastination usually results in indecisiveness and may make a problem more difficult because it has extra time to grow. Procrastination often arises from a fear of failure. It is most prevalent in organisations with a "blame culture" where avoiding mistakes is more important than achieving success. Probably the most effective way of overcoming procrastination is to divide a decision into smaller stages and to set a deadline for the completion of each smaller stage.

Avoiding procrastination does not mean that decisions must be rushed. It means that *unnecessary* delays should be avoided. Impulsive decisions are as bad as delayed ones. In most circumstances it is appropriate to allow time to "sleep" on a decision so that it can be subjected to a reasonable period of reflective thought. Procrastination only arises when a decision is delayed for several days without the prospect of new information.

Anchoring

Anchoring refers to a tendency by decision-makers to give undue importance to information that is received early. It is sometimes called the "primacy effect". Early information tends to act as the standard by which other information is assessed. If later information is contradictory it will tend to be ignored or dismissed. Unfortunately, early information is often inaccurate because it was assembled in a hurry, without the time to perform cross-checks to ensure that it is comprehensive.

Escalation of commitment

A decision may be made on the basis of early information; but as more facts emerge the original decision becomes untenable. By this time a decision-maker may have invested considerable time, effort and prestige in the original decision. To abandon it may appear to be a waste of past commitment and disloyal to their advisers. They may feel that abandoning the original decision would cause them loss of face. Consequently, they may become more and more determined to commit resources to ensuring the success of their initial decision. Up to a point, this may be justified. If a little extra effort is able to produce success then it is reasonable to give a little extra effort. The problem is that a little extra effort may not achieve success – it may require just a little more effort and so on – ad infinitum! There comes a point where it is necessary to cut one's losses and follow another course of action. Some of the worst decisions in history have been the result of the escalation of commitment. In the 1970s America escalated its commitment to the Vietnam war long after it was apparent that the initial decision was flawed. Many government projects have been continued to the point of absurdity because politicians are reluctant to admit mistakes and cut taxpayer's losses. Generally, it is better to avoid these situations by following the example of stock market investors and setting a "stoploss" – a clear point at which they will sell their investment and accept whatever losses they may have incurred.

Groupthink

Participative decision-making has many advantages. A wider range of knowledge or experience and the synergy between members may produce ideas of better quality. However, participative decision-making has a number of disadvantages: it takes extra time, dominant members may distort discussions and the goals of individuals may detract from the goals of the organisation. A further problem with participative decision making is the phenomena of **groupthink**.

Groupthink is a mentality among members of a decision team to suppress their own disbelief in order to show solidarity and maintain agreement at any cost. Members suspend their critical judgements, which could lead to a better decision. Groupthink is particularly prevalent in closely knit groups, whose members come from similar backgrounds and who share similar goals. It is also prevalent in groups that have a high regard for each other. Groupthink is partly produced by the desire to conform. Dissenting members may suspend their personal judgement in favour of what they see as the consensus of the group. Unfortunately, other members may be doing the same. An *illusion* of agreement is created. Those who question this apparent agreement may be ridiculed or have their loyalty questioned. Groupthink often impairs a group's ability to generate a wide range of alternatives and to evaluate them effectively. Many disastrous political decisions such as the Watergate cover-up, the Bay of Pigs invasion and the 1986 *Challenger* launch disaster have been attributed to the negative influence of groupthink.

The effects of groupthink can be so catastrophic that a number of countermeasures have been devised Some organisations only take major decisions after appointing a **devil's advocate** who challenges assumptions and assertions. This forces decision-makers to consider a wider range of solutions. A similar technique is the use of **multiple advocates** where individuals are charged with arguing minority and dissenting viewpoints. Multiple advocacy is used by several governments to ensure that decisions are well argued and take a number of different perspectives into account.

Klein (see Kahneman and Klein, 2010) suggests that organisations should hold a **premortem** before it takes an important decision. Before an important project starts, managers should say "we are looking into a crystal ball and this project has failed; it's a fiasco. Now, everybody, take two minutes and write down the reasons why you think the project failed". Premortums are easy to conduct and they are good at identifying potential problems. They rarely cause decisions to be abandoned but implementation can be "tweaked" in beneficial ways. A premortum is a low-cost, high-payoff management technique.

Communication failure

The final fault in decision-making is failure of communication. It is obvious that a decision needs to be communicated to those involved in its implementation. It is slightly less obvious that it should also be communicated to those, such as suppliers, customers and stakeholders, who will also be affected by the decision. Communication should not be confined to the actual decision. The need, the diagnosis and the range of alternatives underlying the decision must be explained. Particular effort is needed to explain the advantages and the disadvantages of the chosen alternative.

9.6 Decision toolkit

Toolkit

- Do not take decisions by default. Even if nothing is happening or things are going well, decisions may still be needed. Monitor external environment for impending events.

- Clarify and check the main factors involved. Ask "who", "what", "why", "where", "when" and "how" questions. Do not accept the facts as stated to you. Reframe them by looking at then from the other way round.

- Limit risk to a level that your organisation can survive if things go badly.

- If a decision is easily reversed do not procrastinate. Make it quickly.

- Establish standards and measures that you can later use to evaluate important decisions.

- Be creative in producing a number of alternative decisions (e.g. brainstorm).

- If a decision is important, evaluate alternatives using PNI analysis, decision matrices or "hat analysis".

- Communicate decisions extensively.

- Evaluate important decisions against criteria set earlier.

- Avoid groupthink and escalation of commitment.

Activities and further study

Essay plans

Produce essay plans for the following topics:

1 Why do people make bad decisions?
2 How do decisions differ from each other?
3 What different decision-making styles can managers adopt?
4 Is one decision style better than another?
5 What techniques and strategies would you use to ensure that decisions are properly implemented?

Web activities

1 Use the Internet to obtain information about the following decision-making errors. For each error write two sentences about (a) what the error is, (b) why it is important and (c) an example:

- availability heuristic
- base rate fallacy
- loss aversion
- peak-end rule
- representativeness heuristic
- simulation heuristic
- status quo bias

2 Use the Web and other sources to find out about the phenomenon of "Risky shift".
3 Access the following website: http://www.mindtools.com/pages/article/newTED_00.htm. It gives details of the following decision-making tools:

- Pareto analysis
- paired comparison analysis
- grid analysis
- decision trees

- PMI (plus and minus implications)
- six hats analysis

Which tool do you think would be most helpful in making (a) simple, easily reversed decisions and (b) complex decisions with expensive implications?

Experiential activities

1 Think of three managers (or other people you know well) and try to identify their decision-making style. Evaluate their success as decision-makers and summarise their impact on you and others affected by their decisions.

2 Analyse three decisions you have made in the last year. Identify ways that your decision-making process could be improved.

3 Identify an important decision (such as your choice of course options for next year). Perform a grid analysis to establish the best solution to the problem.

Recommended reading

1 Kahneman, E. and Renshon, J. (2007) "Why hawks win", *Foreign Policy*, 158, 34–39. A readable but very informative article by a Nobel prizewinner, which explains why hardliners often influence decision-makers to make a wrong decision.

2 Kahneman, E. and Klein, G. (2010) "When can you trust your gut?", *McKinsey Quarterly*, 0047 5394, issue 2. An easy but an unmissable read where the role intuition should play in decision-making is debated by two top experts.

3 Clydesdale, G. and Tan, J. (2009) "Preparing students for front-line management: non-routine day-to-day decisions", *Journal of European Industrial Training*, **33**(7), 594–613. An article comprising criticisms of the way that decision-making is taught: inappropriate emphasis on models based on physics and too much emphasis on strategy. Highly recommended.

4 Rubinstein, A. (1998) *Modelling Bounded Rationality*, London: MIT Press. This book is freely downloadable. Do not attempt to read all of it. Read section 1.4 (pp. 16–21) which gives excellent evidence that human decision-making is not entirely rational.

5 Chung, J.O.Y., Cohen, J.R. and Monroe, G.S. (2008) "The effect on mood on auditors' inventory valuation decisions", *Auditing: A Journal of Practice & Theory*, **27**(2), 137–159. An empirical example of subjective factors influencing supposedly objective decisions. Do not get bogged down in statistics – skip complicated tables. There are lots of references. This is a good example of reporting empirical studies.

Chapter TEN

Budgeting

Chapter contents

❖ LEARNING OBJECTIVES

After reading this chapter you will be able to understand the importance of budgeting. You will be able to identify the main types of budget and have some understanding of the budgeting process. You will also be able to understand management ratios that are in common use. In particular you will be able to:

❖ **define** a budget and explain the key terms within it

❖ **list** four resources that usually need budgets

❖ **explain briefly** four main types of cash budgets

❖ **draw** and **explain** a cash graph

❖ **explain** the following aspects of budgeting:

  – "top-down" and "bottom up" budgeting

  – zero-based budgeting

  – activity-based costing and budgeting

❖ **explain** the formulae and use of nine different profitability ratios

❖ **explain** the concepts of gearing, leverage and debt ratio

❖ **explain** the formulae and use of four different debt ratios

❖ **explain** the formulae and use of two different operational ratios

It is rare to open the financial pages of a newspaper without seeing at least one article berating some organisational misfortune that was caused by poor budgeting. Case 12.1 illustrates poor budgeting at the BBC.

CASE 12.1: *Bad budgeting at the Beeb*

The BBC is the world's largest broadcasting corporation and has an income of almost £5 billion, raised, compulsorily, from every house in the UK that has a television or radio. You might therefore think that it would have developed a robust system of budgets that would help it use the money wisely. Dream on! In 2010 the National Audit Office investigated the BBC's budgetary system for managing. It found that:

■ There was no cost–benefit analysis of the programming options open to the BBC.

■ It did not have a clear view of the total budget for the coverage of individual events because it has separate budgets for different media, i.e. radio, television and Internet coverage. Further, the fees of some celebrities were hidden among other long-term contracts.

■ It did not compare its costs of covering major sporting and music events with the costs incurred by other broadcasters.

The BBC is not alone in having difficulty with its budgeting process. The government itself has encountered problems – especially in the way that it budgets for major IT projects. A controversial plan to computerise all National Health Service (NHS) patients' records had an original budget of £2.3 billion but the actual cost was in excess of £12.7 billion – a budget overrun in excess of £10 *billion!* Similarly, an IT project to set up a National Offender Management Information System shot up from £2 to £4 million in 2004 to £690 million in 2008 – even though the final system was not as good as the system planned at the start. Further, Fujitsu won a £146 million contract to provide a system for magistrate's courts. Eventually, the system was expected to cost in excess of £500 million – a 352 per cent budget overrun.

Budget overruns also occur in private industry and commerce. However, they are less visible because private organisations can use commercial secrecy to hide them. Budget overruns in government and public corporations have to be paid for or by a taxpayer or licence payer. Budget overruns in private industry or commerce have to be paid for by shareholders (including charities and pension funds). Sometimes bad budgets cause organisations to close down, with the loss of many jobs.

Clearly, budgeting is a vital management process which involves all managers in an organisation. Superficially, similar activities are performed by the finance function. The finance function will help individual managers produce their departmental budgets by providing information and expertise. It then collates individual departmental budgets into a master budget for the whole organisation. However, as Chapter 17 explains, the work of the finance function is more technical and

The finance function
p 409

involves other activities such as issuing stocks and bonds, producing financial reports for investors and ensuring that regulations are followed. It is *helpful* if individual managers have some understanding of these more specialised activities. However, it is *essential* that individual managers can budget the activities of their own departments.

12.1 Definition and concept of budgeting

Distributing an organisation's resources effectively, planning their use carefully and making sure that they are not wasted are vital to adding value. These activities are usually called budgeting. Budgeting may be defined as:

> A single-use, numerical and time-limited plan that commits resources to a project or activity.

This definition has four components:

- **Budgets are plans for future actions.** They are *single-use* plans to meet a situation at a given time – it is highly unlikely that exactly the same plan will ever be used again. Budgets are undoubtedly plans, so Fayol was technically wrong to make budgeting a separate management process. Nevertheless, treating budgets separately has practical advantages: it divides a very large process into two smaller, more manageable, parts and the division emphasises the importance of plans involving money.

Plans and single–use plans p 104

- **Budgets always involve numbers.** This gives greater precision and enables progress to be tracked and controlled with greater accuracy.

- **Budgets have a fixed time interval** – usually a year but other time intervals of one month, three months, six months or two years are quite common. Sometimes, budgets are automatically refreshed and extended about halfway through their time interval. These are called **"rolling" budgets**.

- **Budgets commit resources to specific projects** (such as an advertising campaign) or specific classes of activity (such as travelling expenses).

Nearly always, responsibility for a budget is formally allocated to one person – a **budget holder**. For example, the budget for a whole unit will be the responsibility of the general manager. He or she may then delegate part of the budget to, say, the production director or the sales director, etc. Sometimes budget holders are called **responsibility centres**. In the context of management the word " budget" does not carry the negative connotations of meanness and skimping that are associated with common phrases such as "budget holiday" or "budget jeans". Quite the contrary, some budgets (such as the chairperson's entertainment budget!) might be very generous indeed. Budgets are not just simply plans, *they are also control devices*. Actual expenditure is compared to a budget and remedial action is taken if there

Controlling p 248

is a large "variance". For example, a consultancy organisation will usually compare its budget income against its actual income on a monthly basis. It will take action if the actual income is too low.

Budgets have five main uses. *Planning* the availability and use of money as well as *controlling* the availability and use of money have been noted already. Third, budgets help *co-ordinate* different parts of the organisation. For example, when the production budget and the marketing budget are integrated into a master budget, the activities of the two parts of the organisation will be syncronised. Fourth, budgets *enable managers to delegate many activities* while knowing that they will be performed in a way that is consistent with wider objectives. Fifth, good budgets can also *speed up decision-making*. By referring to the appropriate budget, many decisions can be made without the delay involved in referring them to senior levels.

CASE 12.2: *Banks' advice on budgeting*

Banks are particularly keen to offer advice to new business start-ups. It may mean their customer will grow to use more banking services and pay more charges in the future. New businesses face many challenges in their first year of trading. The main reason so many fail is that they do not budget accurately, so most banks focus on this aspect. Good advice on budgeting may also avoid the heartbreak of a new company becoming bankrupt. A good budget forecasts costs, revenues, sales and how the business is to be financed.

A clear budget is vital. It should be derived from business objectives, and should identify what money is needed, why and where it will come from. Clear, detailed budgets targets help give security by:

- ensuring money is spent on the right things

- identifying loss-making areas

- identifying the need for remedial action if, for example, revenue is not meeting target or if costs are rising

A budget also establishes expected cash flow so the business can assess if its income will cover its expenditure. Difficulty with cash flow is common for new businesses because it takes time to build up a business and win new customers. Good budgeting systems can help manage the business by seeing if customers are slow in settling accounts. Managing cash flow may ultimately keep the business afloat.

12.2 Non-financial budgets

Budgets are used to plan, commit and control many different kinds of resources such as operations, materials, human resources and information. But, above all, they are used to plan, commit and control money and finances. The following section outlines that group of financial budgets. First, this section describes non-financial budgets, in order to emphasise the fact that financial budgets are only one resource that must be planned, allocated and co-ordinated. The main types of **non-financial budgets** concern operations, human resources (HR), materials and intellectual capital.

- **Operations (production) budgets** are detailed plans for the output of production units. They are necessary to ensure an organisation's output matches its sales. Short-term production budgets are often called **production schedules**. Some organisations draw up budgets for new products. For example, major drug companies will try to ensure that they introduce several new drugs to the market every year. This is often called a product pipeline.

- A **materials budget** is a plan for acquiring and storing parts or supplies which need to be available to the production department. It is closely linked with supply chain management.

- **HR budgets** are detailed plans for employees who will be needed to fill various jobs. An HR budget will specify the skills and qualifications that are required by various groups of people. It will need to take into account the likelihood of employees quitting the organisation and the time-lags involved in training their replacements. A specialised HR budget is called a **management succession plan**.

- Some advanced organisations produce budgets for **intellectual capital**. For example, software developers draw up a plan to ensure a steady flow of intellectual property such as patents and new ideas. They may also try to quantify and systematically develop the value of the knowledge possessed by its employees, the value of its brands and the worth of its relationships with customers and suppliers. This is closely linked to knowledge management. It may involve budgets to ensure the intellectual capital of the organisation increases every year.

12.3 Types of financial budget

Money is a vital resource in any organisation. Money is the means by which resources and products are exchanged with the outside world. It is also the means by which the transformation process within the organisation is evaluated. This chapter focuses on the budgets and the way they affect *all* managers – *departmental budgets*. Managing money usually involves the finance function. *Financial budgets* attempt to predict and regulate the flows of money *to* and *from* an organisation, and they are generally constructed by financial experts.

Departmental budgets focus on the flows of money within an organisation and they are generally constructed, and observed, by all types and levels of manager. There are two main types of departmental budget: depertmental expenditure body and departmental capital budgets.

Departmental expenditure budgets

An expenditure budget is a plan showing the money a department can expect to pay out. At the start of a financial period, departmental managers predict what they need to spend.

Expenditure will be detailed into various cost headings, such as labour costs, reorganisation costs, sales, materials, etc. In a large organisation the expense budget will show the anticipated and actual expenses for each responsibility centre such as production unit 1, production unit 2, sales, administration, etc. Departments usually have clearly defined expenditure budgets covering the next 12 months. They may have outline expenditure budgets for future years. Expense budgets will probably specify the outgoings for each month and the actual outgoings will be compared closely with the plan. If actual expenditure exceeds the budget, action, such as cutting costs, will be taken to eliminate the variance. If expenditure is less than the departmental budget, most managers will go on a spending spree to use up their budget so that it will not be cut in future years. The major expenditure budget headings are:

- salaries and benefits
- rent
- utilities (heating, light, power and water)
- business travel
- maintenance of equipment and building
- communications (post, telephone, Internet)
- equipment

Departmental capital budget

The capital budget concerns the investment a department can make in equipment and new buildings. Ideally, these investments are made according to a predetermined plan that anticipates future needs and they will be scheduled in a way that maximises the return on the investment. Usually, an organisation will determine the amount of money it can invest in new building or equipment. It will then ask departments for suggestions on how this money can be invested. The most promising suggestions will be chosen after thorough scrutiny to see if they are practical, related to the organisation's strategy and whether they are likely to give a good return on the investment. Departmental suggestions that survive this scrutiny and which fit within the money available for the organisation as a whole will be given a departmental capital budget. Sometimes, capital expenditure is less controlled. Breakdowns of existing machines, new legislation or unexpected technological developments may force emergency capital expenditure.

12.4 The budgeting process

Departmental budgets (or project budgets) can be prepared in two main ways: a traditional "top-down method" and a more recent "bottom-up method". The **top-down** method of preparing budgets follows the formal lines of authority described by Weber. Senior management set overall budgets which are in line with the organisation's strategy. These overall budgets set out the broad parameters for each department (or project). Departmental managers then prepare more

Weber p 73

detailed budgets, within these limits, for each of their sections – and so on until there are detailed budgets for small units of activity or workers. The top-down method has the big advantage of following established lines of command and it usually produces an integrated set of budgets for the whole organisation. The top down approach to budgeting may use "standard costings" which have been in use since the Industrial Revolution and have been refined in the USA (Fleischman and Tyson, 1998 – a passable read). Standard costs are estimates of outlays such as materials, wages, fuel, etc. needed to produce routine components or services. Standard costs also include an element for overheads. The use of standard costs allows management to control expenditure by identifying situations that cost too much or opportunities where extra value can be added.

Top-down budgeting may appear autocratic and may alienate junior staff. **Bottom-up budgets** aim to remove these disadvantages. Junior members of staff are asked to anticipate their area's income, expenditure and capital needs. Senior management review the departmental budgets to identify crucial factors that will influence or limit departmental budgets. These factors are often termed **principal budget factors** or **limiting factors** or **key factors**. They are factors the organisation cannot change and involve raw materials, labour, finance or legislation. Finally, senior management then integrate all information into a **master budget** which is consistent with the organisation's strategy. The bottom-up approach empowers junior staff. It means that they are more likely to take ownership of the budgets and therefore they are likely to apply them more effectively (see Churchill, 1984).

Most departmental (or project) budgets are now produced by a cyclical process which starts with submissions from their main areas of business activity such as sales or operations, etc. Departmental budgets are synthesised into an initial master budget. The initial master budget is almost certain to be too large and is likely to be sent back to the original departments (or project leaders) with a request to decrease costs. Several iterations may be necessary before departmental budgets and the master budgets converge. This process may seem tedious but it does ensure that many people are involved, and therefore committed, to the final master budget.

Perhaps the easiest way to prepare a departmental (or project) budget is to take last year's budget, and increase each entry by a few per cent to take account of inflation and make other adjustments to accommodate foreseeable changes. This method tends to produce budgets that grow needlessly each year irrespective of needs. **Zero-based budgeting** (Pyhrr, 1973) was introduced to counteract this tendency and it has been adopted by most major organisations because it deploys resources more efficiently than simply adapting last year's budget. In zero-based budgeting all expenditure has to be justified as if it were a new project or activity. The assumption is that any expenditure is unnecessary *unless* a positive case can be made. This means that all activities and the priorities allotted to them are reconsidered at the start of each budgeting cycle. Zero-based budgeting is too radical and takes too much time to apply simultaneously to all budgets within an organisation. Recent history suggests that zero-based budgeting is very susceptible to political influence and pressures. In recent years it has fallen into disuse, at least outside the public sector. Nevertheless, used selectively it does restrain expanding budgets and it reduces the "entitlement mentality" towards budget increases.

Traditionally, budgets were produced on a departmental basis with separate budgets for the purchasing department, the HR department, the production department, and so on.

Since several different responsibility centres will contribute to a given item of production it is difficult to establish the costs or a budget for specific products or services. **Activity-based costing** *and* **budgeting (ABC)** was developed to overcome this difficulty (see Geri and Ronen, 2005 – a passable read; Pare, 1993).

Activity-based costing traces all the costs incurred in generating and delivering a specific product or service. Armed with an accurate picture of the profits generated by a product, managers can expand production of those goods or services that add greatest value. Alternatively, they can try to increase profits by driving down the costs of unprofitable services. In some cases activity-based budgets and costings can point to products or services that should be discontinued. For example, it may be that it costs £20 to buy raw materials and manufacture a product that sells for £40 – a healthy profit of 100 per cent. However, activity-based costing might reveal that the product also requires an average of £10 advertising, £4 storage and £9 for customers' support. These additional costs are normally spread among departmental budgets so that the organisation is unaware that it is making a loss of £3 on each sale. Hoozee and Werner (2010) believe that worker participation and appropriate leadership style are an indispensable element of designing activity-based costing systems (ABCs).

CRITICAL THINKING 12.1 *The problems of budget guesstimates?*

A finished budget, replete with columns of figures, looks authoritative and objective. However, budgets are often political and contain hidden assumptions. When preparing and approving budgets it is often valuable to list such assumptions and to question them. Further, many of the figures contained in a budget are estimates that can sometimes go wildly wrong because of political factors and other "unforeseeable" events. For example, Royal Dutch Shell and its Japanese partners experienced a massive £5.1 billion budget overrun in its project to develop an oilfield near the Russian island of Sakhalin in the Bering Sea, north of Japan. Some of the overrun was caused by Shell and its partners. However, a large proportion of the overrun was the result of political delays and harassment by the Kremlin which was keen to dominate negotiations over ownership of the development. Other expenses were added by the need to re-route a pipeline after environmental groups protested that the original route would damage the breeding grounds of a rare species of whale. Sometimes such factors can be anticipated by making comparisons with budgets from competitors – they may have experienced similar issues. Further, it is worthwhile considering previous budgets in the same organisation. For example, in the building industry there is a chronic tendency for projects to overrun budgets by 100 per cent. For example, the budget in 1997 for conversions to make Holyrood House suitable for the Scottish Parliament was £40 million. The final cost, in 2004, was £431 million – a *1000 per cent* budget overrun.

It is prudent to take such factors into account when preparing budgets (especially budgets for buildings). Experienced managers are aware that budgets are sometimes

> guesstimates. They therefore take a defensive stance by overestimating costs. This conservative approach is likely to give them room for manoeuvre. However, if all managers take this approach a lot of money is reserved unnecessarily and the organisation will not be able to deploy its resources to maximum effect. A number of worthy projects will not go ahead because managers have added a safety margin to their own budgets.

12.5 Management ratios

Financial budgets and outcome figures are usually designed to control individual activities (or projects) at an operational level. Ratios are very useful summaries of aspects of efficiency – but it must be remembered that they are summaries that may hide important details. A list of ratios does not make exciting reading, but this is no reason to ignore them. The following sub-sections describe ratios, of which there are two main types, most frequently used by managers in general describe ratios of which there are two main types, most frequently used by managers in general: labour productivity ratios and operational ratios. There are many other financial ratios that are used by specialists in the finance and accounting function. It is often helpful if managers in general are familiar with them.

Financial ratios p 430

Labour productivity ratios

Labour productivity is the effectiveness with which the efforts of employees are harnessed. There are two main indices: value added per employee and labour productivity. *Value added per employee* yields a monetary figure indicating how much each employee is adds. It is:

$$\text{Value added per employee} = \frac{\text{Net profit}}{\text{Number of employees}}$$

Labour productivity gives a percentage value of how much is added. It is useful because it can be compared with other percentage indicators. It is calculated by the formula:

$$\text{Labour productivity} = \frac{\text{Gross profit}}{\text{Labour costs}}$$

Usually indices of labour productivity are considered alongside indices of return on capital because employees who have lots of capital and equipment at their disposal *should* be expected to be more productive.

CRITICAL THINKING 12.2 *Budget games*

Budgets are supposed to be objective and rational plans for deploying organisational resources – especially financial resources. However, it is quite rare for this to be 100 per cent true. People play budget games. Perhaps the four most common budget games are legacy building, empire building, budget circumvention and "back scratching".

■ The budget game *legacy building* is played by powerful people who want a memorial. They persuade their organisation to divert resources to a charitable institution, or other body, which bears their name, or the name of a cherished one. A classic example was the British magnate and MP, William Greenwood. Many years ago he convinced his cotton company to pay for a research institute, the Shirley Institute in Didsbury, Manchester, on condition that it be named after his daughter, Shirley. Greenwood's company, and the jobs it provided, no longer exist but the work of the Shirley Institute lives on in the Tog Ratings that describe the heat retention of gloves, duvet or anoraks! Powerful people often pre-empt organisational resources to fund a memorial in the form of a building named after them. Examples can be seen in most universities. Most vice-chancellors have an *edifice complex*: they know a new building will be a permanent legacy – unlike an improved education received by students working in a better equipped existing laboratory.

■ The budget game *empire building* is also played by powerful people but also by those who aspire to power. Empire builders manipulate themselves into positions where they hold key information and act as "gatekeepers". By restricting or enhancing the information in a selective way, gatekeepers divert budgets from rational deployment towards that which unnecessarily expands their own area of responsibility. This ploy has the useful function of denying resources to competitors.

■ The game of *budget circumvention* is played by experienced managers at all levels. They know how to get around budget rules. They craftily bring forward certain items of expenditure or income while delaying others. Budget limits can be circumvented by dividing up a large purchase (which would need to be approved by higher authority) into several smaller components and then sanctioning a series of smaller invoices, not needing approval.

■ The full title of the fourth budget game is "*you scratch my back and I'll scratch yours*". It is a non-zero sum team game ubiquitously played at junior management levels. It is also rife at middle management levels. Its simplest form is seen where several junior managers direct similar production lines. One, through circumstances beyond his control, is unlikely to make his budget targets and will be "punished". Another, by happy chance is likely to exceed her targets and is likely to be "rewarded" with higher targets in the next budget round. Neither is stupid. She lends him machines or cedes him priority for

▶

the best jobs – knowing that in a month or two the position is likely to be reversed.

A variation is played by managers who control activities in a production sequence. For example, in banking, one manager may sell a service, the next may process the applications and a third manager may be responsible for delivering the service. If the latter seems to be falling behind their budget, it is highly likely that they contact their comrades. There is a good chance that their comrades agree to trim their activities – knowing that within days the tables may be turned. Back scratching also occurs at middle management levels – especially when budgets are being constructed. One manager may support another's budget "easing" on the basis that their budget may need "easing" next year. The legendary Davy Crockett used the term **logrolling** to mean the same thing. Logrolling is a metaphor of a North American sport where pairs of contestants need to move a floating log from one bank of an icy river to the other bank. It is to the pair's mutual advantage to move their feet in synchrony! Classical managers refer to "back scratching" and "logrolling" as "quid pro quo". It amounts to the same thing!

Seasoned managers know these and many other budget games. They take pains to ensure auditors, accountants and management information systems find it difficult to detect these activities. Budget games mean that any budgetary system is, at best, only 90 per cent accurate. It is wise to accept the imperfection in a tolerant way. Generally, budget games are used to overcome obstacles and inevitable flaws. They help the organisation provided they are played within reasonable limits. Intolerance leads to inflexibility, and may drive budget games underground where they can grow to an unacceptable level and endanger the organisation.

Operational ratios

Operational ratios try to gauge how actively a department or organisation is using its assets. The main operational ratios are the activity ratio and the asset turnover ratio.

The **activity ratio** is sometimes called the "inventory turnover ratio". It is an index of how frequently completed goods or services are replenished ("turned over"). The formula is:

$$\text{Activity ratio} = \frac{\text{Sales turnover}}{\text{Average inventory}}$$

Usually the average inventory is obtained by combining the level of stocks at the start and end of the accounting period and dividing by two. A company that reports a yearly activity ratio of 1 is extremely poor since, on average, finished items languish on shelves a full year before they are sold. In general, a high activity ratio is good.

The **asset turnover ratio** shows how effectively an organisation is using its assets to generate sales. It is calculated by dividing sales revenue by total assets. The formula is:

$$\text{Asset turnver} = \frac{\text{Sales}}{\text{Total assets}}$$

A high figure indicates that the organisation is using assets in an intensive way (Brigham, 1985). However, there are substantial differences between industries. Low-technology operations often yield a high asset turnover because they are labour intensive rather than capital intensive.

Balanced scorecard
p 268

The importance of management ratios in understanding management and managers was emphasised at the start of this section. However, it is equally important to remember that other aspects must be taken into account when arriving at a balanced assessment of an organisation. Taking some kind of corporate action solely on the basis of a collection of ratios is an accident waiting to happen. It is important to draw up a **balanced scorecard** that is made up of both financial and non-financial indicators. Managers often have the motivation and the means to distort and thwart the budgeting process (see Critical thinking 12.2). A safeguard against these aberrations (fraud) is to employ **auditors**. Auditors must be independent of the budgets they examine. They should have no family relations in the unit they are auditing, or any commercial interest in it. External auditors from another organisation, such as an accountancy firm are best, but a great deal of money can be saved by using internal auditors if their independence is guaranteed.

CRITICAL THINKING 12.3 *Disadvantages of budgeting*

Budgets are essential to good management and all managers will need to master the art of preparing and operating a range of budgets and management ratios. However, managers must also be aware of the disadvantages. Three particular disadvantages are costs, manipulation and restricted view:

- Good budgets take a *long time to prepare* and can be very *costly* – especially if the budget is zero based. The budget for a medium-sized department can easily consume four weeks of a manager's time which she or he could be spending on transforming resources rather than on paperwork. Budgets should not cost more than the benefits they bring.

- Unwise implementation of a budget can also lead to *manipulation*. If a manager has an unspent proportion of a budget at the end of an accounting period, there is a strong temptation to spend the residue on unessential purchases in order to make sure that the budget is not cut in future years.

> - Finally, budgets have the disadvantage that they might produce *tunnel vision* or *rigidity* and become an end in themselves. In fact, budgets never account for more than 80 per cent of an organisation's activities. They are a tool to help achieve goals rather than goals in themselves. Budgets should focus on organisational objectives rather than the costs of individual items.

CASE 12.3: *How budgeting helps First Luggage*

Gideon Kasfiner launched First Luggage, a door-to-door luggage collection and delivery service, in 2004. The business now employs nine people and turns over £2 million a year. Here Gideon explains how financial planning has helped him grow his business in a controlled way.

Annual and monthly timetable

"I start doing my annual budgets three months before the year end. I look at the current year and see whether we are going to increase sales, and if we are how it's going to increase our costs, and so on. My accountant actually sets the budgets though, from the figures I give. Then, every month, I sit down with my management accounts. I look at my actual income and expenditure, compare them with my projections and look at the variance. I can see under every budgetary heading where things have gone up or down and I can make appropriate decisions.

So, for example, we may have budgeted sales of £200 000 for one month but only made £170 000. I might, for example, look at the marketing budget and do some more advertising. I might take a service out where costs are high, or even put prices up. It's all about juggling."

Detailed picture business

"I work with as many budget headings as I can. On the sales side, I break the figures down into the different products we deliver – suitcases, prams, golf bags, and so on. Then I can see exactly where revenue is coming from. I'll also look at the top 15 countries I'm delivering to. On the cost side there are all sorts of headings, from transportation to fuel surcharges, office rent, salaries, and PR and marketing. It's not easy doing things this way, but it gives me a better picture of my business and I have more areas to juggle with. Flexibility is very important. Initially, I did the monthly reviews on my own and then I started doing them with a commercial colleague. Ideas are better when you have two heads looking at the same thing."

Basic sensitivity analysis

"After doing the annual budgets, I do them again with a 20 per cent drop in sales to see what the impact would be on the cashflow if there are any changes in the market. I want

> to make sure I'm being as prudent as I can be with my cash. My mind is always looking at the downside as well as the upside. If I have a month that hasn't come up to where it should, my comfort zone is that I can do something about it."

12.6 Budgeting toolkit

- Money is not the only resource which requires a budget. Ensure your organisation has budgets for other resources such as operations, materials and HR. Make sure that *you* have a personal budget for the most precious resource – **time**.
- Make absolutely sure that you have a cash budget that ensures you have enough cash to meet likely bills. Review this budget on a weekly basis.
- Make an expenditure budget so that it shows categories of spending. Review this budget frequently with a view to reducing costs in categories with large expenditure.
- Make a capital budget and review it to ensure that assets under your control are earning a competitive return.
- Involve as many people as possible in the preparation of budgets
- Choose a maximum of seven budget ratios which give appropriate information (your personal dashboard) about how each subunit of your area of responsibility is performing. Build up a time series of these ratios. Review these ratios on a monthly basis. Draw conclusions about the efficiency of your subunits. Check your conclusions after including other information, and then take appropriate action.

Activities and further study

Essay plans

Write essay plans for the following questions:

1 What are the main types of budget used by organisations?
2 Explain in detail the main disadvantages of using budgets within an organisation.
3 Evaluate the advantages and disadvantages of budgets.

Web activities

1 Most organisations view their budgets as commercially sensitive and do not publish them. However you should spend 15–20 minutes trying to locate sites containing some kind of budget. You are most likely to achieve success with international, national and local government sites. These organisations often have a legal obligation to divulge some budgetary information. A good site is: http://www.jointreviews.gov.uk/money/Financialmgt/1-23.html#1-231-councils

2 Locate sites that give guidance on the preparation of budgets. A good site is: http://www.duncanwil.co.uk/cash.html

3 Locate and examine a website with a complicated budget. One possibility is: http://www.enzt.co.nz/~yesweb/_files/Student%20Resources/Finance%203%20 Cash%20 Budget.doc

Experiential activities

1 Obtain budgets for an organisation you know (college, workplace, club, charity). Examine the budgets and compare the range with that given in this chapter.

2 For an organisation you know well, list the budget ratios that would be relevant if you were managing that organisation.

3 Draw up your personal income, expenditure and cash budget for each of the next 12 months.

4 Talk to someone you know well and who trusts you. Ask them what impact budgets have on the way that they work and the methods they use. Enquire what methods they would use to ensure budgets work to their own and their team's advantage.

Recommended reading

1 Fleischman, R.K. and Tyson, T.N. (1998) "The evolution of standard costing in the UK and the US: from decision-making to control", *Abacus*, **34**(1), 92–119. A detailed history of cost accounting showing how managerial techniques evolve in response to problems and pressures of the time.

2 Geri, N. and Ronen, B. (2005) "Relevance lost: the rise and fall of activity-based costing", *Human Systems Management*, **24**, 133–144. A critical review of ABC (pages 134–135): a case study of use of ABC (pages 138–140); and an evaluation of ABC (pages 140–141).

3 Ogden, D.M. (1978) "Beyond zero based budgeting", *Public Administration Review*, **38**(6), 528–530. An old, short, but very useful paper putting zero-based budgeting into context.

Supply Chain

Chapter ELEVEN

The Logistics and Supply Chain Management Disciplines

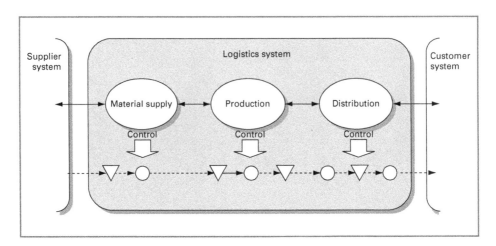

The first part of the book contains three chapters. The first two chapters describe the starting point of, and define different parts and perspectives of, logistics and supply chain management. The third chapter describes how packages, storage, materials handling and freight transport make up the physical flow of material.

Part Contents

1

Introduction to logistics and supply chain management

As consumers, we want to be able to visit a shop or an Internet website to buy clothes, food, furniture, books and so on. In much the same way, industrial companies require access to materials and components in order to manufacture products. Not only do customers demand the right functions and appearance in a product – it must also be available at exactly the place and time demanded and, moreover, at a reasonable price – preferably a very low one. In the case of, for example, clothes, wood products and electronics it is not unusual for raw materials to come from one continent, production to take place in another, and the product sold in a third. Thus, there is a great deal of transportation, handling and storage of the product and its component parts in the supply chain before it reaches the buyer. In the same way a great deal of information will have moved between those involved in activities related to material flows. **Logistics**, or the management of companies' supplies of materials, production and distribution, often plays a decisive role for many businesses in their attempts to satisfy customer needs efficiently, and indeed creates competitiveness.

The purpose of this book is to provide a fundamental understanding of the subject fields of logistics and supply chain management. The focus is on logistics in individual companies and in supply chains. This chapter contains an introduction to the subject and its in-depth treatment in subsequent chapters. Logistics and supply chain management are defined and described in terms of systems. Later, the goals of logistics and what is meant by efficient logistics are taken up, and in what ways contradictory goals may arise. Finally, the role of logistics and its significance in creating competitiveness are discussed.

1.1 What is Logistics and Supply Chain Management?

Logistics may be described as the science of the efficient flow of materials. It is a generic term for all the activities which together ensure that materials and products are at the right place at the right time, that is, create place and time utility. In common with all corporate financial interests, logistics is also aimed at increasing financial gain for the parties concerned. For the individual company this takes place through increased profitability, that is, through more income, lower costs and less working capital. Environmental demands, among others, are made on logistics from the social economic perspective. The term **supply chain management** is sometimes used to describe something similar to but not the same as logistics.

Definitions of logistics and supply chain management

Logistics is often described in terms of an approach, meaning that logistics is not only a number of techniques, methods or tools. Here, the logistics definition of the Council of Supply Chain Management Professionals (CSCMP; www.cscmp.org) is used:

> Logistics management is that part of supply chain management that plans, implements and controls the efficient, effective forward and reverse flow and storage of goods, services, and related information between the point of origin and the point of consumption in order to meet customers' requirements. Logistics management activities typically include inbound and outbound transportation management, fleet management, warehousing, materials handling, order fulfillment, logistics network design, inventory management, supply/demand planning, and management of third party logistics service providers. To varying degrees, the logistics function also includes sourcing and procurement, production planning and scheduling, packaging and assembly, and customer service. It is involved in all levels of planning and execution – strategic, operational, and tactical. Logistics management is an integrating function which coordinates and optimizes all logistics activities, as well as integrates logistics activities with other functions, including marketing, sales, manufacturing, finance, and information technology.

Logistics can be studied as an individual part of one company or as an integrated flow of **materials** through several companies. In the above definition, the flow of materials is from raw materials to end-user and includes the return flow of defective products, reusable packages and the recycling of used products, to name some examples. It is often necessary to have a wider perspective of the logistics system than within an individual company, since there is an interdependence between customers and suppliers, and synergies can be achieved if consideration is taken to the conditions and consequences for those outside the individual company.

Logistics can be divided into issues related to either structure or control. Structural issues are related to how systems for products, distribution, production and supply of materials should be designed for specific conditions. For example, they may dictate how much of the finished product is to be manufactured, the proportions of completed components to be purchased, who the suppliers will be, how deliveries will take place, how production layout and production organisation will be designed, whether the finished products will be stored or distributed directly to customers, and how transportation to customers will take place. The issues of control are related to planning and implementing efficient flows of materials starting with existing structures. Included in that work is the overall planning and execution of inbound deliveries, production and outbound deliveries so that the overall goals of the company and logistics can be achieved. In the shorter perspective this means planning quantities and timing for various items to be delivered to and from stores and production units, and initiating real transportation of materials.

In recent years the concept of supply chain management has come to be used as a similar concept to logistics. The overall aim of using this concept is to emphasise the significance of integrating flows within the individual company with other companies in the supply chain. Intra-organisational supply chains are also discussed – that is, supply chains which integrate flows in several internal units in a company. The Council of Supply Chain Management Professionals (CSCMP) defines supply chain management in a similar way to logistics:

Supply Chain Management encompasses the planning and management of all activities involved in sourcing and procurement, conversion, and all logistics management activities. Importantly, it also includes coordination and collaboration with channel partners, which can be suppliers, intermediaries, third-party service providers, and customers. In essence, supply chain management integrates supply and demand management within and across companies. Supply Chain Management is an integrating function with primary responsibility for linking major business functions and business processes within and across companies into a cohesive and high-performing business model. It includes all of the logistics management activities noted above, as well as manufacturing operations, and it drives coordination of processes and activities with and across marketing, sales, product design, finance and information technology.

In the definition of the Global Supply Chain Forum, "supply chain management is the integration of key processes from end user through original suppliers that provides products, services, and information that add value for customers and other stakeholders (Lambert, 2004)".

The above descriptions and definitions of logistics and supply chain management have the same integrated view of logistics and flows. In the CSCMP definition, however, logistics constitutes one part of the supply chain process. Supply chain management is not only concerned with the integration of material flows over company borders. It also involves more processes and activities in a company than those related to logistics, such as product development, marketing and so on. However, many processes interact and consequently processes not directly related to logistics can have an indirect impact on the logistics.

To create efficient logistics it is necessary to have both efficient and effective internal material flows and efficient and effective flows between companies. The supply chain focus in logistics underlines the significance of these external relationships and flows. Another important point made by CSCMP in their definition is the importance of information flow in creating efficient and effective logistics. The term "supply chain" is slightly misleading since it implies a linearity that is often not the case. The term "supply network" is therefore often used to emphasise that the actual flows are related in networks rather than in chains.

This book on logistics and supply chain management treats all the component areas in logistics, both from an intra-organisational and inter-organisational supply chain perspective. The contents are divided into five parts:

Part 1 – The logistics and supply chain management disciplines: The first part of the book consists of three chapters. The first two chapters describe the starting points of logistics and supply chain management and define the various parts and perspectives of the logistics system. The third chapter describes how storage, handling of materials, transport of goods and packaging affect the physical flow of materials.

Part 2 – Logistics and supply chain goals and performances: The three chapters in the second part treat the performance variables of the logistics system, which represents the goal and measurement system of logistics. The areas of customer service, costs, tied-up capital and environmental aspects are covered.

Part 3 – Logistics and supply chain structures: In the first chapter of the third part, different aspects of the products and items which flow through the supply chain are discussed. The second chapter treats the usual supply strategies and their significance for the logistics system, as well as aspects of choice and design of supplier structures. The third chapter clarifies existing production conditions from the viewpoint of logistics and their significance for achieving efficient and effective flows. Alternative methods of organising production are also described, as are resource strategies in production. This part concludes with a chapter on distribution strategies and distribution structures. The utility values contributed by distributors and the principal alternatives that can be applied to the design of distribution structures are included.

Part 4 – Planning and control of logistics and supply chain systems: This part consists of five chapters. The first describes the customer order process, and processes and methods for forecasting. The second treats materials management and contains different methods and aids to control the flow of materials and stocks. Some general and fundamental starting points and principles for this control are discussed, as well as the de-coupling functions for different types of stocks in the flow of materials. The subsequent two chapters look at different planning and control issues that are specific for manufacturing and distribution companies respectively. Included are principles of production activity control and transport planning. The last chapter describes the purchasing process from a logistics perspective.

Part 5 – Supply chain, IT and improvement aspects of logistics: The last part of the book contains two chapters. The first describes different emerging practices in supply chains. The second is about information systems for logistics and supply chain management. Various planning and execution systems are described, as well as communication and identification systems, and e-commerce. Both chapters support the previous chapters and are closely related to the issues described in Parts III and IV.

Logistics as a system

A system is constructed on subsystems which in turn contain a collection of interrelated **components**. An open system has an exchange with its surroundings, whereas a closed system does not. Logistics is often described as a system. It is always open: that is, it has an exchange with its surroundings. Exactly where the limits of the logistics system lie will vary from case to case. In the same way, the subsystems and components included also vary. If the limits of the logistics system correspond to those of the company then it is common to include the subsystems for supply of materials, production and distribution.

The relationships between the subsystems and components included, and between the system and its surroundings, take the form of co-ordination and exchange of materials and information. The relationships between subsystems and components in the system give rise to synergy effects, meaning that the combination and co-operation of subsystems and components can produce a higher total system effect than that possible from the individual components and subsystems.

The aim of the system is to supply customers efficiently with their required products. Each subsystem controls the size and timing of the flow of materials through the system via storage, transportation and various stages of handling and product value adding, as illustrated in Figure 1.1. In the materials **supply system**, for example, consignments larger than the exact quantity required for manufacturing a batch of products are often purchased. The surplus not used directly when it arrives from the supplier is placed in storage. During the operational steps in the manufacturing process there are also cases of temporary storage in the form of buffers and queues ahead of certain groups of machines. When a product's manufacture is completed it may be placed in finished goods stocks before it is delivered. Efficient distribution may also make temporary storage in central and regional warehouses advantageous. Transportation between storage points takes place, and during the production process value adding is carried out in which materials are processed into components and products. Product value adding sometimes takes place during distribution – for example, in the form of repackaging.

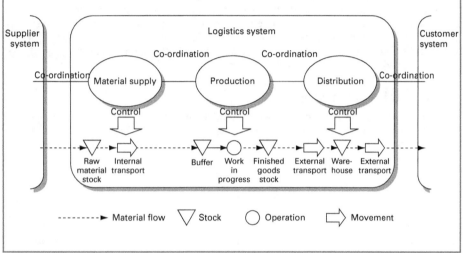

FIGURE 1.1 Logistics systems with the company as a limit. It consists of the subsystems' material supply, production and distribution

The distribution system

Distribution has a close relationship to the overall market strategy, which originates in the market's and customers' needs, and determines what delivery service distribution must achieve, among other things. For example, a market strategy that aims at supplying a number of consumers daily with inexpensive standard products over a large area will require a different distribution structure from one aimed at occasionally distributing complex manufacturing equipment with customer-specific functions to industrial companies. In the first case, consolidated shipment, temporary storage and sales through retail outlets may be necessary to minimise costs and enable sufficiently short delivery times. In the second case, distribution costs and delivery times may be less significant and distribution direct to the customer company and installation in the customer's plant may be part of a suitable distribution structure. If the limits of the logistics system correspond to the limits of the company, then the subsystems of distribution will be main related to the downstream environment – the company's customers. It is necessary to understand that the vending company's distribution must be adapted to customer needs and that commitments do not end on dispatch from the company, but only when the customer's needs have been satisfied. This may mean that distribution is extended as far as the customer's warehouse shelves or production line, or that it continues until the equipment delivered is installed and fully functional.

The production system

From the perspective of logistics, production means those structures and systems that control the flow of materials in production through supplying production resources with information on where and how much is to be produced by machines and personnel, and to ensure access to materials and components. Thus, the logistics of the production system co-ordinates machines, personnel and materials to achieve an efficient production process. The **production system** is closely integrated with the material supply system. When materials are supplied to a raw material store, the interface is set between the two subsystems on outbound delivery from the raw material store. When materials are supplied directly to a production line, materials supply merges into production when the material is accessible at the company premises. The interface with the distribution system is at the inbound delivery of finished products in the finished goods store or, if they are not stored, at the dispatch to customers.

The material supply system

The purpose of materials supply is to supply production with raw materials and components. Materials supply is directly connected with the supplier's distribution system and the individual company's production system. In the same way as in other subsystems, it cannot operate independently of other subsystems and surroundings. Information on the needs of customers and production must be the basis of materials supply. For example, information is required on material needs for future planned production and demands on size of shipments and delivery frequencies to be adapted to assembly work in production. Materials supply must also be adapted to suppliers' distribution and production. If the demand for small and frequent inbound deliveries gives rise to an increase in tied-up capital at the supplier, for example, since the supplier cannot manufacture such small batches as the customer demands, total tied-up capital and costs will increase.

Logistics system and the supply chain

Logistics systems do not only consist of flows of materials, components and products which are processed and distributed to customers, but also include supply chain flows of spare parts and return flows of defective and used products and packaging.

It has become increasingly important to regard the logistics system as a supply chain, not confining the logistics system to the company's boundaries but including the entire material flow from raw material to end-users in the same system. There is a striving towards optimal efficiency and effectiveness in the entire supply chain and not only for individual companies. In practice, however, it is often difficult to identify one clear supply chain. Instead, companies are part of a network of many supply chains. The most common approach is to include direct suppliers and customers in the same logistics system, but not secondary and tertiary level suppliers, as shown

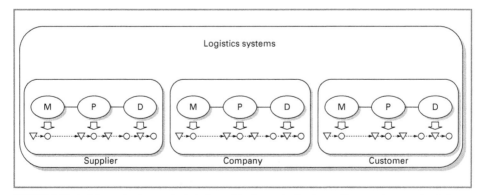

FIGURE 1.2 The logistics system in a supply chain. It consists of several subsystems with companies as system limits

in Figure 1.2. As a result of the interdependence of customers and suppliers, this broader perspective nearly always gives rise to increased efficiency and effectiveness from the individual company's perspective, also. The flow of materials in a supply chain is often compared with a flow of water. If the company being studied is placed in the middle, the flow of materials on the supply side is referred to as upstream, and on the customer side, downstream. Suppliers that deliver directly to the company being studied are called tier 1 suppliers, those that deliver directly to tier 1 suppliers are called tier 2 suppliers, and so on. The boundaries between the logistics system and logistics in supply chains are described in more detail in the next chapter.

1.2 Goals and Performances of Logistics

The purpose of logistics is to create competitiveness and high performance by improving companies' efficiency and effectiveness so as to positively affect profits, but in an environmentally friendly way. Performance can be expressed in terms of different performance variables, each one representing a particular aspect of performance. By setting up goals defined by performance variables, measuring them and following them up, it is possible to formulate a business approach that supports competitiveness and which accords with the company's overall strategy and goals. The logistics system's influence on performance can be expressed with the aid of variables that affect the company's revenue, the company's costs, the company's assets and the environment. There are also variables that indirectly measure the capacity of the logistics system to fulfil performance goals. The system's time and flexibility characteristics are examples of such variables. Logistics' main performance variables and their interrelationships are shown in Figure 1.3. Several of the performance variables are inversely proportional to each other and must be internally prioritised and related to the company's overall goals. The prioritised performance variables then become the starting points when establishing the goals of logistics, and indeed are the basis of a logistics strategy.

Customer service

The influence of logistics on revenues takes place by creating good customer service, which is brought about with the help of activities related to customer contact and delivery of products and services. The logistics system can contribute to **customer service** by creating a good delivery service, supplying information on material flows or other logistics services.

Customer service consists of a mix of different service elements which are more or less important in different situations. In the case of deliveries from finished stocks, the warehouse service level – the extent to which an item is accessible in the warehouse for direct delivery – is

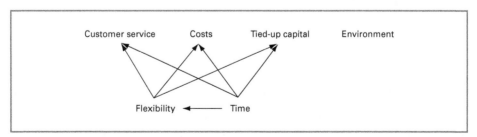

FIGURE 1.3 The logistics system's performance variables. Arrows indicate links between variables

an important measure of the quality of the customer service offered. The period of delivery time and the reliability of promised delivery times are important customer service elements in most situations. **Delivery flexibility** is another service element. This means the capacity to adapt to and comply with changed customer requirements in agreed and ongoing orders. For example, it could mean changing delivery times or ordering quantities at short notice, which is not an uncommon demand for many suppliers.

To create customer service with the help of information on material flows is about enabling the exchange of information with the aim of decreasing uncertainties in planning for the parties involved. Many products are also combined with peripheral services, whose structure can have a positive effect on customer service. It could include giving the product a customer-specific package or label, handling it in the customer's packaging solution, packaging it together with other products, affixing bar codes for subsequent handling by the customer, etc.

Costs

The logistics system influences a number of cost items. The physical handling, moving and storage of materials give rise to costs in terms of personnel, materials, operation and depreciation. The logistics system also incurs costs for administrative personnel and information systems whose purpose is to plan and control the physical flow of materials. **Tied-up capital** along the flow of materials also creates logistics costs. When an order cannot be delivered in accordance with agreement, shortage costs and delay costs arise if measures are necessary to compensate for the missing or late delivery. Warehouse costs, shortage costs and delay costs are to some extent the trade-off for costs in increased capacity. This is the case if buffer stocks are replaced by over-capacity in the production plant to deal with fluctuations in demand.

Tied-up capital

A company's assets can be divided into fixed assets and current assets. Investing in assets ties up capital. Tied-up capital affects a company's cash flow and solvency, but it also incurs costs equivalent to the potential returns on invested capital if it had been used in another way; for example, deposited in a bank account.

Fixed assets are those assets which are utilised over a long time period such as buildings, machines, computer systems and so on. They give rise to costs in the form of depreciation. The degree of capacity utilisation affects the unit cost, since at a lower utilisation level a smaller number of products must bear the same fixed costs of a manufacturing machine.

Current assets refer to assets of a more temporary nature such as materials in stock, in production or transport, and accounts receivable. The capital tied up in accounts receivable is due to the flow of payment, which may partly be affected by logistics. Late deliveries, for example, can give rise to delayed settlement. Tied-up capital from a logistics perspective normally refers to capital involved in the flow of materials, that is, materials that are held in raw material and component stocks, in production, in finished stocks or distribution stocks and in transport.

Flexibility

As described earlier, delivery flexibility is an important part of customer service which can create value for the customer. It has also been mentioned that the capacity to vary production and delivery volumes by deciding to invest in overcapacity may incur flexibility-related costs, which can lead to lower tied-up capital and increased customer service. The flexibility of the logistics system, then, has an indirect influence on the performance variables of customer service, costs and tied-up capital. 'Agility' is a word sometimes used to describe a logistics system that is dynamic and adaptable to rapid external changes, i.e. is flexible. Due to its increasing significance in many logistics systems and its influence on other performance variables, flexibility is dealt with here as a separate performance variable. A distinction is normally made between delivery flexibility, **product mix flexibility** and **volume flexibility**.

- *Delivery flexibility* is an expression of the ability, when required, to make changes in deliveries in order to adapt to customers' changing needs. The ability is determined by factors such as length of promised delivery times, throughput times, set-up times and batch sizes in production.

- *Product mix flexibility* means the ability within the existing capacity to rapidly adapt production and material supplies to shifts in demand between existing products and product variants. This ability is affected by factors such as delivery times for purchase items, size of batches in production and the length of throughput times.

- *Volume flexibility* expresses the ability to rapidly increase or decrease production and delivery volumes independently of any simultaneous mix changes. The ability is determined by delivery times for purchase items, the size of stocks of raw materials, throughput times, batch size in production and the degree of overcapacity, or utilisation of capacity in the existing plant.

Time

The focus on time is central in the logistics system since time influences the other performance variables. Without a time-efficient logistics system it is difficult to create a totally efficient logistics system. The significance of short and reliable delivery times as part of the delivery service and rapid deliveries of spare parts after delivery have already been discussed. Delivery time is sometimes called **time-to-customer (TTC)**.

To make possible short delivery times to customers in the case of engineer to customer order or production to customer order, throughput times and set-up times in business activities must be short. Without short throughput times for those activities which are carried out after receipt of order until dispatch, there is a risk that delivery times will become longer than what is acceptable to customers, more capital will be tied up in the flow and it will take longer to react to changes in customer requirements. The fact that materials with a long throughput time are tied up for longer also increases the risk that the product cannot be sold when it eventually becomes available: in other words, the risk of obsolescence increases. Without short set-up times it is not defensible in terms of cost to manufacture small batches required for manufacturing directly to customer orders. In addition, long set-up times give rise to large manufacturing batches, which in turn result in higher levels of tied-up capital. Short throughput, set-up and delivery times for purchase items also improve all the other flexibility variables, since it is faster and less costly to make changes in orders already accepted.

The innovation capacity of a company is also affected by time. A short product development time, called **time-to-market (TTM)**, or the time from product concept to product launch, can provide a time advantage on the market with respect to competitors. This lead can be increased further with the help of short delivery times.

It is also important to have time-efficient order cycles, which can be achieved through the simplification and automation of parts of the customer order process. Orders of standard items can, for example, be generated automatically in the customer's system when a certain stock level of the items has been reached, and sent to the supplier's system which automatically approves and registers the order. Such a procedure means not only that the order process is faster than a manual process, but that it is also more cost-effective. The logistics system is also dependent on high-quality planning information in the form of sales statistics, forecasts, stock balance information and so on. The quality of information deteriorates when such information is conveyed with time lags. When decision-makers involved have real-time access to necessary information both from their own activities and from other companies' activities in the supply chain, this has a positive influence on efficiency and effectiveness.

Environment

The environmental demands which society, industry, public administration and customers put on industrial and public activities have direct consequences for logistics systems. The environmental impact of logistics systems is through pollution, emissions, noise from transportation, high-energy consumption, poor handling of waste and recycling and so on. The environment is affected by most parts of the logistics system such as production, distribution, after-market, return flows, packaging, product development and overall system design.

An example of logistics-related measures aimed at minimising environmental impact is the adaptation of technical systems through the use of alternative vehicles, engines and fuels which

CASE STUDY 1.1: SCOR MEASURES

The Supply Chain Operations Reference-model (SCOR) was developed by the Supply Chain Council (SCC). As part of the model, five supply chain performance attributes and nine related measures were defined:

Attribute	Measure
Supply chain reliability	*Perfect order fulfillment:* Percentage of orders meeting delivery performance with complete and accurate documentation and no delivery damage.
Supply chain responsiveness	*Order fulfillment cycle time:* Average speed at which the supply chain delivers products to customers.
Supply chain flexibility	*Upside supply chain flexibility:* Number of days an organization requires to achieve an unplanned sustainable 20% increase in quantities delivered.
	Upside supply chain adaptability: Amount of increased production an organization can achieve and sustain in 30 days
	Downside supply chain adaptability: Reduction in quantities ordered sustainable at 30 days prior to delivery with no inventory or cost penalties.
Supply chain costs	*Supply chain management costs (SCMC):* All direct and indirect expenses associated with operating SCOR business processes across the supply chain.
	Cost of goods sold (COGS): Supply chain expenses not measured in supply chain management costs.
Supply chain asset management	*Cash-to-cash cycle time:* Time required for an investment in raw materials to flow back in an organization.
	Return of supply chain fixed assets: Return an organization receives on capital invested in supply chain fixed assets used in plan, source, make, deliver, and return activities.

Source: Supply Chain Council, *Supply-Chain Operations Reference-model Version 7.0.*

are more environmentally friendly. They may also involve combined transport, such as flexible road transportation with environmentally friendly railroad transport, or consolidating goods from several customers with the aim of increasing the load fill rate and decreasing the number of transports. Financial controls may be applied with the purpose of encouraging the logistics system to be more environmentally friendly. Road tolls and environment taxes are examples of such measures.

There are a number of tools and environmental management systems whose purpose is to facilitate, structure and evaluate companies' environment work. Most of them can be utilised to adapt the logistics system to long-term environmental sustainability.

CASE STUDY 1.2: LOGISTICS AND SUPPLY CHAIN GOALS AT VOLVO TRUCKS CORP.

Volvo Truck has nine own assembly plants worldwide. In addition, trucks are assembled at eight plants not owned by Volvo. The company continuously monitors the logistics and supply-chain performances. These are examples of logistics and supply-chain-related goals at Volvo Trucks:

◆ **Leadtime** reduction from order to delivery (average number of days)

◆ Inbound delivery precision (proportion of deliveries on promised day)

◆ "Direct runners" (proportion of totally assembled products without failures direct from assembly)

◆ Product quality (max points based on the number of failures and the criticality of the failures)

◆ Inventory turnover rate (number of days in stock)

◆ Sustainability (e.g. energy consumption)

Logistics and profitability

Since one long-term goal for all companies is to maintain a high return on capital invested in the company, it is natural to view the logistics system as a mechanism for creating high returns. A company's yield is usually measured as annual profits in relation to its total capital tied up in assets and is called profitability or **return on capital employed (ROCE)**, and is calculated using the following formula and expressed as a percentage:

$$\text{Return on capital employed} = \frac{\text{Profit}}{\text{Total capital employed}} = \frac{\text{Revenues} - \text{Costs}}{\text{Total capital employed}}$$

The logistics system affects yield through the variables of customer service, costs and tied-up capital. By focusing on and decreasing the total tied-up capital in stocks, production and transport, it is possible directly to improve the rate of return on capital employed. In a corresponding fashion, decreases in unnecessary costs in the flow of materials caused by long set-up times, unnecessary purchasing administration or low fill rates in transport vehicles would lead to an immediate decrease in return on capital employed. Customer service will also affect a company's yield. By raising service in those areas critical to customers and reducing it in areas which are less crucial – for example, by giving priority to important customer service elements, customers and product groups, the company can offer a better overall delivery service at only a marginally

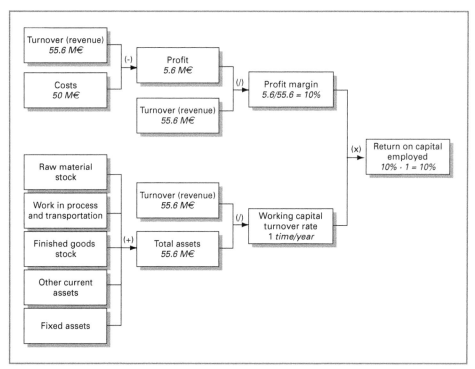

FIGURE 1.4 The DuPont model

higher cost or possibly even a lower cost. The improved delivery service will have an indirect influence on the return on capital employed since it is aimed at creating added value for customers and increasing total revenue in the long term. One way of illustrating these effects on the return on capital employed is to use the DuPont model, as in Figure 1.4. Revenue of €55.6 millions, total costs of €50 millions and total capital tied up in assets of €55.6 millions result in a profit of €5.6 millions, a profit margin of 10 per cent and a working capital turnover rate of one time per year. The return on capital employed is calculated by multiplying the profit margin and working capital turnover rate, in this example 10 per cent multiplied by 1, resulting in 10 per cent return on capital employed.

The return on capital employed is a product of the profit margin (the profit in relation to turnover) and working capital turnover rate (average tied-up capital in relation to turnover). Thus, to achieve a higher return on capital employed percentage it is necessary to increase the profit margin and/or the working capital turnover rate. Customer service and direct cost reductions will influence the profit margin through their effects on profit. Tied-up capital caused by tied-up materials constitutes part of the total capital and therefore exerts an influence on the working capital turnover rate.

In many situations measures for improvement can have a positive impact on both profit margins and working capital turnover rate. Such is the case, for example, when set-up times in production are reduced. If a company succeeds in shortening set-up times the result will be better utilisation of machines' capacity, since less time is taken by non-value-added set-up and

more time can be utilised for production. Through the increase in available capacity it is possible that overtime work and other costly practices can be decreased, which will result in lower
production costs per unit and increased profit margins. Shortened set-up times will also increase
the financial possibility of manufacturing small, customer-specific batches, which can increase
customer service and thereby generate additional sales or make a higher sales price possible.
This will also give rise to increased profit margins. Shortened set-up times will also influence
tied-up capital, since they enable the manufacture of smaller batches. Such measures have an
influence on tied-up capital both during production and storage. The reduction in tied-up capital
results in an increased working capital turnover rate and therefore increased return on capital
employed.

However, it is not the case that all improvements have such a direct and major impact on
both profit margins and working capital turnover rate. It is therefore necessary to give priority to
certain improvements to achieve the best possible effects on profitability. If a company with a
return on capital employed of 10 per cent has a profit margin of 10 per cent and a working

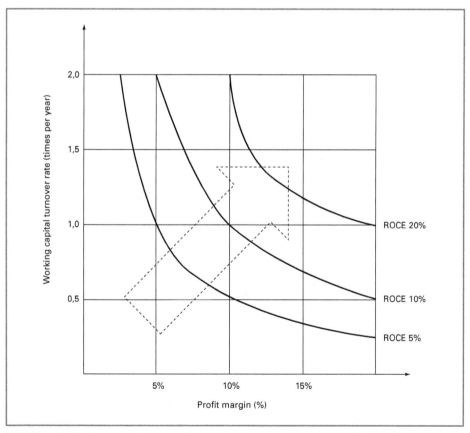

FIGURE 1.5 Example of a profitability diagram showing the relationship between profit margin and working capital
turnover rate
The arrow shows the direction of increased profitability measured as return on capital employed

capital turnover rate equivalent to once per year, a rationalisation of costs that decreases the total annual costs from €50 million to 49 million will mean that the profit margin increases to 11.8 per cent and that the return on capital employed also increases to 11.8 per cent. If, on the other hand, the company was to make the same rationalisation with a return on capital employed of 10 per cent but a profit margin of only 1 per cent and the working capital turnover rate was 10 times per year, the resulting profit margin would be 3 per cent whereas the return on capital employed would be 29.8 per cent. The same decrease in costs in absolute terms results in different levels of profitability improvements. This is because the percentage profit increase is higher in the latter case. In the same way, the influence on profitability of capital rationalisation depends on whether the original working capital turnover rate was high or low. A low working capital turnover rate and a high profit margin require less capital rationalisation in absolute terms than a high working capital turnover rate and a low profit margin. The opposite relationship also exists; when a company has a high working capital turnover rate and a low profit margin, a relatively low absolute increase in profits is required to achieve a relatively high improvement in profitability. The relationship between profit margin and working capital turnover rate is illustrated in Figure 1.5.

Conflicting goals in logistics

The aim of a logistics system is naturally that it should have high quality with respect to goals and performance variables. However, it is necessary to be aware of the conflicting nature of individual variables and that they may be assigned different levels of importance by different people in a company.

A majority of performance variables are, in fact, conflicting. As a result of these inverse relationships, certain priorities must normally be assigned to the variables. It is not a question of optimising one individual performance variable, but rather striving towards the best overall **performance** based on the **trade-off** between several variables. One example of conflicting variables is that high levels of customer service, which can be created through large finished goods stocks, will in turn demand much tied-up capital and high storage costs. Short throughput time in production can be achieved by small manufacturing batches, but this creates low capacity utilisation and high manufacturing cost per unit due to set-up times. It is especially important to balance the trade-offs between customer service, costs and tied-up capital. The three variables have direct profitability impact. The goal should be to create an optimum balance of the three variables, and not to increase one variable at the expense of the other, if that doesn't result in improved total performances.

There are not only goal conflicts between performance variables but also between a company's different departments. The reason is that many companies operate as functional organisations, that is, different departments are specialised and focus on their own well-defined tasks, each striving to minimise its own costs and tied-up capital without considering the whole flow of materials and acting in the best overall interest. Such an approach easily leads to sub-optimisation – individual departments are optimised at the cost of overall performance. Another effect is that employees tend to focus on their own particular tasks to satisfy the manager instead of the customer. The focus then tends to be on efficient use of resources rather than customer value. Table 1.1 provides some examples of common goal conflicts between functions.

One picture of demands which is common for many companies is to have good cashflow, high flexibility, short delivery times and many product variants. At the same time it is becoming more common to have material flows that lead directly from external supplier to component production, from component production to final assembly, and from final assembly to customer without interim storage. In such situations functions become more interdependent, and there are

	Purchasing	Production	Market	Finance
Goal?	Low purchase prices	Low manufacturing costs	High revenues	High profits, good cash flow, low tied-up capital
Customer service?	Large batches and long delivery times to customers are preferable: we then have time for purchases and can gain quantity discounts.	We cannot decrease batch sizes because this causes too much set-up time, which decreases available production capacity.	Customers demand very small and frequent deliveries with short delivery times.	Smaller batches are positive: tied-up capital in stocks decreases, which gives positive effects on cash flow.
Size of stocks?	We can gain quantity discounts if we purchase large quantities.	Large stocks of raw materials decrease the risk of shortages in input material, and since large production batches reduce the number of set-ups, this is preferable.	Customers demand short delivery times, necessitating that all products are available in finished goods stocks.	Large stocks cost too much and cause poor cash flow. They must be kept to a minimum.
Transport and production costs?	"Unnecessary" transportation costs too much. Goods must be consolidated into larger shipments.	By manufacturing larger batches, production costs per unit can be minimised.	Customers demand short delivery times. Consolidated deliveries are not possible since we must send the goods as soon as we get the order. We must be able to manufacture small batches with short leadtimes so that unique customer orders can be quickly supplied.	

TABLE 1.1 Examples of goal conflicts between the functions of purchasing, production, market and finance

higher demands on co-ordination between the different areas of responsibility. The functional organisation, focused on specialisation and use of resources, is seldom the best form of organisation in this case. A more flow-oriented or process-oriented distribution of responsibility and organisation is required, where the focus is on the processes of logistics aimed at efficiently creating value for the customer instead of optimising the use of resources within one particular function. This type of focus normally demands increased co-operation and contributions from many of the traditional functions as in Figure 1.6, where the flow and process orientation illustrates a focus on processes which cut across the functions instead of focusing on individual functions as isolated silos.

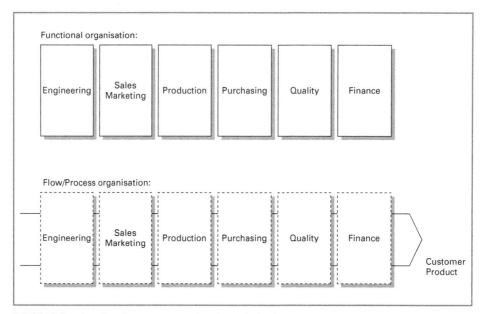

FIGURE 1.6 Function-oriented versus process-oriented organisational structures

1.3 Logistics as a Means of Competition

A well-designed and well-utilised logistics system can create efficiency in different ways for an organisation. However, it is not sufficient only to perform efficient logistics activities. In order to create competitiveness for the company it is also essential that the right type of logistics solutions is performed and the right performance variables are given priority, i.e. the efficiency is turned into effectiveness. Performance variables are variables that impact the efficiency and effectiveness and the success of a company. There is no point in being good at something which is not appreciated by customers or other key stakeholders, such as suppliers, owners and employees. To decide on logistics solutions and how to execute them in order to create competitiveness, the logistics strategy must be aligned with the organisation's other strategies. The starting point for strategic logistics planning is to focus on the customers and group the performance variables into **order-qualifiers** and **order-winners** for products and services.

Order-qualifiers and order-winners

To prioritise different performance variables it is necessary to understand how they influence a company's competitive situation. A common and practical way of doing this is to distinguish between variables which are **order-qualifiers** and those which are order-winners.

Order-qualifies are those variables which open doors to a market but which in themselves do not mean that a customer buys a **product**. They may be seen as a minimum level of performance required for a customer to even consider buying offered products and services. Order-winners are those variables which are decisive for a customer choosing a product or not. It is thus essential to ensure the necessary performance of qualifying variables and to prioritise order-winning variables to be more competitive. For many products and markets, for example, it is necessary to offer almost perfect product quality, short delivery times and a reasonable price, at the same time as it must be simple for a customer to place a purchase order if he is even going to consider buying a product. In such a situation, these variables are order-qualifiers. It may subsequently be the total purchase costs (including the purchase price) and the ability to adapt at short notice to changes in delivery times and delivery volumes that are decisive for whether the customer purchases the product or chooses a competitor. Total costs and delivery flexibility will then be order winners and will determine which supplier the customer finally chooses.

Which variables are order-qualifiers and which are order-winners may vary between a company's different products and sometimes also between different markets for the same product. For a clothes manufacturer, quality and delivery service may be qualifiers and the price an order-winner for a standard garment, whereas a maximum price and delivery service are qualifiers and product characteristics are order-winners for a fashion garment. Logistics with small resources, small stock levels and cost-effective flows of standard fabrics and garments are therefore important logistical challenges for standard garments, whereas being sufficiently cost-effective and being able to adapt very quickly to changes in customer demands for different product models and types of fabric are logistical challenges for fashion garments.

Order-qualifiers and order-winners do not only vary between products and markets. They also change over time. At the start of a new product's lifecycle, when supply is not very large and volumes relatively small, maximum price is often a qualifier and must be held under a certain maximum level so that customers can afford to buy the product. In the same way, delivery service is a qualifier and must not be too poor even if the customer in this situation is prepared to wait for the product. It is the unique product characteristics which are order-winners. When the product has come into the maturity phase of its lifecycle, or when volumes have increased and the competition is tougher, the variables of order-qualifiers and order-winners change. Many of the previous order-winners now become order-qualifiers. Product characteristics are seen as a matter of course and must be offered for the customer to even consider purchasing. Instead it is often costs and certain differentiated customer service characteristics, such as responsiveness, which become order-winners.

Logistics strategy

A strategy consists of those plans or patterns of actions that integrate an organisation's primary goals, policies and activities into a coherent whole. A well-formulated strategy helps to utilise all the resources of an organisation and create value based on its internal competence and shortcomings with respect to the external environment. A strategy may be planned down to the finest detail and far in advance in order to fulfil specific goals. A strategy can also evolve as a consistent pattern of action in business activities, without necessarily having been planned in advance. Most strategies are partly planned and partly evolved.

A logistics strategy consists of those plans or patterns of actions that relate to the flow of materials. It is sometimes called a *functional strategy*. In concert with other functional strategies it is aimed at supporting current order-qualifies and order-winners so that competitiveness can be created according to a defined business strategy, and by extension, so that the long-term goals of growth and yield can be achieved.

A strategy must be focused to some extent, meaning that it is not possible to support too many conflicting performance variables. For example, it is often difficult using the same system to competitively offer both high-volume products demanding low costs at the same time as low-volume products with many variants. The two types of products normally put far too many different demands on the various systems of a business, not least the logistics system. For this reason it is

20 Part 1 The Logistics and Supply Chain Management Disciplines

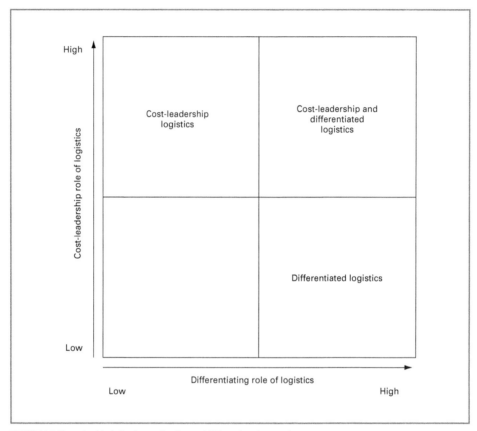

FIGURE 1.7 The role of logistics in cost-leading and differentiated strategies

usually said that a strategy must be focused and aimed at certain performance variables, making it possible to specialise activities. Competitive advantage is achieved by knowing the performance variables relevant for the key stakeholders and developing superior performance on these variables.

A common method of focusing a business strategy is to determine to what extent the company will be a cost-leader or will offer unique, differentiated products and services. Different logistics solutions will be necessary if the business strategy is to be a cost-leader, differentiated with respect to products and customer service commitment, or if it will be a cost-leader at the same time as demands are put on differentiated customer service, as in Figure 1.7. A logistics cost-leadership strategy may focus on minimising the physical logistics costs for transportation, storage, etc. A differentiation strategy may focus on short leadtimes and quick response to fluctuating customer demands. Combining cost-leadership and differentiation may require parallel-focused logistics systems that support different performance variables. For example, outsourced production to low-cost countries could focus on creating cost capabilities for the assortment and volumes with high forecast accuracy, and in-house production close to the markets could focus on creating quick response and flexibility capabilities for the volumes with fluctuating demand.

It is also important to underline the significance of co-ordination of logistics strategies between different organisations that are active in the same supply chain so that they do not use systems with different goals and conditions. The point is not only to align logistics strategies with the company's other strategies, but also to co-ordinate them with customers and suppliers in the supply chain. Superior logistics and supply chain management strategies are often achieved through structural changes of the supply chain, such as specific supplier and customer relationships, allowing for efficient information and material flows or technical developments and innovations. Competitiveness is no longer only conducted between companies. It is to a greater extent groups, chains or networks of companies that together form an enterprise structure and develop competitive advantage and compete with other groups, chains and networks of companies. Thus, competition takes place between supply chains, which calls for supply chain strategies.

1.4 Conclusion and Summary

This chapter has introduced and defined the subjects of logistics and supply chain management, from the starting point of how logistics can create efficiency and effectiveness in a company and supply chain. The goal from a corporate financial perspective is to create profitability through high customer service, low costs, low tied-up capital, high flexibility and short times. From a social economic perspective, environmental aspects are important.

Trade-offs arise between different logistics goals, both between individual performance variables and between goals in the company's different departments. To develop competitive strategies it is important to be aware of these conflicting trade-offs, to consider equally all performance variables and to create forms of organisation which as far as possible eliminate conflicts between departments.

🔒 Key concepts

Components 6	Production system 7
Customer service 9	Product mix flexibility 11
Delivery flexibility 10	Products 18
Distribution system 7	Return on capital employed (ROCE) 13
Leadtime 13	Supply chain management 4
Logistics 3	Supply system 6
Materials 4	Tied-up capital 10
Order-qualifier 18	Time-to-customer (TTC) 11
Order-winner 18	Time-to-market (TTM) 11
Performance trade-off 16	Volume flexibility 11

⬡ Discussion Tasks

1 Some organisations use the terms *value chain, demand chain* and *supply network* as substitutes to logistics and supply chain management. Compare these terms by, for example, searching on the Internet.

2 Goal conflicts are not uncommon between the marketing and production functions of a company. Identify some of these conflicts and give examples of how they could be eliminated.

3 Goal conflicts are not uncommon between different companies in a supply chain. Identify some of these conflicts and give examples of how they could be eliminated.

4 The performance variables with impact on a logistics system vary for different products, markets, and phases of the product lifecycle. Discuss which variables should be order-qualifiers and order-winners for computers, chocolate bars and building materials.

5 A logistics system can be the basis of cost-leading and differentiated strategies. Give examples of a situation (product, market, etc.) in which logistics supports a cost-focused and a differentiated strategy at the same time.

Further reading

Alvarado, U. and Kotzab, H. (2001) "Supply chain management: the integration of logistics in marketing", *Industrial Marketing Management*, Vol. 30, pp. 183–198.

Cooper, M., Lambert, D. and Pagh, J. (1997) "Supply chain management: more than a new name for logistics", *International Journal of Logistics Management*, Vol. 8, No. 1, pp. 1–13.

Hill, T. (1999), *Manufacturing strategy*. McGraw-Hill, New York.

Lambert, D. (2004) "The eight essential supply chain management processes", *Supply Chain Management Review*, Vol. 8, No. 4, pp. 18–26.

Lambert, D., Cooper, M. and Pagh, J. (1998) "Supply chain management: implementation issues and research opportunities", *International Journal of Logistics Management*, Vol. 9, No. 2, pp. 1–19.

Larson, P. and Halldorsson, A. (2002) "What is SCM? And, where is it?", *Journal of Supply Chain Management*, Vol. 38, No. 4, pp. 36–44.

Mentzer, T., Min, S. and Bobbitt, M. (2004) "Towards a unified theory of logistics", *International Journal of Physical Distribution and Logistics Management*, Vol. 34, No. 8, pp. 606–627.

Introduction to logistics and supply chain management **23**

Web links box

The Association for Operations Management (APICS):
www.apics.org
Council of Supply Chain Management Professionals (CSCMP):
www.cscmp.org
European Logistics Association (ELA):
www.elalog.org
Supply Chain Management Council (SCOR):
www.supply-chain.org

Financial Information

Chapter TWELVE

Finance and Accounting

Chapter contents

❖ *LEARNING OBJECTIVES*

After reading this chapter you should be able to appreciate the contribution to an organisation made by the finance and accounting function (FA function). You should be able to identify the four specialist activities that the function performs – over and above the budgeting processes undertaken by all managers. In particular you will be able to:

❖ **describe** how the finance and accounting function:
  – records transactions
  – manages theft and fraud
  – tracks commitments
  – manages information
  – controls costs
  – raises money

❖ **explain in detail** the difference between debt financing and equity financing

❖ **list** five major considerations, including depreciation, that affect investment decisions

❖ **list** four ratios used to evaluate potential investments

❖ **interpret** a company's profit and loss account

❖ **interpret** a company's balance sheet

❖ **interpret** a company's cash-flow statement

❖ **differentiate** between financial reporting and management accounting

❖ **describe** different ways of categorising costs and **give examples** of each category

The finance and accounting (FA) function looks after an organisation's money but is sometimes bitterly resented. Accountants in particular may be castigated "as knowing the cost of everything and the value of nothing". Others dismiss people working in FA function as mere "bean counters", implying that they have a narrow and myopic view. Nevertheless, the function is found in *all* organisations because all organisations need to look after their money. This chapter aims to give non-accountants or non-financial experts a general introduction. As Case 17.1 demonstrates, the FA function is very extensive.

Budgeting p 300

CASE 17.1: *The job of financial accounting*

The Financial Services Skills Council (FSSC) is an employer-led organisation which aims to improve the skills of people who work in finance functions in UK organisations, so it should be in a good position to describe what goes on. It regards financial accounting as a strategic, administrative and support role, involving extracting information from financial records such as budgets and interpreting what they mean. This information is used to help an organisation to see whether it is meeting targets. A true picture of an organisation's finances is an essential basis for strategy and any forward plans which might be available to stakeholders such as shareholders, potential investors, bankers, employees, creditors and government departments.

A chief financial officer (CFO) is likely to have overall control of the financial management systems which control working capital and relationships with debtors, creditors and suppliers. Chief financial officers prepare and sign off the annual reports and need to ensure that the company is complying with all financial legal requirements and professional codes. Specific activities include:

- preparing financial statements and accounts, such as profit and loss accounts or income statements
- monitoring the companyís financial performance on a constant basis
- advising board members and directors on strategic direction and advising managers on daily financial decisions
- advising the business managers and stakeholders about future trends and economic challenges
- reporting on variances between actual performance and budget performance, recommending corrective action
- preparing and reviewing organisational budgets
- advising managers on all aspects of financial policy and control

This chapter gives a deeper explanation of all these activities.

Source: based on Financial Services Skills Council's job profile for "Financial Accountant". The website contains many other profiles such as: Credit Management, Financial Control, Management Accountancy and Anti-fraud.

17.1 Managing the organisation's money

Most people in the FA function will be involved with managing its money. This involves a wide range of activities such as managing credit, recording transactions, tracking commitments, etc.

Managing credit

Most customers obtain goods on credit – either short-term credit (30 days from invoice) or long-term credit where interest is charged and special arrangements are made. One of the main reasons why organisations fail is that a customer goes bankrupt owing a substantial amount. In turn, this loss may force the organisation itself into bankruptcy. In turn this may make a supplier bankrupt . . . and so on. Credit control is clearly a vital activity. The finance and accounting function will be responsible for establishing a system that checks customers' credit ratings quickly but unobtrusively with credit reference agencies such as Experian or Equifax. Credit reference agencies provide information about individuals, companies and organisations. On the basis of this information, a sensible credit limit will be set. If this limit is exceeded the customer will only be supplied if cash is provided. In some industries, such as the building industry (which is notorious for bankruptcies), supplies may only be provided in return for cash.

Recording and expediting transactions

The FA function will also need to keep records of its transactions with customers and suppliers – probably by computer. An organisation must have mechanisms for claiming money from its customers by sending invoices and bills. This must be a systematic process that operates quickly. An organisation can get into financial difficulty by focusing on output but ignoring collecting "money due" until there is a cash crisis. Then it may have difficulty obtaining supplies or it may need to borrow money at a high rate of interest. Invoices for payment therefore need to be sent to customers either at the same time as, or shortly after, they have been sent goods. Some organisations calculate the following ratio to check whether it is paying its bills faster than it is receiving payments from customers:

$$\text{Debt Credit Ratio} = \frac{\text{Debtors}}{\text{Creditors}}$$

Similarly, the FA function must make arrangements to make payments to suppliers (**disbursements**). If these payments are not made promptly the organisation may be refused supplies. In particular wages and taxes must be paid promptly.

Managing theft and fraud

In some organisations, such as supermarkets, large amounts of cash need to be stored and transported. The finance and accounting function needs to ensure the security of cash while it is stored and in transit. In most organisations, prevention of theft and fraud is a major issue. A key element is the fidelity of the staff who handle money. References and other checks must be made to establish trustworthiness. Some organisations take out insurance to guard against embezzlement or fraud by employees who handle money and who have access to financial records. This is often called a "fidelity bond" or a "dishonesty bond". The FA function must also control access to documents such as chequebooks and to computer systems. The use of the Internet by customers and the growing practice of allowing customers and suppliers access to selected parts of an organisation's information system have made computer security particularly important. Key security principles are:

- No one in an organisation should be able to authorise payments to him or her self.

- Large payments must involve authorisation by two independent people.

- Financial records need to be checked (audited) by independent people. **Internal audits** will be conducted by people from the same organisation but who work in a different department or branch and who have no connection whatsoever with the person responsible for maintaining the cash or the records. Internal audits are conducted relatively frequently, say, once every three months. **External audits** are usually conducted by personnel from an accountancy firm or organisation. External audits will be conducted, say, on an annual basis and the external auditors will be required to state whether they believe the accounts and records are an accurate reflection of the true situation.

Tracking commitments

The FA function is responsible for checking that the organisation's commitments are within its ability to pay. Large projects will be tracked individually and require specific authorisation. Smaller, more routine acquisitions will be delegated to managers who will have strict limits of authority. A junior manager, for example, may be permitted to authorise expenditure up to £500 whereas a director may be able to authorise expenditure up to £10 000.

Financial information and budgets

All managers in an organisation will be involved with budgets. A finance and accounting function will give individual managers and departments guidelines and advice. They will also have responsibility for co-ordinating and collating departmental budgets into a master budget. Finally, the accounting and finance function will play the lead role in collecting key financial information and preparing reports for management.

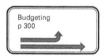

Budgeting
p 300

Controlling costs

Organisations must contain costs. In some organisations there is a separate sub-function to look after "cost accounting". When organisations were small, costs were originally considered as "fixed costs" in the sense that they did not vary with the volume of work – they were much the same during quiet or busy times. For example, a blacksmith's costs of staffing and managing a forge did not change very much according to the number of horses that were shod. However, as organisations became more complex, the importance of "variable costs" was recognised. A workshop producing 20 railway carriages per year would incur more costs than the same workshop producing 10 carriages per year: it would use more materials, consume more power and employ more staff. As organisations, particularly service organisations, became still more complex, a method of "standard costing" was developed. In standard costing, the fixed costs are divided by the number of items produced and the result is then added to the other variable costs to arrive at a cost per item. The method works particularly well when the organisation has only one product or service. Where there are several outputs the allocation of costs is more complicated and requires estimates such as the time spent to produce an item or the percentage of resources used. Some people prefer the terms "**direct costs**" and "**indirect**" costs to the terms "variable" and "fixed" costs. The main variable costs are wages for casual workers and raw materials. A final development in costing has been the use of **activity-based costing**.

This section has outlined the "bread-and-butter" work performed by the FA function. There are, however, other more specialised areas such as raising money, investing money, financial reporting and management accounting.

17.2 Raising money

Often an organisation can profitably use more money than it has to hand. When this occurs, the FA function will be asked to raise money. This is often called "financial management". It generally involves raising capital plus creating and managing an organisation's financial structure. Capital can be raised in two main ways: as debt or equity. The main distinction between them is that debt must be paid back at some time and it increases the organisation's liabilities, whereas equity is not paid back but some of the ownership of the organisation is transferred to the person owning the money.

Debt financing

Debt financing involves a loan for a fixed period at the end of which the money (the principal) is repaid and the lender receives interest during the loan. However, the lender does not gain any ownership rights and debt financing is therefore favoured by people who have strong proprietorial feelings about their organisation. Debt is often classified into **short-term debt** (up to one year – often to cover operating costs such as rents and salaries), **medium-term debt** (between one and five years – often to cover the purchase of new equipment or other medium-sized assets) and **long-term debt** (which is usually used to purchase buildings). Normally, lenders will need to see a credible business plan, a cash-flow forecast and a projection of the financial position in future years. A lender also needs to have confidence in the organisation's senior management. A lender will charge an interest higher than that which could be obtained by leaving the funds on deposit in a government bank. Lenders are "risk averse" and ask for higher rates ("a risk premium") if they believe the risks are greater than leaving their money in a government bank. Main sources of debt finance are:

- Loans from *other parts of the same organisation* which are making lots of money (**positive cash flow**). They are the easiest types of loan to arrange because there is a commonality of interest and the parties to the loan will know each other well.

- Loans from *individuals* such as wealthy people who have assets they do not need for their immediate purposes. These lenders are sometimes called "**Angels**" – especially those lending money to fund a theatrical or cinema production. Individuals making substantial loans are likely to require a formal agreement and guarantee or collateral that, should things go wrong, they can sell to recover their loan. The most usual form of collateral is a claim on buildings or land but it may take other forms such as securities. Owners of small companies are often required to offer their private residence as collateral. Often, very small businesses are set up using loans from family members or friends. In some parts of the world the extended family is *the* main source of funds for small organisations. Loans from family are likely to be informal and impose less rigorous conditions.

- Loans from *finance companies* are also available. Perhaps the most famous finance companies are Warren Buffett's Berkshire Hathaway Investment Company (in 2002 it loaned Wal-Mart $125 million to restructure its finance) and General Electric Capital Fund. Often finance companies specialise in certain industries where they have particular expertise. Finance firms may also specialise in lending to companies at various stages of development. **Venture capitalists** specialise in lending money to business start-ups that have little or no trading history. **Mezzanine capitalists** lend to companies who are likely to seek their stock market quotation in the near future.

- *Banks* are a traditional source of finance and are available in most localities. However, banks have a reputation for being very conservative lenders.

- Loans from *governments* may also be available for organisations in certain areas that meet policy criteria such as maintaining a rural economy or offering work to groups of people who find it difficult to obtain employment.

- Government, local government and very large organisations may be able to raise loans from the *public*. Typically, they are for terms of 10 years or more. Because these loans are usually safe, the interest payable (the **coupon**) will not be high. Government loans are called "gilts" or "consols" (consolidated annuities – an old form of indefinite loans to the British government). Such loans to large companies are often called "debentures".

If the money is needed to acquire an asset such as land, buildings or equipment it can be financed in a rather different way. It can be **leased** rather than bought outright. The organisation never owns the asset but it pays the **lessor** a regular rent. This means that it does not have to find the whole cost "upfront" and the rent can be paid out of current earnings. The length of a lease varies considerably. For equipment such as a photocopier or a computer the lease may be as short as one year. Buildings and land, on the other hand, frequently involve leases as long as 25 or 99 years. Leasing rather than outright purchase may be better. *First*, it reduces the risk of obsolescence. The risk is transferred to the lessor since, if the machinery becomes outdated, it is returned to the lessor and the lease is terminated. *Second*, there may be tax advantages.

Equity finance

With equity finance the loan does not receive interest and there is no promise that it will be repaid. Instead a proportion of the ownership of the organisation is exchanged. If the borrowing organisation is a success there will be a share in the increased value. This may be some combination of an increase in dividends or the value of the share which, ultimately, can be sold to someone else. If the borrowing organisation is a failure, dividends will be cut and the value of the share (equity) will decrease. In equity finance, the lender is taking a risk on the success of the borrower. Consequently, a lender will look for substantial returns. In equity finance, lenders frequently exercise considerable hands-on control of the company. When shares of the company can be bought by members of the public, individual shareholders are often passive investors but their interests are protected by legislation, and big shareholders such as insurance companies who may insist on being represented on the board of directors. A public company must send investors accurate reports and hold a meeting at least once a year (**annual general meetings – AGMs**) in order to appoint directors, approve accounts, approve major changes and appoint auditors. A canny investor could buy one share in 52 companies and dine out every week at a series of well-timed AGMs!

Equity finance has a number of *advantages*. It limits an organisation's exposure to financial risks such as changes in interest rates. New equity partners often bring useful contacts and wider expertise. However, equity finance also has *disadvantages*, especially loss of control. In a private company with only a few equity partners there may be personality clashes between the original owner and investors. There may also be acute difficulties when one equity partner wishes to sell their share of the company. Equity financing is often provided by **venture capitalists** who will seek to achieve high returns within, say, five years. 3i is a classic venture capital organisation.

Larger companies have the option of raising money on a stock market. Usually, these are companies that have outgrown mezzanine finance and their "initial public offering" (IPO) is for the **Alternative Investment Market (AIM)**, which is specifically tailored to the needs of a growing company. The AIM provides the benefits of a public quotation but it has a more flexible approach and fewer formalities than a **full stock market listing**. When a company joins a stock market, the accounting and finance function together with its advisers issue a prospectus that states the maximum number of shares (**share capital**) and the basis of its existence. In the UK the latter consists of a **Memorandum and Articles of Association**. They set out the company's constitution and the rights of shareholders. The shares are given a "nominal value", which is usually £1. The actual value of a share will change immediately they are traded and will be determined by market forces.

There are different types of shares. **Ordinary shares** are closest to the common understanding of shares. They confer ownership of a small part of a company and they carry full voting rights. If the company fails, these shareholders are the last to receive proceeds from its break-up and may receive nothing at all. There is no promise that the shares will ever be redeemed and their value will depend upon what a buyer is prepared to pay. **Preference shares** are a safer investment because there may be a redemption date and they may receive higher dividends. Further, should the company fail, holders of the preference shares are paid before ordinary shareholders. However, preference shareholders are not usually entitled to vote at general meetings unless there has been a default in paying dividends.

CASE 17.2: *3i – The doyen venture capitalist*

Before 1945 it was difficult for small, growing companies to obtain credit. In 1946 the government joined forces with major banks to form "Investors In Industry", subsequently known as 3i. Its job was to lend money to small, promising organisations that were too high a risk for commercial sources of lending. Because it involved several banks and lent to a large number of organisations, the average risk was minimal. Indeed, some of the investments were huge successes. 3i bought shares in the ownership of British Caledonian Airways for £4.5 million and later sold its holding for £100 million. Generally 3i was a huge success and it was floated on the Stock Exchange. It is now a world leader in private equity and venture capital. It has a team of over 250 investment professionals whose work spans three continents. Examples of organisations obtaining venture capital from 3i are given on the company website: www.3igroup.com/shareholders/about/business/venture/venture.pdf.

The accounting and finance function of a publicly quoted company will monitor its share price very closely because it reflects the market's opinion of the company's performance. If the share price "underperforms" the market, the company may become a target for a takeover in which the senior management, including the CFO, may lose their jobs.

When an organisation needs to raise money the FA function will consider the advantages and disadvantages of each source and, with outside specialist help, select the type that is most appropriate. It will then seek to locate a shortlist of specific individuals and organisations. The exact mix of equity finance, long-term debt and the organisation's reserves is known as the "**capital structure**". Probably the most important aspect of an organisation's capital structure is its gearing (leverage). Gearing is a ratio of long-term debt to equity.

Gearing
p 434

17.3 Investing an organisation's money

Types of investment

When an organisation has more money than it needs to meet running expenses, it should spend the surplus wisely on projects that will add value. The FA function will be deeply involved in assessing possible uses. This is often called **"investment appraisal"**. Investments may include:

- plant and equipment
- marketing and brand development
- improved systems, especially IT systems
- stocks of materials or land
- staff training, selection and motivation

Marketing strategy
p 334

Four major investment considerations

Investment projects sometimes arise from current operational demands such as the need to replace existing equipment or move to larger premises. They can also arise from strategic decisions The initial screen of investment projects will involve four major considerations.

The *first* is whether the investment will further the *strategic vision*. Those that lie outside the vision will cause the organisation to lose focus: it may not have the necessary expertise and it may not be able to concentrate on a number of disparate activities.

Second, the likely **rate of return** on the new investment (**ROI**) will be considered. This is effectively the same as **return on capital** (**ROC**) and **Return on Assets** (**ROA**) and its calculation is explained later. **Payback period** is often used to evaluate projects that generate some kind of income. As its name implies, it is the period of time that will need to elapse before the net income received equals the capital invested. Although the concept is simple, the calculations can be quite complex because they involve compound interest. Further, income needs to be discounted to take inflation into account since investment takes place in the present while the income will be received in the future when the money will be worth slightly less. The **net present value** is also based on forecasts of future earnings. Future cash flows are discounted for inflation using present value tables. All the cash flows from a project are then added. If the sum is greater than the initial investment the project goes to the next stage of consideration. If the sum is less than the initial investment, the project is abandoned. If early calculations show that a new investment cannot achieve this target the project is likely to be abandoned.

Return on capital
p 432

The **level of risk** is the *third* major consideration. The finance and accounting function will be asked to forecast outcomes based on three sets of assumptions: unfavourable assumptions, likely assumptions and favourable assumptions. If the results of projections based upon the unfavourable assumptions are dire and suggest that an investment may endanger the whole organisation, it is likely that the project will be abandoned unless some of the risk can be offset by insurance or other means.

Finally, initial considerations of any project will take **affordability** into account. An investment should fit comfortably within the reserves of the organisation – or at least within its borrowing powers. Further, it should not place an unreasonable strain upon the organisation's working capital and cash flow.

Depreciation

The FA function will also estimate the rate at which a proposed investment will depreciate. Equipment will not continue working for ever: it will wear out and become obsolete. The rate at which this occurs plays a crucial role in investment decisions: the costs (which include set-up costs and training, etc.) must be written off by the time the asset comes to the end of its working life. Assets depreciate at hugely different rates. A computer system, for example may need to be written off within three years, while agricultural land may not need to be "written down" at all – indeed, it may appreciate. The rate at which an organisation depreciates its assets is, to some extent, a subjective decision based upon the predicted life of the asset. There are usually regulations governing the rate at which assets can be set against tax liabilities. The level of depreciation is shown on a balance sheet and this may affect an organisation's financial standing.

There are several ratios based upon the rate of return of potential investments. They include **yield**, **discounted rate of return** (**DRR**) and **net present value** (**NPR**). The same measures are used in management accounting to guide managers on how well they are using assets.

17.4 Financial reporting

The finance and accounting function prepare reports on the state of an organisation's finances. Many of these reports are legal requirements. They include tax returns and returns for sales tax or value-added tax. These must be completed correctly and to a deadline otherwise the organisation will incur (in theory) heavy financial penalties. Reports also need to be made to the owners of the organisation so that they can check that the organisation is being managed effectively. For private organisations these reports will be sent to a few people who have a stake in the organisation and they can be in almost any format that these owners consider proper. Charities will need to prepare reports for their trustees. Public bodies will need to prepare reports for the appropriate authority. Companies *must* prepare reports for shareholders and potential investors. Reports, except those for the owners of private companies, are publicly available. The financial reports usually include three specific sets of accounts: profit and loss account; balance sheet; and cash-flow statement.

The profit and loss account

The profit and loss account (also called "**income statement**") is arguably the most important of the three main accounts. It shows the extent to which an organisation is adding value to the resources it consumes. If an organisation is making a healthy profit the chances are that it will also have a healthy balance sheet and cash flow. The profit and loss account also gives some insight into how a company is making its money. An example of a profit and loss account for Tesco is given in Case 17.3.

CASE 17.3: *Tesco profit and loss account*

Tesco's profit and loss account (Table 17.1) is fairly traditional. There is a clear title, date and a statement of the period covered and the units used – £ millions. There are then two columns of figures: present year and previous year. Any significant changes between the years are noted in a narrative report. There are also reference numbers to a series of notes contained elsewhere in the accounts.

The profit and loss account shows that in 2009 Tesco made a healthy and growing after-tax profit of £2166(*) million. This is probably the most important conclusion to be drawn from the profit and loss account. It is also important to note that Tesco contributed £788 million to the community in taxes.

Tesco Group Income Statement (adapted) 53 weeks ended 28 February 2009	Notes	2009 £m	2008* £m
OPERATIONS			
Income from Sales	2	54,327	47,298
Cost of Sales		(50,109)	(43,668)
Gross profit		4,218	3,630
Administrative expenses		(1,248)	(1,027)
Profit arising on property-related items	2/3	236	188
Operating profit	2	3,206	2,791
FINANCE ACTIVITIES			
Share of post-tax profits of joint ventures and associates	13	110	75
Finance income	5	116	187
Finance costs	5	(478)	(250)
Profit before tax	3	2,954	2,803
Taxation	6	(788)¶	(673)
Profit after tax		2,166*	2,130
Non-GAAP measure: underlying profit before tax			
	notes	2009 £m	2008* £m
Profit before tax		2,954	2,803
Adjustments for:			
IAS 32 and IAS 39 'Financial Instruments' - Fair value remeasurements	1/5	88	(49)
IAS 19 Income Statement charge for pensions	28	403	414
'Normal' cash contributions for pensions	28	(376)	(340)
IAS 17 'Leases' - impact of annual uplifts in rent and rent-free periods	1	27	18
IFRS 3 Amortisation charge from intangible assets arising on acquisition	1	32	-
Underlying profit before tax	1	3,128	2,846

TABLE 17.1 Tesco profit and loss 2009

The profit and loss account starts with Tesco's income: its sales of £54 327 million. It then gives the costs of its supplies (£50 109 million). However, there were other costs – administrative expenses of £1248 million. Note that both supplies and expenses need to be subtracted from the money Tesco made, so they are shown in brackets. Tesco manages a great deal of property, buying and selling stores and land as well as granting and taking on leases. In 2009 it made a profit of £236 million. on these activities. The total of all these figures shows the operating profit (£3,206 million). In other words, Tesco's main operations were adding value at a rate of 5.9 per cent. In order to run its business Tesco needs to participate in a number of financial activities. For example it receives profits from partnerships and joint ventures with other organisations (£110 million). On many days it will have spare cash which it can loan to banks and others on a short-term basis (e.g. the **overnight market**) and receive interest (£116 milion). It also has long-term borrowings on which it paid £478 million in interest. These sums are added and subtracted from the operating profit to yield a pre-tax income of £2954 million which falls to £2166 million when tax is extracted.

There are many ways that Tesco could have calculated the figures and presented the results. Adopting its own, idiosyncratic, method could confuse investors. Instead, Tesco prepared its accounts according to standard methods – the **generally accepted accounting principles** (**GAAP**). However, Tesco felt that accounts prepared in this way gave a slightly misleading picture of its underlying profitability. Consequently, it supplied extra information about its pension fund, investments, leases and "payments" made on acquiring new assets. In order to make it easy for investors Tesco has made these additional calculations using proven methods such as the **International Accounting Standard (IAS)** or the **International Financial Reporting Standards (IFRS).** The final result indicates that Tesco's underlying profit before tax was £3128 million – a noticeable increase on the previous year.

Balance sheet

The balance sheet is an essential tool for understanding the financial position of an organisation usually at the end of an accounting period. It is like a snapshot of organisational health. In essence a balance sheet shows what an organisation *owns* and what it *owes*. It indicates whether an organisation is in a position to expand, whether it can handle the normal ebbs and flows of revenues and expenses, and whether it has sufficient cash reserves. It also indicates whether it is collecting debts quickly or whether it is slowing down its payments in order to avoid a cash shortage. Together with profit and loss accounts, balance sheets are the most important reports the accounting and finance function will need to prepare. The profit and loss account of Tesco is explained in Case 17.3.

CASE 17.4: *Tesco balance sheet*

An asset is any item of value owned that could be converted to cash. Like most companies Tesco divides its assets into current assets and non-current assets (Table 17.2).

Current assets are possessions that are expected to be sold or used up in the near future, probably within the next year. In Tesco's accounts current assets are:

- Inventories – stocks of goods waiting to be sold. It is not surprising that Tesco holds £2669 million worth of stock.

▶

- Trade and other receivables – invoices Tesco is expecting to receive from financial institutions for, say, franchises etc. (£1798 million).
- Receivables – it is perhaps surprising that Tesco is owed as much as £4836 million by customers, banks and the taxman in the form of tax credits.
- Short-term investments such as overnight loans to banks are worth £1233 million.
- Cash in the bank to the value of £3509 million is needed to ensure that suppliers are paid promptly.

Clearly, Tesco had plenty of current assets. They totalled £14045 million.

Non-current assets are longer term. They are assets that are likely to be kept longer than, usually, a year. Tesco's non-current assets include:

- goodwill and other intangible assets such as trademarks and intellectual knowledge (£4027 million)
- property, plant and equipment. Tesco has oodles - a whopping £23 152m
- longer-term investments (£1 860m)
- longer-term loans and financial instruments including tax credits (£29 948 million)

Tesco's longer-term assets total £32 008 million. When they are added to current assets, Tesco possesses £46 053 million.

This does not mean that Tesco is worth over £46 000 million, because it also has substantial liabilities. Liabilities are negative. They are usually shown in accounts by enclosing negative figures in brackets. Liabilities are categorised as current or non-current. The main **current liabilities** are:

- invoices and other payable bills to suppliers and for services such as insurance, etc. (£8522 million)
- financial bills such as repayment of loans and financial derivatives (£9508 million)
- a contingency fund of £10 million to guard against various problems and challenges which, individually, are difficult to foresee

In total, Tesco has current liabilities in excess of £18 000 million. Tesco also has **non-recurrent liabilities**. These include:

- *financial liabilities* such as borrowings and financial derivatives (£12 761 million)
- *pension liabilities* (post-employment benefit obligations) of £1494 million
- liabilities that it has been *able to defer* for more than a year (£696 million)
- a *contingency fund* of £67 million to guard against longer-term, unforeseen problems

In total, Tesco has long-term liabilities of £15 018 million. When this is added to the short-term liabilities, the grand total of Tesco's liabilities is £33 058 million. This liability may seem massive. However, it must be remembered that its assets are very, very big. When liabilities are subtracted from the assets it emerges that the net assets of Tesco are £12 995 million – that is what the company was worth on 28 February 2009.

Tesco Balance Sheet (adapted) 28 February 2009	notes	2009 £m	2008 £m
ASSETS			
Current assets			
Inventories	15	**2,669**	2,430
Trade and other receivables	16	**1,798**	1,311
Loans, advances & other assetts	17	**4,836**	411
Short-term investments		**1,233**	360
Cash and cash equivalents	19	**3,509**	1,788
		14,045	6,300
Non-current assets			
Goodwill and other intangible assets	10	**4,027**	2,336
Property, plant, equipment	11	**23,152**	19,787
Investments	12	**1,860**	1,421
Loans and financial instruments	17	**2,969**	320
		32,008	23,864
TOTAL ASSETS		46,053	
LIABILITIES			
Current liabilities			
Trade and other payables	20	**(8,522)**	(7,277)
Financial liabilities (borrowings, liabilities, derivatives)		**(9,508)**	(2,982)
Provisions	26	**(10)**	(4)
		(18,040)	(10,263)
Non-current liabilities			
Financial liabilities		**(12,761)**	(6,336)
Post-employment benefit obligations	28	**(1,494)**	(838)
Deferred tax liabilities	6	**(696)**	(802)
Provisions	26	**(67)**	(23)
		(15,018)	(7,999)

TOTAL LIABILITIES		(33,058)	
BALANCE			
Net assets		12,995	11,902

TABLE 17.2 Tesco balance sheet, 2009

Cash-flow statements

A cash-flow statement indicates how an organisation obtains funds and how it spends them. They are sometimes called "funds flow statements", "sources and uses of funds statements" and "statement of changes in financial position". They should conform to accepted standards such as **IAS7** (**International Accounting Standards 7**) developed by the International Accounting Standards Committee (IASC).

Cash-flow statements are needed because a simple balance might not give a useful picture of an organisation's cash position. It is not uncommon for healthy companies to have a negative cash flow – spending more than their income. It is a nightmare for many smaller organisations. Such companies may be spending a lot of money developing new products and buying new machines. This spending will generate cash in the future. Very unhealthy companies usually have a negative cash flow – they may be wasting resources on opulent offices, champagne receptions and private jets. Without a cash-flow statement it is difficult to differentiate between the two types. Cash-flow statements have two other major uses:

- Indicating whether an organisation is likely to have **enough money to pay future expenses**. If there is more than enough money the organisation should consider how it can use the surplus to add maximum value. If a deficit is likely, the organisation will need to cut costs or arrange extra finance.

- Helping **business planning and control**. A **cash-flow forecast** can be compared with the cash outcomes. This may provide an early warning that things are going wrong. It also helps future planning. The reasons for deviations from the forecast can be identified and incorporated in future plans.

An organisation may yield a 10 per cent profit on its products, but it will need money to buy raw materials, rent premises and pay workers before it receives any money from sales. A company may be fundamentally sound but if it cannot pay its bills promptly its creditors may foreclose. In a more realistic case, the situation will be less dramatic but there will still be some months where expenditure outstrips income, and vice versa. The cash budget is a plan to ensure that money is available when needed to pay bills. Most organisations draw up a cash budget on a monthly basis for a year in advance. Some organisations might budget on a weekly basis and others, especially those in the finance sector, will budget cash very carefully indeed, on a daily basis. The cash flow is sometimes presented as a cash graph. Figure 17.1 gives a cash graph for a holiday company whose cash flow is extremely seasonal.

It can be seen in Figure 17.1 that for the year as a whole, the company will be highly profitable and in most months the cash flow will be positive (colloquially known as "up north"). However, few people take holidays in November and January. The cash flow is likely to "go south" in these months. Indeed, the cash budget indicates that the cash flow will be so negative in these months that it will exceed the organisation's overdraft limit and the CFO must arrange extra credit facilities and place strong constraints upon purchases during November and January. On the other hand, the strong cash flow between June and September means that major purchases should be made at this time and arrangements should be made to invest the surplus "cash pile". Figure 17.1 demonstrates an important point: often, the meaning of financial information is clearer when expressed in a chart.

It is sometimes claimed that cash flow is a better gauge of profitability than reported income. The latter depends on many arguable accounting decisions such as when revenue is recognised and how much to allow for depreciation, etc. Cash flow is more objective – it is the amount of money "in the bank" (and other places) on one specific date minus the money "in the bank" on another specified date. Cash flow is much harder to fudge than reported income.

Types of cash flow

It is customary to organise cash flows under three headings: operating activities, investing activities and financing activities:

- **Operating activities** usually give the largest single flow of cash. The main exceptions to this rule arise in financial organisations such as banks and investment companies. In a healthy company, operating activities provide a positive inflow of cash. Examining the cash flow for operating activities is very important because it may give three clear signals that an organisation may be heading for trouble.

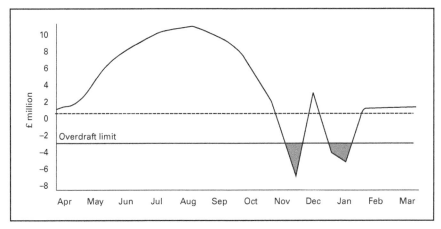

FIGURE 17.1 A cash graph

- If operating cash flow (OCF) is negative the organisation is spending more money than it is creating. This may be justifiable during short periods of expansion and investment. A sustained negative OCF is bad. The organisation may be reporting an income but it may not be making any "real" money.

- If income exceeds cash flow (or if income is increasing while OCF is falling) the organisation is piling up assets that may not be worth what is claimed. For example, it may be counting stocks of unsold goods or income due from customers that have not actually been collected.

- It is often useful to look at OCF alongside sales and accounts payable (money owed to suppliers). If OCF is static or declining while accounts payable are increasing, the organisation may be attempting to ward off difficulties by delaying payments.

Some companies such as Amazon.com emphasise a variant of OCF: the **"free cash flow"**. Ordinary operating cash flow does not usually include capital investments a company must make in premises and equipment in order to stay competitive. Further, for many retail organisations, such as Tesco, growth is mainly in the form of opening up new stores – which takes a lot of cash. Free cash flow takes these factors into account. In essence free cash flow is what is left over from OCF when funds for expansion and continuing operations are subtracted. In Amazon's case, free cash flow is the OCF minus operating interest and the costs of software and website development.

- **Investing activities** include cash received or spent on purchases or sales of land, subsidiaries or equipment. Most companies have some form of long-term investments which are often called "financial instruments". The cash spent when these are bought or received when they are sold is also listed under investing activities. Monies that arise from participation in joint ventures are also usually reported under this heading.

- **Financing activities** include cash obtained by long-term borrowing from the sale of bonds, stocks, shares and preference shares. If these are redeemed payments are shown as a negative cash flow.

17.5 Management accounting

Uses of management accounting

Financial reports (section 17.4) are primarily designed to inform people outside the organisation so that they can decide whether their investments are used correctly and efficiently. However, a great deal of the work of the FA function is concerned with providing people *within* the organisation with information that helps them make day-to-day decisions and manage the organisation in the short and medium terms. This is usually called "management accounting". Management accounting is internal and usually confidential. It is therefore subjected to a lower level of external auditing and legislation. Management accounting often includes subjective data. Because managers need to take frequent decisions, management accounting reports are produced more frequently than financial reports – perhaps on a weekly or monthly basis,

CASE 17.5: *Tesco cash-flow statement*

It can be seen in Table 17.3 there was a healthy inflow of cash (£3960 million) to Tesco from operating activities – even after it had paid interest (£562 million) and corporation tax (£456 million).

However, in 2009 Tesco had a spending spree. It had a massive outflow of £5 974 million to investments. This was largely the result of purchases of property, etc. amounting to £5982 million and investments in joint ventures, etc. (£1263 million). This was a bigger spending spree than the previous year – presumably because Tesco was taking advantage of lower prices caused by the credit crunch. Some of the spending spree was balanced by sales of property, etc. amounting to £1354 million. Money for the spending spree was also obtained from investing activities. It issued more shares (£130 million) and it borrowed a massive £7387 million. However, its total borrowings did not rise by this much because it also repaid £2733 million worth of other borrowing. It also paid £889 million in dividends.

The cash statement ends with a summary. In 2009 Tesco had a net cash flow of £1601 million. This was twice the level of its cash flow in 2008 – mainly because it repaid fewer borrowings. It also had £1788 million cash from the previous year and a useful contribution from gains from changes in the exchange rate. On 28 February 2009 Tesco could lay its hands on cash to the value of £3509 million – more than enough to stop its creditors worrying!

TESCO CASH FLOW STATEMENT (adapted) 53 weeks ended 28 February 2009	notes	2009 £m	2008* £m
Cash flows from operating activities			
Cash generated from operations	33	**4,978**	4,099
Interest paid		**(562)**	(410)
Corporation tax paid		**(456)**	(346)
Net cash from operating activities		3,960	3,343
Cash flows from investing activities			
Purchase of property, plant and equipment, intangible assets,aquisitions		**(5,982)**	(3,769)
Proceeds from sale of property, plant and equipment,investments		1,354	1,056
Increase in loans to joint ventures		**(242)**	(36)
Investments in joint ventures and associates,short-term		**(1,263)**	(421)
Proceeds from sale of short-term investments			
Dividends and interest received		159	216
Net cash used in investing activities		**(5,974)**	(2,954)

Cash flows from financing activities			
Proceeds from the issue of ordinary share capital		**130**	154
Increase in borrowings		**7,387**	9,333
Repayment of borrowings		**(2,733)**	(7,593)
New finance leases		**-**	119
Repayment of obligations under finance leases		**(18)**	(32)
Dividends paid		**(889)**	(795)
Own shares purchased		**(265)**	(775)
Net cash from financing activities		**3,615**	412
Net increase in cash and cash equivalents		**1,601**	801
Cash and cash equivalents at beginning of year		**1,788**	1,042
Effect of foreign exchange rate changes		**120**	(55)
Cash and cash equivalents at end of year	19	**3,509**	1,788

TABLE 17.3 Tesco cash-flow statement, 2009

CRITICAL THINKING 17.1 *Are financial statements accurate? Watch out for restatements and lies*

Hundreds of eminent people have spent thousands of hours working on august committees to produce stringent standards such as the general accepted accounting principles and the international accounting standard. Further, public financial statements are audited and signed off by expensive external experts. There are also huge penalties when executives are discovered "fiddling the books". So you might feel you can rely on the financial statements of large organisations. Maybe, but don't bet your shirt on it. Table 17.4, which is only a small selection of examples, shows that there have been plenty of financial irregularities.

There are plenty of other examples. iSoft is known around the world for its software for the health-care industry. In 2010 Ian Storey, its ex-financial controller, was ordered to pay £20 000 and banned from practising as a chartered accountant for eight years. The granddaddy of financial irregularities was Enron which collapsed in 2002. It employed very gifted accountants to stretch the limits of accounting principles. They were the "smartest guys in the room" and they accumulated bad habits such as:

■ inflating income by adopting *mark to market accounting* by estimating future income and including it in one year's figures

■ *special purpose entries* which hid debt by keeping bad transactions off the balance sheet

▶

- *allowing its own CFO to deal, indirectly in ENRON shares*
- *pressurising its auditors* to apply reckless standards – the firm Arthur Anderson did not want to lose the $50+ million per year it was earning in audit and consultancy fees
- *failing to remove cancelled orders from its balance sheets* – on the basis that official cancellation letters had not been received

Many companies have audit committees to scrutinise their financial statements. It is best not to put too much faith in them. Enron's audit committee included a professor of accounting, a former president of a state bank, a congresswoman and a former UK Secretary of State for Energy!

When finance and accounting scandals come to light, professionals in the function sometimes congratulate themselves that they have revealed fraud! These professionals also have a euphemism for glossing over misleading financial statements; they issue corrections and call them "*restatements* of accounts".

Company	Irregularity	Auditors
AIG (insurance)	Misreporting deals	PricewaterhouseCoopers
Anglo-Irish Bank	Hidden loans	Ernst & Young
AOL	Inflated sales	Ernst & Young
Bristol-Myers Squibb	Inflated income	PricewaterhouseCoopers
Haliburton	Booking unconfirmed agreements	Arthur Anderson
World Com	Overstated cash flow	Arthur Anderson
Xerox	Falsifying results	KPMG

TABLE 17.4 Some irreglarities in financial statements

rather than a yearly or half-yearly basis as for financial reports for shareholders. Management accounting data uses include:

- developing business strategy
- controlling
- improving performance and enhancing value

Cost accounting

Management accounting is closely related to **cost accounting**, which is the process of tracking, recording and analysing costs associated with the activities of an organisation. The quantification and control of costs is a key element in ensuring that managers add value. Often, the first stage of cost accounting is to classify costs. One very simple classification involves dividing costs into materials, labour, power, rent, etc. This information can be collected for individual products and it can be compared with equivalent costs in the past or equivalent competitors. These comparisons point to areas where savings can be made. Many situations benefit from a more sophisticated approach where the costs are subdivided and then grouped according to abstract criteria:

- **Direct costs** are those costs that can be *specifically* and *exclusively* associated with a particular product or service (a **cost object**). For example, the direct costs for a television remote control will include the costs of components (raw materials), the labour costs of the people that assemble the remote control and the costs of packaging, etc. Generally direct costs are objective and easy to measure with great accuracy. **Indirect costs** cannot be identified specifically and exclusively with a cost object (Drury, 2005). Indirect costs are often called "overheads" and they include things like marketing and general expenses such as telephone bills and secretarial costs. Indirect costs also include a special category of **facility-maintaining costs**, which are expenditures on the organisation's infrastructure such as property taxes, lighting and heating. They are completely independent of business volumes but are necessary if the organisation is to stay in business.

- Some organisations allocate indirect costs to products or services using a **blanket overhead rate**. They may calculate the total indirect costs and the total of direct labour hours for the whole organisation and then divide the former by the latter. For example, a large organisation may have indirect costs of £30 million and the direct production of its services may involve 2 million labour hours. Consequently, each labour hour will carry an overhead charge of £15. A service which involves three hours' direct labour will incur a charge of £45 in addition to the direct costs. Blanket overhead rates are sometimes unfair and give a distorted view of true costs – especially where the indirect costs of departments differ drastically. For example, science departments in universities and colleges have much higher indirect costs than arts departments because they require more premises for laboratories, more support staff and higher insurance premiums. It would therefore be wrong to allocate the same blanket overhead rate to each hour of teaching in, say, arts and science.

- **Fixed costs** remain the same irrespective of the number of units produced. They are often closely associated with indirect costs. For example, if the rental of an assembly machine is $1000 a week to produce up to 4999 units, the same rent is paid irrespective of whether it is used to produce one unit or a thousand units. **Variable costs** change with the number of units produced. They are often closely associated with direct costs. For example, if the components for a television remote control cost $1, the variable costs will be $1000 in a week where 1000 remote controls are produced but will be $4999 in a week where 4999 remote controls are produced.

- **Incremental costs** are the extra amount needed to produce one extra item and they are closely related to the variable cost of each item. They are sometimes called **marginal costs**. If something can be sold for the same price and variable costs are low, extra production will mean a substantial increase in profits. Sometimes, however, incremental costs can be so high that extra product will result in a loss. For example, if an assembly machine can produce a maximum of 4 999 remote controls a week at a total cost of $5 999, the production of 5000 remote controls would cost $7000 (6000 plus $1000 to hire another assembly machine). The marginal cost of $1001 indicated by the management accounting system would probably dissuade managers from producing the extra unit.

■ **Opportunity costs** are the value sacrificed when one choice is sacrificed in favour of another. Opportunity costs only apply to scarce resources. For example, an organisation may consider selling a vacant plot of land for a profit of €4 million. If, however it could use the land to build a factory worth €6 million, the opportunity cost of selling would be €6 million. Management accounting information of this kind would help managers make the right decision.

Management ratios

A finance or accounting function may also calculate ratios which indicate an organisation's efficiency. There are many ratios and some, ratios to gauge labour productivity and the likely worth of new investments, have been encountered earlier. These are the ratios that are most useful at the operational level. However, many other ratios are used at a strategic level, to see how well the organisation as a whole is doing. Management ratios are very useful summaries – but it must be remembered that they are summaries that may hide important details.

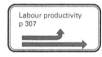

Labour productivity p 307

Clearly, a list of ratios does not make exciting reading, but this is no reason to ignore them. Everyone who is a manager or who needs to communicate with managers needs to be familiar with these indices. They usually form the basis of many senior management decisions and are a dominant influence on the way that senior managers think. If you cannot make sense of a senior management decision it is probable that *you* are at fault because *you* do not know, or understand, the ratios they are using. For example, if an organisation is making a takeover bid for your company it is highly likely that its senior managers have found that your productivity ratios are poor and they think they can make a profit by improving them. If a bank refuses your employer a loan for new machinery it is highly likely that it has computed debt ratios and found them too high. If you dislike figures and you think you can ignore ratios you will not last long as a senior manager – even if you have the charisma of an arch-angel. Scores of management ratios exist. Each has its own purpose. The following subsection contain some of the most frequently used ratios. They can be grouped into two main categories: profitability ratios and debt ratios.

Return on investment p 417

Profitability ratios

Profitability ratios are global indices that show how well an organisation or unit is using resources. The five main global measures of profitability are:

1 **Gross profit**, also called **gross profit margin** or **profitability ratio**, is the organisation's mark-up on the sale price. It is probably the best single measure of an organisation's overall ability to add value when transforming inputs into outputs. It is the most

frequently used measure of profitability. Gross profit is the difference between income from sales and the cost of the goods sold, all divided by the value of the sales and multiplied by 100 to produce a percentage:

$$\text{Gross profit} = \frac{\text{Sales income} - \text{Costs}}{\text{Sales income}} \times 100$$

A comparison of the profit margins over a number of years reveals a great deal about an organisation.

Declining profit margins mean that the organisation is being forced to lower its prices – or is having difficulty in restraining costs, or both. For example, in 2004 the Chinese mobile phone maker, TCL, increased its profit by 30 per cent but its profit margin fell from 27 per cent to 22 per cent. Increased competition had forced it to reduce its prices, hence it was adding less value to each phone it made. Fortunately, TCL was able to sell more phones. In 2009 the bus and train operator, Stagecoach, reported a sharp fall in the gross profit of its train business from a margin of 6.5 per cent to a margin of 2.9 per cent. The company had been hit by falling sales to commuters during the credit crunch (lower income) and higher fuel costs.

Increasing profit margins mean that the organisation is able to command higher prices for its products (perhaps by improving them or shifting to more valuable markets) or is better at controlling its costs. The ideal situation is where a company's profitability increases for several years. This indicates a culture of innovation and cost control. The Compass Group is the largest support service company in the UK. It provides contract catering and other services to many organisations and runs the restaurants in prisons, banks, schools and airports. Its profit margins in 2007, 2008 and 2009 were 5.1 per cent, 5.8 per cent, and 6.5 per cent, respectively. The continuing improvement is attributed to tight control of costs and a move into more profitable markets such as cleaning and reception services. Comparisons of gross profit margins between companies in *the same sector* can indicate which companies have the best management.

2 **Profit after tax**, often known as "net profit margin", is very similar to gross profit margin except that it takes taxes into account. Sometimes it is called "net profit tax". It is a useful index for people who are interested in how much money an organisation is making for itself. It is calculated as follows:

$$\text{Profit after tax} = \frac{\text{Income} - (\text{Costs} + \text{Taxes})}{\text{Income}} \times 100$$

Profit after tax is an index of how well an organisation is able to transform inputs plus the effectiveness with which it is able to arrange its financial affairs in order to minimise tax. Organisations with high net profit margins will have more money to spend on other business operations such as research and development or marketing, or for distribution to shareholders and others. Comparison of the net profit margin for the same company over several years and comparisons between different companies in the same sector are as useful as those involving the gross profit margin. However, such comparisons need to be made with care where the tax regime differs between companies or financial years.

The previous indices focus on sales and revenue. But, in some circumstances sales and revenue are not the crucial factors. A factory which produces a profit margin of 5 per cent using six machines is probably better than a similar factory that has a profit margin of 8 per cent using 20 machines – the former's margin may be lower but each machine is producing a higher number of goods and more value is being created from the money used to buy the machines. In other words the management of the first factory is making capital work harder. A number of indices measure how efficiently capital is used (i.e. productivity). They include rate of return, return on equity, economic value added and payback periods. Indices of labour productivity are also relevant.

Labour productivity
p 307

3 **Return on capital** (**ROC**) is the traditional, most widely used index of how effectively a company is using its capital resources. Return on capital is sometimes called "**return on assets** (**ROA**)" and it is very similar to return on investments. It is calculated using the formula:

Return on
investment p 417

$$\text{Return on capital} = \frac{\text{Net profit}}{\text{Total assets}} \times 100$$

It should the noted that interest on loans is subtracted from net profit and that the index is usually calculated using profits after tax (i.e. net profit). The result depicts the actual benefit to the organisation. However, in some circumstances – when comparing organisations subject to different tax regimes – the index will be computed using the pre-tax figures. Unfortunately, the overall return on capital can sometimes be a misleading index because it includes capital borrowed from other sources. The following index takes borrowing into account.

4 **Return on equity** indicates how well the organisation is transforming the resources provided by the owner. It is calculated by the formula:

$$\text{Return on equity} = \frac{\text{Net profit}}{\text{Owner's equity}} \times 100$$

For example, the owner of a health club may have purchased a gym with £200 000 of her savings plus £100 000 loan from a bank. After deducting costs (including interest to the bank) and taxes, the gym makes a profit of £15 000 per year. This means that the return on equity is 7.5 per cent (15 000/200 000 × 100) which is more than the 5 per cent owner could have earned by leaving her £200 000 in a savings account. However, the extra interest will have been gained by accepting a higher level of risk.

5 **Economic value added** (**EVA**) was developed by Stern Stewart & Co. It compares a company's profitability with a minimum level of profitability elsewhere. It is usually the

difference between the return achieved by an organisation and the rate of interest on a standard loan from the bank (other comparators such as a stock index can be used). Economic value added is often used as an index of how well a company is creating wealth for its owners. The formula for calculating EVA is:

$$\text{EVA} = \text{Net operating profit after tax} - [\text{Capital} \times \text{Rate of interest}]$$

For example, a computer manufacturer in Singapore spent S\$100 million, which it could otherwise invest in securities at 9 per cent, on a new factory. The new factory produced a net operating profit of S\$11 million. An S\$11 million profit seems most acceptable. However, the EVA by the new factory is:

$$\text{EVA} = 11m - [100m \times 0.09] = 11m - 9m = 2m$$

In other words, taking the opportunity costs into account the new factory added an extra 2 per cent value to what could have been earned by keeping the money on deposit – not a big improvement considering the effort and risk involved.

Debt ratios

Debt ratios are just as important as profitability ratios because a large number of organisations operate on credit. This is true of governments, charitable organisations and commercial companies. In itself, debt is not a problem – it can increase productivity. For example, a government may realise that a new school will improve literacy and, in the long run, the welfare of the population. However, it may not have sufficient funds in its current budget and it may be unable to increase taxes. In these circumstances it may make sense to borrow money and make repayments in future years when the benefits start to feed through to the community. Similarly, a bio-technology company may calculate that a new laboratory will be able to obtain a return of 17 per cent on capital employed. A bank may be prepared to lend the capital at 11 per cent. Again, in these circumstances, it would be sensible to borrow money to build the new laboratory. However, debt has its dangers. The greatest danger is that organisations borrow more money than they can repay (service). Debt ratios aim to provide information to help organisations avoid taking on too much debt and to warn lenders against unsound loans. There are four main debt ratios: gearing, interest cover, liquidity and "the acid test".

1   **Gearing** is also called "leverage" or "debt ratio". The basic principles of gearing were described in the previous paragraph: organisations may be able to generate a higher rate of return than the interest they would be required to pay. Gearing indicates the proportion of an organisation's assets which have been purchased on credit. The most usual index of gearing is:

$$\text{Gearing} = \frac{\text{Long-term debt}}{\text{Shareholder's equity}}$$

The level of gearing shows considerable variation from industry to industry. For example, in the transport industry the average gearing ratio is 150 per cent, in the building industry it is about 130 per cent while in a service industry gearing is about 100 per cent. Organisations that operate in very stable, predictable environments, such as public utilities or brewing, can service high rates of debt. On the other hand, lenders will be wary of loans to organisations operating in dynamic but turbulent environments, such as the building industry. A high gearing ratio means that an organisation will experience a greater profit in favourable times. Conversely, high gearing means that an organisation will suffer disproportionately when times are hard and interest rates increase.

2 Sometimes, the level of debt is evaluated using an index known as "**interest cover**" or "times interest earned". This ratio portrays the interest needed to service a debt as a proportion of the organisation's income. The formula is:

$$\text{Interest cover} = \frac{\text{Profit before interest and tax}}{\text{Total interest payments}}$$

Obviously, if the income of an organisation is much greater than its interest payments it is a good proposition for potential lenders.

3 **Liquidity** is a property that allows material to flow freely between one point and another. In financial terms, it refers to the ability to transfer money. Some assets, such as cash, are very liquid and can be transferred from one owner to another in a matter of hours. Other assets, such as property, may take years before a buyer is found and its value can be liberated for transfer. An organisation's liquidity is very important to its debtors because it indicates the organisation's ability to meet its short-term debts. There are several ratios showing an organisation's liquidity. The most important is the **current ratio**:

$$\text{Current ratio} = \frac{\text{Current assets}}{\text{Current liabilities}}$$

Current assets include cash, invoices that have yet to be paid (accounts receivable) and the inventory of goods that lies waiting to be sold to customers. Current liabilities include invoices from suppliers that are waiting payment (accounts payable), accrued expenses and tax liabilities. The current ratio for commercial organisations varies from industry to industry but for manufacturing organisations it is generally about 2.

4 Some organisations apply a stricter liquidity ratio. It is generally called the "**acid test**" but also the "quick ratio" because it indicates how quickly an organisation can make payments, i.e. meet its short-term liabilities without selling its inventory of goods waiting to be sold. The acid ratio is:

$$\text{Acid test} = \frac{\text{Current assets - inventory}}{\text{Current liabilities}}$$

This chapter has only provided a brief introduction to the FA function. However, it has shown that the function is vital to any organisation and the people working in it contribute far more to an organisation than "just counting beans"!

Activities and further study

Essay plans

Write essay plans for the following questions:

1 What measures can an organisation take to protect itself from the risk of bad credit and fraud?

2 What is the role of the finance function in raising money for an organisation?

3 How can the finance function guide an organisation in the investment of its resources?

4 Using the published accounts of an organisation that interests you, explain the organisation's profit and loss account, its balance sheet and its cash-flow statement.

Web activities

1 Look at the sites of professional bodies in finance and accounting such as:

http://www.icaew.co.uk/ (Institute of Chartered Accountants in England and Wales)

www.cipfa.org.uk (Chartered institute of Public and Finance Accounting)

www.icai.ie (The Institute of Chartered Accountants in Ireland).

2 Look up details of finance and accounting scandals, e.g.: http://www.corporatenarc.com/accountingscandals.php

3 Watch some youTube clips on the Enron scandal, e.g. "Enron, the smartest guys in the room" (10 clips), "The effects of Enron Fraud".

Experiential activities

1 It is possible to gain some first-hand experience of finance and accounting with vacation work or, perhaps, a management training scheme with short periods of work in different functions ("Cooks Tours").

2 If possible talk to a manager working in the FA function. Try to get detailed answers to the following questions: What type of organisation is it? What are its goals? What is its basic transformation process? How does the function operate? What are the future challenges the FA function is likely to face?

3 Choose the financial statements contained in the annual report of a company that interests you. Most can be found on the Internet: http://www.hemscott.com/help/company-reports.do. Compare the financial statements with those of Tesco.

Recommended reading

1 Mattessich, R. (2003) "Accounting research and researchers of the nineteenth century and the beginning of the twentieth century: an international survey of authors, ideas and publications", *Accounting Business & Financial History*, **13** (2), 125–170. A reference source rather than a read, this is a good place to start tracing ideas in accounting and finance. Useful for seminars, tutorials and assignments.

2 The Financial Services Skills Council's website.
   www.fssc.org.uk/484808 13.html?i=8. This has a wealth of information on jobs in finance:

   - auditing
   - anti-fraud
   - business advisory
   - corporate finance
   - financial control
   - forensic accountancy
   - insolvency
   - payments and receipts
   - tax accountancy

3 "Tales from the sharp end", *Financial Management*, August 2010, 20–24. Four interesting vignettes of people working in finance and accounting (business consultancy, Africa; orchestra, UK; book-keeping, UK; shipping finance, Sri Lanka), which contain a lot of tacit knowledge.

Quality

Chapter THIRTEEN

Value-chain Management: Functional Strategies to Increase Quality, Efficiency and Responsiveness to Customers

LEARNING OBJECTIVES

After studying this chapter, you should be able to:

- ☑ Explain the role of value-chain management in achieving superior quality, efficiency and responsiveness to customers.
- ☑ Describe what customers want, and explain why it is so important for managers to be responsive to their needs.
- ☑ Explain why achieving superior quality is important.
- ☑ Describe the challenges facing managers and organisations that seek to implement quality management programmes.
- ☑ Explain why achieving superior efficiency is so important.
- ☑ Differentiate among facilities layout, flexible manufacturing, just-in-time (JIT) inventory and process reengineering.

A Manager's Challenge

Bricks, Clicks or Bricks-and-Clicks Supermarkets

How can managers increase operating performance?

The potential uses of IT and the Internet for improving responsiveness to customers became clear to companies in many industries in the late 1990s. One of these industries was the food delivery/supermarket industry. Many supermarkets decided that developing an online ordering system that allowed customers to use the Internet to order their food online and creating an operating system to deliver the food to their homes had enormous potential. An American virtual grocer raised more than £57 million to develop both the information system and the physical infrastructure of warehouses and hot and cold delivery trucks that it needed to deliver food to customers.

However, the world's largest online grocery retailer, the UK-based supermarket giant Tesco, opted for less investment by providing a store-based model. Because Tesco used its already established outlets, it reached a market coverage across England of 90 per cent. This is rivalled only by frozen food retailer Iceland, which has 95 per cent coverage across the UK.

The UK food market is worth between £80 and £100 billion and is dominated by a small number of large supermarket chains. The ongoing competition between Tesco, Sainsbury's, ASDA and Morrisons is only going to intensify away from the 'bricks & mortar' (B&M) of traditional in-store supermarket shopping. The competition has gained momentum; the UK is the global leader in online grocery shopping, overtaking the US and leaving other western European countries such as Spain, France and Italy trailing behind. The e-grocery business in the UK has experienced an annual growth of over 250 per cent; this has already forced smaller retailers such as Budgens and Somerfield to withdraw from selling their groceries online.

One of the first responses by B&M supermarkets was to take steps to make their customers' shopping experience more enjoyable. First, they improved their operations by building large, new, attractive stores that contained a wide variety of produce. Second, they increasingly incorporated IT into their operations to improve customer satisfaction with their stores: most supermarkets, for example, are now offering self-service tills. These IT improvements are seen to help operations because they eliminate lengthy checkout lines and help the company focus more on customer service. These moves have helped B&M supermarkets improve responsiveness to customers and increase the quality of their produce and service. They have also helped reduce operating costs, because customers perform their own services – including of course selecting their own produce and delivering it to their homes.

In Sweden the market share of e-grocers is the largest with approximately 2 per cent, whereby the supply chain model is mainly store-based. The UK has an approximate market share of 0.3–0.7 per cent and in the US the market share is approximately 0.2 per cent. The US operates mainly on a warehouse-based, purely online-based retail model, whereas most UK e-grocers are store-based and associated with established supermarket brands.

However, the question of which operating system is the most successful is difficult to predict. Most online grocery stores do not yet cover all their operating costs, which will, slowly, force some smaller retailers out of the e-grocery market, especially those focusing primarily on online sales. Datamonitor argues that, in order to survive, specialisation in either B&M or online will not be sufficient, and an amalgam of both is needed. Why? First, unlike their well-established B&M rivals, the new e-grocers did not possess the experience and ability to master the complex inventory management, sourcing, transportation, distribution, warehousing and logistics necessary to operate successfully in this market. Second, e-grocers totally underestimated the problems and costs of operating the production and physical delivery service necessary to get products to customers. Tesco opted for a store-based model, arguing that a warehouse-based model would require a minimum of 5,000 orders a week, with each order exceeding £100.

Virtual grocers need to take a careful look at how they are designing their operating systems. While it is still the fastest growing e-commerce market, many players collapsed after initial success in the late 1990s.

Overview

Virtual grocers use IT and the Internet to develop an operating system that may be very responsive to customers but can be very costly and inefficient compared to the systems used by the B&M supermarket chains. Some also failed to develop functional strategies that could have helped their operating systems work more efficiently – such as smaller, warehouse-based e-grocers such as Webvan, an American e-grocer that went bankrupt. The B&M supermarkets, on the other hand, made innovations in their materials management, sales and information systems that allowed them to achieve superior quality, efficiency and responsiveness to customers. Possessing these sources of competitive advantage, they retain control of the £80–£100 billion grocery market.

In this chapter the focus is on **value-chain management** and the functional (or operational) strategies that managers can use to increase the performance of a company's **operating system** – specifically, to improve the quality of a company's goods and services, the efficiency with which they are produced and the level of responsiveness to its customers. By the end of this chapter, you will understand the vital role value-chain management plays in building competitive advantage and creating a high-performing organisation.

Value-chain Management and Competitive Advantage

Value-chain management is the development of a set of functional-level strategies that can increase the performance of the operating system a company uses to transform inputs into finished products and services. An *operating system* is composed of the various different *functional activities* (marketing, materials management or production) an organisation uses to acquire inputs, convert inputs into outputs and dispose of the outputs (products or services). Functional managers are responsible for managing an organisation's operating system; they are the ones who decide what kind of functional strategies each function should pursue to build competitive advantage. Specifically, their job is to manage the value chain to determine where operating improvements might be made to increase quality, efficiency and responsiveness to customers – and so give an organisation a competitive advantage.

The Value Chain

The **value chain** refers to the idea that a company is a *chain of functional activities* that transforms inputs into an output of products or services that are valued by the customer. The process of transforming inputs into outputs is composed of a number of functional operating activities, or an *operating system*, beginning with the need to acquire inputs, to design and control conversion processes and to distribute and sell products and services. Each activity adds value to the product and so increases the price a company can charge for its products. A value chain is illustrated in Fig. 9.1, in which several important functional activities are represented.

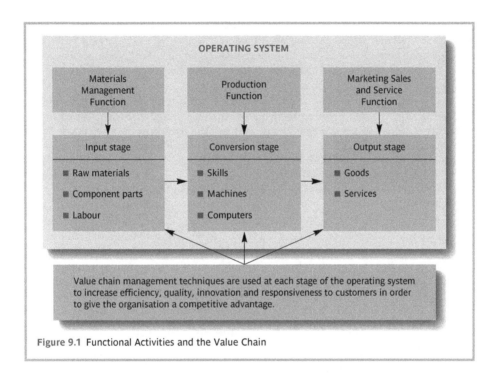

Figure 9.1 Functional Activities and the Value Chain

The **production function** is responsible for the *creation of a product or service*. For physical products, when we talk about production, we generally mean manufacturing. For services such as banking or retailing, production typically takes place when the service is actually delivered to the customer (when a bank provides a loan to a customer, for example it is engaged in 'production' of the loan). By performing its activities efficiently, the production function of a company helps to lower its cost structure. The efficient production operations of some Japanese companies, such as Honda and Toyota, are helping those companies achieve higher profitability relative to competitors such as Volkswagen, Saab or Volvo. The production function of a company can also perform its activities in a way that is consistent with high product quality, which may also lead to differentiation (and higher value) and lower costs.

There are several ways in which the **marketing/sales functions** of a company can help to create value. By *positioning* and *advertising* a brand appropriately, the marketing function can increase the value that customers perceive to be contained in a company's product. As branding aids in creating a favourable impression of the company's product in the minds of customers, they increase value. In the 1980s, the French company Perrier persuaded customers that slightly carbonated bottled water was worth £0.90 for 750 ml, rather than the £0.87 it cost to purchase 5 litres of spring water from the supermarket's own brand. Perrier's marketing function essentially developed marketing strategies that increased the perception of value that customers ascribed to the product. In the 1990s, major companies such as Coca-Cola and PepsiCo rushed to bring out their own bottled-water labels to capitalise on customers' growing appetite for bottled water. The total UK market for bottled water is worth in the region of 50 million litres which equates to about £30 million.

The role of the **service function** is to provide *after-sales service and support*. This function can create a perception of superior value in the minds of customers by solving customer problems and supporting customers after they have purchased the product. DHL, the German-owned logistic company, is able to get its customers' parcels to any point in the world within 24 hours, thereby lowering the cost of their own value-creation activities.

The **materials management function** controls the movement of *physical materials* through the value chain – from procurement through production and into distribution. The efficiency with which this is carried out can significantly lower cost and thus create more value. Wal-Mart, the owner of ASDA supermarkets, has the most efficient materials management function in the retail industry. By tightly controlling the flow of goods from its suppliers through its stores and into the hands of customers, Wal-Mart/ASDA has eliminated the need to hold large inventories of goods. Lower inventories mean lower costs, and hence greater value creation.

Finally, the **information systems function** controls the *electronic systems* for managing inventory, tracking sales, pricing products, selling products, dealing with customer service enquiries and so on. Information systems, when coupled with the communications features of the Internet, are holding out the promise of being able to alter the efficiency and effectiveness with which a company manages its other value-creation activities. Many delivery companies are now allowing you to track your parcels on the Internet, for example. However, the implementation of IT adds value only if all other functions are efficiently and effectively organised.

Functional Strategies and Competitive Advantage

In managing the value chain to create a high-performing operating system, functional managers need to attend to the four major goals discussed in Chapter 1:[1]

1. *To attain superior efficiency*   Efficiency is a measure of the amount of *inputs* required to produce a given *amount* of outputs. The fewer the inputs required to produce a given output, the higher is the efficiency and the lower the cost of outputs. In 1990, it took the average Japanese auto company 16.8 employee-hours to build a car, while the average American car company took 25.1 employee-hours. Japanese companies at that time were more efficient and had lower costs than their western rivals.[2] By 2004, US companies, and many European manufacturers, had adopted more efficient manufacturing methods and narrowed the gap significantly; matching Japanese quality levels, however, has been more difficult.

2. *To attain superior quality*   'Quality' here means producing goods and services that are reliable – they do what they were designed for, and do it well.[3] Providing high-quality products creates a *brand-name reputation* for an organisation's products. In turn, this enhanced reputation allows the organisation to charge a higher price. In the automobile industry, for example, not only does Toyota have an efficiency-based cost advantage over many European competitors, but the higher quality of Toyota's products has also enabled the company to earn more money because customers are willing to pay a premium price for its cars.

3. *To attain superior speed, flexibility and innovation*   Anything new or better about the way an organisation operates or the goods and services it produces is the result of innovation. Innovation leads to advances in the kinds of products, production processes, management systems, organisational structures and strategies that an organisation develops. Successful innovation gives an organisation something *unique* that its rivals lack. This uniqueness may enhance value added and thereby allow the organisation to differentiate itself from its rivals

and attract customers who will pay a premium price for its product. Toyota, for example, is widely credited with pioneering a number of critical innovations in the way that cars are built, and these innovations have helped Toyota achieve superior productivity and quality, the basis of the company's competitive advantage. VW tried a similar innovation by creating their modular consortium plant for the production of HGVs in Brazil.[4] Rather than using a large number of suppliers, an expensive manufacturing process and a large number of employees, VW created an *integrated assembly plant* that incorporated the seven major contributors. Each of those contributors assembled a particular modular for the vehicles, but all seven at the same assembly line. VW's investment was a contribution to the plant and infrastructure and its remaining responsibility was quality control, marketing and sales of the vehicles.

4. *To attain superior responsiveness to customers*   An organisation that is responsive to customers tries to satisfy their needs and give them exactly what they want. An organisation that treats customers better than its rivals provides a valuable service, for which customers may be willing to pay a higher price.

In managing the value chain to add value, or lower the costs of creating value, functional managers need to find ways to attain superior quality, efficiency, innovation and responsiveness to customers. Functional managers are responsible for ensuring that an organisation has sufficient supplies of high-quality, low-cost inputs, and they are also responsible for designing an operating system that creates high-quality, low-cost products that customers are willing to buy. Notice, however, that achieving superior efficiency, quality and innovation is part of attaining superior responsiveness to customers. Customers want value for their money, and an organisation that develops functional strategies that lead to a high-performing operating system creates new high-quality, low-cost products that best deliver this value. For this reason, the chapter begins by discussing how functional managers can design the operating system to increase responsiveness to customers.

Improving Responsiveness to Customers

Organisations create outputs – products or services – that are consumed by customers. All organisations, profit-seeking or not-for-profit, have customers: without customers, most organisations would cease to exist. Because customers are vital to the survival of most organisations, managers must correctly identify their customers and pursue the strategies that respond to their needs. This is why the marketing function plays such an important part in the value chain. Management writers recommend that marketing managers should focus on defining their company's business in terms of the customer needs they are satisfying, and not simply the type of products they make or provide.[5] The credo of the pharmaceutical company Johnson & Johnson, for example, begins: 'We believe our first responsibility is to the doctors, nurses and patients, to mothers and fathers and all others who use our products and services'.[6] Through this credo, Johnson & Johnson's managers emphasise their commitment to exemplary customer service.

In contrast, in the early 2000s, Lucent Technologies, a spin-off of AT&T, decided that, given its expertise in transistor technology, it would focus on producing transistor-based Internet routers that could handle vast quantities of information. When it became clear that customers were choosing optical Internet routers because these routers could transfer information extremely quickly, Lucent lost a large part of its business, and by 2004 had radically altered its strategies to focus on a narrow range of high-speed networking devices that allow Internet service providers to offer their business customers high-speed, secure Internet access.[7]

What Do Customers Want?

Given that satisfying customer demands is central to the survival of an organisation, an important question is: What do customers want? Specifying exactly what they want is usually not possible because wants vary from industry to industry. However, it is possible to identify some *universal product attributes* that most customers in most industries want. Generally, other things being equal, most customers prefer:

1. A lower price to a higher price
2. High-quality products to low-quality products
3. Quick service to slow service (they will always prefer good after-sales service and support to poor after-sales service and support)
4. Products with many features to products with few features (they will prefer a personal computer with a CD-ROM drive, lots of memory and a powerful microprocessor to one without these features)
5. Products that are, as far as possible, customised or tailored to their unique needs.

Of course, the problem is that other things are not equal. Providing high-quality, quick service and after-sales service and support, products with many features and products that are customised raises operating costs and thus the price that must be charged to cover these costs.[8] So customer demand for these attributes typically conflicts with their demand for low prices. Customers must thus make a *trade-off* between price and preferred attributes, and so must managers. This price/attribute trade-off is illustrated in Fig. 9.2.

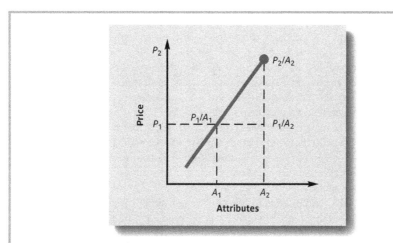

Figure 9.2 The Price–Attribute Relationship

The desired attributes of a product – such as high quality, service, speed, after-sales support, features and customisation – are plotted on the horizontal axis in Fig. 9.2. Price is plotted on the vertical axis. The solid line shows the price–attribute relationship – i.e. the combination of price and attributes an organisation can offer and still make a profit. As Fig. 9.2 illustrates, the higher the price the customer is willing to pay for a product, the more desired attributes the customer is able to get. In other words, the more desired attributes that an organisation can build into its products, the higher is the price that the organisation will have to charge to cover its costs. At price P_1 managers can offer a product with A_1 attributes. If managers offer a product with A_2 attributes at price P_1, they will lose money because the price is too low to cover costs. A product with A_2 attributes needs a price of P_2 to be profitable for the organisation. The nature of the organisation's operating system thus *limits* how responsive managers can be to customers.

Given the limits imposed on managers by their existing operating system, what can the managers of a customer-responsive organisation try to do? They can try to develop functional strategies to push or shift the price–attribute curve to the right (toward the vertical dotted line in Fig. 9.2) by developing new or improved operating systems that are able to deliver either more desired product attributes for the same price, or the same product attributes for a lower price.[9]

Figure 9.3 shows the price-attribute curves for a supermarket chain in the 1990s, before the introduction of customer-oriented IT. The second line represents the same supermarket chain in the 2000s, when new self-service tills and new store design were put in place. By accommodating customer demands for a greater variety of foods, increased quality and quicker customer service, the new operating system allowed the supermarket to offer more product attributes at a similar or even lower price to customers. The shift from a traditional to a modern, IT-oriented store operation thus increased its responsiveness to customers and did so without imposing higher costs.

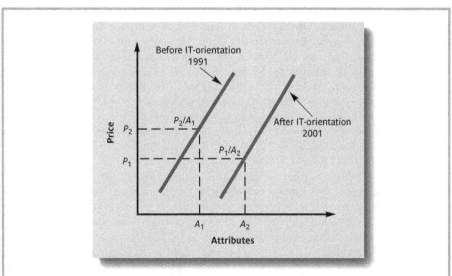

Figure 9.3 Supermarket Price–Attribute Curve

Designing Operating Systems Responsive to Customers

Because satisfying customers is so important, managers try to design operating systems that can produce the outputs that have the attributes customers desire. The attributes of an organisation's outputs – their quality, cost and features – are determined by the organisation's operating system.[10] As discussed earlier, the need to respond to customer demands for competitively priced, quality food drove managers of supermarkets to choose a new store operation system. The imperative of satisfying customer needs shaped Sainsbury's 'production' system. When managers focus on being responsive to their customers, and not just on producing or providing a product, they find new ways to reduce costs and increase quality – such as the introduction of faster self-service tills.

Since the ability of an organisation to satisfy the demands of its customers derives from its operating system, managers need to devote considerable attention to *value-chain management*. Managers' desire to attract customers by shifting the price–attribute line to the right explains their adoption of many new functional strategies to build competitive advantage into their operating systems. These include total quality management (TQM), flexible manufacturing systems, JIT inventory and, of course, new information systems and technologies that can accelerate the sale and delivery of products to customers.

As an example of the link between responsiveness to customers and an organisation's operating system, consider the success of low-cost airlines such as Easyjet or Flybe. One of the most consistently successful airlines, Easyjet expanded rapidly in the early 2000s.[11] One reason for Easyjet's success is that its managers created an operating system uniquely tailored to satisfy the demands of its customers for low-priced, reliable (on-time) and convenient air travel. Easyjet commands high customer loyalty precisely because its operating system delivers products – such as flights from and to most major cities in Europe – that have all the desired attributes: reliability, convenience and low price.

Easyjet's low-cost operating system focuses not only on improving the maintenance of aircraft but also on the company's ticket reservation system, route structure, flight frequency, baggage-handling system and in-flight services. Each of these elements of the operating system is geared toward satisfying customer demands for low-priced, reliable and convenient air travel. Easyjet offers a 'no-frills' approach to in-flight customer service: no meals are served onboard unless you purchase them, and there are no first-class seats. Easyjet does not subscribe to the big reservation computers used by travel agents because the booking fees are too costly, and instead predominantly uses a web-based booking and ticketing system. The airline originally only flew one aircraft, the fuel-efficient Boeing 737, which kept training and maintenance costs down, although they have now added an Airbus model to their fleet. All this translates into low prices for customers.

Easyjet's reliability derives from the fact that it has an extremely fast aircraft turnaround time. An Easyjet ground crew needs only 15–30 minutes to turn around an incoming aircraft and prepare it for departure, a speedy operation which helps to keep flights on time. Easyjet can also deploy their multi-tasking employees to perform a variety of jobs, which keeps employee numbers down. In addition, Easyjet is very strict on closing flights on time to ensure that each flight is able to depart on its allocated slot; every slot missed incurs additional cost.

Easyjet's convenience comes from the scheduling of multiple flights every day between its popular locations and the use of airports that are close to downtown instead of more distant airports (a model that is applied by other no-frills airlines in Europe and North America).[12] Easyjet, unlike other low-cost carriers such as Ryanair, uses main airports that have the infrastructure to allow passengers a quick and efficient onward journey. In sum, Easyjet's excellent value-chain management has given it a competitive advantage in the airline industry.

Although managers must seek to improve their responsiveness to customers by improving their organisations' operating systems, they should not offer a level of responsiveness to customers that is more than can *profitably be sustained*. The company that customises every product to the unique demands of individual customers is likely to see its cost structure become so high that unit costs exceed unit revenues. This happened to Toyota in the 1990s when its managers tried to provide customers with many choices of car models and specifications. This increased costs faster than it generated additional revenues: at one point, Toyota factories were producing literally thousands of variations of Toyota's basic models, such as the Avensis and Corolla. Managers at Toyota concluded that the costs of extreme customisation were exceeding the benefits, and cut back on the number of models and specifications of its cars.[13]

Improving Quality

As noted earlier, high-quality products are reliable, dependable and satisfying. They do the job they were designed for, and meet customer requirements.[14] *Quality* is a concept that can be applied to the products of both manufacturing and service organisations – goods such as a Toyota car or a Tesco ready meal, or services such as Easyjet's flight service or customer service at your local bank. Why do managers seek to control and improve the quality of their organisations' products?[15] There are two reasons (Fig. 9.4).

First, customers usually prefer a higher-quality product to a lower-quality product. So an organisation that is able to provide, *for the same price*, a product of higher quality than a competitor's product is serving its customers better – it is being more responsive to its customers. Often, providing high-quality products creates a brand-name reputation for an organisation's products. In turn, this enhanced reputation may allow the organisation to charge more for its products than its competitors, and thus it makes even greater profits. In 2005, the most reliable car in the UK was a Honda. The only European manufacturers in the Top 10 were Skoda and Mercedes-Benz.[16] The high quality of Honda vehicles enabled the company to charge higher prices for its cars than the prices charged by rival auto makers.

Figure 9.4 The Impact of Increased Quality on Organisational Performance

The second reason for trying to boost product quality is that higher product quality can increase *efficiency* and thereby lower operating costs and boost profits. Achieving high product quality lowers operating costs because of the effect of quality on employee productivity: higher product quality means that less employee time is wasted in making defective products that must be discarded or in providing substandard services, and thus less time has to be spent fixing mistakes. This translates into *higher employee productivity*, which means lower costs.

Total Quality Management

At the forefront of the drive to improve product quality is a technique known as *total quality management* (TQM).[17] TQM focuses on improving the quality of an organisation's products and services and stresses that all of an organisation's value-chain activities should be directed toward this goal. Conceived as an organisation-wide management programme, TQM requires the co-operation of managers in every function of an organisation. The TQM concept was developed by a number of American consultants, including the late W. Edwards Deming, Joseph Juran and A. V. Feigenbaum.[18]

What actions should managers take to implement a successful TQM programme? Ten steps are necessary to make a TQM control system work.

1. *Build organisational commitment to quality*   TQM will do little to improve the performance of an organisation unless all employees embrace it, and this often requires a change in an organisation's *culture*.[19] At Citibank, discussed in detail in Case 9.1, the process of changing culture began at the top. First, a group of senior managers, including the CEO, received training in TQM from consultants from Motorola. Each member of the senior management group was then given the responsibility of training a group at the next level in the hierarchy, and so on down through the organisation until all 100,000 employees had received basic TQM training.

2. *Focus on the customer*   TQM practitioners see a focus on the customer as the starting point.[20] According to TQM philosophy, the *customer*, not managers in quality control or engineering, defines what quality is. The challenge is fourfold: (1) to identify what customers want from the good or service that the company provides; (2) to identify what the company actually provides to customers; (3) to identify the gap that exists between what customers want and what they actually get (the *quality gap*); and (4) to formulate a plan for closing the quality gap. The efforts of Citibank managers to increase responsiveness to customers illustrate this aspect of TQM well (Case 9.1).

Case 9.1: **Citibank uses TQM to increase customer loyalty**

Citibank is one of the leading financial institutions, operating in a large number of countries, including Germany and the UK, where it was voted best Internet bank. Citibank's goal is to become *the* premier institution in the twenty-first century. To achieve this goal, Citibank has started to use TQM to increase its responsiveness to customers, recognising that, ultimately, it is its customer base and customer loyalty that will determine its future success.

As the first step in its TQM effort, Citibank identified the factors that *dissatisfied* its customers. When analysing complaints, it found that most concerned the time it took to complete a customer's request, such as responding to an account problem or getting a loan. So Citibank's managers began to examine how they handled each kind of customer request. For each distinct request, they formed a cross-functional team that broke down a specific request into the steps between people and departments that were needed to complete it. Teams found that many steps in the process were often unnecessary and could be replaced by using the right information systems. They also found that delays often occurred because employees simply did not know how to handle a request: they were not being given the right kind of training. When they couldn't handle a request, they simply put it aside until a supervisor could deal with it.

Citibank's second step to increase its responsiveness was to implement an organisation-wide TQM programme. Managers and supervisors were charged with reducing the complexity of the work process and finding the most effective way to process each particular request, such as a request for a loan. Managers were also charged with training employees to answer each specific request. The results were remarkable. In the loan department the TQM programme reduced the number of handoffs necessary to process a request by 75 per cent. The department's average response time dropped from several hours to 30 minutes. By 2000, more than 92,000 employees worldwide had been trained in the new TQM processes, and Citibank could easily measure effectiveness by the increased speed with which it was handling an increased volume of customer requests.

3. *Find ways to measure quality*   Another crucial element of any TQM programme is the creation of a *measuring system* that managers can consistently use to evaluate quality. Devising appropriate measures is relatively easy in manufacturing companies, where quality can be measured by criteria such as defects per million parts. It is more difficult in service companies, where outputs are less tangible. However, with a little creativity, suitable quality measures can be devised, as they were by managers at Citibank. The common theme is that managers must identify what 'quality' means from a *customer's* perspective and devise some measure that can capture this.

4. *Set goals and create incentives*   Once a measure has been devised, managers' next step is to set a *challenging quality goal* and to create *incentives* for reaching it. At Citibank, the CEO set an initial goal of reducing customer complaints by 50 per cent. One way of creating incentives to attain a goal is to link rewards, such as bonus pay and promotional opportunities, to it.

5. *Solicit input from employees*   Employees can be a major source of information about the causes of poor quality. It is therefore important for managers to establish a framework for soliciting employee suggestions about improvements that can be made. **Quality circles (QCs)** – groups of employees who meet regularly to discuss ways to increase quality – are often created to achieve this goal. Companies also create self-managed teams to further quality improvement efforts. Whatever the means chosen to solicit input from lower-level employees, managers must be open to receiving, and acting on, bad news and criticism from employees.

6. *Identify defects and trace them to their source*   A major source of product defects is the *operating system*. TQM preaches the need for managers to identify defects in the work process, trace those defects back to their source, find out why they occur and make corrections so that they do not occur again. To identify defects, the use of statistical procedures to spot variations in the quality of goods or services may be used, and IT makes the measurement of quality much easier.

7. *Introduce JIT inventory systems*   Inventory is the stock of raw materials, inputs and component parts that an organisation has at its disposal at a particular time. JIT inventory systems play a major role in the process of identifying and finding the source of defects in inputs. When the materials management function designs a JIT inventory system, parts or supplies arrive at the organisation when they are needed, and not before. With a JIT inventory system component parts travel from suppliers to the assembly line in a small-wheeled container known as a *kanban*. Assembly-line workers empty the kanbans and the empty container is then sent back to the supplier as the signal to produce another small batch of component parts, and so the process repeats itself. This system can be contrasted with a *just-in-case* view of inventory, which leads an organisation to stockpile excess inputs in a warehouse just in case it needs them to meet sudden upturns in demand.

Under a JIT inventory system, defective parts enter an organisation's operating system immediately; they are not warehoused for months before use. This means that *defective inputs* can be quickly spotted. Materials managers can then trace the problem to the supply source and fix it before more defective parts are produced.

8. *Work closely with suppliers*   A major cause of poor-quality finished goods is poor-quality *component parts*. To decrease product defects, materials managers must work closely with suppliers to improve the quality of the parts they supply. Managers at Xerox worked closely with suppliers to get them to adopt TQM programmes, and the result was a huge reduction in the defect rate of component parts. Managers also need to work closely with suppliers to get them to adopt the JIT inventory system necessary for high quality.

To implement JIT systems with suppliers, and to get suppliers to set up their own TQM programmes, two steps are necessary. First, managers must reduce the *number of suppliers* with which their organisations do business. Second, managers need to develop *co-operative long-term relationships* with remaining suppliers. Over the years, managers at Dell Computer reduced the number of suppliers they needed to a minimum, which greatly streamlined their interactions with suppliers and led to increased quality and lower-cost inputs. The modular consortium approach adopted by VW also reduced the number of direct suppliers. VW is responsible only for the assembly and quality control so they reduced the number of direct suppliers from over 200 to seven modular manufacturers.

9. *Design for ease of production*   The more steps required to assemble a product or provide a service, the more opportunities there are for making a mistake. It follows that designing products that have fewer parts, or finding ways to simplify providing a service, should be linked with fewer defects or customer complaints. Dell continually redesigns the way it assembles its computers to reduce the number of assembly steps required and to search for new ways to reduce the number of components that have to be linked together. The consequence of these redesign efforts has been a fall in assembly costs and a marked improvement in product quality that has led to Dell's becoming the Number One global PC maker. Dell also has striven to improve its procedures for helping customers who experience problems with their new PCs.

10. *Break down barriers between functions*   Successful implementation of TQM requires substantial co-operation between the different functions of an organisation. Materials managers have to co-operate with manufacturing managers to find high-quality inputs that reduce manufacturing costs; marketing managers have to co-operate with manufacturing so that customer problems identified by marketing can be acted on; information systems have to

co-operate with all of the other functions of the company to devise suitable IT training programmes; and so on.

In essence, to increase quality, all functional managers need to co-operate to develop strategic plans that state goals precisely and spell out how they will be achieved. Managers should embrace the philosophy that mistakes, defects and poor-quality materials are not acceptable, and should be eliminated. Functional managers should spend more time working with employees and providing them with the tools they need to do the job. Managers should create an environment in which employees will not be afraid to report problems or recommend improvements. Output goals and targets need to include not only numbers or quotas but also some notion of quality to promote the production of *defect-free output*. Functional managers also need to train employees in new skills to keep pace with changes in the workplace. Achieving better quality also requires that managers develop *organisational values* and *norms* centred on improving quality.

TQM is now an established model and has been implemented widely across the world. Like other management theories, other models have been developed. Another quality model is the **EFQM model** that was introduced in the early 1990s and has been widely adopted across Europe. It differs from the traditional TQM model as it is an excellence model that focuses on a number of different areas – such as leadership, customer focus, results, employee involvement, continuous learning, partnership involvement and corporate social responsibility. It is a process model that is easily combinable with other quality initiatives such as Investors in People.[21]

Reaction Time

1. What are the main challenges to be overcome in implementing a successful TQM programme?

2. Widespread dissatisfaction with the results of TQM programmes has been reported in the popular press. Why do you think TQM programmes frequently fail to deliver their promised benefits?

Improving Efficiency

The third goal of value-chain management is to increase the efficiency of an organisation's operating system. The fewer the inputs required to produce a given output, the higher will be the operating system's efficiency. Managers can measure efficiency at the organisation level in two ways. The measure known as **total factor productivity (TFP)** looks at how well an organisation utilises all of its resources – such as labour, capital, materials or energy – to produce its outputs. It is expressed in the following equation:

$$\text{TFP} = \frac{\text{Outputs}}{\text{All inputs}}$$

The problem with TFP is that each input is typically measured in *different units*: labour's contribution to producing an output is measured by hours worked; the contribution of materials is measured by the amount consumed (for example, tons of iron ore required to make a ton of steel); the contribution of energy is measured by the units of energy consumed (for example, kilowatt-hours, kWh); and so on. To compute TFP, managers must convert all the inputs to a *common unit*, such as pounds sterling (£), before they can work the equation.

Although sometimes a useful measure of efficiency overall, TFP can obscure the precise contribution of an individual input – such as labour – to the production of a given output. Consequently, most organisations focus on a specific measure of efficiency, known as *partial productivity*, which measures the efficiency of an *individual unit*. For example, the efficiency of labour inputs can be expressed as:

$$\text{Labour productivity} = \frac{\text{Outputs}}{\text{Direct labour}}$$

Labour productivity is most commonly used to draw efficiency comparisons between different organisations. One study found that in 1994 it took the average Japanese automobile components supplier half as many labour hours as the average British company to produce a part such as a car seat or exhaust system.[22] The study concluded that Japanese companies used labour more efficiently than British companies. In the 1990s car companies throughout the world strove to catch up with the Japanese and many, such as Vauxhall and Ford, closed the efficiency gap significantly.

The *management of efficiency* is an extremely important issue in most organisations, because increased efficiency lowers production costs, thereby allowing the organisation to make a greater profit or to attract more customers by lowering its price. In 1990, the price of the average PC was £1,700; by 1995 it was about £1,000; in 2004 it was about £500. This decrease occurred despite the fact that the power and capabilities of the average PC increased dramatically during this period (microprocessors became more powerful, memory increased, modems were built in and multimedia capability was added).

Why was the decrease in price possible? PC makers such as Dell focused on quality and used TQM to boost their efficiency by improving the quality of their components and making PCs easier to assemble. This allowed them to lower their costs and prices and still make a profit.[23] While TQM is an important step in the drive to raise efficiency, several other factors are also important.

Facilities Layout, Flexible Manufacturing and Efficiency

Another factor that influences efficiency is the way managers decide to lay out or design an organisation's physical work facilities. This is important for two reasons. First, the way in which machines and workers are organised or grouped together into workstations affects the efficiency of the operating system. Second, a major determinant of efficiency is the cost associated with setting up the equipment needed to make a particular product. Facilities layout is the process of designing the machine–worker interface to increase operating system efficiency. Flexible manufacturing is the set of techniques, usually IT-based, that attempts to reduce the costs associated with an operating system. This might be the way computers are made on a production line, or the way patients are routed through a hospital.

Facilities layout

The way in which machines, robots and people are grouped together affects how *productive* they can be. Figure 9.5 shows three basic ways of arranging workstations: product layout, process layout and fixed-position layout.

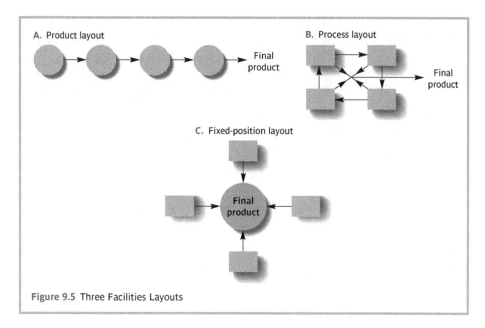

Figure 9.5 Three Facilities Layouts

In a *product layout*, machines are organised so that each operation needed to manufacture a product is performed at workstations arranged in a fixed sequence. Within less tangible products, processes are arranged in a similarly fixed sequence: workers are stationary in this arrangement, and a moving conveyor belt takes the product being worked on to the next workstation so that it is progressively assembled. *Mass production* is the familiar name for this layout, and car assembly lines are probably the best-known example. Product layout used to be efficient only when products were created in large quantities; however, the introduction of *modular assembly lines* controlled by computers is making it efficient to make products in small batches.

In a *process layout*, workstations are not organised in a fixed sequence. Each workstation is relatively self-contained, and a product goes to whichever workstation is needed to perform the next operation to complete the product. Process layout is often suited to manufacturing settings that produce a variety of custom-made products, each tailored to the needs of a different kind of customer. A custom furniture manufacturer might use a process layout so that different teams of workers can produce different styles of chairs or tables made from different kinds of woods and finishes. Such a layout also describes how a patient might go through a hospital from emergency room, to X-ray room, to operating theatre and so on. A process layout provides the flexibility needed to *change* a product, whether it is a PC or a patient. Such flexibility, however, often reduces efficiency because it is expensive.

In a *fixed-position layout*, the product stays in a fixed position. Its component parts are produced in remote workstations and are brought to the production area for final assembly. Increasingly, *self-managed teams* are using fixed-position layouts: different teams assemble each component part and then send the parts to the final assembly team, which makes the final product. A fixed-position layout is commonly used for products such as jet airlines, mainframe computers and gas turbines – products that are complex and difficult to assemble or are so large that moving them from one workstation to another is difficult. The effects of moving from one facilities layout to another can be dramatic (Case 9.2).

Case 9.2: **Paddy Hopkirk improves facilities layout**

Paddy Hopkirk established his car accessories business in Bedfordshire, England, shortly after he had shot to car-racing fame by winning the Monte Carlo Rally. Sales of Hopkirk's accessories, such as bicycle racks and axle stands, were always brisk, but Hopkirk was the first to admit that his operating system left a lot to be desired, so he invited consultants to help reorganise it.

After analysing his factory's operating system, the consultants realised that the source of the problem was the *facilities layout* that Hopkirk had established. Over time, as sales grew, Hopkirk simply added new workstations to the operating system as they were needed. The result was a process layout in which the product being assembled moved in the irregular sequences shown in the 'Before Change' section of Fig. 9.6. The consultants suggested that to save time and effort, the workstations should be reorganised into the sequential product layout shown in the 'After Change' section of Fig. 9.6.

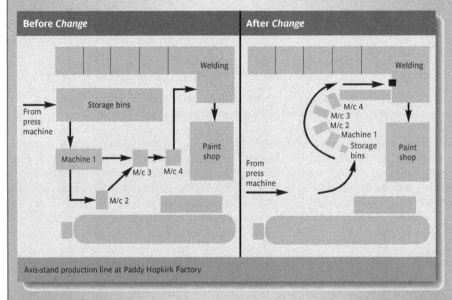

Axis-stand production line at Paddy Hopkirk Factory

Figure 9.6 Changing a Facilities Layout
Source: 'The Application of Kaizen to Facilities Layout', *Financial Times*, 4 January 1994, 12. Reprinted by permission of Financial Times Syndication, London.

Once this change was made, the results were dramatic. One morning the factory was an untidy sprawl of workstations surrounded by piles of crates holding semi-finished components. Two days later, when the 170-person workforce came back to work, the machines had been brought together into tightly grouped workstations arranged in the fixed sequence shown in Fig. 9.6. The piles of components had disappeared and the newly cleared floor space was neatly marked with colour-coded lines mapping out the new flow of materials between workstations.

In the first full day of production, efficiency increased by 30 per cent. The space needed for some operations had been cut in half, and work-in-progress had been cut considerably. Moreover, the improved layout allowed for some jobs to be combined, freeing operators for deployment elsewhere in the factory. An amazed Hopkirk exclaimed: 'I was expecting a change but nothing as dramatic as this . . . it is fantastic'.[24]

Flexible manufacturing

In a manufacturing company, a major source of expenditure is the costs associated with setting up the equipment needed to make a particular product. One of these costs is the cost of production that is forgone because nothing is produced while the equipment is being set up. Components manufacturers often need as much as half a day to set up automated production equipment when switching from production of one component part (such as a washer ring for the steering column of a car) to another (such as a washer ring for the steering column of a truck). During this half-day, a manufacturing plant is not producing anything, but employees have to be paid for this 'non-productive' time.

If setup times for complex production equipment can be reduced, so can setup costs and efficiency will rise. In other words, if setup times can be reduced, the time that plant and employees spend in actually producing the product will increase. This simple insight has been the driving force behind the development of *flexible manufacturing techniques.*

Flexible manufacturing aims to reduce the time required to set up production equipment.[25] By redesigning the manufacturing process so that the production equipment for manufacturing one product can be quickly replaced with the equipment to manufacture another, setup times and costs can be dramatically reduced. Another favourable outcome from flexible manufacturing is that a company is able to produce many more varieties of a product than before, in the same amount of time. Flexible manufacturing thus increases a company's ability to be responsive to its customers.

Increasingly, organisations are experimenting with new designs for operating systems that not only allow workers to be more productive but also make the work process more flexible, thus reducing setup costs. Some Japanese companies are experimenting with facilities layouts arranged as a spiral, as in the letter Y, and as in the number 6, to see how these various configurations affect setup costs and worker productivity. At a camcorder plant in Kohda, Japan, for example, Sony changed from a fixed-position layout in which 50 workers sequentially built a camcorder to a flexible spiral process design in which four workers performed all the operations necessary. This new layout allowed the most efficient workers to work at the highest pace, and it reduced setup costs because workers could easily switch from one model to another, increasing efficiency by 10 per cent.[26]

An interesting example of a company that built a new factory to obtain the benefits from flexible manufacturing is Igus, Inc., headquartered in Cologne, Germany. Igus makes over 28,000 polymer bearings and energy supply cable products used in applications the world over. In the 1990s, Igus' managers realised that they needed to build a new factory that could handle the company's rapidly growing product line. The product line was changing constantly as new products were innovated and old ones became obsolete. At Igus, new products are often introduced on a daily basis, so this need for flexibility is the company's prime requirement:

because many of its products are highly customised, the specific and changing needs of its customers also drive new product development.

Igus' new factory was designed with the need for flexibility in mind. As big as three football fields, nothing in the factory is tied down or bolted to the floor. All the machines, computers and equipment can be moved and repositioned to suit changing product requirements. Moreover, all Igus' employees are trained to be flexible and can perform many of the necessary production tasks. When one new product line proved popular with customers, its employees and production operations were relocated four times as it grew into larger spaces. Igus can change its operating system at a moment's notice and with minimal disruption, and since the company operates seven days a week, 24 hours a day, these changes are occurring constantly.

To facilitate these changes, workers are equipped with power scooters to move around the plant quickly and reconfigure operations. This also allows them to move quickly to wherever in the factory their skills are most needed. Employees are also equipped with mobile phones so that they are always on call.

Igus' decision to create a flexible factory of the future has paid off: in the 1990s its global sales tripled.

Just-in-time Inventory and Efficiency

Although JIT systems, such as Toyota's *kanban* system, were originally developed as part of the effort to improve product quality, they have major implications for efficiency. Major cost savings can result from increasing *inventory turnover* and reducing inventory *holding costs* – such as warehousing and storage costs and the cost of capital tied up in inventory. Although companies that manufacture and assemble products can obviously use JIT to great advantage, so can service organisations. ASDA, one of the biggest grocers in the UK, uses JIT systems to replenish the stock in its stores at least twice a week. Many ASDA stores receive daily deliveries; ASDA can maintain the same service levels as competitors but has a lower inventory holding cost, a major source of cost saving. Faster inventory turnover has helped ASDA achieve an efficiency-based competitive advantage in the retailing industry.[27]

One drawback of JIT systems is that they can leave an organisation without a buffer stock of inventory.[28] Although such stocks can be expensive to store, they can help an organisation when it is affected by shortages of inputs brought about by a supply disruption (such as a labour dispute at a key supplier). Buffer stocks can also help an organisation respond quickly to increases in customer demand – that is, they can increase an organisation's responsiveness to customers.

Self-managed Work Teams and Efficiency

Another efficiency-boosting technique is the use of self-managed work teams.[29] The typical team consists of 5–15 employees who produce an entire product instead of just parts of it.[30] Team members learn all the team tasks and move from job to job. The result is a flexible workforce, because team members can fill in for absent co-workers. The members of each team also assume responsibility for scheduling work and vacations, ordering materials and hiring new members – previously all responsibilities of first-line managers. Because people often respond well to being given greater autonomy and responsibility, the use of empowered self-managed teams can increase productivity and efficiency. Cost savings also arise from eliminating supervisors and creating a 'flatter' organisational hierarchy, which further increases efficiency. The side-effects of self-managed teams are the demise of 'social loafing' and an increase in motivation through the reduction of isolated workers (i.e. workers who usually do not feel part of a team).[31]

The effect of introducing self-managed teams is often an increase in efficiency of 30 per cent or more – sometimes much more. After the introduction of self-managed teams at a UK day surgery unit, a 15-month study showed improvement in patient satisfaction, improvement in staff morale (measured in less absenteeism) and an increase of efficiency of 36 per cent. The day surgery provided more surgeries than national targets dictated and was financially viable.[32]

Process Re-engineering and Efficiency

Think of the value chain as a collection of functional activities or business processes that takes one or more kinds of inputs and transforms them to create an output that is of value to the customer.[33] **Process re-engineering** is the fundamental *rethinking* and radical *redesign* of business processes (and thus the value chain) to achieve dramatic improvements in critical measures of performance such as cost, quality, service and speed.[34] Order fulfilment, for example, can be thought of as a business process: when a customer's order is received (the input), many different functional tasks must be performed to process the order, and then the ordered goods must be delivered to the customer (the output). Process re-engineering boosts efficiency when it reduces the number of order fulfilment tasks that must be performed, or reduces the time they take, and so reduces operating costs.

For an example of process re-engineering in practice, consider the Ford Motor Company. One day, a manager from Ford was working in its Japanese partner Mazda and discovered by accident that Mazda had only five people in its accounts payable department. The Ford manager was shocked, since Ford's operation in other countries had up to 500 employees in accounts payable. He reported his discovery to Ford's managers, who decided to form a task force to figure out why the difference existed.

Ford managers discovered that procurement began when the purchasing department sent a purchase order to a supplier and sent a copy of the purchase order to Ford's accounts payable department. When the supplier shipped the goods and they arrived at Ford, a clerk at the receiving dock completed a form describing the goods and sent the form to accounts payable. The supplier, meanwhile, sent accounts payable an invoice. Accounts payable thus received three documents relating to these goods: a copy of the original purchase order, the receiving document and the invoice. If the information in all three was in agreement (most of the time it was), a clerk in accounts payable issued payment. Occasionally, however, all three documents did not agree, and Ford discovered that accounts payable clerks spent most of their time straightening out the 1 per cent of instances in which the purchase order, receiving document and invoice contained conflicting information.[35]

Ford managers decided to re-engineer the procurement process to simplify it. Now, when a buyer in the purchasing department issues a purchase order to a supplier, that buyer also enters the order into an online database. As before, suppliers send goods to the receiving dock. When the goods arrive, the clerk at the receiving dock checks a computer terminal to see whether the received shipment matches the description on the purchase order. If it does, the clerk accepts the goods and pushes a button on the terminal keyboard that tells the database the goods have arrived. Receipt of the goods is recorded in the database and a computer automatically issues and sends a cheque to the supplier. If the goods do not correspond to the description on the purchase order in the database, the clerk at the dock refuses the shipment and sends it back to the supplier.

Payment authorisation, which used to be performed by accounts payable, is now accomplished at the receiving dock. The new process has come close to eliminating the need for an accounts payable department: in some parts of the company, the size of the accounts payable department has been cut by 95 per cent. By reducing the head count in accounts payable, the re-engineering effort reduced the amount of time wasted on unproductive activities, thereby increasing the efficiency of the total organisation.

Information Systems, the Internet and Efficiency

With the rapid spread of computers, the explosive growth of the Internet and corporate intranets (internal corporate computer networks based on Internet standards) and the spread of high-bandwidth fibre optics and digital wireless technology, the information systems function is moving to centre stage in the quest for operating efficiencies and a lower cost structure. The impact of information systems on productivity is wideranging and potentially affects all the other activities of a company. Cisco Systems has been able to realise significant cost savings by moving its ordering and customer service functions online: the company has just 300 service agents handling its customer accounts, compared to the 900 it would need if sales were not handled online, and the difference represents an annual saving of £11.5 million a year. Without automated customer service functions, Cisco calculates that it would need at least 1,000 additional service engineers, which would cost around £43 million. Dell Computer also makes extensive use of the Internet to lower its cost structure and differentiate itself from rivals, as Case 9.3 shows.

Case 9.3: How to make use of the Internet

By 2004, more than 90 per cent of Dell's computers were sold online.[36] According to Michael Dell: 'As I saw it, the Internet offered a logical extension of the direct [selling] model, creating even stronger relationships with our customers. The Internet would augment conventional telephone, fax and face-to-face encounters, and give our customers the information they wanted faster, cheaper, and more efficiently.'[37]

Dell's website allows customers to customise their orders to get the system that best suits their particular requirements. By allowing customers to configure their orders, Dell increases its customer responsiveness. Dell has also put much of its customer service function online, reducing the need for telephone calls to customer service representatives and saving costs in the process. Each week, some 200,000 people access Dell's troubleshooting tips online. Each of these visits to Dell's website saves the company a potential £8.50, which is the average cost of a technical support call. If just 10 per cent of these online visitors were to call Dell by telephone instead, it would cost the company nearly £9 million per year.

Dell uses the Internet to manage its value chain, feeding real-time information about order flow to its suppliers, which use this information to schedule their own production, providing components to Dell on a JIT basis. Dell's ultimate goal is to drive all inventories out of the supply chain apart from inventory in transit between suppliers and Dell, effectively replacing *inventory* with *information*. In that way, Dell can drive significant costs out of its system.

Companies like Dell use Web-based information systems to reduce the costs of *co-ordination* between the company and its customers and between the company and its suppliers. By using Web-based programmes to automate customer and supplier interactions, the number of people required to manage these interfaces can be substantially reduced, thereby reducing costs. This trend extends beyond high-tech companies. Banks and financial service companies are finding that they can substantially reduce costs by moving customer accounts and support functions online. Such a move reduces the need for customer service representatives, bank tellers, stockbrokers, insurance agents and others. The costs to execute a transaction at a bank, such as shifting money from one account to another, for example, can be reduced by a tenth using online technology.

Managers at all levels thus have important roles to play in developing functional strategies to improve the way a company's value chain operates to boost efficiency. Senior management's role is to encourage efficiency improvements by, for example, emphasising the need for continuous improvement or reengineering. Senior management also must ensure that managers from different functions work together to find ways to increase efficiency. However, while senior managers might recognise the need for such actions, functional-level managers are in the best position to identify opportunities for making efficiency-enhancing improvements to an organisation's operating system. They are the managers who are involved in an organisation's operating system on a day-to-day basis. Improving efficiency, like quality, is an ongoing, never-ending process.

However, not all of those reengineering processes are about the reduction of labour. Most of the time, the expertise that is held by employees is difficult to substitute through technology or better processes. These improvements and increases in efficiency have their roots in the way these changes impact on the interaction of suppliers and manufacturers or service providers. Making those interactions more efficient and customer-focused is a way to improve overall performance.

Value-chain Management: Some Remaining Issues

Achieving improved quality, efficiency and responsiveness to customers often requires a profound change in the way that managers perform the four functions of management. The ways managers plan, organise, lead and control work activities all change as a company searches for ways to increase its competitive advantage. Planning often involves managers at all levels, and customers are brought into the planning process, the use of self-managed teams and empowered workers changes the way that managers lead and organise employees, and employees become responsible for controlling many more dimensions of their work activities.

Obtaining the information necessary to improve the value chain becomes an important and never-ending task for functional managers. It is their job to collect the relevant information about the competitive environment, such as (1) the future intentions of competitors, (2) the identity of new customers for the organisation's products and (3) the identity of new suppliers of crucial or low-cost inputs. They also need to seek out new ways to use resources more efficiently to hold down costs, or to get close to customers and learn what they want.

Two issues that arise from the constant need to improve a company's operating system are, first, the need to use *boundary-spanning roles* to obtain valuable functional information and, second, the need to consider the ethical implications of adopting advanced value-chain management techniques.

Boundary-spanning Roles

The ability of functional managers to gain access to the information they need to improve *value-chain management* is critical. The history of business is littered with numerous once-great companies whose managers did not recognise, and adapt their value chains to respond to, significant changes taking place in the competitive environment. Examples include Digital Equipment, a former leading computer maker now defunct because its CEO believed that 'personal computers are just toys', and Pan-Am, which was unable to survive because of its high operating costs in a competitive airline industry. History is also marked by companies whose managers made the wrong value-chain choices because they misinterpreted the competitive environment. Examples include the Motorola managers who invested more than £1.72 billion in the Iridium satellite project that was abandoned in 2000 and the managers of the thousands of dot-coms, like European online fashion retailer boo.com,[38] who failed to understand the competitive dynamics of the online marketplace and under-estimated the problems associated with delivering online products and services reliably to customers.

Managers can learn to perceive, interpret and appreciate better the competitive environments by practising **boundary spanning** – interacting with individuals and groups outside the organisation to obtain valuable information from the environment.[39] Managers who engage in boundary-spanning activities seek ways not only to respond to forces in the environment but also to *directly influence and manage* the perceptions of suppliers and customers in that environment to increase their organisations' access to resources.

To understand how boundary spanning works, look at Fig. 9.7. A functional manager in a boundary-spanning role in organisation *X* establishes a personal or virtual link with a manager in a boundary-spanning role in organisation *Y*. The two managers communicate and share information that helps both of them understand the changing forces and conditions in the environment. These managers then share this information with other functional managers in their

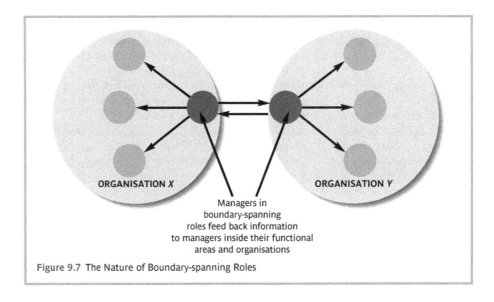

Figure 9.7 The Nature of Boundary-spanning Roles

respective organisations so that all managers become better informed about events outside their own organisation's boundaries. As a result, the managers in both organisations can make value-chain decisions that lead to a higher-performing operating system.

For an example of a manager performing a boundary-spanning role, consider the situation of a purchasing manager for Burger King. The purchasing manager is charged with finding the lowest-cost supplier of low-fat cheese and lettuce. To perform this task, the manager could write to major food companies and ask for price quotes. Or the manager could phone food company managers personally, develop an informal yet professional relationship with them, and, over time, learn from them which food companies are active in the low-fat food and vegetable area and what they envision for the future. By developing such a relationship, the purchasing manager will be able to provide Burger King with valuable information that will allow the purchasing department to make well-informed choices. This flow of information from the environment may, in turn, allow marketing to develop more effective sales campaigns or product development to develop better-looking and better-tasting burgers. Note that *personal communication* is often necessary to supplement the information provided by IT.

What would happen if managers in *all* an organisation's functions performed boundary-spanning roles? The richness of the information available to managers throughout the organisation probably would lead to an increase in the quality of managers' decision making and planning, enabling them to produce goods and services that customers preferred or to create advertising campaigns that attracted new customers.

Searching for and collecting information to understand how changing trends and forces in the environment are affecting a company's operating system is an important boundary-spanning activity. Many organisations employ functional experts whose only job is to scan professional journals, trade association publications and newspapers to identify changes in technology, government regulations, fashion trends and so on, that will affect the way their organisation operates. However, merely collecting information is not enough for the boundary-spanning manager. He or she must interpret what the information means and then practise gatekeeping – deciding what information to allow into the organisation and what information to keep out. The nature of the information that the gatekeeper chooses to pass on to other managers will influence the decisions they make. Accurate information processing is vital, and utilising IT can obviously help here.[40]

Managers as agents of change

Note that although many of the outside forces affecting a company's value chain are independent of a particular organisation (for example, basic advances in biotechnology or microprocessors), the actions managers of a particular organisation take to change their company's operating system can have a significant effect on competition in their industry.[41] The choices functional managers make about which products to produce, and even about how to compete with other organisations, often affect all the companies in an industry. A good example of how the decisions of functional managers (or, in this case, of just one manager) can result in profound changes in the competitive environment is discussed in Case 9.4.

Despite the performance-enhancing advantages of value-chain management, many reports have appeared in the popular press about widespread disillusionment with techniques such as TQM, JIT, flexible manufacturing and reengineering. It is possible that many of the disillusioned organisations are those that have failed to understand that implementing these value-chain techniques requires a marked shift in *organisational culture* – in the way managers think and act.[42]

Case 9.4: IBM's Bill Lowe changes the rules of the game

In 1980, Bill Lowe was a manager at IBM's entry systems division. Lowe had watched the growth of the PC industry – dominated by Apple, Atari and Radio Shack – with growing interest and apprehension. He believed that IBM, the dominant force in the mainframe computer industry, should also be a leading player in the fast-growing PC segment. In mid-1980, acting on his own initiative, he assembled a team of managers to draft a proposal describing how IBM could build a viable PC within a year.

Lowe's plan called for IBM to adopt an open-system architecture for the new PC. This meant that he proposed a departure from the company's normal practice of producing key components and software in-house so that other companies could not buy them. He recommended that IBM buy components 'off the shelf' from other producers. The key components that Lowe proposed to buy included Intel's 8088 microprocessor and a software operating system known as MS-DOS from Microsoft, then a little-known Seattle-based company. The advantage of this approach was that it would enable IBM to get a PC to market quickly. The disadvantage was that it would allow other companies to produce IBM-compatible PCs by simply buying the same Intel microprocessor and MS-DOS operating system. Such a strategy represented a radical departure for IBM, which in the past, as we have seen, had tried to stop imitation of its products by producing all key components in-house.[43]

Lowe's team submitted the plan to IBM's powerful corporate management committee. In August 1980 he received the authorisation to go ahead. Just over a year later the first IBM PC was introduced into the marketplace. It was an overnight sensation and quickly grabbed the market lead from Apple. More important, however, Lowe's decision to go with an open-system architecture enabled a flood of imitators to enter the market.

Within two years, the imitators were producing PCs that were compatible with the IBM standard. The first of these imitators was Compaq Computer. Compaq was soon followed by a myriad of other companies, including current industry stars such as Dell and Gateway. The result was the creation of today's highly competitive PC industry, an industry of which IBM is no longer a part, having exited in 2000 after experiencing huge losses. Lowe's fateful decision to adopt open-system architecture changed competition in the personal computer industry forever.

None of these techniques is a panacea that can be taken once, like a pill, to cure industrial ills. Making these techniques work within an organisation can pose a significant challenge that calls for hard work and years of persistence by the sponsoring managers. Changing the way an organisation works is a difficult and demanding task, and we shall discuss how an organisation can achieve this in later chapters.

Reaction Time

1. What is efficiency, and what are the techniques that managers can use to increase it?
2. Why is it important for managers to pay close attention to their organisation's operating system if they wish to be responsive to their customers?
3. 'Total customer service is the goal toward which most organisations should strive.' To what degree is this statement correct?

Ethical Implications

Managers also need to understand the ethical implications of the adoption of many of the value-chain management techniques discussed in this chapter. Although TQM, JIT, flexible manufacturing and reengineering can all increase quality, efficiency and responsiveness to customers, they may do so at great cost to employees. Employees may see the demands of their jobs increase as the result of TQM – or, worse, may see themselves reengineered out of a job. Toyota is the most efficient car manufacturer in the world, but some of its gains have been achieved at a significant cost to its employees, as discussed in Case 9.5. The example is poignant, as Japan is seen as a superior manufacturer of cars compared to its few remaining European competitors.

Case 9.5: **The human cost of improving productivity**

Hisashi Tomiki is the leader of a four-man self-managed team in a Toyota production plant, 200 miles south of Tokyo, Japan. Tomiki and his team work at a gruelling pace to build cowls (steel chambers onto which the windshields and steering columns are attached). Consider this description of Tomiki at work:

> In two minutes Tomiki fits 24 metal pieces into designated slots on three welding machines; runs two large metal sheets through each of the machines, which weld on the parts; and fuses the two sheets together with two spot welds. There is little room for error. Once or twice an hour a mistake is made or a machine sticks, causing the next machine in line to stop. A yellow light flashes. Tomiki runs over. The squad must fix the part and work faster to catch up. A red button halts the production line if the problems are severe, but there is an unspoken rule against pushing it. Only once this day does Tomiki call in a special maintenance worker.[44]

The experience of workers like Tomiki has become increasingly common – especially in the 2000s when the threat of outsourcing led workers to accept management's demand for a faster work pace. Workers are heard to complain that constant attempts to increase quality and reduce costs really means continuous speedup and added job stress from the increase in the pressure put on employees to perform. Although some pressure is good, beyond a certain point it can seriously harm employees. Consider the following quote from Jerry Miller, whose team of billing clerks reengineered themselves out of a job:

> When we first formed our teams, the company came in talking teams and empowerment and promised that we wouldn't lose any jobs. It turns out all this was a big cover. The company had us all set up for reengineering. We showed them how to streamline the work, and now 9,000 people are gone. It was cut-your-own-throat. It makes you feel used.[45]

Is it ethical to continually increase the demands placed on employees, regardless of the human cost in terms of job stress? It is obvious that the answer is 'no'. Employee support is vital if the organisation is to function effectively. What kinds of work pressures are legitimate, and what pressures are excessive? There is no clear answer to this question; ultimately the issue comes down to the judgement of responsible managers seeking to act ethically.

TIPS FOR PRACTICE

1. Always remember the links between superior customer responsiveness and the production system of an organisation.
2. Think about balancing customer responsiveness with financial viability of the product: if it's too expensive to produce, it's not worth it!
3. Be aware that the organisation needs to ensure that appropriate quality assurance procedures are in place.

Summary and Review

Value-chain management and competitive advantage To achieve high performance, managers try to improve their responsiveness to customers, the quality of their products and the efficiency of their organisation. To achieve these goals, managers can use a number of value-chain management techniques to improve the way an organisation's operating system operates.

Improving responsiveness to customers To achieve high performance in a competitive environment, it is imperative that the operating system of an organisation respond to customer demands. Managers try to design operating systems that produce outputs that have the attributes customers desire. One of the central tasks of value-chain management is to develop new and improved operating systems that enhance the ability of the organisation to economically deliver more of the product attributes that customers desire for the same price. Techniques such as TQM, JIT, flexible manufacturing and process reengineering are popular because they promise to do this. Managers should carefully analyse the links between responsiveness to customers and the operating system of an organisation. The ability of an organisation to satisfy the demands of its customers for lower prices, acceptable quality, better features and so on, depends critically on the nature of the organisation's operating system. As important as responsiveness to customers is, however, managers need to recognise that there are limits to how responsive an organisation can be and still cover its costs.

Improving quality Managers seek to improve the quality of their organisation's output because doing so enables them to better serve customers, to raise prices and to lower production costs. TQM focuses on improving the quality of an organisation's products and services and stresses that all of an organisation's operations should be directed toward this goal. Putting TQM into practice requires having an organisationwide commitment, having a strong customer focus, finding ways to measure quality, setting quality improvement goals, soliciting input from employees about how to improve product quality, identifying defects and tracing them to their source, introducing JIT inventory systems, getting suppliers to adopt TQM practices, designing products for ease of manufacture and breaking down barriers between functional departments.

Improving efficiency Improving efficiency requires one or more of the following: the introduction of a TQM programme, the adoption of flexible manufacturing technologies, the introduction of JIT inventory systems, the establishment of self-managed work teams and the application of process reengineering. Senior management is responsible for setting the context within which efficiency improvements can take place by, for example, emphasising the need for continuous improvement. Functional-level managers bear the prime responsibility for identifying and implementing efficiency-enhancing improvements in operating systems.

Topic for Action

- Ask a manager how quality, efficiency and responsiveness to customers are defined and measured in his or her organisation.
- Go into a local store, restaurant or supermarket and list the ways in which you think the organisation is being responsive or unresponsive to the needs of its customers. How could this business's responsiveness to customers be improved?

Applied Independent Learning

Building Management Skills

Managing an Operating System

Choose an organisation with which you are familiar – one that you have worked in or have used as a customer or one that has received extensive coverage in the popular press. The organisation should be involved in only one industry or business. Answer these questions about the organisation:

1. What is the output of the organisation?
2. Describe the operating system that the organisation uses to produce this output.
3. What product attributes do customers of the organisation desire?
4. Does its operating system allow the organisation to deliver the desired product attributes?
5. Try to identify improvements that might be made to the organisation's operating system to boost its responsiveness to customers, quality and efficiency.

Managing Ethically

Go back and review Case 9.5 on the human costs of Toyota's production system. After implementing efficiency-improving techniques, many companies commonly lay off employees who are no longer needed. Frequently, the remaining employees must then perform more tasks more quickly, a situation that can generate employee stress and other work-related problems.

▶ Questions

1. Either by yourself or in a group think through the ethical implications of using some new functional strategy to improve organisational performance.

2. What criteria would you use to decide what kind of strategy is ethical to adopt and/or how far to push employees to raise the level of their performance?

3. How big a layoff, if any, is acceptable? If layoffs are acceptable, what can be done to reduce their harm to employees?

Small Group Breakout Exercise

How to Compete in the Sandwich Business

Form groups of three or four people, and appoint one member as the spokesperson who will communicate your findings to the whole class when called on by the instructor. Then discuss the following scenario.

You and your partners are thinking about opening a new kind of sandwich shop that will compete head-to-head with Subway. Because this chain has good brand-name recognition, it is vital that you find some source of competitive advantage for your new sandwich shop, and you are meeting to brainstorm ways of obtaining one.

1. Identify the product attributes that a typical sandwich shop customer wants the most.

2. In what ways do you think you will be able to improve on the operations and processes of existing sandwich shops and achieve a competitive advantage through better (a) product quality, (b) efficiency, or (c) responsiveness to customers?

Exploring the World Wide Web

Find a manufacturer who uses TQM and explore how it is employed in that organisation. Find a different organisation that uses EFQM and compare the difference.

Application in Today's Business World

Europe's Fastest Cars

The Continent invented the fast car: It still does it better than anyone

Lavish amenities and high-end appointments are no longer the privilege of luxury cars. These days, even basic Toyotas and low-end Hondas can be equipped with wood trim, heated seats and multi-speaker sound systems at modest consequence to the final cost tally. Korean manufacturers, in particular, are advancing cabin quality in their bargain-basement offerings rapidly enough to startle even the most entrenched auto snob.

But the big European auto makers aren't worried. As the mainstream has moved down-market over the past decade, the biggest (and some of the smallest) in European autos have been working on supercars so powerful, fast and beautiful they zoom past and completely redefine the top end.

The criteria for supercar status is debatable. Indeed, prices range from a mere $250,000 to well over $1 million. Top speeds hover around 200 miles per hour, with a few notable models pushing far past that. Rarity is another important mark of distinction. Many manufacturers produce worldwide runs that number in the mere hundreds.

Rising Stars

If the definition is flexible, it's because there have never been so many supercars to choose from. Nearly every major global brand, from Ford to Ferrari, features at least one high-performance offering. Big European brands have enthusiastically hopped on the speed bandwagon, both for profit and PR.

Newer stars of the superfast firmament include the Porsche Carrera GT and the Mercedes-Benz SLR McLaren, both of which cost more than $500,000. The Carrera's 600-plus horses propel it to over 200 miles per hour, and from 0 to 60 in 3.8 seconds. Mercedes' offering, meanwhile, harkens back to an esteemed racing pedigree, bearing the names of not one but two racing legends – 'SLR' for the famed 1950s model series and 'McLaren' for the Formula 1 giant with which it partners.

But the Germans are treading on hallowed ground. Companies such as Ferrari and Lamborghini have been at the supercar game for decades. Ferrari, in particular, is regarded as the long-haul champ in the arena, having produced classics like the F40, F50 and the current 660 horsepower, V12 Ferrari Enzo.

What's more, the 2006 model year marks what may very well be an apex in supercar history. That's because the long-awaited and much-vaunted Bugatti Veyron will finally be rolling off the assembly line to a lucky few. Its 1,001 horses take it to 60 in 2.5 seconds and make it, most likely, the fastest car in the world – capable of besting 250 miles per hour.

Bully for Billionaires

But why so many new models? For one thing, the supercar market is increasingly lucrative and growing rapidly. Not only do analysts expect annual worldwide sales to increase to $6 billion by 2010 but the number of eligible buyers is expanding as well. Cap Gemini reported that in 2005 the number of high-net-worth individuals – i.e. millionaires and billionaires – grew at a record-setting pace of nearly 10 per cent, to 8.3 million people.

Christoph Grenier, head of sales at Ferrari France, welcomes the growing number of potential supercar customers. 'More and more people have more and more money, which helps us', he says. 'It's true we have many more competitors than before, but to some extent they're all emulating us.' He adds: 'We're a monopoly no more.'

That's partly because the economics of small-run, high-cost vehicles have never been more generous. Phillipp Rosengarten of Global Insight in Frankfurt, Germany, notes: 'The high-quality parts market has never been better or more plentiful. It has become possible for smart manufacturers to return healthy profits from even very small, limited-production runs.'

Plethora of Parts

The availability of performance parts has also led to the rise of small, independent shops – often in unexpected places – that produce vehicles capable of competing with the oldest and most recognized manufacturers. Sweden's Koenigsegg CCR model hails from the snowy land of Volvos and yet holds the Guinness World Record for speed in a production vehicle (see *BW Online*, 'A Revolution in Swede Speed', March 24, 2006). And Holland's Spyker is on an ▶

▶ astonishingly rapid path to profit, announcing that it was doubling production and had increased profits in 2005 by 62 per cent.

Christian von Koenigsegg, the CEO of the company that bears his name and the man behind the marvel of the world's fastest vehicle emanating from Sweden, not Italy, attributes a great deal of his company's success to the availability of high-performance parts. He says: 'They definitely allow us to achieve a performance envelope, from raw horsepower to electronic stabilisation controls, that wasn't possible previously.'

Manufacturers large and small also benefit from significant technological advancements. The use of carbon fibre – which, on average, reduces weight by 60 per cent and fuel consumption by 10 per cent to 30 per cent – is ubiquitous. It's not uncommon to find production materials from jet fighters and the space shuttle being used as well.

California's Cutting Edge

But perhaps the biggest recent change has been the steadily increasing requirements that manufacturers must meet to sell roadworthy cars. Emissions and crash-safety standards – the most restrictive of which happen to emanate from the biggest market in the world, California – force designers to add performance-reducing weight to today's models. Indeed, some contend that the golden age of supercars was 15 years ago, with milestone models like the Jaguar XJ220 and the original McLaren F1 of the early 1990s. Nevertheless, in terms of sheer range and power, today's car cognoscenti have never had so many *à la mode* options.

Ferrari's Grenier sums it up: 'People are following the vogue. And the vogue is towards very fast and very expensive.'

Questions:

1. Why have traditional manufacturers of exclusive high-speed cars lost their monopoly for supercars?

2. How can small producers compete with the traditional supercar manufacturers?

Source: Matt Vella, 'Europe's fastest cars', adapted and reprinted from *BusinessWeek*, April 13, 2006 by special permission. Copyright © 2006 by the McGraw-Hill Companies, Inc.

Notes and References

1 C. W. L. Hill and G. R. Jones, *Strategic Management: An Integrated Approach* (Boston MA: Houghton-Mifflin, 2004).

2 J. Womack, D. Jones and D. Roos, *The Machine That Changed the World* (New York: HarperCollins, 1991).

3 See D. Garvin, 'What Does Product Quality Really Mean?', *Sloan Management Review* 26 (Fall 1984), 25–44; P. B. Crosby, *Quality Is Free* (New York: Mentor Books, 1980); A. Gabor, *The Man Who Discovered Quality* (New York: Times Books, 1990).

4 S. R. I. Pires, 'Managerial Implication of a Modular Consortium Model in a Brazilian Automotive Plant', *International Journal of Operations and Production Management* 18(3) (1998), 221–32.

5 D. F. Abell, *Defining the Business: The Starting Point of Strategic Planning* (Englewood Cliffs, NJ: Prentice Hall, 1980).

6 For details, see 'Johnson & Johnson (A)', Harvard Business School Case, 384–053.

7 www.lucent.com.

8 M. E. Porter, *Competitive Advantage* (New York: Free Press, 1985).

9 According to Richard D'Aveni, the process of pushing price-attribute curves to the right is a characteristic of the competitive process. See R. D'Aveni, *Hypercompetition* (New York: Free Press, 1994).

10 This is a central insight of the modern manufacturing literature. See R. H. Hayes and S. C. Wheelwright, 'Link Manufacturing Process and Product Life Cycles', *Harvard Business Review* (January–February 1979), 127–36; R. H. Hayes and S. C. Wheelwright, 'Competing Through Manufacturing', *Harvard Business Review* (January–February 1985), 99–109.

11 www.easyjet.com.

12 B. O'Brian, 'Flying on the Cheap', *The Wall Street Journal*, October 26, 1992, A1; B. O'Reilly, 'Where Service Flies Right', *Fortune*, August 24, 1992, 116–17; A. Salpukas, 'Hurt in Expansion, Airlines Cut Back and May Sell Hubs', *The Wall Street Journal*, April 1, 1993, A1, C8.

13 K. Done, 'Toyota Warns of Continuing Decline', *Financial Times*, November 23, 1993, 23.

14 The view of quality as reliability goes back to the work of Deming and Juran; see Gabor, *The Man Who Discovered Quality*.

15 See Garvin, 'What Does Product Quality Really Mean?'; Crosby, *Quality Is Free*; Gabor, *The Man Who Discovered Quality*.

16 http://www.jonfry.com/2005/08/what-car-reveals-uks-most-reliable.html.

17 See J. W. Dean and D. E. Bowen, 'Management Theory and Total Quality: Improving Research and Practice Through Theory Development', *Academy of Management Review* 19 (1994), 392–418.

18 For general background information, see J. C. Anderson, M. Rungtusanatham and R. G. Schroeder, 'A Theory of Quality Management Underlying the Deming Management Method', *Academy of Management Review* 19 (1994), 472–509; 'How to Build Quality', *The Economist*, September 23, 1989, 91–92; Gabor, *The Man Who Discovered Quality*; Crosby, *Quality Is Free*.

19 Bowles, 'Is American Management Really Committed to Quality?', *Management Review* (April 1992), 42–46.

20 Gabor, *The Man Who Discovered Quality*.

21 http://www.efqm.org/.

22 J. Griffiths, 'Europe's Manufacturing Quality and Productivity Still Lag Far Behind Japan's', *Financial Times*, November 4, 1994, 11.

23 S. McCartney, 'Compaq Borrows Wal-Mart's Idea to Boost Production', *The Wall Street Journal*, June 17, 1994, B4.

24 R. Gourlay, 'Back to Basics on the Factory Floor', *Financial Times*, January 4, 1994, 12.

25 P. Nemetz and L. Fry, 'Flexible Manufacturing Organizations: Implications for Strategy Formulation', *Academy of Management Review* 13 (1988), 627–38; N. Greenwood, *Implementing Flexible Manufacturing Systems* (New York: Halstead Press, 1986).

26 M. Williams, 'Back to the Past', *The Wall Street Journal*, October 24, 1994, A1.

27 G. Stalk and T. M. Hout, *Competing Against Time* (New York: Free Press, 1990).

28 For an interesting discussion of some other drawbacks of JIT and other 'Japanese' manufacturing techniques, see S. M. Young, 'A Framework for Successful Adoption and Performance of Japanese Manufacturing Practices in the United States', *Academy of Management Review* 17 (1992), 677–701.

29 B. Dumaine, 'The Trouble with Teams', *Fortune*, September 5, 1994, 86–92.

30 See C. W. L. Hill, 'Transaction Cost Economizing as a Source of National Competitive Advantage: The Case of Japan', *Organization Science*, 2, 1994; M. Aoki, *Information, Incentives, and Bargaining in the Japanese Economy* (Cambridge: Cambridge University Press, 1989).

31 http://news.bbc.co.uk/1/hi/uk/341328.stm.

32 V. M. Steelman and N. Quinlan, *AORN Journal* (December 1999).

33 M. Hammer and J. Champy, *Re-engineering the Corporation* (New York: HarperBusiness, 1993), 35.

34 *Ibid.*

35 *Ibid.*

36 www.dell.com.

37   Michael Dell, *Direct from Dell: Strategies That Revolutionized an Industry* (New York: HarperBusiness, 1999), 91.

38   http://news.bbc.co.uk/1/hi/business/752293.stm.

39   J. S. Adams, 'The Structure and Dynamics of Behavior in Boundary Spanning Roles', in M. D. Dunnette, ed., *The Handbook of Industrial and Organizational Psychology* (Chicago: Rand McNally, 1976).

40   For a discussion of sources of organizational inertia, see M. T. Hannah and J. Freeman, 'Structural Inertia and Organizational Change', *American Sociological Review* 49 (1984), 149–64.

41   Not everyone agrees with this assessment. Some argue that organizations and individual managers have little impact on the environment. See Hannah and Freeman, 'Structural Inertia and Organizational Change'.

42   R. X. Cringeley, *Accidental Empires* (New York: HarperBusiness, 1993).

43   For example, see V. Houlder, 'Two Steps Forward, One Step Back', *Financial Times*, 31 October 1994; Kumar Naj, 'Shifting Gears', *The Wall Street Journal*, May 7, 1993, A1; and D. Greising, 'Quality: How to Make It Pay', *BusinessWeek*, August 8, 1994, 54–59.

44   L. Helm and M. Edid, 'Life on the Line: Two Auto Workers Who Are Worlds Apart', *BusinessWeek*, September 30, 1994, 76–78.

45   Dumaine, 'The Trouble with Teams'.

Human Resource Management

Chapter FOURTEEN

Human Resource Management

Chapter contents

❖ LEARNING OBJECTIVES

After you have read this chapter you will have an understanding of the human resource (HR) function and the crucial role it plays in many organisations. You will know the main methods employed by the human resource management (HRM) function to produce an effective workforce. In particular you will be able to:

- ❖ **define** HRM and **differentiate** this function from the process of staffing
- ❖ **explain** how the HRM function should be linked to an organisation's strategy
- ❖ **list** six areas (and give a specific example of each) where there are legal requirements the HRM function must obey
- ❖ **explain in detail** HRM's role in organising pay and compensation
- ❖ **explain in detail** the concept of HR planning and **give** two ratios of employee turnover
- ❖ **explain** the HRM function's contribution to recruitment and selection and training and development
- ❖ **explain in detail** how an HRM function might organise "performance management" and appraisals
- ❖ **explain in detail** HRM's role in employee relations
- ❖ **describe** the welfare role of HRM

The HRM is one of the five major management functions. It is certain to be found in any medium or large organisation, such as the South African publishing organisation, Media24.

CASE 16.1: *The HR function at Media24*

Media24 is Africa's biggest publishing group. It provides entertainment, information and education 24 hours a day. Newspapers (including South Africa's largest, the *Daily Sun*), magazines, books and web publishing and complemented by printing and distribution for private education businesses. Media24 employs about 7100 people in over 60 subsidiaries and divisions.

Each division has an HR function. Typically it has one specialist for every 150 employees who will implement HR policy and provide operational HR support to line managers in fields including recruitment, selection, performance management, employee relations, salary administration and employee relations. The corporate HR function, based in Cape Town, has about 22 specialists. They set the strategic direction and best-practices management across the group. They give specialist HR expertise in the fields of talent management, recruitment, assessment, selection, training, mentoring, succession planning, transformation (specifically black economic empowerment through affirmative action and skills development), remuneration management, payroll administration, employee relations and employee assistance (some of which is outsourced).

The HR function in Media24 is slightly atypical, because Media24 is operated in a strongly decentralised fashion and approaches to HR may differ from business to business within the group. A major challenge is recruiting and developing talented specialists needed to meet a strategy of rapid growth within South Africa and elsewhere on the continent, as well as in Asia.

Source: We are grateful to Shelagh Goodwin of Media24 for providing this case.

Some aspects of HRM are dealt with elsewhere in this book – in Chapter 7 (Staffing – selecting, developing and motivating people) and Chapter 19 (Social responsibility and ethics).

16.1 Definition and history of human resource management

Human resource management is an enabling function that represents "the human side of enterprises" It focuses on the relationships between employees and organisations that add value and help attain goals. Human resource management may be defined as:

> 66 The productive recruitment, development, deployment and motivation
> of people at work in order to achieve strategic business objectives and the
> satisfaction of individual employees. 99

Since people are an integral part of the definition of management, it follows that the function that deals with the human side of the organisation is a pivotal function. All managers play a part in the productive use of people, and in Chapters 7 and 8 we looked at the aspects of managing people – selecting, training, motivating and leading – that involve all managers. The HRM **function** involves a higher level of technical expertise that is only required by *some* managers. In particular the HRM function provides a high-level input to the organisation's *infrastructure for managing people*. In other words:

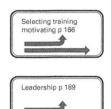

- It formulates policies, strategies and plans concerning the workforce – especially strategies to help organisational change.
- It devises the style and standards of managing people.
- It provides rules and procedures for implementing the two previous activities.
- It provides a service (advice) function for maintaining and improving a workforce.

As an enabling function, the primary mission of HRM is to help other functions – especially the line functions – achieve their goals. Unlike some other functions, HRM is concerned with the whole organisation, so its managers need to know about all parts of the organisation – its strategy, market position, operations, legal requirements, and so

---

CASE 16.2: *The human resource function at Enterprise Rent a Car*

Enterprise Rent a Car is an international company with over 750 000 cars for hire and its success depends upon providing superb customer service. This means that it must ensure it has high-quality, well-motivated staff. The role of its HR function is to make proper arrangements for hiring, training and developing staff, and to ensure proper arrangements for occasions when it is necessary to discipline or dismiss them.

The function goes beyond existing employees: it develops an HRM strategy which is closely linked to the organisation's strategy, anticipating likely developments (e.g. growing into new markets such as truck rental) and technological changes (e.g. global positioning devices for vehicles). The HR function also keeps an eye on likely retirements or promotions, and notes the skills needed by people who will fill the gaps. There is a policy of promoting managers from among existing employees. The workforce planning at Enterprise is developed to take all of these, and other factors into account.

Source: Based on *Times 100 Case Studies*

---

on. While the HRM function is primarily an enabling function, it also has a minor role as a control function. It will usually monitor key indices such as absences, turnover, wage costs and compliance with employment legislation.

There is plenty of evidence that HRM is a function crucial to an organisation's prosperity. There are plenty of CEOs who make comments such as "people are our most important asset". These assertions are backed by empirical research (see Baron and Kreps, 1999; Pfeffer,1998).

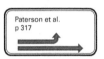

Paterson et al.
p 317

Human management has a long history dating back at least as far as such caring industrialists such as Robert Owen and Joseph Rowntree. Their philosophy of enlightened self-interest led them to provide decent conditions for their employees on the basis that a well cared for worker would be more productive. These efforts were often called "industrial betterment". In 1900 there were about a dozen "professional" welfare workers in the UK, but by 1913 there were about 1300 – enough to form a Welfare Workers' Association. In the inter-war period negotiations with unions became a major issue and these were often conducted by "labour managers" or "employment managers". Large companies such as ICI, Pilkingtons and Marks & Spencer formed specialist personnel departments to manage recruitment and absences among hourly paid workers. During the Second World War the Ministry of Labour insisted that all establishments producing war materials had a welfare worker or a personnel officer.

By 1945 personnel management had taken the form that is just recognisable today. Employment legislation from 1960 onwards added further emphasis to the personnel function. Further, new management techniques for improving worker productivity were suggested by behavioural scientists such as McGregor in the USA. However, personnel management was often seen as a low-status function better suited to amateurs and women! The term "human resource management" began to be used in the USA. The term had useful connotations. It emphasised the fact that human resources were just as important as financial and physical resources, and implied that the people who managed these resources were as important as production managers and finance managers. In addition, the term "human resource management" clearly required personnel managers to take on a strategic role within their organisations. Many people regarded this change of name as superficial spin – "old wine in new bottles!" Others resented the term because it implied that the people in an organisation should be used, manipulated and discarded when necessary like other resources such as metal, machines and a mortgage. As the field of personnel management grew, specialisms started to arise. Larger HR functions may now have special groups devoted to diversity, recruitment, industrial relations or pay.

In the mid-twentieth century many HR departments were highly *centralised*. They formulated a set of procedures that were imposed throughout an organisation. This could mean that policies and procedures would be applied where local conditions made them inappropriate. Moreover, managers often felt alienated by procedures in which they had played no part. It was easy for them to blame their own shortcomings on, say, a subordinate appointed largely at the behest of the centralised HR function.

The HR function in many of today's organisations is *decentralised* and operates in a "devolved" way with general guidelines and advice from the central HR function. This structure has its dangers too. Devolution may mean that complicated procedures are set up and operated by non-specialist staff – some of whom deliver a poor-quality service. The image of the organisation may suffer. Further, devolved units may duplicate the work of other units.

16.2 Components of the human resource function

The components of the HR function can be fitted in a logical framework shown in Figure 16.1

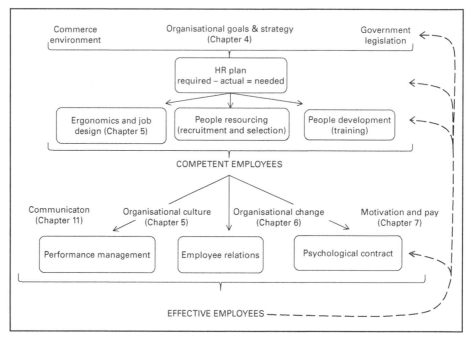

FIGURE 16.1 An idealised HR system

Human resource management starts with organisational goals and strategy that are influenced by both market conditions and government legislation. The HR function must interpret the organisational goals in terms of the numbers of employees, occupations and skills. This interpretation is sometimes called the "people requirement". The HR function then establishes its present number of employees, their mix, occupations and skills. The difference between the future requirements and the present complement is the gap that the HR function must fill. It can be filled in three main ways: ergonomic job design, resourcing people and developing people. Generally it is better to redesign a job ergonomically so that it can be performed by most people – there will then be less need for selection or training and the results are more certain. However, it may be impossible to redesign a job to this extent. The HR department should then attempt to select people who already have the skills and competences needed. This will mean that there is no delay or failure in training people. Unfortunately, selection is not perfect. In many situations the ideal person for a job may not exist and some people offered jobs will turn out not to have the skills they

Job design and ergonomics p 117

claimed. It will be necessary to employ people who have only some of the skills and develop the rest by training.

Well-chosen, well-trained people working in a well-designed job are *competent workers*. They are *able* to do the job, but this does not mean that they *will* do the job. There are a wide range of factors which help transform competent workers into effective workers. Some of these factors, such as organisational climate, motivation and communication, have been covered in earlier chapters. However, the HR function will also need to arrange performance management (e.g. pay, promotion and discipline), and employee relations in order to transform competent workers into effective workers. There are, of course, feedback loops. The success or failure of the HR function to produce effective workers will feed back into the organisation's aims and goals and other aspects of its own function.

People resourcing

People resourcing is known as **recruitment and selection** or **inplacement**. The responsibility for people resourcing lies with individual managers and is a part of the staffing process (see Chapter 7) The HR function must remember that, except when recruiting its own staff, it is offering a service. Responsibility for selecting an employee must lie with the head of the department where he or she will work. So, the main recruitment and selection responsibilities of the HR function are:

- establishing a system for approving and filling a vacancy
- training staff in selection techniques and legal aspects
- advising on a job description and other information for applicants
- preparing and placing advertisements
- approving and liaising with recruitment agencies
- corresponding with applicants (invitations to interview, etc.)
- making arrangements for an interview or other selection methods
- assisting with interview or other selection method
- advising on starting salary and conditions of employment
- communicating the formal job offer and writing to unsuccessful candidates.

People development

People development is also known as **training and development**. Again it must be remembered that, except when training and developing its own staff, it is offering a service. Responsibility for training and developing an employee lies with the head of the department where she or he will work. So, the main development responsibilities of the HR function are:

- establishing and maintaining a system that ensures all employees are fully developed and properly trained
- advising on the development needs of specific individuals
- monitoring and maintaining a list of training providers

- co-ordinating the training offered to employees within the organisation
- developing and providing training courses on topics specific to the organisation or where there are advantages in providing training "in house"
- evaluating the effectiveness of the training

Performance management

Competent employees are generally motivated to perform well and are capable of learning. If suboptimal behaviour is noted and discussed, most workers will improve their behaviour. There are many methods of performance appraisal.

Methods of performance appraisal

In an archetypal appraisal system, a subordinate and his or her boss meet at regular, say three-monthly, intervals to discuss performance. Ideally the meeting will have no other purpose than improving performance; the boss will have an intimate knowledge of the job and the subordinate's actions. Ideally, the subordinate will be totally open, prepared to accept that his or her performance is less than perfect and be willing and able to make substantial changes in the way that he or she works. After "deep and meaningful discussion" the subordinate and the boss will be able to identify the correct way forward and produce a realistic plan that the subordinate will implement with assiduity.

CRITICAL THINKING 16.1 *Why appraisal systems often fail*

There are four main reasons why appraisal systems often fail:

1 Subordinates manipulate information. They are not stupid. They know that, even with assurances that "our conversation will only be used for purposes of your development", information will leak into decisions about pay rises, promotion and, perhaps, dismissal. They will spend time preparing for the appraisal rather than doing their normal work. They will pursue their own targets rather than being a good organisational "citizen".

2 Attribution theory has a big impact on the way an employee interprets, and thus implements, the outcome of appraisals. They almost always attribute good results to their own skill and effort. On the other hand, bad results are attributed to other people or to unfavourable circumstances. Hence a good appraisal merely confirms present behavior while a bad appraisal is likely to focus attention on things that are wrong with the work situation – including the support and effectiveness of the supervisor!

3 A boss will not usually have sufficient time to conduct a comprehensive appraisal. A thorough appraisal, together with the attendant paperwork, might involve a boss in two days' effort. A boss who has, say, eight subordinates will therefore spend 16 days per quarter (about 20 per cent of available time) on

▶

> performance appraisals during which time they need to ignore production crises and other "marginal" matters.
>
> 4 Bosses are rarely fully informed about their subordinates' jobs and their performances; the jobs may have changed quite dramatically since the bosses were promoted from them. The average boss spends less than 10 per cent of their time with any single subordinate. Further, it is difficult for a boss to be objective. They have their own styles and preferences.

Organisations have tried to minimise such problems in two main ways: by making the appraisals more quantitative and obtaining **metrics** by using rating scales.

Although rating scales, especially behaviourally anchored rating scales, look scientific, there is a problem when they are used in appraisal systems. They lack discrimination, because most employees are placed in the top two positions. This is partly because superiors may wish to be kind to subordinates. It may also occur because superiors do not wish to admit that they manage their unit in a way that tolerates average or below-average performance. Furthermore, some managers want to save their time for other activities they consider more productive. They know that any subordinate who receives an average or below-average rating is likely to contest the judgement and they will need to spend hours justifying their view and placating the aggrieved subordinate. Moreover, the aggrieved subordinate will continue to work in their unit. It may be a more cost-effective use of time to give an acceptable rating and invest the time saved in solving another problem.

Problems with superior ratings led to the development of a technique called 360-degree feedback. **360-degree feedback** gets its name from the fact that feedback is provided from all directions (Figure 16.2). Questionnaires are distributed to a range of people including the boss, colleagues, subordinates and perhaps customers.

The questionnaire is completed on a confidential basis and analysed by someone with no vested interest in the results. The average of the ratings will then be fed back to the employee and their boss so that the appropriate lessons are learnt. 360-degree feedback is not without its own problems. People generally dislike rating their colleagues. The actual rating that they give can be distorted in many ways. Sometimes colleagues come to a mutually advantageous agreement that they will not give each other poor ratings. In other cases rivals for promotion can seek to improve their own chances by criticising their competitors.

Consequences of performance appraisal

With luck, a performance appraisal will reveal that a person is working competently and adding value to the organisation but there will be some points that can be improved or developed. The boss and subordinate should note the generally favourable appraisal and produce an action plan to address the development points. This plan should be reviewed after, say, three months to check that the plan has been, or is being, fulfilled. In a minority of cases, an appraisal might reveal problems. This always causes rancour and a great deal of emotion. The subordinate is likely to contend that he or she has been the victim of misunderstandings, bias or stereotyping. These claims may be true and they should be considered fairly.

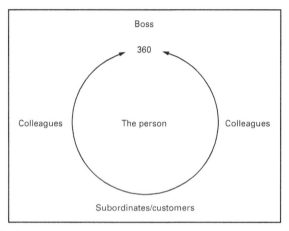

FIGURE 16.2 360° feedback

If the claims are groundless, it is important to tackle the reason for poor performance. If the problem arises from lack of training, additional training can be provided. If the problem arises from a mismatch between a person's abilities and those required by the job, the person can be moved to a more suitable position. A *transfer* that is perceived as demotion will be resented and it is likely that the person will resign from the organisation within a short time. If they remain they are likely to experience frustration, loss of confidence and may transmit discontent to others. Transfers may offer a solution when poor performance arises from poor relationships. For example, if there are frequent personality clashes between colleagues or with a boss it may be better to transfer the person to another job of equal status.

It is quite rare for people to be dismissed for poor performance. Usually *dismissal* only takes place when there has been a clear failure to perform the job. For example, people may be dismissed for *gross misconduct* such as dishonesty, a clear neglect in duty or a blatant refusal to obey an instruction. Dismissal may also occur if a worker *breaches* their *contract of employment* by going on strike, or disrupting the work of others or putting other workers in danger. Dismissal is a major step and normally only taken after considerable thought. The employees should be notified (preferably in writing) of their poor performance, warned of the potential consequences and given reasonable opportunity to make changes. Dismissal procedures and legal requirements must be followed to the letter. In some circumstances, such as theft, drunkenness, the imminent threat of damage to property or the safety of others, it may be possible to **summarily dismiss** an employee without notice. If an employer obstructs an employee and makes it difficult for him or her to do their job, the employee may resign and claim a **constructive dismissal**. This means that the employer has shown that they have no intention of fulfilling their side of the employment contract. The employee may then claim compensation for **wrongful dismissal**.

Pay and compensation

The HR function plays a key role in determining the compensation packages for employees. It will establish a salary structure that other departments must operate. If a salary structure is not in place, different departments will pay different salaries for equivalent work. There will be a great number of anomalies and a lot of time and effort will be spent dealing with complaints. Further, the lack of a sound salary structure is likely to lead to an infringement of employment legislation where different groups are paid different salaries for equivalent work. Most pay structures are based on some form of grading or job evaluation. In the past the tasks involved in a job would be evaluated and allotted points. The number of points would determine the salary band appropriate for the job. Someone's salary would be within that band but other factors such as experience, seniority or recognition for good work would determine the exact placement. Probably the best-known points system for job evaluation is the Hay-MSL system for evaluating senior management jobs.

In the past, a salary system of a large organisation would have many, perhaps seven or more, narrow bands. People would sometimes start employment at the bottom of the lowest band and work their way up to the top of the highest band by the time they retired. **Narrowband** salary structures give workers the sense of progression but they have their disadvantages. First they are complex to administer; every little change in a job's content means the job needs to be regraded. Every time someone moves to a slightly different job they might change salary bands. Because small changes could make a difference to an employee's pay, the HR function was forever wrangling with people who contested the positioning of their job. In recent years there has been a trend towards **broadbanding** where there are fewer, wider bands. As Figure 16.3 shows broadbanding produces a simpler and more flexible salary structure. Some organisations maintain that it is less divisive and more motivating for employees.

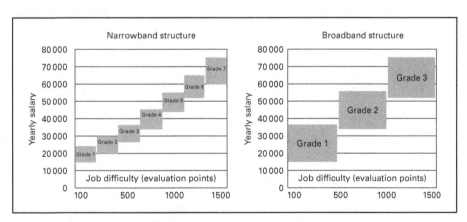

FIGURE 16.3 Narrowband and broadband salary structures

Now it is more likely that jobs are evaluated in terms of the *skills* needed to perform the tasks. Again there is usually a point system. Jobs that demand higher skills, more experience or higher physical demands are generally higher paid. The labour market will also play its part. People in occupations that are in short supply will generally be paid more.

Many firms have moved to a system whereby people are paid according to their *performance*. Such systems are often called *incentive schemes* and they can take many forms, but they are all based on the expectancy theory of motivation. Some jobs are paid on a strict commission basis where there is a direct relationship between salary and output. These schemes produce high motivation for ambitious people who are not concerned about security. However, they have the disadvantage that they encourage selfishness and discourage organisational citizenship. They also encourage people to exploit short-term possibilities and then move on to another job before the long-term consequences are apparent. A less aggressive regime entails a reasonable basic salary plus commission when performance exceeds a pre-set limit. These systems often attract better employees than those solely working on commission. However, they too tend to encourage selfishness and discourage teamwork.

Expectancy theory
p 183

CASE 16.3: *Reckitt Benckiser's remuneration*

Reckitt Benckiser has a remuneration committee which sets the salaries for the company's top managers. It aims to devise a scheme that fosters an innovative and entrepreneurial culture. Top managers' pay consists of three parts: a base salary, short-term incentives and long-term incentives. If a top manager made all their targets, they receive an additional 40 per cent of their base salary. A manager who does extremely well (double targets) can earn a bonus of 144 per cent of the basic salary. Long-term remuneration takes the form of stock options and is based on indices such as three-year corporate growth and earnings per share.

In 2010 the CEO, Bart Brecht, received a basic salary of £987 000 plus a bonus of £3.52 million, making his total salary £4.5 million. In the preceding 10 years he had amassed share options worth £87 million. Bart Brect donated shares worth £110 million to a personal charitable trust that specialises in humanitarian, educational and environmental causes.

(See also Case 2.4 on Reckitt Benckiser's globalisation page 52.)

Performance-related pay (PRP) has many conceptual advantages: in theory, it ties remuneration to the contribution an individual makes to organisational goals. In practice, the achievements of PRP are much less impressive. Outside sales and other readily quantifiable occupations, it is very difficult to assess accurately an individual's contribution to organisational goals – most jobs are too complex and multifaceted. Performance-related pay often engenders distrust. A survey by Towers-Perrin (1999) revealed considerable dissatisfaction in companies that had tried to install the system. Indeed, 84 per cent of companies had experienced problems some writers suggest that PRP reduces employee motivation. A meta-analysis by Perry, Engbers and Jun (2009 – an especially good read for those completing an assignment on PRP) found that recent research largely supported earlier findings that individual financial incentives are ineffective – especially in the public sector. However, contrary to expectations, they found that it could have some effect in lower-paid jobs, where there was a high level of trust and where the appraisal system was objective.

A third system is to pay a basic salary plus a bonus that is based upon the performance of the *team*. In principle, this should promote teamwork while still providing motivation for individuals. Unfortunately, some members of a team may decide that it is better to provide

---

CRITICAL THINKING 16.2 *Why are so many performance-related pay schemes ineffective?*

Performance-related pay schemes were in great favour a few years ago and governments started to introduce them into the public sector in order to drive up productivity. They are now less popular. Many believe that PRP was a major cause of the credit crunch. Many bankers were rewarded by a very aggressive system of PRP and this led them to take enormous risks and to lend unwisely. Furthermore, research findings indicated that, at best, the success of PRP is very patchy. There are four main reasons why PRP schemes may not work:

1 A sizeable minority of employees are very hostile to PRP schemes because they believe the schemes are a tool of management manipulation.

2 The allocation of rewards is perceived as unfair. This is particularly true when appraisals are based on supervisors' opinion and where there is considerable ambiguity in the definition of a job or where the indicators of success are ambiguous or subjective. These situations mean that the links required by the expectancy theory motivation are broken

3 Many employees are already working hard and cannot improve their performance even if offered more pay

4 Performance-related pay might increase motivation but motivation on its own may not be enough to increase performance. Management should first remove other limitations before introducing PRP.

Some people maintain that even the patchy successes of PRP are an artifice because it necessarily involves clarifying employees goals. These sceptics argue that it is the clarification of the goals which produces the partial success or PRP, not the incentives of the payment system.

---

a moderate performance and rely on other members of the team to earn bonuses for them. Another system involves profit, where by employees are given a reasonable basic salary but there is an additional element based on profit in the preceding year.

Other benefits

Benefits are the non-cash rewards that a person receives. They are similar to **perks** or **perquisites** and can form a substantial proportion of the total remuneration. For example, when contribution to state schemes are included, most employers pay employees an additional 15 per cent over and above salary in terms of medical, sickness and retirement benefits. "Benefits in kind" include:

- employee share schemes
- membership of professional bodies
- travel accident insurance
- company car (especially in the UK)
- free car parking
- personal training (e.g. pre-retirement courses)
- counselling
- subsidised childcare
- life insurance
- tuition fees for employees and dependants
- recreational clubs
- subsidised canteens and catering

Benefits can add 30 per cent or more to an employee's total remuneration. Organisations offer these benefits because they help attract and retain people of the calibre they need. Many employees value these benefits more than a marginal increase in salary. They are, therefore, an economical way of motivating employees – especially when benefits receive favourable tax treatment. Some employers offer "flexible benefit packages" where the value of the total remuneration package is fixed but employees have considerable choice about how it is distributed between salary and their own mixture of benefits. An organisation's remuneration system is closely linked to the organisation's maturity, and more details are given in the website that accompanies this book.

Employee relations (industrial relations)

Definition and concept of employee relations

The topic of employee relations (ER) is more widely known as **industrial relations (IR)**. It is also known as **labour relations** and **staff relations**. The term "employee relations" is preferred because in most modern economies only a minority of people work in industry. Similarly, "labour relations" has strong and possibly misleading connotations with physical labour which now forms only a small part of economic activity; the term is more frequently used in the USA. Staff relations implies that the topic is only relevant to people employed in "staff" positions. The term "employee relations" makes it clear that the topic is relevant to everyone who is employed in an organisation. Employee relations may be defined as:

> ❝ The study of institutions and processes controlling the mutual dealings between an organisation and its employees – especially the mutual dealings between an organisation and collective worker groups. ❞

In many situations ER concerns the mutual dealings between an organisation and a trade union, but it also encompasses dealings with staff associations and informal groups. The nature of ER is usually a feature of the management style and the industrial or commercial sector. Generally three main philosophical approaches to ER are distinguished – confrontation, concensus and pluralist:

- **Confrontation** arises from beliefs that organisations and employees have irreconcilable objectives. There is a great deal of mistrust between the two parties. Employee relations are often seen as a battleground in which the employees or the organisation seeks supremacy in dictating terms of employment, etc. Such conflicts can be mutually destructive. For example, workers may strike and picket an organisation with such success that the organisation is forced into bankruptcy and closes, leaving the employees worse off and without employment. Confrontation tends to be seen in traditional organisations with a long history of poor ER – often in traditional and declining industries where competition (perhaps international competition) is fierce. Confrontation is based on a *radical philosophy* derived from Marx: there is a fundamental conflict between employing organisations (capitalists) and the workers (the proletariat). Employers will maximise profits at the expense of the workers. Since employers have more power than an individual employee, workers need to band together so that their collective power is equal to or greater than the power of the employer. The ultimate goal will be for the workers to own the organisation collectivity or to control it by controlling the government. This philosophy was once very prevalent in some trade unions – albeit in a watered down and more sophisticated form.

- **Consensus** is sometimes called the **unitarian approach and** is the mirror image of the confrontation. Employees or their representatives form a genuine partnership working towards mutually beneficial solutions. In practice, a fully consensual approach is very rare and is, perhaps, only seen in co-operatives and small organisations. The consensus approach is based upon a *unitarian philosophy* which believes that there is a set of goals and objectives which serve everyone's interests. The well-being of the organisation is therefore paramount and everyone must work towards pleasing its customers. The **conformity approach** focuses on achieving *harmony between various subgroups of employees* – avoiding demarcation disputes where one group takes industrial action to pre-empt another group trespassing on its traditional territory. The conformity approach tries to set objectives and procedures that allow different groups to rise above their own vested interests. The conformity approach is based on a *pluralistic philosophy* that acknowledges that different workers and groups of workers will have a variety of objectives that may not be totally compatible. Since potential conflict may be mutually harmful, it is necessary to have a system of rules and procedures to resolve it. Workers must conform to the system so that the organisation remains productive.

Employee relations in public service and government are usually based on a pluralistic philosophy.

Employee relations usually involves a sophisticated interplay between *formal* and *informal* systems. The formal part of the system will consist of "official" documents, meetings, agendas and timetables. The formal part of the system legitimises and crystallises ER. However, the formal system is often inflexible and prone to developing into "stand-offs". The informal part of the system consists of networks of respected people in both camps. It often operates via informal meetings in corridors and in "off-the-record" telephone conversations. The informal network oils the informal network and helps it function.

Employee relations usually involves the most senior managers in an organisation. The head of the HR function will have a very important advisory role but final decisions will be made by the CEO or the board of directors. The HR function will play an important role in setting up and maintaining the ER system and may be given executive powers with regard to minor decisions. More information on the people involved in bargaining and the phases of the bargaining process are given in the website that accompanies this book.

Types of unionisation

An organisation will face big disadvantages if its workers are not organised in some way. For example, it will need separate negotiations with each employee or it must ignore employees' wishes. A workforce can be organised in many ways. At the bottom of the scale are **non-union organisations**. Non-union organisations usually occur in small, recently established businesses which are experiencing favourable trading conditions. If the organisation encounters difficulties and employees feel they are ignored they will either join a union or leave the organisation en masse – at a time when the organisation needs to devote its attention to other things. Some non-union organisations establish a **staff association** to represent workers and conduct negotiations. Some organisations try to avoid demarcation disputes between unions by coming to a **single-union agreement** where the whole workforce is represented by one union. It drastically simplifies ER and often means that a more logical and systematic approach to ER can be established. Single-union agreements may be accompanied by **no-strike agreements** whereby both union and organisation agree a method, usually arbitration, of resolving conflicts without strike action.

Many large organisations with a workforce that is very diverse in terms of its skills and trades and which has long history of unionisation are, necessarily, **multi-union**. Multi-unionism can require a great deal of effort managing rivalries between unions. Organisations are usually keen to avoid a sequence of never-ending negotiations where each trade union attempts to impress its own members and poach members of other unions by "leapfrogging" earlier agreements. In these circumstances the organisation may attempt to instigate **single-table negotiations** where all the unions are present and where one comprehensive agreement can be made. Needless to say, single-table negotiations are often very protracted and complicated.

16.3 The psychological contract

The idea of a psychological contract has been around since the 1960s. It is an unspoken understanding between an employee and their employer about what they can expect from each other – "I have promised to do this and my employer has promised me that he or she will do that". Usually the employee understands that she or he has promised effort, loyalty, trustworthiness, etc. in return for training, pay, job security and promotion from the employer. Psychological contracts in the past could be summed up by the phrase "I will give total commitment to the company and the company will look after me until I retire". Robinson and Rousseau (1994) defined the psychological contract in a more long-winded way:

> 66   An individual's belief regarding the terms and conditions of that reciprocal exchange agreement between that focal person and another party . . . a belief that some form of a promise has been made and that the terms and conditions of the contract have been accepted by both parties.   99

Note that it is the individual employee who believes that the contract has been accepted by both parties. An employer may intend to keep the contract but knows full well that it is unenforceable. A new manager installed after a takeover or merger may have no such intention. The HR function plays a crucial role in managing the psychological contract. A classic paper by Sims (1994 – a good read) indicates that the HR function should:

- arrange realistic job previews
- arrange training sessions devoted to the contract during the early stages of employment
- clarify organisational ethics and values

In general, the HRM department should make sure that the contract is communicated as clearly as possible. Guest and Conway (2002 – a good read) discussed the views of 1036 senior managers about the promises made by the organisation and the extent to which the promises were met. Table 16.1 is based on their data and uses an index where 100 is the maximum possible score. The list in the table is a good indication of the areas of employment included in the psychological contract.

It is unsurprising that when fewer promises are made fewer promises are broken. Indeed, when fewer promises are made they tended to be exceeded! Promises are frequently made about training and development, safety, feedback and fairness. Yet in all these areas there are shortcomings in their fulfilment.

Rousseau (1995) identified two main types of psychological contract: transactional and relational. The *transactional psychological contract* is nearest to a normal commercial contract. Workers agree to do certain things such as work overtime or move to a new location in return for a specific reward such as extra money. Transactional psychological contracts are often seen in clearly defined jobs that are relatively short term. They tend to centre upon specific outputs and specific rewards. *Relational psychological contracts*

Aspects of employment	Promises made	Promises kept	Difference
Training and development opportunities	88	63	−25
Safe environment	87	39	−47
Feedback on performance	81	60	−21
Fair treatment	78	49	−29
Open two-way communication	72	67	−6
Fair rate of pay	65	48	−16
Opportunities for promotion	55	67	+12
Avoiding unreasonable demands	54	69	+15
Attractive benefits	54	50	+4
Recognition for innovation and ideas	49	68	+18
Pleasant working environment	49	53	+4
Job security	47	49	+2
Interesting work	43	64	+22

TABLE 16.1 Promises made and promises kept in the psychological contract

are usually seen in long-term employees where the work is only defined in a general way. As their name implies, relational psychological contracts centre upon the way that the parties behave to each other. In the past, this was usually a paternalistic relationship where the employee would be loyal, compliant and adopt the organisation's values in return for secure employment and the knowledge that they would be looked after in times of misfortune. Modern psychological contracts where organisations can no longer offer long-term employment tend to stress a worker providing flexibility and a willingness to learn in return for high pay, the acquisition of marketable skills and a high quality of life.

Although the psychological contract implies a mutual agreement, there is a huge power differential between the two parties – the employer's viewpoint prevails. Workers then feel that the contract has been violated. This happened to large numbers of employees during the downsizing and restructuring of organisations in the 1980s and 1990s. Many workers felt cheated: while they had kept their part of the bargain, many employers had reneged on their part by increasing workloads and making many peoples' jobs redundant. In one study, 54 per cent of graduates claimed that their employers had violated their psychological contracts within the first two years of employment. The most frequent violations involved training, pay and promotion. The reactions of employees who believe that their psychological contract has been violated have been extensively researched. They experience feelings of injustice, deception or betrayal.

There are cultural differences too. For example, workers in Singapore who are used to short-term contracts are less aggrieved by violations than employees in the USA. Violations of the psychological contract usually affect workers' attitudes and behaviour towards their employers. The most obvious response is to leave the organisation and work for another employer. Some people, probably a small minority, complain to their employers. Probably most employees adopt the third option of keeping quiet and focusing tightly on their official duties while cutting back on more discretionary behaviours such as doing extra hours. Some employees attempt to get even. Revenge can take many forms and may include pilfering, neglecting duties that are hard to monitor, denigrating their employers in public, divulging trade secrets and even sabotage or destruction of the employer's property.

CRITICAL THINKING 16.3 *The bizarre nature of the psychological contract*

Lawyers would regard the psychological contract as a very strange contract indeed. It is bizarre in a number of ways:

- *It is rarely written down.* Only a part of the expectations on both sides are made explicit. Some of the expectations are conscious but others are subconscious and the contracting parties may not be aware of their existence.

- *It is based on perceptions.* Consequently, there are as many psychological contracts as there are employees in the organisation.

- *It is dynamic* and will change over time. In a sense the psychological contract is under constant renegotiation.

Because the psychological contract is so dissimilar to other contracts some people believe it needs to be renamed "transitory employee perceptions of their employment". This would emphasise the subjective, individualistic and non-permanent nature of the psychological contract. Guest (1998) complains that, in practice, we should not take the concept seriously because it involves so many variables interacting in unknown ways.

CASE 16.4: *Revenge for reneging on the psychological contract*

Palmer (1999) gives examples of the revenge people can take. Employees sometimes take revenge when employers renege on their psychological contract. For example, one 50-year-old from Wales tells how a new senior position was created in the service department where he had worked alone for more than four years. "I applied in writing for the new position, setting out my achievements. I was not granted even a brief interview despite the fact that I was on the premises. On the last afternoon of my resignation notice I destroyed all the test rigs I had built and the notes I had made to speed up the job. Subsequently I learned that three staff had been taken on to do the work . . . I had previously done myself."

Another example includes a 25-year-old publishing assistant who "rearranged" her boss's files, and did it so effectively that important documents were lost for several months. A final, ingenious example is a disgruntled word-processor operator who changed all the screens in her department to black characters on a black background. The organisation had purchased several replacement monitors before it located the real cause.

16.4 Employee engagement

Employee engagement is a current concern of HR departments yet it has a long history. In 1975 Csikszementkihalyri identified the concept of "flow" – a holistic sensation (presumably a good sensation) that workers feel when they are totally absorbed in their job when there is little difference between their own identity and goals and those of the organisation. Workers in a state of "flow" do not need to make any conscious effort to do the work needed to fulfil the mission and vision of their organisations. In 1990, Kahn coined the term engagement to describe a situation where the very *selves* of organisational members are harnessed to perform their jobs. Engagement integrates the ideas of job satisfaction and organisational commitment. It can be thought of as an employee's involvement with, commitment to and satisfaction with work. Engagement, it is claimed, unlocks people's potential so that they prepared to "run the extra mile" in order to help the organisation. Gatenby *et al* (2009) define engagement as:

> ❝ creating opportunities for employees and their colleagues, managers and wider organization. It is all about creating an environment where employees are motivated and want to connect with their work and really care about doing a good job . . . It is a concept that places flexibility, change and continuous improvement at the heart of what it means to be an employee and employer in the 21st century workplace. ❞

Employee engagement is often measured using a 12-item questionnaire devised by the Gallup organisation. MacLeod and Clarke (2009) report that employee engagement is related to:

- lower pilfering
- lower accidents

- higher productivity
- higher profitability
- higher innovation

Wow! It seems that employee engagement might be an *even* better managerial panacea than leadership! Unfortunately studies suggest that few workers are highly engaged. In high-scoring companies 24 per cent of employees are highly engaged and in low scoring companies only 3 per cent of employees are highly engaged. The main methods of increasing engagement include:

- Give *strong, transparent leadership* which gives employees a clear link between their jobs and the organisational vision.

- Managers who *clearly appreciate the employees' work* and who treat them as individuals. The managers must also be efficient and ensure that workers are equipped and supported to do their job.

- Employees should know that they are *free to express ideas* about how they do their job and how decisions are made in their department. Problems and challenges should be shared. Further, employees should know that their views will be carefully considered.

- The organisation should have a *sense of integrity* and live up to its values.

Unfortunately, there are several barriers to raising the levels of employee engagement. MacLeod and Clarke note that senior managers may not be aware of the need for employee engagement and do not understand the benefits it can bring. Even when senior managers are enthusiastic, middle and junior managers may not share their beliefs. Further, managers may not not know how to increase engagement and they may be ill-equipped to implement engagement strategies. As a result the organisational culture is unable to deliver engagement.

CRITICAL THINKING 16.4 *Doubts about employee engagement*

The arguments in favour of employee engagement seem almost as strong as the arguments that were made by Herzberg in favour of motivators and hygiene factors. Yet, in due course Herzberg's theories were found to be based, to a considerable extent, on methodological flaws (see page 183). MacLeod and Clarke (2009) present a great deal of evidence in favour of employee engagement but, although there is a lot of evidence, much of it has very poor scientific value. There are four main doubts: poor definition, overreliance on case studies, poor quality measures and ambiguous experimental design and analysis.

1 *Definitions of employee engagement are vague.* If those given in MacLeod and Clarke are copied onto file cards and people are asked to nominate the construct

▶

they are defining, a very wide range of answers are obtained. Guest (see MacLeod and Clarke, 2009, p. 8) points out that much of the discussion on engagement tends to get muddled and he suggests that "the concept of employee engagement needs to be more clearly defined . . . or it needs to be abandoned".

2 Much of MacLeod and Clarke's report consists of over 40 repetitive *case studies*. Yet, elsewhere in the this book (page 179) it was noted that case studies are a very weak form of evidence and depend on the background, experience and motives of the writer. There is often a **publication bias** in favour of examples that have worked. After all, what HR director who had invested tens of thousands of pounds in a programme to improve employee engagement that had failed would be keen to allow the results to be published? Many of the case studies are produced by organisations such as consultancies that have a vested interest in promoting employee engagement. It should be remembered that Harvard Business School was using case studies to extol the methods of Enron and the Royal Bank of Scotland.

3 The validity of the scales measuring employee engagement is not high. The most frequently used measure of employee engagement is the Gallup Q12 survey. (http://www.gallup.com/consulting/12153/Employee-Engagement-Overview-Brochure.aspx). A large-scale "in-house" study (Harter *et al.*, 2009) assessed the validity of the Q12 against nine criteria such as customer loyalty, profitability, turnover, safety and quality, etc. The validity correlations were not high. The median coalition was .23 which means that the things measured by the scale captured only 5 per cent of the differences between business units on these outcomes. A validity of .23 can be compared with validities of .58 and .4 for intelligence tests and personality tests, respectively.

4 Many studies of employee engagement are poorly designed and do not differentiate between cause and effect. For example, they show that employee engagement is correlated (slightly) with profitability. However, it is perfectly feasible that working for a profitable company causing people to be engaged rather than the other way round. Further, many studies use weak statistics. For example they divide organisations into high-scoring units and low scoring units. It is virtually certain that employee engagement is a continuum. Analysing a continuum in separate slices wastes information and may produce misleading results.

16.5 The legal background to human resource management

Governments have passed laws concerning the employment of people for almost 200 years. Initially these laws concerned the basic contract between employer and employees such as how wages must be paid (in cash, not in kind) and about the rights of workers to belong to trade unions. Broadly, between, say, 1900 and 1950, governments passed legislation concerning health and safety at work. Since 1960 they have passed legislation concerning social issues and the rights of individuals. As Table 16.2 shows, there is a raft of legislation concerning workers.

Categories of employees
■ Employment of minors – to prevent exploitation of children ■ Part-time workers and fixed-term employees – to prevent their exploitation
Anti-discrimination (to ensure fairness)
■ Race, ethnic origin, colour ■ Gender, pregnancy, sexual orientation ■ Disability, age ■ Rehabilitation of offenders – relatively minor offences need not be disclosed after five years (usually!)
Health and safety
■ Place of work – must be safe, clean and at a reasonable temperature ■ Working hours – must not be excessive ■ Injuries to health
Benefits
■ Form of payment – not as tokens to be exchanged at employer's shop ■ Written statement of wage calculations – to check payment is accurate ■ Minimum Wage Act – to ensure workers are not exploited ■ Holidays – granting minimum statutory (Bank holidays) and other leave ■ Parental leave – paid and unpaid time off work for mother and father ■ Pension benefits – to ensure that people have retirement income ■ Written employment contracts – to ensure clarity about duties and responsibilities ■ Time off for study – to allow people the opportunity to gain qualifications
Redundancy or dismissal
■ Reasons for dismissal – clear, written notification is required ■ Consultation on closure – to ensure that workers' viewpoints are heard ■ Redundancy –prevents victimisation at times of closure or redundancy ■ Period of notice – gives stability of employment ■ Continuation of employment if organisation changes hands (TUPE)
Trade unions
■ Trade union membership – the right to belong or not belong to a trade union ■ Picketing –the circumstances under which picketing may take place

TABLE 16.2 Areas of legislation on the employment of people

Clearly this is not an exhaustive list. Legislation may vary from country to country and from time to time. It is usually the job of the HR function to check the legislation in the territories where they operate. Usually, they maintain a file with this information. They will also give guidance to other managers, perhaps as oral advice, memos on specific cases or periodic guidance notes. Failure to observe the legislation can have serious consequences. Infraction of safety regulations, for example, might result in a temporary closure of the organisation. The organisation might also be fined and its senior managers imprisoned. Failure to uphold employment law may involve an appearance at a tribunal which has the power to fine the organisation, award compensation or order an employee's reinstatement. Cases of this kind are nearly always attended by unfavourable publicity.

CASE 16.5: *Lloyds TSB earns disability benefits*

Lloyds Bank is a venerable institution stretching back to 1765. However, neither its age in nor its size and financial might mean that it can pay lip-service to employment legislation such as the UK's Disability Discrimination Act 2005. This Act covers more than obvious disabilities (e.g. physical impairment). It also covers disabilities that are not visible such as diabetes dyslexia, epilepsy or asthma. The Act means that employers must make "reasonable adjustments" to cope with disability on a person-by-person basis. Lloyds TSB has a strategy to deal with disability which has won numerous awards. The measures which the bank takes to create an inclusive working environments include:

- arranging flexible working hours
- providing software to read Braille
- installing chairs that give extra back support
- personal development programmes for employees with disabilities
- a disability resource toolkit
- software which reads out a computer screen (JAWS)

Such changes have clear benefits. The bank is able to recruit from a wider range of people and, in general, disabled people stay in jobs longer. It also enjoys strategic benefits by making its employees more representative of the community and improving its image – not least among customers who themselves may have a disability.

Source: Based on *Times 100 Case Studies*

16.6 Human resource strategy and manpower planning

An HR plan is often a very complex document. It is often produced in four stages. *First,* the future staffing requirements must be established. The process starts by examining the organisation's strategic plan to establish the impact of any changes, such as:

- new equipment
- expansion or contraction
- new legislation
- centralisation, decentralisation
- new working procedures
- reorganisation or mergers

This establishes the kind of job the organisation will need to fill together with the skills and competences that will be demanded. An organisation may wish, at this stage, to specify the number of various groups such as men, women, ethnic minorities, disabled people it would like to have on the payroll at a future date. At the end of this stage the organisation will have a **future staffing requirement**.

The *second* stage is to establish similar information for the **present staffing levels**. This is sometimes called a **human resource audit** and the result is sometimes called a **workforce profile**. Many organisations conduct HR audits on a systematic basis so that the information will be to hand if it is needed. The information can often be obtained from the organisation's IT system which calculates various indices of labour turnover. The simplest is the **crude percentage turnover** which is calculated according to the following formula:

$$\text{Percentage turnover} = \frac{\text{Number holding posts in year}}{\text{Number of posts}} \times 100$$

Another index of turnover is the **average length of service**. Both the crude index of labour turnover and the average length of service have the disadvantage that a poor result can be produced by the rapid turnover by a few individuals in a few posts. A more sophisticated index that does not suffer this disadvantage is the **labour stability index (LSI)** which is calculated by the formula:

$$\text{LSI} = \frac{\text{Number of people with more than a year's service}}{\text{Number of people employed 12 months before}}$$

Very low labour turnover might indicate a stagnant organisation that is not receiving enough new people and ideas. The problem of a high turnover is even less desirable and more common. An organisation with high turnover will be spending a lot of money recruiting and training people, which is wasted when they leave. Further, a high turnover disrupts the work of the people who stay with the organisation. High turnover is often a symptom of problems elsewhere in the HR function, such as monotonous work, poor communications, poor management style or poor wages. However, labour turnover must be interpreted in the light of information from other comparable organisations. Some industries such as hotel and catering have a notoriously high labour turnover.

It is difficult to determine the exact reason why people leave the organisation unless exit interviews are conducted. **Exit interviews** should be held within a day or two of an employee's resignation. It is no use waiting until the last day when attitudes have mellowed by fond farewells, mending of fences and anticipation of appreciative ceremonies and presents. Exit interviews need to be as close as possible to the point at which an employee decides to leave. They should be conducted by an independent and sympathetic person from the HR function. They *must not* be conducted by line management or people associated with them.

The *third* stage is to subtract the actual staffing levels from the future staffing requirements to produce a "skills gap" – an estimate of the number of new employees that will be needed in order to meet the organisation's strategic plan. Sometimes the comparison of actual and required staffing levels produces a surplus. This can occur if, say, a branch is to be closed or if new equipment will require fewer workers. Identifying surpluses is as important as identifying gaps: it often takes longer to resolve and needs early detection.

In the *fourth* stage gaps or surpluses are carefully inspected and appropriate action taken to ensure that the future supply of workers is equal to the number of workers demanded by the organisation's strategic plan. This is sometimes called "**right sizing**".

It is often possible to fill gaps for junior jobs by recruiting people from outside the organisation, and the time needed to train new employees must be taken into account. Recruitment for jobs with long training times needs to be scheduled ahead of recruitment for jobs with short training times. Senior jobs are often filled by promoting people from within the organisation. This is often a long-term process and it requires careful planning. It is called **succession planning** and almost all large organisations use it. Ironically, succession planning is more important for small organisations. In large organisations there is a much greater probability that someone suitable can be found. Simple arithmetic means that this is much less likely in small organisations, which can be reduced to chaos if a senior member of the management team resigns and no one is ready to take his or her place.

A succession plan starts with the organisational chart and works on a "falling under a bus" basis. This asks the question "who would take over if the CEO fell under a bus tomorrow?" When the successor is identified, other questions are asked: "how ready would the successor be?" and "what extra experience or knowledge would they need?" Of course, there would then be the problem of filling the post vacated by the person promoted to the CEO. Consequently, the process would be repeated for every position within at least two levels of the CEO. A succession plan is completed by drawing up schedules for the training and development of successors.

Succession plans are fraught with problems – which is why they are shunned by many small and medium-sized organisations. If they become public, as they probably will, they become organisational dynamite. The putative successor develops an initial mien of a "crown prince". Rivals to the succession may not acquiesce to their fate. They may set out to undermine the crown prince. They may tear the organisation apart in an attempt to seize the succession.

Staff surpluses often result in retrenchment, which is much less pleasant to deal with than organisational expansion. However, ignoring worker surpluses is great folly. A delay will mean an organisation will decline further, a bigger surplus will accumulate and a further round of unpleasant measures or emergency, traumatic, action will be needed later. It is much better to deal with surpluses promptly.

Potential surpluses can be managed by "freezes on recruitment", early retirements or redundancies. Short-term surpluses can be managed by "overtime bans" or short-time working. A freeze on recruitment may mean that the organisation is cut off from new people and new ideas. Further, unfilled vacancies may accumulate in certain departments that are already overloaded. Bottlenecks that impair the organisation's effectiveness may develop. Early retirement schemes can cause a haemorrhage of valuable expertise.

Redundancy schemes can cause great disruption and cause the motivation of workers to plummet. The HR function may seek to mitigate the effect on morale by offering voluntary redundancy. This too has great dangers. It is virtually certain that the majority of those who volunteer are those the organisation can least afford to lose. Some organisations manage redundancy situations by adopting a policy of last in, first out. At a superficial level this seems fair but it may be that people who have been recruited recently have competencies that are a better match to future needs. Needless to say, all of these problems are easier to solve if they have been detected early and there is plenty of time available to find a solution.

16.7 The welfare role of human resource management

At the start of the chapter it was noted that HRM had some of its roots in the welfare movements of the nineteenth century. The intervening sections of this chapter may have given the picture that HRM is now a mere management tool for controlling and manipulating workers. In fact, HRM has never totally lost its welfare role. In most organisations the HR function has a genuine concern in improving the lives of its employees. The welfare actions an HRM function might take are:

■ Helping employees *solve personal problems*. Employees encountering problems often go to the HR department for help. At its simplest this help might consist of a sympathetic ear plus some common-sense advice. In other situations it might take the form of a transfer, a change in working hours or a modification of the job. At its most sophisticated level the help might take the form of an **employee assistance programme (EAP)**. In an employee assistance programme the workers are given the telephone number or other contact details of a counselling service they can consult if they have personal problems. While the company will pay for the service, the counselling will be totally independent and conducted on a confidential basis. It is argued that the independent nature of an EAP will encourage people to seek help at an early stage before a problem becomes too difficult to solve. An EAP is usually able to help employees who have problems involving debt, marital and family relationships, a poor work–life balance or a drug problem.

■ Help *employees' careers*. Many HR functions try to structure jobs into patterns that provide careers for their employees. They may also offer training that has no direct or immediate relevance to an employee's current job but which will enhance his or her employability. In many cases an HR function will liaise with schools to provide work experience for scholars. Sometimes, the HR function will create temporary posts in order to help unemployed people make the transition into work.

■ When an employee encounters a serious and acute crisis such as illness or bereavement, it is usually the HR function that instigates and *co-ordinates the organisation's compassionate response* such as arranging extra leave or sending condolences. In some countries where there is inadequate health care the HR function may take the lead in raising money to pay for treatment.

■ The HR function usually takes the lead in the *social life of an organisation*. It often manages an organisation's sports and social clubs. Generally, it also organises social events, parties and celebrations. Further, the HR function will usually have responsibility for the organisation's catering services.

All of these contributions are usually considered peripheral activities, but their sum total improves the quality of people's working lives.

A final aspect of the HR function – *its advocacy on behalf of employees* – is often overlooked. In a majority of organisations HR personnel act as a buffer between the demands of other functions and employees. For example, a production manager may, perhaps to further his or her personal career, wish to instigate a very demanding schedule that involves high targets and a great deal of overtime. The marketing and financial functions may lend their support to the changes. It is likely to be someone in the HR function who draws attention to the impact these changes will have on employees. Similarly, the HR director will be present at board meetings where an organisation's strategy and tactics are first discussed. He or she is almost certain to make a significant contribution to ensure that the strategy and tactics are as "employee friendly" as possible.

Activities and further study

Essay plans

Write essay plans for the following questions:

1 What are the main laws that affect employment of people in your country? What steps can the HR function take to ensure that they are observed within an organisation?

2 What is HR planning and how does it contribute to achieving an organisation's goals?

3 What is the role of an HR function in *recruitment and selection* and how does this differ from the staffing procedures performed by managers in other departments?

4 What is the role of an HR function in *training and development* and how does this differ from the staffing procedures performed by managers in other departments?

5 Outline some of the factors that need to be taken into account by an HR function when it sets out to devise a salary and remuneration structure.

6 What are the main approaches and components to employee relations?

7 To what extent does the HR function, in an organisation you know well, still perform a traditional welfare role?

Web activities

1 Look up the website of professional bodies in HRM such as: http://www.cipd.co.uk/default.cipd (Chartered Institute of Personnel and Development) and http://www.nipm.in/ (National Institute of Personnel Management India).

2 Look up postgraduate courses in HRM such as http://www.whatuni.com/degrees/courses/Postgraduate-list/ or Google "HRM postgraduate courses".

Experiential activities

1 It is possible to gain some first-hand experience of HRM with vacation work or, perhaps, a management training scheme with short periods of work in different functions ("Cooks Tours").

2 If possible talk to a manager working in the HR function. Try to get detailed answers to the following questions. What type of organisation is it? What are its goals? What is its basic transformation process? How does the function operate?

3 Write a list of four topics that you think will be particularly relevant to the HR function in the next decade. Consider how they might change the way an HR department is structured.

Recommended reading

1 Perry, J.L., Engbers, T.K. and Jun, S.Y. (2009) "Back to the future? Performance related pay, and the perils of persistence", *Public Administration Review*, **69** (1), 39–52. An analysis of factors relevant to PRP and a review of research that draws practical conclusions.

2 Sims, R.R. (1994) "Human resource management's role in clarifying the new psychological contract", *Human Resource Management*, **33** (3), 373–383. This describes the HR functions's role in clarifying and forming the psychological contract.

3 Guest, D.E. and Conway, N. (2002) "Communicating the psychological contract: an employer perspective", *Human Resource Management Journal*, **12** (2), 22–37. Most research views the psychological contract from the employee viewpoint. This considers it from an employer's viewpoint.

4 Reed-Woodard, M.A. (2010) "Maximising employee value", *Black Enterprise*, **41** (2), 56. An interview with the HR director at Wal-Mart on how it leverages human capital for profits.

Chapter FIFTEEN

Acquiring and rewarding staff

Part contents

Recruiting the right people

Margaret May and Edward Brunsdon

After studying this chapter, you should be able to:

- ☑ **identify** 'broad' and 'narrow' definitions of recruitment in the HR literature

- ☑ **provide** outline descriptions of the procedures involved in 'formative' recruitment

- ☑ **understand** recruitment within its employment law context

- ☑ **recognise** the range of possible sources and methods of recruitment, and assess their comparative strengths and weaknesses

- ☑ **offer** an account as to why organisations use a multisource and multimethod approach to recruitment.

The opening vignette demonstrates how an employer can increase its recruitment pool by getting in touch with the needs of the local community.

NHS Greater Glasgow

Matching people without jobs to employers with vacancies has long been the dream of policy-makers, but has proved surprisingly difficult to achieve. Now a project in Scotland has shown how it can be done. Working for Health in Greater Glasgow, a training and recruitment pro-gramme for long-term unemployed people, has not only succeeded in getting 85 per cent of participants through the programme, but has also placed the majority in jobs. Most of these are among the 2000 or so vacancies the NHS in Greater Glasgow struggles to fill, such as hospital porters, technicians and domestic assistants. This has saved thousands of pounds in recruitment costs, cutting the lead time for filling basic grade hospital jobs from 18 weeks to nothing.

Last year the project involved 149 participants – three-quarters of whom were from deprived areas and had been unemployed for at least six months, some for more than 10 years. The participants spent up to six weeks on a pre-employment programme, which involved life-skills development to build their confidence, support in identifying suitable jobs, job application training and an introduction to the NHS. This included hospital visits, work placements and training in skills such as patient confidentiality and basic hygiene. The programme has now been extended to a maximum of 15 weeks for 2005–06 and aims to cover 350 people, including recent immigrants.

The project is the result of a partnership between NHS Greater Glasgow, JobCentre Plus, the Wise Group (a Glasgow-based charity that helps unemployed people back into work) and other agencies, with the involvement of trades unions. Funded by Scottish Enterprise Glasgow and JobCentre Plus, it arose from the problems facing local hospitals, which were struggling to compete for recruits in an increasingly tight labour market. NHS managers saw the programme as an opportunity to improve health in the community by tackling unemployment. They also aimed to improve staff diversity – 31 per cent of Glasgow's population, but only 12.5 per cent of NHS Greater Glasgow's workforce, live in deprived areas.

Annette Monaghan, care careers programme manager at NHS Greater Glasgow, who leads the project, says all its targets have been met or exceeded, including those on community health; 56 per cent of participants reported an improvement in their general health as a result of the programme, and 82 per cent felt more optimistic.

She stresses the importance of long-term commitment to the health service: 'We're not just looking at jobs, but careers,' she says. 'It's always been theoretically possible for people to work their way up in the NHS, but we are putting a more robust structure and resourcing into that in the coming years.'

Source: adapted from CIPD Annual Conference newspaper,
from *People Management,* 27 October 2005, p. 12.
Reproduced with permission of *People Management.*

Discussion questions

1 Should it be the role of the NHS to reduce local unemployment?

2 Are there differences in recruiting for a job or a career?

Recruitment is an understated and undervalued feature of the HR portfolio. It is given limited space in most publications and, where it is considered, it usually acts as a summary prelude to more detailed discussions of selection. This is something of an irony because, whatever the achievements of selection procedures, they are heavily influenced by the success or otherwise of recruitment. Recruitment supplies the candidates for selection but, more than this, it is very difficult for selection techniques to overcome the failure or limitations of recruitment (Marchington and Wilkinson, 2005). It is therefore of some importance that students of HR understand recruitment procedures in their own right, and be aware of and try to redress their limitations. The opening vignette illustrates how a local hospital can link with the local community for its recruitment needs. This has benefits for both the hospital and the community.

Recruitment: the question of definition

One has only to read the chapters of two or three standard HRM textbooks to recognise that there is no agreed definition of what is meant by the term 'recruitment'. The variations that exist fall into two main types: the 'narrow' and 'broad' definitions, both of which formulate

recruitment

The different activities of attracting applicants to an organisation, and the selection of people to fill vacancies.

recruitment in terms of constituent activities and in relation to selection. The 'broad' definition views **recruitment** as embracing both the different activities of attracting applicants to an organisation and the selection of people to fill vacancies. The 'narrow' definition limits the range of activities to those involved in attracting people to apply for employment in an organisation.

Maund exemplifies the broad definition when she describes recruitment as: 'the term given to ... choosing suitable applicants for job vacancies'. Thus, '[i]ncluded in this process is selection ... [it is] [t]he last part of the recruitment process when the organisation decides who to employ from the candidates available' (Maund, 2001: 151). Bratton and Gold (2003) provide an illustration of the narrow definition when they portray recruitment as: 'the process of generating a pool of capable people to apply for employment to an organisation'. Selection, in their view, is a discrete and subsequent process, 'by which managers and others use specific instruments to choose from a pool of applicants a person or persons most likely to succeed in the job(s), given management goals and legal requirements' (Bratton and Gold, 2003: 221). This division pervades the academic and professional literature. For instance, in similar vein to Maund, several professional writings – for example, the CIPD (2005) article on recruitment and retention and the Acas advisory booklet on the same topic (Acas, 2005) – incorporate selection within a broad conception of recruitment. Against them, a number of academic publications (e.g. Taylor, 2002; Sisson and Storey, 2003; Marchington and Wilkinson, 2005) operate with slightly different formulations of the narrow definition.

It is the narrow definition that will be employed in this chapter, primarily because it is more robust. The broad definition, as it is used by Maund, contains conceptual ambiguities. She wants to use the term 'recruitment' to describe all the activities involved in filling a job vacancy but then see selection as the final part of the process. What is not clear beyond the assertion of this superordinate/subordinate link however is *how* these activities are to be differentiated. It cannot, for example, be in terms of their respective 'goals', since the general goal of filling a job vacancy must incorporate the specific selection goal of 'decid[ing] who to employ from the candidates available'. Again, it cannot be in terms of their constituent activities since the activities of selecting are, in her own terms, also part of recruitment. Again, to try to create a time criterion, as when she describes selection as 'the last part of the recruitment process' (Maund, 2001), does not help because if it is not retrospective, it is too imprecise to allow differentiation.

The narrow definition used by Gold is not subject to these ambiguities. He does not invoke superordinate and subordinate conceptions; recruitment and selection represent distinct but related clusters of activities that *ideally* exist in a temporal sequence. Organisations recruit by generating a pool of suitably qualified applicants for a post or posts;

selection

Consists of sifting through the pool of applicants and making decisions about their appropriateness.

selection consists of sifting through that pool and making decisions about the appropriateness of those applicants. This is not to suggest, however, that his definitions cannot be compromised by real-world situations. For instance, while explicitly designed for selection, it may well be that managers try to use employment interviews to 'sell' their organisation – that is, as a tacit form of recruitment (Taylor, 2002). Again, given that recruitment and selection take place over a period of time, their activities in certain situations could overlap – that is, selection activities could be under way before recruitment has been completed. Such issues, however, are of a different status to those in the Maund type of formulation. They do not undermine the formal definitions so much as convey a warning about the limitations of all definitions and the need to work with them in a cautious, analytical manner.

The recruitment sequence

Within the narrow definition, recruitment is typically seen as occurring in two main stages: the formative work and the recruitment practices (sources and methods) that end with the arrival of applications. Each contains a cluster of activities usually portrayed as a linear sequence (see Exhibit 4-1).

Formative recruitment activities

What triggers the recruitment process? The simple answer is the possibility of acquiring new staff. Whether an organisation is considering additional staff (through expansion or restructuring) or replacing existing staff members who are leaving, the initial phase of formative recruitment involves reviewing the options. What alternatives are there to employing new staff and are they worth pursuing? These might involve restructuring the workforce, changing the technological base, outsourcing the work activities and/or changing the existing working-time arrangements (see Exhibit 4-2).

The alternatives are ideally addressed in broader intra- and extra-organisational contexts. In the case of the former, it is a matter of linking the question of new staff to the organisation's wider human resource strategy and business plans to develop or alter its production and services. With regard to extra-organisational contexts, the focus switches to the question of current labour and product markets and, among other things, ascertaining the availability of people with suitable qualifications and skills at wage levels the organisation is prepared to pay. If, having considered these questions, there is a decision to appoint new staff, the next step is to consider how the vacancy is to be managed.

Managing the vacancy

The work at this point is in deciding who, within the organisation, is going to be responsible for the recruitment and selection activities. Is it to be the line manager, someone within the HR department or a shared activity between the two? Who will provide the administrative support

Major stages	Activities within each stage
Stage 1: Formative recruitment	■ Reviewing the possibility of acquiring new staff and the identification of a vacancy ■ Deciding the management of the vacancy ■ Job analysis, producing a job description and person specification
Stage 2: Recruitment sources and methods	■ Decisions on recruitment sources and methods to be employed ■ Determining the application format (e.g. electronic or paper, formal application or CV) ■ Putting the job vacancy and other publicity materials into the public domain ■ Applications arrive

Exhibit 4–1 Stages and activities in recruitment

Option	Consideration
■ Restructuring the workforce	Can the activities and responsibilities of *current* workers be altered or redefined in order to fill the vacancy?
■ Additional/new technology	Is there a case for buying in additional or new technology to undertake the work rather than employing a new member of staff?
■ Outsourcing	Is it worth outsourcing the work to freelance staff or a third-party organisation?
■ Working time	Can the work be covered with more flexible working arrangements, e.g. allowing some staff to begin earlier/later to provide cover for a longer part of the day? Can it be covered by overtime?

Exhibit 4–2 Possible alternatives to employing new staff

and who will make the final decisions? Once these matters are resolved, a team can be put together, and a realistic time schedule can be set for the completion of recruitment as well as dealing with answers to more specific questions such as who is to undertake the job analysis.

Job analysis

The need for job analysis has been explained by the CIPD in the following way:

> Before recruiting for a new, or existing position, it is important to invest time in gathering information about the nature of the job. This means thinking not only about the content (i.e. tasks) making up the job, but also the job's purpose, the outputs required by the job holder and how it fits into the organisation's structure. It is also important to consider the skills and personal attributes needed to perform the [tasks] effectively.
>
> (CIPD, 2005: 2)

Exhibit 4-3 shows how the different recruitment activities link together and will ultimately lead to the successful selection of the right candidate for the job.

job analysis
Identifying the tasks and skills that make up a job.

Job analysis is important because it provides the information on which two significant recruitment documents are based: the job and person specifications. The *job description* summarises the job's purpose and the activities contributing to that purpose together with lines of responsibility. The *person specification* identifies the characteristics deemed necessary for someone holding that job. In organisations with either buoyant product and service markets and/or high levels of staff turnover it may not be necessary to undertake a job analysis for every vacancy that occurs. In such circumstances, however, it can nonetheless be useful to engage in the more restricted activity of checking whether the existing job description and person specification are appropriate for future needs (Marchington and Wilkinson, 2005).

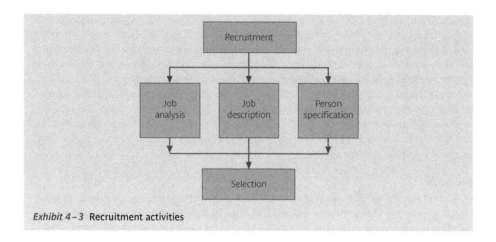

Exhibit 4–3 Recruitment activities

Methods of job analysis

So how is job analysis undertaken? Essentially, it involves collecting systematic information about the job from current incumbents and/or their colleagues (Newell and Shackleton, 2000). The techniques used to gather such information spread across the methodological spectrum from diaries and logs, observations and interviews at the qualitative end, through to the more quantitative forms of analysis such as questionnaires, hierarchical task analysis and repertory grid assessments. Given the range and requirements of each of these methods, it is inevitable that they will differ in terms of their costs, ease of use, sensitivity and sophistication (Searle, 2003). The HR professionals or line managers undertaking the job analysis are thus forced into a 'trade-off' in deciding which of the techniques (or which combination of techniques) to employ. Costs, for example, are a potentially important feature of the calculation in terms of the time, effort and money to be invested. The ability of the techniques to elicit the required information (sophistication) and their accuracy also need to be considered carefully, as do the availability of trained analysts or consultants (convenience), and the willingness of staff to participate (sensitivity). The choice of technique/s is thus determined by the assessed importance of these criteria when evaluated in terms of the jobs to be analysed and the work environment in which the jobs function.

Of the range of techniques, this chapter provides brief synopses of five simply to illustrate what can be involved and the issues that pervade job analysis. (More detailed accounts of all the techniques commonly used can be found in Cooper and Robertson (2002), Cooper *et al.* (2003) and Searle (2003).) Diaries and logs, observation and interviews will be employed as examples of qualitative techniques, and questionnaires and hierarchical task analysis as illustrations of their more quantitative counterparts.

Diaries and logs

These are self-reporting techniques that involve current job-holders recording their activities over a period of time – for example, every working hour over the course of a week. They are simple and non-intrusive ways of collecting information that, in financial terms, can also be relatively cheap. Once the job-holders agree to complete the diaries or logs, the main issues of self-reporting concern the information focus, the process of collecting the information and its accuracy. What, for instance, is being recorded? Is it everything that the employee does or simply specific types of activity? Is there a checklist being employed to aid the employee or do the job-holders log the information in their own terms? Are they to use an actual or electronic diary? Is training being provided? In terms of accuracy, the employees may not complete their log at the required time and, as a consequence, may over- or understate aspects of the tasks. In some instances, they may also choose to exaggerate particular job aspects (perhaps to emphasise their expertise or importance). Diaries and logs rely heavily on the commitment and accuracy of the post-holder completing the record and, as a consequence, have led some job analysts to argue that the technique is best employed in analysing comparatively stable and higher-level managerial or executive posts.

Observation

This is a traditional approach to job analysis in which a trained observer watches the tasks being undertaken and how they are being undertaken. Usually a checklist of factors is employed to ensure that data are gathered against relevant tasks and that there is consistency between observations. This is particularly important if there is a team of observers and/or the observations are carried out over a period of time. The technique is regarded as one of the more accurate ways of obtaining job information and it is generally assumed that it does allow an analyst to detect some required skills (e.g. manual dexterity, computer usage) and aptitudes (e.g. attention to detail, concern for the end-user and safety awareness). However, it is not without its issues. Observation is time-consuming and when employed as the solitary method of analysis may not be able to detect many of the cognitive and intellectual skills invested in some tasks nor provide an insight into their relative level of difficulty. Again, dependent on the period of observation, it may not capture the myriad of tasks involved in some jobs (think, for instance, of firefighters, ambulance personnel, police officers or retail assistants) and observers may well influence the conduct of the job-holders being observed (the 'Hawthorne effect'), leading to inaccurate data. In consequence, observation is often used with other techniques of analysis such as interviewing in order to provide a supplementary source of information.

Interviews

The third form of analysis, these range from structured interviews (with fixed question schedules) through to unstructured interviews (with open-ended question schedules). Fixed question schedules mean that the same questions are asked of each job-holder, thereby enabling easier comparability of the answers. The open-ended questions of unstructured interviews give the interviewer the opportunity to probe for more detailed responses and enable staff to elaborate particular points and, as a consequence, are seen to permit greater accuracy. Trying to draw on the benefits of both types of interview, most job analyses use semi-structured question schedules with some fixed and some open-ended questions. The major strength of interviewing in job analysis is its limited cost, its convenience and the opportunity for rapport to develop between interviewer and job-holder. The major limitations concern the potential variability of interviewer skills and the possible unreliability of the data elicited.

Structured questionnaires

These form one of the more popular ways of obtaining quantitative information about key tasks and aptitudes, and are especially valuable where there is a large job-holder population to cover. While some employers devise their own questionnaire(s), many others will buy in a commercially developed package involving the questionnaires and associated training in their use and analysis. One example of a commercial option is the Work Profiling System (WPS). WPS collects two different sets of job information. The first set concerns the main duties of the job and gathers detailed data about the tasks, their frequency of occurrence and job-holder evaluations of their significance. The second collects information on training and qualification levels, responsibilities, the physical context and the remuneration package (Searle, 2003). Like other structured questionnaires, the WPS provides a systematic way of collecting information and the resultant numerical data can be easily collated and compared using computer analysis. It has a higher reliability than the qualitative job analysis techniques and, once training is completed, can be both cheaper and less time-consuming than, say, interviewing. However, structured question-naires can also have problems. Clearly the quality of data is only as good as the questions asked and the predetermined range of answers. It is therefore vital that the questions are understood by employees and the categories of answer are comprehensive (i.e. they cover all the options).

Hierarchical task analysis

This is a second quantitative technique. Developed some 40 years ago by Annett and Duncan (1967), it defines jobs in terms of their outcomes. The job analyst works with the job-holder to break the job down into its constituent parts – namely plans, subtasks and tasks. The overall aim is to provide a sequential series of activities that will achieve the desired outcomes, whether it's a matter of forklift driving or catering management. The technique involves following a defined set of rules to ensure a clear analysis of the job, the level of performance and the con-ditions under which the tasks are carried out. It is neo-Taylorist in nature and, while producing a methodical picture of the job in terms of a sequence of tasks and subtasks, it is, for many ana-lysts, inflexible and unable to represent the interpretative and situational factors that can influ-ence the achievement of tasks (Cooper *et al.*, 2003; Searle, 2003).

Limitations of the techniques

The limitations of each of these techniques are indicative of more pervasive issues, namely:

- the (empiricist) conception of method underpinning orthodox job analysis
- the assumption of the stability of work.

The empiricist conception of scientific method assumes that there is an objective world to be inves-tigated and that research techniques (such as those employed in job analysis) can be used to gather information from that world in a neutral or value-free way. Thus the job analysis techniques described above are construed as data-gathering instruments that, in themselves, need not and should not have an impact on the information collected. What writers such as Taylor (2002) suggest is that there are major flaws in this viewpoint. Not the least of these is its failure to recognise that all research methods are inherently *social processes*, and are continually subject to the interpre-tations, actions and reactions of researchers, research subjects and others in the context(s) in which data are collected and analysed. In the specific case of job analysis, Searle (2003: 44–48) describes a wide range of potential social influences that include: the respective calculations of job-holder and analyst; the differential skills, work experience and/or social backgrounds within and between researcher(s) and subject(s); the organisational context in which the analysis is undertaken; and even the interpretation of the measurement formats employed in the various job analysis techniques. Empiricism wants to maintain

---

empiricism
Aims to maintain techniques that are inherently neutral and, where social influences exist, considers that they should be treated as 'contamination' or 'bias', and controlled or repressed.

---

that its techniques are inherently neutral and that, where social influences exist, they should be treated as 'contamination' or 'bias' and controlled or repressed through, for instance, research training or the use of more advanced techniques. Its critics suggest that this is not possible and that the data produced by job analysis are always going to contain levels of inaccuracy because of such social factors.

This problem of inaccuracy is compounded by the second pervasive issue – namely the assumption of stability in job analysis. Job analysis techniques take it for granted that 'jobs are relatively stable and subject to limited or no change' (Searle, 2003: 48). This stance basically conflicts with the globalisation of markets and technological change in a number of work areas where jobs are in a continual state of flux with regard to 'content, character and complexity' (Taylor, 2002: 103). The fact that such change is neither unidimensional or unidirectional, simply adds to the case that the products of job analysis – job and person specifications – can quickly become obsolete and thus lose their recruitment and selection value. While there is a counterargument – namely that this should lead to more regular job analysis (for example, through six-monthly or annual appraisals) – it still leaves organisations in a quandary. On the one hand, job analysis is considered central to the recruitment and selection process, often involving a sizeable investment of time, finance and other resources; on the other, its products can quickly become dated and are often based on only partially accurate information. So, what do organisations do? Abandon job analysis and use its resources in a more 'productive' way elsewhere or persevere with a known fallible procedure? Most organisations take the latter course: they see the significance of job analysis and decide to work within its limitations to produce job and person specifications (although in the latter case there has been some enhancement in the form of competency frameworks).

Job descriptions, person specifications and competency frameworks

If written job descriptions and person specifications are the main products of a job analysis, how are they utilised? A job description is used to set out the basic details of the job. It defines its primary purpose, reporting relations, the main activities or tasks carried out, and any special requirements or features. Typically, a job description contains: a job title; a grade and/or rate of pay; a main location; a line manager's name/post; details of any subordinates; summary of the main purpose of the job; a list (and possibly brief descriptions) of principal duties, together with reference to other documents (see the example in Exhibit 4-4 of a job description for an administrative post).

job description
Summarises the job's purpose and the activities contributing to that purpose, together with lines of responsibility; used to set out the basic details of the job.

person specification
Converts the job specification into human terms, specifying the kind of person needed to perform the job described.

Whereas a job description portrays the duties to be under-taken, a person specification 'convert[s] the job specification into human terms, specifying the kind of person needed to perform the described job' (Newell and Shackleton, 2000: 115). Inferences are made about the experience, qualifications, skills and psychosocial characteristics that are necessary for a candidate to become a successful job-holder. The classical versions of person specifications are the seven-point plan constructed by Rodger (in 1952) and its subsequent adaptation by Fraser (1966); these are outlined in Exhibit 4-5. An example of a person specification is given in Exhibit 4-6.

	Job description
Job title	Section secretary
Grade of appointment	Administrative Grade C
Section	Accounts (Moorgate)
Reports to	Administrative manager
Staff responsibilities	None
Job purpose	To provide a full and professional secretarial support service for the three accounts managers in the section including: shorthand, word processing, spreadsheet analysis, diary management, organising meetings, conferences and travel itineraries

The main responsibilities are to:

- produce letters, reports, presentations and other documentation on Word, Excel and PowerPoint from audio tapes, shorthand and copy
- answer telephone queries, redirect or take messages where appropriate
- maintain an effective filing system
- sort and distribute incoming post
- manage three managers' diaries, organise meetings, conferences and travel itineraries
- ensure timely payment of all section invoices and bills
- organise departmental journals and maintain subscriptions
- provide cover for the administrative manager.

For more general working conditions please see the enclosed staff handbook or go to our website at www . . .

Exhibit 4–4 Example of a job description

These specifications have several uses that include: establishing both the essential and desirable criteria against which candidates will be judged; providing a template for subsequent selection procedures; and, together with the job specification, forming the basis for drafting recruitment materials. For successful applicants they are also likely to feature in their future appraisals.

The competency alternative

The inadequacies of the person specification and, in particular, the growing recognition that it is not socially or politically neutral in its construction, have led to attempts to replace it with a competency-based approach. This pays far less attention to personal qualities, characteristics, dispositions or interests, and places much greater weight on what it sees as the effective actions or conduct that are likely to lead to successful individual and organisational performance. **Competency**, then, when employed in recruitment is concerned with *inputs* – in particular, the conduct, skills, knowledge and capacities that applicants

competency
Looks at the effective actions or conduct that are likely to lead to successful individual and organisational performance, rather than qualifications or experience.

Rodger's seven-point plan

1 *Physical make-up*: physical attributes such as ability to lift heavy loads or differentiate between colours

2 *Attainments*: educational or professional qualifications considered necessary for undertaking the work

3 *General intelligence*: ability to define and solve problems, and use initiative in dealing with issues that have arisen

4 *Special aptitudes*: skills, attributes or competencies that are specifically relevant to the particular job

5 *Interests*: both work-related and leisure pursuits that may be relevant to the particular job

6 *Disposition*: attitude to work and to other members of staff and customers, as well as friendliness and assertiveness

7 *Circumstances*: domestic commitments, mobility and family support

Fraser's five-point plan

1 *Impact on others*: this covers much the same sort of issues as 'physical make-up' (above), but is more focused on impact on other employees and customers

2 *Acquired knowledge and qualifications*: see Rodger's second category, above

3 *Innate abilities*: see 'general intelligence', above

4 *Motivation*: a person's desire to succeed in particular aspects of work, and their commitment to achieve these goals

5 *Adjustment*: characteristics specifically related to the job, such as the ability to cope with difficult customers or work well in a team

Exhibit 4–5 Classical views of person specifications
Source: Adapted from Rodger (1952), Fraser (1966).

must possess (or be capable of acquiring) in order to maximise the benefit to the organisation (CIPD, 2004b). Thus, where the person specification for the secretary's post (Exhibit 4-6) may simply ask for someone who is trustworthy, the competency approach would want to express it as a measurable performance such as 'someone capable of dealing with confidential information in an appropriate and sensitive way'. Again, where a person specification for a lectureship might include the requirement of 'self-confidence', the competency approach would seek a measurable input – for example, 'the ability to deliver a cogent and informative lecture to 200 undergraduates'.

The difference between the approaches may, as some suggest, be a matter of emphasis rather than substance (e.g. Newell and Shackleton, 2000). It could, for example, be argued that a secretary needs to be trustworthy if he/she is going to handle confidential information in a sensitive and appropriate manner. Again, a lecturer needs a level of self-confidence if she/he is going to deliver a cogent and informative lecture. Proponents of the competency approach to recruitment, however, maintain that this is not the point. Job and person specifications may well be used in tandem with competency approaches but what the latter provides is the possibility of a clearer statement of expectations of performance that in turn makes the recruitment process fairer and more open. It also enables a clearer set of benchmarks for use in subsequent performance appraisals.

One company that has identified the need to diversify its recruitment strategy is Expedia, as illustrated in the 'Managing diversity' box.

	Job title: Section secretary
Experience	Essential: three years' experience of working in a secretarial role within a large complex organisation; must have provided secretarial support for a team of managers Desirable: previous experience of an accounts department
Qualifications and knowledge	Essential: excellent knowledge of Word, PowerPoint, Excel, shorthand and audio typing Desirable: RSA secretarial qualifications, knowledge of finance/accounts functions
Skills	Essential: accurate typing and well-practised shorthand (60 wpm) Good written and oral communication skills Demonstrates good attention to detail, along with professional presentation and layout of documents Presents a professional and positive image of self and department at all times through written and verbal communication; uses appropriate language and medium when producing written documentation Is good at planning and organising Manages own and others' time and resources effectively, including diary management, a clear filing system and budgetary management A good team worker; works with managers and other administrative staff to ensure the section operates efficiently
Personal qualities and aptitudes	Essential: supportive – capable of demonstrating commitment to the managers and the wider team in the section Proactive: capable of anticipating problems and showing initiative in resolving them and generating new ideas Trustworthy: able to deal with confidential information in an appropriate and sensitive way Flexible: is willing to undertake a range of tasks to ensure the effective running of the section; is willing to work the hours required for the successful completion of tasks

Exhibit 4–6 An illustration of a person specification

The legal context of recruitment

Pertinent to the construction of job, person and competency specifications, and the subsequent processes, is the legal context in which recruitment takes place. When discussed in the HR literature, the focus tends to be on anti-discrimination or equal treatment at work legislation (see, for example, Martin and Jackson, 2002). Prior to 2000, the major initiator of this legislation was the UK Government, which introduced laws, regulations and codes of practice to prohibit direct and indirect discrimination on the basis of someone's gender, disability, race, 'spent' criminal record and trades union membership (see Exhibit 4-7). The abundance of legal activity

managing diversity

Expedia

Expedia is now the largest online travel service in the world, with Expedia.com in the USA and local versions in Europe and Canada. It prides itself on its excellent reputation, both as a profitable business and quality employer, which continues to grow and this, it suggests, makes it an exciting company to have a career with.

It offers a wide variety of career paths with compensation packages that include a competitive salary and excellent benefits. In addition to receiving comprehensive benefits, Expedia suggests that its people enjoy the reward of working for a respected industry leader that continues to innovate and advance.

If this is so, why is it that it finds it so difficult to fill vacancies?

'We're not really making the most of our brand as we still fill 90 per cent of our vacancies through third parties,' Alison Hodgson told *PM*.

Hodgson, who is also chairwoman of the Association of Graduate Recruiters, said the organisation needed to diversify its recruitment strategy by relying less on recruitment agencies to source candidates, and instead conducting research into potential talent pools and advertising more. This year, the company spent on advertising only one-tenth of what it spent on third-party recruitment.

The company, originally set up by Microsoft, currently has 1000 employees in Europe and 3000 in the USA.

'We need to get a healthier balance between the various recruitment methods, and map out how we can access and attract the people we want,' said Hodgson. But she admitted that finding the right people would be a challenge because Expedia operates in the online travel sector.

Hodgson said there was a shortage of candidates with the right combination of merchandising knowledge and online technological acumen that most of Expedia's posts required. 'You don't find the kinds of skills and calibre of people we want in traditional travel firms,' she said.

Another of Hodgson's responsibilities in the newly created role will be to link up separate strands of HR at Expedia, including talent acquisition and succession planning.

Source: Adapted from: 'Expedia needs to use its brand to attract staff', *People Management*, 24 November 2005, p. 14, www.expedia.com.

Discussion questions

1 Could Expedia's inability to recruit be due to its stereotyping of its ideal candidate?

2 How could Expedia make its jobs appeal to a wider audience?

in the first five years of the new millennium, however, has largely emanated from the European Council of Ministers' adoption of the Employment Directive on Equal Treatment in 2000. This required all EU member states to introduce laws prohibiting direct and indirect discrimination at work on grounds of age, race and ethnic origin, sexual orientation, religion and belief, and disability. For the UK this has, in some instances, involved the government in amending existing legislation. In others it has been a matter of creating new legislation as, for example, in the case of the law on age discrimination which will come into force from December 2006.

This is not the place to elaborate on the detail or complexities of these laws, what they cover, their operation or 'policing' nationally and in Europe. What is important for our purposes is to know that the legislation makes it unlawful for organisations to utilise someone's gender, marital status, colour, race, 'spent' criminal record, nationality, disability, religious beliefs,

Equal Pay Act 1970

Rehabilitation of Offenders Act 1974

Sex Discrimination Acts 1975 and 1986

Race Relations Act 1976

Trade Union and Labour Relations (Consolidation) Acts 1992

Disability Discrimination Act 1996

The Sex Discrimination (Gender Assignment) Regulations 1999

The Part-time Workers (Prevention of Less Favourable Treatment) Regulations 2000

The Employment Equality (Amendment) Regulations 2003

The Employment Equality (Religion and Belief) Regulations 2003

Equal Pay (Questions and Answers) Order 2003

The Race Relations Act 1976 (Amendment) Regulations 2003

Disability Discrimination Act 2005

The Age Discrimination Regulations 2006

Exhibit 4–7 UK equal treatment at work legislation since 1970

sexual orientation, trades union membership (and, from December 2006, age) as the basis for making employment decisions. The implications for recruitment are immense. Among the things affected will be: the language and processes of job analysis; job and person specifications; marketing strategy; advertising and application procedures. Managers and HR professionals will be required to reflect on their recruitment strategies, their literature and their performance. Failure to do so adequately could lead to claims of discrimination or unfair treatment, which in turn could mean costly legal cases, fines and damage to the organisation's reputation.

As important as it is in both nature and consequence, equal treatment at work legislation is but one area of employment law impacting on recruitment. There is a range of other UK and European legislation, for instance, on asylum and protection (affecting who can be recruited), health and safety, and the recruitment practices of employment agencies as well as statutes on privacy, access to and the disclosure of information that HR professionals must also understand and observe. To take just one instance of the latter, the Data Protection Act 1998 came into force in March 2000. It is designed to regulate personal data and give effect in UK law to the European Directive on Data Protection (95/46/EC). The Act is concerned with information that employers might collect on any individual who may wish to work, does work or has worked for their organisation. It covers personal data in an electronic, manual or any other format that is readily accessible, as well as all aspects of processing data from collection, holding, access, use and disclosure through to its destruction. There are eight data protection principles that are central to the Act. In brief, they state that personal data should be: processed fairly and lawfully; processed for limited purposes and not in any manner incompatible with those purposes; adequate, relevant and not excessive; accurate; not kept for longer than is necessary; processed in line with applicants' and employees' rights; kept secure; and not transferred to countries that don't protect personal data adequately (www.informationcommissioner.gov.uk).

The Act also gives applicants and employees the right to have a copy of the information that an employer holds about them. It allows them to apply to the courts to obtain an order requiring an organisation or its data control manager to correct inaccurate data, and to seek compensation where damage and distress have been caused as a result of any breach of the Act. Employees may also object to the processing of personal data about them. In some circumstances they can stop employers from keeping certain types of information or from using it in particular ways. Of particular importance here is what is termed 'sensitive personal data', included within which is someone's race or ethnic group, their political opinions, religious or other beliefs, whether they are a member of a trades union or not, their physical or mental health, sexual life, and any court record or allegations of such. Organisations must ensure that both applicants and employees give them explicit consent to process this type of information and/or that the processing has a necessary purpose (for instance, it is a legal requirement or important for monitoring equality of opportunity).

So, what are the implications of this act for recruitment? As with the equal treatment at work legislation, the Data Protection Act has practical consequences for a number of different activities. In terms of recruitment, for example, applicants providing personal information in response to a job advert need to be advised who they are giving the information to and how it will be used. If it is a recruitment agency that is advertising on behalf of an employer, it must explain how the personal data it receives will be employed and disclosed. On receiving identifiable personal details from an agency, an organisation must ensure that applicants become aware that it is now holding their information. With regard to selection, application forms (and subsequent interviews) must seek only personal data that are deemed relevant to the decision to appoint. Organisations must advise applicants how they will verify the information supplied in an application form (or on a CV) and, if sensitive data are collected, explain why this information is sought and how it will be used. The period for retaining personal information in recruitment (and selection) records is not specified in the Act; it simply states that it should not be kept any longer than business need requires and should take account of relevant professional guidelines. The Information Commission (2002), which drew up the Codes of Practice for the Act, recommends that data collected in applications and for checking applications should be kept for no more than six months before being destroyed (although this does not rule out organisations storing information to protect themselves against possible legal action).

This brief discussion of the Data Protection Act has sought to establish that:

- there is a realm of employment law beyond anti-discriminatory legislation that also impacts on aspects of recruitment
- the legislation permeates most aspects of the recruitment process
- a sound knowledge of this area is imperative (non-compliance could lead to legal action – in this instance, to the organisation being prosecuted and/or being subjected to claims for compensation).

Recruitment: sources and methods

With the job analysis completed, and the job description and person specification written up, the next stage of the process is recruitment – that is, considering ways of attracting people who meet the job requirements (Newell and Shackleton, 2000: 116). The HR literature talks in terms of two central types of recruitment: 'internal' and 'external'. The activities contained in each of these categories can be further subdivided in terms of 'source(s)' and 'methods'. This is a subclassification drawn from the employer's perspective in which sources are the differing domains of applicant supply – that is, the part or parts of labour markets from which applicants are sought. 'Methods' are the actual techniques employed both to make individuals aware of vacancies and to make those vacancies attractive to them. They are, in other words, the mechanisms for creating demand for vacancies.

Stop and reflect

Refer to Rodger's seven-point plan and Fraser's five-point plan in Exhibit 4-5. What would be the personal specification of a student? How do the two plans compare in identifying suitable attributes?

Internal recruitment

Internal recruitment methods involve creating a pool of applicants to fill a vacancy from current employees – that is, the organisation operates as its own source of supply. Research suggests that, as a matter of course, most commercial employers attempt to fill vacancies from within their organisation before they consider looking for people outside. The CIPD recruitment survey (2004a), for example, found that 84 per cent of UK organisations surveyed looked to internal applicants in the first instance. They did so by using such methods of communication as internal email or intranet (69 per cent), notice and bulletin boards (68 per cent), team meetings (18 per cent), their staff newsletters or magazines (14 per cent), and by memos, circulars and direct approaches.

internal recruitment
Involves creating a pool of applicants to fill a vacancy from current employees.

According to Taylor (2002: 126), there are several recognised advantages to internal recruitment.

- It is a relatively cheap way of recruiting, vacancies can be advertised at little cost and it can also save time.
- It can lead to a robust internal labour market, and boost employee morale through the opportunities for career development and progression.
- It means that applicants have a better knowledge of the way the organisation operates and what to expect in the job.
- Selection will be based on a better knowledge of the individuals' merits and prospects and is thus less of a risk than external recruiting.

The arguments against internal recruitment are as follows.

- It perpetuates existing ways of thinking and carrying out tasks; external recruits, it is argued, would be more likely to bring in new ways of undertaking tasks.
- It assumes that the 'best' person for the job is currently working for the organisation.
- It recruits in the organisation's current image, hence if ethnic minorities or other disadvantaged groups are not currently well represented, promoting from within will do nothing to create greater diversity.
- Rejecting current employees in an internal recruitment exercise can lead to major morale and confidence issues, possibly leading to further staff turnover.

Exclusive or even regular use of internal recruitment is much less common in public and voluntary sector agencies where stronger equal opportunities policies consistently prevail. In these agencies, whatever the 'strengths' of the internal field, it is considered 'good practice' to create a level playing field in which internal and external candidates can apply for posts.

External recruitment

As Exhibit 4-8 illustrates, an abundance of methods can be employed in **external recruitment**.

---
external recruitment

Identifies possible candidates for recruitment from the labour pool outside the organisation.

Some are used in conjunction with particular labour sources (e.g. employee referral schemes use current staff to refer their friends, family and associates), while others (e.g. advertising) have a broader application. The choice of where and how to look for applicants is related to a range of criteria, such as the organisation's HR strategy, cost and time constraints, the likelihood of the method reaching its anticipated audience, and the volume of applications that each method is likely to yield.

The organisation's own resources

It is common practice, particularly in the commercial sector, for organisations to utilise their own current resources – that is, their employees, their records and databases, and their websites – to create a pool of external applicants for a vacancy. In terms of current staff, the primary method of recruitment is employee referrals – that is, encouraging employees to nominate 'potential recruits through their personal contacts' (Marchington and Wilkinson, 2005: 172). Staff are typically offered a financial incentive to recommend friends or former colleagues for a vacancy in the organisation. Payments for successful recruitment can range from £25 to £5000, and are usually dependent on the type of vacancy. Amazon.com, for instance, pays its staff £200 for new warehouse associates and up to £1500 for managers or 'critical hires', while Capgemini's referral payments range from £500 to £3000, depending on the grade of the person recruited (Income Data Services, 2004).

Employee referral is a narrow search technique in that details of the vacancy are limited to specific individuals or groups known to its staff. Slightly broader are the searches involving the organisation's use of its archives, records and databases. Here it can seek applicants from any combination of prior candidates for posts, its own retirees, former employees working for other organisations (Carrington, 2005), and people who have previously 'walked in' to ask if there are vacancies and left a completed application form or CV. The method involves HR or managers assessing the paper or electronic records against the person or competency specification and inviting the appropriate persons to apply.

According to CIPD research (2004a), a large proportion of the organisations surveyed used these methods of recruitment in the private sector. Employee referral schemes were particularly popular in commercial services, where 71 per cent of companies surveyed and 66 per cent of manufacturing companies used them. In more recent research, some organisations used their schemes to fill as many as 95 per cent of their vacancies (Industrial Relations Services, 2005b). The re-hire of former (or 'boomerang') employees, although not as widespread a practice as in the United States, is also a growth recruitment area. PricewaterhouseCoopers, for instance, has developed its own 'talent bank' that includes former employees with whom it remains in contact through an alumni association. Its use of this bank has led to a 30 per cent reduction in the use of third-party agencies for seeking experienced staff (Carrington, 2005).

However, while the use of organisational sources appears to be popular, opinion is divided among both managers and academics about their value. Some HR management research (e.g. Iles and Robertson, 1997; Income Data Services, 2004) suggests that they can:

- yield a better pool of well-qualified applicants
- contribute to a lower turnover of staff

Sources	Methods
The organisation's resources Current employees Archives and records (past applicants; former employees; retirees and 'walk-ins') Organisation's website	Employee referrals Manual/electronic search of HR records, subsequent HR/manager's decision to inform and/or invite applications Posting the vacancy on its generic or dedicated recruitment site
Educational sources Schools, colleges and universities, careers advisers/Careers Service, tutors	Careers fairs; 'milk-round interviews'; use of student 'work experience/work placements' to assess potential; employer presentations; student sponsorships; advertising in specialist graduate recruitment directories and magazines
Government employment agencies JobCentre Plus Connexions Forces Resettlement Agency	Display cards at the local JobCentre, a quick-call telephone service (Jobseekers Direct) and a website linked to JobPoint; electronic circulation of local, regional, national and international vacancies; focusing on 13–19 year olds, establishing links with 'partnership' employers; two-way information base of available staff and agency searches
Commercial employment agencies Recruitment advertising agencies and consultants Temporary and contract staffing agencies Permanent employment and executive search agencies Cyber agencies	Organisational databases, newsprint advertisements, websites Organisational databases, newsprint advertisements, websites Organisational databases, newsprint advertisements, websites, agency networks Job boards
Professional and industry contacts Professional associations and trades unions; suppliers; customers; works contractors	Conferences, networking, individual contacts
Newsprint sources National and local newspapers Trade and professional journals	Newsprint (often combined with Internet) advertising Newsprint (often combined with Internet) advertising
Other media sources Television, cinema and radio	'Live' advertising

Exhibit 4–8 The sources and methods of external recruitment

- lead to higher levels of employee performance
- contribute to cost reductions (Nationwide, for instance, claims to have saved between £2000 and £10,000 of advertising costs per job by using an employee referral scheme).

Set against these views is the general case that, by using these sources:

- an organisation will only ever reach a limited audience, which is unlikely to reflect the diversity of the wider community
- there is no guarantee that they will generate the best pool of candidates.

In the specific case of employee referral schemes, it is argued that:

- unsuccessful referrals may lead to demotivated staff
- referral schemes can involve an additional administrative HR burden as they have to track both the referrer and applicant, and ensure payment is made correctly and in a timely manner (Income Data Services, 2004).

These critical views seem to hold particular sway in the voluntary and public sectors, where only 34 per cent and 26 per cent of organisations respectively use referral schemes to recruit staff (CIPD, 2004a). The main reason for their aversion seems to be the fact that they tend to favour groups already well represented in the workforce.

A much wider and more speculative use of organisational resources, across the sectors, involves posting vacancies on a generic or dedicated website. This, according to the CIPD survey, is becoming an increasingly popular means of staff recruitment. An estimated 72 per cent of respondents used their own websites to publicise vacancies (CIPD, 2004a). The amount an organisation invests in this source will depend on its e-strategy, available funds and competitor activity. A basic option would simply involve providing a list of vacancies and contact details. A more detailed approach would provide the information normally posted to applicants (e.g. job and person specifications, organisational facilities and benefits, and online application forms). Linked to the person specification, organisations might also provide self-assessment questionnaires or quizzes to assess fitness for the job and cameos of a 'day in the life' nature. Larger organisations often have dedicated sites for particular types of applicant, such as graduates and technical specialists, or have a search facility to view particular types of vacancy.

The main advantages to organisations of recruiting from their websites include the potential to:

- reduce recruitment costs and speed up the recruitment cycle; Woolworths, for example, claims to have reduced its cost per hire by 70 per cent and its time to hire from an average of eight weeks to as little as two days (Smethurst, 2004)
- devote as much space as they wish to 'selling' the job
- make applying easier
- shorten the recruitment cycle
- reach a wide pool of potential applicants
- offer a global audience access to vacancies 24 hours a day, seven days a week
- provide an image of a modern, forward-looking organisation (Industrial Relations Services, 2004).

It is, however, likely to be well-known corporations or organisations with a good reputation within specific labour markets that are likely to reap these benefits as 'small and medium-sized employers will not attract sufficient numbers of hits to their websites to be able to rely on this as a means of finding new recruits' (Taylor, 2002: 138).

Among the possible disadvantages are:

- it tends to be a supplementary rather than first-choice recruitment source for most job-hunters and this may limit the applicant audience
- it obviously excludes those who either cannot access the Internet or do not have software compatible with the website
- organisations may be bombarded with unsuitable applicants because it is so easy to apply online (Industrial Relations Services, 2004)
- the recruitment process becomes impersonal, deterring some applicants
- websites that are not of the highest standard may turn potential applicants away.

Educational sources

Of the wide range of other external sources, educational institutions provide a primary locale for potential recruits. According to the CIPD survey (2004a), links with schools, colleges and universities are used more by the commercial sector (56 per cent of respondents) than the public (38 per cent) and voluntary sectors (40 per cent). This picture might look a little different, however, if data on subgroups of each sector were available. Public agencies (e.g. the Armed Forces, and government departments such as the Inland Revenue and the Treasury), as well as large commercial organisations, invest heavily in national campaigns for university graduates. Because of the costs and relatively small number of recruits required, medium-sized and smaller firms and local authorities are more likely to focus at the area or regional level, seeking young people leaving school, from colleges of further education and local universities.

In seeking graduate applicants of the best calibre, large commercial organisations and national public agencies are prepared to invest in time-consuming and expensive activities such as sending representatives round the country, participating at careers fairs, undertaking presentations for groups of students, performing initial interviews and briefing careers advisers. They are primarily looking for 'management material', and seeking well-qualified, well-motivated, intelligent and mobile graduates. They come 'armed' with glossy literature about their organisation, DVD and PowerPoint presentations, and website addresses with information about future points of contact. It is essentially a 'sales pitch' in a 'war for talent' (Willcock, 2005) in which the representatives attempt to create demand for their jobs by showing students the benefits of working for their organisation. Alongside such methods, the companies and agencies will also advertise in specialist graduate recruitment publications such as the *Prospects* directories, offer work placement opportunities (either as vacation work or as part of a degree programme), and sponsor some students during their studies (on condition that they subsequently join the sponsoring organisation).

Many companies use a global recruitment strategy, as is demonstrated in the 'International perspective' box.

Small and medium-sized organisations operate from a somewhat different platform, with a less direct, lower-cost strategy when looking at schools, further education colleges and local universities (Income Data Services, 1998). Although they offer work experience to students and, in some instances, industry placements for staff, much of what they undertake is designed as a prelude to actual recruitment – that is, they primarily aim to raise the status of the organisation in the community and particularly among the students seeking work in the near future. To this

Shell reaps benefits of global recruitment strategy

Global recruitment initiatives can be transferred to markets around the world while remaining culturally sensitive to local needs, according to Sherri Sheehy, Shell's recruitment manager for Europe, the Middle East, Africa and Russia.

Speaking at the Global Recruiting Forum in Brussels, Sheehy told delegates that Shell's recruitment system was aligned around the world so that it could treat candidates with 'equal fairness'.

She advised companies to develop a global marketing strategy with strong employer branding, designed to give job candidates a clear impression of the firm. 'Companies need to ask themselves: "What do we know about our candidates? Can we offer them what they are looking for?"' she said.

Although there are advantages to working with one global brand and recruitment process, Sheehy said there could be 'creative tension' between headquarters: 'You have to be careful not to be too US-orientated or Eurocentric when dealing with departments in other regions of the world.'

Source: Adapted from S. Overan, 'Shell reaps benefits of global recruitment strategy', *PM Online*, 19 December 2005.

Discussion questions

1 What are the problems with creating a global brand when recruiting locally?
2 Should the head office impose its recruitment strategy on the home country?

international perspective

end, they undertake activities such as sponsoring school/college events, assisting students with projects, running workshops on business understanding, and supporting employees looking to work as school or college governors.

Government agencies

As a resource for other employers, the work of government agencies is primarily a matter of facilitating recruitment. Utilising both direct and indirect methods, this involves providing communication links between employers and their prospective employees, as well as providing training, skills development and, in some instances, financial support to enable people to become either employable or more suitable for a wider range of occupations. The primary institutional vehicle for these activities is the JobCentre Plus network, which, since 2002, has been the lead government agency dealing with jobless people of working age and whose core aim is to put more people into work by helping employers fill their vacancies.

Among the direct methods that it employs are: a one-to-one personal advisory service with benefit claimants; a telephone service, Jobseekers Direct; and a dedicated website listing vacancies linked to JobPoints. Jobseekers Direct sets out to offer a quick and easy telephone service to help the jobless find a temporary or permanent, full- or part-time job. The service advises people of vacancy details and how to apply. It will send them application forms and, wherever possible, will ring the employer to arrange an interview. JobPoints are touch-screen kiosks located in JobCentre Plus offices as well as in supermarkets and libraries. They offer a search facility for different categories of work, and details of local, regional, national and international vacancies. The indirect methods used by the network are typically targeted at those out of work for longer than 26 weeks, although this does vary with the different groups on New Deal schemes. The nature of the assistance ranges from advice and support programmes (e.g. helping people to develop a CV, prepare for an interview, apply for jobs and supplying stamps, stationery and newspapers), through to educational courses (e.g. literacy, numeracy and skills development), sponsored training (e.g. accountancy, computing) and courses leading to qualifications in different trades and services.

Similar programmes geared to a younger age group are provided by another agency – Connexions. Set up in 2001 with a much broader remit, it offers young people between the ages of 13 and 19 information, advice and guidance on health, housing, money, education, work and career topics. In terms of recruitment, it utilises both direct and indirect methods. It helps with applications and CVs, and will organise interviews, but will also offer advice on skills development, guidance on training opportunities and, in partnership with local employers, the opportunity for work experience and careers guidance. Connexions works closely with the Learning and Skills Councils to develop 'work-based routes' for young people looking for vocational qualifications.

More specialist government agencies operate for particular occupational groups. A case in point is the Forces Resettlement Agency, which, as part of its role, offers education, retraining and job opportunities for people retiring from or leaving the Armed Forces. While there is a differentiation of support based on rank and length of service, all service personnel have access to an employment consultant's advice, a job-finding service and access to websites (such as 'Questonline' and 'courses4forces') offering information on jobs and retraining. Those with more than five years' service also have access to career transition workshops and training centres, and the opportunity to gain work experience with civilian employers and receive regular information about job opportunities. Officers have their own job-finding service via the Officers Association.

In addition to providing its own recruitment resource services, the government also sponsors or part-sponsors voluntary agencies. An example here is the Shaw Trust, which is a leading national charity that seeks to create work opportunities for people with disabilities. According to the Office for National Statistics (ONS), over seven million people, or 19 per cent of those of working age, are disabled, of whom only 50 per cent are currently working (ONS, 2004). To increase the number of disabled people in the workforce the Shaw Trust offers a range of work-related services, many of which are funded, under contract, by JobCentre Plus. These services include financial support to buy specialist equipment, advice on training, support in job search and interviews, and arranging 'work tasters' and placements.

Commercial recruitment agencies

Unlike government agencies, whose main aim is to facilitate employment and offer a recruitment service that is free at the point of access, commercial recruitment agencies are companies that undertake part or all of the recruitment process (on behalf of employers) in return for a fee. They form an industry that is heterogeneous in nature, with differing:

- ranges of activity (some agencies specialise in advertising posts, others in the supply of staff, yet others in a complete recruitment package)
- types of staff placement (temporary, fixed-term or permanent staffing)
- ranges of staff supply (from a narrow to a wide variety of occupations)
- catchment areas (e.g. local, regional, national or global suppliers)

- company size, small independent to large multinational (e.g. Reed or Kelly Services)
- business strategy (some agencies have a business model that is high volume/low margins, others a low volume/high margins model).

Recruitment advertising agencies and consultants

Advertising and recruitment consultants are private companies that offer particular sets of services to employers. In the case of the former, recruitment advertising agencies can design, write and place advertisements, produce recruitment materials, advertise on the Internet, build websites and handle responses. Recruitment consultants, by contrast, can take over a larger part of the recruitment process. As well as the advertising, they will also undertake other outsourced aspects of vacancy management, such as getting information to applicants and sifting initial applications to provide employers with a shortlist. The issue always for employers is balancing the costs of outsourcing recruitment activities against the gains of saving company time and using agency expertise, especially in unfamiliar labour markets (Taylor, 2002).

Temporary and contract staffing agencies

The phrase 'temporary and contract staffing agencies' covers the organisations that seek to meet the short-term recruitment needs of employers. The demand for staff may be a consequence of increased productivity, the need to cover a period of extended absence, filling a post while a permanent member of staff is sought or simply the desire to seek a more flexible workforce. Temporary staff are typically selected and paid by the supply agency and offered to employers at an hourly rate. Their length of service may vary from a few days to several months. Contract workers' assignments tend to be longer than those of temporary staff; they are typically taken on for a fixed period of months or on renewable annual contracts. They are usually paid by the employer, with the supplying agency receiving a commission or fee.

There is little in the way of systematic data on temporary and contract staffing agencies; the industry is fragmented and contains both large national and international companies (such as Reed Executive, Adecco and Manpower), and small high-street operations. The majority of agencies are small with fewer than five employees, while the largest in the UK have over 250 employees each (Keynotes, 2004). Traditionally, agencies operated in the clerical and light industrial sectors and, while these areas still provide nearly one-third of their placements, temporary and contract staff are now also supplied to the building and construction, computing/IT, education, financial services, hotel and catering, medical, technical/engineering and professional/managerial sectors. Estimates suggest that there are 12,500 agencies working in the UK temporary and contract staffing market, which placed over one million people in the financial year 2003–04 and generated a turnover of approximately £23 billion (Keynotes, 2004).

The main benefit to employers of recruiting via temporary and contract agencies is the provision of a relatively reliable source of qualified personnel who are available at short notice and can also be laid off relatively cheaply if no longer required. They are 'flexible' both in this sense and in that unsatisfactory or inappropriate workers can quickly be replaced. Employers are outsourcing much of the cost and effort of recruiting, while getting an opportunity to assess staff who might later be offered permanent appointments. Temporary or contract employees similarly get the chance to 'road test' the work environment rather than simply accepting a job based on impressions given at interview or through a tour of the facilities (Taylor, 2002). The main disadvantage of recruiting through temporary and contract agencies is the cost:

> " Hourly rates for agency workers are invariably double those paid to regular employees. In addition, the agency will incorporate charges into the contract that place a financial penalty on employers who make permanent offers of employment to their temps – a practice that is now limited as a result of . . . government regulations [introduced in 2003].
>
> (Taylor, 2002: 145) "

Permanent employment and executive search agencies

The third group of commercial agencies providing recruitment services are those dedicated to identifying candidates for permanent posts. They operate in a smaller market than their temporary and contract counterparts with aggregate annual placements of approximately half a million in 2004 and a turnover of approximately £1.7 billion (Industrial Relations Services, 2005a). Half of these placements were secretarial or clerical staff. Like the temporary and contract market, that for permanent agencies is also fragmented although, in this instance, it has fewer national and international firms and significantly more smaller agencies operating within fairly narrow geographical areas. Adecco (with a UK turnover of £572 million in the year to December 2002) and Brook Street (with a UK turnover of £133 million in the year to December 2003) are the leading permanent employment agencies, but 95 per cent of companies in this sector had turnovers of less than £5 million and half had turnovers of less than £250,000. In terms of staffing, 60 per cent of the VAT-based agencies had fewer than five employees (Keynotes, 2005). They all tend to operate on a 'no sale, no fee' basis. Fees for successful placements typically increase with the seniority, status and salary being paid for the post, and are usually expressed as a percentage of the first year's earnings. They are in the region of 15–17.5 per cent for more junior posts, and can go up to 25–30 per cent for senior posts.

The main benefit that permanent employment agencies offer employers is the opportunity to restrict the cost and outsource the effort of recruitment. To be economically viable, these agencies must therefore be more cost-effective than in-house recruitment options and/or be capable of offering additional services, such as specialist knowledge of the industry sector, advice on the current state of the candidates' market, and pay and benefits packages. Beyond the immediacies of cost, the major issues confronting employers using these agencies are:

- the necessary formative investment in ensuring that job descriptions and person specifications are as accurate as possible
- ensuring that candidates supplied meet both these specifications and the organisation's expected standards of performance
- that delays in the supply of applicants are kept to a minimum (Industrial Relations Services, 2005a).

Executive search agencies (often called 'headhunters') are a subsection of the permanent recruitment market. They focus on supplying suitable candidates for permanent roles as senior directors, managers and executives. They are primarily engaged when:

- the post is of such a senior and sensitive nature that it would be detrimental to the client organisation if it was known to be searching for a senior manager or executive
- there are very few people who could fill the vacancy and the client organisation needs a go-between to see if senior staff in other companies are interested in moving

- the post is at a level where suitable candidates are unlikely to wish to make direct application through normal procedures and may well not read job advertisements.

The major advantage of executive search agencies is that they offer a service that client organisations are unwilling or unable to undertake themselves. In effect, it is a form of soliciting that involves enticing the employees of one organisation to consider moving to another. Each search has its own parameters and is usually undertaken against a strict set of instructions from the client organisation and within an agreed time frame (normally a matter of months). The agencies are expected to remain in continual rapport with their clients, to work speedily and to have the ability to help successful candidates negotiate terms of severance from their current place of employment. Given that the situation is potentially damaging to candidates, their existing companies and the client organisation, discretion and advice on negotiations are of immense importance.

The main issues with engaging executive search agencies are: the problem of poaching; the search consultant's expertise and knowledge of the market; and the pressures of conducting the search within an equal opportunities context. In the case of the first of these, the headhunting agency will get to know one or more of the senior executives of the organisation for which it is working and they, in turn, may be of interest to a third party. Client organisations attempt to preclude this with a 'no poaching' or 'off limits' policy in their contractual agreement with the agency, but this is rarely fireproof. In terms of the second, companies have been known to express their concern about whether search consultants know the market to an appropriate standard and/or whether working within tight time parameters they are capable of finding the *best* possible candidates to shortlist (Industrial Relations Services, 2005a). To counter these types of concern, many of the agencies have adopted a Code of Practice (devised by the Association of Search and Selection Consultants) through which they seek to assure client organisations of the highest standards of service embodied in the code. The third issue, equal opportunities, is a more general matter, and of as much concern to the client organisation as the search agency. In an IRS survey of employers (Industrial Relations Services, 2005a), twice as many public-sector employers as private-sector organisations cited the agency's commitment to equal opportunities as grounds for choosing it to undertake the search for applicants. Although it features in the Code of Practice, if equal opportunities is not a clear commitment for the client, it is unlikely to be a central feature of the agency's search. It is a complex issue for, other than the minimalist stance of refusing to engage in overt discrimination, how can an agency assure a client of equity in what is essentially a closed form of searching?

Cyber agencies

Many permanent and temporary contract agencies also run websites advertising the vacancies of their clients. These compete in the digital world with newspaper websites like Fish4jobs (which is owned by four of the UK's largest newspaper companies – Trinity Mirror, Newsquest, Guardian Media Group and Northcliffe) and what have been termed 'cyber agencies' (Taylor, 2002). Cyber agencies (such as Monster.com) are commercial web companies that operate job boards. In the CIPD survey (2004a) they were used by 39 per cent of respondents primarily to recruit to managerial positions but also to encourage applications to graduate traineeships. Some job boards target specific work sectors – for example, Jobsgopublic – while others are designed for particular occupations (as in the case of people management for HR professionals) or niche markets – such as Jobswithdogs.co.uk, 'your free and friendly destination for all the latest vacancies and news on working with dogs in the UK' (Kent, 2005). Current job boards, however, are not just a service creating an applicant pool by matching job-seekers' CVs with employers' job and person specifications: recent changes in software mean that board operators, or indeed their employer clients, can engage in applicant tracking, skills matching, competency testing and, with the increasing use of broadband, virtual office tours and 'live' employee profiles. They can create, in other words, a much more effective, more informed and informative digital recruitment process than previously possible (Kent, 2005).

The disadvantages of job boards are not dissimilar to those of other websites (see above), however in employers' eyes their primary problem is that they are still not delivering the required quantity or quality of applicants (Industrial Relations Services, 2004). As a consequence, organisations are changing the way they use these boards, employing them more as portals for their own corporate websites. In this way, they gain the marketing potential of the board itself but also have greater control over the quantity and quality of candidates progressing through the recruitment process (Industrial Relations Services, 2004).

Newsprint and other media sources

Newsprint sources offer a more traditional but nonetheless popular way of attracting applicants. Indeed in the CIPD research (2004a), 61 per cent of respondents said that they used national newspapers to advertise some of their vacancies, while an even greater number, 87 per cent, indicated that they advertised in local newspapers – the most frequently used recruitment source in the survey. These aggregate figures do, however, mask quite marked variations in sectoral usage, particularly in the case of national newspapers. Where, for instance, 78 per cent of the sampled public-sector organisations and 72 per cent of the voluntary sector took out advertisements in national newspapers, only 55 per cent of private-sector manufacturing, production and service companies employed the same channel. With local newspapers the variations were narrower, but there was still a difference between public, voluntary and private manufacturing and production, where over 90 per cent of organisations used this recruitment source (94 per cent in the case of public-sector organisations), and the 81 per cent of private-sector services advertising their vacancies in this way.

The choice between national or local newspapers seems to depend largely on the available funds and the target audience. For most posts, local newspapers are considered preferable as they are typically less expensive and reach an audience within travelling distance of the organisation. It is only necessary to meet the higher costs of advertising nationally for relatively specialised posts for which there is a national market (e.g. chief executive of an organisation) or in circumstances where wide trawls of potential applicants are considered desirable (e.g. graduate traineeships for government agencies or national companies). The CIPD survey (2004a) provides supportive evidence. Its research found that local newspaper adverts were primarily utilised in recruiting to administrative, secretarial and manual/craft posts, while those in the national press targeted senior managerial and professional vacancies. It also found that the nature of the advert, in both sources, was beginning to change. To meet with competition from the Internet, 'ads are starting to look different. They are now promoting the employer brand and directing people to their websites' (cited in Arkin, 2004). Thus, rather than being a purely informational base for potential applicants, they are also being employed as a means of marketing the organisation, suggesting why it should be viewed as a 'preferred employer' or 'employer of choice', and how people that apply would benefit from joining.

Trade and occupational journals form the third significant newsprint source, with usage ranging from 71 per cent in private-sector services up to 87 per cent in the public sector (CIPD, 2004a). They provide the medium of choice for advertising professional vacancies in, for instance, engineering, accountancy, legal practice, social work, surveying and human resource management. They are particularly important where the target audience is scattered over a wide geographical area and where the cost of advertising in national newspapers is considered prohibitive. Beyond cost, the major benefit of using this source is that it is aimed at the appropriate professionals and thus the likelihood of responses from unsuitable candidates is reduced. The downside is that such publications often appear only on a fortnightly or monthly basis and, given the time required for creating and placing the advertisement, may lead to costly delays.

Non-newsprint media sources, such as television, cinema and radio, are much less frequently used in recruitment. On average, only 9 per cent of sampled organisations employed these media (CIPD, 2004a). The primary reason is cost: '[t]he cost of preparing and screening a television advertisement is on a par with the whole HR budget for many organisations' (Roberts, 2003: 132). The length of preparation time, however, and the limited availability of 'peak' advertising slots also work to reduce its suitability. Where television advertising has been employed in recent years it has been in government-sponsored campaigns that form part of longer-term recruitment strategies as, for example, in looking to meet the UK shortfall of teachers and nurses, and in attracting personnel to the Armed Forces.

Cinema advertising has also been used in these campaigns and can often provide a lower-cost option than television. It 'is particularly suitable for a younger general target audience and [again] where time is not a problem (for example, the pre-planned recruitment to new businesses). It also offers [more of] an opportunity to localise the advertisement' (Roberts, 2003: 132). Radio recruitment advertising is generally cheaper to prepare and broadcast than its cinema or television equivalents. It is seen to be particularly effective as a complementary form of advertising as, for instance, in prompting people to attend a particular recruitment open day. Like the other non-newsprint sources, it is seen to have a wider coverage than newspapers, and gains attention in ways that newsprint sources cannot. Newspaper advertising: 'will usually be read only by those who are seeking another job, whereas radio advertising at peak commuting time may catch the attention of ... listener[s] driving to and from work and may spark their interest to find out more' (Roberts, 2003: 133). Against this, it is much easier to respond to written advertisements, where all the information on response details are to hand, than to garner the same information from the 'live' advertisements of radio, cinema and television.

Summary

- What this chapter has sought to describe and assess are the major features of formative recruitment and the range of available recruitment sources and methods.

- It should be clear from the discussion that, in both recruitment stages, there are a series of calculations and decisions to be made. These range from how to identify the vacancy, and whether to employ new staff, through to which recruitment sources and methods to deploy to best effect.

- In each instance, the calculations and decisions are linked to both general operational conditions (e.g. the employment law parameters, the competitive nature of the labour market, the organisation's HR strategy), as well as the known imperfections of the methods (in both job analysis and recruitment practice) and the specific circumstances that the organisation faces (e.g. the urgency with which it needs the new staff).

- Other considerations include the amount it can spend on recruiting them, the likelihood of its recruitment methods hitting their anticipated audience and the volume of applications they might yield.

- The explicit risk associated with these calculations and decisions is that they may not generate the best (most appropriate) applicant field for the post – the tacit risks are the problems to which this can lead (e.g. the cost of re-advertising the post or accepting the need to select from a less adequate field with all the potential problematic outcomes this might yield).

- In an attempt to control these risks many organisations, in practice, have turned to multiple recruitment sources and methods in the firm belief that, collectively, they are likely to produce stronger applicant fields (Arkin, 2004).

Personal development

1 **Think about the definitions of recruitment.** In your own words, describe what is meant by the 'broad' and 'narrow' definitions of recruitment. Using HR publications (other than those employed as illustrations in that section of the chapter), try to identify examples of each type of definition in the literature.

2 **Examine how job analysis could be implemented in an organisation.** If you were to engage in job analysis for an organisation, which of the techniques would you choose to employ and why?

3 **Recognise the limitations of job descriptions.** Have you been given job descriptions and person specifications in the jobs for which you have applied? Look at the examples provided in the chapter. Do you think they provide potential applicants with the appropriate information? What more might you want to know about a post before you would consider applying?

4 **Identify how different recruitment methods are implemented by organisations.** Choosing an organisation with which you are familiar, what sources and methods of recruitment does it employ? What other recruitment sources should it consider?

5 **Identify the sources of potential candidates for recruitment.** In your experience of recruitment practices, what sources and methods of recruitment are effective and why?

❓ Discussion questions

1 What alternatives are there to recruiting new staff?
2 Why is job analysis important?
3 In what ways might competency frameworks be seen as an improvement on person specifications?
4 How does employment law impact on the recruitment process?
5 On what grounds do employers use internal recruitment methods? What are the limitations of using these methods?
6 What are the strengths and weaknesses of online recruitment?
7 When might an organisation consider using 'headhunters' in its recruitment practices?
8 In what circumstances might 'live' advertising (e.g. on television and radio) provide an effective form of recruitment?

🔑 Key concepts

recruitment, *p. 107*

selection, *p. 107*

job analysis, *p. 109*

empiricism, *p. 112*

job description, *p. 113*

person specification, *p. 113*

competency, *p. 114*

internal recruitment, *p. 120*

external recruitment, *p. 121*

Individual task

Purpose To apply the information provided in this chapter on formative recruitment and recruitment sources and methods to a practical work situation.

Time 40 minutes

Procedure You are part of a regional HR team for a national DIY company that is planning to open a new branch in Leeds in six months' time. You have been asked to oversee the task of recruiting shopfloor, warehouse and administrative staff for the branch.

- How would you go about this process?
- Describe the sources and methods you would use to recruit the staff.
- What problems might you anticipate in meeting the opening-day deadline?

Team task

Purpose To identify alternatives to the recruitment process.

Time 40 minutes

Procedure Your HR team of four people has been approached by a well-known fast-food burger chain, which is having problems with staffing levels. It operates 24-hour opening, although peak times are during breakfast, lunch and dinner. It is not sure if it can better utilise existing staff or whether it needs to recruit more.

1 Using the chart below, work through the options and identify possible solutions to the problem.
2 What impact could changing the staffing patterns have on the existing workforce?

Option	Consideration
■ Restructuring the workforce	Can the activities and responsibilities of *current* workers be altered or redefined in order to fill the vacancy?
■ Additional/new technology	Is there a case for buying in additional or new technology to undertake the work rather than employing new members of staff?
■ Outsourcing	Is it worth outsourcing the work to freelance staff or a third-party organisation?
■ Working time	Can the work be covered with more flexible working arrangements, e.g. allowing some staff to begin earlier/later to provide cover for a longer part of the day? Can it be covered by overtime?

Chapter SIXTEEN

Selecting the right people

Margaret May and Edward Brunsdon

LEARNING OUTCOMES

After studying this chapter, you should be able to:

- ☑ **outline** the key components of the traditional selection process
- ☑ **review** the grounds for their usage, and their relative merits and drawbacks
- ☑ **discuss** the main contemporary selection instruments
- ☑ **understand** and explain their strengths and limitations
- ☑ **recognise** the value of induction to the selection process.

The opening vignette identifies some of the problems that can be encountered when relying on certain selection methods.

Artificial intelligence and gender bias

Early in 2005, sparks flew when research was published claiming that men were more intelligent than women. The study, by Dr Paul Irwing and Professor Richard Lynn, showed that men were, on average, five points ahead of women in IQ tests. The authors said these results were 'conclusive', as their findings were based on data from 57 other studies that assessed IQ using tests of 'general cognitive ability', which included questions about spatial and verbal ability, among others.

So is it true? And does it matter in a work context? This bias in favour of men is nothing new. For years, research has suggested that traditional IQ tests of general intelligence (rather than assessments of specific aspects of intelligence) often tend to favour certain groups, with white European men frequently outperforming other groups. This suggests an element of bias in the way intelligence is being measured. Often these tests focus on abilities such as spatial awareness, a type of reasoning where men have often been found to outperform women as a result of genetic or educational influences.

The results from Irwing and Lynn's study are therefore not surprising, given the abilities assessed and the format of the tests used. Beyond showing that men are better at general intelligence tests, what use is this information when considering job performance? Not a great deal. IQ is not a good predictor of how someone will perform. Indeed, the authors cite recent statistics indicating that women are increasingly outperforming men, both academically and in the workplace. Their explanation for these statistics is that women have higher levels of motivation and a more conscientious approach to work. They say it is these characteristics, rather than their IQ, that enable women to achieve. This in itself suggests that IQ test results tell us little about how people actually apply their intelligence in 'real life'.

Organisations looking to recruit good performers should therefore use IQ tests at their peril, as they provide only limited information on how an individual is likely to perform.

In our work with organisations, we regularly use a competency-based approach. This gives more valuable information by measuring specific skills, abilities and attributes, such as problem-solving or decision-making. The organisation can then focus on the competencies relevant to the job.

So what differences arise when we assess men and women using a competency-based approach? One client in the pharmaceutical industry asked us to analyse results from an assessment process we designed to recruit salespeople. In contrast to the IQ test study, we found no significant gender differences for any of the 10 competencies against which the managers were assessed. This was despite the roles requiring a range of very different skills, from being hard-nosed and target-driven to being able to display outstanding interpersonal skills. This suggests the assessment process and competencies were free of gender bias and measured attributes that really mattered to these roles.

This carries an important message for assessment, recruitment and selection. We appear to find gender differences only when we look at broad measures – such as those in IQ tests – that do not relate directly to performance. By breaking down intelligence into specific competencies, we can gather more detailed, relevant information and avoid gender bias.

Source: B. Martin and N. Mindell, 'Artificial intelligence',
People Management, 29 December 2005, p. 7.
Reproduced with permission of *People Management*.

Discussion questions

1 Do you think IQ tests should be used as a method of selection?

2 How can employers ensure that selection methods are free from bias?

The opening vignette demonstrates how problems can arise when relying on one selection method.

selection

The process 'by which managers and others use specific instruments to choose from a pool of applicants'.

Selection has been described in the previous chapter as the process 'by which managers and others use specific instruments to choose from a pool of applicants ... [individual(s)] most likely to succeed in the job(s)' (Bratton and Gold, 2003: 221). Like recruitment, selection is a core HRM activity whose importance resides in its consequences. Good selection decisions can provide managers with valuable new members of staff who can contribute additional skills, increase productivity and, perhaps, even change the working ethos. Poor selection decisions can be costly: 'in terms of the management time required to deal with disciplinary cases, in retraining poor performers, and in having to recruit replacements for those individuals who have been selected and/or who quit soon after starting' (Marchington and Wilkinson, 2005: 157).

The traditional selection process

The traditional selection process, or 'classic trio' as it has been called by Cook (1993) and more recently by Taylor (2002, 2005), describes the combined use of three methods of selection: application forms, interviews and references. The key elements of this process are the application form and the interview. References play an important but subsidiary role, operating as either an information and evaluation source for shortlisting and interview questions, or as a check on the interview decision. Sequentially, the process would operate in the following way (see Exhibit 5-1). Having been encouraged by the recruitment material, individuals would apply for details of the vacancy and, by return, receive an application form and additional information such as the job and person specifications. A pool of applicants would be created from those returning the forms (and usually citing one or two referees). These forms would be screened and a shortlist of interviewees created. The appointee would be the candidate considered the best person for the job as ascertained by the application form and interview (and endorsed by references if they had not been used in the shortlisting).

In spite of the growth of an increasingly critical literature, the traditional selection process remains popular. This chapter begins by outlining its constituent instruments, pointing out their drawbacks and thus identifying the grounds for replacing or complementing them. Their limitations centre on what is termed their **predictive validity**. Selection operates from the assumption that applicants can be

traditional selection
Describes the combined use of three methods of selection: application forms, interviews and references.

predictive validity
The appropriateness of the chosen selection method for finding the right candidate.

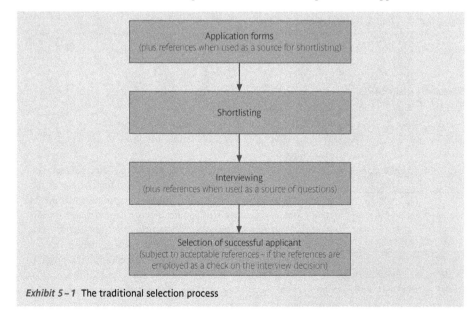

Exhibit 5-1 The traditional selection process

differentiated in terms of their qualities, skills and experience for a particular post. The task of selection instruments, such as application forms, interviews and references, is to facilitate this process – that is, to enable a choice to be made between candidates in terms of who will be most suitable for the job. They should, in other words, act as good 'predictors' of future work performance. Commentators, mainly academic occupational psychologists, maintain that the traditional methods are poor predictors of job performance and, further, that there are better selection methods available today.

Application forms

In its 2005 recruitment survey, the CIPD found that application forms or CVs were still used by over 80 per cent of its sample of organisations. A typical form includes questions asking for personal data, such as name, residence and phone number, 'previous work experience, educational background, vocational training ... and future career aspirations' (Taylor, 2005: 204). They can also include questions seeking information on an applicant's state of health and whether they have criminal convictions. On what is usually a detachable section of the form, there tend to be further questions concerning gender and ethnic background. These are basically for monitoring purposes and are usually removed from the form prior to engaging in the shortlisting procedures.

Application forms are seen to have a number of purposes. Their key functions are to:

- act as the reference document used for the contact address, phone number, and so on, of the candidate
- capture the basic candidate data that enable employers to shortlist for interview
- provide information that can be used in the interview.

Among their supplementary roles, application forms can:

- supply data for good but unsuccessful candidates, which can be stored on a database for future recruitment trawls (providing this meets Data Protection Act 1998 requirements)
- (with the appropriate questions) be used as a means of assessing the effectiveness of the recruitment media
- through their clarity, design, guidance information and questions, convey a positive public image of the organisation (Pioro and Baum, 2005).

Application forms are used extensively in the public and voluntary sectors. They are less prominent in the commercial sector where many companies, particularly smaller firms, encourage applicants to submit a curriculum vitae (hereafter CV) as an alternative (Taylor, 2005). From an employer's viewpoint, there are both benefits and limitations to using application forms and CVs. Among the benefits of using CVs are the following.

- Their design, production and costs are the candidate's rather than the organisation's.
- Applicants can communicate with the prospective employer in their own terms, 'to create a positive impression ... market themselves, indicate [they're] job fit and impress the reader with their skills and abilities' (Searle, 2003: 76).
- They demonstrate the candidate's ability to marshal their thoughts and put together a clear document for a designed purpose (Roberts, 2003: 140).

Among their limitations are that they:

- 'enable ... candidate[s] to construct the application to inflate their strong points and obscure or omit any weakness or concerns' (Roberts, 2003: 140)
- give applicants control over what is presented, which can make shortlisting difficult in terms of both the quantity and comparability of information
- can be written in a style that makes them difficult to verify as, for instance, in claims of the nature that someone is 'an organised manager with good team working skills and proven track record in delivering targets to tight deadlines'
- make the presentation of false information easy – 'CV fraud is rife in all sectors and at all levels' (Smethurst, 2004); among the most common forms of fraud are changing the grade of degrees achieved, claiming qualifications that have not been awarded, and changing employment histories to avoid mentioning dismissals or periods spent in jail; the CIPD recruitment survey (2005a) found that 'one in four companies had to withdraw a job offer because of CV fraud last year, and a similar proportion sacked someone for the same offence' (Smethurst, 2004: 35); to limit such risks, many organisations are now having to pay companies to check the claims made on CVs.

In comparison, the main benefits of application forms are that:

- employers are able to control the information presented to that relevant to the post
- it is harder for applicants to avoid addressing areas of weakness
- they can assist an organisation's equal treatment and fairness policies by creating a 'level playing field' as regards the nature and type of information required and, additionally, the opportunity to provide supportive guidance notes
- it is much easier to assess applicants' answers to questions in this format than via the uneven spread and quality of information submitted in CVs.

Their limitations are as follows.

- Organisations have a choice of either designing a specific form for their vacancy or using a standard application form. Both methods have disadvantages. The first is an expensive route to take and is time-consuming, while the latter may not capture important information about a candidate.
- Poorly designed application forms can appear intimidating and discourage applicants from applying.
- While there is less opportunity than with CVs, there is still a chance of fraudulent claims and thus the cost of vetting application forms.
- Like the CV, much of the information elicited is biographical in nature and commentators question whether it is possible to predict future job performance from such data (Searle, 2003).

Online application forms

Partly in response to the issues of cost and design, many firms have now adopted electronic application forms. Online applications mean that forms can have a more flexible format, overcoming fixed space allocations for particular answers and, once added to the organisation's website, can lead to reduced costs of production and distribution, and improved candidate and employer response times.

Shortlisting

Having obtained the application forms (or CVs), the next stage of the traditional approach is to reduce the applications received to a shortlist of candidates for interview. Shortlisting practice fluctuates from the highly informal to the systematic. On grounds of fairness, most commentators maintain that the systematic approach is the better option (see, for example, Torrington *et al.*, 2005). Drawing shortlisting criteria from the person specification, each application form is assessed and scored against each criterion. The preferred method is for a panel of selectors, operating independently of each other, to scan all the applications and produce their own shortlists. Anyone chosen by all the shortlisters is then invited for interview, while anyone discarded by all is rejected. The panel members then consider the merits of the remaining candidates until they reach an agreement on who should and should not be interviewed (Taylor, 2005).

Police force under fire for axing white males

A soldier who fought in the second Gulf War has spoken of his anger after he claimed he was rejected for a job as a police officer because of his race and sex. Mark Gough, aged 25, who has fought in Iraq and Bosnia, was one of 109 white male recruits cut from Gloucestershire police's recent selection process

The force attracted criticism last week after it emerged that it had given priority to 'females and applicants from minority ethnic backgrounds'.

The move was part of its programme to boost the number of minority ethnic officers within its ranks.

The recruitment drive attracted 301 applicants, of whom 192 could be sent to the police officer assessment centre.

The 109 would-be officers rejected were those who in a questionnaire scored the lowest marks out of the 172 white males who applied.

Mr Gough, a father-of-one from Quedgeley, Gloucestershire, has served in the 3rd Regiment Royal Horse Artillery for six years. He said he had always wanted to become a police officer and had left the Army after the second Gulf War in 2003 so he could prepare for the role.

He said he was shocked at the force's decision to reject him: 'I'm surprised that I quite possibly have been judged on the fact that I am a white male.

'I served with the Army for six years and as a part of my resettlement training I undertook a week with the police and had to take tests at the end, which I passed with ease.'

Civil liberties group Liberty and Law last week reported Gloucestershire Constabulary to the Commission for Racial Equality (CRE) and the Equal Opportunities Commission (EOC) after the men were rejected.

The pressure group also reported Avon and Somerset Constabulary to the CRE and the EOC last November after it emerged that nearly 200 white men had been turned down for jobs with the force because of their skin colour and gender.

A Gloucestershire police spokeswoman said she could not discuss individual applications but all deselected recruits could reapply in the future. Mr Gough will apply again to join the force.

Source: 'Police force under fire for axing white males', *Birmingham Post*, 7 February 2006, p. 6.

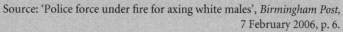

Discussion questions

1 Should this type of discrimination be allowed in order to redress the diversity balance?
2 How can an organisation such as the police appeal to the diverse groups that represent society?

The interview

As intimated above, the primary purpose of the interview is to enable selectors to choose the person best suited to the post from among the shortlisted candidates. It should therefore offer a means of both eliciting information and differentiating candidates. What follows discusses three core dimensions of this process – interview structures, contents and modes of delivery – before addressing the problems associated with this selection instrument.

Interview structures

Presented as a continuum, interviews range from the 'unstructured' to the 'structured' (see Exhibit 5-2). Interviews are unstructured when they are unplanned, non-directed, exchanges that allow free-flowing discussion between applicants and interviewers without pre-set topics or questions. To achieve anything from this interview style requires an immense amount of training, energy and skill on the part of interviewers, who are required to follow up interesting leads or important details that the applicants reveal as the interview unfolds. It seeks to encourage rapport and enable open and frank discussion, but it can also descend into disorder and leave no more than a residue of information for making consistent comparisons between candidates.

At the other end of the continuum are structured interviews. Here the interactions are controlled by the interviewers, who ask pre-set questions, in a particular sequence, on a specific range of topics. Through the structuring the aim is to offer a standardised form of questioning that is reliable and gathers comparable information about candidates. Its downside is that it is

Unstructured →	Semi-structured/focused →	Structured
■ Unplanned ■ Non-directed ■ 'Uncontrolled' ■ Unformatted ■ Bilateral communication flow ■ Flexible	■ Pre-scheduled ■ Interviewer-directed but flexible ■ Major topic areas formatted (focused) and some questions (semi-structured) ■ Communication flows develop to facilitate interview objectives ■ Some flexibility	■ Pre-planned ■ Interviewer directed ■ Standardised ■ Pre-formatted topics and questions ■ Unilateral communication flow ■ Inflexible

Exhibit 5–2 Interview structures
Source: Adapted from Anderson and Shackleton (1993, in Searle, 2003: 104).

inflexible and does not allow for probing or follow-up questioning. Between the two extremes are semi-structured and focused interview structures. Their main difference is that, in focused interviews, the topics for discussion (but not the specific questions) are prescribed, whereas in semi-structured interviews both topics and questions (whether 'closed' or 'open-ended') are prepared in advance. What they share, however, is more than their differences. They possess directed but flexible forms that permit some open and candidate-specific questions, and thus offer the opportunity to explore ambiguous or uncertain features of CVs, application forms or references, as well as giving candidates the chance to ask questions about the job and/or organisation.

Interview content

Within these interview structures, the types of question asked of candidates can also vary. Clearly there is little or no control in unstructured interviews, where much is left to the spontaneity of the situation and the development of the interviewer–applicant rapport. With focused, semi-structured and structured interviews, however, there is an opportunity to plan and control contents, and this has enhanced the development of particular forms of questioning. The four main types are as follows.

biographical questioning
Confirms personal details about candidates and is also employed as a way of putting candidates at their ease.

1 Biographical questioning is often used as the opening gambit in interviews. Other than confirming previous education and qualifications, describing current work experience and exploring the rationale for wanting the post, it is also employed as a way of putting candidates at their ease. Indeed, for some analysts, this latter function is its main value as to ask about: 'hobbies, family background, early childhood and so on [does] not seem to help select the best candidate' (Smith and Smith, 2005: 246).

situational questioning
Requires candidates to respond to hypothetical work-based scenarios.

2 Situational questioning requires candidates to respond to hypothetical work-based scenarios. They are presented with a verbal description of some aspect of the job and asked what they would do in those circumstances. Examples for an HR post might include cameos about sexual harassment or absenteeism in which the applicants are asked how they would go about resolving the problems. The candidates' answers are noted and compared with model answers in a carefully devised marking scheme (Smith and Smith, 2005).

behavioural questioning
Asks questions about problems candidates may have faced in work-based situations.

3 Behavioural questioning comes in slightly different variants. One subtype employs job-relevant cameos and then asks applicants about the nearest situation they have faced to the one described, followed by a series of analytical questions such as ' "What led to the situation?", "What did you do?", "How successful was your response?", "What was the reaction of others?", "What did you learn about the situation?" ' (Smith and Smith, 2005: 246). The second subtype bypasses the cameo and draws on critical incidents from the candidate's experience as the platform for discussing her or his responses to such circumstances. Taylor uses an illustration in which selectors looking to assess candidates' decisiveness, do so by asking them about 'an occasion in which they took a particularly difficult decision or were forced to make an important decision without having as much information as they would have liked' (2005: 216).

stress questioning
A type of questioning that aims to put candidates under pressure, in order to observe how they respond.

4 Stress questioning is less frequently used than the other types of questioning. It is designed to put candidates under pressure by, for instance, deliberately contradicting something they say. The claim by those who use it is that this form of questioning is necessary to observe how applicants *actually* respond to stressful situations rather than listening to them *describing* how they would respond.

Delivery formats

In addition to differences in structure and content, interviews can also vary in terms of their delivery format. In face-to-face interviewing, there are at least four variations linked to the number of selectors and candidates. The *one-to-one interview*, as the name suggests, is where the interview takes place between a single interviewer and the applicant. The *tandem* or *small-group interview* occurs where two or three people interview a candidate together. There may be a division of labour in terms of the aspects of the job they explore, or they may even adopt specific roles for the interview, but they are using the same social interaction to observe the candidate at first hand and reach a joint decision. The *panel interview* operates in a similar way, but with a larger number of assessors – in the case of some senior executive posts there are up to 12 people on the panel. The *candidate group interview* is where several applicants are interviewed together, usually by several assessors. Rarely used in isolation, it is typically employed in conjunction with one-to-one or panel interviews, and to assess social skills and performance in group or team-work settings.

An alternative to the face-to-face delivery format is telephone interviewing (and, in a more advanced form, videoconferencing). Used more as an addition to, than a substitute for, face-to-face interviewing, this has seen considerable growth in the last few years. The CIPD's survey found that, on average, 30 per cent of organisations made use of telephone interviews, a figure that rose to 40 per cent in private-sector services (CIPD, 2005a). This format is employed mainly as a screening procedure and considered particularly valuable in:

- high-volume selection
- filling vacancies where telephone manner and customer contact are an important part of the job (e.g. call and contact centres)
- shortlisting from an international field of applicants (CIPD, 2005f).

Analysts and employers who favour telephone interviewing argue that it is of mutual benefit to applicant and assessor in that: neither has to travel to interview (a particularly important cost consideration when it comes to international selection); the interviews can be arranged and undertaken more speedily; and, it is claimed, 'people are less inhibited than in face-to-face interviews and so the quality of information can be higher' (Martin and Jackson, 2002: 129). Countering these gains, however, are the difficulties of judging how applicants are responding to questions, managing the context in which the interview takes place and the set-up costs (CIPD, 2005f).

There is no logical limit to, or automatic correspondence between, the telephone and face-to-face delivery formats, the contents of interviews and the types of interview structure. It is, for instance, possible to have an unstructured interview conducted by a panel of selectors over the telephone (or via videoconferencing) and a structured interview conducted by a single assessor in a face-to-face situation. In practice, however, there are more, or less, likely combinations.

For example, there is a much greater chance of an unstructured interview being conducted as a one to one (in either delivery format) because it lends itself to relative informality, thus encouraging rapport and producing more open and frank discussions. In similar vein, small groups and panels are more likely to be used in asking situational, behavioural and stress questions in semi-structured, focused and structured interviews. What they lose in informality and flexibility, they gain in control and the likelihood of yielding comparable data.

Problems with interviews

Most commentators agree that there is no such thing as a problem-free interview. Whatever the interview's structure, content or mode of delivery, bias and errors occur that render it an unreliable selection instrument with low predictive validity. In the HR literature, the key sources of these issues are the interviewers themselves. They are the more active and influential party in the conduct of the process but, more than this, it is their interpretations and judgements that determine the selection outcomes. Drawing on the work of Anderson and Shackleton (1993), Taylor lists some of the main errors and sources of bias and distortion that can occur in these interpretations (see Exhibit 5-3).

Stop and reflect

Wanted: Santa

Father Christmas: £8 – £10 an hour; elves or characters in costumes, £6 – £8 an hour

You are responsible for interviewing candidates for the role of Santa and the elves for a shopping centre's Christmas grotto. What would be your selection criteria? How can you ensure you are not breaking any employment laws?

Given this litany of potential bias and distortion, it's surprising not to see interviewing discarded as a major risk to objective selection, but this has not happened. It continues to be a popular instrument, with some 68 per cent of organisations still employing it within the traditional selection process (and 80 per cent in the case of commercial manufacturing and production firms). Some heed has been paid to the assessment of its practice, however, with organisations turning to the more structured types of interviewing and to training their selection teams. The CIPD survey (2005a), for instance, found that 56 per cent of its sample of organisations used structured, panel, interviewing (84 per cent in the case of voluntary sector agencies) and, in terms of content, 41 per cent employed behavioural questions in their structured interviews.

The decline in the use of unstructured interviewing in favour of its more structured counterparts is argued on the grounds that the greater the freedom given to interviewers in terms of structure, content and delivery, the higher the probability of bias and distortion occurring. Unstructured interviews maximise freedom and minimise control; the more structured alternatives delivered by trained individuals, small groups and panels provide greater control and thus better reliability and higher predictive validity. Interview questions can be planned carefully, candidates can be asked a comparable set of items focusing on attributes, skills and competencies, and the answers scored according to agreed rating systems (Taylor, 2005). Training (particularly in the principles of 'fair selection') is seen to be an important ingredient here, both enabling interviews to be conducted appropriately, and controlling the interpretations and

The expectancy effect	When the reading of information in CVs, applications (and perhaps references) may lead assessors to develop (positive or negative) expectations of candidates that influence interview questions and the interpretation of answers
The self-fulfilling prophecy effect	Occurs when interviewers' impressions of candidates are formed in the early stages of interviews, and these permeate subsequent questions and/or evaluations
The attribution (or 'stereotype') effect	Happens when interviewers associate particular groups with specific characteristics and judge individual candidates in these terms; although in the light of recent anti-discrimination legislation much of this stereotyping may be illegal, it is still thought to be widespread
The prototyping effect	When interviewers are impressed by a particular type of person(ality), regardless of job-related factors
The universalist effect	Occurs when interviewers, on the basis of responses to particular questions, rate candidates as 'good' or 'bad' across the board and thus reach very unbalanced decisions
The 'similar to me' effect	Describes situations in which interviewers give preference to candidates they perceive as having a similar background, career history, personality or attitudes to themselves
The information overload effect	Happens when interviewers form judgements based on only a fraction of the data available to them about each candidate
The temporal extension effect	When interviewers assume that candidates' behaviour at interview (e.g. their nervousness) is typical of their general disposition

Exhibit 5–3 **Problems that can arise in interviews**
Source: Adapted from Taylor (2005: 211).

evaluations of the information provided by candidates (Marchington and Wilkinson, 2005). Nonetheless, whether such measures actually eradicate (or even the degree to which they inhibit) interviewer distortion is still a controversial matter. Greater control is sought in the names of fairness and objectivity, but it is far from clear that it can overcome the interpretative (and some would say inherently intersubjective) nature of interviewing (Newell and Shackleton, 2001).

References

References form the final element of the traditional selection process. They differ from both application forms and interviews in that they seek a third-party assessment of the applicant's skills, abilities and character. As with interviews and application forms, they are employed by large numbers of organisations. The CIPD recruitment survey (2005a) revealed that 96 per cent of the sampled organisations asked for references for at least some of their vacancies, while 77 per cent always asked applicants for references.

As suggested earlier in the chapter, references can be employed in different ways at different stages of the selection process.

- They can be requested and used pre-interview, in conjunction with the application form to shortlist and hone interview questions.

- They can be used post-interview as a means of checking: the information provided on the application form, that supplied during the interview and the general impression created by the candidate.

In practice, the survey (CIPD, 2005a) found that 34 per cent of the organisations it sampled took up references pre-interview and thus were able to use them to shortlist and/or as a means of sharpening the interview questions. The majority of the sample, however, chose to employ references post-interview, and primarily as a means of checking the data and impressions of interviews and application forms.

Types of references

References come in many different forms, and include the following.

Employment references

These are requested from current or previous employers, although references from current employers should be sought only with the permission of applicants. This type of reference can either be an open request for information about candidates or, in a more structured form, can ask particular questions about, for example, employment dates, attendance record, responsibilities, competencies and performance.

Personal references

Prospective employers use personal references to ask for assessments of the applicant's character. Again, this can either be an open assessment request or structured in terms of the nature of the job and working conditions, and/or by asking referees to rank or rate particular personal qualities.

Academic references

These normally combine a request to confirm academic achievements with a personal assessment of the candidate's suitability for the post.

Specialist references

Examples of these are credit or medical histories. Credit references are typically undertaken for positions where cash handling or other financial transactions are important. It is now obligatory under the Financial Services and Markets Act 2000 for companies covered by this legislation to provide references for current and past employees. All employers can seek medical references from prospective employees but, as this is considered sensitive personal data by the Data Protection Act 1998, they must obtain the applicant's consent before making such a request.

Problems with references

In spite of their wide usage, references can present problems for both providers and prospective employers. In terms of prospective employers, the following issues apply.

- **Accuracy.** Because a job applicant is being asked to give the names of referees, they are highly unlikely to choose anyone who will give them a bad reference, and therefore inaccuracies or so-called 'leniency errors' may well arise.
- **Authenticity.** Cases of 'fake' references are not unusual. Instances have been recorded in which friends of applicants have posed as line managers and, again, where references have been sent from bogus companies (Smethurst, 2004).
- **Interpretation.** References may require 'interpretation': an exemplary reference could be given because an employer is trying to get rid of a member of staff, a non-committal reference because a line manager is trying to keep a member of staff, and so on.
- **Time delays.** Employers are generally disinclined to invest effort in writing references for former employees or current employees looking to leave the organisation. These are consequently seen as low priority, often leading to delays in the prospective employer's selection schedule (Taylor, 2005).
- **Non-response.** Response rates for reference requests vary between 35 and 85 per cent (CIPD, 2005c) and can cause particular problems for organisations using the references to shortlist or support interviews.
- **Poor prediction of future job performance.** According to Cooper *et al.* (2003: 154), references are 'highly subjective' and 'open to error and abuse'.

In terms of providers, the issues arise primarily from the changing legal status of what is written. The Data Protection Act 1998, and the growth in discrimination legislation and case law have resulted in an increasingly cautious approach to writing references. Referees are seen to owe a 'duty of care' to both prospective employers and applicants. In other words, they are considered culpable if they knowingly deceive recruiting organisations or mislead them into hiring people that they know to be unsuitable. They may also be held liable for losses by applicants if their references contain negligent or defamatory statements.

Attempts to improve references

Most organisations will request written references; this gives referees more time to reflect on the questions, the wording of answers and on the information provided about the job vacancy. Occasionally, however, when it's a senior post, when ambiguities have arisen in the written reference or where references are late, prospective employers may well resort to seeking references by telephone. Doing so is less anonymous, increases the chances of a balanced assessment and, more pointedly, makes it more difficult for ex-employers to avoid giving a reference. A second improvement is the more widespread use of structured questionnaires based on the job and person specifications. While these are seen to require more preparatory work than an 'open' reference, with separate forms for different types of job, they are easier for referees to complete, and permit a more focused and detailed response.

Contemporary methods of selection

Despite their continued usage, the perceived limitations of the traditional selection methods have led both employers and academics to consider alternative ways of selecting. For a few organisations these alternatives act as substitutes; for the majority, however, they are employed to shore up or strengthen the traditional methods. They are seen to:

- reduce the risk of subjective decision-making by increasing the levels of reliability and predictive validity, and

- offer a more comprehensive selection process by measuring factors that could not be adequately assessed using application forms, interviews or references.

Three methods of **contemporary selection** deserve special consideration: biographical profiling, psychological testing and assessment centres.

contemporary selection
Includes biographical profiling, psychological testing and assessment centres.

biographical profiling
The biographic detail of successful job-holders can be used to predict who will be effective in the job in the future.

Biographical profiling

Biographical profiling is held to be both an extension of, and an improvement on, the traditional selection process. It gathers more comprehensive and systematic data than application forms and references and, at the same time, is considered to have greater predictive validity than the interview. This selection method works from three key assumptions:

1 the historicist assumption that the future will be like the past; in other words, that past human action is the best predictor of future human action

2 that individuals differ from each other and these differences can be measured

3 that individual biographic profiles can be matched to job performance.

On this basis, it is argued that the biographic detail of successful job-holders can be used to predict who will be effective in the job in the future. The method starts from the question 'What is it about past and current incumbents that has enabled them to excel at their job?' The answer is sought in demographic, experiential and attitudinal data. This can include anything from simple age, gender and residential information through to 'more intricate details of personal life history and other experiences such as early and late personal relationships, personal habits and attitudes, recreational interests, self-impressions or opinions' (Searle, 2003: 82). Collected through research instruments as varied as structured surveys and qualitative 'life history' essays, the task is to analyse the data in order to establish a link between personal history and successful job performance.

Once this is achieved, the analysis is then used to draft a questionnaire for new job applicants, which sets out to measure whether, and to what extent, they possess the appropriate biographical attributes. The questions used are typically a mixture of hard – in the sense of eliciting easily verifiable information – and 'soft' items – that is, asking for 'judgements, aspirations ... attitudes and expectations' (Searle, 2003: 84). Included within the latter are questions designed to capture the applicant's reactions to specific situations as well as projections on how they would conduct themselves in particular circumstances. As the questions are largely a matter of self-assessment, questionnaires can either be sent to applicants through the post or, as is increasingly the case with other selection tools, presented in an online format.

Although bioprofiling has a long history in the United States (it has been in use there since 1894), only a small number of organisations currently use this method in the UK. It is, however, becoming more popular here (Taylor, 2005). Attracting employers is the fact that bioprofiling:

- is more extensive than an application form and enables information to be collected more economically than by interviewing
- has greater predictive validity than the classic selection format – 'Research evidence indicates that biodata has substantial and generalisable validity. This means that it measures what it claims to measure and is therefore a good predictor of performance (Searle, 2003: 88)
- incorporates independently verifiable data and is thus more difficult for applicants to fake
- is a very efficient way of assessing large numbers of applicants (especially if it is offered as a multiple-choice questionnaire)
- promotes fairness by asking all candidates the same questions and, in large part, assesses their answers on the basis of predetermined responses, thus curtailing the opportunities for assessors to impose their own judgements.

Deterring its use in some instances, however, are specific concerns about:

- the high set-up costs and, in particular, the time and money that would need to be devoted to developing the questionnaire on which the method is based
- its low portability – that is, each type of job would require its own questionnaire; 'A questionnaire that is good at predicting the performance of airline stewards will be very different from one that aims to forecast how effective pilots are likely to be' (Taylor, 2005: 229)
- the speed with which bioprofile questionnaires can become obsolete and thus the need to replace them every few years if they are to retain their predictive value
- how the very nature of the data collection denies the exploration of issues that is available with some other selection methods, such as interviews and assessment centres.

Two more general concerns are also of importance:

- bioprofiling's inherent promotion of the status quo
- the ease with which it could fall foul of anti-discriminatory legislation.

In the case of the former, it is clear that, given the method's use of past and current employees to develop criteria for assessing the likely success of future applicants, it is effectively promoting a very conservative selection strategy. If, for example, a City finance firm has a predominantly young, white, male, Anglo-Saxon employee population, bioprofiling would not, of itself, support greater gender, ethnic or age diversity in selection. With the latter, given the broad-based anti-discriminatory legislation that has developed in the UK and European Union over the last 10 years (see Chapter 11), it is extremely important that the biodata sought are sensitive to the legislative parameters, and to the sense of justice and social fairness on which they are based. Of course, if one is working in another culture then other problems can arise, as can be seen from the 'International perspectives' box.

Juapong Textiles, Ghana

Sometimes, problems can be more to do with local politics than with appropriate selection techniques, as can be seen at Juapong Textiles.

Recruitment of personnel to work at the rejuvenated Juapong Textiles Limited (JTL), scheduled to re-open in April 2006, seems to have created an unprecedented level of anxiety in Juapong, in the North Tongu district of the Volta region, and its immediate environ of Atimpoku in the Eastern Region. This was in consequence of a controversy over who should be responsible for the recruitment of workers and where it should be conducted. While some traditional authorities feel it is the sole right of indigenes of Dorfor traditional area, where the factory is located, some political leaders have maintained that all qualified Ghanaians can be recruited.

The problems seem to stem from the Minster for Trade, who feels that people can be recruited from other regions along the Volta, while the local chief thinks that only people from Juapong should be employed. As a result, he has suggested that local people boycott the factory.

The Deputy Minister for Employment reported that, 'I do not know the criteria for the selection of the right calibre of people. Whatever list anybody is compiling is not automatic because it will have to be screened by a panel', adding that any Ghanaian has the right to seek employment at the factory, irrespective of his or her origin.

The Deputy Minister said that the rejuvenation of the factory should rather be a source of good news to the people of Ghana, and was worried that some leaders had already started judging the good development along ethnic and political lines.

Some of the youth at Juapong said that, in the past, they had enjoyed some sort of priority for work due to the factory's location, expressing the fear that somebody, somewhere, was trying to change the status quo.

Some of them also said that they were staff at the company before its closure, adding that, even though they were paid all their entitlements, they think their friends and colleagues should be considered first in order to maintain the priority reserved for the area.

Source: Adapted from 'Row over job recruitment at "rejuvenated" Juapong Textiles', *Ghanaian Chronicle* (Africa News), 3 February 2006.

international perspective

Discussion questions

1 When working in different cultures, managers often have to adopt different selection procedures. How can they do this and still recruit the right people?

2 How can a manager ensure that selection criteria are transparent?

Psychological testing

psychological testing
Works from the assumption that people differ from each other and that these differences can be measured.

The term 'psychological testing' is usually employed as a synonym for occupational or psychometric testing. Like bioprofiling, it works from the assumption that people differ from each other and that these differences can be measured. Again like bioprofiling, it is rarely used as the exclusive means of making a decision and is typically employed in conjunction with interviewing and assessment centres (see below). It differs from bioprofiling, however, in the range and nature of tests it can call upon and in its popularity. Current estimates suggest that over half a million psychological tests are completed each year by candidates in the UK applying for graduate positions alone (Income Data Services, 2004), and that 70 per cent of firms (Searle, 2003) and 81 per cent of FTSE-100 companies (*People Management*, 2005b) use them in selection. Discussed in much of the HR literature in terms of the selection of managers or graduate applicants, they are in fact employed across a broad spectrum of occupations. B&Q, Vodafone and Asda, for example, utilise them in the selection of their retail staff (*People Management*, 2003; Income Data Services, 2004), while National Car Parks does the same in choosing its parking wardens (*People Management*, 2005a).

Psychological tests can be divided into two main types: those designed to measure applicants' ability and those that set out to assess their psychological disposition (see Exhibit 5-4). Measures are tests of intellectual performance and are usually 'maximal tests' in the sense that 'they aim to find out what is the *best* the test-taker can do' (Searle, 2003: 137). Tests are typically taken under examination conditions with a set time limit and standard instructions. The questions asked have a right answer, and candidates are usually required to select this answer within a multiple-choice format. The goal is to answer the questions as quickly and accurately as possible in the time allowed. In the pen-and-paper version of the tests, they are then marked by trained administrators and the score obtained is matched against a norm group (that is, compared with results gathered from existing employees, applicants or the general population) in order to assess how well the candidate has done. The tests are designed to offer a standardised, objective and structured assessment that is easy to measure and affords simple comparisons.

In contrast, tests of psychological disposition are not usually taken under examination conditions nor are they concerned with maximal performance. Rather, in a structured and standardised way, they seek to gauge and codify the traits or characteristics of applicants with a view to predicting how they will 'fit', perform in or manage a particular work environment. These tests are usually of the self-report type – that is, applicants are asked to record how they see themselves in terms of a range of criteria or characteristics that are typically presented in a questionnaire with multiple-choice or open-ended questions. Answers are plotted on a profile chart and, again, matched against an occupational norm group. Each outcome is typically fed back and discussed with the particular applicant before being reported to the selectors. Selectors are advised by the test administrators as to where there are strong and weak correlations between the applicants' profiles and those described in the job's person specification. They then have the opportunity to decide whether the weak correlations are grounds for rejection or to pursue them with the candidate during the remainder of the selection process.

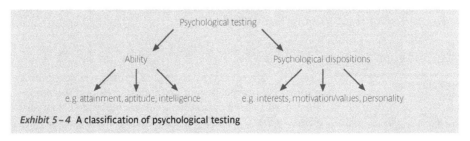

Exhibit 5-4 A classification of psychological testing

Testing ability

Ability is frequently stratified into different fields. Searle (2003) and Roberts (2003), for example, divide it into attainment, aptitude and intelligence. The tests used to measure ability tend to reflect this division primarily in terms of their level of specificity (see Exhibit 5-5). Those measuring attainment operate in particular domains and seek to assess 'present performance, irrespective of how the present capability was acquired or how it might progress …

ability

Frequently stratified into different fields, such as attainment, aptitude and intelligence, and indicates the capability a candidate will have to do a job.

[These] tests are most useful when the selection is made on the basis of who will be the best candidate as soon as they start work' (Smith and Smith, 2005: 192). They are particularly suitable in selection for posts that are unlikely to change in a significant way. Unlike attainment tests, those measuring aptitude gauge the *potential* or propensity to acquire knowledge, competencies or skills in the future. Their aim is to make inferences about future work performance by assessing how well applicants learn a job-related task. They are used in work situations where candidates cannot be expected to possess the requisite skills. In effect, aptitude tests measure the applicant's suitability for training. As an illustration, the psychological test supplier, SHL, has developed the 'Customer Contact Aptitude Series', which is designed to assess whether individuals possess 'the verbal and numerical reasoning required for effectiveness in sales, customer services and call centre roles' (Income Data Services, 2004: 80).

Where attainment and aptitude tests measure specific and often job-related knowledge and skills (see Exhibit 5-6 for illustrations), those tests designed to assess intelligence seek to gauge broad cognitive skills or provide a measure of an individual's overall ability. In Toplis *et al.*'s terms, they assess 'the capacity for abstract thinking and reasoning within a range of different contexts and media (1994: 17). These tests (for example, Raven's Progressive Matrices or the Watson-Glazer Test of Critical Thinking) are usually aimed at graduates, managers or executives (Smith and Smith, 2005). They measure abstract reasoning either through the aggregation of a battery of test scores from specific verbal and non-verbal maximal tests, or by employing a single test that presents complex problems (in words, numbers and diagrams) and then requires candidates to solve them by using logical or lateral thinking.

According to the CIPD survey (2005a), approximately 40 per cent of employers use general ability tests in selection; 50 per cent test for job-specific skills and competencies, and 39 per cent use literacy and/or numeracy tests in choosing at least some of their employees. In both the fields of attainment and aptitude, tests of literacy and numeracy are more likely to be used as

Tests of:	Temporal focus	A measurement of	Breadth
Attainment	Current	Known and controlled experience/ knowledge/skills	Specific test domains
Aptitude	Future potential	Unknown and variable experience/ knowledge	Narrow specific skills, often job-related
Intelligence	Current	Underlying reasoning ability	Broad cognitive skills

Exhibit 5–5 Tests of ability
Source: Adapted from Searle (2003: 144).

Type of test	Application
Verbal/communication	Ranging from attainment tests of spelling and grammar for clerical jobs to tests of verbal/critical reasoning for managers and graduates
Numerical	Ranging from basic arithmetic tests for process workers and clerical administrators to numerical critical reasoning tests for managers and graduate entrants where inferences need to be drawn from business data
Diagrammatic	Tests of logical reasoning presented in the form of shapes and diagrams; often used in occupations involving data processing, and where analytical and problem-solving skills are prevalent
Mechanical	Problem-solving tests, usually in pictorial form; employed in a wide range of apprenticeships and in engineering occupations
Spatial	Used to assess aptitude for posts in design and in occupations that require an understanding of how components fit together
Dexterity	Measure hand speed and fine precision skills and are employed in assessing process and assembly workers, as well as in co-ordination tests (e.g. in the selection of pilots)
Sensory	Measures near or far acuity, sound or colour discrimination; used, for instance, in assessing recruits for the Armed Forces and in construction
Administrative	Measures IT, word-processing speeds, filing and classification skills; used for a range of administrative posts

Exhibit 5–6 The application of measures of attainment and aptitude

'threshold tests' – that is, to eliminate the weaker candidates rather than as a means of choosing between those appointable. The household-to-healthcare company Kimberly-Clark Europe, for instance, uses a numerical reasoning test very early in its selection process for graduate entrants. Those applicants who fail to reach at least the 31st percentile in this test (when compared with an undergraduate norm group) do not progress to the next stage of selection (Income Data Services, 2004: 25).

Advantages of ability tests

Advocates of ability tests suggest that they carry many advantages. Among these are that they:

- measure factors that cannot be assessed using the traditional selection process
- offer a more systematic and more objective selection instrument
- provide organisations with a means of discriminating between large numbers of applicants in a rapid and often cost-effective manner (Searle, 2003)
- are among the best predictors of subsequent job performance (Robertson and Smith, 2001)
- reveal how close an applicant is to the requisite skills level, how much training they might need to reach an acceptable standard and, thus, provide a useful insight into post-hire training costs and on-the-job experience requirements (Searle, 2003)

- are transportable (i.e. they do not have to be constructed for each job)
- once established, they are cheap to run and can be used in a wide variety of selection contexts.

Disadvantages of ability tests

Of their drawbacks, the following are particularly worthy of note.

- The start-up costs are high. These costs would include, for instance:
  - initial training for staff administering and interpreting the tests; ability test training (to British Psychological Society Certificate of Competence Level A) can take up to five days with further one-day training enhancements
  - start-up kits, including one-off costs such as the test user's manual and/or computer software
  - consumables, such as answer sheets for candidates and normative data
  - software packages and licences, where online or computer administration is used (Income Data Services, 2004).
- There is a concern about the validity of the tests themselves, and specifically the degree to which variations in test performance are the product of factors other than ability. Searle (2003: Chapter 6), for instance, suggests that the choice of language, the use of time limits in tests, the emotional state and previous test experience of the test-taker and the environment in which the test occurs can all influence test scores.
- Kandola *et al.* (2000) raise doubts about the universal application of ability testing. They maintain that ability (and particularly intelligence) tests are not suitable for selecting senior managers primarily because factors other than mental ability tend to determine successful job performance at that level of operation.
- At a more overt political level, some analysts have also claimed that ability tests can possess unfair discriminatory features and have an adverse impact on the selection of members of particular social groups. Taylor, for instance, suggests that '[s]ome tests appear to disfavour members of lower socio-economic groups and some ethnic minorities, while others are biased against people whose first language is not English because of the requirement to complete them speedily' (2005: 233–234). Searle expresses her concern in a more focused way, questioning why there has not been more research on the reliability and validity of these selection instruments given the findings indicating 'differences between the performance of Caucasians and African-Americans' (2003: 165).

Testing psychological disposition

Like ability, **psychological disposition** is also divided into different fields of study. The main areas include interests, motivation and values, and personality. Tests employed in these areas (see Exhibit 5-7) look to provide standardised, objective and structured measures that afford simple comparisons of individual applicants. Those assessing interests (e.g. the Rothwell-Miller Interest Inventory) are designed to gauge a person's preferences for specific types of work-related activity. Those measuring motivation and value (e.g. Gordon's Survey of Interpersonal Values and Tarleton's Motivational Styles Questionnaire) are used to map the 'drive' or likely commitment of candidates and to gauge their 'fit'

psychological disposition
Measures are tests of intellectual performance and are usually 'maximal tests' in the sense that 'they aim to find out what is the *best* the test-taker can do'.

within an organisation's culture. Personality assessments also aim to measure applicants' 'fit' along with their likely performance as a team member and their 'match' with the perceived ideal personality for the post. Of the three fields, it is personality assessments that have proven to be the most controversial. There have been disputes about the conception of personality itself and how it is tested (see Smith and Smith, 2005: Chapters 4, 15, 16) and the effectiveness of those tests (see the criticisms below). For some analysts (e.g. Blinkhorn and Johnson, 1990) and employers, the disputes are sufficient reason to avoid current personality assessments in selection procedures. For others, they are grounds for caution in both the application of tests and interpretation of results (Searle, 2003; Taylor, 2005). Figures quoted by the Industrial Relations Services Employment Review (2002) estimated that 26 per cent of employers used personality tests when choosing managers, while the most recent CIPD survey (2005a) indicated that 36 per cent of organisations employed this instrument in selection.

The dominant model of personality in current selection procedures (Cooper *et al.*, 2003; Smith and Smith, 2005) is the 'big five' trait-based framework developed from the conceptual work of McDougall and Norman (Digman, 1990), and the conceptual and methodological work of Eysenck and Cattell (Smith and Smith, 2005). It suggests there are five basic factors, or traits, on which personalities are built and that account for the differences between individuals. Based on Searle (2003: 207–208), these are:

1 emotional stability (measures of which assess the degree to which someone is susceptible to psychological distress)
2 extroversion–introversion (tests here gauge levels of sociability)
3 agreeableness (measures of which assess the extent to which individuals are philanthropic and avoid conflict)
4 conscientiousness (tests here gauge the degree to which individuals are well organised, concerned with meeting deadlines, and the making and implementation of plans)
5 openness to experience (measures of which assess the extent to which individuals are imaginative and show independence of judgement).

Type of test	Purpose
Interests	To identify applicants' preferences for specific types of work-related activity
Motivation and values	To ascertain what 'drives' applicants and what values they think are important; by using these tests, employers look to discover how suitable an applicant is for the job profile and how they might fit within the organisational culture
Personality assessments	To gauge and codify the personal characteristics of applicants in order to predict how well: ■ their personalities match that believed to be ideal for the job, and fit within the organisational culture ■ their disposition complements those of existing team members (Taylor, 2005)

Exhibit 5–7 Tests of psychological disposition

Even among the advocates of personality assessments, these five factors are not assumed to be equally relevant in all selection situations or for all occupations (see Barrick *et al.*, 2001) nor, therefore, are they uniformly strong in predicting job performance (Cooper *et al.*, 2003). Supporters of the tests do, however, see them as providing the basis, the 'building blocks of our personality and explain[ing] the differences between us' (Taylor, 2005: 236).

The uncertain atmosphere surrounding personality assessments has led to a largely solicitous HR literature (e.g. Marchington and Wilkinson, 2005; Taylor, 2005). Replete with warnings about poorly designed tests, the dangers of using untrained analysts to interpret them and unscrupulous test suppliers, it looks to practical guidance from the CIPD and the British Psychological Society (BPS). Both these sources stress the need to train staff in the implementation and interpretation of these tests (to level B of the BPS certificate of competence), urge caution in the inferences drawn from them and recommend that the tests feature as part of a multi-instrument selection process. In their present state of development, their primary role is to enable a more complete picture of an applicant than would otherwise be possible (CIPD, 2005d).

Advantages of tests of psychological disposition

Supporters of the use of tests of psychological disposition maintain that they:

- bring greater objectivity to selection than that afforded by traditional selection methods (Income Data Services, 2004)

- offer employers insights into their candidates that are not available using interviewing, application forms and references

- supply higher predictive validity than the traditional methods

- are relatively easy to use, by a trained administrator, allowing structured comparisons of individuals.

Disadvantages of tests of psychological disposition

Critics of the use of these tests:

- question whether individual jobs can usefully be analysed in terms of more or less desirable personality traits and, relatedly, whether there are ideal personalities that correspond to particular jobs (Newell, 2005)

- ask if a questionnaire that takes 30 to 60 minutes to complete can provide sufficient information about an individual's personality to make meaningful inferences about their suitability for a job

- maintain that the data on which inferences are based are open to faking and distortion by applicants seeking to create a better image and increase their chances of selection (Arthur *et al.*, 2001)

- argue that their predictive validity, although higher than that of traditional methods, is nonetheless relatively low – particularly when compared with ability testing (Robertson and Smith, 2001)

- express concern that some assessments of disposition, particularly those of personality, could discriminate against particular groups, most notably ethnic minorities and women (Newell and Shackleton, 2001; Searle, 2003)

- maintain that initial investment costs are very high for what, essentially, is a supplementary selection instrument.

Online testing

The high initial investment costs for tests of both ability and psychological disposition have led many organisations to seek economies from the outset and opt for an online version of psychological testing. This has particularly been the case with commercial organisations with large numbers of applicants. The perceived benefits include the following.

- **Greater flexibility** for both the organisation and applicants. Applicants can complete their tests at any time and anywhere. Asking them to complete the tests alongside an online application form gives employers access to more information on which to base their short-listing or screening decisions.

- **Time and cost savings.** Without the need for test administrators or finding suitable test venues, the costs of testing and time involved can be greatly reduced. In addition, tests can often be scored automatically, again giving organisations and candidates access to results almost immediately.

- **Improving test content.** Using online technology allows employers to introduce multimedia items into the selection process, permitting both more interactive tests and virtual office tests that are more closely linked to the actual work environment than paper-based methods.

- **Better information management.** Storing test information on computers or CD-Roms provides a much more efficient way of recording test results. Databases make it easier to search and access candidate data, while email technology allows results to be quickly and easily communicated.

- **Feedback.** A number of online tests produce computer-driven narratives that can be supplied to applicants as feedback (Income Data Services, 2004).

The potential drawbacks of online testing include the following.

- **The integrity of candidates' responses.** A major issue confronting employers using online testing is how to ensure that candidates are not cheating (i.e. that they are completing the test themselves and do not have access to reference materials). One way of checking is to re-test those applicants that successfully complete the online screening, although this would clearly counter at least some of the gains of moving to online testing in the first place.

- **Security concerns.** Some employers fear that online tests compromise data security.

- **Regulating test conditions.** Although online tests allow greater standardisation of the instructions given to candidates, test users have no control over the test environment. To help increase consistency, the test instructions should inform candidates of the preferred test conditions (e.g. work area, lighting and noise levels, minimum PC specifications and how the computer should be set up (Income Data Services, 2004).

Assessment centres

assessment centre
Refers to the process of employing a range of work-related tests to assess the aptitude and skills of a group of candidates applying for a position.

The term assessment centre does not refer to a single selection method or to a specific location, but to the process of employing a range of work-related tests to assess the aptitude and skills of a group of candidates applying for a position. It is a multi-method, evidence-based, approach to selection that involves '[T]he utilisation of a number of different selection methods over a specified time period (typically one to four days) in order for multiple assessors to assess many candidates on a range of identified competences or behavioural dimensions' (Newell and Shackleton, 2001: 127).

First used during the Second World War as a tool for selecting military officers, assessment centres have grown in popularity in the UK, particularly for graduate and management selection. In the CIPD recruitment survey (2005a), some 34 per cent of sampled organisations said that they used them for selection purposes (41 per cent in the case of public-sector organisations). Among graduate recruiters, they are used by 52 per cent of employers, while in large organisations with more than 10,000 employees the figure rises to 95.2 per cent (Suff, 2005). Employers' support for assessment centres is in large measure because they allow them to get closer to the selection ideal of observing how applicants *perform* the sort of tasks actually found in the job for which they are being assessed (Income Data Services, 2005a).

Among the exercises utilised for this purpose are group work, written exercises, role-plays and presentations – these are often complemented by interviews and psychological tests (see Exhibit 5-8).

Group work

Group work includes leaderless group discussions, projects and business simulations, and is designed to assess effective communication, problem-solving abilities and interpersonal and

Types of exercise	Competencies and skills
Group exercise (e.g. leaderless projects and discussions, business simulations)	Effective communication; creative problem-solving; leadership; team working; flexibility; organisation skills
Written exercises (e.g. in-tray exercise)	Planning and organising ability; time management; reading and assimilating information; delegation skills; problem analysis; prioritising; decision-making
Presentations (e.g. planned or unplanned)	Effective communication; persuasion skills; ability to work under pressure; knowledge of their topic or the field of presentation
Role-playing (e.g. irate customer exercise, disciplining staff, counselling staff, negotiating with hard-bargaining suppliers, fact-finding interviews)	Communication, listening and interpersonal skills; ability to react in a changing situation; negotiation and problem-solving skills
Complementary activities	
Psychological testing	Usually personality tests, often supplemented with numerical and verbal reasoning exercises
Interviews	Employed for a range of purposes from de-briefings to seeking candidates' assessments of their previous work experience and performance

Exhibit 5–8 Types of assessment centre exercise and their targeted competencies and skills

leadership skills. An example of this type of exercise involves setting a group of applicants a problem to resolve in a specified time period, and monitoring the process of how they set about this task and produce a solution. HM Prison Service, for instance, has used a problem-solving group exercise for its management applicants in which each is allocated an 'employee' for whom they have to negotiate a fair proportion of the organisation's training budget while finding an overall distribution of funds that is acceptable to the rest of the group (Income Data Services, 2005a: 4).

Written exercises

Written exercises are typically individual tests that involve giving candidates a data set and/or information pack about a particular problem or situation, and asking them to produce a written report containing their analysis and recommendations for action. This form of general exercise is seen to provide selectors with a valuable assessment of both analytic and written communication skills. A specific variant of it is the so-called 'in-tray' or 'in-basket' exercise. Here, candidates are given a range of information sources, such as memos, letters, records and other documentary items, and may be asked, for example, to plan and organise their day, prioritise and/or delegate work or respond to enquiries. Some organisations have modernised it by making it an online or 'e-tray' exercise, adding 'a level of reality ... by providing candidates with their own PCs and telephones and simulating the exercise in "real-time"' (Income Data Services, 2005a: 5).

Presentations

Presentations are used to assess applicants' verbal communication skills, their ability to work under pressure and their persuasiveness. The subject matter for this type of activity can range from topics that are highly job specific through to topics of personal interest. For example, an accountant may be asked to present her/his findings on the management accounts or talk about corporate social responsibility, or alternatively, be asked to do a presentation on a topic of their choosing. How much time applicants are given to organise their presentations can also vary. Thames Water advises candidates days or weeks in advance of their assessment centre, whereas applicants to HM Prison Service get just 25 minutes to choose and prepare a topic (Income Data Services, 2005a).

Role-plays

Role-plays offer assessors the opportunity to look at candidates in the kind of situation the latter might encounter in the job for which they are applying. Typical scenarios include asking the candidate to undertake a performance appraisal with an underachieving employee, dealing with an irate customer and negotiating with a hard-bargaining supplier. An assessor usually plays the other role, although some companies bring in actors in the hope of achieving a greater consistency of performance.

Complementary activities

Although not essential, some assessment centres also incorporate psychological tests and interviews as part of their portfolio. Where psychological tests are used, they tend to be personality assessments supplemented by numerical and verbal reasoning tests. In the case of interviews, they range from de-briefings that take place after specific exercises through to the more standard interviews seeking to address candidates' evaluations of their past experience and performance.

The number and types of exercise are always tailored to the job in question, but the assessment centre literature (e.g. Income Data Services, 2005a; Suff, 2005) suggests that, as a general rule, each key skill or competency (as described in the job and person specifications) should be assessed in at least two different exercises and, in each instance, by at least two assessors.

The strengths and limitations of assessment centres

Assessment centres are considered to have a number of advantages over the other modern selection instruments as well as their traditional counterparts. Among the benefits for employers are:

- the consistency and enhanced objectivity they are considered to bring to the selection process through the use of trained assessors employing multiple methods and an evidence-based approach (Income Data Services, 2005a)
- the comprehensive picture of applicants' skills that these methods provide
- the predictive value arising from the use of work-simulation exercises
- their flexibility as selection instruments – 'They are not purchased "off-the-shelf" like [many] psychological tests, and are not as time-restricted as interviews. There is therefore plenty of scope to introduce exercises that are of specific relevance to the job and the organisation involved' (Taylor, 2005: 244)
- the opportunity to convey realistic expectations of the nature and activities of the job.

The potential drawbacks of assessment centres include:

- the expense; 'An effective centre requires a considerable investment in time and resources – the design process alone can take months. The administrative workload can also be heavy and centres are particularly demanding in terms of the time required from assessors, many of whom are relatively senior managers' (Income Data Services, 2005a: 2)
- the opaque nature of how the results of individual exercises are turned into an overall decision; for example, the so-called 'wash-up' process, the aggregation of assessors' candidate scores, can be highly political; it is rarely a straightforward calculative process and much more a meeting of assessors in which the power of individual members prevails
- the quality of training of the assessors, and their ability to assess specific competencies within overall task performance.

However, when these drawbacks are set against the cost of making the wrong recruitment decision, the substantial investment required may seem more reasonable.

Making the appointment: cognisance of the legal framework

Having made the decision on who to appoint and an offer (verbal or written) to the successful candidate, it is then incumbent upon employers to undertake a further set of related activities. It is important, for example, that all the documents pertaining to the selection process are retained for 12 months. This is to enable the organisation:

- to respond to any requests for information under the Data Protection Act 1998 or, where appropriate, the Freedom of Information Act 2000

- to deal with any complaints about the decision or its selection procedures; a number of agencies (e.g. the CRE and the DTI) advise employers to record and store all relevant details, such as their shortlisting schemes, the scores from tests or assessment centres, the interview schedule, interviewers' notes and their ranking of each candidate, discussions and decisions.

Once the offer is accepted by the successful applicant, it becomes a legally binding agreement. While this can be agreed informally, a written statement is clearly of benefit to both parties, not least because it reduces the likelihood of future disputes. In practice, most employers provide a written **contract of employment**. The details of such contracts vary with the nature of the post, with the organisation and, where collective agreements apply, with the terms agreed with the relevant trades unions. For the majority of employees, their terms of engagement are a matter of individual negotiation subject to the employer's compliance with the relevant statute and common law (Lewis and Sargeant, 2004).

contract of employment
The legal contract between employer and employee.

Employers do, however, have a statutory duty to provide new employees with a written statement of **employment particulars** within two months of their start date. Their obligations in this respect are set out in the Employment Rights Act 1996, although in specifying individual terms and conditions, they must also take cognisance of other legal measures, the most important of which are listed in Exhibit 5-9. Collectively, these require employers to provide employees with a written statement detailing:

employment particulars
Details of duties and conditions the employee can expect from the organisation.

- the employer and employee's names
- the date from which the employee's period of continuous employment commenced
- the title of the job or a brief description of the employee's work
- the place of work
- the scale or rate of remuneration and the method of payment
- terms and conditions relating to hours of work and normal working hours
- terms and conditions relating to holiday entitlement and pay.

Equal Pay Act 1970

Rehabilitation of Offenders Act 1974

The Pension Schemes Act 1993

Employment Rights Act 1996

Asylum and Immigration Act 1996

Patents Act 1997

National Minimum Wage Act 1998

The Working Time Regulations 1998

Employment Act 2002

The Information and Consultation of Employees Regulations 2004

Exhibit 5-9 Key legislation relating to employment terms and conditions

In addition, they are also required to provide either in the written statement or in an accompanying document details of:

- the period of notice to be given by the employer and the employee
- the period for which any non-permanent employment is expected to continue or, if it is for a fixed term, the date when it is to end
- the terms and conditions relating to incapacity for work due to sickness or injury, including any sick pay provisions
- pensions and pension schemes
- any collective agreements that directly affect the terms and conditions of employment
- the length of time, the currency in which the salary will be paid, additional remuneration and benefits (e.g. flights home, schooling), and the terms and conditions for returning to work in the UK where an employee is required to work outside the UK for more than one month
- dismissal, disciplinary and grievance procedures.

In terms of good practice, many employers provide more detailed specifications either in the contract or in accompanying documents, such as, for instance, staff handbooks. Such documents cover particular organisational practices, including restrictive covenants protecting intellectual property, probationary periods, business travel and expenses, and Internet and email use. While these, as employment lawyers emphasise (Lewis and Sargeant, 2004), may not form part of the contract, they nonetheless frame the employment relationship. Ensuring that employees are fully aware of the terms and conditions of their employment and what is expected of them is thus a key element in successful selection. The major tool in this familiarisation process is the final phase of selection: induction.

Induction

Induction comes into play once the successful applicants have been chosen, offers made, and the contractual terms and start dates agreed. Its general purpose is 'to ensure the effective integration of staff into or across the organisation for the benefit of both parties' (CIPD, 2005e: 1). Starting a new job can clearly be stressful. New recruits need to learn about their employing organisation, employment conditions, their colleagues, line managers and 'the way things are done'. Induction provides the employer with the opportunity of welcoming new colleagues, giving them the information they require to operate in their new work environment and to support their acclimatisation. From an employer's or manager's perspective, it is a critical phase. Poor induction could wipe out all the potential selection gains, leading to:

induction
'To ensure the effective integration of staff into or across the organisation for the benefit of both parties.'

- discord within work teams
- low morale, particularly for new employees
- loss of productivity and, in extreme cases, the avoidable costs of finding further staff if the new recruits leave or are dismissed.

The latter is not a point to be underestimated, the CIPD recruitment survey (2005a) estimates that some 13 per cent of leavers had less than six months' service.

The nature of induction varies in content, length and ethos according to the size of the organisation and type of recruit. 'Good practice' guides (e.g. Acas, 2005; CIPD, 2005e) suggest that they should, at a minimum, include:

- details of the organisation's history, its products and services
- a site map/description, describing the location of different facilities
- an organisational orientation, showing how the employee(s) fit into team and wider organisational structures
- job requirements
- terms and conditions
- health and safety information – required by law under the Health and Safety at Work Act 1974.

Reid *et al.* (2004: 225–227) add two further items, suggesting that the portfolio should also include:

1 company rules and policies (e.g. disciplinary and grievance procedures, equal opportunities policies)
2 employee development opportunities, sports and social amenities, and other employee benefits.

How this information is conveyed will also vary. For small- and medium-sized organisations, induction might involve a combination of one-to-one discussions with senior and line managers, an information pack, staff handbook, job shadowing and perhaps the allocation of a mentor or 'buddy' over the first few weeks. In larger organisations there is a greater likelihood of a formal induction programme, over days or weeks, combining an induction event with classroom-based training, presentations from senior managers and existing staff, support literature (e.g. information pack, staff manuals and handbooks), job shadowing, mentoring and e-learning facilities such as the organisational intranet (see the 'Team task' on Arup at the end of this chapter).

The main advantages of formal induction programmes (Income Data Services, 2005b) are that they:

- enable a spread of information inputs over a longer period, allowing a more gradual assimilation by the new recruits
- enable economies of scale in terms of time and costs in dealing with group rather than individual inductions
- ensure a consistency of information and enable a common positive message to be conveyed in a variety of media
- facilitate the development of work relationships through team-building events and more informal socialising (CIPD, 2005e).

Among their potential drawbacks are that:

- good inductions are difficult and time-consuming to achieve (Taylor, 2005; 261)
- they can be impersonal and remote if they rely heavily on HR and senior managers rather than colleagues and line managers (Industrial Relations Services, 2003)
- there is a continual danger of information overload if the induction programme is too intensive

- they can raise expectations beyond that which the organisation and/or the specific job can deliver, leading to low morale or disillusionment
- recruits may well vary in what they need from induction programmes, so putting everyone through a standardised programme could well be counterproductive (Taylor, 2005: 262).

Whether it's a matter of inappropriate programmes or simply negligence, the damage that poor induction can do means that organisations should regularly:

- review what they think new starters need
- attempt to tailor induction programmes where possible and appropriate
- deliver them in the right way and according to the right time scale.

Summary

- This chapter has focused on a core element of HRM: the use of effective selection instruments. Given the manifold costs of an inappropriate appointment, it is clearly important that HR advisers are aware of the relative merits and drawbacks of the selection tools available to them.
- To this end the chapter has outlined the main components of the traditional selection process and reviewed contemporary selection instruments such as bioprofiling, psychological testing and assessment centres.
- As should be clear from the discussion, none of these is problem free.
- Some, however, are seen to possess greater predictive validity than others, or to be more appropriate for certain types of job or levels of employment.
- They also vary in the costs, training and time involved.
- Employers are therefore faced with a series of decisions as to what best meets their operational exigencies and sustains their competitive edge within a complex legislative framework.

Personal development

1 **Understand the selection process.** Define the term 'selection' in your own words and summarise why it is a core HRM task. How would you explain the concept of 'predictive validity' to a colleague? Can you identify the different methods of selection? Reflect on the ways in which an organisation can ensure that it operates a fair selection process.

2 **Develop an understanding of how interviews are conducted.** What are the main constituents of (a) traditional and (b) contemporary methods of selection? How would you account for the emergence of the latter?

3 **Identify when psychological tests can be used.** What are the main types of question used in structured interviews? Using the typology provided on pp. 145–146, draw up an interview schedule for a sales representative for a pharmaceutical company. To further your understanding of these types of questions, look at several graduate traineeship application forms (either online or via your institution's Careers Service). How would you classify the questions used? How would you draw on your own experience to answer them?

4 **Identify the limitations of psychological testing.** What are the main types of psychological test used by selectors? Review the differing perspectives on the testing of psychological dispositions. Why do you think such tests are so controversial? Summarise in your own words what is meant by maximal and typical response tests, giving examples of each and the types of employment for which they might be used as selection tools.

5 **Identify how selection tools are used in organisations.** Revisit your responses to question 1 of the 'Personal development' section at the end of Chapter 1. Think again of an organisation with which you are familiar, either through your own employment or that of a friend or a member of your family. What selection tools does it utilise? Were you (or they) aware of the selection criteria for the post? Was an application form required? How was it structured? Did you/they also submit a CV? Were you/they interviewed? Who conducted the interview and what types of question were asked? Were references required? When and in what form? Looking back at the experience, how would you/they evaluate it? In the light of your reading of this chapter what could have been done to improve the process?

6 **Identify an organisation's selection strategy.** Thinking about a workplace with which you are familiar, consider whether it uses contemporary methods of selection. If so, which ones and for what type of job? How would you explain its selection strategy?

7 **Understand how interviewees can improve their performance.** Have you, or someone you know, ever been unsuccessful in your application for a job? Were you given feedback as to why you were unsuccessful and how you might have improved your chances? Consider why organisations are often advised to provide feedback, particularly if they use assessment centres as a method of selection.

8 **Identify effective induction techniques.** Have you ever attended an induction programme, either as an employee or a student? How effective did you find the arrangements? Think about your ideal job. If you were about to start it, what information and support would help you to settle in?

❓ Discussion questions

1 What are the most important aspects to consider when designing an application form? What questions would you place on an application form for a graduate traineeship?

2 What are the advantages and disadvantages of asking applicants to complete an application form rather than submit a CV?

3 What are the main drawbacks of face-to-face interviews? Why, despite these drawbacks, have they retained their popularity as a selection tool? How might organisations seek to maximise their effectiveness?

4 What are the main ways in which references might be sought? Which would you recommend and why?

5 In what circumstances would you recommend the use of bioprofiling in the selection process?

6 What are the main types of ability test? What types of job could these tests be used for? What are their main merits and drawbacks as selection tools?

7 Why would a selector want to know about an applicant's personality? What problems do personality tests present? How can these be minimised?

8 What selection criteria and methods would you recommend to an NHS Hospital Trust wishing to recruit an HR adviser? Why?

9 Draw up a business case for induction, and design an induction checklist for (a) management-level staff and (b) sales assistants in a supermarket chain. How would you organise an induction for each group?

10 What are the main areas of law affecting selection and appointment? How does an organisation ensure that its selection and appointment processes are within the law?

🔑 Key concepts

selection, *p. 139*	biographical profiling, *p. 151*
traditional selection, *p. 140*	psychological testing, *p. 153*
predictive validity, *p. 140*	ability, *p. 155*
biographical questioning, *p. 145*	psychological disposition, *p. 157*
situational questioning, *p. 145*	assessment centre, *p. 160*
behavioural questioning, *p. 145*	contract of employment, *p. 164*
stress questioning, *p. 146*	employment particulars, *p. 164*
contemporary selection, *p. 151*	induction, *p. 165*

Individual task

Purpose To understand the role and constituents of an assessment centre, and the issues confronted in designing and using it in the selection process.

Time 60 minutes

Procedure Construct an assessment centre for UK firefighters, summarising and justifying the selection instruments you would employ.

Team task

Graduate Induction at Arup

Arup, the consulting engineering group, recruits some 200 graduates each year, half of whom are destined for its different European operations. For their induction, this European-based cohort are expected to undertake:

- a three-day general event, supported by
- a skills week
- a local induction, and
- online induction material.

The three-day event is devoted to two goals: developing an understanding of the company, its history, global operations and values; and team-building activities designed to facilitate work networks that will help the graduates through both their first few months and subsequent Arup careers. The introduction to the company has involved the chairman of Arup Group welcoming the new recruits to the event and describing the global nature of the company and its values. The team-building activities have centred on problem-solving. The cohort is divided into different groups, each with a mix of engineering disciplines. Each group is set a construction task (e.g. building a bridge from planks and barrels or making a hot-air balloon to a client's brief). The supportive environment in which these tasks are undertaken is expected to enable the formation of social networks that are going to be of benefit to both the individuals and the company.

Following the three-day event, the graduates attend one of six skills weeks. This predominantly classroom-based element of the induction looks to provide the graduates with the means of translating their academic engineering base into a practical project-based contribution through the acquisition of the software, tools and processes employed in Arup: 'Typically, the week is built around a specific project seen through from beginning to end to put their learning into context' (Income Data Services, 2005b: 26).

After their skills week, the new recruits are allocated to posts in Arup's European offices. The local HR managers are responsible for ensuring that the core workplace induction activities (e.g. health and safety) are covered. Once they have settled in their new locations, the recruits are then encouraged to take some responsibility for the furtherance of their education and training at their own pace. The company provides a 'Welcome to Arup' website that has an array of information sources on company values, and information on pay and benefits. The website also provides access to e-learning modules and in-house courses.

Source: Adapted from Income Data Services (2005b: 26).

Discussion questions

1 If you were responsible for designing an induction scheme for graduate recruits at a multinational legal services firm, what lessons could you draw from this case study?

2 What would you do differently?

3 How would you convince senior managers of the importance of having an induction scheme?

4 How would you evaluate it?

Chapter SEVENTEEN

Remuneration and reward

The opening vignette reflects one of the debates around pay and reward today. Although the government sets the national minimum wage, many people realise that it is not always a living wage and, to attract the best employees, they need to take action.

The rise of the living wage

HSBC has become the second big bank to agree to pay cleaning staff a 'living wage'. Could this signal the start of a trend and the end of the national minimum wage?

Last month HSBC followed Barclays to become the second big east London employer to agree to pay cleaning staff a 'living wage'. The living wage is being campaigned for by community action group The East London Communities Organisation (Telco), and trades unions including Unison. Telco commissioned research to find out the level required to enable a family of two parents and two children, with one parent working full-time and one part-time, to live above the poverty line without state benefits. The initial level was set at £6.30, and is now £6.70 an hour.

The concept seems to be gathering pace. The latest move has seen Ken Livingstone, Mayor of London, agreeing to set up a living wage unit at the Greater London Authority (GLA) and set a £7.70 per hour living wage level for those employed in the GLA's workforce.

These moves have potentially far-reaching consequences for employers with outsourcing contracts. The packages set a new standard for cleaning contractors. And by providing better basic pay, plus other benefits such as pensions, holiday and sick pay, these organisations have made it clear that they see good employment conditions for contractors as their responsibility.

This was not HSBC's stance earlier this year. In January 2004, Adrian Russell, public relations officer at the bank, said: 'We are sympathetic towards Telco's ultimate objective, which is better lives for the people they represent, but we cannot support the way they are trying to achieve it. We support the minimum wage, which is £4.50, but believe it is for the government, not HSBC, to set that level.'

Indeed, when cleaner Abdul Durrant appealed to HSBC's chairman, Sir John Bond, to renegotiate the contract with cleaning contractor OCS, Bond replied: 'We are sympathetic but we are running a business and to do that we have to get the best deal for our shareholders. What OCS pays staff is its own matter.'

But the organisation's most recent announcement shows how far its standpoint has moved. 'Corporate social responsibility (CSR) runs through much of what we do as an organisation. Certainly, we wish to be viewed as a good neighbour and a responsible employer and purchaser of contracts,' said an HSBC spokesperson in June 2004. 'We are happy to support the living wage and what OCS is willing to do for their cleaning staff. They deserve credit for listening to their staff and being prepared to make changes.'

Barclays told *PM* that the bank recognised the business benefits of paying a living wage. 'It is a CSR issue in that we want to be fair across the board, but it's also an HR issue because we want to attract the right people as well. It's about getting the right people to work for us,' said spokesman George Hulbert.

Paul Sellers, policy adviser at the TUC, believes the establishment of the living wage by the Mayor's office moves the campaign to a new level. 'It should enable the concept to spread to other parts of the country,' he said.

Barclays is already extending the deal across its London branches, with plans to go UK-wide before long, but Sellers believes that, while the initiative is so new, the private sector may be worried about how the deal will go down with shareholders looking for the biggest return on their investment – usually reflected in employing the cheapest labour.

'Once the benefits can be seen and the case can be defended against any shareholder criticism, companies will be keen to advertise the living wage as a real part of their CSR armoury,' said Sellers.

And he believes that this will come very soon. The business case for the living wage is that it brings a better standard of employee who will be more satisfied with his or her work. This leads to lower staff turnover and less absenteeism. Productivity levels rise and the higher morale means a greater commitment to the company.

So does this mean, as some campaigners have argued, that a national minimum wage is redundant?

Telco believes that the latest developments, particularly Livingstone's active involvement, will lead to the minimum wage becoming redundant in London at least.

'The Mayor's action should ensure that the minimum wage becomes irrelevant, with all good employers in London following his civic example. It will be up to the Mayor to then use his procurement powers to police the living wage,' said Neil Jameson, a co-ordinator with Telco.

▶   He believes that the living wage is now seen as a real social responsibility issue. 'People are looking at what low pay does to British people in comparison to the effects of, say, bad labour practices on children making trainers in Thailand,' said Jameson.

Telco is keen for the issue to move up the CSR agenda. The next stage would see firms agree to sign up to a CSR contract of employment. Some companies, such as Richer Sounds, an independent UK hi-fi retailer, have already shown interest. Telco also says that Stephen Timms, the minister responsible for CSR, has met with them and given his support to the project.

As a result the group plans to draw up, with the involvement of these stakeholders, a three-tier benchmark of low, middle and good performance in employment conditions of support services contracts. This would include wages, at least some employer contribution to pensions, sick pay, bank holidays and training.

This, combined with the examples of HSBC and Barclays, suggests that a living wage is now seen as a CSR policy that other firms, particularly in the financial services sector in London, will consider adopting in the not too distant future.

Source: Paul Donovan, *People Management*, 15 July 2004, p. 14.
Reproduced with permission of *People Management* and Paul Donovan.

Discussion questions

1 Who do you think should take responsibility for ensuring that employees are paid a living wage?

2 As an HR manager, how could you persuade senior managers about the benefits of a living wage as opposed to paying the minimum wage?

Definitions of remuneration and reward

Remuneration and reward are an important part of the HR function and can link directly to the organisation's strategic goals. Many organisations view compensation as one of the strategies that drives their business. The remuneration and reward package offered can not only help to attract and retain employees, it can also be used as a powerful tool to motivate staff, which in turn can increase competitiveness, profitability and competitive advantage. **Reward** can be either monetary or non-monetary, and is something that is given or received in exchange for services. In the case of employees, this means being rewarded for work performed. **Remuneration** refers to the monetary aspect of rewarding an employee for their performance. Monetary rewards are clearly important, as few people can afford to work for no pay; however, it is also important that any remuneration is fair and equitable. Yet money does not necessarily make people work harder. In other words, it is not necessarily a motivator.

reward
Compensation given to an employee in return for performance. It can be monetary, in the form of remuneration, or non-monetary.

remuneration
The monetary aspect of rewarding an employee for performance.

It is often the non-monetary awards that employees value more, such as career and social awards. Opportunities for job security, career growth, praise and recognition may be far more important to an employee than a high income in a boring, repetitive or undervalued job.

Therefore, it is important for employees to be aware of the total reward system that can be offered to an employee, as can be seen in Exhibit 6-1.

Monetary compensation is important, however, as it ensures that:

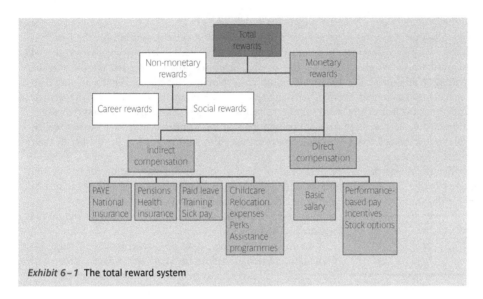

Exhibit 6 – 1 The total reward system

- the pay is sufficient to attract the right people to the organisation
- the pay is perceived as equitable so that good employees can be retained
- the rewards ensure that the organisation can maintain its competitive advantage
- the rewards are available to increase productivity and profitability
- legal obligations are met, such as equal pay for equal work
- the organisational pay structure is clearly defined and transparent to avoid criticism that could lead to legal action.

The appropriate monetary compensation can ensure harmony in several aspects of the organisation and can also have wider implications. Through the external environment it ensures that employees can be attracted to the organisation and good relationships with employee unions can be maintained while ensuring that pay is competitive. In the internal environment, pay can be linked to increased performance through performance-related pay, which can link into the business strategy. The human resource functions of job analysis, recruitment and selection, and performance management can all be linked to the type of monetary rewards on offer.

Payment structure

How much to pay staff is an important consideration for managers. In most organisations pay, benefits and staffing costs often total 23 per cent of income and, in some organisations, this can be as much as 50 per cent. This is especially true in organisations requiring a high level of personal service, such as the hotel industry.

For employees, the wages they are paid affects their standard of living and also their status in the eyes of their community, therefore it is important for pay decisions to be managed carefully. Employees also evaluate their pay decisions against awards made to other employees in an organisation.

When deciding pay levels the organisation also needs to consider the competition in the marketplace for the product or services it is providing and the competition for the labour it requires. The competition for the product means that organisations have to compete on several dimensions, such as quality, service and price. Therefore, production costs are likely to be important. If an organisation has higher labour costs than its competitors then it will more than likely have to charge higher prices for its product, which means it could be less competitive. Competition for labour is also an important factor, as organisations have to compete against each other for the best employees. Organisations that fail to offer competitive salaries will be unable to attract and retain the best employees, which in turn may affect the quality of their product or service.

When deciding what to pay, organisations need to analyse the competition for labour and decide whether it is in their interests to pay above the market average in an attempt to attract the top talent, at the risk of adding to their costs. Information about pay per sector can be obtained from the Equal Opportunities Commission and on the website statistics.gov.uk.

pay structures
The criteria used to establish the worth of a job and how much should be paid.

One method of establishing **pay structures** is through job evaluation, which, according to Acas (2003), is the process of 'determining the relative worth of a job to the organisation'.

The CIPD (2004a) suggests that job evaluation is used when:

- determining pay and grading structures
- ensuring a fair and equal pay system
- deciding on benefits provision (e.g. bonuses and cars)
- comparing rates against the external market
- undergoing organisational development in times of change
- undertaking career management and succession planning
- reviewing all jobs post-large-scale change, especially if roles have been changed.

Job evaluation needs to be based on detailed job descriptions, as discussed in Chapter 4.

job evaluation
The process of measuring the size and significance of a job in an organisation.

points rating
A system of breaking a job into key elements, factors and components, and awarding points based on the complexity of tasks.

factor comparison
A system of basing a job on an assessment of factors involved.

Job evaluation is important in ensuring that a fair payment system is in place, which is transparent and can be communicated to all employees. When there are no pay structures in place, employees may see themselves as being treated unfairly if they are paid less than their colleagues. This will be discussed in more detail later in this chapter.

Two methods of job evaluation are **points rating** and **factor comparison**. Points rating is the most commonly used method and breaks the key elements of the job into factors, which are in turn broken down into components. Each factor is allocated points according to the level needed for the job. The more demanding the job, the higher the number of points it is allocated, and therefore the higher the pay. Examples of factors that are measured frequently can be seen in Exhibit 6-2.

The factor comparison, on the other hand, is based on an assessment of factors without the allocation of points. The use of factor analysis is not as widespread as that of points rating, as most jobs have to be done on an individual basis, while the allocation of points allows a large number of jobs to be ranked at one time.

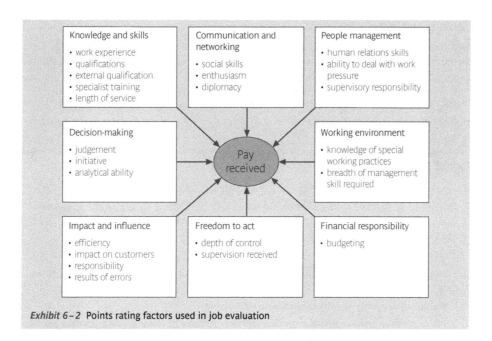

Exhibit 6 – 2 Points rating factors used in job evaluation

Other methods of job evaluation, which are seen as less objective but cheaper to implement, are job ranking, paired comparisons and job classification.

job ranking
Placing jobs in order of importance in a hierarchy. Pay is then matched to task difficulty.

- **Job ranking** involves ranking jobs in order of their importance to the organisation. This would include level of difficulty and their value to the organisation. Sometimes these are clearly defined, such as in a hairdressing salon – the stylist who cuts hair would be paid more than the person who does only washing and drying, however the latter may be paid more than the person who is on reception. Judgements are made about the skill level, task complexity and level of autonomy used to do the job. The jobs are then ranked in a hierarchy, which is made transparent to all employees.

paired comparison
Uses a ranking form to allocate points to jobs, which are then compared to other jobs.

- **Paired comparisons** uses a ranking form to allocate points to a job to compare each job with others in an organisation. It is more transparent than job ranking but takes longer. When comparing jobs with each other, two points will be allocated if a job is considered of higher value, one if of the same value and none if of lower value. The points are then added up and an overall ranking given.

job classification
Also known as job grading, based on the requirements of the job and levels of responsibility.

- **Job classification** (also known as job grading) involves allocating jobs to an agreed number of grades (usually between four and eight) based on the requirements of the job and levels of responsibility.

Broad banding

Broad banding refers to classifying jobs into a broad banded pay structure, with a large gap between the bottom and top rates of pay. Pay progression through each band is often related to performance or market pay rates. Broad banding is used when organisations decide to redesign or modernise pay structures, and want to address recruitment and retention difficulties by grouping jobs into a job family or moving employees to a team-based approach to work. This enables related tasks to be grouped together and employees to be encouraged to move through the band by acquiring new skills.

Armstrong (2000) suggests using the following 12 steps for developing a broad banded pay structure.

1 Reach an agreement that it is the most appropriate pay structure for progression.

2 Provisionally estimate the number of bands that will be required by analysing the organisation's structure and the various roles carried out at each level.

3 Decide on the width of bands, the degree of overlap (if any), the anchor points and pay zones.

4 Carry out a job evaluation exercise to define band boundaries, and revise the band structure as appropriate.

5 Conduct a pay survey to establish market rates.

6 Position roles in bands (singly or in clusters) on the basis of relative size as established by job evaluation results and market.

7 Decide on the basis for progressing pay within zones and for adjusting pay levels following a change in role.

8 Decide on the role of job evaluation in defining band boundaries, guiding band positioning decisions and dealing with new roles or equal value queries.

9 Examine existing rates of pay for employees, identify any increases and establish any cases where pay protection may be necessary.

10 Draw up procedures for managing the structure, including the allocation of roles to bands. Include the use of job evaluation, the conduct of pay reviews, fixing salaries for recruitment purposes or following a change in role, maintaining data on market rates and the use of performance management processes to assist in making pay review decisions.

11 Brief and train managers on the new structure and their roles in managing pay.

12 Communicate to staff the details of the new structure and how it affects them.

The advantages of broad banding are that it is more suited to flatter and leaner organisations, giving more scope for career development and more flexibility for organisations. It can simplify pay systems by grouping more jobs within the same band, which can reduce problems of inequity. It is ideal for linking with performance, which means it can in turn be linked to strategic goals.

However, there are also disadvantages with such a system, in that it needs to be carefully monitored to ensure awards are not made on the subjectivity of managers, and to guard against discrimination. Rates of pay also need to be monitored continually to ensure that they are in keeping with market rates, especially if broad banding is in response to recruitment and selection problems. There is also a resource issue, as time is needed to train managers in its implementation to ensure that it is not seen as producing inequity.

Job families

Job families group jobs with similar characteristics into categories. The job families reflect different levels of responsibility and have an individual pay structure.

Jobs within families can be linked by:

- occupation
- nature of work
- function.

The CIPD (2000) identified four key reasons as to why organisations use job families. These are:

1 to map career paths
2 to achieve greater flexibility
3 to identify groups of employees that can be linked to the market
4 to provide rewards based on personal contribution and progress.

The distinction between job families and traditional grading schemes is that each job family has completely separate pay arrangements and is allowed to set its own pay and grading bands. This means that separate families are able to compete with market expectations. For example, the accountancy department of an organisation would have a different pay structure from that of the purchasing department and this would reflect the market expectations of employees in that department. Job families can, therefore, be linked to broad banding and the market: employers have the scope to place jobs in families that reflect market conditions and provide a broad banded pay structure that allows the employee to progress either through further training or improved performance.

Market competition

Organisations need to be able to sell their goods or services at a competitive price in the marketplace. Therefore, the cost of labour will be an important factor in developing pay levels. Organisations with higher labour costs than their competitors will have to charge higher prices for their products. For example, a company selling family cars with a labour cost of 30 per cent will either need to sell more cars than a company with labour costs of 25 per cent, or will have to be prepared to make less profit. The loss of profit may be unacceptable to shareholders, which could mean that the organisation's value decreases. Therefore, it is important for managers to ensure that they get it right. At the other end of the scale managers also need to ensure that they do not pay too little, otherwise they may be unable to attract staff.

Deciding what to pay

Since employees are a resource it is important for managers to ensure that they are able to get a return on their investment. Pay policies are one of the most important resource tools available to HR managers to enable them to encourage desirable behaviours and discourage undesired ones. Therefore, it is important that managers evaluate their reward system not just in terms of cost but also in terms of return on investment: in other words, how they attract, retain and motivate a high-quality workforce.

Although organisations need to take into account external competition they still have some discretion in setting their pay levels. Deciding whether to pay higher or lower than average, or average wages needs to be decided at strategic level. Paying above the market average has the benefits of being able to attract and retain top talent, which should lead to an effective and productive workforce despite the extra cost. To determine how beneficial paying higher wages could be when compared to the higher costs, researchers Lambert and Larcker (1989) developed the efficiency wage theory, which compares wages paid and productivity. They found that, where organisations need highly skilled employees or where employees are responsible for managing themselves,

---

efficiency wage theory

The comparison of wages to productivity.

---

organisations may wish to pay an above-average wage as an incentive to maintain or improve performance. The theory suggests that employees who are paid more will want to retain their salary and will therefore work harder, although it should be remembered that pay is not the only motivator and the quality of the working environment is often more important than an increased pay packet.

Market surveys

---

benchmarking

Comparing aspects of performance with the same aspects in other organisations.

Pay surveys are a useful tool to enable organisations to benchmark their practices against those of the competition. Benchmarking is typically carried out through the use of pay surveys, which provide important insights into the average rates of pay for different sectors. When using surveys it is important to identify:

- which employers should be used as a comparison
- which jobs should be used for the comparison, and are they similar in function, level and market segmentation
- if different surveys are used, how are they applicable to the organisation concerned?

What organisations are paying may be only one side of the story. It is also useful to compare ratios such as turnover to employees and turnover to labour cost, although it should be remembered that different sectors are likely to have different labour ratios and therefore like should be compared with like.

Rate ranges

Many jobs in the public sector, such as nurses, teachers and clerical officers, are attached to a salary scale. The employee starts at a fixed point on the scale, often dependent on qualifications, experience and age. They then progress annually until they reach the top of the scale. Promotion usually enables them to move on to a different scale. The advantages of such schemes are that they are transparent, everyone knows what the scale is and colleagues of equal status will be paid the same. The disadvantage is that there is no incentive to work harder as extra effort is not rewarded with increased pay.

Both nurses and police enter at an initial level and receive incremental pay rises each year until they reach the top of their grade. They can move to different grades through examination and/or training and promotion. It is also interesting to note that, while both nursing and the police are funded by the public sector, there is a great discrepancy between the pay scales of jobs that have in the past been seen as traditional female jobs (nursing) and traditional male jobs (policing). These pay scales also demonstrate the value society places on such jobs. For example, a police constable commencing service in 2005 could expect to receive £19,803 while an auxiliary nurse would expect £10,375.

Some organisations are attempting to bridge the gap with enhanced pay for enhanced performance, usually linked to an appraisal system. There is considerable debate at the moment concerning public-sector pay reform, with government economists arguing for pay to be set at the local level in line with that of private companies. However, this is not always the case, with large national employers such as Barclays and Tesco often using nationally set pay scales but enhancing them in areas where there is a higher cost of living, such as London and the south-east.

Research by Hatchett (2004) suggests that there are several myths about how regional and national pay is set, as can be seen in Exhibit 6-3.

Payment concepts

When determining which payment system to use, an organisation needs to decide whether payment will be linked to the reward system or not. As all aspects of reward will ultimately be a cost to the organisation, the employer needs to decide whether the type of reward offered will lead to improved performance.

Myth 1

There is a significant amount of regional variation in pay outside London and the south-east. In fact, the average earnings data show that differences are minimal

Myth 2

Pay in large private-sector companies is set by myriad individual-level decisions, when in fact there are national structures and systems. Firms frequently often allow variation from the norm, under certain controls, but within defined systems and budgets

Myth 3

There is minimal influence on pay from collective bargaining, with most pay decisions set at management's discretion, based on local cost of living factors. In fact, unions have significant influence in large organisations

Myth 4

Local cost of living factors now outweigh skill levels or competencies. In fact, managers look at skill levels and grading across their organisations rather than just locally. There are complex versions of what might have been termed a 'rate for the job', whether set by job evaluation or job weight, or by sectoral or national benchmarking

Myth 5

Pay in the public sector is set by rigid national agreements, with no scope for flexible interpretation. In reality there is scope for local flexibility to deal with recruitment and retention issues, although these have not always been well funded. Some of the new measures in London, such as pay spines for school teachers, are an example. The recent report of the Local Government Pay Commission found there was adequate flexibility in local determination within a national framework

---

Exhibit 6–3 Myths about regional and national pay
Source: A. Hatchett, 'What next for local pay?', *People Management*, 12 February 2004, p. 15.

Traditional pay

Traditional pay follows the principles of scientific management developed by Taylor (1914) and discussed in more detail in Chapter 1. To Taylor, measuring work meant that the job could be broken down into steps that could be timed and rated for difficulty and expertise. This allowed pay to be linked directly to performance and became the basis of pay systems, especially for low-skilled manual labour. Managers had overall control, and pay would be linked to performance in an attempt to increase productivity. However, there were consequences for the social aspect of work, which was ignored by Taylor and often meant that the workforce became demotivated. This was characterised by Wood (2000), who felt that this type of performance-related pay could alienate the workforce and cause workers to disengage.

traditional pay
Pay linked to task complexity and completion time.

New pay

New pay is a term coined by Lawler (2000), and developed by Zingheim and Schuster (1995), popular in the USA. New pay involves using a combination of traditional pay and non-traditional elements such as skill-based pay and/or recognition for training and performance. This could mean that employees who are keen to develop their skills would be compensated. New pay can also include an element of variable pay, where employees are compensated for achieving organisational goals. It may be paid in the form of a cash bonus or share options.

new pay
Pay linked to personal development and task performance, and ultimately organisational goals.

According to Heery (1996), new pay should also be linked to both organisational performance and individual performance.

Heery (1996) characterises new pay as follows:

- an increased awareness of the need to link pay to organisational strategy
- the use of reward systems to reflect the flexibility of the organisation
- the use of variable pay based on both individual performance and personal development.

The concept of new pay is gaining ground in the USA, with many large companies now offering compensation packages that include elements of basic pay and variable pay, often linked to performance appraisal. Although not as popular in the UK some companies are now exploring its benefits.

Merit pay

Merit pay ties performance to add-on rewards. Often a base salary or hourly wage is provided and then an incentive or bonus offered, based on output. Output could be measured by volume, quality of production or cost savings. Sales representatives and call centre operators often have a basic salary with commission for sales or successful calls. To improve performance the rewards have to be seen to be achievable and desirable, and when tied to performance should be seen as motivational. However, where every employee is out to make their targets, merit pay can detract from teamwork, and there could also be the problem of employees' expectations differing from the employer's. Therefore, merit pay needs to be clear and measurable to avoid problems.

merit pay
Increasing pay by adding on rewards based on improved performance.

Bonuses and profit sharing

Compensation plans are often based on the overall performance of the organisation rather than an individual's performance. **Profit sharing** is one method of ensuring that employees are

profit sharing
A method of rewarding employees when an organisation does well, through issuing shares or paying bonuses.

rewarded when a company does well. One such organisation, the John Lewis Partnership, rewards business performance by distributing profits back to its employees. For John Lewis, profit sharing is a major part of the employee compensation package. To qualify for the scheme, employees need to have spent at least a year at the organisation; they are then eligible for a percentage

of profit. The John Lewis scheme makes the organisation one of the leading employers in the retail sector, and this is often reflected in the quality of customer service found in its stores.

bonuses
Additional rewards, usually monetary, paid to employees for improved organisational performance.

In many other organisations it is the director's compensation package that is loaded with **bonuses**, share options and other additions, often totalling several times the base salary, and incurring much criticism from employees and shareholders, although some companies do attempt to distribute rewards throughout

the workforce. Both Body Shop and Johnson & Johnson have devised schemes that compensate employees with share options. Research by Crystal (1995) into 15 high-performing and 15 low-performing companies suggested that there was no positive relationship with performance between directors who received substantial shares and those who did not.

When implementing share plans organisations need to be clear about how they are implemented. Fergusson (2003) suggests that they can do this by ensuring that:

- their share plans are operated in accordance with any employee contractual rights
- share plan discretions are exercised fairly and reasonably
- share plan rules have a full exclusion clause to rule out implied contractual rights
- all communications relating to share plans contain appropriate exclusion wording
- employment contracts do not give employees a contractual right to participate in share plans.

Gainsharing plans

Gainsharing encourages employees at all levels of the organisation to be responsible for

gainsharing
A pay-for-performance system that shares financial rewards among employees, based on performance improvements for the organisation.

improving organisational efficiency. Gainsharing plans link financial rewards for all employees to improvements in business performance. It is being seen as an increasingly popular motivational tool to improve performance and is summarised in Exhibit 6-4.

The idea is that gainsharing can make employees more cost conscious. One example of its success was found in the post room of a gas company, where an employee noticed that by changing delivery times to 10.30 am the next day instead of 10 am postal costs could be cut by 43 per cent. This resulted in a 2 per cent bonus for all employees.

HR managers also need to be aware of the impact of rewards on motivation, as a motivated workforce is likely to be more productive.

Survey research has revealed seven fundamental reasons why gainsharing continues to grow as a method of rewarding performance.

1 The basic design of jobs is undergoing a fundamental change from individuals into teams
2 Other performance-related pay systems often lead to disappointing results, especially those that reward individuals; this is because it is often difficult to untangle individual performance from the contributions of other employees
3 Gainsharing is easy to sell to top management because payouts are often modest and any gains are shared with the organisation
4 Gainsharing has a long history, which makes it easy to imitate successful plans
5 There are many specialist consultants who can help implement such plans
6 Gainsharing provides flexibility in choosing pay-off criteria from such diverse factors as profitability, labour costs, material savings, safety records, reject rates, meeting deadlines and customer satisfaction
7 Gainsharing complements the move towards participative management and employee involvement, as many plans incorporate committee structures to evaluate and act on employee recommendations

Exhibit 6–4 The popularity of gainsharing plans
Source: Adapted from Welbourne and Gomez-Mejia (1995).

Reward and motivation

Equity theory

The **equity theory** of motivation demonstrates what can happen when employees perceive their treatment to be inequitable. Equity theory puts forward the idea that motivation can be affected by perceived fairness or discrepancies between the contribution and rewards of employees. Adams (1965) popularised the idea that employees would work better if they perceive a fairness among effort, performance and reward relationships. There are two basic dimensions to the equity process: the ratio of personal outcomes to inputs, and external comparisons.

equity theory
The idea that motivation is moderated by perceived fairness or discrepancies between contributions and rewards.

Ratio of personal outcomes to inputs

People often think in terms of the ratio of their personal outcomes to work inputs. In other words, their perceptions of fair treatment depend on how they answer the question 'What is the pay-off to me in terms of money, status, benefits, recognition, promotion and job assignments, relative to my inputs of effort exerted, skills, job knowledge and actual task performance?' Although this applies to all aspects of employee reward, payment is a major factor in assessing equitable treatment.

External comparisons

Employees are also likely to compare their own outcomes and inputs ratio to those they perceive for other people doing comparable work. These comparisons are often made on three levels.

1 Comparisons to specific individuals: if two people are performing at the same level, then they could both expect to receive the same pay and recognition.

2 Comparisons to another reference group: workers in one department may compare themselves to workers in another department. If they are getting the same deal then treatment may be seen as equitable, however if their deal is perceived to be not as good, then it is seen as inequitable and is likely to lead to dissatisfaction.

3 Comparisons to general occupational groups: people may compare themselves to other people in similar positions in other organisations, or with those of a similar educational level. For example, nurses, who are now often university graduates, may compare themselves with accountants and find discrepancies in pay and conditions inequitable.

Equity issues are not just concerned with undercompensation, they can also apply when employees see themselves as being overcompensated compared with their reference group. Attempts are then made to close the equity gap. For example, those who feel they are overcompensated may increase their performance to justify increased compensation levels, while those who perceive themselves to be undercompensated may reduce effort, leave the organisation or find alternative comparisons.

Perceived fairness

Perceived fairness is a powerful motivational tool and involves a focus on both **distributive justice**, which refers to the amount of compensation an employee receives, and **procedural justice**, which refers to the perceived fairness of how managers arrive at decisions with regard to pay and reward. Folger and Konovsky (1989) identified that distributive satisfaction has a major influence on job satisfaction and attitudes to pay and promotion decisions, whereas procedural justice reflects more on organisational outcomes such as employee commitment and trust in management. When the distribution of rewards is perceived to be inequitable and the criteria to arrive at that distribution are believed to be unfair then mounting feelings of injustice are likely to arise at work, which can easily lead to resentment. Equity therefore begins with fair procedures, which means that the pay and reward system must be seen as transparent. Even if employees are dissatisfied with levels of pay, as long as the organisation's procedures treat them fairly they are more likely to remain committed to the organisation.

distributive justice
The perceived fairness of the amount and allocation of rewards among individuals.

procedural justice
The perceived fairness of the means used to determine the amount and distribution of rewards.

Expectancy theory

The **expectancy theory** of motivation focuses on a person's beliefs about the relationships among effort, performance and rewards for doing a job. Vroom (1982) suggests that people will be motivated to achieve a desired goal as long as they expect that their actions will achieve that goal.

Expectancy theory was originally expressed as a probability relationship among three variables labelled expectancy, instrumentality and valence.

expectancy theory
A theory of motivation based on a person's beliefs about effort–performance–outcome relationships.

- Expectancy is the probability from 0 to 1 that an individual believes his or her work effort directly affects the performance outcome of a task.

- Instrumentality is the probability from 0 to 1 that an individual anticipates that an attained level of task performance will have personal consequences.

- Valence is the value from positive to negative that a person assigns to the personal consequences that follow work performance.

Using expectancy theory, an employee will decide whether the expected reward is available and worth it. Wanous *et al.* (1980) argue that this measurement, while useful for psychologists, can not always be implemented by managers.

To help implement his theory Vroom developed the following equation:

$$\text{Force (F)} = \text{Valence (V)} \times \text{Expectancy (E)}$$

For employees to understand their motivations, according to Bloisi *et al.* (2003), they need to ask themselves three questions.

1 **Does how hard I work really affect my performance?** Vroom argues that, to be motivated, you must have a positive answer to this expectancy question. Employees need to believe that their personal efforts make a positive performance difference. The employee must have the capacity for internal attribution, or a willingness to take personal credit or blame for their performance. Positive task motivation begins when employees see the link between personal effort and task performance.

2 **Are personal consequences linked to my performance?** To answer this instrumentality question, you must believe that task performance results enable you to attain pay-offs. Increased motivation is possible when an employee perceives they will receive a positive personal consequence arising from satisfactory task performance.

3 **Do I value the consequences available to me?** Answers to this valence question will depend on how much you value a particular expected outcome or pay-off. If employees really do not care about the potential reward then they will have little incentive to work harder. A person must value the pay-off if the expectancy loop is positive and motivational.

Vroom recognises the importance of individual needs and motivations, and that individuals have personal goals that may differ from those of the organisation. Managers need to understand that, to achieve a motivated workforce, organisational and individual goals need to be harmonised.

Another theory of motivation, developed by Herzberg, recognises that other aspects of work can be motivators, and managers need to be aware of this as part of their strategy for motivating employees.

Herzberg's dual-factor theory

A needs-based model intended to provide direct managerial applications evolved from Frederick Herzberg's research into the sources of job-related satisfaction and dissatisfaction. Herzberg (1966) carried out 203 interviews with accountants and engineers using the critical incident method. They were asked two questions: What made them feel good about their job and what made them feel bad. The interviewees were asked to relate the sequence of events leading up to the feelings. The responses revealed that there were two different factors affecting motivation and work. From the research Herzberg concluded that:

- job satisfaction and job dissatisfaction derive from different sources
- simply removing the sources of dissatisfaction will not cause a person to be motivated to produce better results.

dual-factor theory
Herzberg's motivation content theory, based on two independent needs: hygiene and motivator factors.

Herzberg blended these two premises into a dual-factor explanation of motivation. **Dual-factor theory** refers to two different types of need:

1 hygiene factors, which involve working conditions and can trigger dissatisfaction if inadequate

2 motivator factors, which originate from the nature of the job itself and can create job satisfaction.

Dissatisfiers as hygiene factors

hygiene factors
Job context factors such as working conditions and benefits that cause dissatisfaction if inadequate.

Herzberg drew the term hygiene factors from his public health experience. **Hygiene factors** are those basic factors surrounding the job – job security, working conditions, quality of supervision, interpersonal relationships, and adequacy of pay and fringe benefits – that, if lacking, can cause dissatisfaction. Such factors are largely *extrinsic*, or external to the nature of the job itself, and can therefore be thought of as job context features.

Hygiene factors do not produce job satisfaction. If adequate, they simply produce neutral feelings with the realisation that basic maintenance needs are taken care of. Like a city's water and sanitation systems, these factors do not cause people to be healthy and robust; they simply prevent disease and unhealthy conditions – they provide good hygiene.

Satisfiers as motivator factors

According to Herzberg (1993), only when a person feels the potential for satisfaction is he or she able to muster significant work motivation. **Motivator factors** such as job challenge, responsibility, opportunity for achievement or advancement, and recognition, provide feelings of satisfaction. These are associated with job content and are *intrinsic*, or unique to each individual in his or her own way.

motivator factors
Job content factors such as responsibility and achievement that provide feelings of satisfaction when experienced.

Herzberg's dual-factor theory suggests that if motivators are not present in a job, a person will not necessarily be dissatisfied. However, that person will simply not be in a position to experience satisfaction, since nothing about the work itself is a motivational turn-on. When motivator factors are inherent in the job, satisfaction is perceived as possible and work-directed energy is aroused or sustained. Only then can a person be consistently motivated, according to Herzberg. Exhibit 6-5 presents the four alternative combinations of hygiene and motivator factors derived from the theory.

To improve motivation to work, managers are first advised to provide an adequate job context of working conditions and benefits for their people. This will satisfy lower-level hygiene needs, which, if not met, cause dissatisfaction. But to arouse work interest and promote self-directed task motivation, managers also need to ensure that the content of the job itself is reasonably satisfying – that jobs contain responsibility, challenge, and the opportunity to learn and advance.

The 'Stop and reflect' box gives you the opportunity to think about what you would like from your job.

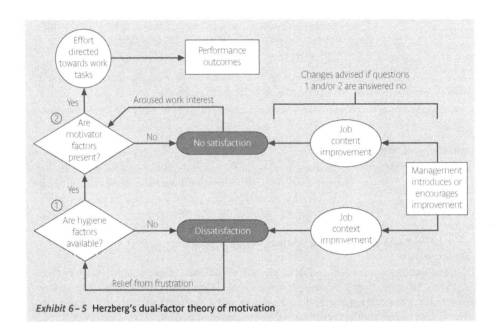

Exhibit 6–5 Herzberg's dual-factor theory of motivation

Stop and reflect

What do you want from your job?

Rank the following 16 work-related rewards and outcomes from 1 (most important) to 16 (least important) to you.

Good health insurance and other benefits   _____
Interesting work   _____
Job security   _____
Opportunity to learn new skills   _____
Having a week or more holiday   _____
Being able to work independently   _____
Recognition from co-workers   _____
Regular hours (no weekends, no nights)   _____
Having a job in which you can help others   _____
Limiting job stress   _____
High income   _____
Working close to home   _____
Work that is important to society   _____
Chances for promotion   _____
Contact with a lot of people   _____
Flexible hours   _____

Which of these rewards do you receive now?
Which of them can you control to increase your probability of satisfaction?

Source: Adapted from Bloisi *et al.* (2003).

A reward strategy

Research by the CIPD (2004a) found that two-thirds of organisations took a strategic approach to reward and had a written reward strategy. One of the main concerns for managers was the ability to pay the market rate in order to attract and retain the best people. For most organisations, the top priorities of a reward strategy are as follows:

- reward business goals
- recruit and retain high performers
- control pay costs
- ensure equity.

The 'International perspective' box illustrates how a reward strategy can improve employee performance.

Total rewards

total rewards
The reward strategy that brings together all components of reward, including monetary, non-monetary, learning and development.

Total rewards is a strategy which recognises that pay, although important, is not the only motivator, and that there are other tangible and non-tangible rewards that can encourage a more committed workforce. HR professionals need to recognise that total reward can be a powerful tool for aligning HR with business strategies and ensuring competitive advantage.

According to the CIPD (2004a):

> Total reward is the term that has been adopted to describe a reward strategy that brings additional components such as learning and development, together with aspects of the working environment into the benefits package. It goes beyond company culture, and is aimed at giving all employees a voice in the operation, with the employer in return receiving an engaged employee performance.

The advantages of a total reward scheme are, according to Thompson and Milsome (2001):

- easier recruitment of better-quality staff
- reduced wastage from staff turnover
- better business performance
- enhanced reputation as an employer of choice.

However, there can also be problems in creating a total reward package, in that it is always bespoke and needs to be specially designed for the organisation. Although there are consultants who specialise in developing total reward packages, they can be very expensive to set up. The cost of such a scheme needs to be matched with the potential benefits of increased employee commitment and increased competitive advantage.

Exhibit 6-6 demonstrates how financial rewards and non-financial rewards link together to form total rewards.

There are several total reward models. However, according to Thompson and Milsome (2001), they tend to share the following characteristics.

- Holistic: they focus on all aspects of the organisation, from recruitment to selection, retention, pay and reward, and are designed so that employees can contribute to the success of the organisation.

international perspective

In corporate India, it pays to reward performers

Gone are the days of across-the-board pay hikes. Today, Indian companies are going in for performance pay structures, a norm that has been in practice for several years among multinational companies (MNCs) operating in the country.

A recent study by Hewitt bears out this fact. It shows that almost 87 per cent of Indian companies are looking at retaining top talent and are using performance pay to do it. 'The results of the study, in fact, reveal that an outstanding performer earns on an average twice the salary increase earned by an average performer,' says Mr Nishchae Suri, measurement practice leader, Hewitt Associates.

According to him, Indian companies are practising the concept of performance-linked rewards widely. 'While the outstanding performers of these companies got a hike that was almost 4.7 per cent higher than the low performers last year, this year the percentage grew by 6 per cent.'

Mr Suri adds, 'As corporate revenues and budgets stagnate or even reduce, the companies are also realising the need to retain their best talent in order to drive better business results.'

Agreeing with Mr Suri, Mr Sunit Mehra, managing director of Hunt Partners, says, 'Almost all progressive companies that I am aware of have a performance pay plan in place or are implementing it. Instead of remunerating everyone equally, the Indian companies have started remunerating the performers more. The advantage to both parties is that overall salary costs are contained and it also helps to motivate the better performers.'

Mr Mehra also points out that, although this structure has definitely helped to improve the efficiency of employees, in order to make the plan effective, companies need to have simple, effective, realistic and transparent metrics to evaluate performance.

Mr Ulhas Deshpande, vice-president, human resources, IDBI Bank, says, 'Ever since we switched over to the performance-reward structure, it has helped in enhancing the efficiency and effectiveness of our employees. Just as a large number of employees have exceeded expectations, quite a few underachievers have also worked in earnest and shown significant change for the better. Overall, it has helped to improve employee productivity and quality.'

Mr Deshpande says across-the-board hikes not only result in a wider distribution of rewards but also dilute the quantum for each employee and this results in building a mindset of complacency. He adds, 'Moreover, contributors who add significant value are left with a feeling that there is no premium on performance and hence either get demotivated and leave or start underperforming. As far as the non-performer is concerned, he continues to get some increase, which is a good enough incentive to continue in the system and not improve. Therefore, the Indian companies are rightly focusing on differentiation and targeted rewards linked to results.'

Source: Ajita Shashidhar, *Hindu Business Line*, 14 March 2000, New Delhi.

Discussion questions

1 How can organisations encourage non-performers to improve their performance?

2 Does performance-related pay reward a few at the expense of the majority?

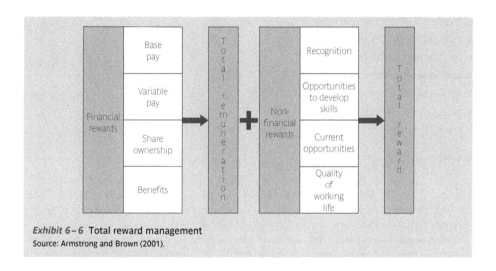

Exhibit 6–6 **Total reward management**
Source: Armstrong and Brown (2001).

- Best fit: they are adapted to fit the organisation, therefore different organisations will design their total reward packages to meet the needs of their individual business goals and organisational climate.
- Integrative: rewards are integrated into policies and practices according to the needs of the employees.
- Strategic: reward is linked to business strategy with the view that the total rewards on offer will improve performance.
- People centred: as people form the basis of organisations, it is important that the reward packages not only meet their needs but also encourage greater commitment.
- Customised: flexible rewards offer choice and meet the needs of employees. Younger employees often have different needs and aspirations to those of older employees and this is reflected in the package they are offered.
- Distinctive: the total reward package sets the organisation apart from others and therefore can be used as a powerful tool in attracting and retaining employees.
- Evolutionary: the total reward process should evolve over time to meet the needs of the organisation.

In the past the promise of a job for life was often enough to attract and retain workers, and financial benefits may have included shares or bonuses linked to company performance. However, with a more diverse workforce, employees are requesting different returns at work, which not only need to be varied but also flexible, so that when circumstances change the employee is able to pick and mix different benefits.

The elements included in the total reward package may, according to the CIPD (2004a), include some of the following aspects:

- flexible benefits
- access to training courses
- a challenging work role

- freedom and autonomy at work
- opportunity for personal growth
- recognition of achievements
- preferred office space
- preferred office equipment and mobile phone
- flexible working hours
- secretarial support.

Flexible benefits

According to the CIPD (2004c), there has been a distinct move towards providing a more flexible system of benefits, with 10 per cent of employers moving to such a system in the last five years. Flexible benefit schemes, also known as a 'cafeteria of benefits', allow employees to pick and choose their rewards, depending on their circumstances.

Flexible benefits form part of the total reward package and are beginning to take off as a key element of the reward package despite having been around for the last 20 years. The reason for such an interest is that employers have finally recognised that their employees prefer to choose their benefits rather than have a scheme imposed on them, and there are several consultants with sufficient expertise to enable organisations to design and deliver such schemes. Employees can now decide if they want a company car, private medical insurance, pension contributions or extra holiday. An example of one such successful scheme has been implemented in the public sector by housing association Poplar Harka, which wanted to be able to distinguish itself from other public-sector organisations to enable it to attract and retain high-calibre staff. Under the scheme employees are able to choose a mix of benefits such as medical and dental insurance, health checks, extra holiday or a home computer. Other reasons for a move to flexible benefits are the changes in tax benefits to encourage pension plans and increase in taxes to discourage company car use.

flexible benefits
A pick and mix of rewards that employees can choose depending on their wants and needs.

The advantages and disadvantages of implementing a flexible benefits scheme can be seen in Exhibit 6-7.

Incentives

Incentives are one method of recognising good performance and showing employees that they are valued and appreciated. In the past they were often linked to targets but now they are seen much more as an expected part of the rewards system. To be effective, incentive schemes need to be flexible and exciting and able to motivate a diverse workforce. However, if handled badly, they can cause serious dissatisfaction.

incentives
Mechanisms to encourage and recognise good performance.

Whatever incentives are used, they need to be suitable for the recipients. Tony Kilcoyne, a corporate gifts manager from Fraser Hart Awards and Incentives, suggests that organisations need to look at the diversity of their workforce. A young workforce, such as often found in call centres, is more likely to prefer electrical goods, while older workers may prefer holidays or gift vouchers. Employers, however, do need to remember that many incentives come with tax implications for employees which, to avoid any negative impact, they would have to pay.

Advantages of flexible benefits schemes
■ Employees choose benefits to meet their needs, and value these benefits more highly
■ Employers and employees share the responsibility for providing benefits
■ During periods of change (including mergers and acquisitions), flexible benefits help to harmonise rewards
■ Employers provide benefits at a known cost that is fixed regardless of the choices that employees make, so allowing them to cap future benefit costs
■ Employees have a true idea of the full worth of the benefits package they receive and employers do not provide benefits that are not valued
■ Employees are given a sense of control and involvement by having a choice
■ Dual-career couples avoid having benefits duplicated by their respective employers
■ Employers are seen to be more responsive to the needs of an increasingly diverse, demanding and ageing workforce
■ A competitive benefits package is valuable in attracting and retaining key personnel
■ The awarding of benefits such as company cars becomes less divisive
■ Employers' demands for flexible working practices are more justifiable if employees enjoy flexible benefits
■ Helps to align the total reward strategy to the HR and business strategies
Disadvantages of flexible benefits schemes
■ Employers find them complex and expensive to set up and maintain (although new technology is reducing both the cost and administrative burden)
■ The choices made may cause problems, both for employers and employees

Exhibit 6–7 Advantages and disadvantages of flexible benefits

Individual pay

This focuses on rewarding the right people for the right things. The idea is that pay can be a motivator and that, to motivate:

- a reward must be perceived as worth working for
- the reward must have a clearly perceived connection with the work results
- work goals must be seen to be achievable.

Traditional pay schemes are rarely able to do this and tend to pay employees regardless of their performance. One way round this is to link pay to performance through an appraisal and performance-related pay system. However, this must be robust and employees need to have a high level of trust in the appraisal system.

Performance-related pay

Performance-related pay (PRP) is often linked to performance appraisal: employees are rewarded for meeting targets, set either by themselves or their managers. PRP enables organisations to link an employee's performance to the organisational strategy and reinforce strategic goals. Often, this is an attempt to change the culture of an

performance-related pay
Pay linked to performance to encourage greater productivity.

organisation in order to improve productivity. The problem with performance-related pay is that it sends a message to employees that, to earn more they have to perform. Often, this means that it is the strongest who survive, which could result in lower performers underachieving as they have no incentive to try.

To avoid this, PRP can be linked not only to performance objectives but also to development objectives. If employees undertake training or skills development they too can be rewarded. In implementing PRP managers need to ensure that they have evaluated the need for improved performance and identified the following issues.

- Do employees value pay?
- What are the objectives of a PRP system?
- Does implementing PRP conform to the organisational values already in place?
- How can employees be encouraged to accept the system?
- What training will be given to managers on implementing the system?
- How will performance be measured and will it be accurate?
- Will there be different levels of reward depending on achievement of targets?
- How will differing contributions be assessed?
- Are there sufficient financial resources to allow payments to be made?
- How will the system be monitored?
- What happens if increased performance does not increase competitive advantage?
- How will the organisation ensure that awards are fair and equitable?

Effective PRP can substantially improve performance; however, poorly implemented systems can alienate employees. As one education union announced: 'We've performed, you pay.' In other words, we are already doing our job to the best of our ability and therefore should be rewarded properly. To be effective, PRP should specify and measure performance, specify the reward and gain employee acceptance.

One example of the negative impacts of PRP was found by a study at Aston University, where 22 organisations were examined. It was found that in the majority of cases PRP was used to encourage staff to make as many transactions in the shortest time possible. The result was that customers who went over the three minutes were cut off. Another example was a directory enquiries company, where one member of staff gave out the number of the local pizza restaurant to every caller in an attempt to minimise call times. Kent County Council, in an attempt to overcome such problems, has attempted to redress the balance by rewarding staff for their customer care, instead of whether they answer the phone in four rings. The advantages and disadvantages of PRP are summarised in Exhibit 6-8.

Team pay

Although few organisations implement team-based pay, according to the CIPD (2004b) managers who believe that their teams make a significant contribution to performance believe the teams deserve to be rewarded financially as well as being given scope to manage themselves. If the workplace is moving towards self-managed teams, then it makes sense that managers reward the team rather than the individual. Research suggests that senior managers are the ones most likely to be rewarded for their team's performance and that the rewards are not always filtered down to other employees.

Advantages	Disadvantages
■ It can retain and attract good performers	■ Reinforces management control
■ If properly implemented, it can improve both individual and organisational performance	■ Can cause pay inequality
■ Job roles and duties are clarified by linking PRP to job descriptions and performance outcomes	■ Reinforces power hierarchies
	■ Difficult to implement effectively in practice
	■ Undermines team working as it is individually based
■ It can improve communication	■ Can involve subjective rather than objective evaluations by managers
■ It can improve motivation	
■ It reinforces management control where in the past it may have been weak	■ External factors may mean employees are unable to control or achieve desired performance
■ It identifies developmental objectives	
■ It reinforces the individual employment relationship rather than the individual	■ Fast-changing work environments may mean objectives become obsolete
■ It rewards individuals without the need to promote them	■ It can discourage creative thinking
	■ Budgetary constraints can affect ratings
	■ Employees may ignore their weaknesses in order to receive increased pay, and therefore not develop
	■ Managers may reward all staff regardless of performance in order to remain popular
	■ The pay bill increases but productivity may not

Exhibit 6 – 8 Advantages and disadvantages of performance-related pay

The CIPD (2004b) believes that **team pay** works best if teams:

team pay
Rewarding the team rather than the individual for team performance.

- stand alone with agreed targets and standards
- have autonomy
- are composed of people whose work is interdependent
- are stable
- are well established and make good use of complementary skills
- are composed of flexible, multiskilled team players who are capable of expressing a different point of view if it is for the good of the whole.

For team pay to be accepted as a reward, the CIPD (2004b) also suggests that:

- everybody must understand and accept the targets
- the reward must be clearly linked to effort and achievement
- the reward must be worth striving for
- performance measures must be fair, consistent and acceptable
- everybody must be able to track performance in relation to targets and standards
- the team must influence its performance by changing behaviour or decisions
- the incentive formula must be easily understood

- reward must closely follow accomplishment
- the scheme must be appropriate
- the scheme should be carefully designed, installed, maintained and adapted to meet changing circumstances.

Another question for managers is what type of reward should be offered that would be acceptable for all members of the team. This could be monetary rewards, or team-based rewards such as away-days in luxury hotels. Research suggests they prefer team rewards, such as recognition and celebrations, rather than monetary rewards. Whatever type of reward is offered it is important to ensure that there is the right mix and that employees are aware of the distinction between individual rewards and team rewards. To be successful, both managers and teams need to understand that they have responsibilities, as can be seen in Exhibit 6-9.

Team-based pay has both advantages and disadvantages (see Exhibit 6-10) and needs to be managed carefully to ensure its success.

Organisations that have consulted thoroughly with their employees and that have a well-thought-out system will find that team pay may well enhance the performance of organisational teams, but they need to remember that there are alternatives to team-based pay that may work equally well.

Managers need to:	Teams need to:
<ul><li>conduct an initial needs analysis</li><li>analyse current practice</li><li>define individual and team reward philosophies</li><li>consider team pay reinforcement and non-financial rewards</li><li>create a collaborative climate</li><li>identify critical success factors</li><li>involve all employees</li><li>communicate the benefits</li><li>train employees and team leaders to optimise team performance</li><li>provide team-building training</li><li>help individuals improve their skills</li><li>monitor and evaluate</li><li>audit the costs and ensure the scheme is self-financing</li><li>promote the value of non-financial rewards</li><li>recognise team accomplishments with appropriate action</li></ul>	<ul><li>participate in the scheme's design and modification</li><li>define critical success factors and performance measures</li><li>set objectives</li><li>identify accomplishments</li><li>monitor and evaluate team performance</li><li>establish priorities</li><li>analyse the financial rewards and decide on improvements</li><li>conduct peer reviews of individuals</li><li>identify training and development needs</li><li>suggest improvements to the scheme</li><li>promote non-financial rewards</li></ul>

Exhibit 6–9 Manager and team responsibilities
Source: CIPD (2004b).

Advantages	Disadvantages
Team pay can: ■ encourage co-operative work and behaviour ■ clarify goals and priorities at team and organisational level ■ emphasise a flatter and more process-based organisation ■ act as a lever for organisational change ■ encourage flexible working and multiskilling ■ offer a fairer perceived payment system ■ collectively improve performance and team processs ■ encourage the less effective to meet team standards ■ develop self-managed and directed teams	Team pay can: ■ diminish individual self-worth ■ mask individual team contributions ■ compel individuals to conform to oppressive group norms ■ result in low output that is sufficient only to gain a reasonable reward ■ cause difficulties when developing performance measures that are fair ■ shift problems of unco-operative behaviour from individuals in teams to the relationships between teams ■ prejudice organisational flexibility – cohesive and high-performance teams may be unwilling to change

Exhibit 6–10 The advantages and disadvantages of team-based pay
Source: CIPD (2004b).

Legal aspects

In the UK there is a variety of legislation in place to protect the worker and ensure that they are treated fairly. This includes the:

■ Equal Pay Act 1970
■ The Equal Pay Amendment (Regulations) 1983
■ Employment Rights Act 1996
■ Social Security Contributions and Benefit Act 1992
■ National Minimum Wage Act 1998

Equal Pay Act 1970

The purpose of this act is to ensure that women and men doing the same or broadly similar work, receive the same pay. The Act states that there is a right to equal pay between men and women. Although in most instances prosecution under the Act has been on behalf of women, it applies equally to men.

The Equal Pay Act 1970 applies to all employees and is not only concerned with the equality of pay but also with the provision of equal benefits such as bonuses, holidays and hours of work.

The tests used to check whether a person is entitled to equal pay are where:

■ a person is employed in like work with a person of the opposite sex in the same employment
■ a person is employed on work rated as equivalent to that of a person of the opposite sex in the same employment
■ a person is employed in work of equal value to that of a person of the opposite sex in the same employment.

The Equal Pay Amendment (Regulations) 1983

The Equal Pay Amendment (Regulations) 1983 added to the Equal Pay Act 1970 a further category of work of 'equal value'. This came about from European Law, Article 119, and the Equal Pay Directive, as the 1970 Act did not fully comply with work of 'equal value'. The procedure involved in bringing a complaint under this act can be time consuming. It involves an independent expert, usually appointed by Acas, to visit the place of work and observe the complainant at work. This involves negotiation with the employer to access the premises, and interviewing managers and employees. The burden of proof is on the complainant to show that comparable jobs are of equal value.

Employment Rights Act 1996

The Employment Rights Act 1996 consolidates much of the previous employment rights legislation. This includes the right to an itemised pay statement for every employee who works more than eight hours. The pay statement should include details of:

- the gross amount earned
- any tax and National Insurance deductions
- any fixed deductions agreed by the employee such as pension payments
- the amount of net pay.

The Act also protects employees from unlawful deductions. For example, they cannot have their pay docked for breakages or missing stock unless it is an agreed part of their contract, but they can have their pay docked if the deductions are a result of strike action or of an overpayment in wages.

The Act also covers guarantee payments where an employee who has been paid for more than one month has the right to be paid if they are temporarily laid off due to a diminution in the employer's requirements for labour.

Social Security Contributions and Benefits Act 1992
Sick pay

All employees are entitled to receive a basic amount of sick pay. Often employees provide increased benefits, and these need to be written into the terms and conditions of employment.

Under the Social Security Contributions and Benefits Act 1992 all employees are entitled to receive statutory sick pay for the first 28 weeks of their illness. To qualify for sick pay the employee must be:

- suffering from some disease/physical or mental disability that renders him/her incapable of work, and
- the period of incapacity must be a period of four or more consecutive days.

Statutory sick pay is the responsibility of the employer and cannot be claimed back unless the sick pay exceeds 13 per cent of their National Insurance contributions each month. Some organisations, such as Tesco and British Airways, in an attempt to discourage absences, do not pay employees for the first three days of sickness, which although unpopular with staff and unions does nevertheless comply with legislation.

managing diversity

Tesco acts to reduce staff sick days

Britain's biggest private-sector employer has launched an experiment to reduce sick days with a mixture of sticks and carrots (or at least vouchers to buy them). One pilot scheme launched by Tesco rewards those staff who have an exemplary record for turning up with extra holiday. Another one gives them reward vouchers, and another fails to give them sick pay for their first three days off.

The supermarket chain's initiative reflects a belief among many employers that a large proportion of sick days are not caused by genuine illness: 51 per cent of human resource professionals believe that more than half the days employers lost to stress were not genuine, a survey by the Health & Safety Executive and *Personnel Today* magazine suggested last year.

A survey of GPs published this year by Norwich Union, the insurer, found that more than a third of the sick notes they issued every year might be bogus.

The CBI employers' organisation has estimated that staff absence costs business £11.6bn a year.

There are even signs that fear of 'sickies' may be exacerbating the problem of genuine sickness. More than four in ten private-sector businesses in the HSE/*Personnel Today* survey said they did not want to raise the profile of stress in case this encouraged increased reporting of it.

Under Tesco's extra holiday scheme, all staff are given three more days over the year. For every day off sick, they lose one of these extra days – though they can never lose more than three. Tesco said no worker had been compelled to take part in the pilots.

Usdaw, the shopworkers' union, which represents Tesco workers, is co-operating with the pilots. Its acquiescence contrasts sharply with the bitter opposition from the Public and Commercial Services Union to plans by management at the Department for Work and Pensions for a crackdown on sick days.

Under a proposed bonus scheme, workers whose general performance qualified them for extra cash would lose some of it if they took five days off a year, apart from annual holiday.

Source: David Turner, *Financial Times*, 17 May 2004, p. 4.

Discussion questions

1 What impact do you think these different schemes could have on employee motivation?

2 Which scheme, if any, would motivate you to work harder and which would demotivate you?

National Minimum Wage Act 1998

The National Minimum Wage Act 1998 became effective in 1999 and was designed to alleviate poverty in the low-earning sector of the workforce. The national minimum wage is the same regardless of job location, job type, size or industrial sector. Therefore someone living in London would be paid the same as someone living in Newcastle, despite substantial differences in living costs. The reasons put forward to support a national minimum wage (NMW) cover three broad areas:

1 **social** – a minimum wage would attack low pay and poverty

2 **equity** – a minimum wage reduces exploitation, protects employers against undercutting on wages, and cuts the cost to taxpayers of topping up low incomes via the social security system

3 **economic** – extra demand in the economy would increase employment; a minimum wage could also boost investment and productivity.

In commenting on the report of the Low Pay Commission, the then Secretary of State emphasised four key messages. The NMW (2004) would:

1 begin to end the 'scandal of poverty pay'
2 form part of an overall package to make work pay
3 produce a more committed and productive workforce
4 encourage competition based on quality not 'sweatshop labour'.

To comply with legislation, employers have to display details of the hourly minimum wage on the payslip and in the workplace (LPC, 2004).

The NMW has established the following rates:

- **standard rate £5.35** – payable to people aged 22 and over
- **development rate £4.45** – payable to people aged 18 to 21 years, whether or not they are receiving 'accredited training'; payable to people aged 22 and over who start a new job with a new employer and receive 'accredited training' for first six months
- **youth rate £3.30** – payable to 16 and 17 year olds (above the compulsory school leaving age); this new rate was introduced on 1 October 2006.

Low pay

The minimum wage has increased by 50 per cent since its introduction in 1999, and while some employers, such as Asda, welcome it, the Confederation for British Industry (CBI) has criticised it for stifling British industry and making it hard for businesses to be competitive. The minimum wage, as it suggests, is a minimum and many people still find it hard to make ends meet, especially if they live in London. As discussed in the opening vignette, some organisations have moved on from the minimum wage to the idea of a living wage.

The idea of a living wage originated in the USA where cities including Boston, Los Angeles and Chicago have adopted living wage ordinances, meaning that they will not employ people or contract with those who pay their staff less than a living wage. The idea is now gathering pace in the UK and already the cleaners at the Houses of Parliament are paid a living wage as are staff at Barclays and HSBC. Although some jobs are contracted out, some local authorities, such as the Greater London Authority (GLA), are implementing rules which mean that contractors will have to commit to pay the living wage if they want to work for the GLA.

Transparency and equity

To avoid any unpleasantness from employees, it is good practice for employers to ensure that an organisation rewards employees fairly. In other words, employers provide equal pay for equal work. Employers are responsible for ensuring this happens and therefore it is desirable that pay systems are clear and transparent. A structured pay system is more likely to provide such transparency than a system that relies on an employer's discretion.

In building a pay system, it is necessary for the organisation to carry out an equal pay review that involves all levels of staff, management and their representatives. According to the Equal

Opportunities Commission (EOC), 'an equal pay review involves comparing the pay of women and men doing equal work, investigating the causes of gender pay gaps and closing any gaps that can not be satisfactorily explained on grounds other than sex'. The EOC recognises that the equal pay review is concerned only with a narrow aspect of sex discrimination at work and does not take into account other aspects of inequality such as the glass ceiling. Nevertheless it does try to address the issue of disparity of a 19.5 per cent pay gap between men and women working full-time and the 40 per cent gap between men working full-time and women working part-time.

The EOC suggests following a five-step process, as illustrated in Exhibit 6-11.

Employers who ignore such advice do so at their peril. In a recent case an employee was awarded a £1,000,000 settlement that was largely the result of management's 'behind closed doors' bonus culture. Even if payouts are less substantial, an employer could still be liable for six months' back pay if found guilty of discrimination.

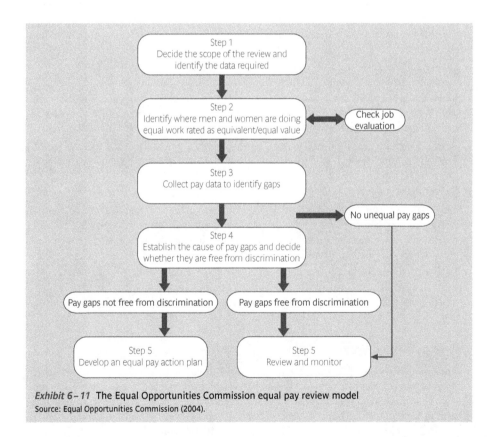

Exhibit 6–11 The Equal Opportunities Commission equal pay review model
Source: Equal Opportunities Commission (2004).

Summary

- Remuneration and reward are an important part of the HR function, as they link directly to an organisation's strategic goals. Remuneration refers to the monetary aspect, whereas rewards can be monetary or non-monetary and should be designed to show employees that they are valued.
- Payment structures are developed to ensure that employers pay the market rate, which enables them to attract and retain employees, and to demonstrate that employees are rewarded fairly and equitably.
- There are various methods that can be used to evaluate jobs, such as job ranking, paired comparisons and job classification. Information about deciding what to pay can be gathered from market surveys.
- Traditional pay was linked to the principles of scientific management and was closely controlled by managers. New pay combines traditional pay with personal development, and recognises that it should be linked to both the organisation and the individual.
- Rewards can take several forms, such as merit pay, bonuses, profit sharing and gainsharing plans.
- Reward can be linked to motivation to improve performance by ensuring that rewards meet employees' expectations and that employees are treated equitably.
- A total rewards system recognises that pay is only one aspect of motivation and there are other rewards that can improve performance. These rewards should be linked to the business strategy to enable competitive advantage.
- Flexible benefits allow employees to match their rewards to their needs, and these can form part of the total reward package. Flexible benefits can include incentives, pensions, company cars, extra holiday, and childcare vouchers.
- Legislation helps to ensure that employers meet their obligations to their employees and that workers are protected and treated fairly.
- Performance-related pay links improved performance to pay, often through the appraisal system, and is designed to encourage employees to develop skills that would enable the organisation to become more effective.
- Team pay reflects the idea that teams make a significant contribution to performance and, as such, should be rewarded. There are both advantages and disadvantages of such a system. Managers considering team-based pay need to consult their employees to ensure that it will enhance organisational performance and not diminish it.

Personal development

1 **Understand the role of remuneration and reward.** If you work for an organisation, what types of reward are you offered? What makes you work harder? How flexible are the rewards? If you are young, would you prefer a pension or a company car? You may also want to look around at your colleagues: what are their needs and how do these differ from yours? Can your organisation meet the different needs of its employees?

2 **Recognise the importance of payment systems.** Does the organisation you work for have a payment structure? Can you identify how this has been developed? Does this reflect the market conditions? If yes, how does this make employees feel? If no, why are people still working there? Does the payment system allow for recognition of achievement or perform-

ance, and who is responsible for recognising the achievement? Is it at the whim of the manager or more consistent? Do you progress because of your ability or on length of service, and is this fair?

3 **Determine the impact of bonus systems.** If you had a good idea at work and it saved the company a considerable amount of money, would you like to be rewarded? Should it only be you who receives the reward, or should it be evenly distributed? Gainsharing is one example of how employees can benefit by improving organisational efficiency. Alternatively, would you prefer a profit-sharing plan? Which scheme would encourage greater commitment to the organisation?

4 **Understand the impact of motivation on employee performance.** If you were paid less than your colleague for doing the same job, how would you feel? Would you want to work harder in the hope that your pay would be increased, or would your performance deteriorate as you became less motivated? Managers need to understand the importance of motivation to performance. Treating employees equitably not only ensures fairness, it also ensures that organisations protect themselves from legal action. Employees also have expectations: in other words, if they work harder then they may well expect promotion; if this doesn't happen, is performance likely to increase or decrease?

5 **Recognise the need to work within the legal framework.** HR practitioners need to familiarise themselves with their legal obligations. This means ensuring that employees are not discriminated against on the grounds of race, gender or disability. Other legal obligations relating to pay are concerned with the types of deduction an employer can make, and ensuring that minimum wages are paid. Legislation provides a minimum requirement. Many employers go beyond legislation to value diversity or ensure employees are paid a living wage, rather than a minimum wage.

6 **Recognise the implications of team pay.** Many people today work in leaner and flatter organisational structures, where teamwork is valued. You may well work in such a team. If so, would you like to be rewarded as part of the team or as an individual? It may be that you play sport; if so, how would you feel if every time a goal was scored, the scorer received extra pay despite it being a team effort? Team pay aims to reward team effort as opposed to individualism.

? Discussion questions

1 Define the terms 'reward' and 'remuneration'.

2 'We perform, you pay.' What are the arguments for and against performance-related pay?

3 What does an organisation need to consider when developing a pay structure?

4 What is the difference between 'new pay' and 'traditional pay'?

5 How could gainsharing plans be implemented as part of the reward system?

6 Why is it important for managers to have an understanding of motivation when rewarding employees?

7 What are the characteristics of a total reward system?

8 How can managers successfully implement flexible benefits while meeting the needs of the organisation?

9 What are the advantages and disadvantages of team pay?

10 How can pay and performance be linked to the strategic aims of the organisation?

❶ Key concepts

reward, *p. 178*	bonuses, *p. 187*
remuneration, *p. 178*	gainsharing , *p. 187*
pay structures, *p. 180*	equity theory, *p. 188*
job evaluation, *p. 180*	distributive justice, *p. 189*
points rating, *p. 180*	procedural justice, *p. 189*
factor comparison, *p. 180*	expectancy theory, *p. 189*
job ranking, *p. 181*	dual-factor theory, *p. 191*
paired comparison, *p. 181*	hygiene factors, *p. 191*
job classification, *p. 181*	motivator factors, *p. 191*
efficiency wage theory, *p. 184*	total rewards, *p. 193*
benchmarking, *p. 184*	flexible benefits, *p. 196*
traditional pay, *p. 186*	incentives, *p. 196*
new pay, *p. 186*	performance-related pay, *p. 197*
merit pay, *p. 186*	team pay, *p. 199*
profit sharing, *p. 187*	

Individual task

Purpose To gain an understanding of job evaluation, one of the techniques available for determining pay.

Time 40 minutes

Procedure A points ranking system can be one method of job evaluation used to determine the level of pay. Note down the following headings:

Knowledge and skills
Decision-making
Impact and influence
Communication and networking
Freedom to act
Working environment
People management
Financial responsibility

(More detailed descriptions can be found in Exhibit 6-2.)

Now rank the following jobs in order of importance, using 1 to denote the most important and 20 the least.

Nurse	_____	Childcare assistant	_____
Cleaner	_____	Paramedic	_____
Secretary	_____	Police officer	_____
Receptionist	_____	Soldier	_____
Porter	_____	Shop assistant	_____
Doctor	_____	Call centre operator	_____
Teacher	_____	Computer technician	_____
Artist	_____	Accountant	_____
Lawyer	_____	Journalist	_____
Postman/woman	_____	HR manager	_____

What influenced your decision?

How does this compare to the rankings given by other members of the group and why are there differences?

Team task

Purpose To identify the different wants and needs people have in life, and to link them to a flexible reward system.

Time 50 minutes

Procedure Working individually, develop a list of approximately 10 rewards you would like from a job. Try to include those you would like now and those you may want later in life. Decide which rewards are essential and which desirable.

Divide into groups of four and compare which needs are similar and which different.

What are the implications for organisations who want to design a flexible benefits system?

How would you decide whether the types of reward were equitable when compared to each other?

What could happen if people see their rewards as inequitable to those given to others?

Chapter EIGHTEEN

Developing people

Part contents

Learning, training and development

LEARNING OUTCOMES

After studying this chapter, you should be able to:

- ☑ **understand** the nature and process of learning
- ☑ **identify** different styles and approaches to learning
- ☑ **understand** the education and training debate
- ☑ **identify** strategies for training
- ☑ **understand** the relationship between competence and performance.

The opening vignette demonstrates the importance of training as a means of improving business performance.

Education can keep the car industry ahead: Japanese customers' demands have sparked a training explosion

When Nissan asked to see the training centre at a small Sutton Coldfield toolmaking company, it threw Colin Sarson, the managing director, into a panic.

Negotiations for Mr Sarson's business to become a supplier to the Sunderland plant of Japan's second largest car maker were at a delicate stage – and enormously important to the company.

But, as with hundreds of similar companies in the West Midlands vehicle heartland, it had never occurred to the toolmaker to have a training centre, something expected by the Japanese car maker.

However, after identifying a suitable room, the company won the contract, but Mr Sarson got rather more than he had bargained for. 'Somehow, word got round the plant that we had a proper learning centre,' he says, slightly guiltily. 'And all of a sudden, entirely on their own initiative, there were people off the shopfloor coming into the room actually looking for training.'

After this incident in 1991, training programmes are now embedded in the business. The Japanese-inspired culture of continuous improvement permeates every activity. Mr Sarson intends virtually all his 400 employees to have earned a National Vocational Qualification (NVQ) before long.

All this is music to the ears of Mike Beasley, former managing director of Jaguar Cars, Graham Broome, a former Rover executive who since 1996 has been chief executive of the Society of Motor Manufacturers and Traders' (SMMT) Industry Forum, and David Cragg, head of the Learning and Skills Council's own Automotive Forum in the Midlands.

The trio are spearheading the biggest ever initiative – backed by industry leaders, government departments, regional authorities and the academic establishment – to increase skills within the UK's 250,000-strong vehicle industry workforce and help it to sustain global competitiveness.

They are not undertaking it in isolation from those who set the benchmarks for competitiveness: the car makers of Japan. The chairman of the SMMT's Industry Forum is Alan Jones, the long-time managing director of Toyota's manufacturing operations in the UK. Nissan and Honda, the UK's other Japanese 'transplants', are also represented.

'Supply them and you can supply anyone' is the message delivered, to the components sector in particular, by the initiative.

Under the title of Skills4Auto, the venture also aims to convince the young that the motor and engineering industries can provide enjoyable and attractive careers.

It has already created a task force with the Engineering Employers' Federation (EEF) in the West Midlands to promote the industry in schools. The scale of the problem is outlined by Ian Smith, the regional EEF's managing director. He estimates that a minimum of 2000 apprentices a year are needed in the region's manufacturing and engineering centres.

Skills4Auto itself is the first product of another initiative: an 'automotive academy' first outlined in mid-2003 by Sir Nick Scheele, the former Jaguar chairman who is now chief operating officer of parent company Ford.

'To stay ahead in the future we need people who are trained to the highest level and we aim to make that happen,' says Nick Barter, former development head at Jaguar and Land Rover, who last year was named launch director of the academy.

Skills4Auto is already identifying and evaluating training opportunities and making education and training providers more aware of the industry's needs. Chosen training schemes are being prepared as further 'spokes' are created.

Mr Beasley says: 'For the first time we have a training and development plan devised by the industry for the industry; training materials accredited by the industry; and training providers to work to the highest global standards.'

Programmes under development are at many levels: the academy itself, for example, has teamed up with the University of Cambridge to help train and educate some of the next generation of industry chief executives. But the main thrust is the creation of a range of so-called Business Improvement Techniques NVQs.

That there is a need for the initiative is not in doubt, observes Kevin Whale, Vauxhall's chairman and managing director: 'We have a shortage of application skills at technical levels as well as higher-level engineering support. So we critically need to improve training at that level.'

The seriousness of the issue in its international context is underlined by Digby Jones, director-general of the Confederation of British Industry, who warns that there is a real risk of investment in training, research and development slipping behind that of China and India.

So far, five colleges in the region, the SMMT's Industry Forum and the Sector Skills Council have collectively developed and launched more than 50 NVQ modules on business and process improvement techniques. Some 500 businesses have already been exposed to the skills programmes.

The Learning and Skills Council's David Cragg points to one company's reduction in lead times from 16 days to 12 hours, and what he describes as 'huge upskilling' at BMW's nearby Hams Hall engine plant.

As for widely aired business views critical of the quality of much of the country's NVQ programme, Mr Broome insists that the motor programmes have achieved what he regards as the three essential ingredients for NVQ integrity: 'Get the content right [and] the trainers properly validated and make sure the assessors are competent.'

Source: Adapted from John Griffiths, in the *Financial Times*, 16 March 2004, p. 12.
Reproduced with permission of the *Financial Times*.

Discussion questions

1 What does this case suggest about the importance of training for an organisation?

2 Many organisations fail to train their workers. Why do you think this happens, and what are the implications for the organisation and for the country?

The opening vignette shows the importance of a planned training programme. Many organisations fail to see the significance of this and as a result suffer from a lack of skills, which ultimately leads to an inability to compete in the global marketplace. This chapter focuses on the importance of training and gives an insight into how organisations can implement training strategies.

In some people's minds there is a clear distinction between training, education and development. To others the processes become blurred. Even if there is no formal training process all new members coming to an organisation will go through some form of socialisation.

Socialisation refers to teaching the organisational culture and philosophies to enable an employee to fit in and operate effectively. On entry to a new organisation an employee needs to 'learn the ropes' – in other words, how things are done in the new environment. This would include not only written policies and procedures, which can often be found in employee manuals, but also unwritten expectations, which an employee would need to understand in order to survive and progress in the organisation. Socialisation follows the recruitment and selection process and, as part of this process, applicants may already have gone through rigorous vetting procedures to ensure they are suitable for the organisation and the job. Before starting work, employees are often required to take part in a socialisation, also known as work orientation or induction, process. This often involves an introduction to the organisation's norms and values, where employees are introduced to company folklore, stories and symbols that form part of the organisational culture.

Whether training is planned or ad hoc, organisations that have a coherent training and development policy are more likely to be at the cutting edge and able to develop competitive advantage through their people.

The advantages of learning, training and development

Organisations that encourage learning, training and development make an intentional effort to improve not only current performance but also the future performance of employees.

By encouraging an employee to learn new skills and develop, employers can:

- ensure that their staff have the capabilities and skills to enable them to be more effective in the workplace
- create an understanding of how to work more effectively as part of a team, and the employee's role in contributing to the organisation
- ensure that the organisation's culture emphasises innovation, creativity and learning
- increase their knowledge of competitors and how employees learning new skills can lead to competitive advantage
- ensure employees are flexible and able to respond to change, which in turn provides them with increased job security as they can move around the organisation when their jobs become obsolete
- encourage acceptance of diversity so that employees have a greater understanding of each other.

The education and training of employees not only helps them to learn new skills but is also essential for their motivation, and will help organisations to attract and retain a highly motivated workforce.

education
The behavioural process of learning that applies to the whole person rather than specific skills.

Education versus training

Education and training both involve the process of learning and have been given the following definitions by the MSC (1981).

Education is defined as:

> activities which aim at developing the knowledge, skills, moral values and understanding required in all aspects of life rather than a knowledge and skill relating to only a limited field of activity. The purpose of education is to develop an understanding of the traditions and ideas influencing the society in which [people] live and to enable them to make a contribution to it. It involves the study of their own cultures and of the laws of nature, as well as the acquisition of linguistic and other skills which are basic to learning, personal development and communication.

training
The process of change used to develop specific skills, usually for a job.

Training is defined as:

> a planned process to modify attitude, knowledge or skill behaviour through learning experience to achieve effective performance in an activity or range of activities. Its purpose, in the work situation, is to develop the abilities of the individual and to satisfy the current and future needs of the organisation.

This means that training refers to a planned intervention by an organisation to improve an employee's job-related competencies. The role of training is to enable employees to master the necessary knowledge, skills and behaviours that will enable them to improve their performance on the job, whereas education is more general and provides the conditions to enable learning to take place.

The distinction between education and training is becoming increasingly blurred as qualifications such as National Vocational Qualifications (NVQs) and General National Vocational Qualifications (GNVQs) have been developed to enable parts of the education system to be more vocationally orientated.

High-leverage training links training to strategic business goals. It is used to encourage a learning organisation, where employees are required not only to acquire new skills and knowledge, which can then be applied to their job, but are also expected to share this information with other employees.

Before deciding on what type of education or training programme to offer it is a good idea to gain an understanding of how people learn.

How do people learn?

Individuals must be able to learn new knowledge and skills in order to survive in both society and the workplace. In today's fast-changing world, everyone who works is periodically required to learn new knowledge and skills. This is even more apparent from the mushrooming uses of the Internet, as it changes the ways people perform routine functions and discover new ways of obtaining and acting on information.

An important distinguishing characteristic of human beings is their ability to store information and to learn. **Learning** is the acquisition of knowledge, skill or values through study, practice or experience. Learning is usually considered to lead to relatively permanent changes in behaviour, as the learner develops capabilities for functioning in his or her environment.

learning
The acquisition of knowledge or skill through study, practice or experience.

The learning process takes place primarily in the brain. One useful metaphor for the brain is a computer. It has the capacity to receive inputs, organise and store them, and respond to some calls for retrieval. New data can be entered and existing data can be reorganised or deleted. Memory is similar to computer files, and perception and learning are the processes through which new data are added and old data revised.

intelligence
The ability to adapt to novel situations quickly and effectively, use abstract concepts effectively, and grasp relationships and learn quickly.

Computers differ in their capacity to receive, store, process and retrieve information quickly, and to manipulate the data in order to solve problems. These differing capacities are somewhat analogous to different individuals' intelligence and ability to think. Intelligence is a fuzzy concept. Generally, **intelligence** includes three different aspects:

1 the ability to adapt to novel situations quickly and effectively

2 the ability to use abstract concepts effectively

3 the ability to grasp relationships and to learn quickly.

Goleman (1994) has identified another aspect of intelligence, which he labels 'emotional intelligence'. It reflects the functioning of a person's emotional brain, which generates and regulates feelings. Goleman suggests that emotional intelligence relates to a person's ability to get along with others, exert control over their own life, and think and decide clearly.

Individuals differ in terms of their memory, intelligence and ability to learn. Now you have the opportunity to learn some of the basic theories of how individuals learn. The main theories we will consider are:

1 behavioural conditioning

2 social learning

3 cognitive discovery.

We will also look at different individual styles of learning, because people tend to differ from one another in how they learn.

Behavioural conditioning

The development of learning theory began in the early twentieth century when the Russian physiologist Ivan Pavlov found he could condition dogs to salivate in response to the sound of a tuning fork, a previously neutral stimulus. Pavlov's work led to the development of classical conditioning, which is an experimental approach that associates a conditioned stimulus with an unconditioned stimulus to achieve a conditioned response.

classical conditioning
An experimental approach that associates a conditioned stimulus with an unconditioned stimulus to achieve a conditional response.

Dogs and other animals naturally salivate (*unconditional response* – R) when they are hungry and food (*unconditional stimulus* – S) is present. Pavlov experimented by preceding the presentation of food with the sound of a tuning fork (*conditional stimulus* – S') and, over time, taught the dogs to salivate (*conditional response* – R') at the sound alone. His experiments provided the intellectual basis for an empirical approach to the study of learning.

People experience classical conditioning in their everyday lives without realising it. For example, assume you frequently walk by a bakery early in the morning and smell (S) the freshly baked bread. If you have not had breakfast, you are likely to salivate and feel hunger pangs (R). The odour is an unconditioned stimulus, and your physical reaction is an unconditioned response. Assume this happens frequently. Then one day you drive by the bakery and cannot smell the bread, but you salivate and feel hungry anyway. The sight of the shop (S') has become a conditioned stimulus and your physical response, which now occurs without the actual odour, is also conditioned (R') (Pavlov, 1927).

Conditioning through management of reinforcement

The psychologist B.F. Skinner (1964) extended the work of Pavlov and others to develop operant conditioning, which is learning in which reinforcement depends on the person's behaviour. In operant conditioning, the critical learning element is the direct linkage of significant contingent consequences to an operant behaviour.

operant conditioning
Learning in which reinforcement depends on the person's behaviour.

A *contingent consequence* is a reinforcer; it may be positive, negative or neutral. The term *operant* simply means that the individual 'operates' in his or her environment to obtain some desired consequences and avoid adverse or negative consequences. Individuals learn to anticipate or expect a certain consequence following specific behaviours. They learn to behave in ways that achieve positive consequences. The more frequently we get the desired consequences or avoid undesirable ones, the firmer the learning.

For example, assume Donna works extra hard on a special project to meet a tight deadline. Her boss is appreciative of her efforts, gives her special praise and celebrates by treating her to lunch at an upmarket restaurant. Donna enjoys the recognition and is likely to work hard again to receive the desired compliments. If she gets no response at all, she will probably feel less inclined to work hard. If Donna is late with her report and is reprimanded, she is likely to work harder the next time to avoid the negative consequence.

According to Thorndike (1913), the basic assumption underlying conditioning theory is simple: people tend to repeat those behaviours that lead to desirable consequences and avoid those that lead to negative results. Conditioning theory underlies many of the behaviours managers and teachers use in an attempt to motivate people and teach them to behave in certain ways. Today, Skinner's principles of operant conditioning are commonly applied in organisational settings to help change many types of human behaviour: drug addicts, students with learning disabilities, smokers, sex offenders and phobics, as well as employees.

Self-management of contingencies

It is possible for a person to manage his or her own contingencies. For example, one principle of time management has evolved from the premise that a person will complete 'have to' tasks quite expediently if the reward (positive reinforcement) is engaging in tasks that are more creative, enjoyable or satisfying. The psychologist, Premack (1959), formalised this self-management strategy of pairing tasks or events.

Premack principle
The pairing of disagreeable tasks with enjoyable tasks or events to hasten their completion.

The Premack principle is based on the finding that, when tasks are paired, the more probable (more pleasurable) behaviour will tend to reinforce or bring about the less probable behaviour. For example, complete the report, then play football or tennis. Well-organised students and workers may find they have adopted the Premack principle without even knowing it had a name. If you have not used it for self-management, try it.

Social learning theory

Behaviourist psychologists believe that operant conditioning or reinforcement theory is the most valid explanation for how people learn. However, many researchers disagree with Skinner's (1971) contentions that humankind is simply an instrument of society, and that people are passively subject to shaping by environmental events and by those in control.

Unwilling to accept the fact that reinforcement alone is the answer, Bandura (1974, 1977)

social learning theory
The belief that we learn many behaviours by observing and imitating others.

and others have researched the social learning aspects of human development. Social learning theory is based on the process of observational learning through modelling and imitation. It holds that, rather than learning exclusively through reinforcement and the shaping of successive approximations towards a desired behaviour, we acquire much behaviour simply through imitation. Imitation is especially strong when the learner identifies with and desires to be like the role model or mentor. Imitators are in conscious control of whether or not to act like the model. As one application, research has found that the success of corporate ethics programmes is most strongly linked to top management's commitment to ethical behaviour – employees will model what they see in leaders.

anticipatory control
Bandura's suggestion that people are capable of choosing how they will respond in various situations.

Bandura (1974) suggests that people are capable of **anticipatory control** – of choosing how they will respond in various situations. Because people are capable of observing the effects of their behaviours, they can anticipate consequences across a variety of circumstances. For example, George's boss may say something in a meeting that angers him. George can choose whether or not to express his anger publicly. He is capable of anticipating his boss's response, based on his experiences with the boss and others in authority positions. He may let it pass based on anticipatory self-control.

Even though the organisational world acts on them, adults at work still choose what situations to get involved in and how to act in them to produce a desired outcome. We learn through social observation to expect that certain socially desirable behaviours will be reinforced, and we learn the value of the reinforcer. While social learning theory acknowledges and builds on many principles of reinforcement, it moves closer to the concept of learning cognitively through insight and self-discovery.

The cognitive view: new patterns of thought

The perceptual-cognitive view of learning focuses on what happens within the individual: motives, feelings, attitudes, memory and cognition (thought). Sensory mechanisms are of primary importance in the key cognitive activity, which is observation based. Through speech and knowledge of language, humans form abstract concepts for organising perceptions and manipulating ideas. Thus, **cognitive learning** involves selective interpretation of perceptual data organised into new patterns of thoughts and relationships. A manager who asks a subordinate if he has a few minutes to talk illustrates this kind of learning. The latter says, 'Well,... OK [voice dropping].' Although the words indicate consent, the boss notices a look of frustration and reads into the pause and tone of voice a strong unwillingness. The boss's ability to observe multiple stimuli and to interpret the non-verbal along with the verbal communication can be learned through training and experience.

cognitive learning
Selective interpretation of perceptual data organised into new patterns of thoughts and relationships.

Human beings are capable of rearranging thought patterns into new configurations, or gestalts. **Gestalt** is a German word meaning 'shape, configuration or the arrangement of relationships in a total situation.' Patterns of concepts and relationships may occur suddenly, through insight, or they may evolve gradually as elements are linked together with new data.

gestalt
A German word meaning 'shape, configuration or the arrangement of relationships in a total situation'.

Insight

Often known as the Eureka! ('I've found it!') or aha! experience, **insight** is best described as the sudden discovery of the answer to a problem. We achieve insight into a situation, relationship or problem when we suddenly grasp an idea or see a relationship that helps us to understand the situation better or solve the problem. Insight often comes while doing something and observing what happens.

insight
The sudden discovery of the answer to a problem.

Kohler (1925) presented the first experimental evidence on insight in the 1920s, when he demonstrated the results of his work with a chimpanzee named Sultan. The turning point in Kohler's research occurred when he enclosed Sultan and a short stick inside a barred cage, outside of which he placed a longer stick and a banana – both too far away for Sultan to reach.

Sultan first picked up the short stick and attempted to rake in the banana. However, the elusive banana remained beyond the chimp's extended reach. Unable to obtain results, Sultan sat cowering in the cage, gazing at the objects around him. Suddenly he jumped up and reached for the short stick. With it he raked in the long stick, then he used the long stick to rake in the banana. Eureka! The chimp had discovered a solution. Today we know that two of the learning processes involved in the phenomenon of insight are discrimination and generalisation.

Discrimination

Sometimes called differentiation, **discrimination** is the process by which universal or previously unstructured elements are placed into more specific structures. People learn to read by discriminating among symbols – first individual letters, then groupings of letters (words), and finally meaningful groupings of letters separated by spaces and punctuation. Discrimination also occurs when three cars are seen as a Mercedes, a Volkswagen and a Porsche, or considered in terms of their components: tyres, engines, doors, seats. Managers discriminate a general concept such as 'organisation' into people, positions, structures, policies, power, leadership, and so on (Bloisi *et al.*, 2003).

discrimination
The process by which universal or previously unstructured elements are placed into more specific structures.

Generalisation

When concepts, functions, objects and events are grouped into categories, generalisation is at work. **Generalisation** is the means through which we transfer learning from one situation to another as well as categorise information. Whereas discrimination breaks down the general into the specific, generalisation unites previously separate elements into meaningful universal themes or clusters. Generalisation helps people map out and programme their memories so that not every event has to be experienced as something totally new.

generalisation
The means through which we transfer learning from one situation to another, as well as categorise information.

Managers generalise when they categorise an organisational behaviour problem as one of communication, for example, or of conflict, motivation, job design or leadership. Then they differentiate its possible causes and probable solutions. They remember the consequences of attempted actions and apply that learning when diagnosing current problems and deciding how they will act. The ability to discriminate, generalise and develop insight is vital to conceptual skill, which is critically important for successful managers, accountants, analysts, scientists and other knowledge workers.

Because insight is a human resource, a manager may draw others into a group problem-solving process. An idea offered by Simon may trigger a thought by Sheila, which prompts a creative suggestion from Susan. One insight tends to generate another in the search for an effective group solution.

How do people differ in how they learn?

One of the most important abilities an individual can possess is the ability to learn. A manager's long-term success depends more on the ability to learn than on the mastery of specific skills or technical knowledge. However, people learn in different ways. We now discuss two ways of differentiating how people learn: one based on behavioural styles, the other on brain dominance.

Experiential learning styles

What is now a research classic by Kolb (1976) indicates that managers favour a style of learning that differs from that of many other professionals. Managers learn most readily from direct experience and by actively testing the implications of concepts to new situations. Kolb's findings are based on a model of learning that involves four different abilities; these combine to form four distinct styles.

Kolb's experiential learning model distinguishes two primary dimensions of the learning process. If we visualise his model in the form of a compass, one dimension ranges from north (the concrete experiencing of events) to south (abstract conceptualisation of ideas). The other dimension extends from west (active experimentation or testing) to east (reflective observations).

These two dimensions are combined to suggest four main learning abilities or processes. As shown in Exhibit 7-1, a complete pattern of learning flows in a circular direction. Beginning at the top: (1) the learner becomes actively involved in new concrete experiences, and (2) through reflective observation examines these experiences from different perspectives (3) to form abstract concepts and generalisations, which (4) lead to theories or assumptions that can be used for active experimentation in problem-solving and decision-making.

Most people become highly skilled at one or two processes rather than all four. When two adjacent processes are emphasised, a dominant learning style emerges. The four characteristics identified in Exhibit 7-1 – divergence, assimilation, convergence and accommodation – represent distinct personal learning styles.

The diverger

Divergers learn best by reflecting on specific experiences and drawing new inferences. The diverger tends to be highly imaginative, excels at brainstorming and likes involvement in the generation of creative ideas. Divergers have an uncanny ability to view concrete situations from many perspectives. Academically, such learners are often interested in the liberal arts, humanities and fine arts. Human resource managers are often divergers.

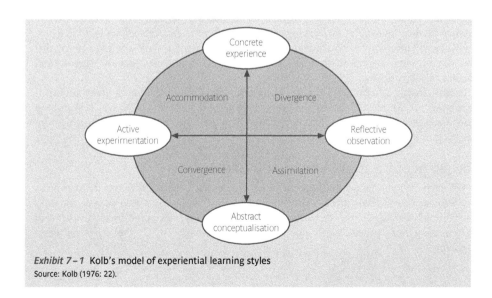

Exhibit 7–1 Kolb's model of experiential learning styles
Source: Kolb (1976: 22).

The assimilator

With their capability to combine reflective observation and abstract conceptualisation, assimilators are good at creating theoretical models. Inductive reasoning is the forte that permits integrating diverse observations into a coherent explanation. Dealing with abstract ideas is the assimilator's domain, more so than seeking practical applications or working with people. Individuals who adopt this learning style are attracted to basic research; in business, you may find them staffing corporate research and planning departments.

The converger

Convergers use abstract concepts as a basis for active experimentation. They focus on specific problems, looking for answers and solutions. Like the assimilator, the converger prefers working with ideas and specific tasks to working with people. Convergers tend to do well in the physical sciences and engineering.

The accommodator

This style focuses on doing. The accommodator's domain is active experimentation and the carrying out of plans that lead to real experiences. Such people are risk takers, able to adapt quickly to new situations. If a theory does not fit the situation, the accommodator discards the concept and works from the facts. Although at ease with people, accommodators tend to be impatient and assertive. Accommodation is often the dominant style of individuals trained for the business world, especially those who gravitate towards action-orientated management or sales jobs.

The need to combine skills and styles

Kolb's research finds that managers tend to be orientated towards learning by active experimentation and concrete experience. Many managers are accommodators. By contrast, many business school faculties tend to be strong on reflective observation and abstract conceptualisation. This makes them assimilators. Because accommodator managers tend to make fewer inferences from data and are less consistent in their actions than assimilators, both learning styles are necessary within organisations. To blend styles within an organisation, Kolb (1976) offers two recommendations.

First, managers and organisations should value and consciously seek learning from experience by budgeting time for the learning process. Second, managers and organisations should value and include those with different learning styles and perspectives. Action-orientated people should be combined with those who are reflective, and those involved in concrete experience should be joined with those who are analytical. Learning can be enhanced when style differences are valued, just as it can by integrating people from different cultures and ethnic backgrounds. (To increase your own awareness of learning style preferences and the need to develop complementary abilities, complete the 'Individual task' at the end of this chapter.)

Honey and Mumford (1992) built on Kolb's theory and defined four major categories of learning. As can be see from Exhibit 7-2, these correspond with Kolb's learning styles.

Honey and Mumford (1992) describe the people strong in the four styles of reflector, theorist, pragmatist and activist as follows.

Reflector

Prefers to stand back and think about experiences and observe them from many different perspectives. These people will collect data, analyse it and look at all angles before coming to a decision. They tend to be cautious and thoughtful, and when they act it is as part of the wider picture.

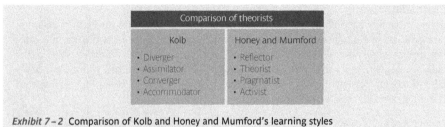

Exhibit 7–2 Comparison of Kolb and Honey and Mumford's learning styles

Theorist

Thinks problems through in a logical step-by-step sequence. These people assimilate disparate facts into a coherent theory. They tend to be perfectionists and prefer logic and rationality to reach a decision.

Pragmatist

Keen to try out new ideas, theories and techniques to find out if they work in practice. These people respond to problems and opportunities as a challenge. They tend to be impatient and will act quickly to try out new things that interest them.

Activist

Activists involve themselves in new experiences. They are open minded and tend to be enthusiastic about anything new. They tend to act first and consider the consequences later. They move quickly from one activity to another, and are often considered outgoing and gregarious.

The concept of learning styles is important as it helps us plan how different people are likely to respond to training programmes. This is illustrated in Exhibit 7-3.

Depending on the preferred style of the individual they will start at different points in the learning cycle. For example, a salesperson may start with experience and accompany a person

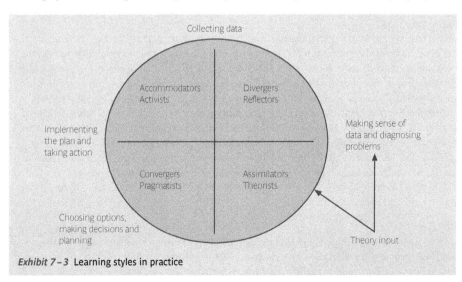

Exhibit 7–3 Learning styles in practice

making a sale; this will involve collecting data. Once they have made a sales call they may reflect on it and think about: What went well? What didn't go well? The next stage would be referring to theory either as directed by their trainer or from their own deliberations. They would then move on to planning the new behaviour: How will they make the sale next time? From here it moves back to experience. The learning cycle is continuous and as new experiences are tried out, so they are reflected on, refined and re-evaluated.

An understanding of learning styles can be really helpful for managers designing training programmes, although this is not the only explanation for differences in learning, as can be seen from studies of the two hemispheres of learning.

Two hemispheres of learning

Another explanation of differences in learning is based on brain-hemisphere dominance. Neurologists and psychologists have long known that the left hemisphere of the brain controls movements on the right-hand side of the body, and vice versa. Ornstein (1973) and others have carried this further by suggesting that our dominant brain hemisphere may play a significant role in how we learn.

The linear/systematic left

The brain's left hemisphere assimilates information in ordered, systematic ways. The process of analysis and planning (usually a central theme of the business school curriculum) is linear in structure. Accounting systems and management-science quantitative models are based on rational logic. Their underlying assumption is that if data are channelled into a formula or model, a working solution can be found.

The left hemisphere of the brain handles quantification and written language. Many organisational activities are well served by predictability and logic. In stable environments, structured, planned behaviour is likely to be effective. However, organisations do not survive and grow without creativity and change.

The holistic/relational right

Mintzberg (1976) suggests that, when it comes to running organisations, planning occurs on the left side, managing on the right. He writes, 'it may be that management researchers have been looking for the key to management in the lightness of logical analysis whereas perhaps it has always been lost in the darkness of intuition'. In drawing insights from observing managers' behaviours, Mintzberg adds, 'effective managers seem to revel in ambiguity; in complex, mysterious systems with relatively little order'.

The world of the right-hemisphere-dominant manager involves holistic, simultaneous, creative learning. In addition, it emphasises learning from face-to-face verbal exchanges rather than from written reports. Through verbal communication, managers can interpret non-verbal cues and act simultaneously on real-time data. Synthesis of soft data – impressions, feelings, intuition – provides the basis for acting more than hard-data analysis does.

Hunches and judgement are mental processes from which insights and new possibilities spring forth. With brief time sequences for processing information, action – not reflection – is more the executive norm. Orderly agendas are atypical in a world beset with interruptions and unplanned activities.

In an article on why and how to develop right-hemisphere intuitive powers, Agor (1984) cited the experiences of a number of executives who relied heavily on intuitive decisions.

Stop and reflect

Looking at the table below, rank in order of importance the skills that you think are necessary for an HR manager.

Then, looking at the right-hand column and using a scale of 1 to 5, where would you rate each skill?

	Order of importance				
	I am good at this			I need to improve	
Verbal communication	1	2	3	4	5
Managing time and stress	1	2	3	4	5
Managing individual decisions	1	2	3	4	5
Recognising, defining and solving problems	1	2	3	4	5
Motivating and influencing others	1	2	3	4	5
Delegating	1	2	3	4	5
Setting goals and articulating a vision	1	2	3	4	5
Self-awareness	1	2	3	4	5
Team building	1	2	3	4	5
Managing conflict	1	2	3	4	5

Lifelong learning

Both the Kolb and Honey and Mumford models of learning styles and the notion of brain-hemisphere specialisation emphasise the ongoing nature of individual learning. Life is a series of learning episodes and processes. Those who are managers will find that their jobs involve knowing both how to learn themselves and how to influence the learning of others.

Now that you are familiar with the different ways of learning, you can probably see for yourself why no one theory works all the time across all situations. Applied behaviour modification principles, for example, are best used in situations in which reinforcing environmental consequences can be structured. Those who learn best through direct experience are not likely to become reflective/conceptual learners. Each approach and style has its essential place in organisations.

Designing effective training programmes

To be effective, training needs to follow a systematic process, as can be seen in Exhibit 7-4.

- **Assessing needs** identifies the type of training needed; this may be through an organisational analysis, a person analysis or a task analysis.
- **Trainee acceptance** involves the employee accepting the need for training, and having the motivation and basic skills to be able to master the training content.
- **Learning environment** refers to identifying whether the factors are available to enable learning to occur. This will identify the learning aims and objectives to be achieved, the materials available, feedback, evaluation processes and other administrative processes.
- **Training methods** identify how the training will take place, such as on or off the job. The training method needs to be appropriate for the learning environment.

Changing attitudes in a business culture that is often endemically corrupt is an ongoing campaign and a challenge for Mexico City's Business School

Few business schools have as clear or as distinct a mission as Mexico City's Ipade. Part of the Panamerican University, it provides senior executives with training to US standards, but has always had a broader agenda: aiming to make the nation competitive on a global level and instilling ethics in a business culture that is often endemically corrupt.

As head of Ipade's marketing department, Mr Gutierrez has already begun promoting the school differently. He is working on raising its media profile, encouraging faculty to participate in conferences outside the traditional business arena. The primary aim is to demonstrate the data's relevance to businesses.

'Often the client of a researcher is another researcher, and the client of an academic is another academic,' Mr Gutierrez says. 'For the businessman, what matters is: "What am I going to do [to find solutions] with marketing or finance or control or accounting?" It's for that reason that they come to Ipade. We are very close to our clients.'

This is in line with the mission of the school, which trains mostly managers and executives, and graduates approximately 70 MBA students per year.

The MBA course was the last to be added, and the training of higher executives is a clear priority. 'Our mission isn't to sell more, it's to sell better. It's not to train lots of people, it's to train them well,' Mr Gutierrez says. 'It's not informative, it's formative, designed to sustain enthusiasm.'

Within Mexico's largest companies, 20 to 25 per cent of chief executives report having taken a course at Ipade.

Ipade sees the rounded development of executives as part of its mission. 'We look for more human development of executives than other business schools, to develop them as a whole person, with integral training,' Mr Gutierrez says, proposing more supplementary seminars in music and arts appreciation.

Within his own marketing classes, Mr Gutierrez has discussed the ethics of raising the price of umbrellas during rain storms or that of cold drinks during heatwaves. 'When students say "It's supply and demand", I ask them: "Are the laws of supply and demand and its results ethical?" and that makes students freeze.'

The national election in 2000 brought new business opportunities and ethical challenges. While President Vicente Fox promised to increase tax collections, open the energy sector to private investment and make social spending more effective, such change has been elusive.

He pledged to combat corruption in all its forms, hiring Ipade graduates to help him, but principled stances are not always easy when doing business in Mexico.

Much of the culture of doing business is unchanged and corruption is considered the oil that keeps the wheels moving.

Mr Gutierrez believes Ipade has a role to play in bringing change to Mexican business culture and in helping Mexico become an entry point for doing business in the rest of Latin America.

Along with other schools, Ipade is contributing case studies to a database at the Latin American Research Center at Harvard Business School. 'Even if a company doesn't export, we can learn from the cases and experience of other companies in other nations,' he says.

international perspective

▶

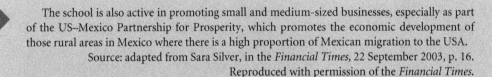

> The school is also active in promoting small and medium-sized businesses, especially as part of the US–Mexico Partnership for Prosperity, which promotes the economic development of those rural areas in Mexico where there is a high proportion of Mexican migration to the USA.
> Source: adapted from Sara Silver, in the *Financial Times*, 22 September 2003, p. 16.
> Reproduced with permission of the *Financial Times*.

Discussion questions

1 This example refers to education rather than training. What are the differences between them?

2 Ethics is seen as an important part of the education programme. Do you think ethical behaviour can be taught?

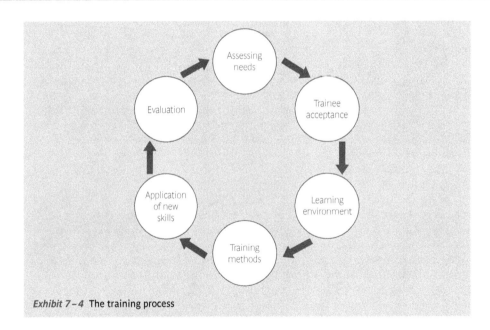

Exhibit 7–4 The training process

- **Application of new skills** ensures that trained employees are able to apply their new skills to the job, and should involve self-management strategies and peer and management support.

- **Evaluation** determines whether training has achieved its objectives of changed behaviour and improved performance.

Steps in training

The needs analysis

The needs analysis identifies the specific skills required for performance and productivity, as can be seen in Exhibit 7-5.

The needs analysis looks at the organisation and identifies reasons that could affect the performance of the organisation. The next step is to identify whether training is the most appropriate solution for the organisation. This would involve determining the appropriateness of

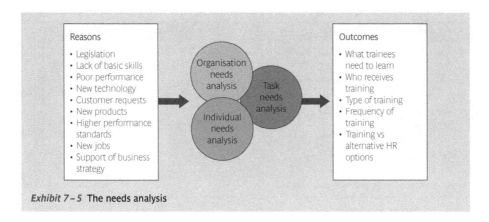

Exhibit 7–5 **The needs analysis**

training in relation to the organisation's business strategy, the financial and physical resources available and the support for training from both managers and employees.

The individual needs analysis helps to identify:

- current performance against desired performance, and the gaps in ability, skills and knowledge
- whether poor performance is a result of lack of knowledge, skill ability, or a motivational or work design problem
- who it is that needs training
- the readiness of the employee to accept training, as resistance may mean training interventions are ineffective.

The task analysis includes identifying the elements that make up the task, in terms of the knowledge, skill and behaviours that need to be emphasised in the training process.

Training is expensive, therefore managers need to ensure that they have fully assessed the situation to establish whether training is the answer. Once they have decided on a training strategy then training policies are the next stage.

Training policies

The training policy should be linked to the organisation's strategy and can have the characteristics demonstrated by Hackett (2003) in Exhibit 7-6.

Whether the training policy is implicit or explicit, most organisations have an underlying philosophy or belief about the value of training and will decide what type of training will be implemented, to whom, and where the training will be undertaken. This may also be in response to government initiatives such as development of a national skills base through Learning and Skills Councils (LSCs), which are responsible for achieving national training targets, through initiatives such as Investors In People (IIP) or National Vocational Qualifications (NVQs).

National Vocational Qualifications (NVQs)

National Vocational Qualifications (NVQs) were developed from a government initiative dating from 1985, as an attempt to rationalise and co-ordinate qualifications, which would

Either	Or
■ Based on careful analysis of organisational needs, best practice and relevant law ■ Formally written down as a basis for future decisions ■ Communicated to all employees to guide decision-making ■ Prescriptive and all embracing ■ Supported by operating procedures ■ Part of an internally consistent framework (e.g. personnel policy, public relations policy)	■ Intuitive ■ Inferred from the pattern of decisions previously made ■ Referred to after the event to justify specific decisions ■ Allow considerable discretion ■ Unsupported ■ Stand-alone

Exhibit 7–6 Policy characteristics (Hackett, 2003)

enable employers to have a greater understanding of the levels of qualifications and make them more skills-relevant. By 1999 a framework of over 800 NVQs had been developed covering 500 occupations. This was further developed by offering General National Vocational Qualifications (GNVQs), which covered general occupational areas rather than specific industry skills. This enabled them to be delivered in schools and colleges as part of the curriculum. NVQs are offered over five performance levels, which can be seen in Exhibit 7-7. The qualifications and standards are monitored by the Qualifications and Curriculum Authority (QCA).

NVQs
National Vocational Qualifications, used to measure competence in specific skills in the workplace.

NVQs focus on competencies, which is the ability to do something, rather than broader-based knowledge or behaviours. This means that training can be carried out in the workplace rather than traditional education establishments. Many large employers implement NVQs in liaison with their industry lead body or professional association. This means that the role of training has become more integrated into organisational life, with employees at different levels working towards different levels of NVQs, as well as supervisors and managers gaining training qualifications to enable them to assess candidates. This also links into National Learning Targets.

National Learning Targets

National Learning Targets
Targets set by the government to increase the achievement of skills both at school and in the workplace.

The National Learning Targets are one way of measuring the progress of the Department for Education and Skills (DfES). They help focus efforts to increase participation and achievement in both school and workplace learning.

The aim is to ensure that all young people gain the necessary abilities for a secure foundation for lifelong learning. There is a particular focus on improving literacy and numeracy skills in primary schools and pupil achievement in secondary schools.

The Targets also aim to develop a general commitment to lifelong learning, and to encourage employers to invest in the training and development of their employees.

Level	Performance
1	Competence that involves the application of knowledge and skills in the performance of a range of varied work activities, most of which may be routine and predictable
2	Competence that involves the application of knowledge and skills in a significant range of varied work activities, performed in a variety of contexts. Some of the activities are complex or non-routine, and there is some individual responsibility or autonomy. Collaboration with others, perhaps through membership of a work group or team, may often be a requirement
3	Competence that involves the application of knowledge and skills in a broad range of varied work activities performed in a wide variety of contexts, most of which are complex and non-routine. There is considerable responsibility and autonomy, and control or guidance of others is often required
4	Competence that involves the application of knowledge and skills in a broad range of complex, technical or professional work activities performed in a wide variety of contexts and with a substantial degree of personal responsibility and autonomy. Responsibility for the work of others and the allocation of resources is often present
5	Competence that involves the application of skills and a significant range of fundamental principles across a wide and often unpredictable variety of contexts. Very substantial personal autonomy and often significant responsibility for the work of others and for the allocation of substantial resources feature strongly, as do personal accountabilities for analysis and diagnosis, design, planning, execution and evaluation

Exhibit 7–7 Levels of NVQ performance
Source: QCA's *Data News* (May 1998).

The Learning and Skills Council

The Learning and Skills Council (LSC) has been in place since March 2001. It replaced the training functions of Training and Enterprise Councils (TECs) and the funding responsibilities of the Further Education Funding Councils (FEFCs) within England.

It brings a new coherence to all post-16 education and training, excluding higher education. The LSC is governed by a National Council, which is advised by two statutory committees (one covering adult learning and one covering young people), and operates through 47 local offices.

The Learning and Skills Council has an annual budget of around £6bn and the responsibility for funding around five million learners each year in England.

The Learning and Skills Council is responsible for the funding, planning and quality assurance of further education, school sixth form, work-based training for young people, workforce development, adult and community learning, information, advice and guidance for adult learners, and education business links.

The role of the Learning and Skills Council is to:

- assess national learning and skills needs, and advise the government on the National Learning Targets

- develop plans and strategies to meet the National Learning Targets

- set a clear agenda for workforce development, working with business, trades unions and Sector Skills Councils (SSCs)
- tackle adults' poor basic skills, accessibility of learning for the socially disadvantaged and those with learning difficulties, and promote equal opportunities
- develop national partnerships to understand needs and agree strategies for working together
- allocate budgets to the local Learning and Skills Councils.

Local Learning and Skills Councils

Local Learning and Skills Councils are responsible for annual budgets of £100m and for the funding of over 100,000 local learners. Their role is to ensure that the needs of local communities, businesses and individuals are met through Learning and Skills Council-funded provision and, for delivering national priorities at local level, to allocate Learning and Skills Council funding within a national framework with local flexibility, and deploy significant local discretionary budgets including funds to:

- increase the quality of local provision and support local initiatives that otherwise would not attract mainstream funding
- develop local workforce development plans that direct local action to encourage employers and small firms to invest in developing their workforce, and promote business benefits to work with SSCs in the development of the sector workforce development plan
- work closely with Regional Development Agencies (RDAs), local authorities, learning partnerships, the Connexions service, Small Business Service (formerly Business Links), University for Industry (UFI) and others to ensure coherent action is taken to achieve goals.

National committees

The Learning and Skills Council is advised by two national committees: the Young People's Committee and the Adult Learning Committee.

The Young People's Committee is responsible for advising the national council on the best means of achieving the National Learning Targets for young people. This includes strategies for increased participation from young people to remain in education until the age of 19. The committee also works alongside the Connexions service (formerly the Careers Service) to improve employability and personal development.

The Adult Learning Committee is responsible for advising the Learning and Skills Council on achieving National Learning Targets for adults, and for raising attainment and improving basic skills among adults. The Committee also works closely with the Small Business Service to encourage businesses to invest in their workforce.

Identifying training needs

As stated earlier, training is the bridge that fills the gap between where an individual is and where the organisation wants them to be. To identify such gaps, Boydell and Leary (2002) suggest that the organisation needs to identify three levels of performance, which are:

Level 1 **implementing** – bridging the gap between present and desired performance, measured against existing standards

Level 2 **improving** – to enable a continual raising of standards

Level 3 **innovating** – doing new and better things to enable change and a continuous learning organisation.

A good place to start is by examining job descriptions and job specifications, which are discussed in Chapter 3, along with techniques for analysis. These can then lead into a training specification, which, according to the Manpower Services Commission (MSC, 1981) is a 'detailed statement of what a trainee needs to learn, based on a comparison between the job specification and the individual's present level of competence'. This can be identified through comparison with expected performance standards or through the appraisal system, which is discussed in Chapter 8.

Determining training objectives

Reid and Barrington (1999) suggest that the first step in implementing training is to identify training objectives. Once the objectives have been established the next step is to identify how best to achieve them, select a strategy, then plan, implement and evaluate the training. The training objectives should identify the learning or behavioural objectives to be achieved. It is not enough just to identify the training; this must be linked to the expected change in behaviour.

This means that, in compiling the objectives, thought needs to be given as to how they will be measured, under what type of conditions and to what standard.

Determining the training strategy

Once the training objectives have been established, the type of training needs to be identified. This will usually fall into the following main categories:

- on-the-job training
- in-house programmes
- external courses
- external bespoke programmes
- self-managed learning.

On-the-job training

This might involve 'sitting next to Nellie', where a new employee is trained by an existing employee. This often means that training is not regulated and that bad habits are passed on as well as good ones. Alternatively, on-the-job training can include detailed training procedures, in line with Modern Apprenticeship schemes. On-the-job training accounts for half of all training carried out in organisations. The success of such schemes depends on:

'sitting next to Nellie'
A method of training where a trainee learns new skills by copying a more experienced worker.

- the competence of the trainers, not only in the job skills but also their training skills
- the recognition of the need for trained trainers
- adequate preparation of structured training sessions
- health and safety issues being adequately incorporated into the sessions
- regular monitoring and evaluation of performance against targets.

In-house programmes

In-house training programmes are run by the organisation. These may be provided to enhance understanding of specific topics or as development for future managers. Many organisations also run competence-based programmes, such as NVQs, that are specifically designed for their organisation. The advantage of in-house programmes is that they can be designed solely to meet organisational needs and can be delivered at a time convenient to the employer. Problems with in-house training can involve the initial cost of suitable resources and the development of train-ers. There is also the need for support from management to allow employees time for training.

External courses

There are many further and higher education colleges that offer a variety of courses, often voca-tionally related. The advantages of external courses are that they allow participants to mix with people from other organisations and share ideas. As they are delivered outside the organisation they do not involve internal resources such as in-house specialist staff or rooms and equipment. Often, employees are able to work towards qualifications that can enhance their own develop-ment and career prospects. As with all training, if the company is prepared to allow employees to attend a course, it also needs to ensure that they are given time to study.

External bespoke courses

Many training organisations will offer tailor-made programmes for organisations. Some of these courses may also be externally recognised by examination or professional associations. Before embarking on such a scheme, managers need to ensure that the course:

- is organised by people qualified to deliver such a course
- meets the organisational objectives
- meets a training need that can be measured and assessed
- has a cost that is related to the expected benefits
- is being run by a training organisation that can provide references from other satisfied organisations.

Self-managed learning

Self-managed learning needs to be part of the overall organisational strategy. To be effective, the following conditions need to be present:

- learning must be seen to be valued by the organisation
- opportunities are made available for employees to learn through their work
- individual appraisal helps to identify development opportunities, which are then sup-ported by the organisation
- managers, coaches, mentors and colleagues also provide assistance for the development of learning.

Reid and Barrington (1999) suggest that:

> The culture of a learning organisation recognises that any learning is beneficial to the development of the whole person, and that the gain would ultimately be fed back to the organisation in the form of [the] increased maturity and learning capacity of its personnel.

As can be seen from the 'Managing diversity' box, training needs to reflect the need of the people in the organisation and it is the organisation who can help direct employees to achieve new skills when in the past they may not have thought this possible.

Training techniques can take several different forms and managers need to ensure that they constantly evaluate their training objectives, policies and practices.

Evaluation of training

Training is about improving performance, and therefore training programmes need to be measured to ensure that this is what they have done. Training evaluation should look at four basic categories.

1 **Reaction** – the trainee's views on the programme. Did they find it useful? Was it worthwhile?

2 **Learning** – have they learned the skills they were supposed to learn? Will they now be able to do their job better?

3 **Behaviour** – has this now changed due to the training programme? Are they able to work more effectively with colleagues and customers?

4 **Results** – are the trainees now more productive? Has performance improved? Is it of better quality?

Managers who fail to evaluate training will never know if the training has been effective. As has been said before, training is expensive and managers need to know that they are getting a return on their investment.

Nearly three million UK workers may be affected by dyslexia, but there is still widespread ignorance about the condition; what are employers doing to break down the barriers?

His teachers considered him slow, unsociable and a dreamer, and he apparently didn't learn to read until he was eight or nine. Yet Albert Einstein went on to make some of the most important scientific discoveries of the twentieth century – even though it is widely believed that he was dyslexic.

He is certainly not alone. The list of successful dyslexics includes the likes of children's author Hans Christian Andersen, entrepreneur Sir Richard Branson and actor Tom Cruise.

The British Dyslexia Association (BDA) estimates that between 4 and 10 per cent of the population is dyslexic and, according to a recent report by the TUC, *Dyslexia in the Workplace*, up to 2.9 million workers may be affected. Nevertheless, the report claims that many employers do not appreciate the link between dyslexia and common performance problems. As a result they often judge dyslexic employees unfairly, even though the condition is recognised as a disability under the Disability Discrimination Act, which since October 2004 has covered all employers, regardless of size.

While most people have heard of dyslexia, there are misconceptions about what it entails. This became apparent to Aaron Tyler, a machine supervisor at Konica Minolta, when he first told his colleagues he had been diagnosed as dyslexic.

The BDA describes dyslexia as a 'combination of abilities and difficulties' – the key word here being 'abilities'. Aside from often having high IQs, dyslexics can be very creative and good at practical tasks, while also showing strengths in areas such as problem-solving, innovation and lateral thinking. Carol Youngs, policy and communications director at the BDA, says dyslexic

managing diversity

▶ people can often see the bigger picture, even though they may not be as good at certain processes.

But if dyslexia has not been diagnosed, or if an employee is afraid to disclose their problems, then all too often any resulting poor performance is dealt with as a disciplinary matter. 'There are people who don't know they are dyslexic and are struggling. Then there are those who are trying to hide their condition because of fear they will lose their job. We need to break down both of these areas,' explains Shirley Cramer, chief executive of the Dyslexia Institute.

Peter Purton, policy officer at the TUC, agrees. He says that if employers are to benefit from the many strengths that dyslexic people can offer, they need to become more knowledgeable about the condition and take steps to harness individuals' strengths, rather than penalise them for their weaknesses. With the right support, it is possible for dyslexic people to develop strategies and alternative methods to overcome what weaknesses they do have.

Of course, the common fear among many employers, especially smaller ones, is that additional support will cost them money. But this is not necessarily the case. Kirsten Knight, a producer at BBC Radio 4, explains that some of her support will be funded by Access to Work, which she describes as the 'best piece of hidden disability support the government provides'.

Peter Purton agrees it is a key initiative that needs to be more powerfully promoted. Administered by JobCentre Plus, Access to Work can provide a grant of between 80 and 100 per cent towards any approved extra employment costs that result from a person's disability.

With or without external funding, many of the adjustments employers can make do not need to be costly. According to specialist training company Dyslexia Works, supporting a dyslexic employee may mean as little as offering some flexibility in working environment and practices – and small things can make a difference. For example, providing information on coloured paper will enable some dyslexic people to read it more easily.

Judy Greevy, head of diversity and corporate responsibility at Centrica, says that about 18 months ago the company became aware that it needed to do more around the issue of dyslexia. It now provides guidance on the subject as part of the general information made available for managers.

Centrica is also looking to put in place an e-learning package on diversity for all staff, which uses dyslexia as an example. Greevy explains that this will help people to move away from the idea that disabilities involve only physical or mobility issues.

Hampshire Constabulary, meanwhile, is delivering awareness training for one particular group of managers who have dyslexic staff reporting to them.

The plan is to ensure that all line managers and tutor constables eventually go through this training. Recruitment manager Valerie King says the Constabulary is also working hard to ensure that dyslexic applicants are treated fairly during the recruitment process. The organisation has forged links with a local further education college to help people with dyslexia or other learning difficulties prepare for their police entry assessments – for which they are also given extra time.

One employee who has particularly benefited from Hampshire's positive approach is Sarah McCabe, a recruiting assistant in the personnel department. She didn't reveal she was dyslexic until two weeks into the job because she was afraid of what the reaction would be. But McCabe explains that her colleagues responded positively and are more than willing to help her with things like emails and letters.

'If someone had told me a few years ago that I would be working in recruitment administration, I would have laughed,' she says. 'Now I think, if I can do this, what else can I do?'

Source: Catherine Edwards, *People Management*, 24 March 2005, p. 38.
Reproduced with permission of *People Management*.

Discussion questions

1 How can training programmes meet the needs of dyslexic employees?

2 Why is diversity an important issue when developing education and training programmes?

The learning organisation

Learning organisations, according to Senge *et al.* (1995), are organisations that focus energy and resources on learning from mistakes as well as opportunity seeking. They are likely to 'learn faster than the competition, change before they're forced to, and always try to marry personal and financial performance'. Senge has popularised the concept of the learning organisation. A **learning organisation** develops tools and methods to analyse, change and re-evaluate its organisational systems so that employees respond more effectively and quicker to the same work-related stimulus than they did in the past, and to novel stimuli almost as quickly.

learning organisation
A deliberate effort by organisational members to develop models, tools and techniques for their organisation to change and grow faster than competitors.

One successful learning organisation, Royal Dutch Shell, became committed to systematising learning when its research into older companies found that learning was their key to survival. Christensen and Overdorf (2000) suggest that the alternative is to be plagued with 'learning disabilities', which retard adaptiveness to change and can be fatal, causing organisations to prematurely shorten their life span. Like individuals, organisations that do not know how to learn to maximise the effectiveness of appropriate capabilities may survive but never live up to their potential. Those firms that become effective learners are the ones most likely to succeed in increasingly turbulent, competitive global markets.

Garvin (1993) suggests that a learning organisation is skilled at creating, acquiring and transferring knowledge, and at modifying its behaviour to reflect new knowledge and insight. Below are examples of how two managers view the power of learning within their organisations.

- Ron Hutchinson, vice president of customer service for Harley-Davidson Motor Company, Inc., says: 'To be effective long term, we must have an organisation in place that understands what caused prior mistakes and failures – and most importantly what caused successes. Then, we need to know how we can inculcate the successes and inculcate the preventive measures to avoid additional failures.'

- Human resources manager Laura Gilbert says her Educational Computing Company has become 'a place that has a proactive, creative approach to the unknown, encouraging individuals to express their feelings, and using intelligence and imagination instead of just skills and authority to find new ways to be competitive and manage work.'

The characteristics of learning organisations

Senge (1990) identified five characteristics required for a learning organisation. These are summarised in Exhibit 7-8. They are personal mastery, mental process models, shared vision,

- **Systems thinking:** members perceive their organisation as a system of interrelated processes, activities, functions and interactions. Any action taken will have repercussions for other variables in the system. It is important to see the entire picture in the short and long run
- **Shared vision:** belief and commitment towards a goal deeply desired by all. Sublimation of competing departmental and personal interests for the achievement of the shared vision
- **Personal mastery:** continual learning and personal growth by all organisational members. Individuals are willing to give up old ways of thinking and behaving to try out possible better ones for themselves and the organisation
- **Mental process models:** shared internal images of how individuals, the organisation and the world work. Willingness to reflect on the reasoning underlying our actions and to change these assumptions when necessary to create a more appropriate process for doing things
- **Team learning:** organisation members openly communicate across departmental and hierarchical boundaries to help all members solve problems and learn from each other. Decreasing the need for personal wins in order to increase the search for the truth for the good of the entire team

Exhibit 7-8 Characteristics of a learning organisation

team learning, and systems thinking. Systems thinking is the most important because all the others are a part of it. In a learning organisation, people are willing to let go of old defences and ways of behaving in order to learn with others how their organisation really works. Then they can form a common vision of where they want to go, develop mental models of how organisational processes work, design a plan to get there, and implement it as a committed team.

Armed with these characteristics, learning organisations are better equipped to cope with the traditional organisational constraints of fragmentation, competition and reactiveness. Instead of separating different organisational functions into competing fragments, learning organisations emphasise the total system and how each function contributes to the whole process. Instead of competing for resources and trying to prove who is right or wrong, learning organisations promote co-operation and sharing of knowledge for the benefit of all. Finally, instead of reacting to problems like a firefighter, learning organisations encourage innovativeness and continual improvement so that problems don't occur in the first place, or will not recur in the future.

Types of organisational learning

As discussed in the previous chapter, individuals prefer different learning styles. So do organisations. Research by Rheem (1995) has identified four basic types of organisational learning: competence acquisition, experimentation, continuous improvement, and boundary spanning.

1 **Competence acquisition:** organisations that learn by competence acquisition cultivate new capabilities in their teams and individuals – capabilities including resources, processes and values. They demonstrate public commitment to learning by continuously seeking new ways to work, and by promoting learning as a fundamental part of their business strategies.

2 **Experimentation:** organisations that learn by experimentation try out new ideas. They are innovators who attempt to be the first to market with new processes or products.

3 **Continuous improvement:** organisations that learn by continuous improvement strive to master each step in the process before moving on to the next. Their goal is to become the recognised technical leader for a particular product or process.

4 **Boundary spanning**: organisations that learn by boundary spanning continuously scan other companies' efforts, benchmarking their processes against those of competitors. Like many organisations that learn from others, Porsche sent engineering teams to Japanese car factories to compare assembly times and discover how to improve its own processes.

Rheem (1995) found that, in general, companies that learn by experimentation are better able to compete and change than those that rely on the other learning methods. This doesn't mean that experimentation is best for all companies. To maximise competitiveness, an organisation's dominant type of learning should match its culture. For instance, a bureaucratic organisation proud of tradition would have a difficult time trying to learn by experimentation.

Creating learning organisations

How can a traditional reactive organisation be changed into a continual learner? Richards (1994) suggests that instituting any process that enlarges the organisation's knowledge base and improves the way knowledge is interpreted and put to use will help. Four specific actions are to establish a learning strategy, redesign the organisational structure, infuse enterprise resource planning systems, and modify the organisation's culture.

1 **Establish a learning strategy**: management needs to develop and make explicit a strategic intent to learn. This includes a commitment to experimentation, a willingness to learn from experiences, and a willingness to implement necessary changes in the spirit of continuous improvement. One strategy worthy of elaboration in the closing part of this section is the stimulation of double-loop learning rather than conventional single-loop learning.

2 **Redesign the organisational structure**: traditional hierarchical organisational structures, which emphasise authority, separate departments into competing domains and enforce formal communication networks, impede organisational learning. To enhance organisational learning, communication can be increased by encouraging informal face-to-face interaction and electronic distribution to all concerned parties. Competition can be replaced with co-operation through the establishment of common performance measures and rewards. Authority levels are reduced by instituting cross-functional teams and eliminating departmental boundaries.

3 **Infuse enterprise resource planning systems**: enterprise resource planning (ERP) systems are software packages (such as SAP-R3 or Peoplesoft) that integrate all facets of a business, including manufacturing, accounting, procurement, human resources and sales. ERP and other forms of integrative software are increasingly web-based, designed to permit anyone who has a need to know to call up real-time information. Such instant access to data sources of information promotes learning by enabling people throughout the organisation to analyse situations and to make timely, more informed decisions. Peters (2000) refers to enterprise software as 'white-collar robots', saying that they will transform organisational productivity in the early twenty-first century, much as robots and mechanised automation transformed blue-collar efficiency in the latter half of the twentieth.

4 **Modify the organisation's culture**: learning happens best in the context of organisational cultures that value growth, openness, trust and risk taking. Known as the regenerative climate, emphasis is on high openness, trust and owning of responsibility. Managers

promote experimentation, trying new things, constructive criticism, learning from past mistakes and bringing functional disagreements into the open. Management establishes regenerative climates by publicising what is desired, acting accordingly themselves, and rewarding desired behaviours. The organisational development process is concerned with developing learning organisations to improve individual and organisational effectiveness.

Single-loop to double-loop learning

From research involving 6000 people across a wide variety of countries, ages, ethnic identities, educational levels, power levels, experience and from both sexes, Argyris (1994) concluded that many modern techniques that promote communication between managers and employees are dysfunctional. Techniques such as total quality management, management by walking around, focus groups and organisational surveys inhibit learning if used in a one-dimensional way.

Single-loop learning displaces employees' responsibility

According to Argyris (2000), when learning is of a single-loop character, the responsibility for learning and action shifts from subordinate to manager. Argyris emphasises: 'single-loop learning asks a one-dimensional question to elicit a one-dimensional answer' wherein outcome responsibility resides with the manager doing the asking.

single-loop learning
Occurs when a manager shifts responsibility from employees to himself or herself by asking simple, unidimensional questions that produce simple, impersonal responses.

For example, the manager who asks others to identify the major obstacles to faster product innovation actually shifts accountability for innovation from the employee to the manager. Although on the surface it may appear as if employees are being empowered because their opinions are being asked for, the implication is that the manager takes responsibility for acting on the advice.

Double-loop learning keeps accountability on followers

To enter into double-loop learning, the leader would have to shift accountability back to employees. This might be done by asking tough questions, such as: How long have you known about these problems? What goes on in this company that prevented you from questioning these practices and getting them corrected or eliminated? Double-loop learning turns questions back on people in the form of follow-ups – to ask not only for facts, but also for the motives and action implications behind the facts, with the implication that changing the situation is their responsibility.

double-loop learning
Shifts accountability for actions and learning to employees by having a manager ask complex questions about the employee's motivation for solving a problem.

Managers often contribute to the problem if they have been trained to emphasise positive regard of others, being considerate and employee morale. Such motives and attitudes deprive employees of the opportunity to take responsibility for their own behaviour by learning to understand it. According to Argyris (2000), because double-loop learning depends on questioning one's own assumptions and behaviour, 'this apparently benevolent strategy [of single-loop learning] is actually *anti-learning*'.

All too often, managers use socially 'upbeat' feedback and behaviour to unconsciously inhibit learning, when honesty and candour would produce more responsible behaviour. Organisational members learn a set of rules to deal with difficult situations in ways that do not embarrass or threaten psychological well-being. Managers end up sending mixed messages when they reply along the lines of 'your recommendation is a good one, but I have to overrule it because...'. By saving face with subordinates while nevertheless thinking the idea is not a good one, managers are telling employees that their job is to make suggestions, and the manager's job is to make decisions and act. Rather than confront others with candour and forthrightness, managers who absolve others are talking the talk but not walking the walk. Rather than promoting the empowerment of others, they are creating dependence. Argyris (2000) writes:

> Once employees base their motivation on extrinsic factors – [such as] the CEO's promises – they are much less likely to take chances, question established policies and practices, or explore the territory that lies beyond the company vision as defined by management. They are much less likely to learn.
>
> A generation ago, business wanted employees to do exactly what they were told, and company leadership bought their acquiescence with a system of purely extrinsic rewards ... Today ... managers need employees who think constantly and creatively about the needs of the organisation. They need employees with as much intrinsic motivation and as deep a sense of organisational stewardship as any company executive.

Summary

- Socialisation refers to the process an employee goes through to fit into an organisation.
- Education is the development of knowledge and skills, as well as moral values related to all aspects of life.
- Training is the planned acquisition of particular skills to perform an activity.
- Training managers need to know how people learn, as different learning styles and preferences can have an impact on the success of training schemes.
- Lifelong learning means that people continue to learn throughout their life and managers need to ensure that employees also have an opportunity to develop new skills and knowledge.
- Training programmes should fill the gap between present performance and desired future performance.
- Competence refers to the ability to perform a task or job. NVQ qualifications test competence to set standards.
- Training strategy needs to be linked to business strategy to ensure the organisation's goals are met.
- Organisations should aim to develop a learning organisation that, by definition, will be flexible and more able to respond to change.

Personal development

1 **Recognise the difference between education and training.** Think about the different methods of learning you use when studying at college or when learning a skill for a new job. What processes do you use? How are they different and how are they the same?

2 **Match abilities to aptitudes.** Develop a list of your abilities and a list of your aptitudes (where you have the capacity to learn). Where you have aptitudes that are not yet fulfilled with abilities, write a plan of what you need to do to develop abilities. Distinguish between what you can do while still a student and what you can better learn while working over the next five years or so.

3 **Apply the Premack principle of reinforcement.** When deciding on the sequence of your 'to do' list, pair tasks and do the less satisfying one first. Do something that is more enjoyable or fulfilling as reinforcement for having done the one that is more of a chore.

4 **Follow the flow of experiential learning styles.** Refer back to Exhibit 7-1 and using the descriptors for Kolb's four styles of learning, identify the one that is most characteristic of you. As each style represents the combination of two learning abilities, observe the two alternative abilities you seem to use less frequently. Practise following the flow of the model when you are learning something complex. That way, you will include the less developed abilities and complete the learning loop.

5 **Plan for lifelong learning.** How can you plan for continuous development throughout your career? What is the impact for the individual and the organisation when learning is not valued?

6 **Develop competence.** It is one thing to know what tasks involve but another to carry them out effectively. How do you know when you are competent? How can you develop competence?

❓ Discussion questions

1 Describe the process a new employee may go through as part of socialisation into an organisation. What can be planned and what can be unplanned?

2 What are the differences between training and education?

3 Why should a manager be concerned with lifelong learning?

4 What does a training manager need to consider before implementing a training programme?

5 What are the advantages and disadvantages of the following: (a) on-the-job training; (b) in-house programmes; (c) external courses; (d) external bespoke programmes?

6 How can managers encourage self-managed learning?

7 Why is it important for the training strategy to link with the business strategy?

8 Give an example of how the manager of an e-commerce unit might apply each of these three learning theories: (1) behavioural conditioning, (2) social learning theory, and (3) cognitive theory.

❶ Key concepts

education, *p. 218*	gestalt, *p. 222*
training, *p. 218*	insight, *p. 222*
learning, *p. 219*	discrimination, *p. 223*
intelligence, *p. 219*	generalisation, *p. 223*
classical conditioning, *p. 220*	NVQs, *p. 232*
operant conditioning, *p. 220*	National Learning Targets, *p. 232*
Premack principle, *p. 221*	'sitting next to Nellie', *p. 235*
social learning theory, *p. 221*	learning organisation, *p. 239*
anticipatory control, *p. 222*	single-loop learning, *p. 242*
cognitive learning, *p. 222*	double-loop learning, *p. 242*

Individual task

Reflections on learning styles

Continual learning is fundamental to functioning successfully within organisations. Therefore, those who aspire to careers in organisations should be aware of how they prefer to learn, and work to develop complementary learning skills where those abilities are low. To think more personally about learning processes, begin by answering the following questions. Circle the number that best describes you for the eight questions below. (This entire activity can be completed in about 5 to 7 minutes.)

1 I enjoy venturing into new experiences and relationships to see what I can learn.

This describes me			*This does not describe me*	
1	2	3	4	5

2 I actively participate in here-and-now experiences that enable me to become aware of how I affect my environment and others.

This describes me			*This does not describe me*	
1	2	3	4	5

3 I am a careful observer of events and people, and find myself reflecting on what I see and hear from what goes on about me.

This describes me			*This does not describe me*	
1	2	3	4	5

4 I find myself talking with others about our recent experiences so that I can make sense of what people say and do, and of why events turn out as they do.

This describes me			*This does not describe me*	
1	2	3	4	5

5 I like to manipulate abstract ideas and symbols to visualise how concepts and things are related.

This describes me			*This does not describe me*	
1	2	3	4	5

6 I find myself engaging in 'what if?' forms of reasoning and synthesising ideas into hypotheses for future testing.

This describes me			*This does not describe me*	
1	2	3	4	5

7 I enjoy taking risks by testing my ideas on others or in actions to see if they work.

This describes me			*This does not describe me*	
1	2	3	4	5

8 I am decisive, a practical problem-solver who enjoys putting plans into action.

This describes me			*This does not describe me*	
1	2	3	4	5

There are no right or wrong answers to the above questions. The questionnaire is not intended to be a scientifically valid instrument, but simply to serve as a stimulus to your thinking and learning. To interpret your answers, add your 'scores' for each pair of questions (1 + 2, 3 + 4, etc.) in the table below:

Scores from questions	Learning processes (abilities)
1 _____ + 2 _____ = _____	Concrete experience
3 _____ + 4 _____ = _____	Reflective observation
5 _____ + 6 _____ = _____	Abstract conceptualisation
7 _____ + 8 _____ = _____	Active experimentation

Your lowest score(s) suggest the learning processes that you tend to favour. The higher the score, the less inclined you are to use that process or ability.

Now turn back to Exhibit 7-1 and write your total scores on each of the four processes next to the appropriate label in the diagram. Are your two lowest scores adjacent to one another in the flow process (for example, 'concrete experience' and 'reflective observation')? If so, circle the learning style indicated by the combination of the two (such as 'divergence' for the above example). This is suggestive of your dominant style of learning. Read again the description of this style and reflect on whether you believe that it appropriately describes you.

If you do have a dominant style, is the total of your other two processes at least twice as high as your two lowest scores? If so, you might want to strengthen them as this suggests they are seldom used. Write down three action steps you could take to activate learning using these process alternatives. Then seek to practise them.

You may want to compare results with those of a classmate. If the two of you differ in learning styles, you can learn from one another how to strengthen your less used abilities.

Team task

Purpose To encourage students to think about how they learn, and their role in the learning experience.

Time 40 minutes

1 Think about past learning experiences, which (a) made you feel good, and (b) made you feel bad. Write down what it was that made it a good or bad learning experience.

2 In pairs, share good/bad learning experiences and see if there are any similarities or differences.

3 In fours, collectively write notes on a flip chart under the following headings: 'Things that encourage learning' and 'Things that inhibit learning'.

4 Feed back your findings to the whole group. How do these items relate to what you know or expect from your current course?

Marketing Management

Chapter NINETEEN

Marketing

Chapter contents

❖ LEARNING OBJECTIVES

After reading this chapter you should understand some of the purposes and the position of the marketing function within organisations. You should be familiar with ways of analysing markets and understand the ideas behind the marketing mix. You should also be familiar with some of the general criticisms of the marketing function. In particular you should be able to:

❖ **define** both markets and marketing and explain key terms such as size, niches, segmentation and relationship marketing

❖ **explain** concepts such as competition, barriers to entry and exit and market dynamism

❖ **discuss in detail** market strategy and market positioning

❖ **contrast** briefly markets research and marketing research

❖ **list** seven uses and four methods of market research

❖ **discuss in detail** each of the five main components of the marketing mix

❖ **differentiate** between marketing and public relations

❖ **outline** some of the techniques and methods used in advertising

❖ **evaluate** at least four criticisms of marketing

In theory at least, marketing has prime place in the sequence of management functions because it identifies needs an organisation can exploit with a product or service. Once this need has been recognised, the other functions – operations, human resource management (HRM), finance function, etc. – can work together to produce the product or service. In fact, the marketing function also plays an important part at the end of the process – selling the finished product. Some people find it difficult to distinguish between marketing and sales. As a simplification, marketing is "having something you can get rid of" while selling is "getting rid of what you have!"

CASE 14.1: *Marketing Red Bull*

You are late for a lecture, and feeling exhausted after last night's party. What you need is a pick-me-up. You pop into the nearest corner shop and scan the fridge which is full of cans of various fizzy drinks. You soon see that the shop has a promotion on a brand of cola (buy one get one free), but it's not your preferred choice. Luckily, it does sell your favourite energy drink which you eagerly buy, even though the smaller can represents relatively poor value. After a few swigs, the caffeine kicks in and you're feeling almost human again.

When you're shopping like this, do you ever wonder why does this shop sell one type of fizzy drink but not another? Do you wonder why they packaged the drinks in that way, or why one costs more than another? All these decisions have been made as part of somebody's marketing strategy, involving a complex mix of pricing, competition, promotion and positioning. And Red Bull is an excellent example of this.

In the early 1980s, Dietrich Mateschitz came across products known as "tonic drinks" while travelling in the Far East, including one, from Thailand which local workers used to stay awake during their shifts. It was called Krating Daeng or "Red Bull". Mateschitz bought the foreign licensing rights and decided to target young professionals, rather than factory workers, as they were more affluent and open to trendy marketing campaigns. The firm focused on "buzz marketing" or word of mouth, and the brand image was linked to youth culture and extreme sports, such as motor sports, mountain biking, snowboarding and dance music. Red Bull's target consumer segment began to adopt nicknames for the product such as "liquid cocaine" or "speed in a can", thus spreading its "left-field" appeal. Red Bull is now a leading player in the energy drinks field, yet still maintains an anti-corporate image.

The marketing of Red Bull involves a lot more than spotting a gap in the market and then developing an excellent brand image. It also included developing a marketing strategy based upon a great deal of market research. A sophisticated marketing mix was also developed to make Red Bull a competitive product. Last, but by no means least, it needed a large and well-motivated salesforce to get the product "on the shelves" so that the ultimate consumers could make their purchases. This chapter gives a greater understanding of all these aspects of marketing.

Source: based on: http://www.bized.co.uk/compfact/redbull/redbullindex.htm

14.1 Definition of marketing

Typical definitions assert that marketing is:

> An organisational function and set of processes for creating, communicating and delivering value to customers and for managing customer relationships in ways that benefit the organisation and its stakeholders.
>
> *(American Marketing Association, 2004)*

> Responsible for identifying, anticipating and satisfying customer requirements profitably.
>
> *(Hannagan, 2005)*

> The management process responsible for identifying, anticipating and satisfying customer requirements profitably.
>
> *(Chartered Institute of Marketing [UK], 2010)*

Each of the definitions has disadvantages. The first is so megalomanic that it includes practically everything in an organisation. It does not differentiate between marketing and other essential functions such as production or finance. Two of the definitions imply, quite wrongly, that marketing only applies to commercial, profit-making, organisations. A definition which escapes these problems and which commands some consensus is:

> A product or service's conception, pricing, promotion and distribution in order to create exchanges that satisfy consumers, organisational objectives and the interest of other stakeholders.
>
> *(See, for example, Health Advantage, 2004; Pride and Farrell, 2000; Quintessential Careers, 2004)*

This definition has a number of key features:

- It centres on the exchange relationship between consumers (in the broadest sense) and organisations.
- It emphasises that these exchanges should be satisfactory to all parties.
- It specifies the activities which constitute marketing.
- It implicitly accepts that other functions in the organisation play an important part in a satisfactory exchange.

Many writers emphasise the importance of adopting a marketing orientation where everyone in an organisation has a marketing role. For example, when a driver of a company van parks discourteously it tarnishes the company's image and affects its relationship with a customer. Similarly, an operative making a poor-quality product, an off-hand customer service assistant, a tardy accounts clerk and an arrogant chief executive all affect an organisation's relationship with customers and clients. The management guru, Peter Drucker (1999) takes the view that:

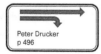

Peter Drucker
p 496

> 66 The purpose of business is to create and keep customers . . . it has only two functions – marketing and innovation. The basic function of marketing is to attract and retain customers at a profit. 99

This view is overstated. It makes marketing synonymous with everyone in an organisation so the term is therefore redundant. Further, there are many non-profit organisations where customer satisfaction is not the only organisational objective (e.g. the prison service). Nevertheless, most organisations need to have a **market orientation**. This is also called being "consumer centred" or being "consumer driven".

14.2 Successive views of the marketing function

Robert Keith (1960) argued that marketing functions had experienced a revolution. His ideas have been updated: current "periodisation" divides the marketing revolution into five phases (see below), and plentiful examples of of each phase still exist. Petkus (2010) suggests that practical outcomes can arise from a study of marketing history:

- **Production** orientation was the first phase – at its height from, say, 1870–1950. This marketing strategy emphasised producing as much of any product as cheaply as possible so that as many people as possible would buy it. This orientation is appropriate when a large, under-supplied market exists and where consumer tastes do not alter very quickly. A classic example would be Sunlight Soap, developed in 1884. There was a huge market but incomes were low. Further, there was not an over-supply of soap; there was a credo that "cleanliness is next to godliness" and smoke-filled skies guaranteed continuing demand. The manufacturers, Lever Brothers, only had to make huge quantities of soap at a low price and get it to the shops. They and their workers in Port Sunlight were "well off".

- **Product** orientation was very prominent from, say, the 1920s until the 1960s. This strategy emphasised the quality of a product in the belief that well-made products would dominate. This strategy is appropriate when a market is aspirational, incomes are rising and where other products are of dubious quality. A classic example would be the Hoover vacuum cleaner whose quality features included a "beater bar" and a headlight.

- **Selling** orientation was important during the 1950s and 1960s. It emphasised high sales and promoting products as much as possible – with relatively little attention to product design. It required good salespeople, advertising and points of display. A classic example would be the selling of washing powders where there was little difference between the products but they were heavily advertised in order to gain brand recognition and to encourage consumers to perceive the differences.

- **Marketing** in its current form gained importance in the 1970s. It is the dominant orientation today. It focuses on detecting and satisfying consumer needs. It is characterised by high levels of market research and good customer services. *Societal marketing* is now considered a major aspect of the marketing orientation. It emerged in the 1960s and is based on the idea that products should meet the needs of customers and also promote the well-being of society by refraining from products or selling methods that would be harmful. A good example of societal marketing would be the development of the Fair Trade organisation and the development of investments that are ethical. Much of the rest of this chapter is based on this orientation. However, the next edition of this text will probably need to include a section on academic advances in galactic marketing!

■ **Relationship marketing** stresses satisfying, and preferably long-lasting, links with customers. Quality products which satisfy customer needs remain important, but consultants and academics advise that a positive customer experience engendered by close attention to customers and good customer service is paramount. The aim is to develop customer loyalty so they repeat their purchases. A classic example of relationship marketing is Marks & Spencer's emphasis on good quality products, which used to be made in Britain for use by British people, at a sensible price and with good customer service which would not make exchanges or refunds difficult. Marks & Spencer's ubiquitous phrase "Your M&S" clearly exemplifies *they* have "bought into" relationship marketing. It is often thought that relationship marketing emerged during the 1970s but it has been present longer (see, Tadajewski and Saren, 2009).

CRITICAL THINKING 14.1 *Are "stages" marketing's own QWERTY keyboard?*

The stages of the marketing "revolution" are reproduced in most contemporary textbooks. Yet, decades ago, Fullerton (1988) and Hollander (1986) disputed them. A recent analysis by Jones and Richardson (2007) shows that the other marketing orientations were clearly in existence during the period known as the production era. Jones and Richardson attribute the persistence of periodisation to "sloppy scholarship to plagiarising the work of other textbook authors". Perhaps there is an analogy with keyboard production. As noted earlier, while it is known that the QWERTY keyboard is very inefficient, it is so familiar that no manufacturer would dare to be the first to market something better – what a pity for us all!

14.3 Markets

A market (in contrast to *marketing*) may be defined as:

> 66   The actual or potential buyers of a product.   99

This means a market is wider than individuals: it includes private and public sector organisations, supplier groups and purchasing groups. It is also wider than present or past buyers: it includes anyone or any organisation that is reasonably likely to buy a product in the future. Kotler (1986) defined a product broadly as:

> 66   anything that can be offered to a market for attention, acquisition, use or consumption that might satisfy a want or need. It includes physical objects, services, persons, places, organisations and ideas.   99

An organisation that hopes to sell its product needs to study its market very carefully and may commission extensive market research. It needs to examine the characteristics of its market such as:

Market research
p 335

- the *people* and *organisations* that make up the market
- the *product* or *service* it offers
- the *purpose* for which the product is bought and the *needs* it satisfies
- the *times* and *occasions* (e.g. birthdays, setting up a new home or everyday purchases) when the product is bought
- the *method used to buy* the product (e.g. retail outlet, regular order, telephone order or Internet shopping)

People and organisations do not buy products for their own sake. Products are bought because they *solve a problem* or confer *benefits* upon their owners. For example, organisations do not purchase a car for a sales representative because they want to own a car. It will be purchased because the organisation believes it will benefit from the sales representative's ability to visit more customers and it can be sure its image will not be damaged by its representative arriving in a clapped-out old banger.

Markets can differ in many ways. The main differences are size, competition, barriers and dynamism.

Size, niches and market segmentation

Markets differ markedly in size. Some markets, such as detergents and cleaning materials, are vast and international. Global companies such as Proctor and Gamble have developed to meet the needs of such markets. In principle, large markets are good and lead to very cost-effective products because development costs are shared among millions of customers. However, these benefits accrue only if the large market is *homogeneous* (every consumer is quite similar and has comparable needs). It is difficult to mount an effective marketing campaign for a large, *heterogeneous* market (where there are distinctive groups with distinctive needs). It is usually better to target a smaller, more homogeneous group. by focusing upon a restricted range of products or consumers, i.e. a niche market.

A **niche market** is "a portion of a market whose needs are met by a restricted range of specialised products". A classic example is the Tie Rack chain. It operates within a wider market for clothing, but it sells only ties, scarves, handkerchiefs and other accessories. Appropriately, many of Tie Rack's outlets occupy physical niches at airports or railway stations. WesternGeco, a subsidiary of the American company Schlumberger, also operates within a niche market. It provides technically sophisticated seismic imaging services for oil companies. Catering for a niche market means an organisation can develop highly specialised expertise and project a distinctive image.

Another way to produce a homogeneous market is *market segmentation* where a wider market is divided into subgroups whose members have similar needs. Typical methods of market segmentation divide customers according to factors such as loyalty, age, gender, neighbourhood or social economic status.

Perhaps the most important way to segment a market is to divide it into *past customers* (i.e. loyal customers) and *new customers*. In the late 1990s there was a craze to focus upon past customers. The craze arose because, with the development of the Internet, customers had a much greater ability to "shop around" and become "promiscuous consumers". Many organisations therefore concentrated on establishing a dedicated base of existing customers and developing a long-term relationship that would prevent loyal customers switching to other suppliers. This is called "relationship marketing". It was supported by claims such as:

- Costs of acquiring a new customer are 10 times higher than keeping an existing customer.
- Loyal customers spend more than new customers.
- Past, satisfied customers tell others about their satisfaction.
- Past customers are more profitable because they are willing to pay a premium for a service they know.

The principles of relationship marketing were embraced by organisations trading with other organisations. For example, a computer software company would develop a close marketing relationship with its customers. Specific programmers would be devoted to specific clients so personalised assistance would be available if needed and they would help establish a deep, long-term and profitable relationship. Initially these concepts were applied to business organisations (**B2B transactions**). However, their relevance to retail transactions was quickly appreciated. Very successful examples of **customer management** and relationship marketing include the Tesco Clubcard scheme and Airmiles. A fundamental aspect of customer

B2B transactions
p 450

management is the concept of **client life-cycle**. A new client needs to be welcomed, perhaps by email, and assured that they have made the correct choice. An established customer needs to be told that they are important and that the organisation wishes to attend to their needs. A long-established client needs to be made aware of new products.

Some of these basic beliefs have not withstood scrutiny. Werner and Kumar (2002) suggest that loyalty is not as profitable as the gurus of the 1990s suggested. For example, long-term customers tend to demand more favourable contracts. Further, many long-term customers make disproportionate demands in terms of customer support.

Market segmentation by *age* is also very common. Classic examples are the UK travel organisation Club 18–30 which markets lively Mediterranean holidays to youthful consumers, and the SAGA Group which markets holidays and financial products to people aged over 50 years. Market segmentation by age is widespread in the fashion and entertainment industries.

Market segmentation by *gender* is widespread in the publishing industry. For example magazines such as *Woman's Weekly* and *Cosmopolitan* are marketed for women, while *FHM* and *What Car* are marketed for men. Similarly, cars offered by major manufacturers will include some cars designed to appeal to women and other cars designed to appeal to men.

Market segmentation by *neighbourhood* is very common. For example, billboards in prosperous areas will depict luxury goods purchased out of discretionary income, while billboards in less affluent areas will advertise basic products. Probably the most extensive classification of residential areas is the ACORN system (CACI, 2010). Readers in the UK can obtain the ACORN classification of where they live by visiting the Internet site http://www.caci.co.uk/acorn-classification.aspx. The ACORN classification starts with five major categories:

1 wealthly achievers
2 urban prosperity
3 comfortably off
4 moderate means
5 hard-pressed

These are then subdivided into 17 major groups. For example, the wealthy achievers are subdivided into three groups: wealthy executives, affluent greys and flourishing families. The hard-pressed are divided into four groups: struggling families, burdened singles, high-rise hardship and inner-city adversity. The groups are further divided into subgroups. For example, the affluent greys, who comprise 7.7 per cent of the British population, are subdivided into older affluent professionals (1.8 per cent), farming communities (2.0 per cent), old people in detached homes (1.9 per cent) and mature couples (2.0 per cent). A manager marketing sophisticated financial products such as shares or annuities would target neighbourhoods containing many affluent greys, while a government department trying to ensure proper take-up of welfare benefits might target neighbourhoods containing many people experiencing high-rise hardship.

Markets are often segmented by *socio-economic status*. This system classifies markets according to the work performed by the head of the household. The categories are:

- A upper middle-class (e.g. directors, senior managers and senior civil servants)
- B middle-class (e.g. lawyers, doctors, middle managers and higher professional workers)
- C1 lower middle-class (e.g. teachers, nurses, junior managers and lower professional workers)
- C2 skilled workers including technologists and many engineering workers
- D working class
- E subsistence workers and unemployed people

Market segmentation by socio-economic status groups consumers who have similar spending power and preferences. This discussion covers only the most popular ways of dividing a large market into homogeneous groups. Many other methods exist. Markets are often segmented by lifestyle using categories with cute acronyms such as "YUPPIES" (young upwardly mobile persons), "DINKIES" (dual income no kids) or "GRUMPIES" (grown-up mature persons).

Competition

In a captive market customers must purchase from a single supplier or do without. For a supplier a captive market is ideal because very little effort is needed to sell products. But, captive markets are like magnets to other organisations that set up in competition. Captive markets are very rare. A market is generally regarded as being a captive when there are fewer than four suppliers. Sometimes captive markets are called **monopolies** or **duopolies**. A market which has, say, more than 12 suppliers is generally called a "fluid market".

Barriers to entry and exit

Captive markets exist in situations when it is difficult for competitors to enter. For example, in the aerospace industry there are often only one or two suppliers (e.g. Boeing or Airbus). Few organisations can afford the immense costs of setting up huge and complicated factories or build up the technical knowledge and expertise. **Barriers to entry** also exist in the form of laws and regulations such as patent laws, copyright laws and planning permissions. Distribution channels can also constitute entry barriers. Commercial practices by competitors may present further entry barriers – especially the practice of **predatory pricing** (OECD, 1989), whereby a large, established business cuts its price below its costs so that new competitors must sell at a loss and therefore eventually be driven out. **Exit barriers** prevent organisations withdrawing from markets. Usually they wish to exit because a market because it is unprofitable or it is no longer fits an organisation's strategy. Typical exit barriers include losing the capital already invested, the costs of making staff redundant, loss of prestige or government pressure.

CASE 14.2: *Rockefeller's predatory pricing*

A classic case of predatory pricing is given by John D. Rockefeller's oil interests (Tarbell, 1950). A new entrant, the Pure Oil Company, was driven out of business when Rockefeller's Standard Oil Company drastically lowered its price, knowing that its vast reserves could survive a short-term loss in order to reap a long-term benefit of having the market to itself. Another example of predatory pricing is the way established airlines cut the price of their air fares in the 1970s to force a new entrant, Laker Airways, out of the transatlantic passenger market.

Dynamism

A growing market is called an "expanding market". A market that is shrinking is called a "declining market" and one that stays the same is called a "static" or "stagnant market". It is generally easiest to operate in an expanding market. Organisations operating in a declining market need to pay very close attention to costs in the hope that they will be able to drive out less efficient competitors.

These characteristics are not the only factors that differentiate markets. In order to predict and anticipate markets it is necessary to understand six further influences such as those indicated by a PESTLE analysis. **Cultural factors** are also important characteristics of markets. For example, the French culture and traditions made it much more difficult for the McDonald's hamburger chain to enter the French market.

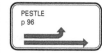
PESTLE
p 96

14.4 Market strategy and market positioning

Organisations often consciously decide, the type of market they prefer to serve. This is called "**market strategy**", "**market positioning**" or "**portfolio planning**". PESTLE analysis was developed to aid market positioning. Other schemes include the Boston matrix, the General Electric matrix and the Anscoff matrix.

The **Boston Consulting Group Matrix** (**BCG matrix**) focuses on two aspects of a market, its *dynamism* (growth rate) and relative *share of a market*. This allows products or services to be categorised into the four types shown in Figure 14.1.

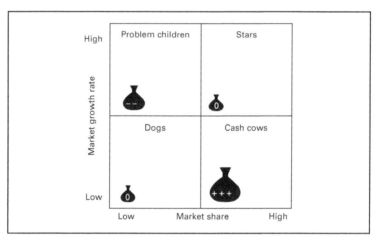

FIGURE 14.1 The BCG matrix

If a product has a low market share in a slow-growing market, the product is classified as "a dog" because it is doing poorly in a weak market. The outlook is poor and an organisation might be well advised to consider eliminating the product from its range – preferably by selling it to someone else or, in the worst case, shutting it down. If the product has a low market share but operates in an expanding market, the organisation has a "problem child" because the outlook is mixed. The expanding market bodes well but the low market share implies a struggle to keep up with market leaders who will be able to obtain greater economies of scale. In these situations an organisation must decide whether to inject substantial resources. This may be risky. Sometimes, products categorised as "problem children" are called "cash hogs" because, like some adolescents, their potential is uncertain but they require large and frequent injections of cash. A product which commands a high share of a slowly growing market is categorised as a "cash cow". Its high market share means that economies of scale are achieved and a lot of money is generated. This money can be used to promote other projects such as "a problem child" or a "star". Organisations may become complacent about their "cash cows" and pay more attention to new products. Because of lack of investment the "cash cows" lose their competitiveness and turn into "dogs". A "star" is a product that has a high share of an expanding market. Generally, it will generate most of the funds needed for its own development and promotion but, from time to time, this may need supplementing by injections of resources from a "cash cow".

CRITICAL THINKING 14.2 *What is wrong with the Boston matrix?*

The Boston matrix provides a reasonable basis for the allocation of development funds. However, it has its disadvantages (Morrison and Wensley, 1991). It oversimplifies markets by focusing upon just two aspects: market growth and market share. This may lead an organisation to ignore other important aspects (Haspeslagh, 1982). Moreover, the Boston matrix simplifies the two dimensions into just two crude categories; high and low.

The **General Electric matrix** is also known as "The Industry Attractiveness/ Business Strength" matrix or the "Directional Policy" matrix. It overcomes some of the disadvantages of the Boston matrix by incorporating *more factors* and allowing *three levels* for each dimension. The General Electric matrix has two composite dimensions: "industry attractiveness" and "business strength". **Industry attractiveness** is an amalgam of five characteristics, resembling PESTLE:

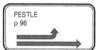

PESTLE
p 96

- *market forces* – size, growth, price sensitivity and bargaining position
- *competition* – as types of competitors or substitution by new technology
- *financial and economic factors* – economies of scale, profits, entry and exit barriers
- *technology* – market maturity, patents, copyrights and manufacturing technology
- *socio-political factors* – pressure groups, legal constraints and unionisation

The General Electric matrix then evaluates on factors reflecting **business strength**. Using these two dimensions an appropriate strategy is determined. In practice, this process is quite complicated because an intricate system of weights is applied to the characteristics of the industry and the strengths of the business or product. Figure 14.2 indicates appropriate strategy for products or sevices in each cell.

For example, a weak product in an unattractive market should be discontinued, preferably by its sale to another organisation. A strong product in a similarly unattractive market should be milked for all the cash it can generate. The case of a weak product in an attractive market is interesting. The organisation should either quit or take a gamble and invest many resources in the hope the product or service can be a market leader. It is similar to the "problem child" category of the BCG matrix.

Unfortunately, even a system as sophisticated as the General Electric matrix does not capture the full complexity of product positioning. For example, an established market leader can be positioned in a number of ways. It could try to obtain an even greater market

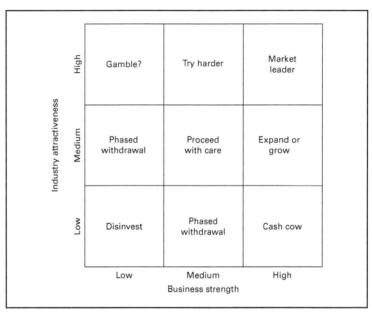

FIGURE 14.2 The General Electric matrix

share. Alternatively, the product can be adjusted so that it appeals to a new market. Ansoff (1989) developed a matrix to aid these decisions. An Ansoff matrix focuses upon whether both the markets and the products are new or established. Figure 14.3 shows Anscoff's recommendation for each combination.

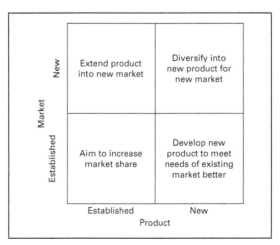

FIGURE 14.3 The Ansoff matrix

Once a suitable market has been identified it is necessary to decide the organisation's position. It is often assumed that organisations should be market leaders or **pioneers** – devising new methods, opening up new markets and devising new products (Pettinger, 1997). They frequently have a high esteem. However, being a pioneer can be risky. There may be unknown difficulties. Pioneers carry substantial development costs. If the ideas are successful they can be copied, at less cost, by other organisations. An alternative, often more successful, marketing strategy is to adopt a "follow the leader" approach: keeping a keen eye on developments and maintaining a capability to quickly exploit the advances made by others. Other organisations adopt a strategy of building up a competitive advantage through **technical excellence**, or quality.

A marketing function must consider the maturity of their organisation's products or services and try to ensure their portfolios contain goods at different stages of the product life cycle. In general, product life cycles have five main phases, as shown in Figure 14.4.

The continuous line shows the "natural" progression of sales. When a new product or service is introduced, there is a period of slow growth of sales, followed by a rapid increase as the product or service is adopted by opinion leaders and then a wider range of consumers. At maturity, growth is either slow or there is a small decline as the product loses some of its "novelty value". At this point the product has wide acceptance. During the saturation phase, sales may decline because, although the market may be expanding, new competitors emerge. Finally, the product declines and sales generate little cash. This pattern varies greatly. In fashion items and children's toys, the whole life cycle is less than a year. In other cases such as "big ticket" items (e.g. televisions) the life cycle can be more than a decade. Organisations try to predict the life cycle of their products or services to ensure that they have new products "in the pipeline" to replace saturated or declining products. The life cycle

Advertising and product life cycle p 342

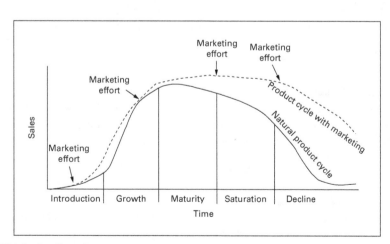

FIGURE 14.4 Product life cycle

of products is particularly important in industries such as pharmaceuticals where it can take decades to develop new medicines. Marketing functions monitor the life cycles of products for a second reason. By mounting a marketing effort, such as advertising, new packaging or restyling at key times, sales can be boosted to extend the product life cycle. The effect of a marketing effort on a product life cycle is demonstrated by the dotted line in Figure 14.4.

14.5 Understanding markets (market research)

Market research is defined by the American Marketing Association (2004) as:

> *the function that links the consumer, customer and public to the marketer through information – information used to identify and define marketing opportunities and problems; generate, refine and evaluate marketing actions; monitor marketing performance; and improve understanding of marketing as a process.*

The terms "market research", "markets research" and "marketing research" sound very similar. **Market research** refers to *any* information about markets. **Markets research** is looks at the characteristics of markets. **Marketing research** looks at information concerning a specific product or service. It is useful to divide market research into two main activities: *markets research* and *marketing research*.

Markets research

Research on markets is sometimes called "market intelligence". It obtains information, usually quantitative, on the size of a market, its growth, its use of technology, its dynamism and the level of competition. Often markets research is based on existing (secondary) data compiled by government and industry sources such as census figures, the retail price index and the value of imported goods. It may also use journal and newspaper articles to build up a picture of competitors.

Marketing research

Marketing research is information that will be useful to organisations who wish to sell specific products. It is the research which, say, the brand manager for Coca-Cola uses to devise an advertising campaign. Marketing research overlaps with research on markets but its focus is narrower and is closer to the point of sale. Marketing research can, perhaps, best be considered under two headings: usage and methods.

Uses of marketing research

Marketing research can play a vital role in bringing to market a product valued by customers and which is presented to them in an enjoyable way. Marketing research's main uses include:

- *Product generation* – identifying new products by listening to consumers, brainstorming sessions with designers and marketing executives.
- *Product improvement and embellishment* – again, the source of suggestions can be consumers or brainstorming. Ideas may also be generated by examining competitors' products or even products and services in other markets.
- *Product testing and refinement* – prototypes of products and services can be tested on small groups of consumers. Their reactions and comments are usually incorporated in a modified product.
- *Consumer targeting* – pinpointing the people who are most likely to buy the product or use a service.
- *Sales forecasting.*
- *Packaging and advertising design* – various suggestions for packaging or adverts can be tested on consumers and the most effective chosen.
- *Point-of-sale displays and procedures* – developing and then refining point of sale displays, brochures, etc.

Marketing research methods

The main sources of marketing research are:

- **Existing internal data** – sales records, call reports and especially quotations that have been not been taking up by customers. Customer loyalty schemes routinely gather vast amounts of information on consumers. **Surveys** have many forms. The simplest is a questionnaire returned by a purchaser when she or he registers a guarantee. Many organisations also use **questionnaire surveys**. Questionnaire surveys are administered by market researchers who approach customers, who fit their **quotas**, as they visit shopping malls, etc. Alternatively, they may be administered in a more rigorous way to a **random sample** of people. Random samples are much more expensive than quota samples. Questionnaires *may also* be distributed via the post but this method may result in a very poor response rate. The telephone and the Internet are also used to administer questionnaires. However, the sample of respondents may be very unrepresentative.
- Questionnaires need to be constructed to ensure that questions are "neutral". A series of questionnaires administered to the same group of people is called **consumer panel**. Consumer panels have the advantage that they can track changes in customer preferences. Unfortunately, repeated questioning of the same people can sensitise them to issues so that they gradually become unrepresentative. Some unscrupulous organisations use questionnaires as a way of introducing themselves to people, getting them to divulge information and then attempting to sell them a product. This is called "SUGGING" (selling under the guise). Charities also use surveys as a ruse to raise funds. This is called "FRUGGING" (fund-raising under the guise). Both practices are unethical.
- **Focus groups** or **group discussions** are frequently used in market research – especially when customers' underlying attitudes to new or changing situations are relevant. Focus groups consist of, say, 12 people representing different types of consumers plus a leader who ensures they cover the required topics. Focus groups may attempt to assess "emotions" and "deep attitudes". Some techniques are exotic and perhaps

silly. Participants, might be asked to nominate a type of tree that they associate with a certain public figure. In better situations, a focus group is asked to taste a new drink and compare it to existing drinks. **Experiments** are used infrequently. Usually they are employed to study the impact of advertisements and packaging and they often take the form of observing consumer behavior. For example, a supermarket may stock shelves in a different ways and videotape the behaviour of customers. The videotape will be analysed to establish which shelf layout generates most purchases.

14.6 The marketing mix

Successful marketing involves an appropriate combination of five main factors. This combination is called the **marketing mix** and is based on the "5 Ps": **p**roduct or service, **p**rice, **p**ackaging, **p**romotion and **p**lace of purchase.

Products

A product can be either a physical entity or a service. Ownership of a physical entity changes hands when a *product* is purchased. When a *service* is purchased ownership is not transferred. From a marketing viewpoint, the most important feature of either is the *benefit* it bestows upon the customer. An engineer, a technologist, and a design specialist may eulogise about the product's features or its technical sophistication. However, these are only important if the consumer believes that they confer some benefit. Benefits may be a saving of time, enabling a previously impossible task, a feeling of well-being and attractiveness or an increase in status. In other words a product or service must solve or ease a problem for the consumer. For example, consumers do not buy computers because they can add up numbers quickly or because they are high technology. They buy computers because the machines solve problems such as communicating with others, writing assignments, keeping accounts or storing information. If a product or service confers benefits its competitors do not, the product has a "**unique selling-point**".

Consumers frequently judge products on the basis of their **quality** – freedom from imperfections and an implication of exclusivity or "class". Marketeers imply quality when they offer "fine wines", "prime beef", "select cheeses", "high-calibre education", and so on. Generally products must also offer **durability** – functioning satisfactorily for an acceptable time. However, in some products (razors, pens, live entertainment, etc.) durability is not expected.

Brand is important. Marketing functions give their brands close attention. Brands started when farmers burnt distinctive marks into the flesh of their cattle so that they could be identified should they stray or be stolen. Farmers who produced good cattle were particularly keen on branding because their brand would be recognised at market and their cattle would command a higher price. In the early days of mass production good producers of products such as cornflakes (Kelloggs) or soap (Pears) would mark their products with a distinctive mark. As the brands of cornflakes or soap became better known, manufacturers took steps to ensure other people could not use the same mark. They also promoted brands via advertising that made them instantly recognisable and invoked positive associations in consumer's minds. Kellogg's, for example, developed a brand which is associated with freshness, sunshine and vitality. Today, most major products carry brands, some of which are so well known that they are very valuable. Some of the most famous brands in the USA include Coca-Cola, Ford, McDonald's, Microsoft and GAP. Other world-famous brands include BP, Cadbury, IKEA, Nintendo, Qantas and Rip Curl.

The major advantage of brands is that they add benefits to a product. A classic experiment by Penny, Hunt and Twyman as long ago as 1974 neatly demonstrates the point. They asked consumers who normally used brand B to try two products without knowing their brand. A majority (61 per cent) preferred brand A while 39 per cent preferred brand B. Another group also tried the same two products. For this group the brands were known. 35 per cent were found to prefer brand A while 65 per cent preferred brand B. A brand may be defined as:

> 66 A symbolic construct created by a marketeer to represent a collection of information about a product or group of products. This symbolic construct typically consist of a name, identifying mark, logo, visual images or symbols or mental concepts which distinguish the product or service. 99

A brand projects a product's "promise" and differentiates it from competitors, and may attempt to give a product a "personality". To be successful, a brand must have several characteristics (see iboost, 2005). These include:

- *Simple, clear messages*. A campaigning message or one which seems to go against the "Establishment" (e.g. the themes of the Benetton and FCUK branding) are often a "cheap" way to success.
- *Credibility* – so claims are believed.
- *Motivation of customers* which increases the enjoyment of purchasing products with the brand. This makes it more likely that purchases will actually take place.
- *Creation of strong user loyalty*. This is, perhaps, the most important aspect of branding.

Once a brand has been established, it can be extended to other products. This reduces the cost of a new project gaining a place in the market. However, extension to weak or inappropriate new products can cause significant damage to a brand image.

Price

As a broad generalisation, a marketing function will set the price of its goods at a *level* above its costs and as much as the product or service can command.

Exceptions to this rule are almost as many as adherents. The ability and willingness of consumers to pay for a product is important. It is pointless marketing a product or service at a price beyond the means of customers. The variation in supermarket and petrol prices from region to region or town to town is a clear example of how the ability of the consumer to pay influences prices: in affluent areas prices are usually higher than in poorer areas. Luxury goods are a classic example where people are willing to pay substantially more than the production costs. The price of diamonds, for example, has, for over a century, been maintained at an artificially high level. Superb branding (a diamond is forever) and a superb cartel (DeBeers) meant that the price of diamonds could be controlled so that the very affluent and starry-eyed men would pay high prices (*see* Economist, 2004).

Sales of some products respond very quickly to changes in price while the sales of other products change very little if the price increases or decreases (this is called **price sensitivity** or **elasticity of demand**). The price of vegetables such as broccoli is very price sensitive because people will switch to another vegetable such as cauliflower if there is a small price increase. On the other hand, many medicines are price insensitive. People will cut back on other purchases in order to have money to buy medicines that might save their life. If a product or service has an inelastic demand, the marketing function of an organisation can engage in **price-skimming** – supplying only the upper fraction (those who can afford high prices) of the market. They can charge very high prices which quickly recover development and production costs. Price-skimming enables an organisation to build a considerable surplus so that, should a competitor enter the market, they can afford to engage in predatory pricing. Branding can also raise prices. Classic examples are the pharmaceutical industry where branded, well-advertised products supported by an excellent sales force can cost several times more than an equally effective generic medication. For example, the painkiller Neurofen costs more than the equally effective generic drug Ibuprofen. However, the generic drug Ibuprofen does not have to bear the marketing, sales and advertising costs incurred by the branded version.

The price of products is heavily influenced by marketing strategy. For example, new products, such as plasma screen televisions, are introduced at a very high price to establish an aspirational position at the top of the market. This confers prestige that will help sustain a higher price among naive and impressionable consumers.

The price of a product or service may be concealed. For example, people can visit many tourist attractions such as museums, parks or educational "lectures" without any fee. However, someone, somewhere, will be paying higher taxes to sustain their enjoyment. In fact, a marketing function's dream is to separate the person who uses the product from the person or organisation that pays – that way the demand will stay high despite high prices.

Packaging

Packaging is not often considered as a separate aspect of the marketing mix and it is usually subsumed under the heading of "promotion". In practice, the marketing function of most organisations will pay considerable attention to the way goods are packaged because it can make a very substantial difference to sales. Further, packaging has the important purpose of ensuring a product is delivered in prime condition. Packaging can also be used to increase the perceived benefit. For example, some items are packaged in an oversized box in an attempt to make the customer believe that the product is bigger than its actual size. Similarly, some products such as jewellery, are packaged in grossly expensive cases made of embossed leather and silk in order to enhance the perceived value of their contents.

The characteristics of good packaging include:

- *It is distinctive* from its competitors.
- *The colours are appropriate to the product's benefits*. For example, the packaging of a valuable item is likely to be coloured in gold and silver, while the packaging of a fun item is likely to be coloured in vivid reds, oranges and yellows.

- It *displays the brand name* in a prominent position.
- It contains a *flattering picture of the product* where happy people (sometimes, animals) clearly enjoy the benefits of a purchase.

Promotion

Promotion is also called "**marketing communications**" and may be defined as:

> Any type of persuasive communication between the marketing function and one or more of its present customers, potential customers or stakeholder groups which aims, directly or indirectly, to increase the likelihood that time, product or service will be purchased.

This definition has four important components. *First*, it emphasises the central concept of persuasive communication. *Second*, the aim of communication is to increase purchases. *Third*, communications are directed at a target that is wider than the organisation's present customers. *Finally*, some communications may be closely linked to the sales process in the short term, while other communications may be designed to have an indirect, longer-term effect.

Public relations

Public relations (PR) is also known as "**perception management**" and critics such as Chomsky (2002) have called it "manufacturing consent", "media control" or "spin". It may be defined as:

> A part of the promotional mix that communicates with stakeholders, the media and the public in general in order to achieve broadly favourable and supportive attitudes towards a product, organisation or cause.

A shorter and less technical definition for public relations might be "the management of an organisation's image". Both definitions emphasise that public relations is a general activity and is only loosely tied to the sale of a specific product. It aims to obtain a generally favourable attitude so that subsequent, more specific communications are likely to succeed. Often, an organisation's marketing function will employ specialist public relations consultants to maintain its image. Public relations experts use six main methods:

- **Press conferences** are public or quasi-public events where speakers provide information on newsworthy items. They are stage-managed and attended by selected journalists and television reporters.
- **Press releases** are also called "news releases" and may consist of short fax statements sent to the media.
- **Publicity events** are contrived situations designed to attract media attention. Outrageous publicity events are sometimes called "**guerrilla marketing**".
- **The circuit** refers to the "talk-show circuit" where public relations consultants attempt to get their clients or spokespersons to appear on these programmes.

- **Books, brochures** and other writings are sometimes commissioned and published on behalf of clients.
- **Press contacts** are developed assiduously so that they can be fed information about the organisation in the hope that the reporter will write a favourable story.

Public relations experts often identify opinion leaders and powerful people ("movers and shakers"). They then attempt to develop friendships by offering corporate hospitality at events such as the Chelsea Flower Show, the Happy Valley racecourse in Hong Kong or Australia's prestigious Telstra motor rally.

Sometimes public relations organisations engage in "cause-related marketing" – giving a proportion of their profits to a good cause in the hope that their generosity will reflect positively on them.

CASE 14.3: *Cause-related marketing*

A classic example of cause-related marketing is given by Christmas card manufacturers who hope to promote their sales by promising to give 10 per cent of their profits to charities. A clever and ingenious example of this is provided by Tesco's "Computers for Schools" campaign in which shoppers are given vouchers to pass to their local school. However, cause-related marketing can backfire. In 2003 Cadbury sold chocolate bars with tokens which a school could exchange for sports equipment. The scheme caused uproar. It was criticised by the Food Commission for encouraging obesity rather than a healthy, sporty lifestyle.

Internal promotion

Internal promotion aims to alter the attitudes of the organisation's own workforce. It is particularly relevant when new products are being launched. Internal communications tend to foster the "team spirit" within an organisation. Further, staff become an unofficial salesforce who talk about the new product with their relatives, friends and acquaintances.

CASE 14.4: *Guerrilla marketing*

A good example of guerrilla publicity occurred in August 2002 when Vodafone arranged for two men to "streak" at an international rugby game with the Vodafone logo painted on their backsides. The men's magazine *FHM* provides another good example of guerrilla marketing. The magazine cover featured a nude photograph of a former children's television presenter. After doctoring the photograph to preserve her modesty, *FHM* projected it onto one of the towers of the Houses of Parliament. Both stunts earned considerable free publicity. World Cup authorities take guerrilla marketing very seriously indeed. Perhaps

▶

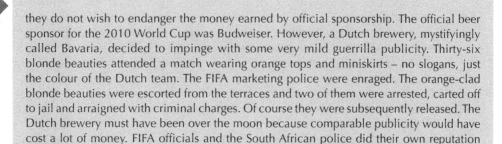

they do not wish to endanger the money earned by official sponsorship. The official beer sponsor for the 2010 World Cup was Budweiser. However, a Dutch brewery, mystifyingly called Bavaria, decided to impinge with some very mild guerrilla publicity. Thirty-six blonde beauties attended a match wearing orange tops and miniskirts – no slogans, just the colour of the Dutch team. The FIFA marketing police were enraged. The orange-clad blonde beauties were escorted from the terraces and two of them were arrested, carted off to jail and arraigned with criminal charges. Of course they were subsequently released. The Dutch brewery must have been over the moon because comparable publicity would have cost a lot of money. FIFA officials and the South African police did their own reputation some harm.

In 2010 the British Conservative Party anticipated the route that the outgoing prime minister would take on the way to seek the Queen's approval for a general election. They also anticipated that the media would film his progress from helicopters. So, they arranged supporters to be along the route. They held aloft big placards promoting the Conservative cause. Few television newscasts could resist the images.

Advertising

Advertising *promotes specific goods and services*. It may be defined as:

> 66   Attracting public attention to a product, service or issue using non-personal methods of communication with a view to persuading the targets to adopt certain behaviours or thought patterns. Usually the desired behaviour is to purchase a product and the advertising organisation usually pays for the advertisement to be put before the target audience. 99

It should be noted that advertising is impersonal. There is no one-to-one contact between buyer and seller. This distinguishes advertising from selling. Moreover, advertising concerns specific products or services. This distinguishes it from public relations.

An advertising campaign can have a number of objectives depending upon a product's position in the product life cycle. If the product is new, the campaign is likely to focus on making target customers aware that the product exists. It may also try to establish the new product's position in the market and its brand. Advertising a new product will also emphasise its unique benefits and appeal to people's needs for novelty and the status from being an early adopter. During the growth stage, advertising may seek to reassure tentative purchasers and boost confidence in the product.

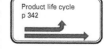

Product life cycle
p 342

In the maturity and saturation stages, advertising will seek to differentiate one brand from another. At this stage the main objective will be to increase, or at least preserve, market share. Organisations may engage in either defensive or offensive advertising. Offensive advertising ("knocking copy") points out weaknesses of competitors' products.

Advertisers use many media including: **billboards** ("poster hoardings") (lorries, taxis or buses); **leaflets** (also known as "flyers") (distributed in the street); **direct mail** (magazines) newspapers, skywriting, Web-banners; **radio, cinema** and **television**. The exact choice depends on the product and target audience. For example, luxury goods are unlikely to be advertised using leaflets distributed in the street. They are more likely to be advertised in upmarket magazines.

An advertisements first job is to **a**ttract attention, then develop the **d**esire for the product and finally to encourage consumers to take **a**ction and purchase the product (ADA). Methods may include:

- *Repetition* – very important with new products where the aim is to make people remember the name.
- *Bandwagon campaigns* implying everyone is purchasing the product or service and to be without it would be odd. This tactic is frequently used during a product's growth stage.
- *Testimonials* appeal to people's propensity to obey authority. They may quote sources of authority such as "five out of six doctors eat product X".
- *Pressure campaigns* often take the form of "buy now, before stocks are gone" or "buy now, before a tax increase". This tactic is frequently used during a product's maturity stage.
- *Association campaigns* try to link products with desirable things and attractive or famous people. Association campaigns are often used in conjunction with testimonials.

CASE 14.5: *Misleading advertisements*

In 2002 the Chinese State Drug Administration estimated that 89 per cent of advertisements for drugs and medical services were illegal. Specific examples of misleading advertisements are found throughout the world. In 2003 the American Federal Drug Agency (FDA) ordered Purdue Pharma to withdraw advertisements for a painkiller, OxyCotin, because they failed to mention a fatal side effect. A rather different criticism was levelled against the American milk industry's campaign "got milk" featuring celebrities with "milk moustaches". Physicians complained that the advertisements ignored data linking high milk consumption with heart disease and prostate cancer. Their complaints were supported by the Department of Agriculture (USDA).

Place

Place is the fifth and final component of the marketing mix. It is the location where ownership of goods is transferred or where a service is performed. The place where a product is marketed depends on two main factors: distribution channels and customer expectations.

Distribution and place

Transporting goods to market, storing them until requested by a customer, employing sales staff and providing a setting which the customer finds conducive can cost as much as the production of an article or service. Few organisations can afford to provide these facilities on a national or regional basis; hence they need to rely on other people, wholesalers and retailers. Since wholesalers and retailers act on behalf of many producers the costs can be shared. Moreover, wholesalers and retailers develop specialist expertise so distribution costs are minimised. Historically, the location of the transfer of goods and services happened in marketplaces at the centre of towns and cities. Then it took place in shops in the centre of towns and cities. Now, with motor transport, goods and services are exchanged for money in an often purpose-built **shopping mall** or **retail park** on a motorway circling a large town.

However, a traditional *shop* or a *department store* is not always appropriate or convenient. **Catalogue sales**, for example, are more convenient for people in isolated communities or those who are confined to homes by disability. Some organisations have deliberately developed alternatives to the traditional chain of retail distribution. Tupperware developed a new distribution structure by *selling its products in people's homes* at Tupperware parties. This reduced costs and used social pressures. **Catalogue showrooms**, pioneered by Argos, reduce the need for space to display merchandise. Consequently catalogue showrooms offer a wider range of products at a keen price. However, they require superb logistics to ensure that a replacement article is sent from a central store on the same day one is sold. With the Internet a growing number of transactions take place in *cyberspace*.

E-commerce p 446

Customer experience and place

Customers have clear images and expectations about where they will buy goods. If these expectations are not met they do not buy. They expect to buy cabbages at a greengrocer and not at a newsagent. They expect to buy expensive jewellery in a plush setting where they receive a great deal of personal attention. Consequently, a marketing function will pay great attention to the image of the place where its goods or services are exchanged, This is known as the "**merchandise assortment**". The merchandise assortment must be consistent with the ideas of the consumer otherwise they are unlikely to enter the store to find a suitable article. Another important factor image is *location*. People expect stores to be located among other stores selling similar or complementary products. For example, it is expected that a store selling chairs and tables will be near a store that sells carpets, which in turn will be near a store that sells curtains. Stores arranged in a line next to a large parking area are called a "strip". Stores that are arranged around a central area designed for sitting, strolling and perhaps taking light refreshments are called, especially in America, a "mall".

The interior of a store will be laid out so it gives a customer an experience which is consistent with the image of the organisation. The physical characteristics such as decor, displays and layout are called "atmospherics" or "ambiance". Most important, the exterior atmospherics, which indicate the type of things a store will sell, exert a strong influence on a customer's willingness to enter. Interior atmospherics, which may include music, influence a customer's movement and mood. A primary concern will be to draw potential consumers to the back of a store by using a particularly attractive display or moving image. Once drawn to the back of a store a customer will be encouraged, perhaps by appropriate music or exotic displays, to tarry. As they tarry, they are more likely to make a purchase. A way for supermarkets to draw customers to the further reaches of their stores is to place essential items such as bread at the furthest distance from the entrance. Supermarkets have long appreciated the importance of layout. For example, sales are increased if essential items are positioned either on high shelves or on low ones. Discretionary items are placed on shelves at eye level. As consumers reach for essential items they are likely to see, and purchase, discretionary products. Similarly, supermarkets know that the ends, between aisles, are positions where products are most likely to be selected.

CRITICAL THINKING 14.3 *The charges against marketing*

Marketing is more controversial than other management functions. Its intentions – to interpret and fulfil customer demand – are impeccable. It also plays an undeniable role in creating mass markets which bring economies of scale that in turn drive prices down to the benefit of most people. However, its critics also have a strong case. Their indictment includes misleading advertisements, manipulation, encouragement of antisocial behaviour, creation of false markets and dumbing down.

Use of *misleading advertisements* is a frequent criticism. The malpractice seems to be particularly prevalent in the pharmaceutical and food industries where advertisements may claim spurious health benefits. In some countries the problem seems endemic. The marketing function is often accused of *underhand manipulation*. Advertisements may not openly state a product's benefits. They may be implied by information of which the consumer is unaware. In other words, consumers are induced to buy products by messages outside their awareness or logical control. This reflects an imbalance in power and resources. A consumer buying an everyday product can only devote seconds to their choice. A multinational organisation marketing the same product to millions of individuals can devote a team of a dozen or more experts for several months to devise ways to induce a consumer to make a purchase. One tactic is to target people with fewer evaluative powers. For example, makers of a breakfast cereal may *target adverts at children* knowing that, in turn, they will pressurise their parents.

Another tactic might be **subliminal advertising**, which involves projecting a message at a very low level so that people are not conscious of the message being there. For example, an advertiser might project a very faint advertisement during a soap opera programme. The advert is so faint that the viewer does not realise it is there but the message is registered subconsciously. Initial experiments showing subliminal advertising could be effective were seriously flawed. Modern research shows that subliminal advertising does not work. Subliminal advertising is illegal in many countries. Underhand manipulation is not limited to the use of children or

▶

subliminal adverts. It can arise from non-verbal messages. An advertisement may not explicitly state that a product will bring wealth and power. It may, however, imply these benefits by including images of wealthy and powerful people. For example, a business school prospectus might include photographs of successful business people boarding an aeroplane en route to a meeting on international strategy. However, it may know, full well, that most of its MBAs work within the domestic economy. One of the first people to note manipulation by the marketing function was Packard (1957).

Criticisms of the marketing function for using misleading advertisements are by no means restricted to the pharmaceutical or food industries. The travel industry, especially companies selling air fares, is frequently admonished for misleading, bait and switch tactics. Hectares of Sunday newspapers are covered with offers of cheap flights. Yet, when even the nimblest consumer telephones, there are no remaining seats at the cheapest rates. They are encouraged to switch to more expensive, and presumably more profitable, flights.

Some people criticise marketing for *encouraging antisocial behaviour*. Attracting attention is a major problem. There is so much advertising and so much media coverage that an organisation's message may get lost. An easy solution is shock tactics. But many shock tactics involve antisocial behaviour. For example, an organisation producing crisps (chips) might draw attention to its product with an advertisement depicting a pupil successfully deceiving a teacher during a mathematics lesson to eat crisps. The advertisements would probably increase the sales of the crisp manufacturer. However, it would make classroom discipline more difficult. It might mean the skills of a future generation are impaired so that a country has a reduced ability to provide social goods such as transport or health care.

The marketing function will usually seek to maximise the benefit for its own organisation rather than the community. It may benefit the organisation to develop and market a new product that is unnecessary and which will, in the long term, damage people and their society. In essence, this criticism accuses the marketing function of *developing and exploiting unnecessary and dangerous consumer needs*. For example, the market research of the company Masterfoods (MARS) revealed a marketing opportunity for a large wafer, chocolate caramel cream confectionary bar for women. It developed a product, Mars Delight, which was launched in Ireland. A marketing spend of £15 million was devoted to promoting this product. However, in the light of increasing obesity in the developed world, Mars was criticised for developing a needless and, possibly dangerous, product.

Perhaps the most important criticism against the marketing function is its *impact on society*. Because of its economic power and its expertise, the influence of the marketing is very widespread and pervasive. This leads to two further criticisms. First, it promulgates a capitalist, market ethos which ignores other social, cultural and aesthetic considerations. Probably more important is the impact on intellectual standards – *dumbing down*. The marketing function will

▶ wish to appeal to as many people as possible. This behaviour might lead to a society with low standards.

Many of these criticisms may be unfair because they are directed at the image of the marketing function. The marketing function may be partly responsible as a victim of its own hype. Further, many countries have enacted legislation that curb marketing's worst excesses.

14.7 The sales function

The sales function is ignored by many textbooks. However, practising managers such as Henry Ford knew the value of the sales function. He is reported to have said that *nothing* has value until it is actually sold. Strategy can be superb, production can be lean, finance can be sophisticated and the human resources function can be inspirational, but a commercial organisation will die unless it sells its products or services.

CRITICAL THINKING 14.4 *Why do textbooks shun sales?*

Most management textbooks wax lyrical about marketing and marketing strategy and devote endless chapters to them, but sales is all but ignored except for a brief mention of sales promotion. This is clearly unbalanced since many of the top organisations such as Marks & Spencer, Tesco, B&Q, Amazon, John Lewis, IKEA, Carphone Warehouse and DSG (formerly Dixons) are predominantly sales organisations. How does this imbalance come about? Why do academics and researchers tend to shun the sales function? There are at least three possible reasons:

1 Academics and researchers work in universities and colleges where income is provided by the state and the sales function, if any, is small. They are unaware of its importance.

2 They have a negative view of sales as the mere pursuit of profit and lucre – this, they believe, is so much less worthy than the pursuit of truth, knowledge and learning.

3 The topic of sales is less congenial to academic study. An understanding of sales requires more than reading a few books and research papers. It may need some actual experience. Further, sales requires more than analysis and contemplation. It requires practical, emotional and social skills.

A cynic might maintain that people who are interested in sales avoid academic life, with its writing and research, because so much more money can be earned working in sales than writing about it.

The sales function covers a huge range of situations – from someone on a street corner selling the *Big Issue* to a very high-powered executive selling an inter-continental computer system. There are many instances of heinous sales methods. The techniques to sell timeshares and the methods employed by consultants and advisers in the finance and pension industries are sometimes very questionable indeed. Often, the common link in bad sales is a highly geared bonus or commission system. Nevertheless, these examples of sales give an inaccurate caricature. The vast majority of sales staff are oriented to providing a service to provide a benefit to the community. For example, without the activities of pharmaceutical company's sales representatives many GPs would remain ignorant of medications that would be good for their patients.

Most sales situations can be fitted into one of two categories: B2C (business to customer) and B2B (business to business) sales There are at least two general approaches to **B2C sales**. At the lower end, where the product is worth less than, say, £2, or where local enthusiasts for a charity aim to raise contributions, a pushy approach may yield benefits. People will contribute £1 or £2 to avoid hassle. However, a pushy sales approach soon reaches its limits. Sales people selling big-ticket items need to adopt a much more thoughtful approach. Within seconds, they need to evaluate the best way to approach a customer and to elicit their likely needs. It is often said that a good salesperson sells with their ears, not with their mouths! When needs are clarified a salesperson needs to suggest appropriate purchases and the **benefits** that the purchases will provide. Inexperienced sales staff often make the mistake of pointing out the technical features of a purchase such as a television screen with a faster refresh rate. An experienced salesperson, on the other hand, emphasises the benefits of a better viewing experience of, say, a soccer match where a football in flight is smooth rather than juddering. The sales function will be responsible for training sales staff. Much of this training will be on-the-job training but most sales staff will attend a course on selling techniques. Many different approaches are available. Perhaps the best known is the AIDA method which has four stages:

E-commerce B2C and B2B p 450

- First, **Attract** the customer's attention in a pleasant and civilised way.
- Second, **Interest** the customer in a product.
- Third, develop the customers **Desire** to own the product (anticipating the benefits).
- Finally, induce the customer to take a vital **Act** of making the purchase.

Business-to-business sales can be very sophisticated. In essence, a sales representative will aim to establish a long-term relationship where they are regarded as a trusted adviser. Again there are many methods and training courses. Perhaps the best known is "**the seven steps of the sale**" which is also known as PSS – professional selling. The seven steps are:

1 *Plan the approach carefully*. The larger the organisation the greater the need for research about its structure, suppliers and the organisation's strategy, etc. Gaining access can be a major problem. It is usually vital to establish a good rapport with a decision-maker's personal assistant since they can grant or deny access. They can also provide information that is very useful at a later stage.

2 *Prepare a friendly, professional and confident introduction* to the first meeting and set the scene by asking how much time is available and if it is acceptable to start by asking questions and taking notes. In some situations a *brief* description of your own organisation and its capabilities might be appropriate at this stage.

3 *Use thoughtful questions* to determine the needs of the organisation. Often there is a major need plus subsidiary ones. Questioning should be done with empathy and the responses should be listened to most carefully. Body language is important. Questions should also cover how the organisation might prefer to develop your relationship. *Make a presentation* which focuses upon how the benefits of the product match the needs of the organisation. The presentation should also show an understanding of the organisation. *Overcome* objections and comments. Often the first response should be to clarify the issue by asking questions such as "what makes you say that?" Many objections are merely requests for further information. Use questions and objections to develop a constructive discussion.

4 *Close the sale* – but not too early! A standard closing is, "Are you happy that we've covered everything and would you like to go ahead?" – but many other ploys exist.

5 *Follow-up* depends on the type of product or service. At the very least it should be a call to confirm that they customer is happy with the product and its delivery. Follow-up may provide good opportunities for extending a network of contacts.

Business-to-business sales may involve other activities. It may, for example, include advising customers how to display your products. It may involve explaining the product to your customer's staff and perhaps training them to use it. Above all else, sales representatives gather a great deal of intelligence about the market – its trends and opportunities – which the marketing function and the organisation as a whole might exploit.

14.8 The marketing plan

Many marketing functions formalise their intentions into a marketing plan for the next three or more years. The process is a special version of planning in general, which was explained in Chapter 4. Typically, the plan starts with the corporate mission which is translated into a future strategy incorporating customer needs and the resources, especially financial technological and human, available. Marketing strategy is usually formed after reviewing:

Planning
p 89

- the marketing environment
- the organisation's marketing mix
- the organisation's marketing function – its experience and capabilities

This information is used to devise an appropriate marketing mix which will contain specific targets for major objectives. Tactical plans are constructed to enable the achievement of the major objectives. They will include goals such as advertising campaigns, sales efforts and, say, point-of-sale material. Finally, there will be operational plans to determine, for example, exactly which advertisements will be placed in which magazines on what dates. The process is rarely so linear. For example, a strategic marketing plan is revised when operational plans make it apparent that there is no realistic prospect of achieving a strategic objective.

CASE 14.6: *Sleigh Bells' marketing plan*

Sleigh Bells is a new American duo who specialise in noise, dance punk and lo-fi. The contract is with Columbia Studios which are owned by Sony. In 2010 they released their debut album, *Treats*. Marketing is a vital component in the success of performers. A label will have a strategic marketing plan that involves maintaining existing stars and launching a number of new performers each year (launch pipeline).

The marketing department at Columbia devised a tactical marketing plan for Sleigh Bells – only parts of which are public. The department went into top gear to implement its front-line tactical marketing. A lead single was planned to step up publicity in preparation for the release of an album. The next tactical event was a campaign in the UK where the awareness of the duo was thought to be strong – partly because the plan had staged a series of events and articles with *NME*, *Sunday Times Culture* and *Q*. Specialist radio support was scheduled to include John Kennedy at XFM, Zane Lowe and and Huw Stephens at Radio One. A whole year was a careful marketing plan.

Marketing plans and, indeed, the whole of the marketing function are useless unless they are properly implemented and the product or service is formed. This can be a complicated operation. The next chapter therefore gives details of the operations function.

Activities and further study

Essay plans

Write essay plans for the following questions:

1 How might markets differ?
2 What models might organisations use to locate a profitable market? To what extent are these models consistent with each other and how useful might they be in practice?
3 Why do organisations undertake market research? What methods could they use?
4 What is meant by "the marketing mix"?
5 What are the main criticisms against marketing? To what extent are these criticisms valid?

Web activities

1 Look up the websites of:
Chartered Institute of Marketing – http://www.cim.co.uk/home.aspx
 Marketing Week – http://www.marketingweek.co.uk/
 Marketing Institute Singapore – http://www.mis.org.sg/
 Marketing Association of Australia and New Zealand – http://www.marketing.org.au/
2 Look up postgraduate courses in marketing such as:
 http://www.prospects.ac.uk/
 http://www.whatuni.com/degrees/courses/Postgraduate-list/Marketing
 http://www.masterstudies.com/MBA-MSc-Masters-Degree/Business-Economics-and-Administration/Marketing/Sweden/

Experiential activities

1 It is possible to gain some first-hand experience of marketing or sales with vacation work or, perhaps, a management training scheme with short periods of work in different functions ("Cooks Tours").
2 Talk to a manager who works in marketing or sales. Try to get detailed answers to the following questions: what type of organisation is it? What are its goals? What is its basic

transformation process? What are the future challenges marketing and sales functions are likely to face?

Recommended reading

1 Smith, M. (2002) "Derrick's Ice Cream Company: applying the BCG matrix in customer profitability analysis" *Accounting Education*, **11** (4), 365–376. A practical example of how the BCG matrix can be used.

2 Friel, M. (1999) "Marketing practice in small tourism and hospitality firms", *International Journal of Tourism Research*, **1**, 97–109. A description of the way small firms in the English tourist industry market themselves.

3 Cooper, L. (2010) "Small business digs in deep into marketing mix", *Marketing Week*, **33** (28), 26–29. Discusses the marketing activities of small and medium-sized businesses.

Chapter TWENTY

Marketing Research and Information Systems

Chapter Outline

The importance of marketing research

Types of marketing research

Ad hoc research

Continuous research

Approaches to conducting marketing research

Stages in the marketing research process

Marketing information systems

Learning Outcomes

By the end of this chapter you will understand:

1 the importance of marketing research
2 the different types of marketing research available
3 the approaches to conducting research
4 the stages in the marketing research process
5 the nature and purpose of marketing information systems.

Marketing Spotlight

Searching for 'cool'

Trend spotting is one of the biggest marketing research challenges facing companies marketing to the 16–34 age group. It is sometimes described as the search for 'cool', which is an invisible, intangible but very valuable commodity. Marketers know that if 'cool' people start talking or eating or dressing or shopping in a certain way, then 'non-cool' people will follow them. Understand what cool people are doing today and you can see what everyone else will be doing a year from now.

But cool is an elusive quality. And it will not be discovered through conventional market research techniques such as surveys or focus group interviews. Many leading companies employ professional trend spotters ('cool hunters') to seek it out. In what might sound like the ideal job, trend spotters, who are usually in their 20s, spend their time going to parties, making new friends online, travelling to far-flung destinations and hanging out in 'cool' places like New York's Soho district. They are then responsible for providing regular reports on the latest happenings in music, fashion, lifestyle and technology. Perhaps the biggest challenge for both the trend spotter and their employer is to sift through the mass of

information that is available to truly identify the drivers of youth behaviour. Separating fads from real trends is not easy, as the obsession with everything online demonstrated in the late 1990s. In addition, there are now a variety of boutique research firms providing trend-spotting services—including, for example, the Zandl Group and www.trendwatching.com.

One company that uses trend spotters to maintain its cool positioning in the marketplace is the urbanwear brand, Diesel. The Diesel brand started out in Italy in 1975 and has since grown to annual global sales levels in the region of US$680 million. The company employs 50 25-year-old trend spotters from around the world who travel wherever they want to research and seek out new trends and ideas. Maintaining its cool image is extremely important to a brand that is now so large that it has become mainstream. Therefore it must constantly seek to be innovative in its product design— for example, producing a new line like 55 DSL, which targets skateboarders and snowboarders, as well as being creative in its advertising and online marketing (www.diesel.com).[1]

The importance of marketing research

Marketing research is enormously important. Truly market-led companies recognize that they need to always be in touch with what is happening in the marketplace. Customer needs are continually changing, often in ways that are very subtle. For some companies, no major strategic decisions are made without first researching the market. But this activity goes far beyond commercial organizations. For example, organizations ranging from political parties to record companies are heavy users of marketing research and often stand accused of over-dependence on it to shape everything from manifestos to new albums. Marketing research can play a role in many different activities. Research can be useful to help understand what customers want, to decide whether to launch a new product or not, to get feedback from customers about ongoing levels of service, to measure the effectiveness of a sponsorship campaign, and so on.

The marketing research industry is massive, estimated to be worth over US$24 billion globally in 2006 and US$10,597 million in Europe, or nearly half the total global spend. Table 4.1 provides details of levels of marketing research expenditure throughout the world. Market research also tends to follow market development. For example, some of the highest growth rates for market research have been in countries like Latvia and Bulgaria, whose growing economies have attracted the interest of marketers.[2] Defining the boundaries of marketing research is not easy. Casual discussions with customers at exhibitions or through sales calls can provide valuable informal information about their requirements, competitor activities and future happenings in the industry. More formal approaches include the conduct of marketing research studies or the development of marketing information systems. This chapter focuses on these formal methods of information provision. First, we will describe the different types of marketing research and the approaches used to conduct research studies. Then we will look at the process of marketing research and its uses in more detail. Finally, we examine the development of marketing information systems and the ethics of market research.

Types of marketing research

In the first instance we need to distinguish between ad hoc and continuous research.

Table 4.1 Global marketing research expenditure 2006 (selected countries)

Country	Turnover in US$ million	Spend per capita in US$
UK	2369	39.19
Sweden	335	36.92
France	2214	35.33
USA	8232	27.49
Norway	126	27.10
Germany	2206	26.73
Australia	532	25.76
Denmark	131	24.11
Finland	125	23.96
Switzerland	166	22.76
Netherlands	346	21.17
New Zealand	86	20.76
Canada	652	20.04
Ireland	84	19.97
Belgium	167	16.06
Luxembourg	6	13.09
Singapore	55	12.23
Italy	706	12.16
Japan	1380	10.79
China	583	0.44

Source: Esomar Global Market Research, 2007

Ad hoc research

Ad hoc research focuses on a specific marketing problem, collecting data at one point in time from one sample of respondents. Examples of ad hoc studies are usage and attitude surveys, product and concept tests, advertising development and evaluation studies, corporate image surveys and customer satisfaction surveys. Ad hoc surveys are either custom-designed or omnibus studies, and these account for over 60 per cent of market research expenditure globally.

Custom-designed studies

This type of study is based on the specific needs of the client. The research design is based on the research brief given to the marketing research agency or internal marketing researcher. Because they are tailor-made, such surveys can be expensive.

Omnibus surveys

An alternative to the custom-designed study is the **omnibus survey** in which space is bought on

Exhibit 4.1 Face-to-face interviews and telephone surveys are two of the most popular ways to conduct ad hoc research

The rapid growth of online blogs and discussion forums has given rise to a variant on the traditional customer panel. These types of discussion boards are everywhere on the internet, discussing anything from the fat content of potato crisps to the merits of new electronic gadgets. In most instances, they have not been formally created by corporations but the frank nature of the debate that often takes place on them makes them appealing to managers. Some companies track these discussion groups to see what is being said about their brands and what trends are emerging. It is also a very cost-effective form of research as much of the monitoring can be done electronically. However, because this monitoring is generally covert, it may be disturbing for participants to learn that what they have to say is being studied by companies.

questionnaires for face-to-face or telephone interviews (see Exhibit 4.1). An interview may cover many topics, as questionnaire space is bought by a number of clients, who benefit from cost sharing. Usually the type of information sought is relatively simple (e.g. awareness levels and ownership data). Often the survey will be based on demographically balanced samples of 1000–2000 adults. However, more specialist surveys covering the markets for children, young adults, mothers and babies, the 'grey' market and motorists exist.

Continuous research

Continuous research involves the interviewing of the same sample of people repeatedly. The main types of continuous research are consumer panels, retail audits and television viewership panels.

Consumer panels

When large numbers of households are recruited to provide information on their purchases over time, together they make up a **consumer panel**. For example, a grocery panel would record the brands, pack sizes, prices and stores used for a wide range of supermarket brands. By using the same households over a period of time, measures of brand loyalty and switching can be achieved, together with a demographic profile of the type of person who buys particular brands. Recent years have seen a significant growth in the use of technology in consumer panel research, with studies being conducted online or over the telephone as well as face to face. Once participants are familiar with the researchers and have indicated a willingness to participate then these more remote research approaches can work very effectively.

Retail audits

Another type of continuous research is the **retail audit**. By gaining the co-operation of retail outlets (e.g. supermarkets), sales of brands can be measured by means of laser scans of barcodes on packaging, which are read at the checkout. Although brand loyalty and switching cannot be measured, retail audits can provide an accurate assessment of sales achieved by store. A major provider of retail audit data is ACNielsen. For example, its BookScan service provides weekly sales data on over 300,000 titles collected from point-of-sale information from a variety of retailers.

Television viewership panels

A television viewership panel measures audience size on a minute-by-minute basis. Commercial breaks can be allocated ratings points (the proportion of the target audience watching)—the currency by which television advertising is bought and judged. In the UK, the system is controlled by the Broadcasters' Audience Research Board (BARB) (www.barb.co.uk), and run by AGB and RSMB. AGB handles the measurement process and uses 'people meters' to record whether a set is on/off, which channel is being watched and, by means of a hand console, who is watching. Because of concerns about the extent to which viewers actually watch advertising, audience measurement companies are now providing measures of the viewership of advertising breaks as well as programmes. Technological developments continue to revolutionize TV audience measurement. Personal video recorders (PVRs), build up a profile of viewers' likes and dislikes, and record their favourite programmes automatically, but the box also relays every button press on its remote control back to the manufacturer, providing exact details of what programmes people watch on what channels.

Exhibit 4.2 Loyalty card schemes are used extensively by organizations to build up databases of customers

Marketing databases

Companies collect data on customers on an ongoing basis. The data are stored on marketing databases, containing each customer's name, address, telephone number, past transactions and, sometimes, demographic and lifestyle data. Information on the types of purchase, frequency of purchase, purchase value and responsiveness to promotional offers may be held (see Chapter 10). For example, retailers are encouraging the collection of such data through introducing loyalty card schemes, which are popular with supermarkets, department stores and petrol retailers (see Exhibit 4.2). Customers collect points that can be redeemed for cashback or gifts while at the same time the retailer collects valuable information about the customer each time the card is used.

Banks have become heavy users of this type of information as they seek to manage more carefully consumers that have taken on debts such as mortgages and credit cards. Banks get information from a number of sources, including their own records, their links to other payment organizations, such as Visa and Mastercard, and specialist credit checking agencies. Through the examination of this information, they can develop relatively accurate predictions of which customers are likely to default on a loan, or they can intervene earlier before debts become significant. For example, if consumers have switched more of their regular shopping, such as groceries, from cash to credit cards, this may indicate a cash shortage and the increased risk of a missed payment on a loan.

Customer relationship management (CRM) systems

A potential problem with the growth of marketing databases is that separate ones are created in different departments of the company. For example, the sales department may have an account management database containing information on customers, while call centre staff may use a different database created at a different time also containing information on customers. This fragmented approach can lead to problems, when, for example, a customer transaction is recorded on one but not the other database. Issues like this have led to the development of customer relationship management (CRM) systems where a single database is created from customer information to inform all staff who deal with customers. CRM is a term for the methodologies, technologies and e-commerce capabilities used by companies to manage customer relationships[3] (see Chapter 10). Companies such as Tesco make some of their CRM data available to suppliers in order that they can respond better to the needs of their ultimate customer: the grocery shopper.

Website analysis

Continuous data can also be provided by analysing consumers' use of websites. Measurements of the areas of the site most frequently visited, which products are purchased and the payment method used can be made. Indeed one of the challenges of website analysis is coping with the vast volumes of data that can be produced. Whatever the challenges of measuring the size of the audience from an advertising point of view, there are several aspects of how consumers behave while visiting a website that owners should record and monitor. First, where did they come from —for example, did they come via a search engine or from a link on another site? Second, where do they go once they are on the site? What options are selected, what visuals are viewed, and so on. Did they respond to particular offers, promotions or site design changes? And, if the company is an online retailer, what percentage of consumers proceeded to the checkout and, for those that didn't, at what stage in the process did they drop out? Some of the challenges of measuring website audiences are discussed in Marketing in Action 4.1.

Approaches to conducting marketing research

There are two main ways for a company to carry out marketing research, depending on the situation facing it. It might either carry out the work itself or employ the services of a market research agency. The advantage of using an agency is that it will have the specialist skills and experience of conducting studies; these advantages may be offset, however, by the prohibitively high cost of using the agency's services. Where the study is small in scale, such as gathering information from libraries or interviewing a select number of industrial customers, companies may choose to conduct the work themselves. This is

Marketing in Action 4.1: Website audience measurement

> **Study guide:** Below is a review of some of the key metrics used to measure website audiences. Read it and consider the advantages and disadvantages of each measure.

Internet advertising is the fastest-growing sector of the advertising industry, but before you decide where to advertise you need to be able to estimate how many people are likely to see your advert. Fortunately websites are rich in the data they provide but, unfortunately, they produce so much that it makes the selection decision very difficult. Should you go by hits, unique users, time spent on a site, or indeed by click-through, impressions, sessions, queries or engagement? The internet advertising planner is faced with some very difficult decisions.

In the early days of e-commerce, many internet companies proudly trumpeted the number of hits their websites received. A hit is recorded when a web user clicks on any one element (such as an image, text, etc.) of one web page. However, this was an easy figure to manipulate—simply increasing the number of graphics on a page increased the number of hits. Page views (the number of pages a visitor looks at) became the next currency by which websites were measured, but this is equally suspect. Many modern websites use a technology that allows pages to update parts of themselves, such as a share-price ticker, without having to reload and redraw the rest of the page. But the problem is that a user spending the entire day on Yahoo!Finance, for example, counts as only one page view. Unique users (when a person visits a website) is another popular metric. But it, too, is problematic because 2 million unique users could mean anything from 2 million people visiting the site once, to one person visiting it 2 million times. It is impossible to know for sure. As websites like MySpace and YouTube have become more interactive, advertisers have become more interested in other measures. 'Duration' and 'time spent' suggest how long one or more people are interacting with a page, which in turn gives an indication of how 'engaged' they are.

Basic customer behaviour patterns on a website are tracked through technologies such as logfiles, which are a record of all activity on a site, and cookies, which are files located on the visitor's hard drive. For example, click-through or click-stream analysis looks at logfiles to see where users go when they visit a site. Web analytics combines these basic metrics with demographic and subscription information to provide a more detailed analysis of visitor behaviour. Website owners can know a lot about what visitors to their site do but getting this information requires careful planning.

Based on: Anonymous (2007);[4] Guenther (2003);[5] Phippen, Sheppard and Furnell (2004)[6]

particularly feasible if a company has a marketing department and/or a marketing research executive on its staff. Other companies prefer to design the research themselves and then employ the services of a fieldwork agency to collect the data. Alternatively, where resources permit and the scale of the study is larger, companies may employ the services of a market research agency to conduct the research. The company will brief the agency about its market research requirements and the agency will do the rest. The typical stages involved in completing a market research study are described next; full-service agencies generally conduct all the activities described below.

The leading marketing research firms in the world are shown in Table 4.2.

Stages in the marketing research process

Figure 4.1 provides a description of a typical marketing research process. Each of the stages illustrated will now be discussed. Some leading companies' different approaches to research problems are discussed in Marketing in Action 4.2.

Initial contact

The process usually starts with the realization that a marketing problem (e.g. a new product development or advertising decision) requires information to aid its solution. Marketing management may contact internal marketing research staff or an outside agency. Let

Table 4.2 World's leading marketing research firms, 2006

Name	Country	Employees	Turnover (US$m)
The Nielsen Company	USA	39,517	3,696.0
IMS Health, Inc.	USA	7,400	1,958.6
Taylor Nelson Sofres plc	UK	14,570	1,851.1
The Kantar Group	UK	6,900	1,401.4
GfK AG	Germany	7,900	1,397.3
Ipsos Group SA	France	6,503	1,077.0
Synovate	UK	5,726	739.6
IRI	USA	3,600	665.0
Westat, Inc.	USA	1,906	425.8
Arbitron, Inc.	USA	1,045	329.3

Source: Esomar, Global Market Research, 2007

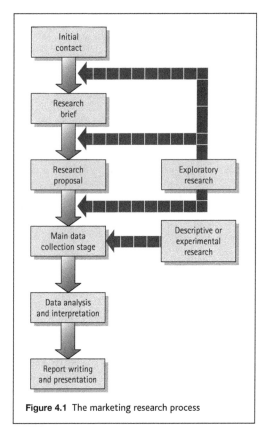

Figure 4.1 The marketing research process

us assume that the research requires the assistance of a marketing research agency. A meeting will be arranged to discuss the nature of the problem and the client's research needs. If the client and its markets are new to the agency, some rudimentary exploratory research (e.g. a quick online search for information about the client and its markets) may be conducted prior to the meeting.

Research brief

At a meeting to decide what form the research will need to take, the client explains the marketing problem and outlines the company's research objectives. The marketing problem might be the need to attract new customers to a product group, and the research objectives to identify groups of customers (market segments) who might have a use for the product and the characteristics of the product that appeal to them most.

Other information that should be provided for the research agency includes the following.[7]

1 *Background information*: the product's history and the competitive situation.
2 *Sources of information*: the client may have a list of industries that might be potential users of the product. This helps the researchers to define the scope of the research.
3 *The scale of the project*: is the client looking for a 'cheap and cheerful' job or a major study? This has implications for the research design and survey costs.
4 *The timetable*: when is the information required?

The client should produce a specific written **research brief**. This may be given to the research agency prior to the meeting and perhaps modified as a result of it but, without fail, should be in the hands of the agency before it produces its **research proposal**. The research brief should state the client's requirements and should be in written form so that misunderstandings are minimized. In the event of a

Marketing in Action 4.2: Getting to know customers

> **Study guide:** Below are some examples of how firms use market research to solve business problems. Read them and think of other examples of ways in which companies can get close to their customers.

When it comes to trying to understand customers, organizations can take a variety of different approaches. For example, one of the world's largest retailer's, Wal-Mart, has had a tradition of doing very little consumer research. It preferred to test-market items from suppliers in its stores and then simply ordered those that sold well. But in recent years, as its sales growth has slowed and it has faced intense competition from other retailers like Target, it has begun to invest more heavily in market research. In early 2004, it carried out a study of 6000 existing customers and found that a significant number wanted more in terms of fashion items and contemporary styles from the organization. In response, it created the Metro 7 sub-brand, which is targeted at fashion-conscious female customers with an urban lifestyle. Metro 7 is located in about 500, mostly urban, Wal-Mart stores as well as on the company's website. In keeping with the fast-fashion trends in this sector, its range is refreshed monthly to reflect evolving styles. As well as meeting the needs of its customers, more fashionable clothing is also attractive to Wal-Mart as these kinds of products are more profitable than many of its grocery and household lines. It is also increasing its investment in market research and consumer insights to identify further growth opportunities and to try to move away from its heavy reliance on an 'every day low prices' approach.

Retailers generally are in a very good position to know a lot about customers, particularly through the analysis of shopping patterns and also by monitoring how consumers respond to sales promotions. This in turn has put pressure back on manufacturers to ensure that they also try to get to know their customers better. Companies like confectionery manufacturer Mars have begun to take novel approaches to this problem. For example, Mars has opened seven café-style outlets in Chicago, which include 'chocolate lounges' where a wide range of premium chocolates are available for purchase. Essentially, Mars has ventured into retailing in order to get closer to its customers. It has also conducted focus-group interviews with potential customers to get a better understanding of what they would like to see in the cafés. One of the earliest insights to emerge from this research is that consumers expressed a preference for dark chocolate for its perceived health benefits. Whether on the part of manufacturers or retailers, it is clear that there is an increasing emphasis on trying to understand our tastes and preferences.

Based on: Birchall (2005);[8] Grant (2005)[9]

---

dispute later in the process, the research brief (and proposal) form the benchmarks against which it can be settled. It is typical to brief two or three agencies as the extra time involved is usually rewarded by the benefits of more than one viewpoint on the research problem . . . and a keener quote!

Research proposal

A research proposal lays out what a marketing research agency promises to do for its client, and how much this will cost. Like the research brief, the proposal should be written in a way that avoids misunderstandings. A client should expect the following to be included.

1. *A statement of objectives*: to demonstrate an understanding of the client's marketing and research problems.
2. *What will be done*: an unambiguous description of the research design—including the research method, the type of sample, the sample size (if applicable) and how the fieldwork will be controlled.
3. *Timetable*: if and when a report will be produced.
4. *Costs*: how much the research will cost and what, specifically, is/is not included in those costs.

When assessing a proposal, a client needs to ensure that it is precise, jargon-free and that it addresses all the issues the client expects.

Exploratory research

Prior to the main data collection stage, **exploratory research** is employed to carry out the preliminary exploration of a research area. This usually occurs between acceptance of the research proposal and the main data collection stage, but can also take place prior to the client/agency briefing meeting and before submission of the research proposal, as an aid to its construction. Exploratory research techniques allow the researcher to understand the people who are to be interviewed in the main data collection stage, and the market that is being researched. The main survey stage can thus be designed with this knowledge in mind rather than being based on the researcher's ill-informed prejudices and guesswork.

A project may involve all or some of the following exploratory research activities:

- secondary research
- qualitative research (group discussions and depth interviews)
- observation.

Secondary research

Because the data come to the researcher 'second-hand' (i.e. other people have compiled it), this type of study is known as **secondary research**. (When the researcher actively collects new data—for example, by interviewing respondents—this is called primary research.) Secondary research should be carried out before primary research. Without the former, an expensive primary research survey might be commissioned to provide information that is already available from secondary sources. Increasingly a significant amount of market information is available for purchase through companies like Mintel, Euromonitor and others.

Secondary data can be found via examination of internal records and reports of research previously carried out for a company. External sources include government and European Commission statistics, publishers of reports and directories on markets, countries and industries, trade associations, banks, newspapers, magazines and journals. Given the amount of potential sources of information that are available globally, for many the first port of call is an internet search engine. The search engine business has grown dramatically in recent years and has led to expressions such as 'to google', after the popular search engine Google, entering the general lexicon. The range of sources of information available to researchers in the European Union is included in Appendix 4.1 (at the end of this chapter), which lists some of the major sources classified by research question.

Qualitative research

Group discussions and depth interviews are the main types of **qualitative research**. This kind of research aims to establish customers' attitudes, values, behaviour and beliefs.

Group discussions, sometimes referred to as **focus groups**, involve unstructured or semi-structured discussions between a moderator or group leader, who is often a psychologist, and a group of consumers (see Exhibit 4.3). The moderator has a list of areas to cover within the topic, but allows the group considerable freedom to discuss the issues that are important to them. By arranging groups of six to twelve people to discuss their attitudes and behaviour, a good deal of knowledge may be gained about the consumer. This can be helpful when constructing questionnaires, which can be designed to focus on what is important to the respondent (as opposed to the researcher) and worded in language the respondent uses and understands. Sometimes focus groups are used to try to generate new product ideas, through the careful selection of participants who have a flair for innovation or a liking for all things new.

The traditional focus group takes place face to face, but the rise of the internet has led to the creation of online focus groups. The internet offers 'communities of interests', which can take the form of chatrooms or websites dedicated to specific interests or issues. These are useful forums for conducting focus groups or at least for identifying suitable participants. Questions can be posed to participants who are not under time pressure to respond. This can lead to

Exhibit 4.3 Focus group interviews such as this one are a very popular form of market research

richer insights since respondents can think deeply about the questions put to them online. Another advantage is that they can comprise people located all over the world at minimal cost. Furthermore, technological developments mean it is possible for clients to communicate secretly online with the moderator while the focus group is in session. The client can ask the moderator certain questions as a result of hearing earlier responses. Clearly, a disadvantage of online focus groups compared with the traditional form is that the body language and interaction between focus group members is missing.[10]

Depth interviews involve the interviewing of individual consumers about a single topic for perhaps one or two hours. The aims are broadly similar to those of the group discussion, but depth interviews are used when the presence of other people could inhibit the expression of honest answers and viewpoints, when the topic requires individual treatment (as when discussing an individual's decision-making process) and where the individual is an expert on a particular topic. For example, depth interviews have been used to conduct research on wealthy Americans to try to understand their attitudes and opinions on money and how they spend it. This was deemed to be a method that was superior to focus groups or surveys, where it was felt that respondents would be reluctant to talk about these issues. A technique called 'snowballing' was also used, where interviewees would recommend others that they thought would be willing to participate in the research.[11]

Care has to be taken when interpreting the results of qualitative research because the findings are usually based on small sample sizes, and the more interesting or surprising viewpoints may be disproportionately reported. This is particularly significant when qualitative research is not followed by a quantitative study.

Qualitative research accounts for 14 per cent of all expenditure on marketing research, of which 70 per cent is spent on group discussions, 15 per cent on in-depth interviews and 15 per cent on other qualitative techniques. Because of its ability to provide in-depth understanding, it is of growing importance within the field of consumer research.[12]

Observation

Observation can also help in exploratory research when the product field is unfamiliar, and may be either informal (where marketers take note of shopping patterns, etc.) or formal (where an observation study is designed and conducted). Observation studies can have a number of advantages. First, they do not rely on the respondent's willingness to provide information; second, the potential for the interviewer to bias the study is reduced; and, third, some types of information can be collected only by observation (for example, a traffic count). Observation studies can be conducted either by human or mechanical means, such as video recording, and may be conducted with or without the customer's knowledge. Camera phones are the latest technology to be used for observation studies, with problems arising when they are used covertly. Samsung, the world's leading manufacturer of camera phones, has even banned their use in its factories, fearing industrial espionage.[13] Observation studies are particularly popular in the retail trade where a great deal can be learned by simply watching the behaviour of shoppers in a supermarket or clothing shop. The growth of observation as a research technique has given rise to the development of the field of **marketing ethnography** (see Marketing in Action 4.3).

The objective of exploratory research, then, is not to collect quantitative data and form conclusions but to become better acquainted with the market and its customers. This allows the researcher to base the quantitative survey on informed assumptions rather than guesswork.

The main data collection stage

The design of the main data collection procedures will be done following careful exploratory research. The most usual approach is to undertake survey research to describe customers' beliefs, attitudes, preferences, behaviour, and so on. In general, the research design will be based on the following framework.

- Who and how many people to interview: the sampling process.
- How to interview them: the survey method.
- What questions to ask: questionnaire design.

The sampling process

Figure 4.2 offers an outline of the **sampling process**. This starts with the definition of the population—that is, the group that forms the subject of study in a particular survey. The survey objective will be to provide results that are representative of this group. Sampling planners, for example, must ask questions like 'Do we interview purchasing managers in all software development firms or only those that employ more than 50 people?'

Once the population has been defined, the next step is to search for a sampling frame—that is, a list or other record of the chosen population from which a sample can be selected. Examples include the

Marketing in Action 4.3: Marketing ethnography

> **Study guide:** Below is a review of the use of ethnographic techniques in researching markets. Read it and then conduct your own small-scale ethnographic study to see what insights you can generate.

One of the criticisms of research techniques like focus-group interviews is that they are somewhat contrived. Groups of people, who may or may not know each other, are brought together in boardroom-type settings and expected to provide insights into their thoughts, feelings and opinions. In such settings consumers may find it difficult or be unwilling to fully engage. As a result, many research companies are borrowing from the kinds of techniques that are employed by anthropologists and biologists, which place an emphasis on the observation of species in their natural settings. This emerging field is known as marketing ethnography.

In ethnographic studies, researchers decide what human behaviours they want to observe. They then go out into the field and record what consumers do, how they live their lives, how they shop, and so on. Having recorded these activities, consumers are interviewed to try to gain insights into the motivations and attitudes that underpin their actions. When all these data have been collected, they are analysed using qualitative software packages that search for common patterns of behaviour and generate clusters of consumers. Finally, the presentation of research findings via video can be very powerful. This allows marketing executives to know consumers in a more intimate way than other forms of research, such as the focus group. More importantly, it provides a mechanism for senior executives to get close to consumer groups they may never come into contact with in their own daily lives because of physical distance and/or social class disparities.

Several leading companies are extensive users of ethnographic research. For example, Procter & Gamble has used it to understand party planning in American homes. Researchers observed both adults planning a dinner party and teenagers planning a gathering, and generated over 100 general insights that enabled the company to plan products and services. Specific themes that emerged from the research included: making parties fun for the host, overcoming unpleasant surprises and ensuring that the party met preconceived expectations. Technology companies like Xerox and Intel use the technique to try to understand the different ways in which technology is used around the world. For example, Xerox researchers examining mobile phone use found that one Malaysian man used the GPS function on his phone every day to find Mecca; this is typical of the kind of unexpected findings that ethnography can uncover. Intel's research in China revealed that parents saw PC use as a distraction for young children, which resulted in its development of a computer aimed at the home educational market. Employed in a business setting, ethnography has some key strengths. It provides an unbiased record of key variables such as what is happening, where is it happening, the order in which it happens, as well as who is doing what and what is being communicated verbally and non-verbally.

Based on: Berner (2006);[14] Durante and Feehan (2006);[15] Thomas (2005)[16]

electoral register and the *Kompass* directory of companies. Researchers then choose between three major sampling methods: simple random sampling (where the sample is drawn at random and each individual has a known and equal chance of being selected); stratified random sampling (where the population is broken into groups and a random sample is drawn from each group); and quota sampling (where interviewers are instructed to ensure that the sample comprises a required number of individuals meeting pre-set conditions, such as a set percentage of small, medium-sized and large companies).

Finally, the researcher must select an appropriate sample size. The larger the sample size the more likely it is that the sample will represent the population. Statistical theory allows the calculation of sampling error (i.e. the error caused by not interviewing

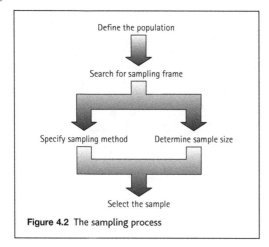

Figure 4.2 The sampling process

everyone in the population) for various sample sizes. In practice, the number of people interviewed is based on a balance between sampling error and cost considerations. Fortunately, sample sizes of around 1000 (or fewer) can provide measurements that have tolerable error levels when representing populations counted in their millions.

The survey method

Four options are available to those choosing a survey method: face-to-face interviews, telephone interviews, mail surveys or internet surveys. Each method has its own strengths and limitations; Table 4.3 gives an overview of these.

A major advantage of face-to-face interviews is that response rates are generally higher than for telephone interviews or mail surveys.[17] It seems that the

personal element in the contact makes refusal less likely. Face-to-face interviews are more versatile than telephone and mail surveys. The use of many open-ended questions on a mail survey would lower response rates,[18] and time restrictions for telephone interviews limit their use. Probing for more detail is easier with face-to-face interviews. A certain degree of probing can be achieved with a telephone interview, but time pressure and the less personalized situation will inevitably limit its use.

Face-to-face interviews do, however, have their drawbacks. They are more expensive than telephone and mail questionnaires. Telephone and mail surveys are cheaper because the cost of contacting respondents is much less expensive, unless the population is very concentrated. The presence of an interviewer can cause bias (e.g. socially desirable answers) and lead to the misreporting of sensitive information. For example, O'Dell[19] found that only 17 per cent of respondents admitted borrowing money from a bank in a face-to-face interview compared to 42 per cent in a comparable mail survey.

In some ways, telephone interviews are a halfway house between face-to-face and mail surveys. They generally have a higher response rate than mail questionnaires but a lower rate than face-to-face interviews; their cost is usually three-quarters of that for face-to-face but higher than for mail surveys; and they allow a degree of flexibility when interviewing. However, the use of visual aids is not possible and there are limits to the number of questions that can be asked before respondents either terminate the interview or give quick (invalid) answers in order to speed up the process. The use of computer-aided telephone interviewing (CATI) is growing. Centrally

Table 4.3 A comparison of survey methods

	Face to face	Telephone	Mail	Internet
Questionnaire				
Use of open-ended questions	High	Medium	Low	Low
Ability to probe	High	Medium	Low	Low
Use of visual aids	High	Poor	High	High
Sensitive questions	Medium	Low	High	Low
Resources				
Cost	High	Medium	Low	Low
Sampling				
Widely dispersed populations	Low	Medium	High	High
Response rates	High	Medium	Low	Low
Experimental control	High	Medium	Low	Low
Interviewing				
Control of who completes questionnaire	High	High	Low	Low/high
Interviewer bias	Possible	Possible	Low	Low

Table 4.4 Relative levels of expenditure on survey methods, 2006 (selected European countries)

Country	Face-to-face	Telephone	Mail	Internet	Other	Total*
Denmark	9	27	15	14	0	65
Finland	7	22	10	10	45	94
France	19	16	2	10	38	85
Ireland	50	12	0	3	0	65
Italy	39	35	1	3	2	80
Netherlands	13	19	8	22	14	76
Spain	31	26	2	10	13	82
Sweden	6	34	10	22	16	88
Switzerland	20	55	4	6	1	86
UK	26	18	6	13	17	80

*Total is the total for quantitative market research expenditure; the remainder is accounted for by qualitative techniques such as focus-group interviews
Source: Esomar, Global Market Research, 2007

located interviewers read questions from a computer monitor and input answers via the keyboard. Routing through the questionnaire is computer-controlled, thus assisting the process of interviewing.

Given a reasonable response rate, mail survey research is normally a very economical method of conducting research. However, the major problem is the potential for low response rates and the accompanying danger of an unrepresentative sample. Nevertheless, using a systematic approach to the design of a mail survey, such as the Tailored Design Method (TDM),[20] has been found to have a very positive effect on response rates. The TDM recommends, as ways of improving response rates, both the careful design of questionnaires to make them easy to complete, as well as accompanying them with a personalized covering letter emphasizing the importance of the research. Studies using the TDM on commercial populations have generated high response rates.[21]

The internet has become a very popular medium for conducting survey research. Online research expenditures exceeded US$3 billion in 2006, a rise of over 14 per cent on the previous year, with the largest growth being recorded in the UK, which rose by over 90 per cent on the previous year.[22] The internet questionnaire is usually administered by email or signals its presence on a website by registering key words or using banner advertising on search engines to drive people to the questionnaire. The major advantage of the internet as a marketing research vehicle is its low cost, since printing and postal costs are eliminated, making it even cheaper than mail surveys. In other ways, its characteristics are similar to mail

surveys: the use of open-ended questions is limited; control over who completes the questionnaire is low; interviewer bias is low; and response rates are likely to be lower than for face-to-face and telephone interviews.

When response is by email, the identity of the respondent will automatically be sent to the survey company. This lack of anonymity may restrict the respondent's willingness to answer sensitive questions honestly. A strength of the internet survey is its ability to cover global populations at low cost, although sampling problems can arise because of the skewed nature of internet users. These tend to be from the younger and more affluent groups in society. For surveys requiring a cross-sectional sample this can be severely restricting.

The relative levels of expenditure on the different research methods are shown in Table 4.4.

Questionnaire design

To obtain a true response to a question, three conditions are necessary. First, respondents must understand the question; second, they must be able to provide the information; and, third, they must be willing to provide it. Figure 4.3 shows the three stages in the development of the questionnaire: planning, design and pilot.

The planning stage involves the types of decision discussed so far in this chapter. It provides a firm foundation for designing a questionnaire, which provides relevant information for the marketing problem that is being addressed.

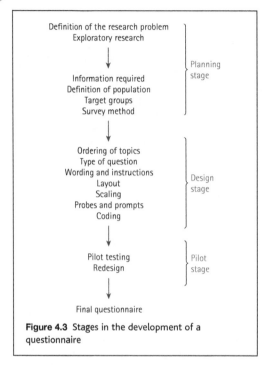

Definition of the research problem
Exploratory research

↓

Information required
Definition of population
Target groups
Survey method

} Planning stage

↓

Ordering of topics
Type of question
Wording and instructions
Layout
Scaling
Probes and prompts
Coding

} Design stage

↓

Pilot testing
Redesign

} Pilot stage

↓

Final questionnaire

Figure 4.3 Stages in the development of a questionnaire

The design stage deals with the actual construction of the survey instrument and involves a number of important decisions. The first relates to the ordering of topics. It is sensible to start with easy-to-answer questions, in order to relax the respondent, and leave sensitive questions until last. Effective questionnaires are well structured and have a logical flow. Second, the type of question needs to be decided. Generally, three types are used: dichotomous questions (allow two possible answers, such as 'Yes'/'No'), multiple-choice questions, which allow more than two answers, and open questions, where the respondents answer by expressing their opinions.

Great care needs to be taken with both the wording and instructions used in the questionnaire and its layout. Questionnaire designers need to guard against asking ambiguous or leading questions, and using unfamiliar words (see Table 4.4). In terms of layout, the questionnaire should not appear cluttered and, where possible, answers and codes should each form a column so that they are easy to identify.

The use of 'scales' is very common in questionnaire design. For example, respondents are given lists of statements (e.g. 'My company's marketing information system allows me to make better decisions') followed by a choice of five positions on a scale ranging from 'strongly agree' to 'strongly disagree'. 'Probes' are used to explore or clarify what a respondent has said. Following a question about awareness of brand names, the exploratory probe 'Any others?' would seek to identify further names. Sometimes respondents use vague words or phrases like 'I like going on

Exhibit 4.4 The Whiskas brand used a play on market research with its famous slogan '8 out of 10 cats prefer Whiskas' and has continued this theme

Table 4.5 Poorly worded questions

Question	Problem and solution
What type of wine do you prefer?	'Type' is ambiguous: respondents could say 'French', 'red' or 'claret', say, depending on their interpretation. Showing the respondent a list and asking 'from this list...' would avoid the problem
Do you think that prices are cheaper at Asda than at Aldi?	Leading question favouring Asda; a better question would be 'Do you think that prices at Asda are higher, lower or about the same as at Aldi?' Names should be reversed for half the sample
Which is more powerful and kind to your hands: Ariel or Bold?	Two questions in one: Ariel may be more powerful but Bold may be kinder to the hands. Ask the two questions separately
Do you find it paradoxical that X lasts longer and yet is cheaper than Y?	Unfamiliar word: a study has shown that less than a quarter of the population understand such words as paradoxical, chronological or facility. Test understanding before use

holiday because it is nice'. A clarifying probe such as, 'In what way is it nice?' would seek a more meaningful response. 'Prompts', on the other hand, aid responses to a question. For example, in an aided recall question, a list of brand names would be provided for the respondent. Coding involves the assignment of numbers to specific responses in order to facilitate analysis of the questionnaire later on.

Once the preliminary questionnaire has been designed it should be piloted with a representative subsample, to test for faults; this is known as the 'pilot stage'. Piloting tests the questionnaire design and helps to estimate costs. Face-to-face piloting, where respondents are asked to answer questions and comment on any problems concerning a questionnaire read out by an interviewer, is preferable to impersonal piloting where the questionnaire is given to respondents for self-completion and they are asked to write down any problems found.[23] Once the pilot work proves satisfactory, the final questionnaire can be administered to the chosen sample.

Data analysis and interpretation

Computers are invariably used to carry out the quantitative analysis of questionnaire data. Basic marketing analyses can be carried out using such software analysis packages as Microsoft Excel on a personal computer. More sophisticated analyses can be conducted using packages such as SPSS-PC and NUD.IST.

Basic analysis of questionnaire data may be at the descriptive level (e.g. means, frequency tables and standard deviations) or on a comparative basis (e.g. t-tests and cross-tabulations). More sophisticated analysis may search for relationships (e.g. regression analysis), group respondents (e.g. cluster analysis), or

establish cause and effect (e.g. analysis of variance techniques used on experimental data).

When interpreting marketing research results, great care must be taken. One common failing is to infer cause and effect when only association has been established. For example, establishing a relationship that sales rise when advertising levels increase does not necessarily mean that raising advertising expenditure will lead to an increase in sales. Other marketing variables (e.g. salesforce effect) may have increased at the same time as the increase in advertising. A second cautionary note concerns the interpretation of means and percentages. Given that a sample has been taken, any mean or percentage is an estimate subject to 'sampling error'—that is, an error in an estimate due to taking a sample rather than interviewing the entire population. A market research survey which estimates that 50 per cent of males but only 45 per cent of females smoke, does not necessarily suggest that smoking is more prevalent among males. Given the sampling error associated with each estimate, the true conclusion might be that there is no difference between males and females.

Report writing and presentation

Crouch suggests that the key elements in a research report are as follows:[24]

1 title page
2 list of contents
3 preface—outline of agreed brief, statement of objectives, scope and methods of research
4 summary of conclusions and recommendations
5 previous related research—how previous research has had a bearing on this research
6 research method
7 research findings

8   conclusions
9   appendices.

Sections 1–4 provide a concise description of the nature and outcomes of the research for busy managers. Sections 5–9 provide the level of detail necessary if any particular issue (e.g. the basis of a finding, or the analytical technique used) needs checking. The report should be written in language the reader will understand; jargon should be avoided.

Marketing information systems

By carefully following each of the stages described above, researchers can improve the quality of the market information they collect. However, the variety of information that is currently available to companies means that it is sensible to set up a **marketing information system**. A marketing information system has been defined as:

> . . . a system in which marketing information is formally gathered, stored, analysed and distributed to managers in accord with their informational needs on a regular planned basis.[25]

The system is built on an understanding of the information needs of marketing management, and supplies that information when, where and in the form that the manager requires it. Marketing information system (MkIS) design is important since the quality of a marketing information system has been shown to influence the effectiveness of decision-making.[26] The MkIS comprises four elements: internal continuous data, internal ad hoc data, environmental scanning, and marketing research (see Figure 4.4).

Companies possess an enormous amount of marketing and financial data (internal continuous data) that may never be used for marketing decision-making unless organized by means of an MkIS. This includes, for example, information that is available from the company's salesforce, such as number of accounts opened, customer attitudes, etc., as well as financial data such as that regarding sales and profitability.

Company data can also be used for a specific (ad hoc) purpose (this is known as internal ad hoc data). For example, management may look at how sales have reacted to a price increase or a change in advertising copy. Although this could be part of a continuous monitoring programme, specific one-off analyses are inevitably required from time to time. Capturing the

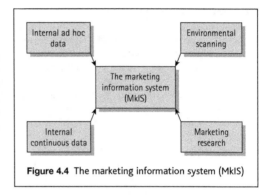

Figure 4.4 The marketing information system (MkIS)

data on the MkIS allows specific analyses to be conducted when needed.

The environmental scanning procedures discussed in Chapter 2 also form part of the MkIS. Although often amorphous in nature, environmental analysis—whereby the economic, social, legal, technological and physical forces are monitored—should be considered part of the MkIS. These are the forces that shape the context within which suppliers, the company, distributors and the competition do business. As such, environmental scanning provides an early warning system for the forces that may affect a company's products and markets in the future. In this way, scanning enables an organization to act upon, rather than react to, opportunities and threats.

As discussed in this chapter, marketing research is primarily concerned with the provision of information about markets and measuring the reactions of consumers to various marketing actions.[27] As such it is a key part of the MkIS because it makes a major contribution to marketing mix planning.

The use of marketing information systems and marketing research

It is important to understand the factors that affect the use of marketing information systems and marketing research. Systems and marketing research reports that remain unused have no value in decision-making.

Marketing information systems should be designed to provide information on a selective basis (for example, by means of a direct, interactive capability).[28] Senior management should conspicuously support use of the system. These recommendations are in line with Ackoff's view[29] that a prime task of an information system is to eliminate irrelevant information by tailoring information flows to the individual manager's needs. It also supports the prescription of Piercy and

Evans that the system should be seen to have top management support,[30] and is consistent with Kohli and Jaworski's view that a market orientation is essentially the organization-wide generation and dissemination of, and responsiveness to, market intelligence.[31]

One of the biggest challenges facing the modern marketing company is the sheer volume of customer information available to it. For example, when continuous data like internal sales records, loyalty card data and website analysis data are combined, the amount of information held about customers can grow very quickly. For example, a US study found that France Telecom's databases held 29.2 terabytes of data, which was equivalent to the printed collection of the Library of Congress six times over.[32] Converting this data into usable and timely information for managers is a critical management challenge.

Marketing research is more likely to be used if researchers appreciate not only the technical aspects of research, but also the need for clarity in report presentation and the political dimension of information provision. It is unlikely that marketing research reports will be used in decision-making if the results threaten the status quo or are likely to have adverse political repercussions. Therefore, perfectly valid and useful information may sometimes be ignored in decision-making for reasons other than difficulties with the way the research was conducted.

Ethical Debate 4.1: Market research—fact or fiction?

Market research is one of the most visible faces of marketing. At some stage or other, nearly everyone participates in a survey, whether it is in a retail environment, a university or at home via telephone, post or, increasingly, by pressing the red button on their television remote controls. Consumers are also invited to participate in focus groups, depth interviews and ethnographic research. While all this research provides answers, it also seems to be raising some very fundamental questions.

The first concerns the widespread usage to which research is being put. It is virtually impossible now to pick up a newspaper or watch the television without seeing the results of some survey or other being presented. It may be about the most mundane of matters, such as how much time is spent cleaning the kitchen floor or who people think is the most eligible film star. The more outrageous the survey or its findings, the more likely it is to be picked up by news bulletins or discussed on talk radio shows. In other words, surveys have become the news and for 24-hour news channels they represent a relatively cheap and useful time filler. For example, many people missed the irony of Sky News charging viewers to vote by text on whether they thought they were paying too much for their mobile phone bills.

The sheer prevalence of surveys and their findings raises two other fundamental questions: who sponsored the study and how was it conducted? The former is crucial because it demonstrates that many of the surveys in the media are, in truth, public relations pieces being put out by particular companies or brands. For example, our floor cleaning survey is likely to have originated from a cleaning products company; that the majority of workers favour emailing colleagues over face-to-face meetings is likely to come from a business communications company, and so on. Sometimes, this can be relatively harmless fun but in other instances it can be very serious if the subject matter relates to food, family health and the like. The surfeit of visual, audio and print media means that there is always an outlet for these kinds of PR exercises. The consumer should take care to know who sponsored any study that receives media coverage.

After reading this chapter, you should also be critical of how studies are being conducted. What was the sampling frame and the sample size? What questions were asked, and were they unbiased or leading questions? For all the survey findings that are presented regularly, this type of background detail rarely is. In its absence, it is impossible to conclude that the research was conducted scientifically. Unfortunately, time-pressed consumers rarely seek out this information and tend to take survey results at face value.

Market research suffers from other problems, too. In some instances it is used to gather competitor intelligence. Questionable practices include using student projects to gather information without the student revealing the identity of the sponsor of the research, pretending to be a potential supplier who is conducting a telephone survey to understand the market, posing as a potential customer at an exhibition, bribing a competitor's employee to pass on proprietary information, and covert surveillance such as through the use of hidden cameras. The practice of selling in the guise of marketing research, commonly known as 'sugging', also occurs from time to time. Despite the fact that it is not usually practised by bona fide marketing research agencies but, rather, unscrupulous selling companies who use marketing research as a means of gaining compliance to their requests, it is the marketing research industry that suffers from its aftermath.

Market research is an important vehicle by which organizations can learn more about their customers, and develop products and services that meet their needs. Properly conducted, it can yield invaluable insights, and can be the difference between success and failure in business. But its reputation is being sullied by the prevalence of 'bogus' surveys and other questionable practices. This raises the issue of whether research deals with the facts or is an exercise in fiction.

Summary

This chapter has examined the nature and role of marketing research and marketing information systems. The following key issues were addressed.

1. The importance of marketing research: marketing research is key if an organization is to be truly market-led. It can provide answers to all sorts of marketing questions that the organization may face.

2. The types of marketing research: marketing research can be either ad hoc (to solve specific problems at a point in time) or continuous (to gather information on an ongoing basis). Ad hoc research is more popular, but a range of continuous research techniques, such as online consumer panels, loyalty cards and website analysis, provides firms with a steady stream of consumer information.

3. The approaches to conducting research: marketing research can be conducted either by the organization itself or by employing the services of a professional marketing research firm. Large-scale, complex research work is best conducted by a professional firm.

4. The stages in the market research process: these include initial contact, the research brief, the research proposal, exploratory research, the main data collection phase, data analysis and report writing/presentation.

5. Qualitative research techniques: these comprise focus groups, depth interviews and observation. The latter, combined with the use of ethnographic techniques, is an increasingly popular way of collecting customer information.

6. The four main survey methods, namely face-to-face, telephone, mail and internet: each has its unique advantages and disadvantages, and the decision as to which to use should be guided by the nature of the study, the respondents and the cost.

7. The nature of marketing information systems: these are systems in which marketing information is formally gathered, stored and distributed on a regular, planned basis.

Key terms

ad hoc research a research project that focuses on a specific problem, collecting data at one point in time with one sample of respondents

consumer panel household consumers who provide information on their purchases over time

continuous research repeated interviewing of the same sample of people

depth interviews the interviewing of consumers individually for perhaps one or two hours with the aim of understanding their attitudes, values, behaviour and/or beliefs

exploratory research the preliminary exploration of a research area prior to the main data collection stage

focus group a group, normally of six to eight consumers, brought together for a discussion focusing on an aspect of a company's marketing

marketing ethnography the study of consumer behaviour in its naturally occurring context, through observation and/or discussion

marketing information system a system in which marketing information is formally gathered, stored, analysed and distributed to

managers in accordance with their informational needs on a regular, planned basis

marketing research the gathering of data and information on the market

omnibus survey a regular survey, usually operated by a market research specialist company, which asks questions of respondents

qualitative research exploratory research that aims to understand consumers' attitudes, values, behaviour and beliefs

research brief written document stating the client's requirements

research proposal a document defining what the marketing research agency promises to do for its client and how much it will cost

retail audit a type of continuous research tracking the sales of products through retail outlets

sampling process a term used in research to denote the selection of a subset of the total population in order to interview them

secondary research data that has already been collected by another researcher for another purpose

Study questions

1. What are the differences between secondary and primary data? Explain the roles played by each.
2. Outline the main stages in the marketing research process, identifying particularly the kinds of difficulties that might be faced at each stage.
3. Market research is being trivialized by the number of surveys that are being reported in the media. Discuss
4. Discuss recent developments in the measurement of website audiences.
5. What is meant by a marketing information system? Discuss, using examples, the main components of such a system.
6. Visit www.surveymonkey.com and learn about how to create and administer a survey.

Suggested reading

Carson, D., A. Gilmore and **K. Gronhaug** (2001) *Qualitative Marketing Research*, London: Sage Publications.

Cooke, M. and **N. Buckley** (2008) Web 2.0, Social Networks and the Future of Market Research, *International Journal of Market Research*, **50** (2), 267–92.

Fahy, J. (1998) Improving Response Rates in Cross-Cultural Mail Surveys, *Industrial Marketing Management*, **27**, 459–67.

Grossnickle, J. and **O. Raskin** (2001) *The Handbook of Online Marketing Research: Knowing Your Customers Using the Net*, New York: McGraw-Hill.

Lorange, P. (2004) Memo to Marketing, *Sloan Management Review*, **46** (2), 16–20.

Ulwick, A. and **L. Bettencourt** (2008) Giving Customers a Fair Hearing, *Sloan Management Review*, **49** (3), 62–68.

102 Foundations of Marketing

References

1. **Grossman, L.** (2003) The Quest for Cool, *Time Canada*, **162** (10), 44; **Langer, J.** (2001) Forecasting Traps can Trip up Trend Spotters, *Advertising Age*, **72** (14), 18; **Terazono, E.** (2003) Squaring the Mainstream Circle, *Financial Times: Creative Business*, 24 June, 2–3; **Wood, D.** (2004) Up on What's Going Down, *Financial Times*, Creative Business, 4 May, 6.

2. **Fielding, M.** (2007) Explore New Territory, *Marketing News*, 1 March, 25–8.

3. **Foss, B.** and **M. Stone** (2001) *Successful Customer Relationship Marketing*, London: Kogan Page.

4. **Anonymous** (2007) Many Ways to Skin a Cat, *Economist*, 1 December, 72–3.

5. **Guenther, K.** (2003) Nothing Measured, Nothing Gained, *Online*, **27** (6), 53–5.

6. **Phippen, A., L. Sheppard** and **S. Furnell** (2004) A Practical Evaluation of Web Analytics, *Internet Research*, **14** (4), 284–93.

7. **Crouch, S.** and **M. Housden** (1999) *Marketing Research for Managers*, Oxford: Butterworth Heinemann, 253.

8. **Birchall, J.** (2005) What Wal-Mart Women Really Really Want, *Financial Times*, 10 October, 11.

9. **Grant, J.** (2005) The Search for Dark Secrets, *Financial Times*, 29 November, 14.

10. **Gray, R.** (1999) Tracking the Online Audience, *Marketing*, 18 February, 41–3.

11. **Birchall, J.** (2005) Rich, But Not Fortune's Fools, *Financial Times*, 13 December, 13.

12. **Goulding, C.** (1999) Consumer Research: Interpretive Paradigms and Methodological Ambiguities, *European Journal of Marketing*, **33** (9/10), 859–73.

13. **Harper, J.** (2003) Camera Phones Cross Moral, Legal Lines, *Washington Times*, Business, 15 July, 6.

14. **Berner, R.** (2006) The Ethnography of Marketing, *Businessweek.com*, 12 June.

15. **Durante, R.** and **M. Feehan** (2006) Watch and Learn, *Marketing News*, 1 February, 59–61.

16. **Thomas, K.** (2005) Anthropologists Get to the Bottom of Customers' Needs, *Financial Times*, 24 August, 9.

17. **Yu, J.** and **H. Cooper** (1983) A Quantitative Review of Research Design Effects on Response Rates to Questionnaires, *Journal of Marketing Research*, 20 February, 156–64.

18. **Falthzik, A.** and **S. Carroll** (1971) Rate of Return for Close v Open-ended Questions in a Mail Survey of Industrial Organisations, *Psychological Reports*, **29**, 1121–2.

19. **O'Dell, W.F.** (1962) Personal Interviews or Mail Panels?, *Journal of Marketing*, **26**, 34–9.

20. **Dillman, D.** (1978) *Mail and Telephone Surveys: The Total Design Method*, New York: John Wiley & Sons.

21. See **Fahy, J.** (1998) Improving Response Rates in Cross-cultural Mail Surveys, *Industrial Marketing Management*, 27 (November), 459–67; **Walker, B., W. Kirchmann** and **J. Conant** (1987) A Method to Improve Response Rates in Industrial Mail Surveys, *Industrial Marketing Management*, 16 (November), 305–14.

22. **Esomar** (2007) *Global Market Research, 2007*, www.esomar.org.

23. **Reynolds, N.** and **A. Diamantopoulos** (1998) The Effect of Pretest Method on Error Detection Rates: Experimental Evidence, *European Journal of Marketing*, **32** (5/6), 480–98.

24. **Crouch, S.** (1992) *Marketing Research for Managers*, Oxford: Butterworth Heinemann, 253.

25. **Jobber, D.** and **C. Rainbow** (1977) A Study of the Development and Implementation of Marketing Information Systems in British Industry, *Journal of the Marketing Research Society*, **19** (3), 104–11.

26. **Van Bruggen, A., A. Smidts** and **B. Wierenga** (1996) The Impact of the Quality of a Marketing Decision Support System: An Experimental Study, *International Journal of Research in Marketing*, **13**, 331–43.

27. **Moutinho, L.** and **M. Evans** (1992) *Applied Marketing Research*, Colorado Springs, CO and Wokingham: Addison-Wesley, 5.

28. **Jobber, D.** and **M. Watts** (1986) Behavioural Aspects of Marketing Information Systems, *Omega*, **14** (1), 69–79; **Wierenga, B.** and **P.A.M. Oude Ophis** (1997) Marketing Decision Support Systems: Adoption, Use and Satisfaction, *International Journal of Research in Marketing*, **14**, 275–90.

29. **Ackoff, R.L.** (1967) Management Misinformation Systems, *Management Science*, **14** (4), 147–56.

30. **Piercy, N.** and **M. Evans** (1983) *Managing Marketing Information*, Beckenham: Croom Helm.

31. **Kohli, A.** and **B. Jaworski** (1990) Market Orientation: The Construct, Research Propositions and Marketing Implications, *Journal of Marketing*, **54**, 1–18.

32. **London, S.** (2004) Choked by a Data Surfeit, *Financial Times*, 29 January, 17.

When you have read this chapter, log on to the Online Learning Centre for *Foundations of Marketing* at **www.mcgraw-hill.co.uk/textbooks/jobber**, where you'll find multiple-choice test questions, links and extra online study tools for marketing.

Appendix 4.1

Sources of European marketing information

Is there a survey of the industry?

Euromonitor GMID Database has in-depth analysis and current market information in the key areas of country data, consumer lifestyles, market sizes, forecasts, brand and country information, business information sources and marketing profiles.

Reuters Business Insight Reports are full-text reports available online in the sectors of healthcare, financial services, consumer goods, energy, e-commerce and technology.

KeyNote Reports cover size of market, economic trends, prospects and company performance.

Mintel Premier Reports cover market trends, prospects and company performance.

Snapshots on CD-Rom The 'Snapshots' CD series is a complete library of market research reports, providing coverage of consumer, business-to-business and industrial markets. Containing 2000 market research reports, this series provides incisive data and analysis on over 8000 market segments for the UK, Europe and the United States.

British Library Market Research is a guide to British Library Holdings. It lists titles of reports arranged by industry. Some items are available on inter-library loan; others may be seen at the British Library in London.

International Directory of Published Market Research, published by Marketsearch.

How large is the market?

European Marketing Data and Statistics Now available on the Euromonitor GMID database.
International Marketing Data and Statistics Now available on the Euromonitor GMID database.
CEO Bulletin
A–Z of UK Marketing Data
European Marketing Pocket Book
The Asia Pacific Marketing Pocket Book
The Americas Marketing Pocket Book

Where is the market?

Regional Marketing Pocket Book
Regional Trends gives the main economic and social statistics for UK regions.
Geodemographic Pocket Book

Who are the competitors?

British companies can be identified using any of the following.
Kompass (most European countries have their own edition)
Key British Enterprises
Quarterly Review—KPMG
Sell's Products and Services Directory (Gen Ref E 380.02542 SEL)

For more detailed company information consult the following.
Companies Annual Report Collection Carol: Company Annual Reports online at www.carol.co.uk
Fame DVD (CD-Rom service)
Business Ratio Reports
Retail Rankings

Overseas companies sources include:
Asia's 7,500 Largest Companies
D&B Europa
Dun's Asia Pacific Key Business Enterprises
Europe's 15,000 Largest Companies
Major Companies of the Arab World
Million Dollar Directory (US)
Principal International Businesses

What are the trends?

Possible sources to consider include the following.
The Book of European Forecasts Now available on the Euromonitor GMID database.
Marketing in Europe
European Trends
Consumer Europe Now available on the Euromonitor GMID database.
Consumer Goods Europe
Family Expenditure Survey
Social Trends
Lifestyle Pocket Book
Drink Trends
Media Pocket Book
Retail Business

Mintel Market Intelligence
OECD (Organisation for Economic Co-operation and Development)

EU statistical and information sources
'Eurostat' is a series of publications that provide a detailed picture of the EU; they can be obtained by visiting European Documentation Centres (often in university libraries) in all EU countries; themes include general statistics, economy and finance, and population/social conditions
Eurostat Yearbook
European Access is a bulletin on issues, policies, activities and events concerning EU member states.
Marketing and Research Today is a journal that examines social, political, economic and business issues relating to Western, Central and Eastern Europe.
European Report is a twice-weekly news publication from Brussels on industrial, economic and political issues.

Abstracts and indexes
Business Periodicals Index
ANBAR Marketing and Distribution Abstracts
ABI Inform
Research Index
Times Index
Elsevier Science Direct
Emerald
Wiley Interscience and Boldideas

Guides to sources
A great variety of published information sources exists; the following source guides may help you in your search.
Marketing Information
Guide to European Marketing Information
Compendium of Marketing Information Sources
Croner's A–Z of Business Information Sources
McCarthy Cards: a card service on which are reproduced extracts from the press covering companies and industries; it also produces a useful guide to its sources: *UK and Europe Market Information: Basic Sources*

Statistics
Guide to Official Statistics
Sources of the Unofficial UK Statistics

Sources: the authors thank the University of Bradford School of Management Library for help in compiling this list

Case 4 Inchydoney Island Lodge and Spa

Exponential growth in spas has occurred in Ireland over the last five years, with much of this growth being represented in the hotel or resort spa sector. The growth is not only in response to changing consumer expectations but is also playing a key role in educating consumers with regard to spa experiences. Within a short period of time, the health and wellness industry has grown from offering a few select, dedicated health farms and spas to offering a significant choice to the consumer, including:

- destination spa or purpose-built facility, whose sole purpose is to offer a comprehensive, full-service wellness spa experience for overnight or day guests
- dedicated full-service spa in a hotel or resort, which offers a dedicated and comprehensive full-service wellness spa experience separate to the hotel business
- other hotel spas with small but well-appointed spas offering spa services and pampering packages
- specialized retreats and health farms, which differ from a spa and offer specialized services including holistic treatments and experiences.

Trends in the market

People visit spas for a variety of reasons, including pampering, relaxation, fitness, health and spirituality. What appears to unite all customer groups is the desire to feel better, but it is how they seek to feel better that varies. Some of the motivations of those who visit spas include the following.

- A desire to feel better via pampering and indulgence: outer beauty is a key draw for the majority of spa-goers, who assume that cosmetic treatments (e.g. facials, manicures) will be available at all spa facilities.
- A means of escape: consumers generally feel better when removed from the normal day-to-day environment and circumstances. Many people visit spa facilities to relieve or reduce stress, or simply to indulge their senses.
- A desire to gain a holistic approach to well-being: for those who are looking for serenity, understanding and self-acceptance.
- A desire for improved wellness, to feel better by changing one's spirit or body: for those who want to discover how lifestyle choices can lead to optimal health.
- Rehabilitation: for those who need to recover after an illness.

- Expert advice: on skincare and diet, products and techniques to use at home to recreate the spa experience.
- A way to achieve fitness: for people who want to get in shape by attending fitness classes, or adopting a healthier lifestyle.

Over the past few years, an upmarket spa has become a prerequisite for many Irish hotels as they attempt to attract customers in an increasingly competitive market. One hotel that has excelled in the area of providing a top-quality spa experience is Inchydoney Island Lodge and Spa.

The Inchydoney Island Lodge and Spa

The Inchydoney Island Lodge and Spa is an award-winning hotel located near Clonakilty in County Cork. In a setting overlooking two beaches, it has become renowned as Ireland's most exclusive and tranquil retreat. The Lodge and Spa combines its great location, luxurious accommodation, unique seawater therapies and top-class dining to create an attractive offering to customers. It was voted Best Four Star Hotel at the Hotel and Catering Review Gold Medal Awards 2006, and was voted Ireland's Leading Spa Resort at the World Travel Awards in 2004 and 2007.

Spa retreat

The spa at the Inchydoney Island Lodge and Spa hotel specializes in thalassotherapy. Thalassotherapy comes from the Greek word for 'sea', and refers to a variety of treatments that use seawater and seaweed, each designed to tone, moisturize and revitalize the body and skin, and in many cases improve circulation. Other marine and ocean derivatives feature in thalassotherapy too, including algae, mud and sand. All are cleaned and purified before use. Different forms of thalassotherapy have different effects, helping users to:

- relax
- tone muscles
- cleanse skin
- reduce the appearance of cellulite
- boost the immune system
- improve sleep quality.

Thalassotherapy is also thought to help people with circulatory problems (such as hypertension and arteriosclerosis), respiratory conditions (such as asthma and bronchitis), post-traumatic disorders (such as muscle atrophy) and chronic inflammations (such as rheumatic arthritis). Interestingly, there is no scientific evidence for the efficacy of thalassotherapy, although many people give anecdotal evidence about how it has helped them.

The Inchydoney Island Lodge and Spa has a fully equipped thalasso pool that is split into two parts—one for swimming and the other for water massage. It offers a wide array of thalassotherapy treatments, such as mud baths, underwater showers, hydro-massage, aromatherapy, and seaweed, mud and algae wraps, as well as massage and beauty therapies. Guests at the hotel can enjoy unlimited use of the heated seawater therapy pool, with its bubble seats, micro jets and massage jets, as well as the sauna, steam room, gym and relaxation room. In the competitive spa market, one of Inchydoney's key competitive advantages is that it is home to Ireland's only accredited thalassotherapy spa. There are a number of thalassotherapy spas in Britain and many more across luxurious hotels in European countries, such as the Mare Nostrum in Greece, the Trianon Palace and Spa, Westin Hotel in France, and the Sheraton Fuerteventura Beach, Golf and Spa Resort in Spain.

Despite this advantage, competition is intense. Spa treatments in Ireland are now more varied than ever. Some take inspiration from their beautiful natural surroundings using home-grown products including seaweed, peat, seawater and local plant extracts. Others have imported spa services from around the world. It is not unusual to find Ayurveda, reiki, lomi lomi massage and balneotheraphy all at one spa. Some of Inchydoney's most significant competitors in Ireland include the following.

- The Aghadoe Heights Hotel and Spa: a luxurious five-star hotel located overlooking the Lakes of Killarney. This spa applies customized treatments using particular specialist brands, such as Aveda, Biodraga, Neom and Futuresse.
- ESPA at the Ritz-Carlton, Powerscourt, County Wicklow: the luxurious treatments here are inspired by Eastern philosophies and use the award-winning ESPA product range. ESPA has also created a selection of signature experiences unique to the Ritz-Carlton, Powerscourt, including the 'Garden of Inspiration Body Ritual' and the 'Garden of Inspiration Botanical Facial Ritual'. It is the first ESPA-branded spa to launch at a Ritz-Carlton in Europe.
- Sheraton Fota Island Golf Resort and Spa, located on Fota Island in County Cork: the spa

offers an extensive range of signature treatments, hydrotherapy, thermal suites, as well as holistic relaxation and pampering.

- Park Hotel Kenmare, County Kerry: here the Sámas Experience comprises three elements—thermal suite, holistic treatment of your choice and 'Pure Relaxation'.
- Molton Brown Spa Killarney Plaza: located in the heart of Killarney Town at the gateway to the Ring of Kerry. The treatments offered here reflect the impulse of the seasons—whether one is in need of renewal (spring), radiance (summer), replenishment (autumn) or regeneration (winter).
- Muckross Park Hotel and Cloisters Spa: situated in Killarney's National Park with 25,000 acres of forest, mountains and lakes. Cloisters Spa offers itself as a sanctuary for mind and body, with 12 treatment rooms, a vitality pool and thermal suite including a herbal sauna.

In light of these changes in the spa market, two issues emerge as critical to the future development of marketing strategies for Inchydoney.

1. How important is thalassotherapy to Irish consumers when choosing a destination spa?
2. What differentiates Inchydoney from other leading thalassotherapy spas across Europe?

Inchydoney Island Lodge and Spa recognizes that marketing research needs to be conducted to generate the answers to the above questions. It is envisaged that the information gathered will enable the marketing team to develop marketing strategies that will be effective in attracting and meeting consumers' needs, both nationally and internationally.

Questions

1. Develop specific research objectives for Inchydoney Island Lodge and Spa.
2. Identify potential sources of secondary data that could be used to research the Irish and international markets.
3. Develop a research plan to meet the research objectives that you have set. In particular, provide details of and justify the data collection methods you would use and any sampling procedures that you would employ.

This case was prepared by Rose Leahy and Nollaig O'Sullivan, Cork Institute of Technology, from published sources as a basis for class discussion rather than to illustrate either effective or ineffective management.

Planning and Strategy

Chapter TWENTY ONE

The Manager as a Planner and Strategist

LEARNING OBJECTIVES

After studying this chapter, you should be able to:

☑ Describe the three steps of the planning process and the relationship between planning and strategy.

☑ Explain the role of planning in predicting the future and in mobilising organisational resources to meet future contingencies.

☑ Outline the main steps in SWOT analysis.

☑ Differentiate among corporate-, business- and functional-level strategies.

☑ Describe the vital role played by strategy implementation in determining managers' ability to achieve an organisation's mission and goals.

A Manager's Challenge

How to Compete in the Soft-Drink Business

What is the best way to compete in an industry?

Coca-Cola and Pepsi-Cola are household names worldwide. Together they control over 70 per cent of the global soft-drink market. Their success can be attributed in part to the overall strategy that Coca-Cola and PepsiCo developed to produce and promote their products. Both companies decided to build global brands by manufacturing the soft-drink concentrate that gives cola its flavour and then selling the concentrate in a syrup form to bottlers throughout the world. Coca-Cola and PepsiCo charge the bottlers a premium price for the syrup; they then invest part of the proceeds in advertising to build and maintain brand awareness. The bottlers are responsible for producing and distributing the product. They add carbonated water to the syrup, package the resulting drink and distribute it to vending machines, supermarkets, restaurants and other retail outlets.

The bottlers leave all the advertising to Coca-Cola and PepsiCo. In addition, the bottlers must sign an exclusive agreement that prohibits them from distributing competing cola brands. A Coke or Pepsi bottler cannot bottle any other cola drink. This strategy has two major advantages for Coca-Cola and PepsiCo. First, it forces bottlers to enter into exclusive agreements, which create a high barrier to entry into the industry; any potential competitors that might want to produce and distribute a new cola product must create their own distribution network rather than use the existing network. Second, the large amount of money spent on advertising (in 2003, both companies spent over £287 million each) to develop a global brand name has helped Coca-Cola and PepsiCo differentiate their products so that consumers are more likely to buy a Coke or a Pepsi rather than a lesser-known cola. This is further enhanced by using celebrity endorsements that are relevant for each country (for example the use of David Beckham, who, during the 2002 World Cup, was advertising both soft drinks[1]), or Pepsi's football table advert, using a number of famous international players that widens the country-specific appeal. Brand loyalty allows both companies to charge a premium or comparatively high price for what is, after all, merely coloured water and flavouring. This differentiation strategy has made Coca-Cola and PepsiCo two of the most profitable companies in the world.

In the last decade the global soft-drink environment has undergone major changes due to the entrepreneurial skills of the then CEO of Cott Corporation, Gerald Pencer. Cott is one of the world's largest suppliers of retailer-branded carbonated soft drinks and supplies some of the biggest food retailers and wholesalers in the UK, as well as a large number of leading retailers throughout Europe. It has 19 manufacturing facilities in Canada, the US, Mexico and the UK and a syrup concentrate production plant in Columbus, Georgia, that supplies most of the private-label grocery stores, chemist outlets, mass-merchandising and convenience store chains in these countries. In successfully capturing the retailer brands, Cott has created a leadership position in the international soft drinks market by providing high-quality retailer brand drinks to the benefit of discerning customers.[2]

The UK/European division of Cott now employs over 700 employees and operates three beverage production facilities in the UK. In 2005 Cott UK/Europe led the company's sales growth with an increase of 30 per cent with sales of £228 million. This was partly due to a diversification strategy of including the production of Hi-energy drinks and a premium organic fruit carbonate. Such changes led to the acquisition of Macaw Soft Drinks Company in 2005 and Cott grossed £163 million at the year end. The UK CEO, John Sheppard, announced that '2006 will be an important transition year, as we are pursuing a number of specific initiatives including a disciplined and strategic approach to pricing, sourcing and supply chain efficiencies etc.'.

In the early 1990s Pencer came up with a new plan for competing in the cola market and created a new strategy to attract customers. Pencer's strategy was to produce a high-quality, low-priced cola, manufactured and bottled by the Cott Corporation, and sell directly to major retail establishments (such as supermarket chains) as a private-label 'house brand', thus bypassing the bottlers. Retailers were attracted to Cott's cola and other soft-drink flavours because its low cost allowed them to make more profit than they received from selling Coke or Pepsi while building their store brand image.

To implement his strategy, Pencer decided to spend no money on advertising (so that he could charge a lower price for the soft drinks) but instead took advantage of efficient national distribution systems that giant retailers such as ASDA have created in recent years. This low-cost strategy enabled Cott to circumvent the barrier to entry created by the exclusive distribution agreements that Coca-Cola and PepsiCo had signed with their bottlers. Pencer went on to supply an international market by offering to sell soft-drinks concentrate at prices lower than Coca-Cola and PepsiCo charged. In April 1994, for example, Cott launched a cola product in Britain for Sainsbury's, one of Britain's largest supermarkets. The product was sold as 'Sainsbury's Classic Cola' and was priced 30 per cent below Coke and Pepsi.[3]

Overview

As the beginning of the chapter suggests, there is more than one way to compete in an industry, and to find a viable way to enter and compete in an industry, managers must study the way other organisations behave and identify their strategies. By studying the strategies of Coca-Cola and PepsiCo, Cott were able to devise a strategy that allowed them to enter the cola industry and take on these global giants; so far, Cott has had considerable success.

In an uncertain competitive environment, managers must engage in thorough planning to find a strategy that will allow them to compete effectively. This chapter explores the manager's role both as *planner* and as *strategist*. The different elements involved in the planning process will be discussed, including its three major steps: (1) determining an organisation's mission and major goals, (2) choosing strategies to realise the mission and goals and (3) selecting the appropriate way of organising resources to implement the strategies. Further discussion points in this chapter concern two important techniques that managers can use in their analysis of situations: scenario planning and SWOT analysis. By the end of this chapter, you will understand the role managers play in the planning and strategy making process to create high-performing organisations.

The Nature of the Planning Process

Planning, as was noted in Chapter 1, is a process that managers use to identify and select appropriate goals and courses of action for an organisation.[4] The *organisational plan* that results from the planning process details the goals of the organisation and specifies how managers intend to attain them. The cluster of decisions and actions that managers take to help an organisation attain its goals is its **strategy**. Planning is thus both a goal making and a strategy making process.

In most organisations, planning is a three-step activity (Fig. 8.1). The first step is determining the organisation's *mission* and *goals*. A **mission statement** is a broad declaration of an organisation's overarching purpose, intended to identify an organisation's products and customer base, as well as distinguish the organisation in some way from its competitors. The second step is *formulating strategy*. Managers analyse the organisation's current situation and then conceive and develop the strategies necessary to attain the organisation's mission and goals. The third step is *implementing strategy*: managers decide how to allocate the resources and responsibilities that are required to implement the strategies for people and groups within the organisation.[5] In subsequent sections of this chapter, each of these steps will be examined in detail. The general nature and purpose of planning, which is one of the four managerial functions identified by Henri Fayol (p. 5), will also be revisited.

Levels of Planning

In large organisations, planning usually takes place at three levels of management: corporate, business or division and department or functional. Figure 8.2 shows the link between the three

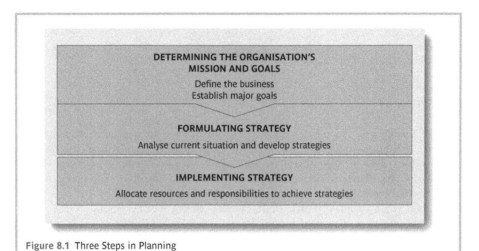

Figure 8.1 Three Steps in Planning

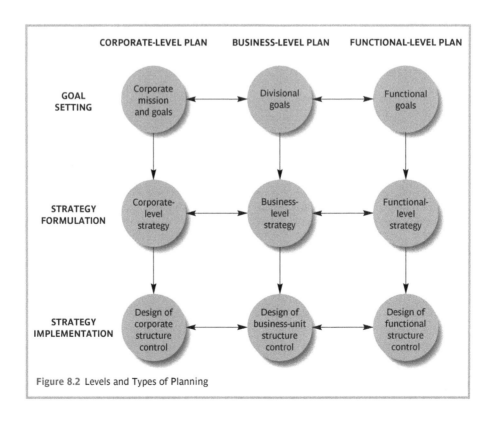

Figure 8.2 Levels and Types of Planning

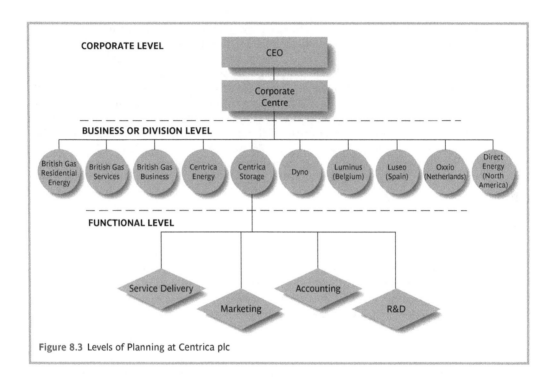

CORPORATE LEVEL

CEO

Corporate Centre

BUSINESS OR DIVISION LEVEL

British Gas Residential Energy | British Gas Services | British Gas Business | Centrica Energy | Centrica Storage | Dyno | Luminus (Belgium) | Luseo (Spain) | Oxxio (Netherlands) | Direct Energy (North America)

FUNCTIONAL LEVEL

Service Delivery | Marketing | Accounting | R&D

Figure 8.3 Levels of Planning at Centrica plc

steps in the planning process and these three levels. To understand this model, consider how Centrica, a large UK-based organisation that competes in many different businesses, operates.[6]

Centrica provides many different products and services, from gas and electrical to insurance and telephone services across Europe. Centrica has three main levels of management: corporate level, business level and functional level (Fig. 8.3). At the Board or corporate level are the Chairman Roger Carr and CEO, Sir Roy Gardener, three other senior directors and non-executive directors. Below the Board level is the business or **division** level: *a division* is a business unit that competes in a distinct industry.

Each division has its own set of **divisional managers** and its own set of **functions** or **departments** – manufacturing, marketing, human resource management (HRM), R&D and so on. British Gas which is part of BG Group plc, for example, has its own marketing function, as do Transco (part of Centrica plc) and Dyno (part of British Gas).

At Centrica, as at other large organisations, planning takes place at each level. The **corporate-level plan** contains senior management's decisions pertaining to the organisation's mission and goals, overall (corporate-level) strategy and structure (Fig. 8.2). **Corporate-level strategy** indicates in which industries and national markets an organisation intends to compete. One of the goals stated in Centrica's corporate-level plan is to be the leading supplier of energy and related services throughout the UK and Europe. With this overall goal in mind and the 2003 EU Energy Directives enabling open competition for the energy market across Europe by 2007, Centrica has already started to extend its energy supply business.[7] It now has a joint energy supply business in Belgium with the creation of Luminus Energy. It has entered Spain where it has created a Spanish subsidiary company (Centrica Energia SL) who supply electricity to SMEs across Spain. With the acquisition of Oxxio (a low-cost energy supplier in the Netherlands) another step in the development of Centrica's European long-term strategy has taken place. A large conglomerate such as Centrica has to respond and plan at a corporate level for divisional goals as well as changes across the industry. If a division cannot attain its goals then a company may be sold or demerged. Once gas supply became competitive in May 1998, British Gas plc demerged and formed two separate companies: Centrica plc is responsible for gas trading and supply, and BG plc focuses on gas transportation, storage, exploration/production and R&D.

The corporate-level plan provides the framework within which divisional managers create their **business-level plans**. At the business level, the managers of each division create a *business-level plan* that details (1) the long-term goals that will allow the division to meet corporate goals and (2) the division's **business-level strategy** and structure. The *business-level strategy* states the methods that a division or business intends to use to compete against its rivals in an industry. For example, Bruce Walker, the Managing Director of Centrica Storage, was committed to meeting the highest achievable health, safety and environmental standards in operations, both offshore and onshore. This was aligned with the company's priority of improving the reliability of facilities and in excess of £20 million was spent over 2004–05 in capital and revenue projects. Centrica Storage has benefited from this high-level investment as they are ahead of their competitors in that all firm-storage capacity for 2006 has been sold and customers are now focusing on requirements for 2007–08.

A *function* is a unit or department in which people have the same skills or use the same resources to perform their jobs: examples include manufacturing, accounting and sales. The business-level plan provides the framework within which **functional managers** devise their plans. A **functional-level plan** states the goals that functional managers propose to pursue to help the division attain its business-level goals – which, in turn, allow the organisation to achieve its corporate goals. The **functional-level strategy** sets out the actions that managers intend to take at the level of departments such as manufacturing, marketing and R&D to allow the organisation to attain its goals.

An important issue in planning is ensuring *consistency* in planning across the three different levels. Functional goals and strategies should be consistent with divisional goals and strategies, which in turn should be consistent with corporate goals and strategies. Once complete, each function's plan is normally linked to its division's business-level plan which, in turn, is linked to the corporate plan. Although few organisations are as large and complex as Centrica, most plan as Centrica does and have written plans to guide managerial decision making.

Who Plans?

In general, corporate-level planning is the primary responsibility of senior managers.[8] At Centrica, the corporate-level goals of being a leader in energy supply and related services were the vision of CEO Sam Laidlaw. The CEO and his corporate-level management team decide in which industries Centrica should compete. Corporate-level managers are responsible for approving business- and functional-level plans to ensure that they are consistent with the corporate plan.

Corporate planning decisions are not made in a vacuum: other managers have input. At Centrica, and many other companies, divisional and functional managers are encouraged to submit proposals for new business ventures to the CEO and senior managers, who evaluate the

Contemporary Management, European Edition

THE NATURE OF THE PLANNING PROCESS

proposals and decide whether or not to fund them. Thus, even though corporate-level planning is the responsibility of senior managers, lower-level managers can be, and usually are, given the opportunity to become involved in the process.

This approach is common not only at the corporate level but also at the business and functional levels. At the business level, planning is the responsibility of divisional managers, who also review functional plans. Functional managers also typically participate in business-level planning. Similarly, although the functional managers bear primary responsibility for functional-level planning, they can and do involve their subordinates in this process. Thus, although ultimate responsibility for planning may lie with certain select managers within an organisation, all managers and many non-managerial employees typically participate in the planning process.

Time Horizons of Plans

Plans differ in their **time horizons**, or intended durations. Managers usually distinguish among *long-term plans*, with a horizon of five years or more; *intermediate-term plans*, with a horizon between one and five years; and *short-term plans*, with a horizon of one year or less. Typically, corporate- and business-level goals and strategies require long- and intermediate-term plans, and functional-level goals and strategies require intermediate- and short-term plans.

Although most organisations operate with planning horizons of five years or more, it would be inaccurate to infer from this that they undertake major planning exercises only once every five years and then 'lock in' a specific set of goals and strategies for that time period. Most organisations have an *annual planning cycle*, which is usually linked to the annual financial budget (although a major planning effort may be undertaken only every few years).

Although a corporate- or business-level plan may extend over five years or more, it is typically treated as a *rolling plan*, a plan that is updated and amended every year to take account of changing conditions in the external environment. Thus, the time horizon for an organisation's 2006 corporate-level plan might be 2011; for the 2007 plan 2012; and so on. The use of rolling plans is essential because of the high rate of change in the environment and the difficulty of predicting competitive conditions five years in the future. Rolling plans allow managers to make *mid-course corrections* if environmental changes warrant, or to change the thrust of the plan altogether if it no longer seems appropriate. The use of rolling plans allows managers to plan flexibly, without losing sight of the need to plan for the long term.

Why Planning Is Important

Essentially, planning is ascertaining where an organisation *is* at the present time and deciding where it *should be* in the future, and how to move it forward. When managers plan, they must consider the future and forecast what may happen in order to take actions in the present and mobilise organisational resources to deal with future opportunities and threats. As discussed in Chapter 6, however, the external environment is uncertain and complex, and managers must typically deal with *incomplete information* and *bounded rationality*. This is one reason why planning is so complex and difficult.

Almost all managers engage in planning, and all should participate because they must try to predict future opportunities and threats. The absence of a plan often results in hesitations, false steps and mistaken changes of direction that can hurt an organisation or even lead to disaster. Planning is important for four main reasons:

1. Planning is a useful way of getting managers to participate in decision making about the *appropriate goals and strategies* for an organisation. Effective planning gives all managers the opportunity to participate in decision making. At Intel, for example, senior managers, as part of their annual planning process, regularly request input from lower-level managers to determine what the organisation's goals and strategies should be.

2. Planning is necessary to give the organisation a *sense of direction and purpose*.[9] A plan states what goals an organisation is trying to achieve, and what strategies it intends to use to achieve them. Without the sense of direction and purpose that a formal plan provides, managers may interpret their own tasks and roles in ways that best suit themselves. The result will be an organisation that is pursuing multiple and often conflicting goals and a set of managers who do not co-operate and work well together. By stating which organisational goals and strategies are important, a plan keeps managers on track so that they can use the resources under their control effectively.

3. A plan helps co-ordinate managers of the different functions and divisions of an organisation to ensure that they *all pull in the same direction*. Without a good plan, it is possible that the members of the manufacturing function will produce more products than the members of the sales function can sell, resulting in a mass of unsold inventory. Implausible as this might seem, it happened to the high-flying Internet router supplier Cisco Systems in the early 2000s. The company suddenly found it had over £1.2 billion of unsold routers because of the combination of an economic recession and customers' demands for new kinds of optical routers that Cisco did not have in stock.

4. A plan can be used as a device for *controlling managers* within an organisation. A good plan specifies not only to which goals and strategies the organisation is committed, but also who is responsible for putting the strategies into action to attain the goals. When managers know that they will be held accountable for attaining a goal, they are motivated to do their best to make sure the goal is achieved.

Henri Fayol, the originator of the model of management (Chapter 1), said that effective plans should have four qualities: unity, continuity, accuracy and flexibility.[10] *Unity* means that at any one time only one central guiding plan is put into operation to achieve an organisational goal; more than one plan to achieve a goal would cause confusion and disorder. *Continuity* means that planning is an ongoing process in which managers build and refine previous plans and continually modify plans at all levels – corporate, business and functional – so that they fit together into one broad framework. *Accuracy* means that managers need to make every attempt to collect and utilise all the available information at their disposal in the planning process. Of course, managers must recognise the fact that uncertainty exists and that information is almost always incomplete (for the reasons discussed in Chapter 7). Despite the need for continuity and accuracy, however, Fayol emphasised that the planning process should be *flexible* enough so that plans can be altered and changed if the situation changes: managers must not be bound to a static plan.

Scenario Planning

One way in which managers can try to create plans that have the four qualities that Fayol described is by utilising **scenario planning**, one of the most widely used planning techniques. Scenario planning (also known as *contingency planning*) is the generation of multiple forecasts of future conditions followed by an analysis of how to respond effectively to each of them.

As noted previously, planning is about trying to forecast and predict the future in order to be able to anticipate future opportunities and threats. The future, however, is inherently *unpredictable*. How can managers best deal with this unpredictability?

Scenario planning was first developed by Pierre Wack and Edward Newland for strategic purposes at Royal Dutch/Shell in 1971.[11] Research revealed that Shell's survival depended upon its senior management teams being able to pre-empt changes in the market and act accordingly, and be able to 'learn quicker than their competitors'.[12] However, little research has been done on how scenario planning can affect company performance over time.[13]

At the World Economic Forum in January 2005, the Chief Executive of Royal Dutch Shell, Jeroen van der Veer, stated that global scenario planning was vital for energy companies that are highly complex. World events such as 11 September 2001, the fall of Enron, terrorism, etc. have highlighted the *vulnerability* of our globalised world. This has led Shell to re-think their 'futures planning' in an attempt to promote continuity and flexibility for strategic planning in a complex and changing environment. Since the 1970s, Shell have developed *Global Scenarios* in order to identify emerging challenges and foster adaptability to change. The current Global Scenarios to 2025 (released in 2005) took a more robust view and addressed broader planning and strategic requirements. They have moved from a three-year planning cycle to an annual one, and van Der Veer has adopted a new analytical framework involving three potential Global Scenarios. The first is known as 'Low Trust Globalisation' which emphasises security and efficiency. The second possible futures scenario is 'Open Doors', which emphasises social cohesion and efficiency where the market provides 'built-in' solutions to the crises of trust and security within the industry. The third, called 'Flags', is a scenario where security and community values are emphasised at the expense of efficiency.[14]

Because the future is unpredictable, the only reasonable approach to planning is first to generate 'multiple futures' – or scenarios of the future – based on different assumptions about conditions that *might* prevail in the future and then to develop different plans that detail what a company *should* do in the event that one of these scenarios actually occurs. Scenario planning is a *learning tool* that raises the quality of the planning process and can bring real benefits to an organisation.[15] Shell's success with scenario planning has influenced many other companies to adopt similar systems: by 1990, more than 50 per cent of Fortune 500 companies were using some version of scenario planning, and the number has increased since then.[16] The great strength of scenario planning is its ability not only to anticipate the challenges of an uncertain future but also to educate managers to think about the future – to *think strategically*.[17]

TIPS FOR PRACTICE

1. Even if it is not always appropriate, try to use some of the structured techniques, such as scenario planning, when planning your work. The more you use it, the easier it gets.

2. Don't feel that plans are rigid. They are guides to action, but need to be flexible enough to be adaptable if changes in the environment occur.

3. Always ensure that your plans match and are compatible with those at the other organisational levels. The aim of an organisation is to achieve a common goal, so all plans need to move in the same direction.

4. Be as participative as possible when planning. This ensures commitment and allows for a broad range of perspectives to inform your plans.

Reaction Time

1. Describe the three steps of planning. Explain how they are related.
2. How can scenario planning help managers to predict the future?

Determining the Organisation's Mission and Goals

Determining the organisation's mission and goals is the first step of the planning process. Once the mission and goals are agreed upon and formally stated in the corporate plan, they guide the next steps by defining which strategies are appropriate and which are inappropriate.[18]

Defining the Business

To determine an organisation's mission, managers must first *define its business* so that they can identify what kind of value they will provide to customers. To define the business, managers must ask three questions: (1) Who are our customers? (2) What customer needs are being satisfied? (3) How are we satisfying customer needs?[19] These questions identify the customer needs that the organisation satisfies and the way that the organisation satisfies those needs. Answering these questions helps managers to identify not only the customer needs they are satisfying now but the needs they should try to satisfy in the future and who their true competitors are. All of this information helps managers plan and establish appropriate goals. Case 8.1, on the Lego Group, shows the important role that defining the business has in the planning process.

Case 8.1: Ups and downs at The LEGO Group

LEGO was founded in 1932 in Denmark and in 2000 the LEGO brick was announced the 'toy of the century' by the British Association of Toy Retailers. However most toy manufacturers and suppliers have recently witnessed difficult times, primarily due to rapid changes in consumer behaviour through the escalation of technology. Consumer electronics, MP3 players, video games and interactive soft toys have overtaken 'imaginative playing' and children now tend to grow out of traditional toys at a younger age. Consequently, LEGO has had to change its strategy in order to keep up with competitors, as well as think about how they are going to tackle the future. After suffering financial losses in 2003–04, the company changed its CEO and the corporate management team has developed and implemented new strategies which are now beginning to bear fruit. Initially, LEGO decided to cut their labour costs and closed down factories in Korea along with some closures in Denmark and Switzerland. By outsourcing their labour to Eastern Europe they were able to cut production costs considerably.

Throughout the 1990s the LEGO group launched a constant flow of new products including the LEGO Technic, LEGO Belville (fairytale toys for girls) and LEGO Primo (LEGO designed for 0–2 year olds). During this period they also opened a number of LEGOLAND parks (in the US, Denmark, the UK and a fourth in Germany in 2002). This diversification was boosted by a licensing agreement with Lucas-film Ltd, which allowed LEGO to develop, manufacture and market a series of LEGO based on the Star Wars trilogy. Further expansion included the BIONICLE range, which was a whole building system using LEGO in the development of story themes using construction and action figures. Financial losses made the company 'rethink its strategy', to rationalise its business in terms of defining exactly on what it was going to concentrate. LEGO has now reverted to what it knows best in terms of production and is focused once again on the core business, 'the LEGO brick'. The new corporate team made up of Chairman, Vice Chairman and CEO stated in their 2005 annual report that 'LEGO has for generations given children a very special playing experience and stirs children's imagination'.[20]

LEGO has developed its markets around these values and has concentrated on building good quality, effectively costed bricks. A third strategy has been to develop financial stability. LEGO decided to sell assets, including its majority shareholding in the LEGOLAND parks, thus releasing financial and management resources so that the group could survive. Since 2006 they have downsized the structure of the company in order to increase focus on both the operational and strategic challenges that the company still faces. Jorgen Vig Knudstorp, LEGO Group CEO, commented that 'it is important for us to build on the unique advantages we have. The LEGO brick and system are proving their ability to cater for the modern world – continuing to represent creativity, fun and quality and these are precisely the values that consumers associate with the LEGO brand.'[21]

In the fast-paced toy market where customers' needs change and evolve, and where new groups of customers emerge as new technologies result in new kinds of toys, toy companies like LEGO must learn to define and redefine their businesses to satisfy such needs (see Table 8.1). The results of the company's radical strategic planning has turned the LEGO group around and having suffered a £154 million loss in 2004 they announced pre-tax profits of £64 million in 2005. The CEO maintains that nurturing and building good customer relationships and continuing to adapt the Group to the changing market conditions is the key to enabling them to achieve their medium-term goal of creating sustainable value and increasing profitability.

Table 8.1 Three mission statements

Company	Mission statement
LEGO[22]	Our mission is to nurture the child in each of us, and this means that we actively encourage self-expression through creation, thus enabling children of all ages to bring endless ideas to life. The LEGO® experience is playing, learning, interacting, exploring, expressing, discovering, creating and imagining – all with a heavy dose of fun. We will do this as the world leader in providing quality products and experiences that stimulate creativity, imagination, fun and learning.
ASDA[23]	Our customers have always expected us to deliver a great range of quality goods and services at our famous 'everyday low prices' . . . but not at any cost. That's why we believe we have a responsibility not only to 'do the right thing' for our customers and colleagues, but also for the wider community.
IKEA[24]	The IKEA Concept is based on offering a wide range of well-designed, functional home furnishing products at prices so low that as many people as possible will be able to afford them. Rather than selling expensive home furnishings that only a few can buy, the IKEA Concept makes it possible to serve the many by providing low-priced products that contribute to helping more people live a better life at home.

Establishing Major Goals

Once the business is defined, managers must establish a set of *primary goals* to which the organisation is committed. Developing these goals gives the organisation a sense of direction or purpose. In most organisations, articulating major goals is the job of the CEO, although other managers have an input into the process.

The best statements of organisational goals are ambitious – they stretch the organisation's imagination and require that managers improve its performance capabilities.[25]

In 2005 the CEO of Britain's oldest family-owned jam maker outlined some very challenging goals.[26] Mark Duerr, of F. Duerr & Sons, had to face a shrinking market of 'jam eaters'. Since the 1950s, British jam manufacturing has declined from over 40 companies to three in 2006, one of which is Duerr & Sons, still remaining independent. The reasons for such rapid decline in jam sales have been factors such as increased awareness of obesity in both adults and children, competition with other foods such as snacks, cereal bars, etc. and the general consciousness of people about reducing sugar intake. The challenge for this small company was how to expand when sales were falling. Fortunately Duerr was forward-thinking in his strategy, and saw such changes in the environment coming and changed the emphasis of his business from making jam under his own name to making jams and other products under own-label supermarket names such as Morrisons, Tesco and Sainsbury's, which now makes up 60 per cent of Duerr's business. At the top end of the jam market, branded names are still popular, and profit margins are higher; however, costs in production are high due to the investment in machinery and marketing. The competition, particularly from European companies (e.g. Bonne Maman), also has a stronghold in this market.

Duerr has therefore used a *diversification strategy* and begun making other products such as peanut butter and condiments: peanut butter sales have increased dramatically since the 1980s and now represent 20 per cent of Duerr's sales. Duerr has survived so far, but realises that any diversification will remove him from his core strengths. Another way that Duerr has strategically enhanced its business arm is to embark on a joint venture with a Welsh spring water company to make unfrozen spring-water ice-cubes, to encourage consumers to make their own ice-cubes but with the added benefit of using spring water. Duerr owns 51 per cent of the company and they already have contracts with the four main British supermarkets. Duerr is still an independent family-owned business that is self-funded, but if these latest strategies do not succeed the company may be tempted to sell out or merge.

Although goals should be challenging, they should also be *realistic*. Challenging goals give managers an incentive to look for ways to improve an organisation's operation, but a goal that is unrealistic and impossible to attain may prompt managers to give up.[27] For example, Duerr set the challenging, realistic goal of being able to increase sales by diversifying by maintaining their main product but reducing costs and increasing profit margins by producing own-label products for larger conglomerates. Duerr is a small company, but it is surviving due to forward planning and innovative strategies, while keeping their main product intact. The time period in which a goal is expected to be achieved should be stated. Time constraints are important because they emphasise that a goal must be attained within a reasonable period; they inject a sense of urgency into goal attainment and act as a motivator.

Formulating Strategy

In **strategy formulation**, managers analyse an organisation's current situation and then develop strategies to accomplish its mission and achieve its goals.[28] Strategy formulation begins with managers analysing the factors within an organisation and outside (in the global environment) that affect or may affect the organisation's ability to meet its goals now and in the future. SWOT

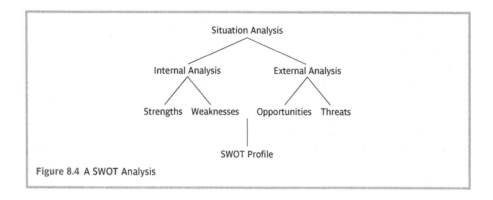

Figure 8.4 A SWOT Analysis

analysis and the five forces model (p. 255) are two useful techniques that managers can use to analyse these factors.

SWOT Analysis

SWOT analysis is a simple framework for generating strategic alternatives from a situation analysis. SWOT stands for Strengths, Weaknesses, Opportunities and Threats. The SWOT framework was formulated in the late 1960s[29] and focuses on issues that have potentially most impact. It is a useful tool when a very limited amount of time is available to address a complex strategic situation.

Figure 8.4 shows how a SWOT analysis fits into a strategic situation analysis.

The internal and external situation analysis can produce a large amount of information, much of which may not be highly relevant. The SWOT analysis can serve as an *interpretative filter* to reduce the information to a manageable quantity of key issues. The SWOT analysis classifies the internal aspects of the company as strengths or weaknesses and the external situational factors as opportunities or threats. *Strengths* can serve as a foundation for building a competitive advantage, and *weaknesses* may hinder it. By understanding these four aspects of its situation, an organisation can better leverage its strengths, correct its weaknesses, capitalize on opportunities and deter potentially devastating threats.

The internal analysis is a comprehensive evaluation of the internal environment's potential strengths and weaknesses. An evaluation of areas across the organisation may include factors such as:

- Company culture
- Company image
- Organisational structure
- Key staff
- Access to natural resources
- Position on the experience curve
- Operational efficiency
- Operational capacity
- Brand awareness

- Market share
- Financial resources
- Exclusive contracts
- Patents and trade secrets.

The SWOT analysis summarises the internal factors of the firm as a list of strengths and weaknesses.

Within an organisation, opportunities that may arise to introduce a new product or service are often the result of a change in the external environment. Such changes can sometimes be seen as threats to the market position of existing products and may necessitate a change in product specifications or the development of new products in order for the company to remain competitive. Changes in the external environment may be related to:

- Customers
- Competitors
- Market trends
- Suppliers
- Partners
- Social changes
- New technology
- Economic environment
- Political and regulatory environment.

Based on a SWOT analysis, managers at the different levels of the organisation select the corporate-, business- and functional-level strategies to best position the organisation to achieve its mission and goals (Fig. 8.5). SWOT analysis is the first step in strategy formulation at any level and is examined first, before turning specifically to corporate-, business- and functional-level strategies.

In Chapter 6 forces in the task and general environments that have the potential to affect an organisation were discussed. It was noted that changes in these forces can produce opportunities that an organisation might take advantage of and consider threats that may harm its current

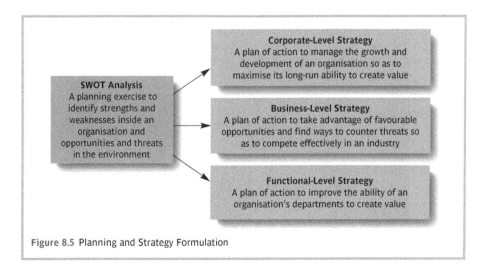

Figure 8.5 Planning and Strategy Formulation

situation. The first step in SWOT analysis is to identify an organisation's strengths and weaknesses. Table 8.2 lists many important strengths (such as high-quality skills in marketing and in R&D) and weaknesses (such as rising manufacturing costs and outdated technology). The task facing managers is to identify the strengths and weaknesses that characterise the *present state* of their organisation.

The second step in SWOT analysis begins when managers embark on a full-scale SWOT planning exercise to identify potential opportunities and threats in the environment that affect the organisation at the present, or may affect it in the future. Examples of possible opportunities and threats that must be anticipated (many of which were discussed in Chapter 5) are listed in Table 8.2.

Table 8.2 Questions for SWOT analysis

Potential strengths			
Well-developed strategy?	Expand core business(es)?	Poorly developed strategy?	Attacks on core business(es)?
Strong product lines?	Exploit new market segments?	Obsolete, narrow product lines?	Increase in domestic competition?
Broad market coverage?			
Manufacturing competence?	Widen product range?	Rising manufacturing costs?	Increase in foreign competition?
Good marketing skills?	Extend cost or differentiation advantage?	Decline in R&D innovations?	Change in consumer tastes?
Good materials management systems?	Diversify into new growth businesses?	Poor marketing plan?	Fall in barriers to entry?
R&D skills and leadership?	Expand into foreign markets?	Poor materials management systems?	Rise in new or substitute products?
HR competencies?	Apply R&D skills in new areas?	Loss of customer goodwill?	Increase in industry rivalry?
Brand-name reputation?		Inadequate human resources?	New forms of industry competition?
Cost of differentiation advantage?	Enter new related businesses?	Loss of brand name?	Potential for takeover?
Appropriate management style?	Vertically integrate forward?	Growth without direction?	Changes in demographic factors?
Appropriate organisational structure?	Vertically integrate backward?	Loss of corporate direction?	Changes in economic factors?
Appropriate control systems?	Overcome barriers to entry?	Infighting among divisions?	Downturn in economy?
Ability to manage strategic change?	Reduce rivalry among competitors?	Loss of corporate control?	Rising labour costs? Slower market growth?
Others?	Apply brand-name capital in new areas? Seek fast market growth?	Inappropriate organisational structure and control systems?	Others?
	Others?	High conflict and politics? Others?	

With the SWOT analysis completed and strengths, weaknesses, opportunities and threats identified, managers can begin the planning process and determine strategies for achieving the organisation's mission and goals. The resulting strategies should enable the organisation to attain its goals by taking advantage of opportunities, countering threats, building strengths and correcting organisational weaknesses. To appreciate how managers can use SWOT analysis, consider how Douglas Conant, CEO of Campbell Soup, has used it to try to find strategies to turn around the troubled food products maker (Case 8.2).

Case 8.2: **Douglas Conant is in the soup**

Campbell Soup Co. is one of the oldest and best-known companies in the world. However, in recent years it has seen demand for its major products such as condensed soup plummet as customers have switched from high-salt, processed soups to healthier low-fat, low-salt varieties. Indeed, its condensed soup business fell by 30 per cent between 1998 and 2004. By the early 2000s Campbell's market share and profits were falling, and its new CEO Douglas Conant decided it was necessary to devise a three-year turnaround plan to help the company maintain its market position.

One of Conant's first actions was to initiate a thorough SWOT planning exercise. An analysis of the environment identified the growth of the organic- and health-food segment of the food market and the increasing number of other kinds of convenience foods as a threat to Campbell's core soup business. The analysis of the environment also revealed three growth opportunities: (1) the growing market for health and sports drinks, in which Campbell was already a competitor with its V8 juice, (2) the growing market for salsas, in which Campbell competed with its Pace salsa and (3) chocolate products, where Campbell's Godiva brand had enjoyed increasing sales throughout the 1990s.

With the analysis of the environment complete, Conant turned his attention to his organisation's resources and capabilities. His internal analysis of Campbell identified a number of major weaknesses. These included staffing levels that were too high relative to its competitors and high costs associated with manufacturing its soups because of the use of outdated machinery. Conant also noted that Campbell had a very conservative culture in which people seemed to be afraid to take risks – something that was a real problem in the fast-changing food industry where customer tastes are always changing and new products must constantly be developed. At the same time, the SWOT analysis identified an enormous strength. Campbell enjoyed huge economies of scale because of the vast quantity of food products that it makes. It also had a first-rate R&D division that had the capability to develop exciting new food products.

Using the information gained from this SWOT analysis, Conant and his managers decided that Campbell needed to use its product development skills to revitalise its core products and modify or reinvent them in ways that would appeal to increasingly health-conscious and busy consumers who did not want to take the time to prepare old-fashioned condensed soup. Moreover, it needed to expand its franchise in the health-, sports-, snack- and luxury-food segments of the market. Another major need that managers saw was to find new ways to deliver Campbell's products to customers. Campbell's needed to tap into new food outlets, such as corporate cafeterias, college dining halls and other mass eateries to expand consumers' access to its foods. Finally, Conant decided that it was necessary to decentralise authority to managers at lower levels in the organisation and give them the responsibility of bringing new kinds of soups, salsas and chocolate products to the market. In this way, he hoped to revitalise Campbell's slow-moving culture and speed the flow of improved and new products to the market.

Conant put his new plan into action – sales of soup started to rise and he began to put more emphasis on sales of soup at outlets such as Subway and less on supermarket sales.[30] By 2004, analysts felt that he had made a significant difference in Campbell's performance but that there was still a lot to do as operating margins were still shrinking. Carrying on the SWOT analysis, Conant decided Campbell should produce more products to meet the challenge of the 'low-carb diet', such as new kinds of low-carb bread and cookies. He also decided to shrink the company's operations to lower costs. His goal is to raise profit margins to the level of his major competitor (Kraft) by 2007, using a new three-year plan based on his SWOT analysis.[31]

The Five Forces Model

A well-known model that helps managers isolate the particular forces in the external environment that are potential threats is Michael Porter's five forces model (the first four of which were discussed in Chapter 5). Porter identified these five factors as major threats because they affect how much profit organisations competing within the same industry can expect to make:

- *The level of rivalry among organisations in an industry*   The more that companies compete against one another for customers – for example, by lowering the prices of their products or by increasing advertising – the lower is the level of industry profits (low prices mean less profit).

- *The potential for entry into an industry*   The easier it is for companies to enter an industry – because, for example, barriers to entry, such as brand loyalty, are low – the more likely it is for industry prices (and therefore industry profits) to be low.

- *The power of suppliers*   If there are only a few suppliers of an important input, then suppliers can drive up the price of that input, and expensive inputs result in lower profits for the producer.

- *The power of customers*   If only a few large customers are available to buy an industry's output, they can bargain to drive down the price of that output. As a result, producers make lower profits.

- *The threat of substitute products*   Often, the output of one industry is a substitute for the output of another industry (plastic may be a substitute for steel in some applications, for example; similarly, bottled water is a substitute for cola). Companies that produce a product with a known substitute cannot demand high prices for their products, and this constraint keeps their profits low.

Porter argued that when managers analyse opportunities and threats they should pay particular attention to these five forces because they are the major threats that an organisation will encounter. It is the job of managers at the corporate, business and functional levels to formulate strategies to counter these threats so that an organisation can respond to its task and general environments, perform at a high level and generate high profits. At Campbell, Conant performed such an analysis to identify the opportunities and threats stemming from the actions of its food industry rivals.

Formulating Corporate-level Strategies

Corporate-level strategy, as previously discussed, is a *plan of action* concerning the industries and countries in which an organisation should invest its resources to achieve its mission and goals.

In developing a corporate-level strategy, managers must ask: how should the growth and development of the company be managed in order to increase its ability to create value for its customers (and thus increase performance) over the long run? Managers of most organisations have the goal of growing their companies, and actively seek out new opportunities to use the organisation's resources to create more goods and services. Examples of organisations growing rapidly are Google, Hyundai, Innocent Drinks and Toyota, whose managers pursue any feasible opportunity to use their companies' skills to provide customers with new products.

In addition, some managers must help their organisations respond to threats due to changing forces in the task or general environment. Customers may no longer be buying the kinds of goods and services a company is producing (bulky computer monitors or televisions), or other organisations may have entered the market and attracted away customers (this happened to Intel when AMD began to produce more powerful chips). Senior managers aim to find the best strategies to help the organisation respond to these changes and improve performance.

The principal corporate-level strategies that managers use to help a company grow, to keep it on top of its industry and to help it retrench and reorganise to stop its decline are (1) concentration on a single business, (2) diversification, (3) international expansion and (4) vertical integration. These four strategies are all based on one idea: an organisation benefits from pursuing any one of them only when the strategy helps *further increase the value of the organisation's goods and services for customers*. To increase the value of goods and services, a corporate level strategy must help an organisation, or one of its divisions, differentiate and add value to its products either by making them unique or special, or by lowering the costs of value creation.

Concentration on a Single Business

Most organisations begin their growth and development with a corporate-level strategy aimed at concentrating resources in one business or industry in order to develop a strong competitive position within that industry. Innocent Drinks started as a stall at a music festival, and has now become a major player in the healthy-drinks market, with an annual growth of 50–60 per cent.[32]

Concentration on a single business can become an appropriate corporate-level strategy when managers see the need to reduce the size of their organisations to increase performance. Managers may decide to get out of certain industries, for example, when particular divisions lose their competitive advantage: managers may sell off those divisions, lay off workers and concentrate remaining organisational resources in another market or business to try to improve performance. This happened to electronics maker Hitachi when it was forced to get out of the CRT computer monitor business. Intense low-price competition existed in the computer monitor market because customers were increasingly switching from bulky CRT monitors to the newer, flat, LCD monitors. Hitachi announced it was closing three factories in Japan, Singapore and Malaysia that produced CRT monitors and would use its resources to invest in the new LCD technology. In contrast, when organisations are performing effectively, they often decide to enter new industries in which they can use their resources to create more value.

Diversification

Diversification is the strategy of expanding operations into a new business or industry and producing new goods or services.[33] Examples of diversification include Tesco or Sainsbury's which diversified into financial products, or British Petroleum (BP), which diversified into convenience stores on the US West coast. There are two main kinds of diversification: related and unrelated.

Related diversification

Related diversification is the strategy of entering a new business or industry to create a competitive advantage in one or more of an organisation's existing divisions or businesses. Related diversification can add value to an organisation's products if managers can find ways for its various divisions or business units to share their valuable skills or resources so that *synergy* is created.[34] Synergy is obtained when the value created by two divisions co-operating is greater than the value that would be created if the two divisions operated separately. For example, suppose two or more divisions within a diversified company can utilise the same manufacturing facilities, distribution channels, advertising campaigns and so on. Each division that shares resources has to invest less in the shared functions than it would have to invest if it had full responsibility for the activity. In this way, related diversification can be a major source of cost savings.[35] Similarly, if one division's R&D skills can be used to improve another division's products, the second division's products may receive a competitive advantage.

Procter & Gamble's disposable diaper and paper towel businesses offer one of the best examples of the successful production of synergies. These businesses share the costs of procuring inputs such as paper and developing new technology to reduce manufacturing costs. In addition, a joint sales force sells both products to supermarkets and both products are shipped by means of the same distribution system. This resource-sharing has enabled both divisions to reduce their costs, and as a result, they can charge lower prices than their competitors and thus attract more customers.[36]

In pursuing related diversification, managers often seek to find new businesses where they can use the existing skills and resources in their departments to create synergies, add value to the new business and hence improve the competitive position of the company. Alternatively, managers may acquire a company in a new industry because they believe that some of the skills and resources of the acquired company may improve the efficiency of one or more of their existing divisions. If successful, such skill transfers can help an organisation to lower its costs or better differentiate its products because they create synergies between divisions.

Unrelated diversification

Managers pursue *unrelated diversification* when they enter new industries or buy companies in new industries that are not related in any way to their current businesses or industries. One main reason for pursuing unrelated diversification is that, sometimes, managers can buy a poorly performing company, transfer their management skills to that company, turn around its business and increase its performance, all of which creates value.

Another reason for pursuing unrelated diversification is that purchasing businesses in different industries lets managers engage in a *portfolio strategy*, which is apportioning financial resources among divisions to increase financial returns or spread risks among different businesses. For example, managers may transfer funds from a rich division to a new and promising division and, by appropriately allocating money between them, create value. Though used as a popular explanation in the 1980s for unrelated diversification, portfolio strategy ran into increasing criticism in the 1990s.[37]

Indeed, more and more companies and their managers have abandoned the strategy of unrelated diversification because there is evidence that too much diversification can cause managers to lose control of their organisation's *core business*. Management experts suggest that although unrelated diversification may initially create value for a company, managers sometimes use portfolio strategy to expand the scope of their organisation's businesses too much. When this

happens, it becomes difficult for senior managers to be knowledgeable about all of the organisation's diverse businesses. Managers do not have the time to process all of the information
required to adequately assess the strategy and performance of each division objectively, and
organisational performance often suffers.

Thus, although unrelated diversification can create value for a company, research evidence
suggests that many diversification efforts have reduced value rather than created it.[38] As a consequence, there was a trend during the 1990s among many diversified companies to divest many
of their unrelated divisions. Managers sold off divisions and concentrated organisational resources
on their core business, focusing more on related diversification.[39]

International Expansion

As if planning the appropriate level of diversification were not a difficult enough decision,
corporate-level managers must also decide on the appropriate way to *compete internationally*.
A basic question confronts the managers of any organisation that competes in more than one
national market: to what extent should the organisation customise features of its products and
marketing campaign to different national conditions?[40]

If managers decide that their organisation should sell the same standardised product in each
national market in which it competes, and use the same basic marketing approach, they adopt
a **global strategy**.[41] Such companies undertake very little, if any, customisation to suit the specific
needs of customers in different countries. However, if managers decide to customise products
and marketing strategies to specific national conditions, they adopt a **multi-domestic strategy**.

Matsushita, with its Panasonic brand, has traditionally pursued a global strategy, selling the
same basic TVs and VCRs in every market in which it does business and often using the same
basic marketing approach. Unilever, the European food and household products company, has
pursued a multi-domestic strategy. To appeal to German customers, Unilever's German division
sells a different range of food products and uses a different marketing approach than its North
American division or even its UK division.

Global and multi-domestic strategies have both advantages and disadvantages. The major
advantage of a global strategy is the significant cost savings associated with not having to customise products and marketing approaches to different national conditions. For example, Rolex
watches, Ralph Lauren or Tommy Hilfiger clothing, Chanel or Armani accessories or perfume,
Dell computers, Chinese-made plastic toys and buckets, and US-grown rice and wheat are all
products that can be sold using the same marketing across many countries by simply translating it into a different language, saving companies a significant amount of money. The major
disadvantage of pursuing a global strategy is that, by ignoring national differences, managers
may leave themselves vulnerable to local competitors that do differentiate their products to
suit local tastes. This occurred in the British consumer electronics industry. Amstrad, a British
computer and electronics company, began by recognising and responding to local consumer
needs. Amstrad captured a major share of the British audio market by ignoring the standardised
inexpensive music centres marketed by companies pursuing a global strategy, such as Sony and
Matsushita. Instead, Amstrad's product was encased in teak rather than metal and featured a
control panel tailor-made to appeal to British consumers' preferences. To remain competitive in
this market, Matsushita had to place more emphasis on local customisation of its Panasonic and
JVC brands.

The advantages and disadvantages of a multi-domestic strategy are the opposite of those
of a global strategy. The major advantage of a multi-domestic strategy is that by customising

product offerings and marketing approaches to local conditions, managers may be able to gain market share or charge higher prices for their products. The major disadvantage is that customisation raises production costs and puts the multi-domestic company at a price disadvantage because it often has to charge prices higher than the prices charged by competitors pursuing a global strategy. Obviously, the choice between these two strategies calls for *trade-offs*.

Managers at Gillette, the well-known razor blade maker, created a strategy that combined the best features of both international strategies. Gillette was a global company from the beginning, as its managers quickly saw the advantages of selling its razor blades abroad. By 2004, 65 per cent of Gillette's revenues came from global sales, and this percentage was expected to increase.[42] Gillette's strategy over the years was pretty constant: find a new foreign country with a growing market for razor blades, form a strategic alliance with a local razor blade company and take a majority stake in it, invest in a large marketing campaign and then build a modern factory to make razor blades and other products for the local market. When Gillette entered Russia after the break-up of the Soviet Union, it saw a huge opportunity to increase sales. It formed a joint venture with a local company called Leninets Concern, which made a razor known as the Sputnik, and then with this base began to import its own brands into Russia. When sales growth rose sharply, Gillette decided to offer more products in the market and built a new plant in St Petersburg.[43]

Today, Gillette operates 50 manufacturing facilities in more than 20 countries.[44] It establishes its factories in countries where labour and other costs are low and then distributes and markets its products to countries in that region of the world. In this sense it pursues a global strategy. However, all of Gillette's research and development and design take place in one location. As it develops new kinds of razors, it equips its foreign factories to manufacture them when it decides that local customers are ready to trade up to the new product. So Gillette's latest razor, for example, may be introduced in a foreign country years later than in the US. Gillette is customising its product offering to the needs of different countries and also pursuing a multi-domestic strategy. By pursuing this international strategy, Gillette can achieve low costs and still differentiate and customise its product range to suit the needs of each country or world region. This strategy has proved very effective, and the company's global sales and profits continue to increase.

Choosing a way to expand internationally

As discussed above, a more competitive global environment has proven to be both an opportunity and a threat for organisations and managers. The opportunity is that organisations that expand globally are able to open new markets, reach more customers and gain access to new sources of raw materials and to low-cost suppliers of inputs. The threat is that organisations that expand globally are likely to encounter new competitors in the foreign countries they enter, and must respond to new political, economic and cultural conditions.

Before setting up foreign operations, managers of companies such as Amazon.com, Lands' End, Toys 'R' Us and Volkswagen needed to analyse the forces in the environment of a particular country (such as Korea or Brazil) in order to choose the right method to expand and respond to those forces in the most appropriate way. Four basic ways to operate in the global environment are importing and exporting, licensing and franchising, strategic alliances and wholly owned foreign subsidiaries. Each one will be briefly discussed, moving from the lowest level of foreign involvement and investment required of a global organisation and its managers, and the least amount of risk, to the high end of the spectrum (Fig. 8.6).[45]

Figure 8.6 Four Ways of Expanding Internationally

Importing and exporting

The least complex global operations are **exporting** and **importing**. A company engaged in *exporting* makes products at home and sells them abroad. An organisation might sell its own products abroad or allow a local organisation in the foreign country to distribute its products. Few risks are associated with exporting because a company does not have to invest in developing manufacturing facilities abroad. It can further reduce its investment abroad if it allows a local company to distribute its products.

A company engaged in *importing* sells at home products that are made abroad (products it makes itself or buys from other companies). For example, most of the products that IKEA or ALDI sell are made abroad, and in many cases the appeal of a product is that it is made abroad. The Internet has made it much easier for companies to inform potential foreign buyers about their products; detailed product specifications and features are available online and informed buyers can communicate easily with prospective sellers. The way in which Levi Strauss was forced to change its international approach from exporting to importing (Case 8.3) illustrates how the growth of low-cost manufacturing abroad has changed competition in many industries.

Case 8.3: **Levi Strauss's big problems**

Levi Strauss, the well-known jeans maker, was once the global leader in the apparel industry. Its jeans commanded a premium price as customers the world over perceived that the value or status of wearing Levi jeans was worth paying extra for. Indeed, in Europe and Asia, Levi jeans were often sold at double or triple their US price. No more: Levi is now fighting to lower its costs to be able to survive in the fast-changing jeans industry.

Levi's problems arose because of changes in the international strategies of other jeans makers and apparel companies. In the early 1990s, other jeans makers such as VF Corp (which makes Wrangler jeans), Calvin Klein and Polo outsourced the production of jeans to countries abroad where labour costs were lowest. With their lower costs, these companies then began to charge lower prices for their products and customers began to switch to buying their jeans. Then, in a significant move, companies such as ASDA and Matalan began to wonder why they should pay Levi a premium price for selling its jeans when they could sell jeans under their own labels at a lower price and still make more profit than if they sold Levi's jeans. So they contracted with low-cost foreign producers to make jeans under their own in-house labels. The result was that sales of Levi jeans plummeted as many customers began to buy jeans on the basis of their price.

Levi, because it still produced most of its jeans in the US and exported them abroad, was caught unprepared and found it could no longer compete. It lost billions of dollars in the 1990s. To survive, it was forced to change from exporting its jeans to importing its jeans from abroad – it outsourced all production to manufacturers abroad. Since 1997 it has closed all 35 of its US manufacturing facilities and laid off over 30,000 employees.

Once it outsourced production abroad, Levi was able to reduce its prices to be competitive. Indeed, its prices fell so low that ASDA began to sell Levi jeans as part of its range in its stores. However, low prices mean low profits, and Levi's problems have continued into the 2000s as it struggles to find a way to compete successfully in a global market dominated by ruthless low-cost/price competition.

Licensing and franchising

In licensing, a company (the *licenser*) allows a foreign organisation (the *licensee*) to take charge of both manufacturing and distributing one or more of its products in the licensee's country or world region in return for a negotiated fee. German chemical maker BASF might license a local factory in India to produce glues. The advantage of licensing is that the licenser does not have to bear the development costs associated with opening up in a foreign country; the licensee bears the costs. The risks associated with this strategy are that the company granting the licence has to give its foreign partner access to its technological know-how, and so risks losing control over its secrets.

Whereas licensing is pursued primarily by manufacturing companies, franchising is pursued primarily by service organisations. In franchising, a company (the *franchiser*) sells to a foreign organisation (the *franchisee*) the rights to use its brand name and operating know-how in return for a lump-sum payment and share of the franchiser's profits. Hilton Hotels might sell a franchise to a local company in Chile to operate hotels under the Hilton name in return for a franchise payment. The advantage of franchising is that the franchiser does not have to bear the development costs of overseas expansion and avoids the many problems associated with setting up foreign operations. The downside is that the organisation that grants the franchise may lose control over the way in which the franchisee operates and product quality may fall. Franchisers, such as Hilton, Europcar and McDonald's, then risk losing their good names. Customers who buy McDonald's hamburgers in Korea may reasonably expect those burgers to be as good as the ones they get at home. If they are not, McDonald's reputation will suffer over time. Once again, the Internet facilitates communication between partners and allows them to better meet each other's expectations.

Strategic alliances

One way to overcome the loss-of-control problems associated with exporting, licensing and franchising is to expand globally by means of a strategic alliance. In a strategic alliance, managers pool or share their organisation's resources and know-how with those of a foreign company, and the two organisations share the rewards or risks of starting a new venture in a foreign country. Sharing resources allows a company, for example, to take advantage of the high-quality skills of foreign manufacturers and the specialised knowledge of foreign managers about the needs of local customers and to reduce the risks involved in a venture. At the same time, the terms of the alliance give the company more control over how the good or service is produced or sold in the foreign country than it would have as a franchiser or licenser.

A *strategic alliance* can take the form of a written contract between two or more companies to exchange resources, or it can result in the creation of a new organisation. A *joint venture* (JV) is a strategic alliance among two or more companies that agree to jointly establish and share the ownership of a new business.[46] An organisation's level of involvement abroad increases in a JV because the alliance normally involves a *capital investment* in production facilities abroad in order to produce goods or services outside the home country. Risk, however, is reduced. The Internet and global teleconferencing provide the increased communication and co-ordination necessary for partners to work together on a global basis. In 2001, for example, Coca-Cola and Nestlé announced that they would form a JV and co-operate in marketing their teas, coffees and health-oriented beverages to more than 50 countries in the world.[47] British Petroleum (BP), Amoco and Italy's ENI announced in the same year that they would form a JV to build a £1.4 billion gas-liquefaction plant in Egypt.[48]

Wholly-owned foreign subsidiaries

When managers decide to establish a wholly-owned foreign subsidiary, they invest in establishing production/service operations in a foreign country independent of any local direct involvement. For example, UK's Lloyds Pharmacy Ltd is a wholly-owned subsidiary of GEHE AG, now Celesio AG, Europe's largest pharmaceutical wholesaler based in Germany.[49] Being a subsidiary allows the pharmacy to compete on economies of scales.

Operating alone, without any direct involvement from foreign companies, an organisation receives all of the rewards and bears all of the risks associated with operating abroad.[50] This method of international expansion is much more expensive than the others because it requires a higher level of foreign investment and presents managers with many more threats. However, investment in a foreign subsidiary or division offers significant advantages. It gives an organisation high potential for returns because the organisation does not have to share its profits with a foreign organisation, and it reduces the level of risk because managers have full control over all aspects of their foreign subsidiary's operations. Moreover, this type of investment allows managers to protect their technology and know-how from foreign organisations. Large, well-known companies like Scottish Power and Gillette, which have ample resources, make extensive use of wholly-owned subsidiaries. No matter what means they choose to expand globally, however, companies have to be careful to design and select the right kind of information systems and websites to allow customers to buy their products.

Vertical Integration

When an organisation is doing well in its business, managers often see new opportunities to create value by either *producing* their own inputs or *distributing* their own outputs. The Spanish clothes retailer ZARA felt it was a waste of resources to source all its products from different suppliers such as H&M, who uses approximately 900 suppliers. In order to be more efficient, more than 50 per cent of its clotheslines are now made in-house, integrating marketing, design and manufacturing.[51]

Vertical integration is the corporate-level strategy through which an organisation becomes involved in producing its own inputs (*backward* vertical integration) or distributing and selling its own outputs (*forward* vertical integration).[52] A steel company that supplies its iron ore needs from company-owned iron ore mines is engaging in backward vertical integration. A PC company that sells its computers through company-owned distribution outlets has engaged in forward vertical integration.

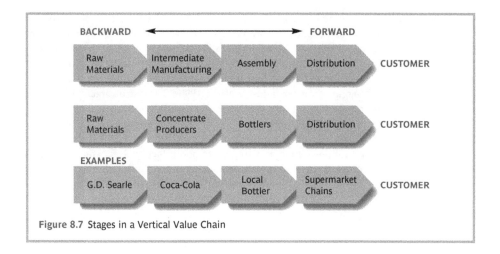

Figure 8.7 Stages in a Vertical Value Chain

Figure 8.7 illustrates the four main stages in a typical raw-material-to-consumer value chain: value is added at each stage. Typically, the primary operations of an organisation take place in one of these stages. For a company based in the assembly stage, backward integration would involve establishing a new division in intermediate manufacturing or raw-material production, and forward integration would involve establishing a new division to distribute its products to wholesalers or to sell directly to customers. A division at one stage receives the goods produced by the division in the previous stage, transforms it in some way – adding value – and then transfers the output at a higher price to the division at the next stage in the chain.

As an example of how the value chain works, consider the cola segment of the soft-drink industry. Raw-material suppliers include sugar companies and the manufacturer of the artificial sweetener NutraSweet, which is used in diet colas. These companies sell their products to companies that make concentrate – such as Coca-Cola and PepsiCo – which mix these inputs with others to produce the cola concentrate that they market. In the process, they add value to these inputs. The concentrate producers then sell the concentrate to bottlers, who add carbonated water to the concentrate and package the resulting drink – again adding value to the concentrate. Next, the bottlers sell the packaged product to various distributors, including retail stores such as Sainsbury's and ASDA and fast-food chains such as McDonald's. These distributors add value by making the product accessible to customers. Value is thus added by companies at each stage in the raw-material-to-consumer chain.

A major reason why managers pursue vertical integration is that it allows them either to add value to their products by making them special or unique or to lower the costs of value creation. For example, Coca-Cola and PepsiCo, in a case of forward vertical integration to build brand loyalty and enhance the differentiated appeal of their colas, decided to buy up their major bottlers to increase control over marketing and promotion efforts, which had been handled by the bottlers.[53] An example of using forward vertical integration to lower costs is Matsushita's decision to open company-owned stores to sell its Panasonic and JVC products and thus keep the profit that otherwise would be earned by independent retailers.[54]

Although vertical integration can help an organisation to grow rapidly, it can be a problem when forces in the environment counter the strategies of the organisation and make it necessary for managers to reorganise or retrench. Vertical integration can reduce an organisation's flexibility to respond to changing environmental conditions. IBM used to produce most of its own components for mainframe computers; while this made sense in the 1970s it became a major handicap in the fast-changing computer industry of the 1990s. The rise of organisation-wide networks of personal computers meant slumping demand for mainframes, as demand fell, IBM found itself with an excess-capacity problem not only in its mainframe assembly operations but also in component operations. Closing down this capacity cost IBM over £2.8 billion.[55]

When considering vertical integration as a strategy to add value, managers must take care because vertical integration can sometimes actually reduce an organisation's ability to create value when the environment changes. This is why so many companies now *outsource* the production of component parts to other companies. IBM, however, has found a new opportunity for forward vertical integration in the 1990s.[56] It decided to provide IT consulting services to mainframe users and to advise them on how to install and manage any software packages they chose on their mainframes. Providing such IT services was so profitable for IBM that by 2000 it had recovered its market position.

A second type of integration is called horizontal integration. This type of integration usually refers to an organisation that is expanding its business activities at the same level, mostly through mergers or acquisitions (M&As). While BP may own a number of distribution networks (vertical integration), it has also bought the German-based petrol stations chain ARAL; it has therefore bought into the same type of industry. The advantages of horizontal integration are economies of scale and greater market power. The disadvantages are similar to those associated with M&As – i.e. problems of the *realisation of economies of scale*.

Formulating Business-level Strategies

Michael Porter, the researcher who developed the five forces model discussed on p. 255, also formulated a theory of how managers can select a *business-level strategy*, a plan to gain a competitive advantage in a particular market or industry.[57] According to Porter, managers must choose between two basic ways of increasing the value of an organisation's products: *differentiating* the product to add value or lowering the costs of *value creation*. Porter also argues that managers must choose between serving the *whole* market and serving just one *segment* or *part* of a market. Based on those choices, managers choose to pursue one of four business-level strategies: low cost, differentiation, focused low cost, or focused differentiation (Table 8.3).

Low-Cost Strategy

With a low-cost strategy, managers try to gain a competitive advantage by focusing the energy of all the organisation's departments or functions on driving the organisation's costs down below the costs of its rivals. This strategy requires that manufacturing managers search for new ways to reduce production costs, R&D managers focus on developing new products that can be manufactured more cheaply and marketing managers find ways to lower the costs of attracting customers. According to Porter, organisations pursuing a low-cost strategy can sell a product for less than their rivals sell it and yet still make a profit because of their lower costs. Organisations that pursue a low-cost strategy thus hope to enjoy a competitive advantage based on their low prices. ALDI, the German supermarket discounter, for example, is able to offer low prices by

Table 8.3 Porter's business-level strategies

Strategy	Many	Few
Low cost	✓	
Focused low cost		✓
Differentiation	✓	
Focused differentiation		✓

only stocking a limited number of products and being able to exert pressures on its producers through economies of scale. This has led to Theo and Karl Albrecht, the owners of ALDI, being amongst the richest entrepreneurs in Europe.[58]

Differentiation Strategy

With a *differentiation strategy*, managers try to gain a competitive advantage by focusing all the energies of the organisation's departments or functions on distinguishing the organisation's products from those of competitors on one or more important dimensions, such as product design, quality or after-sales service and support. The process of making products unique and different is often expensive, and this strategy often requires that managers increase spending on product design or R&D to differentiate the product, and costs rise as a result. Organisations that successfully pursue a differentiation strategy may be able to charge a *premium price* for their products – a price usually much higher than the price charged by a low-cost organisation. The premium price allows organisations pursuing a differentiation strategy to recoup their higher costs. Large fashion brands like Gucci and Armani are some of the many well-known companies that pursue a strategy of differentiation. They spend enormous amounts of money on advertising to differentiate, and create a unique image for, their products. However, just because companies can differentiate their products does not mean that there cannot be intense competition between them, as Case 8.4 suggests.

Case 8.4: **Strategy in the world package delivery business**

In 1971, Federal Express (FedEx) turned the package delivery world upside down when it began to offer overnight package delivery by air. Its founder, Fred Smith, had seen the opportunity for next-day delivery because both the US Postal Service and United Parcel Service (UPS) were, at that time, taking several days to deliver packages. Smith was convinced there was pent-up demand for overnight delivery, and he was also convinced that customers would be willing to pay a high premium price to get such a unique new service, at least about £10 a package at that time.[59] Smith was right: customers were willing to pay high prices for fast, reliable delivery. By discovering and tapping into an unmet customer need, he redefined the package delivery industry.

Several companies imitated FedEx's new strategy and introduced their own air overnight service. None, however, could match FedEx's state-of-the-art information system that allowed continuous tracking of all packages in transit, and several of its competitors went out of business. A few, like Airborne Express, managed to survive by focusing or *specialising* on serving the ▶

▶ needs of one particular group of customers – corporate customers – and by offering lower prices than FedEx.

The well-known road delivery package company UPS initiated an overnight air delivery service of its own in 1998.[60] UPS managers realised that the future of package delivery lay both on the road and in the air because different customer groups, with different needs, were emerging. It began to aggressively imitate FedEx's state-of-the-art operating and information systems, especially its tracking system. Slowly and surely UPS increased the number of overnight packages that it was delivering. In 1999, UPS announced two major innovations. First, it introduced a new tracking and shipping information system that matched, and even exceeded, the sophistication of the FedEx system because it could work with any IT system used by corporate customers. (By contrast, customers had to install and use FedEx's proprietary IT, an approach that caused more work and cost for them.) Second, UPS integrated its overnight air service into its nationwide delivery service and created a seamless interface between these two different aspects of its business. This gave it a differentiation advantage over FedEx because UPS could deliver short-range and mid-distance packages, those being shipped within about 500 miles, more quickly than FedEx, as well as matching the speed and reliability of FedEx's long-range operations.

Competition between FedEx and UPS became intense in the early 2000s. Then, in 2003, both companies received a shock when the largest global package delivery company, the now German-owned DHL, announced that it would purchase Airborne Express and would thus become a direct competitor of FedEx and UPS. When DHL began a marketing campaign to emphasise the extent of its global reach and the speed of its operations, all three companies started to fight for customers and find new ways of differentiating their products. In 2003 FedEx announced that it would purchase Kinko's Copies and make each Kinko's store a base for its delivery operations. In doing so, it was following UPS' approach; UPS had purchased a chain of packaging stores and turned them into UPS stores. The fight is ongoing, and which company will turn out to be the global leader is still unclear.

'Stuck in the Middle'

According to Porter's theory, managers cannot simultaneously pursue both a low-cost strategy and a differentiation strategy. Porter identified a simple correlation: differentiation raises costs and thus necessitates premium pricing to recoup those high costs. If ALDI suddenly began to advertise heavily to try to build a strong global brand image for its products, costs would rise; the stores would then no longer make a profit simply by pricing their products lower than other supermarkets. According to Porter, managers must choose between a low-cost strategy and a differentiation strategy. He refers to managers and organisations that have not made this choice as being 'stuck in the middle'. Organisations 'stuck in the middle' tend to have lower levels of performance than do those that pursue either a low-cost or a differentiation strategy. To avoid being 'stuck in the middle', senior managers must instruct departmental managers to take actions that will result in either low cost or differentiation.

However, exceptions to this rule can be found. In many organisations managers have been able to drive costs below those of rivals and simultaneously differentiate their products from those offered by them.[61] Toyota's production system is reportedly the most efficient in the world. This efficiency gives Toyota a low-cost strategy *vis-à-vis* its rivals in the global car industry. At the same time, Toyota has differentiated its cars from those of rivals on the basis of superior design and quality. This superiority allows the company to charge a premium price for many of its popular models.[62] Toyota thus seems to be simultaneously pursuing both a low-cost and a differentiated business-level strategy. This example suggests that although Porter's ideas may be valid in most cases, very well managed companies such as Toyota may have both low costs and differentiated products.

Focused Low-cost and Focused Differentiation Strategies

Both the differentiation strategy and the low-cost strategy are aimed at serving many or most segments of a particular market, such as that for cars or computers. Porter identified two other business-level strategies that aim to serve the needs of customers in only one or a few market segments.[63] Managers pursuing a **focused low-cost strategy** serve one or a few segments of the overall market and aim to make their organisation the lowest-cost company serving that segment. For example, Cott Corporation is the world's leading supplier of retailer-brand-name carbonated soft drinks. With production facilities in North America and the UK, Cott produces, packages and distributes a wide selection of retailer-brand beverages for grocery, mass-merchandise and convenience store chains. All Sainsbury's soda sold under its own brand name is made by Cott, for example. However, while Cott is the world's leading supplier of retailer-brand-name sodas, it is focusing on a *low-cost strategy*: It makes no attempt to compete with Coke and Pepsi which, as noted earlier, pursue a differentiation strategy and whose brand-name sodas dominate the global soda market.

By contrast, managers pursuing a **focused differentiation strategy** serve just one or a few segments of the market and aim to make their organisation the most differentiated company serving that segment. BMW, for example, pursues a focused strategy, producing cars exclusively for higher-income customers. By contrast, Toyota pursues a differentiation strategy and produces cars that appeal to consumers in almost all segments of the car market, from basic transportation (Toyota AYGO), through the middle of the market (Toyota Avensis) to the high-income end of the market (Lexus).

As these examples suggest, companies pursuing either of these focused strategies have chosen to *specialise* in some way by directing their efforts at a particular kind of customer (such as serving the needs of babies or affluent customers) or even the needs of customers in a specific geographic region (customers in Eastern Europe or Western Europe).

Zara, the Spanish manufacturer of fashionable clothing, provides an excellent example of how a company can pursue both a low-cost and a differentiated focused strategy at the same time by using new IT. Well-known fashion houses like Channel, Dior and Armani can charge thousands of pounds for the fashionable collections of suits and dresses that they introduce twice yearly in the autumn and in the spring. Only the rich can afford such differentiated and expensive clothing, and this has opened up a gap in the fashion market for companies that can supply fashionable clothes at lower prices. Essentially, these companies have the capabilities to pursue a focused differentiation and cost-leadership strategy.

While many clothing companies, such as the The Gap and England's Jaeger and Laura Ashley, have attempted to supply fashionable clothes at lower prices, none has succeeded as well as Spanish clothes maker Zara, whose sales have soared in recent years.[64] Zara has managed to position itself as the low-price/cost leader in the fashion segment of the clothing market because of the way it uses IT. It has created an information system that allows it to manage its design and manufacturing process in a way that minimises the inventory it has to carry – the major cost borne by a clothing retailer. However, its IT also gives instantaneous feedback on which clothes are selling well and in which countries, and this gives it a competitive advantage from differentiation.

Zara can manufacture more of a particular kind of dress or suit to meet high customer demand, decide which clothing should be sold in its rapidly expanding network of global stores and constantly change the mix of clothes it offers customers to keep up with fashion. Moreover, it can do this at relatively small output levels, something which is also a part of a specialised, focused strategy. This is partly possible as Zara has *vertically integrated* some of its production.

Zara's IT also allows it to manage the interface between its design and manufacturing operations more efficiently. Zara only takes five weeks to design a new collection and then a week to make it. Other fashion houses, by contrast, can take six or more months to design the collection and then three more before it is available in stores.[65] This short *time to market* gives Zara great flexibility and allows the company to respond quickly to the rapidly changing fashion market in which fashions can change several times a year. Because of the quick manufacturing-to-sales cycle and just-in-time (JIT) fashion, Zara can offer its clothes collections at relatively low prices and still make a profit that is the envy of the fashion clothing industry.[66]

Formulating Functional-level Strategies

Zara has developed many kinds of strengths in functions such as clothing design and IT that have given it a competitive advantage. A *functional-level strategy* is a plan of action to improve the ability of an organisation's functions to create value. It involves the actions that managers of individual functions (such as manufacturing or marketing) can take to add value to an organisation's goods and services and thereby increase the value customers receive. The price that customers are prepared to pay for a product indicates how much they value an organisation's products: the more customers value a product, the more they are willing to pay for it.

There are two ways in which functions can add value to an organisation's products:

1. Functional managers can lower the costs of creating value so that an organisation can attract customers by keeping its prices lower than its competitors' prices.
2. Functional managers can add value to a product by finding ways to differentiate it from the products of other companies.

If customers see more value in one organisation's products than in the products of its competitors, they may be willing to pay a premium price. There must be a fit between functional- and business-level strategies if an organisation is to achieve its mission and goal of maximising the amount of value it gives customers. The better the fit between functional- and business-level strategies, the greater will be the organisation's *competitive advantage* – its ability to attract customers and the revenue they provide.

Each organisational function has an important role to play in the process of lowering costs or adding value to a product (Table 8.4). Manufacturing can find new ways to lower production costs or to build superior quality into the product to add value. Marketing, sales and after-sales service and support can add value by, for example, building brand loyalty (as Coca-Cola and PepsiCo have done in the soft-drink industry) and finding more effective ways to attract customers. Human resource management (HRM) can lower the costs of creating value by recruiting and training a highly productive workforce. The R&D function can lower the costs of creating value by developing more efficient production processes. R&D can also add value by developing new and improved products that customers value over established product offerings.

Creating value at the functional level requires the adoption of many state-of-the-art management techniques and practices that are discussed at length in Chapter 9. As discussed here, it

Table 8.4 How functions can lower the costs and create value or add value to create a competitive advantage

Value-creating function		
Sales and marketing	■ Find new customers	■ Promote brand-name awareness and loyalty
Materials management	■ Find low-cost advertising methods	
R&D		■ Tailor products to suit customers' needs
Manufacturing	■ Use JIT inventory system/ computerised warehousing	
HRM	■ Develop long-term relationships with suppliers and customers	■ Develop long-term relationships with suppliers to provide high-quality inputs
	■ Improve efficiency of machinery and equipment	■ Reduce shipping time to customers
	■ Design products that can be made more cheaply	■ Create new products
		■ Improve existing products
	■ Develop skills in low-cost manufacturing	■ Increase product quality and reliability
	■ Reduce turnover and absenteeism	■ Hire highly skilled employees
		■ Develop innovative training programmes
	■ Raise employee skills	

is the responsibility of managers at the functional level to identify these techniques and develop a functional-level plan that contains the strategies necessary to develop them. The important issue to remember is that all of these techniques can help an organisation achieve a competitive advantage by lowering the costs of creating value, or by adding value above and beyond that offered by rivals.

Reaction time

1. What is the role of divisional and functional managers in the formulation of strategy?
2. Why is it important for functional managers to have a clear grasp of the organisation's mission when developing strategies within their departments?
3. What is the relationship among corporate-, business- and functional-level strategies, and how can they create value for an organisation?

Planning and Implementing Strategy

After identifying the appropriate strategies to attain an organisation's mission and goals, managers must confront the challenge of putting those strategies into action. *Strategy implementation* is a five-step process:

1. Allocating responsibility for implementation to the appropriate individuals or groups
2. Drafting detailed action plans that specify how a strategy is to be implemented
3. Establishing a timetable for implementation that includes precise, measurable goals linked to the attainment of the action plan
4. Allocating appropriate resources to the responsible individuals or groups
5. Holding specific individuals or groups responsible for the attainment of corporate, divisional and functional goals.

The planning process goes beyond the mere identification of strategies; it also includes actions taken to ensure that the organisation actually puts its strategies into action. It should be noted that the plan for implementing a strategy may require radical redesign of the organisation's structure, the development of new control systems and the adoption of a programme for changing the organisation's culture. These are all issues that are addressed in Chapters 9–11.

TIPS FOR PRACTICE

1. Always remind yourself of the primary business of your organisation. Ask questions about how well the organisation is achieving this, and use this to decide future goals.
2. Make SWOT an automatic and integral part of any planning process.

Summary and Review

The nature of the planning process Planning is a three-step process: (1) determining an organisation's mission and goals; (2) formulating strategy; (3) implementing strategy. Managers use planning to identify and select appropriate goals and courses of action for an organisation and to decide how to allocate the resources they need to attain those goals and carry out those actions. A good plan builds commitment for the organisation's goals, gives the organisation a sense of direction and purpose, co-ordinates the different functions and divisions of the organisation and controls managers by making them accountable for specific goals. In large organisations planning takes place at three levels: corporate, business or divisional and functional or departmental. Although planning is typically the responsibility of a well-defined group of managers, the subordinates of those managers should be given every opportunity to have input into the process and to shape the outcome. Long-term plans have a time horizon of five years or more; intermediate-term plans, between one and five years; and short-term plans, one year or less.

Determining the organisation's mission and goals and formulating strategy Determining the organisation's mission requires that managers define the business of the organisation and establish major goals.

Formulating strategy Strategy formulation requires that managers perform a SWOT analysis and then choose appropriate strategies at the corporate, business and functional levels. At the corporate level, organisations use strategies such as concentration on a single business, diversification, international expansion and vertical integration to help increase the value of the goods and services provided to customers. At the business level, managers are responsible for developing a successful low-cost or differentiation strategy, either for the whole market or for a particular segment of it. At the functional level, departmental managers strive to develop and use their skills to help the organisation either to add value to its products by differentiating them or to lower the costs of value creation.

Planning and implementing strategy Strategy implementation requires that managers allocate responsibilities to appropriate individuals or groups, draft detailed action plans that specify how a strategy is to be implemented, establish a timetable for implementation that includes precise, measurable goals linked to the attainment of the action plan, allocate appropriate resources to the responsible individuals or groups and hold individuals or groups accountable for the attainment of goals.

Topic for Action

- Ask a manager about the kinds of planning exercises he or she regularly uses. What are the purposes of these exercises, and what are their advantages or disadvantages?
- Ask a manager to identify the corporate-, business- and functional-level strategies used by his or her organisation.

Applied Independent Learning

Building Management Skills

How to Analyse a Company's Strategy

Pick a well-known business organisation that has received recent press coverage and for which you can get the annual reports from their website. For this organisation, do the following:

1. From the annual reports, identify the main strategies pursued by the company over a 10-year period (if that many reports are available).
2. Try to identify why the company pursued these strategies. What reason was given in the annual reports, press reports and so on?
3. Document whether and when any major changes in the strategy of the organisation occurred. If changes did occur, try to identify the reason for them.
4. If changes in strategy occurred, try to determine the extent to which they were the result of long-term plans and the extent to which they were responses to unforeseen changes in the company's task environment.
5. What is the main industry that the company competes in?

▶

▶ 6. What business-level strategy does the company seem to be pursuing in this industry?

7. What is the company's reputation with regard to productivity, quality, innovation and responsiveness to customers in this industry? If the company has attained an advantage in any of these areas, how has it done so?

8. What is the current corporate-level strategy of the company? What is the company's stated reason for pursuing this strategy?

9. Has the company expanded internationally? If it has, identify its largest international market. How did the company enter this market? Did its mode of entry change over time?

Managing Ethically

A few years ago, IBM announced that it had fired the three senior managers of its Argentine division because of their involvement in a scheme to secure a large contract for IBM to provide and service the computers of one of Argentina's largest state-owned banks. The three executives paid millions of the contract money to a third company, CCR, which then paid nearly half to phantom companies. This money was then used to bribe the bank executives who agreed to give IBM the contract.

These bribes are not necessarily illegal under Argentine law. Moreover, the three managers argued that all companies have to pay bribes to get new business contracts, and they were not doing anything that managers in other companies were not doing.

Questions

1. Either by yourself or in a group decide if this business practice of paying bribes is ethical or unethical.

2. Should IBM allow its foreign divisions to pay bribes if all other companies are doing so?

3. If bribery is common in a particular country, what effect would this likely have on the nation's economy and culture?

Small Group Breakout Exercise

Low Cost or Differentiation?

Form groups of three or four people, and appoint one member as spokesperson who will communicate your findings to the class when called on by the instructor. Then discuss the following scenario.

You are a team of managers of a major national clothing chain, and you have been charged with finding a way to restore your organisation's competitive advantage. Recently, your organisation has been experiencing increasing competition from two sources. First, discount stores such as Wal-Mart and Target have been undercutting your prices because they buy their clothes from low-cost foreign manufacturers while you buy most of yours from high-quality domestic suppliers. Discount stores have been attracting your customers who buy at the low end of the price range. Second, small boutiques opening in malls provide high-price designer clothing and are attracting your customers at the high end of the market. Your company has become 'stuck in the middle', and you have to decide what to do.

Should you start to buy abroad so that you can lower your prices and begin to pursue a low-cost strategy? Should you focus on the high end of the market and become more of a differentiator? Or should you try to do both and pursue a low-cost strategy and a differentiation strategy?

1. Using scenario planning, analyse the pros and cons of each alternative.
2. Think about the various clothing retailers in your local malls and city, and analyse the choices they have made about how to compete with one another along the low-cost and differentiation dimensions.

Exploring the World Wide Web

Go to the corporate website of Google (www.google.com/corporate/execs.html), click on 'corporate info', and explore this site; in particular, click on 'Google's history' and 'The 10 Things' that guide Google's corporate philosophy.

1. How would you describe Google's mission and goals?
2. What is Google's business-level strategy?
3. What is Google's corporate-level strategy?

Application in Today's Business World

Volkswagen Slips Into Reverse

It has been a rough ride for Bernd Pischetsrieder since the former BMW boss took over as chief executive at Volkswagen (VW) in April 2002. VW's share price has fallen nearly 50 per cent since then, wiping out $11 billion in market capitalisation as profits plummeted at the $150 billion company.

On 23 July 2004, Pischetsrieder delivered more bad news – a 36 per cent net profit drop in the first half of the year. Profits for all of 2003 were already down by more than half, and just to take even more air out of VW's tyres the boss issued a grim earnings warning for 2004. In three years – just half a model life cycle in the auto business – the world's fourth-largest car maker had gone from Europe's showcase turnaround to major-league laggard.

What went wrong? Volkswagen's vaunted brand premium – the implicit guarantee of quality and innovation that for long allowed it to charge as much as 8 per cent more than the competition for mass-market cars – is eroding fast. French, Asian and even US rivals are improving quality, bolstering manufacturing efficiency and besting VW at design. The Golf compact lost out in 2003 to the Peugeot 206 as Europe's best-selling car for the second year in a row. The all-new, richly priced Golf is running neck-and-neck with its ageing French rival in 2004. To counter slow sales of its Golf in Europe, VW was forced in January to offer a $1,500 air-conditioning system for free and hefty dealer rebates on used-car trade ins. In the US, meanwhile, VW has slapped a $3,000 rebate on its ageing Passat and joined the 0 per cent financing game. US losses were expected to reach $1.4 billion in 2004, due to falling sales and the weak dollar's impact on reported earnings.

▶   Another nasty surprise was in China, which until recently accounted for up to 24 per cent of VW's operating profit. In late May 2004, General Motors Corp., keen to dethrone VW as China's market leader, cut prices by 11 per cent. VW matched the move. GM's sales doubled in the first half of 2004, while VW's fell 4.2 per cent. VW commanded half the mainland market in 1999; now it controls just over a quarter. Pischetsrieder now expected China sales to grow only 5 per cent to 7 per cent in 2004, down from over 30 per cent in recent years. 'Our prime objective is profitability, not maintaining market share,' he said in a 23 July 2004 conference call with financial analysts and journalists.

What is the way out? Pischetsrieder has launched a cost-savings programme called ForMotion aimed at trimming $2.6 billion over two years, on top of the company's existing effort to squeeze costs by $1.1 billion a year. The plan seeks to cut $970 million in purchasing costs, $600 million in reduced staffing and $360 million in restructured sales activities. VW is also beefing up its lucrative auto-finance business by buying a leading Dutch car-leasing company.

More models are coming, too: a souped-up Golf was due later in 2004, with the debut of Passat and Jetta remakes. In China, Pischetsrieder is investing $6 billion over the next four years and aims to double VW's production capacity, to 1.6 million cars, by 2008. VW is also introducing fresher models to the Chinese market – the Touareg sport utility, the Phaeton luxury sedan, the Audi A6 and a car that will be expressly designed for China. Pischetsrieder is shifting decision making from VW's Wolfsburg headquarters to Beijing and sending out experienced managers.

Pischetsrieder also has a winner in the Audi, VW's $28 billion-in-revenue premium brand. Strong sales of Audi's luxury A8, the new A6 midsize sedan and the hot A3 compact helped drive a 10 per cent increase in operating profit, to $666 million, in the first half of 2004. Audi introduced the rugged Pike's Peak SUV in 2005.

Cost cuts, new models, new focus, a strong luxury brand: sounds good. So why aren't investors impressed? Analysts who had expected 2004 to be a comeback year now say that earnings will remain anemic through 2006. 'VW is a huge ship. You can't turn it for miles and miles,' says George C. Peterson, president of AutoPacific, Inc. in Tustin, CA.

One problem is that achieving big efficiencies is like shooting at a moving target. Pischetsrieder's cuts will help, but analysts say the effort pales in comparison with the thorough streamlining already achieved at Renault, Peugeot and Chrysler. Besides, 'VW has never faced up to its fundamental cost problem. It has never faced up to the unions,' says John Wormald, a partner at London-based consultant Autopolis. While rivals retooled, VW dallied. Labour costs at VW's factories are 17.4 per cent of revenues, versus a European average of 15 per cent, according to a 27 July 2004 report by Dresdner Kleinwort Wasserstein. Since closing a plant in Germany is politically impossible, analysts say, Pischetsrieder needs to accelerate cost-cutting dramatically and boost sales while improving plant flexibility. 'The group is far from being on a sound recovery path,' says Bruno Lapierre, an Exane BNP Paribas analyst, in a 23 July 2004 report.

VW has also blundered by neglecting to develop a stable of minivans and SUVs, which make up over 54 per cent of industry sales in the US. So far, VW's only offering is the Touareg SUV. 'In the United States, it's playing with one hand behind its back. It has no lineup to match Honda and Toyota,' says Peterson. 'How did that escape them?'

Slow-Moving Managers

Pischetsrieder, who has a consensus-driven management style, is making little headway against a bureaucracy that is resistant to change. Insiders say that VW's chronically weak management and poor execution were aggravated by the nine-year tenure of former CEO Ferdinand K. Piëch, a brilliant but autocratic engineer. 'Of the top 100 managers, 50 are not used to making their own decisions or thinking on their own. They wait for the phone to ring to get their orders. They are used to being told what to do,' says an auto-industry expert who is close to the company.

Pischetsrieder has sought to set up more democratic decision-making structures, but many say the pace of change is glacial. 'What Pischetsrieder wants to do is right – to transform the organisation, processes and behaviour,' says one consultant. 'The question is whether there is enough time to survive the tough period ahead.' Looks like it's time for a radical shift of gears.

Questions

1. What is the source of Volkswagen's problems?

2. What strategies is it adopting to solve these problems?

Source: Gail Edmundson and Dexter Roberts, 'Volkswagen Slips into Reverse', adapted and reprinted from *BusinessWeek*, August 9, 2004 by special permission. Copyright © 2004 by the McGraw-Hill Companies, Inc.

Notes and References

1 *Evening Standard*, 'Pepsi vs Coke over Beckham', April 2002.

2 www.cott.com, 2004.

3 htpp://www.cnw.ca/en/releases/archive/January2006/26/c0838.html; http://www.cott.com/.

4 A. Chandler, *Strategy and Structure: Chapters in the History of the American Enterprise* (Cambridge, MA: MIT Press, 1962).

5 *Ibid.*

6 http://www.centrica.co.uk/index.asp?pageid=5.

7 www.edf.fr.

8 F. J. Aguilar, 'General Electric: Reg Jones and Jack Welch', in F. J. Aguilar, *General Managers in Action* (Oxford: Oxford University Press, 1992).

9 H. Fayol, *General and Industrial Management* (1884; New York: IEEE Press, 1984).

10 *Ibid.*

11 P. Wack, 'Scenarios – Shooting the Rapids', *Harvard Business Review* 85. (November–December 1985), 131–50; P. Wack, 'Scenarios – Uncharted Waters Ahead', *Harvard Business Review* 85 (September–October 1985), 73–89.

12 A. P. De Geus, 'Planning as Learning'. *Harvard Business Review* 88 (March–April 1988), 70–74.

13 R. Phelps, C. Chan and S. C. Kapsalis, 'Does Scenario Planning Affect Performance? Two Exploratory Studies', *Journal of Business Research*, 51(3) (2001), 223–32.

14 http://www.shell.com/home/Framework. http://www.shell.com/static/royal-en/downloads/scenarios/exsum_23052005.pdf.

15 Wack, 'Scenarios – Shooting the Rapids'.

16 P. J. H. Schoemaker, 'Multiple Scenario Development: Its Conceptual and Behavioral Foundation', *Strategic Management Journal* 14 (1993), 193–213.

17 Phelps, Chan and Kapsalis, 'Does Scenario Planning Affect Performance?'.

18 J. A. Pearce, 'The Company Mission as a Strategic Tool', *Sloan Management Review*, (Spring 1992), 15–24.

19 D. F. Abell, *Defining the Business: The Starting Point of Strategic Planning* (Englewood Cliffs, NJ: Prentice Hall, 1980).

20 http://www.lego.com/info/pdf/annualreport2005UK.pdf.

21 http://www.lego.com/info/pdf/annualreport2005UK.pdf. http://www.lego.com/eng/info/default.asp?page=pressdetail&contentid=18853&countrycode=2057.

22 G. Hamel and C. K. Prahalad, 'Strategic Intent', *Harvard Business Review*, (May–June 1989), 63–73.

23 *Sunday Times*, 6 March 2005.

24 www.lego.com.

25 www.asda.co.uk.

26 http://franchisor.ikea.com/showContent.asp?swfId=concept2.

27 E. A. Locke, G. P. Latham and M. Erez, 'The Determinants of Goal Commitment', *Academy of Management Review* 13 (1988), 23–39.

28 K. R. Andrews, *The Concept of Corporate Strategy* (Homewood, IL: Irwin, 1971).

29 Edmund P. Learned, C. Roland Christiansen, Kenneth Andrews and William D. Guth, *Business Policy, Text and Cases* (Homewood, IL: Irwin, 1969).

30 G. Mulvihill, 'Campbell Is Really Cooking', San Diego Tribune.com, August 5, 2004.

31 W. D. Crotty, 'Campbell Soup Is Not So Hot', MotleyFool.com, May 24, 2004.

32 http://www.bcentral.co.uk/startingup/formingacompany/innocent-drinks.mspx.

33 E. Penrose, *The Theory of the Growth of the Firm* (Oxford: Oxford University Press, 1959).

34 M. E. Porter, 'From Competitive Advantage to Corporate Strategy', *Harvard Business Review* 65 (1987), 43–59.

35 D. J. Teece, 'Economies of Scope and the Scope of the Enterprise', *Journal of Economic Behavior and Organization* 3 (1980), 223–47.

36 M. E. Porter, *Competitive Advantage: Creating and Sustaining Superior Performance* (New York: Free Press, 1985).

37 For a review of the evidence, see C. W. L. Hill and G. R. Jones, *Strategic Management: An Integrated Approach*, 5th ed. (Boston: Houghton Mifflin, 2003), Chapter 10.

38 V. Ramanujam and P. Varadarajan, 'Research on Corporate Diversification: A Synthesis', *Strategic Management Journal* 10 (1989), 523–51. See also A. Shleifer and R. W. Vishny, 'Takeovers in the 1960s and 1980s: Evidence and Implications', in R. P. Rumelt, D. E. Schendel and D. J. Teece, *Fundamental Issues in Strategy* (Boston: Harvard Business School Press, 1994).

39 J. R. Williams, B. L. Paez and L. Sanders, 'Conglomerates Revisited', *Strategic Management Journal* 9 (1988), 403–14.

40 C. A. Bartlett and S. Ghoshal, *Managing Across Borders* (Boston: Harvard Business School Press, 1989).

41 C. K. Prahalad and Y. L. Doz, *The Multinational Mission* (New York: Free Press, 1987).

42 www.gillette.com, 2004.

43 'Gillette Co.'s New $40 Million Razor Blade Factory in St Petersburg Russia', *Boston Globe*, June 7, 2000, C6.

44 www.gillette.com, 2004.

45 R. E. Caves, *Multinational Enterprise and Economic Analysis* (Cambridge: Cambridge University Press, 1982).

46 B. Kogut, 'Joint Ventures: Theoretical and Empirical Perspectives', *Strategic Management Journal* 9 (1988), 319–33.

47 'Venture with Nestle SA Is Slated for Expansion', *The Wall Street Journal*, April 15, 2001, B2.

48 B. Bahree, 'BP Amoco, Italy's ENI Plan $2.5 Billion Gas Plant', *The Wall Street Journal*, March 6, 2001, A16.

49 http://www.lloydspharmacy.co.uk/home-page/about-us/who_are_we.htm.

50 N. Hood and S. Young, *The Economics of the Multinational Enterprise* (London: Longman, 1979).

51 http://www.betterproductdesign.net/npi/products/zara.htm.

52 M. K. Perry, 'Vertical Integration: Determinants and Effects', in R. Schmalensee and R. D. Willig, *Handbook of Industrial Organization*, 1 (New York: Elsevier Science, 1989).

53   T. Muris, D. Scheffman and P. Spiller, 'Strategy and Transaction Costs: The Organization of Distribution in the Carbonated Soft Drink Industry', *Journal of Economics and Management Strategy* 1 (1992), 77–97.

54   'Matsushita Electric Industrial (MEI) in 1987', Harvard Business School Case, 388–444.

55   P. Ghemawat, *Commitment: The Dynamic of Strategy* (New York: Free Press, 1991).

56   www.ibm.com.

57   M. E. Porter, *Competitive Strategy* (New York: Free Press, 1980).

58   http://archives.cnn.com/.

59   www.federalexpress.com.

60   www.ups.com.

61   C. W. L. Hill, 'Differentiation Versus Low Cost or Differentiation and Low Cost: A Contingency Framework', *Academy of Management Review* 13 (1988), 401–12.

62   For details, see J. P. Womack, D. T. Jones and D. Roos, *The Machine That Changed the World* (New York: Rawson Associates, 1990).

63   Porter, *Competitive Advantage*.

64   www.zara.com.

65   C. Vitzthum, 'Just-in-Time-Fashion', *The Wall Street Journal*, May 18, 2001, B1, B4.

66   www.zara.com.